HARDPRESS.NET
HOME OF HARD-TO-FIND BOOKS

The Select Works of Benjamin Franklin
by Benjamin Franklin

The select works of Benjamin Franklin

Benjamin Franklin, E. Sargent

Ar 599.

THE

Select Works

OF

BENJAMIN FRANKLIN.

"FRANKLIN had at once genius and virtue, happiness and glory. His life, always felicitous, is one of the best justifications of the laws of Providence. Not only great, he was good; not only just, he was amiable. A sage full of indulgence, a great man full of simplicity, so long as science shall be cultivated, genius admired, wit relished, virtue honored, and liberty prized, his memory shall be one of the most respected and most cherished." — MIGNET.

"NOT half of Franklin's merits have been told. He was the true father of the American Union. It was he who went forth to lay the foundation of that great design at Albany; and in New York he lifted up his voice. Here among us he appeared as the apostle of the Union. It was Franklin who suggested the Congress of 1774; and but for his wisdom, and the confidence that wisdom inspired, it is a matter of doubt whether that Congress would have taken effect. It was Franklin who suggested the bond of the Union which binds these States from Florida to Maine. Franklin was the greatest diplomatist of the eighteenth century. He never spoke a word too soon; he never spoke a word too much; he never failed to speak the right word at the right season." — BANCROFT.

H.W. Smith.

The Select Works of Franklin.

EDITED BY

Epes Sargent.

BOSTON:
PHILLIPS, SAMPSON & CO.

THE

SELECT WORKS

OF

BENJAMIN FRANKLIN;

INCLUDING

His Autobiography.

WITH NOTES AND A MEMOIR

BY EPES SARGENT.

BOSTON:
PHILLIPS, SAMPSON AND COMPANY.
NEW YORK: J. C. DERBY.
1855.

Stereotyped by
HOBART & ROBBINS,
NEW ENGLAND TYPE AND STEREOTYPE FOUNDRY,
BOSTON.

PREFACE.

FRANKLIN'S personal celebrity has so eclipsed his literary fame, that justice has hardly been done to him as a writer and an essayist; and yet he has himself confessed that he was indebted mainly to his pen for his advancement in public life. He was singularly indifferent, however, to any reputation or profit that might accrue from his writings, and left it to his friends to collect and republish them as they might please. The consequences of this indifference are manifest even to the present time, in the absence of any cheap popular edition of his select works. He has been posthumously fortunate, however, in having so able an editor as Mr. Sparks, whose ten volumes of the Works of Franklin, with a memoir and notes, leave nothing to be desired in the way of an ample and accurate collection.

But Franklin's is a name so eminently and intimately popular, that the want of a collection of his best works, more generally accessible in respect to size and cost, has long been experienced; and to supply this want the present edition is offered. In the introductory memoir, the editor

has been indebted for some new facts to the French me-
moirs by Mignet and Sainte-Beuve; and the works of John
Adams, recently published, have supplied many interesting
details, not embraced in any other biographical account.
All Franklin's purely literary productions of merit are
contained in the present collection, with liberal specimens
of his philosophical writings, and the choicest of his letters.
Much that he wrote was of merely local and temporary
interest, designed to affect provincial legislation; and,
though valuable to the historian, is unprofitable to the general reader of a subsequent time.

The fine portrait, forming the frontispiece, is from the
painting in the gallery of Versailles, and is now, it is believed, engraved for the first time.   It is supposed to have
been taken some eight years before that by Duplessis, a
copy of which, cut on wood, is placed in juxtaposition.

CONTENTS.

MEMOIR OF FRANKLIN.

HIS AUTOBIOGRAPHY.

HIS POLITICAL PAPERS.

HIS PHILOSOPHICAL PAPERS.

HIS MORAL AND MISCELLANEOUS PAPERS.

HIS CORRESPONDENCE.

MEMOIR

OF

BENJAMIN FRANKLIN.

I.

No memoir of Franklin can be a successful substitute for
his Autobiography. In the present sketch, we shall aim at
little but a review of such facts as are too lightly touched
on in his own charming narrative, or as are needed to complete the account of his useful and eventful life. The First
Part of his Autobiography, addressed in the form of a letter
to his son, William Franklin, Governor of New Jersey, was
written in England, in the year 1771, during the author's
sojourn at Twyford, the seat of Dr. Shipley, Bishop of St.
Asaph. In this Part, he brings down the narrative of his
life to the year 1730; and of it there were an original
draft and a copy taken with a machine. The original manuscript was given to M. Le Veillard, of Passy, who was
guillotined during the French revolution, when it fell into
the possession of his daughter. The copy became the property of Franklin's grandson, William Temple Franklin.

By M. Veillard this First Part was translated into
French, and published together with a collection of Franklin's Essays. It is a curious circumstance, that an English
translation having been made from this French version for

a similar collection, published in London, shortly after
Franklin's death, this translation of a translation has been
repeatedly republished, both in England and this country, as
the life of Franklin, written by himself.   What renders the
fate of it still more singular is the fact that the English
re-translation, translated back into French, was published in
Paris in 1798.   The Autobiography as originally written,
and as printed in the present volume, was first published in
1818, by William Temple Franklin.

The occurrence of the American revolution interrupted
Franklin's autobiographical task, and he did not resume it
till twelve years later, while resident at Passy, near Paris,
in France.   The Second, and last, Part of his Autobiography, terminates with his arrival in London, in 1757, as the
agent of the Pennsylvania Assembly, in their dispute with
the descendants of Penn, the "proprietaries," as they were
called, of the territory ceded to their ancestor.

Such is the graceful and unaffected candor of Franklin's
style, that his story is ever best told in his own words.
"His confessions of his faults," says Sainte Beuve, "have
an air of sincerity and simplicity, which leave us in no
doubt as to the genuineness of the sentiment he expresses.
When Rousseau, in his *Confessions*, makes similar avow-
als, he vaunts, even while he accuses himself.   Franklin,
who has few but venial faults to reveal, accuses himself less
vehemently and does not vaunt at all."

We shall give a brief summary of the events related in
the Autobiography, and then take up the thread of Franklin's history where he drops it.

Benjamin Franklin was born in Boston, January the
17th, 1706.   His father, who had emigrated from England,
was a tallow-chandler.   Benjamin was the fifteenth of
seventeen children, and the eighth of ten by a second wife.
He was named for an uncle, who emigrated to Boston in the
year 1715.   This uncle had the poetical faculty in no
ordinary degree, as may be inferred from the following
pieces, which, while they are marked by the fashionable
quaintnesses of the religious poets of the seventeenth century, give evidence of considerable literary culture.   The
first bears the title of an "Acrostic sent to Benjamin
Franklin, in New England, July 15, 1710."

> " Be to thy parents an obedient son ;
> Each day let duty constantly be done ;
> Never give way to sloth, or lust, or pride,
> If free you 'd be from thousand ills beside ;
> Above all ills be sure avoid the shelf
> Man's danger lies in, — Satan, sin and self !
> In virtue, learning, wisdom, progress make ;
> Ne'er shrink at suffering for thy Saviour's sake.

> " Fraud and all falsehood in thy dealings flee;
> Religious always in thy station be ;
> Adore the Maker of thy inward part ;
> Now 's the accepted time, give Him thy heart ;
> Keep a good conscience, — 't is a constant friend ;
> Like judge and witness this thy acts attend !
> In heart, with bended knee, alone, adore
> None but the Three in One forevermore."

From the following lines, "sent to Benjamin Franklin, 1713," when he was only seven years old, it would seem that his literary tendencies were developed even earlier than his own account would lead us to suppose :

> " 'T is time for me to throw aside my pen,
> When hanging sleeves read, write, and rhyme like men.
> This forward spring foretells a plenteous crop ;
> For, if the bud bear grain, what will the top ?
> If plenty in the verdant blade appear,
> What may we not soon hope for in the ear ?
> When flowers are beautiful before they 're blown,
> What rarities will afterward be shown !
> If trees good fruit unnoculated bear,
> You may be sure 't will afterward be rare.
> If fruits are sweet before they 've time to yellow,
> How luscious will they be when they are mellow !
> If first years' shoots such noble clusters send,
> What laden boughs, Engedi-like, may we expect in the end !"

At twelve years of age, Benjamin was apprenticed to his elder brother, James, a printer, and publisher of the *New England Courant*, a newspaper in Boston. Benjamin had a passion for reading, and he now found means of gratifying it. He was also tempted to try his skill in literary composition, and wrote some anonymous pieces for his brother's journal, which were published and approved. Some political articles in the *Courant* having offended the Legislative Assembly of the colony, the publisher was imprisoned and forbidden to continue his journal. To elude this prohibition, young Franklin was made the nominal editor, and his indentures were temporarily cancelled. After the

2*

release of his brother, he availed himself of this act to assert his freedom, and thus escaped from a position which had been irksome in consequence of the ill treatment to which he was subjected. Franklin subsequently blamed himself for thus taking advantage of his brother's difficulty, and set down his own conduct on this occasion as one of the *errata* of his life.

He now secretly embarked, without means or recommendations, on board a small vessel bound to New York. Not finding employment there, he set out for Philadelphia, where he arrived on foot, with a penny-roll in his hand, and one dollar in his purse. Here he obtained employment as a compositor, and, having attracted the notice of Sir William Keith, Governor of Pennsylvania, was, through his promises, induced to visit England, for the purpose of purchasing the materials for establishing himself in business as a printer. On reaching London, in 1725, he found himself entirely deceived in his promised letters of credit and recommendation from Governor Keith; and being, as before, in a strange place, without credit or acquaintances, he went to work once more as a compositor.

In 1726, after a residence of about eighteen months in London, he returned to Philadelphia, soon after which he entered into business as a printer and stationer; and in 1728 established a newspaper. In 1732 he published his "Poor Richard's Almanac," which became noted for its pithy maxims,— some original, but mostly taken from various sources, ancient and modern. In 1736 he was appointed clerk to the General Assembly of Pennsylvania, and the year following postmaster of Philadelphia. In the French war, in 1744, the Governor having in vain importuned the legislature, a majority of whom were Quakers, to pass a militia law, and adopt other precautions for defence, Franklin proposed to accomplish the object by a voluntary subscription; and he set forth its importance in a pamphlet entitled "Plain Truth," which did not fail of effect.

About the year 1746, he commenced his electrical experiments, and made several important discoveries. In 1747 he was chosen a representative of the General Assembly, in which situation he distinguished himself by several acts of public utility. By his influential exertions a militia bill was passed, and he was appointed colonel of the Philadelphia regiment. In 1757 he was sent to England as agent for Pennsylvania.

II.

FRANKLIN'S second visit to England was made under auspices very different from those which had attended his first. Then he went a poor printer, relying upon the imaginary influence of the graceless Sir William Keith, who had amused him with chimerical promises, and cajoled him with sham letters of recommendation. Now it was Franklin, the eminent philosopher and discoverer, the gifted writer and sagacious statesman, who took up his temporary residence in London. His electrical discoveries had been promulgated some ten years before. His first letter on the subject was communicated ·March 28, 1747, to Peter Collinson, a member of the Royal Society. In this and his subsequent letters, Franklin makes known the power of points in drawing and throwing off the electrical matter,—a fact which had hitherto escaped the attention of electricians. He also made the discovery of a *plus* and *minus*, or of a *positive* and *negative*, state of electricity.

"Besides these great principles," says Dr. Stuber, " Franklin's letters on electricity contain a number of facts and hints which have contributed greatly towards reducing this branch of knowledge to a science. His friend, Mr. Kinnersley, communicated to him a discovery of the different kinds of electricity excited by rubbing glass and sulphur. The philosophers were disposed to account for the phenomena rather from a difference in the quantity of electricity collected ; and even Du Faye himself seems at last to have adopted this doctrine. Franklin at first entertained the same idea ; but, upon repeating the experiments, he perceived that Mr. Kinnersley was right, and that the *vitreous* and *resinous* electricity of Du Faye were nothing more than the *positive* and *negative* states which he had before observed ; that the glass globe charged *positively*, or increased the quantity of electricity on the prime conductor ; whilst the globe of sulphur diminished its natural quantity, or charged *negatively*. These experiments and observations opened a new field for investigation, upon which electricians entered with avidity ; and their labors have added much to the stock of our knowledge."

In 1749 he suggested an explanation of the aurora borealis and thunder-gusts on electrical principles. The same year he conceived the project of testing the truth of his theory in respect to lightning, by means of sharp-pointed iron rods, raised into the region of the clouds. But it was not till the summer of 1752 that he resorted to the expedient of a common - kite, and by means of it converted what was theory into scientific truth.

While waiting for the construction of a spire from which to try his experiment, it occurred to him that he might secure the desired contact with the clouds by means of a kite. He prepared one of a silk handkerchief, as being less likely to be affected by rain than paper. To the upright stick of the frame he attached an iron point. The string was, as usual, of hemp, except the lower end, which was of silk ; and where the hempen and silken cords were united, he fastened a metallic key.

With this apparatus, he went forth, with his son, into the fields, as a thunder-storm was coming on, to try the experiment, the memory of which was to be immortal. Well knowing the ridicule which scientific experiments, when unsuccessful, often call forth, he kept his intentions a secret from all but his companion. He placed himself under a shed, to avoid the rain. His kite was raised. A thunder-cloud passed over it. No sign of electricity appeared. Franklin began to despair of success, when suddenly he saw the loose fibres of his string in motion, and bristling, in an upright position, as if placed on a conductor. On applying his knuckle to the key, he experienced a smart shock, accompanied by a bright spark. Here was his theory verified ! As the string became wet with the rain, it operated better as a conductor, and he was enabled to collect an abundant supply of electricity, with which he charged a jar.

This experiment was made in June, 1752. It had been successfully performed, according to Franklin's original plan, by means of a pointed bar of iron, about a month previous, in Paris, by M. De Lor ; but Franklin had not been apprized either of the attempt or the result at the time of making his experiment with the kite. He afterwards had an insulated rod constructed to draw the lightning into his house, with a bell attached, in order to inform him when the rod was affected by electricity. By means of this apparatus he was enabled to collect a considerable quantity of electric fluid, on which to experiment at his leisure.

Franklin's letters to Collinson, narrating his electrical experiments, were at first received with incredulous raillery by the Royal Society, and regarded as unworthy of being printed among its transactions. The scientific men of France, however, did ample justice to Franklin's merits, and at length the experiment of procuring lightning from the clouds by a pointed rod having been verified in England, the Royal Society made amends for its neglect by choosing him a member, exempting him from the customary admission fee of twenty-five guineas, and, in 1753, presenting him with the gold medal of Sir Godfrey Copley.

"The fame of Franklin," says Mignet, "rapidly spread with his theory over the whole world. His Treatise, published by Dr. Fothergill, a member of the Royal Society, was translated into French, Italian, German and Latin. It produced a scientific revolution throughout Europe. The experiments of the American philosopher, which Dalibard had made simultaneously with him at Marly-le-Roi, were repeated at Montbard, by the great naturalist Buffon; at Saint Germain, by De Lor, before Louis XV., who wished to be a witness of them; at Turin, by Father Beccaria; in Russia, by Professor Richmann, who, receiving too powerful a discharge, fell lightning-struck, and gave to science a martyr. Everywhere conclusive, these experiments caused the new system to be adopted by acclamation; and it was styled *Franklinian*, in honor of its author.

"Thus all at once distinguished, the Philadelphia sage became the object of universal regard, and was abundantly loaded with academic honors. The Academy of Sciences of Paris made him an associate member, as it had Newton and Leibnitz. All the learned bodies of Europe eagerly admitted him into their ranks.* To this scientific glory,

---

* Emmanuel Kant, the celebrated German philosopher, spoke of Franklin, in 1755, as "the Prometheus of modern times."

which he might have extended if he had consecrated to his favorite pursuits his thoughts and his time, he added high political distinction. To this man, happy because he was intelligent, great because he had an active genius and a devoted heart, was accorded the rare felicity of serving his country skilfully and usefully for a period of fifty years; and, after having taken rank among the immortal founders of the positive sciences, of enrolling himself among the generous liberators of the nations."

With a scientific and literary reputation familiar to all Europe, Franklin was hospitably received in England on the occasion of his second visit, which lasted from July 27, 1757, to the latter part of August, 1762. At this time Dr. Johnson was publishing his *Idler;* Burke had just given to the world his "Essay on the Sublime and Beautiful," and was editing the *Annual Register* for Dodsley; Hume was about completing his History of England; Sterne was publishing his Tristram Shandy; Swedenborg was residing obscurely in London, engaged upon his mystical writings; Goldsmith was just launching upon a literary career in the same great metropolis; Garrick was electrifying the town with his acting; and the brothers Wesley were engaging in their extraordinary labors for the establishment of a re-formed Protestantism. Sir Isaac Newton had died thirty years before. Franklin, when in London before, had been promised a sight of him, but the promise was not kept. It does not appear that Franklin ever became personally acquainted with any of these distinguished persons, excepting Hume, Garrick and Burke.

After partaking of the hospitality of his friend and correspondent, Mr. Collinson, he took lodgings at a house in Craven-street, a few doors from the Strand, which had been recommended to him by some of his Philadelphia friends. It was kept by a Mrs. Stevenson, "a very discreet, good gentlewoman," and Franklin did not change his quarters during the whole period of his stay in England. Many of his best philosophical papers were addressed to Miss Mary Stevenson, a daughter of his landlady, and a young lady of decided taste for scientific investigation. With this family he maintained the most affectionate relations during his long life.

Among the acquaintances of Franklin at this time was John Baskerville, whose improvements in printing and type-founding had commended him to the literary world. He was born the same year with Franklin, and similarity of mechanical tastes brought them together. William Strahan, king's printer, and a member of Parliament, was one of Franklin's most intimate associates and admirers, and his regard seems to have been reciprocated. "He was very urgent with me," says Franklin, in a letter to his wife, "to stay in England, and prevail with you to remove hither with Sally. He proposed several advantageous schemes to me, which appeared reasonably founded." In a letter to Mrs. Franklin, dated London, December 13, 1757, Mr. Strahan writes of her husband:— "I never saw a man who was, in every respect, so perfectly agreeable to me. Some are amiable in one view, some in another,—he in all." It is a painful example of the estrangements produced by war to read, in connection with this, the following letter (by some supposed not wholly serious) from Franklin to Strahan, written some eighteen years afterwards:

Philad., July 5, 1775.

MR. STRAHAN: You are a Member of Parliament, and one of that majority which has doomed my country to destruction. You have begun to burn our towns and murder our people. Look upon your hands;— they are stained with the blood of your relations! You and I were long friends,—you are now my enemy; and I am

After the independence of the Colonies, the friendly intercourse of Franklin with Strahan was renewed, and old ties were reknit with added warmth on both sides.

In the autumn of 1757 Franklin had an attack of illness, resulting in a violent cold and fever; during which, as he writes to his wife, he was "now and then a little delirious." "They cupped me," he continues, "on the back of the head, which seemed to ease me for the present. I took a good deal of bark, both in substance and infusion; and, too soon thinking myself well, I ventured out twice, to do a little business and forward the service I am engaged in, and both times got fresh cold and fell down again. My good doctor grew very angry with me for acting contrary to his cautions and directions, and obliged me to promise more observance for the future." The "good doctor" here alluded to was Doctor Fothergill, who attended Franklin very carefully and affectionately during his illness, which lasted nearly two months.

Franklin entered into the objects of his mission with his usual alacrity and fidelity of attention. A brief review of these objects will be appropriate in this place.

By the death of the widow of William Penn, and of Springett Penn, son and heir of William Penn the younger, the territorial rights of the province were reünited, under the will of William Penn, the founder, in John, Thomas, and Richard, his sons by his second wife. John, the eldest, born in Pennsylvania during his father's last visit, possessed a double share. By John's death, without issue, his half of Pennsylvania descended to his next brother, Thomas, who thus became "Proprietary" of three-fourths of the province, his brother Richard being the "Proprietary" of the remainder.

To extend their influence, these Proprietaries had claimed the appointment of judicial and other officers. They had forbidden all other persons to purchase lands of the natives, — thus establishing a monopoly in their own favor; and they had insisted on the exemption of their immense estates from taxation. In an address to the Proprietaries in 1751, the General Assembly urge the old complaint, that the Province was at the sole expense of Indian treaties, of which the chief benefit resulted to the Proprietaries in the cession of lands. Disputes ensued on these controverted claims between the General Assembly and the Governor, who was the nominee of the Proprietaries, and the representative of their interests. The ready pen and clear judgment of Franklin were frequently called into requisition in drawing up reports and representations in reply to the Proprietaries and their advocates; and, at last, having showed himself more than a match for the writers on the other side, the Assembly sent him as their agent, as already mentioned, to represent their case to the king.

On his arrival in England he found that the newspapers were mostly in the Proprietary interest, and that "intelligence from Pennsylvania," evidently manufactured with a view to prejudicing public opinion, represented the inhabitants of the province as actuated by a selfish and refractory spirit; although they merely withstood the claim of the Proprietaries to an exemption from a taxation which was as necessary to the defence of their own estates as to the general safety. One of Franklin's first steps was to reform an erroneous public opinion, through the same medium by which it had been created,— namely, the press. It having been stated in a newspaper called *The Citizen, or General Advertiser*, that ravages had been committed by the Indians on the inhabitants of the western part of the province, and that the Assembly's pertinacious disputes with the Governor prevented anything being done for the public protection, Franklin caused a reply to be inserted in the same newspaper. over the signature of his son, William Franklin, and dated from the "Pennsylvania Coffee-house, London, Sept. 16, 1757." In this communication a circumstantial denial is given to the charges brought against the Assembly, and more especially the Quaker portion of that body.

With a view to enlightening public opinion still further in regard to the rights of the people of Pennsylvania, as opposed to the claims of the two sons of William Penn, in the beginning of 1759 an anonymous work was published, entitled "An Historical Review of the Constitution and Government of Pennsylvania from its origin." The motto was as follows: "Those who give up essential liberty to purchase a little temporary safety deserve neither liberty

3

nor safety." The authorship of this work was at once charged upon Franklin, although by some it was attributed to his old comrade, James Ralph, then resident in London. The volume was dedicated to Arthur Onslow, Speaker of the House of Commons; and, in his dedication, the writer says, " The cause we bring is, in fact, the cause of all the provinces in one. It is the cause of every British subject in every part of the British dominions. It is the cause of every man who deserves to be free, everywhere."

Following the dedicatory epistle is an "Introduction," in which Thomas Penn is referred to as "an assuming landlord, strongly disposed to convert free tenants into abject vassals, and to reap what he did not sow." As an excuse for bringing before the British public " the transactions of a Colony till of late hardly mentioned in our annals," the author remarks : " But then, as there are some eyes which can find nothing marvellous but what is marvellously great, so there are others which are equally disposed to marvel at what is marvellously little, and who can derive as much entertainment from their microscope, in examining a mite, as Dr. —— in ascertaining the geography of the moon, or measuring the tail of a comet." The author does not presume that "such as have long been accustomed to consider the Colonies in general as only so many dependencies on the Council-board, the Board of Trade, and the Board of Customs, or as a hot-bed for causes, jobs, and other pecuniary emoluments, and as *bound as effectually by instructions as by laws*, can be prevailed upon to consider *these patriot rustics* with any degree of respect. Derision, on the contrary, must be the lot of him who imagines it in the power of the pen to set any lustre upon them." And he eloquently concludes in these words : " But how contemptibly soever these gentlemen may talk of the Colonies, how cheap soever they may hold their Assemblies, or how insignificant the planters and traders who compose them, truth will be truth, and principle principle, notwithstanding. Courage, wisdom, integrity, and honor, *are not to be measured by the sphere assigned them to act in*, but by the trials they undergo, and the vouchers they furnish; and, if so manifested. need neither robes nor titles to set them off."

The Proprietaries were much incensed by the language applied to them in this work. The belief that it was from the pen of Franklin was so fixed and general, that he made no public disavowal of the authorship,— partly, perhaps, through a willingness to incur all the odium of it, and partly because he was really responsible for the publication and for many of the facts. In the Philadelphia edition of his works, published as late as 1840, the "Historical Review " is inserted entire, as from his pen. It appears, however, from a letter to David Hume, dated September 27, 1760, that the work was incorrectly attributed to him. In this letter (first published by Mr. Sparks) he says : "I am obliged to you for the favorable sentiments you express of the pieces sent to you ; though the volume relating to our Pennsylvania affairs was not written by me, nor any part of it, except the remarks on the proprietor's estimate of his estate, and some of the inserted messages and reports of the Assembly, which I wrote when at home, as a member of committees appointed by the House for that purpose. The rest was by another hand." The "Historical Review," though anonymous, appears to have been of considerable service in gaining friends for the Assembly, in opposition to the Proprietaries.

In conformity with directions from the Assembly, Franklin had an interview with the Proprietaries, resident in England, and discussed the points of difference. The Messrs. Penn would not relax in their arbitrary claims. They seemed ambitious of holding the whole population of the province in a state of vassalage. Not only did they claim political privileges, insisting on giving such instructions to their deputy governor as made him a mere puppet in their hands, and trammelled him in a manner to render him powerless for good to the people, but they looked sharply after their pecuniary interests, and continued to chaffer with the Assembly for an exemption of their princely domains from taxation.

While the quarrel was pending, the Assembly passed a law taxing the proprietary estates, which law was approved by Governor Denny. This and several other laws, having a similar sanction, were so displeasing to the Proprietaries, that they removed the Governor from office. The laws being sent over to England for the King's approval, the Penns petitioned for a veto on them; and the whole question being brought before the Board of Trade, was at length decided in June, 1760, Franklin having been detained some three years in the prosecution of his mission.   By this decision the right of the Assembly to tax the proprietary estates was admitted, and their suit, so far as related to the main point of the controversy, was triumphantly terminated. The Board of Trade, however, in their decision, commented in severe terms on an inferred collusion between the Assembly and Governor Denny, evinced by a grant to the latter of a distinct sum of money for consenting to the several acts objected to by the Proprietaries.   Some modifications of the act taxing the Proprietaries were also required; and, as these were not important, Franklin readily concurred in them, and the controversy for the time was settled, much to his reputation as a prudent and faithful negotiator.   The powerful influence of Lord Mansfield had been given in favor of the Assembly's demand that the lands of the Proprietaries should be taxed.

The war with France, in which Great Britain was at this time involved, occupied much of Franklin's concern, and he was, at an early period, convinced of the policy of changing the theatre of hostilities from Europe to Canada. His views on this subject were drawn from him by Messrs. Potter and Wood, secretaries of Lord Chatham, then prime minister, and probably had some weight in determining the enterprise which resulted in Wolfe's brilliant victory. and the final retention of the Canadian provinces.   About the year 1760, Franklin, assisted by his friend Richard Jackson, wrote a pamphlet entitled " *The Interest of Great Britain considered with regard to the Colonies, and the Acquisition of Canada and Guadaloupe.*"   In this work he demonstrated in a clear and forcible manner the advantages that would accrue to Great Britain from the proposed addition to her provincial territory.

His prediction that " *there can never be manufactures to any amount or value in America* " did not look to the possibility of a protective tariff.   " Manufactures," he says, " are founded in poverty : it is the multitude of poor without land in a country, and who must work for others at low

wages or starve, that enables undertakers to carry on a
manufacture, and afford it cheap enough to prevent the
importation of the same kind from abroad, and to bear the
expense of its own exportation.   But no man, who can have
a piece of land of his own, sufficient by his labor to subsist
his family in plenty, is poor enough to be a manufacturer,
and work for a master.   Hence, while there is land enough
in America for our people, there can never be manufactures
to any amount or value."   Could the writer have looked a
century into the future, he would have been startled at the
contradiction which time would give to these speculations.

The idea of the independence of the American Colonies
does not appear to have been seriously entertained by him
at this time.   He alludes to it as "a visionary danger."
Of these Colonies, which American Independence and the
American Constitution subsequently united in a harmonious
system, he says : "Their jealousy of each other is so great,
that, however necessary an union of the Colonies has long
been for their common defence and security against their
enemies, and how sensible soever each Colony has been of
that necessity, yet they have never been able to effect such
an union among themselves, nor even to agree in requesting
the mother country to establish it for them."   He repudi-
ates the idea of a union of the Colonies against the mother
country, but prudently adds a qualification in these words :
"When I say such an union is impossible, *I mean, without the most grievous tyranny and oppression.*"

The Proprietaries appear to have found in him a steady
and vigilant antagonist.   When the annual share of the
Parliamentary grant due for military and other expenses to
Pennsylvania and the Delaware Colonies, and amounting
to about thirty thousand pounds, became payable, he was
employed by the Assembly to receive and invest the amount.
The Proprietaries interfered to prevent this disposition of
the money, claiming that their deputy, the Governor, ought
to have a hand in the management of the fund.   Here they
were again baffled by Franklin ; for the ministry took his
view of the matter, and decided that the money ought to be
paid to the Assembly's agent.

Notwithstanding Franklin's opposition to the usurpations
of the Proprietaries, the latter were forced to admit that his

course was fair and unexceptionable. "I do not find,"
writes Thomas Penn, "that he has done me any prejudice
with any party. I believe he has spent most of his time in
philosophical, and especially in electrical, matters, having
generally company in a morning to see those experiments,
and musical performances on glasses, where any one that
knows him carries his friends." The musical performances
here referred to were on the Harmonica, an instrument contrived by Franklin, being an improvement on the mode of
using musical glasses. It was quite in vogue at one time
in London.

"He was gifted," says Mignet, "with the spirit of
observation and inference above all other endowments.
Observation conducted him to discovery, and inference to a
practical application of it. Was he traversing the ocean, he
made experiments upon the temperature of the waters, and
proved that the warmth of the water in the Gulf Stream
was much greater than that of the water on each side of it.
He thus revealed to mariners a simple mode of discovering
when they were in the Gulf Stream. Was he listening to
sounds produced by glasses put in vibration, he remarked
that these sounds differed according to the size of the glass,
and the relations to its width, capacity and contents. From
these observations resulted the suggestion of a new musical
instrument, and Franklin invented the Harmonica.* Did
he chance to examine the loss of heat through the aperture
of chimneys, and the imperfect combustion in a closed stove,
he invented, from this double examination, by combining
both means of heating, a chimney-place which was as
economical as a stove, and a stove which was as open as a
chimney-place. This stove, which is in the chimney-place
form, was very generally adopted, and Franklin refused a

---

* Franklin possessed a strong natural taste for music. Leigh Hunt,
speaking of his own mother, a Philadelphia lady, says : "Dr. Franklin
offered to teach her the guitar, but she was too bashful to become his
pupil. She regretted this afterward ; partly, no doubt, for having missed
so illustrious a master. Her first child, who died, was named after him. I
know not whether the anecdote is new, but I have heard that, when Dr.
Franklin invented the Harmonica, he concealed it from his wife till the
instrument was fit to play, and then woke her with it one night, when she
took it for the music of angels." In one of his letters to his wife, Franklin presents his best respects to "dear, precious Mrs. Shewell," who was
Leigh Hunt's grandmother.

patent for the exclusive sale. But his most glorious and important discovery was that of the nature of lightning and the laws of electricity."

The fact of the production of cold by evaporation, unfamiliar at the time to science, was illustrated by him on several occasions, while in England. Some curious experiments, by which an extraordinary degree of cold, even to freezing, might be produced by evaporation, had been previously communicated to him by Professor Simpson, of Glasgow. One of these was by wetting the ball of a thermometer with spirit of wine, thus causing the mercury to sink. Being at Cambridge, Franklin mentioned this to Dr. Hadley, professor of chemistry, and several interesting experiments were tried, of which an account is given by Franklin, in a letter to Dr. Lining. In another, to Dr. Heberden, he communicated some discoveries which he had made, to test a disputed question, in regard to the electrical peculiarities of the tourmaline, a stone found chiefly in the East Indies, and the chief constituents of which are silica and alumina. The transparent colored varieties are very beautiful. It was known to the ancients under the name of *lyncurium*. It was the opinion of Æpinus that the tourmaline is always endowed with a positive and negative electricity at the same moment, these different states being confined to opposite sides of the fossil. Franklin satisfied himself that this account was well-founded. He also observed that the warmth of his finger, when he wore the stone, was sufficient to give it some degree of electricity, so that it was always ready to attract light bodies. He thought that experiments might have failed, in many instances, in consequence of the stones having been improperly cut by the lapidaries, or through omission to impart to them the full heat given by boiling water.

In a letter to Alexander Small, of London, he communicates reasons, which he had long entertained, for the opinion that our north-east storms in North America begin first, in point of time, in the south-west parts : that is to say, the air in Georgia begins to move south-westerly before the air of Carolina, the air of Carolina before that of Virginia, and so on. Among his reasons for believing this, was the fact that, some twenty years before, having been prevented by a

north-east storm from witnessing an eclipse of the moon at
Philadelphia, he subsequently learned that the eclipse was
distinctly observed in Boston, and that the storm did not
begin there till four hours after it had begun in Philadelphia.   The conjecture deduced from this and similar facts
has been abundantly confirmed by later experience; the
telegraph now frequently reporting that a north-easterly
storm is raging in Philadelphia, while the weather is yet
clear in Boston.   Franklin explained the phenomenon by
supposing that, to produce our north-east storms, some
great heat and rarefaction of the air must exist in or about
the Gulf of Mexico; the air thence rising has its place supplied by the next more northern, cooler, and therefore
denser and heavier air; that, being in motion, is followed
by the next more northern air, &c., in a successive current,
to which current our coast and inland ridge of mountains
give the direction of north-east, as they lie north-east and
south-west.   In a letter from London to Peter Franklin, he
speculates on the saltness of sea-water, and inclines to the
opinion that all the water on this globe was originally salt,
and that the fresh water we find in springs and rivers is
the produce of distillation.

Several letters, written about this time to his landlady's
intelligent daughter, Miss Stevenson, exhibit Franklin in a
most amiable light.   The mixture of playfulness with
gravity, of the light-hearted pleasantry of the humorist
with the profound insight of the sage, which they exhibit,
is a combination as rare as it is charming.   In one of these
letters, in reply to the question from the young lady, *why
the water at Bristol, though cold at the spring, becomes
warm by pumping*, he says that it will be most prudent in
him to forbear attempting to answer, till, by a more circumstantial account, he is assured of the fact; and he adds:
" This prudence of not attempting to give reasons before
one is sure of facts I learnt from one of your sex, who, as
Selden tells us, being in company with some gentlemen that
were viewing and considering something which they called
a Chinese shoe, and disputing earnestly about the manner
of wearing it, and how it could possibly be put on, put in
her word, and said, modestly, ' Gentlemen, are you sure it
is a shoe ?   Should not that be settled first ? ' "

In another letter to the same lady, after alluding to the study of entomology, and illustrating its importance by an anecdote, he advises a prudent moderation in the pursuit, lest more important things be sacrificed; "for," he says, "there is no rank in natural knowledge of equal dignity and importance with that of being a good parent, a good child, a good husband or wife, a good subject or citizen, — that is, in short, a good Christian. Nicholas Gimcrack, therefore, who neglected the care of his family to pursue butterflies, was a just object of ridicule, and we must give him up as fair game to the satirist."

After being present, by invitation, at the Commencement at Cambridge, the beginning of July, 1758, Franklin went through Huntingdonshire into Northumberlandshire, in search of some of his own and his wife's English relatives. Although they were all in humble spheres of life, he seems to have taken genuine pleasure in finding them out and making himself known. "At Wellingborough," he says, in a letter to his wife, "on inquiry, we found still living Mary Fisher, whose maiden name was Franklin, daughter and only child of Thomas Franklin, my father's eldest brother; she is five years older than Sister Douse, and remembers her going away with my father and his then wife, and two other children, to New England, about the year 1685. We have had no correspondence with her since my Uncle Benjamin's death, now near thirty years. I knew she had lived at Wellingborough, and had married there to one Mr. Richard Fisher, a grazier and tanner, about fifty years ago, but did not expect to see either of them alive, so inquired for their posterity. I was directed to their house, and we found them both alive, but weak with age, — very glad, however, to see us; she seems to have been a very smart, sensible woman. They are wealthy, have left off business, and live comfortably." From Wellingborough, Franklin and his son went to Ecton, about three or four miles, where his father was born, and his father, grandfather and great-grandfather, had lived. He visited the old family house, which he describes as "a decayed old stone building, but still known by the name of Franklin House." Here he made the acquaintance of the rector of the village and his wife, "a good-natured, chatty old lady," who remembered a good deal about the family. She led the way into the church-yard, "and showed us several grave-stones, which were so covered with moss that we could not read the letters till she ordered a hard brush and basin of water, with which Peter scoured them clean, and then Billy copied them."

A group for a picture this! Franklin, his son, and the "chatty old lady," and Peter scrubbing the moss and dust from the grave-stones of the philosopher's ancestors, "the rude forefathers of the hamlet"!

The rector's wife told diverting stories of Thomas Franklin, Mrs. Fisher's father, who was a conveyancer and a bit of a lawyer, and was looked upon as something of a conjurer by some of the villagers. He was a leading man in county affairs,—set on foot a subscription for having chimes in the steeple, proposed an easy method to prevent the village meadows from being submerged, and, in short, exhibited many of the traits afterwards more conspicuously developed in the character of his illustrious nephew. "He died," says Franklin, "just four years before I was born, on the same day of the same month." Perhaps a notion of transmigration slid into Franklin's brain, as he noted this coincidence.

From Ecton, he went to Birmingham, where, upon inquiry, he found out some of his wife's, "and Cousin Wilkinson's, and Cousin Cash's relations." One was a button-maker, and another a turner; and one was a "lively, active man, with six children;" and they were all very glad to see any person that knew their relatives in America; and Franklin was well pleased with them and with his visit. Returning to London, he found out a daughter of his father's only sister, very old, and never married; "a good, clever woman, but poor, though vastly contented with her situation, and very cheerful." Happening to hear that the child of a distant relation was in a destitute state, he took her home, and educated and maintained her till she was married.

In February, 1759, the University of St. Andrew's conferred upon Franklin the degree of Doctor of Laws; and in the summer of that year, accompanied by his son, he made a visit to Scotland, with which he seems to have been highly gratified. He here formed the acquaintance of David Hume and Dr. Robertson, the historians, Lord Kames and other eminent scholars and writers. In a letter some months afterwards to Lord Kames, he alludes to his six weeks spent in Scotland as a period of "the *densest* happiness" he had met with in any part of his life; and he adds : "The agreeable and instructive society we found there in such plenty has left so pleasing an impression on my memory, that, did not strong connections draw me elsewhere, I believe Scotland would be the country I should choose to spend the remainder of my days in." On hearing that Franklin was about to return to America, David Hume wrote to him : "I am very sorry that you intend soon to leave our hemisphere. America has sent us many good things, — gold, silver, sugar, tobacco, indigo (?), &c.; but you are the first philosopher, and, indeed, the first great man of letters, for whom we are beholden to her." During a second visit to Scotland, in 1771, Franklin passed some three weeks in Edinburgh, during which he lodged with David Hume.

Academic honors, similar to those awarded by the University of St. Andrew's, were conferred on Franklin by the Universities of Oxford and Edinburgh ; and, by the former of these last, the degree of Master of Arts was conferred on his son William. Another distinction awaited the latter. Through the influence of Lord Bute, he was appointed Governor of New Jersey.*

* Franklin was subjected to some uncharitable attacks in consequence of this appointment. A caricature of him, published in Philadelphia, contained these lines :

> " All his designs concentre in himself,
> For building castles and amassing pelf ;
> The *public* 't is his wit to sell for gain,
> Whom *private* property did ne'er maintain."

False in spirit and in fact, these lines indicate the malevolence of his enemies, and the abuse to which Franklin, in common with Washington and other great men, was subjected.

William Franklin was born in 1731. He was a captain in the French and English war, and fought bravely under Abercrombie at Ticonderoga. He was for a time popular as Governor of New Jersey ; but, taking sides with the ministry, he was declared by the Congress of New Jersey to be an enemy to liberty, and was seized in his own house at Perth Amboy, and conveyed a prisoner to Connecticut. In 1778, he was exchanged and released. He went to England at the close of the war, where he resided until his death, in November, 1813, in the receipt of a pension from the

III.

AFTER a sojourn of more than five years in England, Franklin sailed for home, the latter part of August, 1762. His vessel, being under convoy of a man-of-war, was obliged to touch at Madeira, and remained there a few days; so that it was the first of November before he arrived in Philadelphia. He was welcomed with enthusiasm by his many political and personal friends. He found his wife and daughter well; "the latter grown quite a woman, with many amiable accomplishments acquired in my absence, and my friends as hearty and affectionate as ever; with whom my house was filled for many days, to congratulate me on my return." During his absence he had been annually elected a member of the Assembly; and now that body passed a vote of thanks "as well for the faithful discharge of his duty to that province in particular, as for the many and important services done to America in general, during his residence in Great Britain." They voted him also a more substantial testimonial, in a compensation of three thousand pounds sterling for his six years' service.

John Penn, son and presumptive heir of Richard Penn, one of the joint proprietors, succeeded Hamilton as governor in October, 1763. He entered upon his official duties at a time when the back settlers of Pennsylvania were in a state of great excitement, because of the depredations of the confederated tribes of Indians, under the instigation of Pontiac, upon the frontiers of that province; hundreds of persons had been plundered and slain, families driven from their homes, and a state of constant disquiet and alarm produced among the settlers, who were goaded to exasperation by the cruelties that had been practised. The Pennsylvania borderers were chiefly Presbyterians of Scotch and Irish descent, and religious antipathy and fanaticism concurred to inflame their resentment. The scriptural

British government of four thousand dollars per annum. He left a son, William Temple Franklin, who edited his grandfather's works, and died at Paris in 1823. In his will, after making a few inconsiderable bequests to his son, Franklin remarks: "The part he acted against me in the late war, which is of public notoriety, will account for my leaving him no more of an estate he endeavored to deprive me of."

command, that Joshua should destroy the heathen, was conveniently construed into an injunction to Pennsylvanians to exterminate the Indians.

In December, 1763, a band of Indian haters from Paxton, a little town on the east bank of the Susquehannah, made an excursion to Conestoga, some distance above, and slaughtered, in cold blood, six poor Indians, chiefly women and old men, belonging to a remnant of twenty of the Iroquois tribe, living in a peaceable manner under the superintendence of Moravian missionaries. After this outrage, the other Indians belonging to the settlement, and who did not happen to be in the village at the time of the massacre, were lodged for safety in Lancaster jail. The Governor issued a proclamation denouncing the massacre, and offering a reward for the guilty parties. But the Paxton men, instead of being intimidated, ventured upon an aggravation of their crime. On the 27th of December, a party of about fifty ruffians rode at a gallop into Lancaster, broke into a yard adjacent to the jail where the Indians were assembled, and slaughtered them all, without regard to age or sex. Another proclamation was issued by the Governor ; but so audacious had the rioters become, that a number of them marched in arms to Philadelphia to pursue some other friendly Indians, who had taken refuge in that city. This was towards the end of January, 1764. The detachment of rioters numbered from five to fifteen hundred men. They were inflamed by exasperation at once against the Indians and the Quakers, looking upon the latter, through their opposition to defensive measures, as aiders and abettors of the barbarities inflicted by the former. There was a considerable class in Philadelphia who sympathized with the rioters. Franklin was now, as ever, found arrayed on the side of humanity and justice. The persecuted and detested Indians found in him a zealous champion and protector. He wrote a pamphlet, giving a narrative of the massacre, and calling earnestly on "all good men " to " join heartily and unanimously in support of the laws." The Assembly having passed a vote extending the English riot-act to the province, he organized, at the Governor's request, military companies composed of the citizens, and exerted himself most effectually in giving the right direction to a divided

4

public sentiment. In a letter to Lord Kames, relating to this period, he says: "Near one thousand of the citizens accordingly took arms. Governor Penn made my house for some time his head-quarters, and did everything by my advice; so that, for about forty-eight hours, I was a very great man, as I had been once some years before, in a time of public danger. But the fighting face we put on, and the reasonings we used with the insurgents (for I went, at the request of the Governor and Council, with three others, to meet and discourse with them), having turned them back and restored quiet to the city, I became a less man than ever, for I had by this transaction made myself many enemies among the populace; and the Governor (with whose family our public disputes had long placed me in an unfriendly light, and the services I had lately rendered him not being of the kind that make a man acceptable), thinking it a favorable opportunity, joined the whole weight of the Proprietary interest to get me out of the Assembly."

The rioters having advanced as far as Germantown, within six miles of Philadelphia, Franklin, with three other influential citizens, was deputed to go out and confer with them. The deputation was received with respect, and prevailed upon the rioters to abandon their hostile project. Franklin's conduct was the more creditable throughout this affair, as it exposed him to the abatement of his popularity among a class from whom he had hitherto derived much political support.

He was at this time a member of the Board of Commissioners for the disposal of the public money in carrying on the war against the Indians, and his labors in this capacity were quite arduous. He still held the office of Postmaster-general. In the spring of 1763 he made a tour through the northern colonies, to inspect and regulate the post-offices. He travelled some sixteen hundred miles, and did not get home till the beginning of November. He was accompanied, during a considerable part of the journey, by his daughter, on horseback.

Governor Penn was no more fortunate than his predecessors in avoiding collisions with the Assembly. Franklin, who had resumed his place in that body, was still the leader of the opposition. A militia bill, which he had framed, was vetoed by the Governor, who claimed the appointment of officers, and made other arbitrary demands which were inadmissible. The Paxton riots showed the danger of the absence of an organized military force. Franklin published an account of the loss of the militia bill, and he did not spare the Proprietary party in his animadversions. · Other difficulties ensued between the Assembly and the Governor, in which the latter showed himself intractable. Persuaded that the evils of the Proprietary system were incurable, Franklin, in the early part of 1764, published a tract entitled "Cool Thoughts on the Present Situation of Public Affairs," in which he proposed the substitution of a Royal for a Proprietary government. Numerous petitions to the king in favor of the change were sent in to the Assembly. A petition from the Assembly to the king, to the same effect, was drafted by Franklin, and warmly discussed. John Dickinson, a wealthy lawyer of Philadelphia, was one of the ablest supporters of the Proprietary interest. It being proposed to send Franklin to England as bearer of the petition, Dickinson remarked, in a speech to the Assembly: "The gentleman proposed has been called here to-day *a great luminary of the learned world.* Far be it from me to detract from the merit I admire. Let him still shine, but without wrapping his country in flames. Let him, from a private station, from a smaller sphere, diffuse, as I think he may, a beneficial light; but let him not be made to move and blaze like a comet, to terrify and distress."

Norris, Speaker of the Assembly, was also opposed to Franklin's project, and, refusing to sign the petition, he resigned his seat, and Franklin was chosen in his stead, and signed the petition as Speaker. He was ably seconded in his opposition to the existing system by Joseph Galloway, an eminent lawyer. A speech which the latter delivered in reply to Dickinson was published with a preface by Franklin, which is one of his most adroit and caustic political essays.

At the annual election, in the autumn of 1764, the Proprietary party made great efforts to defeat him; and, after having been elected to the Assembly fourteen successive years, Franklin lost his election by a majority of about twenty-five votes. The Proprietary party were much elated at this result, but their joy was of very transient duration. It was found that the anti-Proprietary party were in a large majority in the Assembly, notwithstanding Franklin's defeat. One of their first acts was to choose him their agent to take charge of their petition to the king for a change of government. Great was the consternation of the Proprietary party on finding that, in excluding Franklin from the Assembly, they had placed him in a position where his powers of opposition were incalculably enlarged. They were greatly enraged at being "headed off" in this unexpected manner. They signed a solemn Protest, which they presented to the Assembly, against Franklin's appointment; but it was refused admission upon the minutes. The vindictive personal opposition raised on this occasion against him was hardly allayed during his whole protracted public career. Wherever slander was busiest, it might be traced to some old grievance connected with the movement against the Proprietary system. Before departing for England on this second mission, he wrote some remarks in reply to the Protest. The opposition to him had come from men with whom he had long been associated both in public and private life. He felt their estrangement deeply. They were men "the very ashes of whose former friendship," he said, he "revered." "I am now," he remarked, in conclusion, "to take leave — perhaps a last leave — of the country I love, and in which I have spent the greatest part of my life. *Esto perpetua!* I wish every kind of prosperity to my friends, and I forgive my enemies."

On leaving Philadelphia to embark for England, he was escorted by a cavalcade of three hundred of his friends to Chester, where he was to go on board his vessel. He sailed the next day, but was detained a night in the Delaware. He arrived at Portsmouth, in England, after a voyage of thirty days. Proceeding at once to London, he established himself in his old quarters at Mrs. Stevenson's. This was in December, 1764.

IV.

In opposition to the remonstrances of Franklin and the agents in England of Massachusetts and Connecticut, a bill for collecting a stamp tax was brought into Parliament early in the year 1765. In reply to a notification, in the winter of 1763–4, that a stamp duty was intended, it was urged by Franklin, in the Assembly of Pennsylvania, that the Colonies had always granted liberally to his majesty on the proper requisitions being made; that they had granted so liberally during the late war that the king had recommended it to Parliament to make them some compensation, and the Parliament accordingly returned them two hundred thousand pounds a year, to be divided among them; that the proposition of taxing them in Parliament was, therefore, both cruel and unjust; that, by the constitution of the Colonies, their business was with the *king* in matters of aid. So far from refusing to grant money, as had been asserted, the Pennsylvania Assembly passed a resolution to the effect that, as they always had, so they always should think it their duty, according to their abilities, to grant aid to the crown whenever required of them in the usual constitutional manner. A copy of this resolution Franklin brought with him to England, and presented it to Mr. Grenville, before the Stamp Act was brought in. Similar resolutions had been passed by other colonies. "Had Mr. Grenville," said Franklin, subsequently, "instead of that act, applied to the king in council for such requisitional letters to be circulated by the Secretary of State, I am sure he would have obtained more money from the Colonies by their voluntary grants than he himself expected from his stamps. But he chose compulsion rather than persuasion, and would not receive from their good-will what he thought he could obtain without it."

The passage of the Stamp Act called forth one unanimous voice of reprobation and protest from the Colonies. The act had been most strenuously opposed by Franklin; but he was subjected, notwithstanding his efforts against it, to charges of having given it his approval. Tucker, Dean of Gloucester, in a book on the colonial troubles, spoke of "a certain American patriot" who had applied for the

4*

appointment of stamp officer in America. It was under stood that the allusion was to Franklin, and he thought it of sufficient importance to notice, which he did in a respect-ful letter to the dean, in which he says : " I beg leave to request that you would reconsider the grounds on which you have ventured to publish an accusation that, if believed, must prejudice me extremely in the opinion of good men, especially in my own country, whence I was sent expressly to oppose the imposition of that tax." All the foundation for the charge appears to have been the simple circumstance that Franklin, in common with other American agents, was drawn in to nominate, at the request of the minister, suitable persons in the Colonies for the proposed new offices. Frank-lin, never imagining that his compliance with this request would be construed into a proof of his approbation of the Stamp Act, nominated Mr. Hughes for the province of Pennsylvania. In concluding his letter to Dean Tucker, Franklin says :

"I desire you to believe that I take kindly, as I ought, your freely mentioning to me ' that it has long appeared to you that I much exceeded the bounds of morality in the methods I pursued for the advancement of the supposed interests of America.' I am sensible there is a good deal of truth in the adage that *our sins and our debts are always more than we take them to be ;* and though I cannot at present, on examination of my conscience, charge myself with any immorality of that kind, it becomes me to suspect that what has *long appeared* to you may have some found-ation. You are so good as to add, that ' if it can be proved you have unjustly suspected me, you shall have a satisfaction in acknowledging the error.' It is often a thing hard to *prove* that suspicions are unjust, even when we know what they are ; and harder, when we are unacquainted with them. I must presume, therefore, that in mentioning them you had an intention of communicating the grounds of them to me, if I should request it ; which I now do, and, I assure you, with a sincere desire and design of amending what you may show me to have been wrong in my conduct, and to thank you for the admonition."

To this reasonable request Franklin never received any reply.

There was a change of ministry in July, 1765, and Mr. Grenville was succeeded in office, as First Lord of the Treasury, by the Marquis of Rockingham. The subject of a repeal of the Stamp Act was the agitating topic before Parliament. Mr. Pitt, afterwards Earl of Chatham, took high ground against the right of the kingdom to lay a tax upon the Colonies. Taxation, he contended, was no part of the governing or legislative power. The taxes were the voluntary gift and grant of the Commons alone. The Commoners of America, represented in their several Assemblies, alone had the constitutional right of giving and granting their own money. Mr. Grenville was one of the principal speakers in reply. His argument was, that protection and obedience being reciprocal, since Great Britain protected America, America was bound to yield obedience.

On the third of February, 1766, Franklin was summoned before the House of Commons, and subjected to an examination upon facts relative to the repeal of the Stamp Act. He was plied with questions by Grenville and his friends and Charles Townshend. Without preparation, he submitted to a series of very close inquiries, various in their character, and demanding very extensive information in the respondent. The promptitude, sagacity and independence of his replies, with the simple and expressive diction in which they were conveyed, and his self-poised but unassuming deportment, commanded the respect of all parties. In answer to the interrogatories addressed to him, he said that there was not gold and silver enough in the Colonies to pay the stamp duty for one year; that it was not true that America was protected by Great Britain, and paid no part of the expense ; that the Colonies raised, clothed and paid, during the last war, near twenty-five thousand men, and spent many millions ; that the temper of America towards Great Britain, before the year 1763, was the best in the world, and to be an *old England man* was of itself a character of some respect, and gave a kind of rank among Americans ; but that their temper now was very much altered.

To the inquiry whether he thought the Americans would submit to pay the stamp duty if it were lessened, he replied, " No, never ! unless compelled by force of arms." " May not a military force carry the Stamp Act into execution ? " asked one of his interrogators. Franklin replied : " Suppose a military force sent into America ; they will find nobody in arms ; what are they, then, to do ? They cannot force a man to take stamps who chooses to do without them. They will not *find* a rebellion ; they may, indeed, *make* one." " Supposing the Stamp Act continued and enforced, do you imagine that ill-humor will induce the Americans to give as much for worse manufactures of their own, and use them in preference to better of ours?" "Yes, I think so. *People will pay as freely to gratify one passion as another,— their resentment as their pride.*" "Would the people at Boston discontinue their trade?" "The merchants are a very small number, compared with the body of the people; and must discontinue their trade, if nobody will buy their goods." "What are the body of the people in the Colonies?" "They are farmers, husbandmen, or planters." "Would they suffer the produce of their lands to rot?" "No; but they would not raise so much. They would manufacture more, and plough less." "I do not know a single article," he subsequently affirmed, "imported into the northern Colonies, that they cannot either do without or make themselves."

In less than three weeks after Franklin's examination, a motion for leave to bring in a bill for the repeal of the American Stamp Act was introduced into the House of Commons. It was vehemently opposed by Grenville. "Do not die," he said, "from the fear of dying. With a little firmness, it will be easy to compel the colonists to obedience." In the course of this debate, Burke made his first speech in the House of Commons. It was in behalf of the colonists, and drew from Mr. Pitt a warm encomium. In spite of much influential opposition, a bill to repeal the Stamp Act was introduced on the 26th of February. It received the royal assent on the 18th of March. But the tranquillizing effect of this repeal among the colonists was marred by the simultaneous passage of a declaratory act, as it was called, by which it was asserted that the king, with the consent of the Lords and Commons in Parliament assembled, had undoubted power and authority to make laws of sufficient force "to bind the Colonies and people of America in all cases whatsoever." This declaration was as absurd and supererogatory as it was offensive; and it only added fuel to the flames of resentment which the passage of the Stamp Act had kindled, and which its repeal, in consequence of this ungracious asseveration, did not suffice to extinguish.

Franklin had been instructed by the Pennsylvania Assembly to solicit the repeal of the restraints laid upon the issue of paper money as a legal tender. Finding that the time for urging the repeal was unpropitious, and fearing lest the agitation of the question might lead to the adoption on the part of the ministry of a scheme, entertained by Mr. Townshend, for the manufacture by the British government of paper money for the Colonies, he recommended to the Assembly that some means should be resorted to by which the credit of issues of paper money could be supported without making it a legal tender. The principal object of his mission was not meanwhile forgotten. The question of purchasing from the Proprietaries of Pennsylvania their right of jurisdiction, leaving to them their lands, was discussed in the British cabinet, but the continued warlike tone of the colonists interrupted and soon rendered nugatory the consideration of the subject. There began to be a prospect that the difficulties with the Proprietaries would be settled simultaneously with those with the "mother country," and in a like summary manner.

By correspondence with friends in both countries, Franklin did much to enlighten public opinion in regard to the claims and rights of the Colonies, and the injustice of the ministerial policy. "The British empire," he contended, "was not a single state; it comprehended many; and, though the Parliament of Great Britain had arrogated to itself the power of taxing the Colonies, it had no more right to do so than it had to tax Hanover. The Colonies had the same king, but not the same legislatures." To Lord Kames he wrote in 1767 : "Every man in England seems to consider himself as a piece of a sovereign over America; seems to jostle himself into the throne with the king, and talks of *our subjects in America*." "America, an immense territory, favored by nature, with all advantages of climate, soils, great navigable rivers, lakes, &c., must become a great country, populous and mighty ; and will, *in a less time than is generally conceived*, be able to shake off any shackles that may be imposed upon her, and perhaps place them on the imposers."

V.

THE act of Parliament for quartering troops in the Colonies had caused great dissatisfaction. The chancellor of the Exchequer, Charles Townshend, in January, 1767, brought forward a new scheme for raising a revenue in America, including not only the maintenance of a standing army, but the provision of permanent salaries for the governors and judges, rendering them independent of the Colonial Assemblies. This scheme was adopted by Parliament with little opposition. A Board of Revenue Commissioners for America, to have its seat at Boston, was established; and not only tea, but several articles of British produce, were made objects of custom-house taxation in the Colonies. These measures were there regarded as quite as odious as the Stamp Act; for it was contended by the leading colonists that "taxes on trade, if designed to raise a revenue, were just as much a violation of their rights as any other tax." This position was advocated by Franklin's old political opponent, John Dickinson, in his celebrated "Farmer's Letters," a work which Franklin, forgetting all former differences, caused to be reprinted and circulated in London, prefacing the edition with commendatory remarks of his own. Although he had at first made a distinction between taxes on imported commodities and internal taxes, and was of opinion that the American grievance was not that Britain put duties upon her own manufactures exported to the Colonies, but that she forbade the latter to buy the like manufactures from any other country, he finally adopted the views advanced by Dickinson in Pennsylvania, and which were eloquently maintained by James Otis in Massachusetts.

The ministerial measures were met with a determined opposition in the Colonies, especially in Boston, where the newly-appointed revenue commissioners had to fly for their lives. New supplies of British troops were now poured into that refractory town to quell the spirit of resistance. "The Boston *Gazette* has occasioned some heats, and the Boston resolutions a prodigious clatter," writes Franklin to his son, under date of London, January 9th, 1768; "I have endeavored to palliate matters for them as well as I can. I send you my manuscript of one paper, though I think you take the *Chronicle.* The editor of that paper, one Jones, seems a Grenvillian, or is very cautious, as you will see by his corrections and omissions. He has drawn the teeth and pared the nails of my paper, so that it can neither scratch nor bite. It seems only to paw and mumble." The piece in the *Chronicle,* to which Franklin here alludes, was entitled *Causes of the American Discontents.* Two other pieces, one on *Smuggling,* and the other on the *Laboring Poor,* were published about this time; the former in the *Chronicle,* and the latter in the *Gentleman's Magazine.*

On the change of ministry in 1768, the office of Secretary for the Colonies was created, and given to Lord Hillsborough, "a little alert man of business, but passionate and headstrong," as Franklin describes him. "I am told there has been a talk of getting me appointed under-secretary to Lord Hillsborough," he writes to his son; "but with little likelihood, as it is a settled point here that I am too much of an American." Indeed, according to his own expression, he had rendered himself suspected, by his impartiality, "in England of being too much of an American, and in America of being too much of an Englishman." Instead of being appointed to a new office, there was now a motion to deprive him of his deputy-postmastership for the Colonies. "If Mr. Grenville," he writes to his son, "comes into power again in any department respecting America, I must refuse to accept of anything that may seem to put me in his power, because I apprehend a breach between the two countries; and that refusal might give offence. So that you see a turn of a die may make a great difference in our affairs. We may be either promoted or discarded."

A report that Franklin was intriguing for office under the ministry reached Pennsylvania, and was readily entertained by his political adversaries. Did not the whole tenor of his life and correspondence contradict it? A moment's consideration will show that he was in such a position that he had only to give in his adhesion to the ministry to obtain any office that he might in reason covet.

He made two visits to the continent, while affairs were

ripening between Great Britain and her Colonies.   One of these visits was in the summer of 1766, and the other in September, 1767.   In both he was accompanied by his "steady, good friend, Sir John Pringle."   He was gone eight weeks on his first excursion, and visited Gottingen, Hanover, and some of the principal cities of Germany.   In the second visit, he went to Paris, and was received with marked attention.   At Versailles he was presented to the king and his sisters, and in Paris he formed the acquaintance of many distinguished men of science.   He subsequently told John Adams that, during this visit, Sir John Pringle "did all his conversation for him, as interpreter, and that he understood and spoke French with great difficulty" until his official visit in 1776.   If this were so, Franklin must have acquired his proficiency in French after his sixty-first year.   He again visited Paris in the summer of 1769, passing several weeks there.

In 1768 he was appointed agent for Georgia; and, two years later, for Massachusetts.   He has given an amusing account of his interview with Lord Hillsborough, on going to present his credentials as agent for the last-named province.   Franklin had checkmated his lordship in several political movements, and had been in the habit of writing very freely to his correspondents in both countries in relation to ministerial measures.   An indiscreet or treacherous use was undoubtedly made of some of his letters, by publishing them, or forwarding them to the ministers.   The threat was thrown out that he would lose his appointment in the American post-office.   He repudiated the idea that every man who holds an office should act with the ministry, and he continued to be independent in this regard.   "Possibly," he said, "they may remove me; but no apprehension of that sort will, I trust, make the least alteration in my political conduct.   My rule, in which I have always found satisfaction, is, never to turn aside in public affairs through views of private interest; but to go straight forward in doing what appears to me right at the time, leaving the consequences with Providence."

On Franklin's introducing himself to Lord Hillsborough as the authorized agent of Massachusetts, his lordship interrupted him with, "I must set you right there, Mr. Franklin; you are not agent." "I do not understand your lordship. I have the appointment in my pocket." His lordship remarked that the bill had not received the assent of Governor Hutchinson. "There was no bill, my lord. It was by a vote of the House." His lordship summoned his secretary, and asked for the Governor's letter ; but, on examination, found that it contained nothing in relation to the agent. "I thought it could not well be," said Franklin, "as my letters are by the last ships, and they mention no such thing. Here is the authentic copy of the vote of the House appointing me, in which there is no mention of any *act* intended. Will your lordship please to look at it?" His lordship took the paper reluctantly, and, without condescending to read it, launched into a rebuke of the practice of appointing agents by vote of the Assembly, without the Governor's assent. Franklin suggested that, inasmuch as the agent was employed to transact the business of the people and not of the Governor, the people had a right to appoint their agents, independently of him, through their representatives. His lordship would not be convinced against his will. He handed back to Franklin his credentials unread ; and Franklin, whose demeanor thus far had been marked with the most imperturbable good-humor, notwithstanding his provocations, took his leave, sarcastically remarking to his lordship that it was plainly "of very little consequence whether the appointment was acknowledged or not, for it was clear to his mind that, as affairs were now administered, an agent could be of no use to any of the Colonies."

In 1772, Lord Hillsborough gave in his resignation, a step which Franklin had done much to accelerate, by overruling his Report on a proposed grant of land in Ohio, and thus exhibiting to the king and ministers his lordship's incompetency to manage colonial affairs. To a question put by a person high at court to Franklin, whether he could name another person likely to be more acceptable to the Colonies, he replied : "Yes, there is Lord Dartmouth ; we liked him very well when he was at the head of the board formerly, and in all probability should again." Lord Dartmouth was appointed to succeed Lord Hillsborough.

Prior to Lord Hillsborough's resignation, Franklin was

5

entertained by him, at his place in Ireland.   In a letter to
Thomas Cushing, Franklin writes : "Being in Dublin at
the same time with his lordship, I met with him accidentally at the Lord Lieutenant's, who had happened to invite
us to dine with a large company on the same day.   As
there was something curious in our interview, I must give
you an account of it.   He was surprisingly civil, and urged
my fellow-travellers and me to call at his house in our
intended journey northward, where we might be sure of
better accommodations than the inns would afford us.   He
pressed us so politely, that it was not easy to refuse without
apparent rudeness, as we must pass through his town,
Hillsborough, and by his door ; and, therefore, as it might
afford an opportunity of saying something on American
affairs, I concluded to comply with his invitation.   His
lordship went home some time before we left Dublin.   We
called upon him, and were detained at his house four days,
during which time he entertained us with great civility, and
a particular attention to me, that appeared the more extraordinary, as I knew that just before we left London he had
expressed himself concerning me in very angry terms, calling me a republican, a factious, mischievous fellow, and the
like.

"He seemed attentive to everything that might make my
stay in his house agreeable to me, and put his eldest son,
Lord Killwarling, into his phaeton with me, to drive me a
round of forty miles, that I might see the country, the seats
and manufactures, covering me with his own great-coat, lest
I should take cold.   In short, he seemed extremely solicit-
ous to impress me, and the Colonies through me, with a good
opinion of him.   All which I could not but wonder at,
knowing that he likes neither them nor me ; and I thought
it inexplicable but on the supposition that he apprehended
an approaching storm, and was desirous of lessening beforehand the number of enemies he had so imprudently created.
But, if he takes no steps towards withdrawing the troops,
repealing the duties, restoring the Castle,* or recalling the
offensive instructions, I shall think all the plausible behavior
I have described is meant only, by patting and stroking the

* Castle William, in Boston Harbor.

horse, to make him more patient, while the reins are drawn tighter, and the spurs set deeper into his sides."

On his return to London, Franklin waited on Lord Hillsborough, to thank him for his civilities in Ireland, and to discourse with him on a Georgia affair. "The porter," says Franklin, "told me he was not at home. I left my card, went another time, and received the same answer, though I knew he was at home, a friend of mine being with him. After intermissions of a week each, I made two more visits, and received the same answer. The last time was on a levee day, when a number of carriages were at his door. My coachman, driving up, alighted and was opening the coach-door, when the porter seeing me, came out, and surlily chid the coachman for opening the door before he had inquired whether my lord was at home ; and then turning to me, said, ' My lord is not at home.' I have never since been nigh him, and we have only abused one another at a distance."

Franklin was destined to experience still another instance of his lordship's caprice. Being at Oxford with Lord Le Despencer, Lord H. called upon Lord Le D., who was occupying the same chamber with Franklin, in Queen's College. "I was in the inner room, shifting," writes Franklin, in a letter to his son, "and heard his voice, but did not see him, as he went down stairs immediately with Lord Le D., who mentioning that I was above, he returned directly, and came to me in the pleasantest manner imaginable. ' Dr F.,' said he, ' I did not know till this minute that you were here, and I am come back *to make you my bow*. I am glad to see you at Oxford, and that you look so well,' &c. In return for this extravagance, I complimented him on his son's performance in the theatre, though, indeed, it was but indifferent,—so that account was settled. For as people say, when they are angry, if he *strike me*, I'll strike him again ; I think sometimes it may be right to say, *if he flatters me, I'll flatter him again*. This is *lex talionis*, returning offences in kind. His son, however (Lord Fairford), is a valuable young man, and his daughters, Ladies Mary and Charlotte, most amiable young women. My quarrel is only with him, who of all the men I ever met with is surely the most unequal in his treatment of people, the most insincere, and the most wrong-headed."

In April 1770, Parliament repealed the whole of Townshend's act for raising a revenue in America, excepting the tax on tea. But as the exception involved the whole principle against which the Colonists were contending, their dissatisfaction was increased, rather than abated, by this partially retrograde legislation. Franklin had, for the last three years, urged upon Americans the adoption of resolutions to forego the use of imported goods. To a committee of Philadelphia merchants he writes: " I hope you will — if backed by the general honest resolutions of the people to buy British goods of no others, but to manufacture for themselves, or use colony manufactures only — be the means, under God, of recovering and establishing the freedom of our country entire, and of handing it down complete to posterity." In reply to questions addressed to him, in November 1769, by his friend William Strahan, member of Parliament, he had given it as his opinion that a repeal of the revenue laws, excepting the duty on tea, would *not* fully satisfy the Colonists,— an opinion which was soon abundantly verified. He was now the commissioned agent of four of the American Colonies, namely, Pennsylvania, Georgia, Massachusetts and New Jersey, and his time was fully occupied.

VI.

NOTWITHSTANDING the absorbing nature of his political business, Franklin gave much of his attention to scientific and economical questions of public utility. He corresponded with Dr. Cadwallader Evans, of Philadelphia, in regard to the culture of silk, and earnestly recommended a trial of the experiment in America. He hoped that our people would not be disheartened by a few accidents; "by diligence and patience the mouse ate in twain the cable." In 1771 he made an excursion through various parts of England, Wales, Ireland and Scotland. At Leeds, he visited his attached friend Dr. Priestley, at Manchester, Dr. Percival, and at Litchfield, Dr. Erasmus Darwin, the celebrated poet and naturalist. In Ireland, he was handsomely entertained "by both parties, the courtiers and the patriots." The Irish Parliament being in session, he was, by a formal vote, admitted within the bar of the House, as a member of the Pennsylvania Assembly. In Scotland, he passed some days with Lord Kames and David Hume, and received many civilities from Dr. Robertson, Sir Alexander Dick, and other distinguished men. At Preston, in Lancashire, he met, for the first time, his son-in-law, Mr. Richard Bache, by whose deportment and character he was agreeably impressed. With his old friend, Dr. Shipley, Bishop of St. Asaph, he passed some weeks. Miss Georgiana Shipley, a daughter of the "good bishop," was subsequently one of Franklin's favored correspondents.

We gather, from his letters to his son about this time, that, though well pleased with his residence in England, he had a strong inclination to return to America. He writes :

"Nothing can be more agreeable than my situation, more especially as I hope for less embarrassment from the new administration. A general respect paid me by the learned — a number of friends and acquaintance among them, with whom I have a pleasing intercourse ; a character of so much weight, that it has protected me when some in power would have done me injury, and continued me in an office they would have deprived me of ; my company so much desired, that I seldom dine at home in winter, and could spend the whole summer in the country-houses of inviting friends, if I chose it. Learned and ingenious foreigners that come to England almost all make a point of visiting me (for my reputation is still higher abroad than here); several of the foreign ambassadors have assiduously cultivated my acquaintance, treating me as one of their *corps*, partly, I believe, from the desire they have from time to time of hearing something of American affairs, an object become of importance in foreign courts, who begin to hope Britain's alarming power will be diminished by the defection of her colonies ; and partly, that they may have an opportunity of introducing me to the gentlemen of their country who desire it. The king, too, has lately been heard to speak of me with regard. These are flattering circumstances ; but a violent longing for home sometimes seizes me, which I can no otherwise subdue, but by promising myself a return next spring, or next autumn, and so forth. As to returning hither, if I once go back, I have no thoughts of it. I am too far advanced in life to propose three voyages more. I have some important affairs to settle at home ; and, considering my double expenses here and there, I hardly think my salaries fully compensate the disadvantages. The late change, however (of the American minister), being thrown into the balance, determines me to stay another winter."

In the summer of 1769 Franklin was one of a committee appointed by the Royal Society, to consider the best method

5*

of protecting the cathedral of St. Paul's from lightning
The committee recommended the application of electrical
conductors, and their report was adopted. In August,
1772, another committee of the Royal Society, of which
Franklin was a member, visited, under the direction of the
government, the powder magazines at Purfleet, for the purpose of considering the most effectual means for protecting
them from lightning. Franklin drew up a report, which
was accepted, in which the erection of pointed rods was
advised. A controversy, of some notoriety in its day, grew
out of the dissent of one member of this committee, a Mr.
Wilson, who contended that the conductors ought to be
blunt, inasmuch as if pointed they would attract the lightning. To this Franklin replied that the attraction was the
very thing desired, for the charge is thereby silently and
gradually drawn from the building, and conveyed without
danger to the earth. Mr. Wilson still clung to his theory
in regard to blunt conductors, and persuaded the king to
change his pointed ones for blunt, at Buckingham House.
One of Franklin's friends (Dr. Ingenhousz, a member of
the Royal Society) wrote of Wilson's charlatanry in so
heated a manner, that Franklin wittily remarked: "He
seems as much heated about this *one point* as the Jansen-
ists and Molinists were about the five." The following
clever epigram, upon the subject of the king's yielding to
Wilson's arguments in opposition to Franklin's, appeared
about this time :

> "While you, great GEORGE, for safety hunt,
>   And sharp conductors change for blunt,
>   The empire 's out of joint ;
>   Franklin a wiser course pursues,
>   And all your thunder fearless views,
>   By keeping to the point."

In 1773, while at the summer residence of his friend,
Lord Le Despencer, Franklin assisted that gentleman in
preparing an abridgment of the Book of Common Prayer.
He wrote a Preface, in which he expresses his belief that
"this shortened method, or one of the same kind, better
executed, would further religion, remove animosity, and
occasion a more frequent attendance on the worhip of
God." The Catechism he abridged by retaining of it only

the two questions, "What is your duty to God? What is your duty to your neighbor?" with answers. "The Psalms," he tells us, "were much contracted by leaving out the repetitions (of which I found more than I could have imagined) and the imprecations, which appeared not to suit well the Christian doctrine of forgiveness of injuries, and doing good to enemies. The book was printed for Wilkie, in St. Paul's Church-yard, but never much noticed. Some were given away, very few sold, and I suppose the bulk became waste paper."

A fifth edition of Franklin's philosophical writings appeared about the same time in London. Two French editions had been published in Paris, and a third was now issued, the translation of which was executed by his friend, Barbeu Dubourg, described by John Adams as "a physician, a bachelor, a man of letters, and of good character, but of little consequence in the French world;" "a jolly companion, and very fond of anecdotes."

Besides some philosophical pieces, chiefly on electrical subjects, written about this time, Franklin published anonymously his "Rules for Reducing a Great Empire to a Small One," and his "Edict by the King of Prussia." Much literary skill is apparent in the construction of these *jeux d'esprit*. Of the first, Lord Mansfield remarked, it was "very able and very artful indeed." Of the effect of the latter, Franklin gives the following pleasant account, in a letter to his son:

"What made it the more noticed here was, that people, in reading it, were, as the phrase is, *taken in*, till they had got half through it, and imagined it a real edict, to which mistake I suppose the King of Prussia's *character* must have contributed. I was down at Lord Le Despencer's when the post brought that day's papers. Mr. Whitehead was there, too (Paul Whitehead, the author of Manners), who runs early through all the papers, and tells the company what he finds remarkable. He had them in another room, and we were chatting in the breakfast-parlor, when he came running in to us, out of breath, with the paper in his hand. 'Here!' says he, 'here's news for ye! Here's the King of Prussia claiming a right to this kingdom!' All stared, and I as much as anybody; and he went on to read it. When he had read two or three paragraphs, a gentleman present said, 'Hang his impudence! I dare say we shall hear by next post that he is upon his march with one hundred thousand men to back this.' Whitehead, who is very shrewd, soon after began to smoke it, and looking in my face said, '*I'll be hanged if this is not some of your American jokes upon us.*' The reading went on, and ended with abundance of laughing, and a general verdict that it was a fair hit: and the piece was cut out of the paper, and preserved in my lord's collection."

VII.

EARLY in 1774 Franklin was dismissed by the ministry from his office of Deputy Postmaster of the Colonies. The immediate cause was his agency in communicating to the public certain original letters, written in Massachusetts, by Governor Hutchinson, Lieutenant-governor Oliver, and others, and addressed to Mr. Thomas Whately, a member of Parliament. These letters, recommending coërcive measures against the Colonists, and intimately affecting their interests, were transmitted by Franklin to Thomas Cushing, chairman of the Massachusetts Committee of Correspondence. In the Colonies they excited the deepest indignation towards the writers, and gratitude to Franklin for exposing what seemed a course of treachery on the part of the Governor and Lieutenant-governor of Massachusetts. The House of Representatives agreed on a petition and remonstrance to his majesty, in which they charged those functionaries with giving private, partial and false information, and prayed for their speedy removal from office.

In transmitting this correspondence to Mr. Cushing, Franklin says: "I am not at liberty to tell through what channel I received it; and I have engaged that it shall not be printed, nor copies taken of the whole, or any part of it; but I am allowed to let it be seen by some men of worth in the Province, for their satisfaction only. In confidence of your preserving inviolably my engagement, I send you enclosed the original letters, to obviate every pretence of unfairness in copying, interpolation or omission." He added a request that they should be returned. Three individuals, besides himself, one of whom was Mr. John Temple, were aware of their transmission.

The news being received in England of the publication of these letters in Boston, a duel ensued between Mr. Temple and Mr. William Whately, brother of the deceased member of Parliament to whom they had been addressed. Mr. Temple had obtained permission to examine certain papers in the possession of Mr. William Whately, and the latter now charged him with having taken occasion to procure these letters. Mr. Whately was wounded, though not dangerously, in the duel; and Franklin, who had not anticipated any such quarrel, fearing a renewal of the duel, addressed an explanation to the *Public Advertiser*, in which he exonerated Mr. Temple, and took upon himself the responsibility of having "obtained and transmitted to Boston the letters in question;" adding that they were never in Mr. Whately's possession. A stupendous clamor was hereupon raised against Franklin by the ministerial party. Mr. Whately, acting, probably, under the ministerial nod, though he had been indebted to Franklin for the recovery of a considerable property in Pennsylvania, now "clapped a chancery suit on his back," praying the Lord Chancellor that Franklin might "be obliged to discover how he came by the letters, what number of copies he had printed, and to account with him for the profits, &c. &c.," in allusion to which Franklin ironically says : "Those as little acquainted with law as I was (who, indeed, never before had a lawsuit of any kind) may wonder at this as much as I did; but I have now learned that, in chancery practice, though the *defendant* must swear to the truth of every point in his answer, the *plaintiff* is not put to his oath, or obliged to have the least regard to truth, in his bill, *but is allowed to lie as much as he pleases.* I do not understand this, unless it be for the encouragement of business."

. Franklin's answer, upon oath, was : "That the letters in question were given to him, and came into his hands, *as agent for the House of Representatives of the Province of Massachusetts Bay ;* that when given to him he did not know to whom they had been addressed,—no address appearing upon them,— nor did he know before that any such letters existed; that he had not been for many years concerned in printing ; that he did not cause the letters to be printed, nor direct the doing it; that he did not erase any address that might have been on the letters ; nor did he know that any other person had made such erasure; that he did, as agent to the Province, transmit (as he apprehended it his duty to do) the said letters to one of the committee, with whom he had been directed to correspond, inasmuch as, in his (Franklin's) judgment, they related to matters of great public importance to that Province, and were put into his hands for that purpose," &c.

The chancery suit, instituted for the purpose of disgracing Franklin, was finally dropped. "You can have no conception," he writes to Thomas Cushing, "of the rage the ministerial people have been in with me, on account of my transmitting those letters." Their vindictiveness was somewhat abated by Wedderburn's scurrilous attack upon him, at the hearing before the Privy Council, to which body the king had referred the petition against Hutchinson and Oliver. This hearing had been fixed for January 11, 1774, "at the Cockpit,"— name ominous of the quality of that vituperation with which Wedderburn, the King's Solicitor, was charged. At the appointed time Franklin appeared, and then for the first time learned that Wedderburn was present as counsel for Hutchinson and Oliver. Franklin remarked that, as he had supposed the question to be rather one "of civil and political prudence" than one involving any point of law or right, he had omitted to engage counsel in behalf of the petition; but he now requested that he might employ counsel. To this the Chief Justice assented, and the hearing was deferred three weeks.

Meanwhile the grossest abuse was launched at Franklin. Hints were even thrown out that there were some thoughts of apprehending him, seizing his papers, and sending him to Newgate. Confident that "time would soon lay the dust which prejudice and party had raised," he gave himself little concern. He engaged for the Assembly's counsel the celebrated John Dunning and Mr. John Lee. The scene before the Privy Council, at the next consideration of the petition, is thus described by Franklin:

"Notwithstanding the intimations I had received, I could not believe that the Solicitor-general would be permitted to wander from the question before their lordships, into a new case, the accusation of another person for another matter, not cognizable before them, who could not expect to be there so accused, and therefore could not be prepared for his defence. And yet all this happened, and in all probability was preconcerted; for all the courtiers were invited, as to an entertainment, and there never was such an appearance of privy counsellors on any occasion,— not less than thirty-five, besides an immense crowd of other auditors.

"The hearing began by reading my letter to Lord Dartmouth enclosing the petition, then the petition itself, the resolves, and lastly the letters, the Solicitor-general making no objections, nor asking any of the questions he had talked of at the preceding board.   Our counsel then opened the matter, upon their general plan, and acquitted themselves very handsomely; only Mr. Dunning, having a disorder on his lungs, that weakened his voice exceedingly, was not so perfectly heard as one could have wished.   The Solicitor-general then went into what he called a history of the province for the last ten years, and bestowed plenty of abuse upon it, mingled with encomium on the Governors.   But the favorite part of his discourse was levelled at your agent, who stood there the butt of his invective ribaldry for near an hour, not a single lord adverting to the impropriety and indecency of treating a public messenger in so ignominious a manner, who was present only as the person delivering your petition, with the consideration of which no part of *his* conduct had any concern.   If he had done a wrong in obtaining and transmitting the letters, that was not the tribunal where he was to be accused and tried.   The cause was already before the Chancellor.   Not one of their lordships checked and recalled the orator to the business before them, but, on the contrary, a very few excepted, they seemed to enjoy highly the entertainment, and frequently burst out in loud applauses.   This part of his speech was thought so good, that they have since printed it, in order to defame me everywhere, and particularly to destroy my reputation on your side of the water; but the grosser parts of the abuse are omitted, appearing, I suppose, in their own eyes, too foul to be seen on paper; so that the speech, compared to what it was, is now perfectly decent.   I send you one of the copies.   My friends advise me to write an answer, which I purpose immediately.   The reply of Mr. Dunning concluded.   Being very ill, and much incommoded by standing so long, his voice was so feeble as to be scarce audible.   What little I heard was very well said, but appeared to have little effect.

"Their Lordships' report, which I send you, is dated the same day.   It contains a severe censure, as you will see, on the petition and the petitioners, and, as I think, a very unfair conclusion, from my silence, that the charge of surreptitiously obtaining the letters was a true one; though the Solicitor, as appears in the printed speech, had acquainted them that that matter was before the Chancellor; and my counsel had stated the impropriety of my answering there to charges then trying in another court. In truth, I came by them honorably, and my intention in sending them was virtuous, if an endeavor to lessen the breach between two states of the same empire be such, by showing that the injuries complained of by one of them did not proceed from the other, but from traitors among themselves."

It should be remembered that these letters, which Wedderburn represented as "private and confidential," were addressed by public officers to a public officer, with the view of affecting public measures, and producing (to use Hutchinson's own words) "an abridgment of English liberties in the Colonies."

Wedderburn, with his facile assumption of indignation, instead of defending the defendants, entered upon a bitter and carefully-prepared invective against Franklin. "The letters," said the adroit lawyer, "could not have come to Dr. Franklin by fair means." "I hope, my lords, you will mark and brand the man, for the honor of this country, of Europe, and of mankind." "He has forfeited all the respect of societies and of men. Into what companies will he hereafter go with an unembarrassed face, or the honest intrepidity of virtue? Men will watch him with a jealous eye; they will hide their papers from him, and lock up their escritoires. He will henceforth esteem it a libel to be called a man of letters, *homo trium literarum.*"* "Amidst these tragical events, of one person nearly murdered, of another answerable for the issue,— of a worthy governor hurt in his dearest interests, the fate of America in suspense,— here is a man, who, with the utmost insensibility of remorse, stands up and avows himself the author of all. I can compare it only to *Zanga* in Dr. Young's *Revenge:*

> ' Know, then, 't was I ;
> I forged the letter — I disposed the picture —
> I hated — I despised — and I destroy.' "

* That is, the word fur (or *thief*).

Such was the clever clap-trap, gravely substituted for rational argument, uttered before a body of men assembled to consider the application of a provincial legislature for a change of local rulers! Franklin's demeanor, during this indecent invective, was calm and dignified. Dr. Priestly, who was present with Edmund Burke, says that "the real object of the court was to insult Dr. Franklin;" but that he stood "without the least apparent emotion" during the whole of Wedderburn's ribald attack. The lords of the council seemed to enjoy it highly, however. All of them, with the exception of Lord North, "frequently laughed outright" at the abuse heaped upon the venerable sage, then in his sixty-ninth year, whose life had been so largely devoted to the advancement of the interests of humanity. He had been the zealous and vigilant champion of the political rights of the Colonists; and this their lordships could not forgive. He had insisted upon his countrymen's participation in all the rights of Englishmen; and this their lordships were not disposed to allow. He had vindicated the character and courage of Americans; and it was the *ton* among the "hereditary legislators" of England to speak of them as a cowardly and inferior race. It was not, therefore, a matter of surprise to anybody, that the decision at which their lordships arrived was adverse to the Assembly and to Franklin. The Assembly's petition was pronounced "groundless, vexatious and scandalous," "founded upon resolutions formed on false and erroneous allegations," and "calculated only for the seditious purpose of keeping up a spirit of clamor and discontent" in the Province. As for Franklin, he was the next day dismissed from his office of Deputy Postmaster for the Colonies. Their lordships were resolved that no effort on their part should be wanting to "mark and brand" him as Wedderburn had recommended. The British press sedulously lent its aid, and public opinion was so generally prejudiced against him, that David Hume, with whom he had lodged in Edinburgh, on the most friendly terms, wrote, under date of February 3, 1774, to a correspondent: "Pray what strange accounts are these we bear of Franklin's conduct? I am very slow in believing that he has been guilty in the extreme degree that is pretended; *though I always knew him to be a very factious*

6

man,— and a faction, next to fanaticism, is of all passions the most destructive of morality. How is it he got possession of these letters? I hear that Wedderburn's treatment of him before the Council was most cruel, *without being in the least degree blamable.*" In spite of Hume's amateur republicanism, he seems to have found it difficult, in his imagination, to reconcile a person's opposition to the ministry with freedom from factious motives.

Through this storm of obloquy and detraction, Franklin bore himself with the tranquillity of a philosopher and the moderation of a Christian. "I made," he says, "no justification of myself from the charges brought against me. I made no return of the injury, by abusing my adversaries, but held a cool, sullen silence, reserving myself to some future opportunity; for which conduct I had several reasons, not necessary here to specify." "As I grow old, I grow less concerned about censure, when I am satisfied that I act rightly." He was content to bide his time, confidently though not vindictively. He never divulged the mode in which he came into possession of the letters which were made the subject of so much controversy; but that he came by them honorably we have his own ample assurance, fortified by concurrent circumstances. He lived to see the parties who had exulted in the temporary obscuration of his reputation suing for his influence to avert the consequences which he had long predicted as the result of ministerial arrogance and infatuation. In less than a year after the scene at the Council Board, Lord Howe appealed to his magnanimity not to consider his ill treatment by the ministry; that "some of them were ashamed of it, and sorry it had happened; *which he supposed must be sufficient to abate resentment in a great and generous mind.*"*

---

* In a letter to Dr. Hosack, John Adams states that Sir John Temple told him, in Holland, that he had furnished the Hutchinson and Oliver letters to Dr. Franklin. Mr. Adams adds, however, his belief that they were delivered through the hands of a third person, a member of Parliament. This is consistent with Franklin's own account.

VIII.

FRANKLIN, if he did not originally suggest the plan of a Continental Congress, was among its earliest approvers. In a letter, dated July 7, 1773, to Thomas Cushing, of Massachusetts, he says: "It is natural to suppose, as you do, that, if the oppressions continue, a Congress may grow out of that correspondence. Nothing could more alarm our ministers; but, if the Colonies agree to hold a Congress, I do not see how it can be prevented." In a letter of the same date, to be read to the Assembly, he says: " Perhaps it would be best and fairest for the Colonies, in a general Congress, now in peace to be assembled, or by means of the correspondence lately proposed, after a full and solemn assertion and declaration of their rights, to engage firmly with each other, that they will never grant aids to the crown, in any general war, till those rights are recognized by the king and both houses of Parliament; communicating at the same time to the crown this their resolution. Such a step, I imagine, will bring the dispute to a crisis." From these passages ·it would seem that the scheme had been already agitated. It grew naturally out of the exigences of the times, and probably no Province or individual can rightly claim the merit of its origin.

The First Continental Congress assembled at Philadelphia, September 17, 1774. In December following, their petition to the king was forwarded under cover to Franklin. It was transferred by the king to Parliament, by which body it was contemptuously rejected. It was the last tender of the olive-branch, and it was spurned. Franklin now began to think of returning to America. He was regarded with a good deal of distrust by the ministry, who, it was privately intimated to him, entertained some thoughts of arresting him as a fomenter of rebellion in the Colonies. A coalition on the American question being talked of among the opposition in Parliament to the ministry, he endeavored to promote it, and, in conversation with members of the minority in both Houses, he "besought and conjured them most earnestly not to suffer, by their little misunderstandings, so glorious a fabric as the present British empire to be demolished by these blunderers." But the "blunderers" blundered on, although some eloquent voices were raised in Parliament to deter them; among others, that of Lord Chatham, whose intrepid words, "I rejoice that America has resisted," though they elicited a cry of horror from the ministerial benches, thrilled like a trumpet-note through the hearts of the Colonists.

Franklin had long admired Lord Chatham at a distance. Circumstances now brought them together, and their intercourse was throughout of a character honorable to both parties. His lordship's noble vindication of Franklin from the aspersions of Lord Sandwich in the House of Lords is a tribute that outweighs all the abuse ever lavished upon the American sage by the supporters of the ministry. Franklin's own account of his acquaintance with Lord Chatham will be found in another part of this volume.

An aspersion upon his personal truthfulness is contained in Lord Mahon's recent History of England, based upon an apparent discrepancy in Franklin's assurance to Lord Chatham that "America did not aim at independence," and the statement of Josiah Quincy, Jr., that Franklin's ideas were "extended upon the broad scale of total emancipation."*
A little attention to dates would have satisfied his lordship, in spite of his strong tory bias, of the rank injustice of his charge against Franklin of playing "a double game." Franklin's assurance to Lord Chatham was given in August 1774, and was unquestionably sincere. The letter of Josiah Quincy, Jr., containing the expression quoted to give countenance to the imputation of duplicity, bears date November 24, 1774. During the interval between these two dates, the probabilities of a reconciliation between Great Britain and the Colonies had greatly diminished. A general election had taken place, which had given Lord North and his colleagues an overwhelming majority in Parliament. Hopes of redress from that quarter were therefore at an end. Franklin began to see that a contest was inevitable,

* Under date of London, November 24, 1784, Josiah Quincy, Jr., wrote home to Boston: "Dr. Franklin is an American in heart and soul. You may trust him; his ideas are not contracted within the narrow limits of exemption from taxes, but are extended upon the broad scale of total emancipation."

and that "total emancipation" must now be the object of the Colonists. If he had entertained contrary views a few months before, he entertained them in common with Washington, John Adams, Jay, Jefferson, Madison, and other foremost men of the Revolution. The attempt of Lord Mahon to show that there was any prevarication in his course is confuted by notorious facts.

Several negotiations were set on foot by agents of the ministry to secure the good offices of Franklin to bring about a settlement with the Colonies. To this end, his friend Dr. Fothergill and David Barclay interceded with him. At their request he drew up a plan, in the shape of hints for conversation, seventeen in number, as the terms to which the Colonists would probably assent. This paper was communicated by Mr. Barclay to Lord Hyde, and by Dr. Fothergill to Lord Dartmouth. Lord Hyde thought the propositions too hard. Lord Dartmouth, while he admitted that some of them were reasonable, regarded others as inadmissible or impracticable. The Speaker of the House of Commons thought it would be very humiliating to Britain to be obliged to submit to such terms.

At the request of Lord Howe, who, with ex-Governor Pownall, aspired to the appointment of Commissioner to America to settle difficulties, and who hoped to take Franklin with him, the latter sketched another plan; but this, too, involved concessions which the ministry were not ready to allow. Several attempts were made to renew these informal negotiations. It was evidently supposed that Franklin, though he disclaimed all authority to act, was well aware of the terms that Congress would accept. Any concessions which he might make were relied upon as certain to be obtained; but the ministry were rapacious, and he was unyielding. After repeated interviews with Mr. Barclay and Dr. Fothergill, Lord Howe and Lord Hyde, for the purpose of devising some plan of settlement, the attempt was abandoned.

One of the manœuvres resorted to by friends of the ministry to bring about a private intercourse with Franklin is thus described by him:

"The new Parliament was to meet the 29th of November (1774). About the beginning of that month, being at the Royal Society, Mr. Raper, one of our members, told me there was a certain lady who had a desire of playing with me at chess, fancying she could beat me, and had requested him to bring me to her.   It was, he said, a lady with whose acquaintance he was sure I should be pleased, — a sister of Lord Howe's, — and he hoped I would not refuse the challenge.   I said I had been long out of practice, but would wait upon the lady when he and she should think fit.   He told me where her house was, and would have me call soon, and without further introduction, which I undertook to do ; but thinking it a little awkward, I postponed it, and on the 30th, meeting him again at the feast of the society election, being the day after the Parliament met, he put me in mind of my promise, and that I had not kept it, and would have me name a day, when he said he would call for me and conduct me.   I named the Friday following.   He called accordingly.   I went with him, played a few games with the lady, whom I found of very sensible conversation and pleasing behavior, which induced me to agree most readily to an appointment for another meeting a few days afterwards, — though I had not the least apprehension that any political business could have any connection with this new acquaintance.''

On the evening appointed, Franklin attended his "second chess party with the agreeable Mrs. Howe."

"After playing as long as we liked, we fell into a little chat, partly on a mathematical problem, and partly about the new Parliament, then just met, when she said, 'And what is to be done with this dispute between Great Britain and the Colonies ?   I hope we are not to have a civil war.' 'They should kiss and be friends,' said I ; 'what can they do better ? Quarrelling can be of service to neither, but is ruin to both.'   'I have often said,' replied she, 'that I wished government would employ you to settle the dispute for them ; I am sure nobody could do it so well.   Do not you think that the thing is practicable ?'   'Undoubtedly, madam, if the parties are disposed to reconciliation ; for the two countries have really no clashing interests to differ about.   It is rather a matter of punctilio, which two or three reasonable people might settle in half an hour.   I thank you for the good opinion you are pleased to express of me ; but the ministers will never think of employing me in that good work ; they choose rather to abuse me.'   'Ay,' said she, 'they have behaved shamefully to you.   And, indeed, some of them are now ashamed of it themselves.' ''

Franklin looked upon this, at the time, as an accidental conversation ; but it was the prelude to informal negotiations, to which members of the ministry were a party behind the curtain.   It led to his acquaintance with Lord Howe, who assured him that "there was a sincere disposition in Lord North and Lord Dartmouth to accommodate the differences with America, and to listen favorably to any propositions that might have a probable tendency to answer that salutary purpose."   He then asked Franklin's opinion in regard to sending over a Commissioner to inquire into grievances and compose differences. "I wish, brother," said Mrs. Howe, "you were to be sent thither on such a service; I should like that much better than General Howe's going to command the army there." "I think, madam," said Franklin, "they ought to provide for General Howe some more honorable employment."

Overtures were made to Franklin, in the hope of finding some accessible point on the side of his ambition or self-interest, where a breach could be effected, through which ministerial favors might be thrust, in anticipation of influence exerted by him in the desired direction. In the conversations between him and Mr. Barclay, the latter hinted that from Franklin's coöperation in promoting a settlement with the Colonists he might expect "not only the restoration of his old place, but almost any other he could wish for;" upon which Franklin, writing to his son, remarks: "I need not tell you, who know me so well, *how improper and disgusting this language was to me.*" He replied to Mr. Barclay: "The ministry, I am sure, would rather give me a place in a cart to Tyburn than any other place whatever."

Lord Howe, also, threw out lures. though in a more guarded and delicate manner. After remarking that "he was thought of to be sent Commissioner for settling the differences in America," in which event he hoped to take Franklin with him, giving him a "generous and ample" appointment, he asked, "in order that the ministry might have an opportunity of showing their good disposition" to Franklin, that the latter would give him leave to procure the payment of the arrears of his salary as agent for New England. "My lord," said Franklin, "I shall deem it a great honor to be in any shape joined with your lordship in so good a work; but, if you hope service from any influence I may be supposed to have, drop all thoughts of procuring me any previous favors from ministers; my accepting them would destroy the very influence you propose to make use of; they would be considered as so many bribes to betray the interest of my country." On another occasion, Lord Howe, in alluding to the contingency of Franklin's lending his services to the ministry to bring about a settlement, remarked to him, that he should not think of influencing him by any selfish motive, but certainly he (Franklin) might, with reason, expect "any reward in the power of government to bestow." "This to me," says Franklin, "was what the French vulgarly call spitting in the soup."

IX.

AFTER prolonging his stay in England to await the result of the Continental Congress, Franklin made his preparations for returning home. Happening to be at the House of Lords to hear Lord Camden on American affairs, he was "much disgusted" by many "base reflections," from the ministerial side, "on American courage. religion, understanding, &c., in which we were treated with the utmost contempt as the lowest of mankind, and almost of a different species from the English of Britain;" some of the lords asserting "that we were all knaves, and wanted only by this dispute to avoid paying our debts." Under the excitement occasioned by hearing these aspersions on his country, he wrote a Memorial, which he gave to his friend Mr. Thomas Walpole, a member of the House of Commons. Walpole looked at him as if he apprehended he were a little out of his senses, and, after taking the Memorial to show to Lord Camden, he returned it to Franklin, with the remark that it "might be attended with dangerous consequences to his person, and contribute to exasperate the nation."

Before leaving England, Franklin received news of the death of his wife, Deborah Franklin, which took place at Philadelphia, December 19, 1774. Their relations to each other appear to have been thoroughly affectionate. From his letters to her it would seem that while abroad he was continually sending little presents for her use and gratification. He generally addresses her as "my dear child," or "my dear love," and she sometimes responds in the same terms. In a letter dated London, 6 January, 1773, he writes: "My Dear Child: I feel some regard for this sixth of January, as my old nominal birthday, though the change of style has carried the real day forward to the seventeenth, when I shall be, if I live till then, sixty-seven years of age. It seems but the other day since you and I were ranked among the boys and girls, so swiftly does time fly! We have, however, great reason to be thankful that so much of our lives has passed so happily, and that so great a share of health and strength remains as to render life yet comfortable." "O! my child," writes Mrs. Franklin to her husband, "there is a great odds between a man's being at home and abroad; as everybody is afraid they shall do wrong, so everything is left undone." In a letter, some years afterwards, to a young female friend, Franklin writes: "Frugality is an enriching virtue; a virtue I never could acquire myself; but I was once lucky enough to find it in a wife, who thereby became a fortune to me."

Franklin had now two children left to him; his son, William, estranged by political differences, and his daughter, Sarah, married to Mr. Bache. A second son, Francis Folger, died when four years old. The recollection of him always seemed to touch a tender spot in Franklin's heart. "Though now dead thirty-six years," he writes, "to this day I cannot think of him without a sigh."

Leaving directions with Mrs. Stevenson to deliver to Arthur Lee, the newly-appointed agent for Massachusetts, all the papers relating to that province, Franklin sailed for Philadelphia the 21st of March, 1775, and arrived there on the 5th of May. During the voyage, he occupied himself in writing out a full account of his political negotiations in London. The weather was all the while so moderate "that a London wherry might have accompanied us all the way." He made some experiments with a thermometer in crossing the Gulf Stream, which afforded a valuable hint to navigators for discovering, by the temperature of the water, when they were in the Stream.

The scenes of Lexington and Concord had transpired, and the Second Continental Congress was in session. "I got home in the evening," writes Franklin to Dr. Priestley, "and the next morning was unanimously chosen by the Assembly of Pennsylvania a delegate." To the same friend, a few weeks after, alluding to the action of Congress, he wrote: "It has been with difficulty that we have carried another humble petition to the crown, to give Britain *one more chance* — one opportunity more — of recovering the friendship of the Colonies; which, however, I think she has not sense enough to embrace, so I conclude she has lost them forever." In the same letter he says: "My time was never more fully employed. In the morning, at six, I am at the Committee of Safety, appointed by the Assembly to put the Province in a state of defence, which committee holds till near nine, when I am at the Congress, and that sits till after four in the afternoon."

On the 26th of May, 1775, the committee of the whole reported, and Congress resolved that hostilities had been commenced by Great Britain; and it was voted that the Colonies ought to be put in a posture of defence. The " humble petition "— the "one more chance "— to which Franklin alludes was the petition to the king carried by John Dickinson, and others of the moderate party, against the views of John Adams and others, who thought that the time for " humble petitions " had gone by. The first sketch of a plan of confederation ever presented to Congress is due to Franklin, who brought it forward the 21st of July, 1775. It practically involved independence, but differed in many particulars from the plan ultimately adopted. The name which he proposed for the confederacy was " The United Colonies of North America." About this time Congress established a post-office system of its own, and appointed Franklin Postmaster General.

On all the most important committees, public or secret, formed by Congress, Franklin was placed, and he entered into the duties of them with all the buoyancy and activity of youth. As chairman of the Committee of Safety, he projected the chevaux-de-frise in the Delaware, for the protection of Philadelphia, then the residence of Congress. When the Continental paper-money system was under discussion, he recommended that the bills should bear interest; and it was a matter of regret, when too late, that his advice had not been adopted. In October, 1775, Franklin was one of a committee appointed by Congress to consult with Washington at his head-quarters at Cambridge, near Boston, in relation to a new organization of the army. General Greene writes, October 16, 1775: "The committee of Congress arrived last evening, and I had the honor to be introduced to that very great man, Doctor Franklin, whom I viewed with silent admiration during the whole evening. Attention watched his lips, and conviction closed his periods."

Besides serving in Congress, Franklin, at this period, represented the city of Philadelphia in the Pennsylvania Assembly, and was at the same time a member of the Congress Committees of Safety and of Secret Correspondence. Early in 1776, he was appointed, with Samuel Chase and Charles Carroll, a commissioner to Canada to obtain the coöperation of the inhabitants. He was nearly a month in accomplishing the journey to Montreal, and suffered considerably in his health, from the hardships of the route. It was not till June that ه got back to Philadelphia. Having resigned his places in the Assembly and the Committee of Safety, he now devoted himself to the important business before Congress, and was appointed one of a committee of five, including Thomas Jefferson, John Adams, Roger Sherman and Robert R. Livingston, to prepare a Declaration of Independence. The original draft, by Jefferson, of this momentous document, contains interlineations in the handwriting of Franklin. The Declaration was finally adopted by Congress the fourth of July, 1776. It is related that when Franklin and others were signing their names to this immortal document, John Hancock remarked, " We must be unanimous,— we must all hang together; " to which Franklin replied, " Yes, if we would not hang separately."

A characteristic anecdote is related by Jefferson. Alluding to the mutilations made in his draft of the Declaration in committee of the whole, he says: "I was sitting by Dr. Franklin, who perceived that I was not insensible to these mutilations. ' I have made it a rule,' said he, ' whenever in my power, to avoid becoming the draftsman of papers to be reviewed by a public body. I took my lesson from an incident which I will relate to you. When I was a journeyman-printer, one of my companions, an apprentice-hatter, having served out his time, was about to open shop for himself. His first concern was to have a handsome sign-board, with a proper inscription. He composed it in these words: *John Thompson, hatter, makes and sells hats for ready money*, with a figure of a hat subjoined. But he thought he would submit it to his friends for their amendments. The first he showed it to thought the word *hatter* tautologous, because followed by the words *makes hats*, which showed he was a hatter. It was struck out. The next observed that the word *makes* might as well be omitted, because his customers would not care who made the hats; if good and to their mind, they would buy, by whomsoever made. He struck it out. A third said he thought the words *for ready money* were useless, as it was not the custom of the place to sell on credit. Every one who purchased expected to pay. They were parted with, and the inscription now stood: *John Thompson sells hats.* "*Sells* hats?" says his next friend; "why, nobody will expect you to give them away. What, then, is the use of that word?" It was stricken out, and *hats* followed, the rather as there was one painted on the board. So his inscription was reduced, ultimately, to *John Thompson*, with the figure of a hat subjoined.' "

Franklin was president of the Pennsylvania convention for forming a constitution; but he was unable to give that time to its deliberations which was desirable. By the instrument finally adopted, religious toleration was partially secured, and the right of suffrage extended. His hand may be recognized in the feature of a single Legislative Assembly, by which he thought the process of legislation would be simplified and accelerated. He used to illustrate the inconveniences of a double chamber by comparing them to those of a double-headed snake, who would be in an unpleasant dilemma, if it should be travelling among bushes, and one head should choose to go on one side of the stem of a bush, and the other head should prefer the other side, and neither of the heads would consent to come back, or give way. This theory of a single chamber was abandoned by Pennsylvania, and is not now incorporated in any one of our state constitutions. But it found favor in France, where it was adopted in the National Assemblies which sprang from the revolutions of 1789 and 1848.

The plan of a confederation being before Congress, Franklin was a strenuous opponent of the proposition for giving states an equal vote, without regard to their population. He contended that the article allotting one vote to the smallest state, and no more to the largest, was unjust and injurious.   As president of the Pennsylvania convention, he drew up a Protest on this subject, but forebore to urge it, in consideration of the state of the country.

Early in 1776 the British Parliament passed a somewhat incongruous act, one provision of which was to "prohibit and restrain" the trade of the "refractory Colonies," and the other to enable persons appointed by the king to grant pardons.   With a view to the latter object, Lord Howe, who was at the head of the British fleet in North America, was in May appointed joint commissioner with his brother, General William Howe.   Lord Howe wrote a private letter to Franklin, which the latter answered.   "Your lordship," he wrote, "may possibly remember the tears of joy that wet my cheek, when, at your good sister's in London, you once gave me expectations that a reconciliation might soon take place."   After the battle of Long Island, Lord Howe expressed to General Sullivan, who had been taken prisoner and liberated on parole, a desire to confer with a delegation from Congress.   That body accordingly appointed Benjamin Franklin, John Adams and Edward Rutledge, a committee of conference.   They met Lord Howe at Staten Island, opposite Amboy, within the British lines.   His lordship received and entertained them politely, but acquainted them that he could not treat with them as a committee of Congress, although his powers enabled him to consult with them as private gentlemen of influence in the Colonies.   Finding, however, that no accommodation was likely to take place, he put an end to the conference, and the committee returned and reported the result to Congress.   This conference with Lord Howe took place September 11, 1776.   John Adams has left an amusing account of the journey of the committee from Philadelphia to Staten Island.

"The taverns," he says, "were so full, we could with difficulty obtain entertainment.   At Brunswick but one bed could be procured for Dr. Franklin and me, in a chamber little larger than the bed, without a chimney, and with only one small window.   The window was open, and I, who was an invalid and afraid of the air in the night, shut it close. 'O!' says Franklin, 'don't shut the window,— we shall be suffocated.'   I answered I was afraid of the evening air. Dr. Franklin replied, 'The air within this chamber will

7

soon be, and indeed is now, worse than that without doors.
Come, open the window and come to bed, and I will convince you. I believe you are not acquainted with my theory of colds.' Opening the window and leaping into bed, I
said I had read his letters to Dr. Cooper, in which he had
advanced that nobody ever got cold by going into a cold
church or any other cold air, but the theory was so little
consistent with my experience, that I thought it a paradox.
However, I had so much curiosity to hear his reasons, that I
would run the risk of a cold. The Doctor then began a
harangue upon air and cold, and respiration and perspiration, with which I was so much amused that I soon fell
asleep, and left him and his philosophy together; but I
believe they were equally sound and insensible within a few
minutes after me, for the last words I heard were pronounced as if he was more than half asleep. I remember
little of the lecture, except that the human body, by respiration and perspiration, destroys a gallon of air in a minute;
that two such persons as were now in that chamber would
consume all the air in it in an hour or two; that by breathing over again the matter thrown off by the lungs and the
skin we should imbibe the real cause of colds, not from
abroad, but from within.''

In December, 1775, Franklin, as one of the Committee
of Secret Correspondence, had written to his friends abroad,
and particularly to M. Dumas, in Holland, requesting
information as to whether any of the European courts were
disposed to afford assistance to the American Colonies in
their struggle for independence. It being decided to make
an application to France for aid, three commissioners —
namely, Benjamin Franklin, Silas Deane and Arthur Lee
— were appointed by Congress to negotiate with that power.
Two of the commissioners were already in Europe. Franklin, accompanied by his two grandsons, William Temple
Franklin and Benjamin Franklin Bache, left Philadelphia
October 26, 1776, proceeded to Marcus Hook, and, the next
day, embarked in the United States sloop-of-war Reprisal,
mounting sixteen guns, and commanded by Captain Wickes.
The sloop was chased several times by British cruisers, but,
though prepared for action, the captain obeyed orders, and
shunned an engagement. When near the coast of France,

however, he seized two British vessels, with cargoes, one from Bordeaux, and the other from Rochefort. Early on the morning of November 28th, he came in sight of Belle-isle, and, having taken a pilot, he ran the sloop the next day into Quiberon Bay, where she continued till December 3d. The winds being against her entering the Loire, Franklin and his grandsons went on board a fishing-boat, which had come along-side, and were put on shore at Auray, so that they did not reach Nantes till December 7th. Here they stayed eight days, being fêted and treated with the utmost distinction. No announcement of Franklin's coming had reached France; nor was it known in Europe that Congress had decided on any application for aid. But it was now generally surmised that he was present on some official errand, and he found himself none the less welcome on that account. It was the 21st of December, 1776, when he arrived in Paris. Here he found his colleagues, Messrs. Deane and Lee. On the 1st of January following, Congress directed Franklin to proceed to Spain, there to transact such business as might be intrusted to him. This mission he declined, and it was arranged among the commissioners that Mr. Lee should undertake it.

X.

THE diplomatic career of Franklin in France extends over a period of nearly nine years. He had made two previous visits to Paris, in 1767 and 1769. His reputation in that metropolis at those periods had been great,— greater than it was either in England or America; but it was now matured by the lapse of time, and he was received with a degree of distinction rarely accorded to any foreigner. After remaining a week or two in Paris, he established himself at Passy, a village about three miles from the central part of the city. He took up his abode in a large and handsome house, belonging, with its extensive garden, to M. Le Ray de Chaumont. In regard to the rent, John Adams wrote, some months afterwards, that he never could discover it; "but," he adds, "from the magnificence of the place, it was universally suspected to be enormously high."

It appeared, however, as he himself confessed, that there was much exaggeration in this suspicion. The owner of the estate, a stanch friend of America, was content to have Franklin occupy his house on very moderate terms, and, after our revolution. to receive his pay from our government in grants of the public land.

Franklin's prompt attention was given to the great object of his mission. Previous to his arrival, the French court, which was not yet prepared for an open breach with England, had secretly advanced, through M. Beaumarchais, the celebrated dramatist, about two hundred thousand dollars for the remission of arms and military stores to America, it being arranged that Congress should send tobacco and other produce in return. The three American commissioners were received in their private capacity very kindly by Vergennes, minister for foreign affairs; but it was thought advisable to defer, for the present, any open recognition of their diplomatic character. It was arranged, however, that they should receive, ostensibly from a private source, though really from the king's treasury, for the use of Congress, a quarterly allowance, amounting in the whole to about four hundred thousand dollars; and half as much more was advanced on loan by the "farmers general," to be repaid by remittances of tobacco. Being thus at once supplied with upwards of half a million of dollars, they sent home arms and equipments, fitted out armed vessels, and supplied the American cruisers touching at French ports.

Meanwhile the British ambassador at Paris, Lord Stormont, was loud in his remonstrances, complaining of the underhand aid afforded to the insurgents, their fitting out vessels of war from French ports, bringing in prizes and effecting sales, &c. Vergennes made a show of rebuking the commissioners, but the latter do not seem to have been deterred by it from their operations. They wrote to Lord Stormont relative to an exchange of prisoners. His lordship pompously replied: "The king's ambassador receives no application from rebels, unless they come to implore his majesty's mercy." Franklin's reply, signed also by Deane, to this impertinence, was: "My Lord: In answer to a letter, which concerns some of the most material interests of humanity, and of the two nations, Great Britain and the

United States of America, now at war, we received the enclosed indecent paper as coming from your lordship, which we return for your lordship's more mature consideration." The British ministry, finding the balance of prisoners against them, were soon glad to accept the proposition thus magnificently put aside by Lord Stormont.

Although the sympathies of the French court seemed to be heartily with the Americans from the first, it abstained from committing itself openly until the news of Burgoyne's surrender to the Americans under Gates,* at Saratoga, October 17th, 1777, was received in France. That event decided the French cabinet in its course. "The capitulation of Burgoyne," writes Franklin, "has caused the most general joy in France, as if it were a victory won by her own troops over her own enemies. Such is the universal ardent and sincere good-will and attachment of this nation for us and our cause." He availed himself of this moment of enthusiasm to promote the interests of his country.

On the 7th of December, Vergennes informed the American commissioners that his majesty was disposed to establish more direct relations with the United States. Two treaties were signed February 6, 1778; one of amity and commerce, the other of alliance for mutual defence, by which the king agreed to make common cause with the United States, should England attempt to obstruct the commerce with France; and guaranteed to the United States their liberty, sovereignty and independence. "The king," writes Franklin, "has treated with us generously and magnanimously; taken no advantage of our present difficulties to exact terms which we would not willingly grant when established in prosperity and power." "England is in great consternation." The intelligence of the signing of these treaties, which were at once ratified by Congress, was received with the greatest rejoicing throughout the United States. In England it created much dissatisfaction, and led to the recall of her ambassador from Paris.

* This surrender gave occasion to Sheridan's mischievous epigram upon Burgoyne, who aspired to be a dramatist as well as a military commander:

"Burgoyne surrendered? O, ye fates!
Could not that Samson carry Gates?"

7*

The American commissioners now appeared at court on a footing with the representatives of other independent powers. Franklin was presented by Vergennes to Louis the Sixteenth at Versailles, and was received with the clapping of hands and other tokens of welcome from the surrounding courtiers. He appeared at this royal audience very simply attired, with straight, unpowdered hair, a brown cloth coat, and round hat. A crowd had collected to see him. His age, his venerable aspect, his simple dress, contrasted with the finery around him, the recollection of his services to science and humanity, all combined to waken the utmost enthusiasm of the spectators. The king received him with much cordiality, charging him to assure the United States of his friendship, and expressing his satisfaction with the conduct of their commissioner during his residence in France. On his withdrawing from this audience, the crowd in the passage-ways received Franklin with renewed manifestations of welcome, and followed him for some distance. The enthusiasm of which he had been the object at Versailles was renewed at Paris. Voltaire had recently arrived there, after an absence of thirty years. He was in his eighty-fifth year. Franklin called upon him, and was received with evident pleasure. Voltaire at first accosted him in English; but, having lost the habit of speaking it, he resumed the conversation in French, adroitly remarking, "I could not resist the temptation of speaking for a moment the language of Franklin." The Philadelphia sage then presented his grandson to the patriarch of Ferney, and asked his blessing upon him. "God and liberty!" said Voltaire, raising his hands over the young man's head; "that is the only benediction appropriate to the grandson of Franklin."

A few days after this interview, the same parties met at the Academy of Sciences, and were placed side by side. The sight of these distinguished old men elicited another outbreak of Parisian enthusiasm. The cry arose that they should embrace. They stood up, bowed, took each other by the hand, and spoke. But this was not enough. The clamor continued. "Il faut s'embrasser à la Française," was the cry; whereupon they kissed each other on the cheek,—and not till then did the tumult subside. The scene was classically compared, by the *litterateurs* of the day, to "Solon embracing Sophocles." Voltaire lived only a month after this second encounter with his American contemporary.

Franklin was greatly annoyed at this time by applications for employment in the service of the United States. In a letter to a friend he says: "Frequently, if a man has no useful talents, is good for nothing, and burdensome to his relations, or is indiscreet, profligate and extravagant, they are glad to get rid of him by sending him to the other end of the world; and for that purpose scruple not to recommend him to those they wish should recommend him to others, as 'un bon sujet — plein de merite,' &c. &c. In consequence of my crediting such recommendations, my own are out of credit, and I cannot advise anybody to have the least dependence on them." And he humorously adds: "You can have no conception how I am harassed. All my friends are sought out and teased to tease me. Great officers of all ranks, in all departments, ladies great and small, besides professed solicitors, worry me from morning to night. The noise of every coach now that enters my court terrifies me. I am afraid to accept an invitation to dine abroad, being almost sure of meeting with some officer or officer's friend, who, as soon as I am put in good humor by a glass or two of champagne, begins his attack upon me."

There was one illustrious exception to the annoyances he received from applications for letters to America. The following passage is from a letter to Congress, signed by him and Mr. Deane: "The Marquis de Lafayette, a young nobleman of great family connections here, and great wealth, is gone to America in a ship of his own, accompanied by some officers of distinction, in order to serve in our armies. He is exceedingly beloved, and everybody's good wishes attend him. We cannot but hope he may meet with such a reception as will make the country and his expedition agreeable to him."

Most of the business of the commission was, for tne first eight or nine months, transacted by Franklin and Deane, Mr. Arthur Lee being absent the greater part of the time in Spain and Germany. The feelings of this gentleman towards his colleagues do not seem to have been of a character that promised harmony of action. Thinking that Mr.

Deane had taken the negotiation with Beaumarchais out of his hands, he had quarrelled with him incontinently. Towards Franklin his malevolence seems to have commenced in London, on account of the prolongation of Franklin's stay there as agent for Massachusetts, while he himself was expecting the reversion of the office. Petulant, irritable and distrustful, he seems to have been one of that class of persons who think that nothing can be well carried out in which they do not have a ruling hand. Returning to Paris, he found fault with all that his colleagues had done or left undone during his absence; criticized their contracts; charged them with squandering, if not embezzling, the public money; and intimated that where they had not favored themselves in the disposition of it, they had used it for the benefit of their friends. In replying to one of his letters, Franklin writes : "It is true that I have omitted answering some of your letters, particularly your angry ones, in which you, with very magisterial airs, schooled and documented me, as if I had been one of your domestics. I saw in the strongest light the importance of our living in decent civility towards each other while our great affairs were depending here. I saw your jealous, suspicious, malignant and quarrelsome temper, which was daily manifesting itself against Mr. Deane, and almost every other person you had any concern with. I, therefore, passed your affronts in silence; did not answer, but burnt, your angry letters ; and received you, when I next saw you, with the same civility as if you had never wrote them." On the subject of personal expenses, Franklin adds: "If you think we should account to one another for our expenses, I have no objection, though I never expected it. I believe they will be found very moderate. I answer mine will, having had only the necessaries of life, and purchased nothing besides, except the Encyclopedia, nor sent a sixpence worth of anything to my friends or family in America."

Not content with scolding his colleagues on the spot, Arthur Lee wrote home injurious letters respecting them to members of Congress, charging them with peculation and indifference to the public interests. He did not have the craft, however, to conceal his ambitious motive. In the same letter in which he casts these aspersions upon his colleagues, he proposes that he should be retained at the court of France, Franklin sent to Vienna, and Deane to Holland. An ally, in the person of Mr. Ralph Izard, soon appeared on the scene, from whom Mr. Lee received comfort and countenance in his acrimonious course towards his colleagues. Mr. Izard had been appointed by Congress commissioner to the Court of Tuscany. He preferred to remain in Paris, and claimed a voice in the negotiations with the court of France. Franklin does not seem to have encouraged the claim, and this was Mr. Izard's first grievance. His second was, that Franklin, through whom the public drafts were negotiated, after having paid to Mr. Izard some twelve thousand dollars as commissioner to Tuscany, declined paying him any more until there was a prospect of his getting to Tuscany, or, at least, until he was otherwise instructed by Congress. Mr. Izard, who was a passionate though not ungenerous man, took mortal offence at this refusal to open the public purse-strings, and was profuse thenceforward in his denunciations of Franklin. To the annoyances resulting from the personal hostility of Messrs. Lee and Izard, the brave old man submitted with his habitual equanimity and good temper. To Mr. Izard he writes : "I must submit to remain some days under the opinion you appear to have formed, not only of my poor understanding in the general interests of America, but of my defects in sincerity, politeness, and attention to your instructions. These offences, I flatter myself, admit of fair excuses, or will be found not to have existed."

Mr. Deane did not exercise due caution in the matter of engaging foreign officers ; and as Congress began to feel some inconveniences from his imprudence in this respect, they recalled him, and appointed John Adams his successor. Mr. Adams arrived in Paris April 8, 1778. It appears, from his recently published diary while in France, that his sentiments towards Franklin were far from friendly. He writes : "The first moment Dr. Franklin and I happened to be alone, he began to complain to me of the coolness, *as he very coolly called it*, between the American ministers." "Franklin's cunning will be to divide us," says Mr. Adams on another occasion. And again : "Thinking this to be the best course I could take, to become familiar with the

language and its correct pronunciation. I determined to frequent the theatres as often as possible. Accordingly, I
went as often as I could, and found a great advantage in it,
as well as an agreeable entertainment. But as Dr. Franklin
had almost daily occasion for the carriage, and I was determined the public should not be put to the expense of another
for me, I could not go so often as I wished."

The truth was, that Franklin's reputation in France so
towered above that of his colleagues, that the latter found
themselves mere ciphers by his side, both in society and in
diplomatic encounters. Mr. Adams candidly admits this.
"On Dr. Franklin," he says, "the eyes of all Europe are
fixed, as the most important character in American affairs in
Europe; neither Lee nor myself is looked upon of much
consequence." To men of spirit, in their country's service,
this absorption of their diplomatic individualities in another
must have been galling in the extreme. Adams felt it, as
well as Lee; but, instead of intriguing to have Franklin displaced, he simply wrote home to a member of Congress, representing the inconveniences resulting from the multiplicity
of ministers, and recommending the continuance of one only.
This he did, after considering, as he tells us, that the consequence of his plan would be that Franklin "would, undoubtedly, *as he ought*, be left alone at the court of Versailles," and that for himself the alternative would be to
return to America. These representations had their weight
with Congress, and on the 14th of September, 1778,
Franklin was appointed minister plenipotentiary to the
court of France. His enemies had created some little opposition to him in Congress, and, at one time, on a proposition
for his recall, among thirty-five members, eight voted in
favor of it, and twenty-seven against it. He took no trouble
to contradict malevolent reports, but relied upon the justice
of Congress to take no step without giving him an opportunity of exculpation; and his reliance was justified by the
result. Some years afterwards, he wrote to John Jay:
"I have, as you observe, some enemies in England, but
they are my enemies as an *American ;* I have also two or
three in America, who are my enemies as a *minister ;* but
I thank God there are not in the whole world any who are
my enemies as a *man ;* for by His grace, through a long

life, I have been enabled to conduct myself that there does not exist a human being who can justly say, ' *Ben Franklin has wronged me.*' This, my friend, is, in old age, a comfortable reflection."

As the British government had now a prospective war with France and Spain on their hands, they began to be desirous of making terms with the United States. Several secret agents, selected generally on account of their personal acquaintance with Franklin, were sent over to Paris to confer with him on the subject of a negotiation. James Hutton, secretary to the society of Moravians, and whom Franklin addresses as "his dear old friend," came first; then followed Mr. Pulteney, a member of Parliament, who assumed in Paris the name of Williams; and finally came Mr. David Hartley, also a member of Parliament, affectionately regarded by Franklin. To all these informal negotiators he replied that every proposition implying a return on the part of the United States to a dependence on Great Britain was now become impossible; but that a peace, on equal terms, undoubtedly might be made. Finding that he could get little satisfaction for the ministry from Franklin, Mr. Hartley, in a letter of April 23, 1778, wrote to him: "If tempestuous times should come, take care of your own safety; events are uncertain, and men may be capricious." To which Franklin replies: "I thank you for your kind caution, but, having nearly finished a long life, I set but little value on what remains of it. Like a draper when one cheapens with him for a remnant, I am ready to say, 'As it is only the fag-end, I will not differ with you about it; take it for what you please.' Perhaps the best use such an old fellow could be put to is to make a martyr of him."

In June, 1778, he received from a supposed secret agent of the British ministry, signing himself Charles De Weissenstein, a letter, declaring the impossibility of their recognizing the independence of the Colonies; proposing that America should be governed by a Congress of American peers, and that Franklin, Washington, Adams and Hancock, should be of the number. "Ask our friend if he should like to be a peer?" writes John Adams to Elbridge Gerry, in ridicule of the proposition. "Dr. Franklin, to

whom the letter was sent," he adds, "as the writer is supposed to be a friend of his, sent an answer, in which they
have received a dose that will make them sick." Still
another effort to conciliate Franklin was made by the
British ministry. In May, 1779, his friend, the estimable
William Jones, afterwards the distinguished Sir William,
author of the celebrated ode, "What Constitutes a State,"
and translator of various poems from Asiatic languages,
visited Paris, and made an ingenious communication to
Franklin, which, under the guise and title of "A Fragment
of Polybius," indirectly proposed an arrangement by
which the Colonies would gain everything except independence. This attempt was as fruitless as those that had
preceded it.

About this time the celebrated naval adventurer, John
Paul Jones, was in France He is described by John
Adams as "the most ambitious and intriguing officer in the
American navy. His voice is soft; his eye has keenness,
and wildness, and softness." In compliment to Franklin,
whose "Poor Richard's Maxims" were quite popular in
France, he named the forty-two gun-ship of the mixed
French and English squadron of which he had the command the Bon Homme Richard. His victory in this ship
over the Serapis obtained for Jones the present of a gold-
hilted sword from the French king.

The commission to France having been dissolved, John
Adams returned to America, but was, in September 1779,
appointed by Congress commissioner to negotiate a peace
with Great Britain whenever an opportunity might offer.
This measure had been recommended by M. Gérard, the
French minister in the United States, and by his successor,
M. Luzerne. We are told, in Mr. Adams's fragmentary
autobiography, that it had been the expectation of the French
ministry "in both cases, that Franklin would be elected;"
and that "in this respect Congress disappointed them."
It was soon evident that Congress did not act with wisdom
in this. Mr. Adams possessed little of that suavity of manner so important in personal negotiations. Franklin wrote
of him, that, though "always an honest man, and often a
wise one, he was sometimes, and in some things, absolutely
out of his senses." Adams himself tells us that Mr. David

Hartley spoke of him as " the most ungracious man he ever saw." Arriving in Paris on his second mission in February, 1780, Adams soon found himself uncomfortable at the French court, having given offence to Vergennes in his correspondence. Franklin had confidence in the upright and generous intentions of the court, and wrote to the president of Congress, — " Mr. Adams, on the contrary, who, at the same time, means our welfare and interest as much as I or any man can do, seems to think a little apparent stoutness, and a greater air of independence and boldness in our demands, will procure us more ample assistance." Finding that he could bring little to pass in Paris, Adams proceeded to Holland, where he had been authorized to negotiate a loan, but where he at first failed in his object, and was obliged to resort to Franklin's influence with the French court to provide for the heavy drafts which Congress had made on their commissioner for a peace, in the expectation of the success of his financial application to the Dutch.

There can be little doubt that the liberal and timely aid rendered by France to the United States was due, in a great measure, to the personal influence and the diplomatic address of Franklin. Hostility to Great Britain was an element that entered largely into the policy which supplied this aid; but that hostility would not have availed to induce that policy, had it not been that the United States had an envoy on the spot, who personally commended his country's cause to the French court and people, in a manner the most ample and impressive. We have Franklin's own testimony to the fact that Vergennes never promised him anything " which he did not punctually perform." Franklin accordingly carried into his diplomatic intercourse the unsuspicious manners which his conviction of the sincerity of the party with which he was dealing made easy; and he obtained, through the personal regard of the king and ministry for himself, concessions and loans for his country which would not have been granted to him in his public capacity, unsustained by the influences which his private reputation and demeanor had created. He seems to have been deeply impressed with " the noble and generous manner " in which France, " without stipulating for a single privilege," had " afforded us aid in our distress; "

8

and though there were many then who undervalued our
obligations, and though there are many still who speak
slightingly of them, no one can study intimately the history
of those times without admitting that the aid of France was
most timely and important, and that the news of her alliance was better than an army in sending confidence and
joy through our dwindling ranks.   It was reported to his
prejudice, in the United States, that Franklin had been so
flattered in France that he was ready to favor that country
at the expense of his own.   But time has fully exposed the
absurdity of the suspicion, and justified him in his un-
wavering confidence in the good faith of our allies.   In the
summer of 1780, Count Rochambeau arrived at Newport,
Rhode Island, with a French army of six thousand men;
and, in 1781, Franklin procured from France an additional
loan of three millions of livres, and the sum of six millions,
not as a loan, but as a free gift.

On the 12th of March, 1781, being then in his seventy-sixth
year, he wrote to the President of Congress, requesting his
recall.   John Adams speaks of this as a "pretended request;"
but there is no evidence to sustain the idea of simulation.
" I do not know," writes Franklin, "that my mental faculties are impaired; perhaps I shall be the last to discover
that; but I am sensible of great diminution in my activity,
a quality I think particularly necessary in your minister for
this court.   I find, also, that the business is too heavy for
me, and too confining. . . . . I purpose to remain here at
least till the peace; perhaps it may be for the remainder
of my life."   To a friend, who wrote, urging him, in complimentary terms, to continue at his post, Franklin, who
was never at a loss for an illustrative story, replied : "Your
comparison of the *key-stone of an arch* is very pretty,
tending to make me content with my situation.   But I suppose you have heard our story of the *harrow :* if not, here
it is : — A farmer in our country sent two of his servants
to borrow one of a neighbor, ordering them to bring it between them on their shoulders.   When they came to look
at it, one of them, who had much wit, said, 'What could our
master mean by sending only two men to bring this harrow? No two men upon earth are strong enough to carry it.'
'Poh!' said the other, who was vain of his strength, 'what do

you talk of two men, — one man may carry it; help it upon my shoulders, and you shall see.' As he proceeded with it, the wag kept exclaiming, 'Zounds! how strong you are! I could not have thought it! Why, you are a Samson! There is not such another man in America. What amazing strength God has given you! But you will kill yourself! Pray put it down and rest a little, or let me bear a part of the weight.' 'No, no,' said he, being more encouraged by the compliments than oppressed by the burden; 'you shall see I can carry it quite home.' And so he did. In this particular I am afraid my part of the imitation will fall short of the original." But to Franklin's application for a release, Congress replied, the following June, by appointing him one of a commission of five, including John Adams, Jay, Jefferson * and Laurens, to negotiate a treaty of peace. Finding his health "considerably reëstablished," Franklin accepted the new appointment.

The preliminary conditions, which he laid down, as essential to any treaty with Great Britain, were, the independence of the United States full and complete, a satisfactory boundary, and a participation in the Newfoundland fisheries. It has been stated that he was not decided in regard to the last-named condition. But the evidence to the contrary is most explicit. Both Mr. Adams and Mr. Oswald, the British negotiator, testify that Franklin insisted on the condition as essential; and Mr. Jay, in a letter to Franklin, says, "I do not recollect the least difference of sentiment between us respecting the boundaries or fisheries."

Notwithstanding the liberal conduct of France towards the United States, and the fact that the American commissioners had positive instructions to undertake nothing without her concurrence in negotiating a peace, a treaty with Great Britain was signed on the 30th of November, 1782, without the coöperation or knowledge of our generous ally. In a letter, dated the 5th of the following month, and addressed to Robert R. Livingston, Franklin writes:

"The arrival of Mr. Jay, Mr. Adams and Mr. Laurens, relieved me from much anxiety, which must have continued if I had been left to finish the treaty alone; and it has given me the more satisfaction, as I am sure the

* In consequence of his wife's illness, Jefferson did not go to France till after the treaty of peace was signed.

business has profited by their assistance.   Much of the summer was taken up in objecting to the powers given by Great Britain, and in removing those objections.   The using any expressions that might imply an *acknowledgment* of our independence seemed, at first, industriously to be avoided. But our refusing otherwise to treat at length induced them to get over that difficulty : and then we came to the point of making propositions.

" The British ministers struggled hard for two points,—that the favors granted to the royalists should be extended, and our fishery contracted. We silenced them on the first, by threatening to produce an account of the mischiefs done by those people ; and as to the second, when they told us they could not possibly agree to it as we required it, and must refer it to the ministry in London, we produced a new article to be referred at the same time, with a note of facts in support of it, which you have, No. 3. Apparently it seemed that, to avoid the discussion of this, they suddenly changed their minds, dropped the design of recurring to London, and agreed to allow the fishery as demanded.

" We communicated all the articles, as soon as they were signed, to Mons. le Comte de Vergennes (except the separate one), who thinks we have managed well, and told me that we had settled what was most apprehended as a difficulty in the work of a general peace, by obtaining *the declaration of our independence.*"

Vergennes was chagrined, not without cause, at the course of the commissioners.   " I am at a loss, sir," he wrote to Franklin, " to explain your conduct and that of your colleagues on this occasion.   You have concluded your preliminary articles without any communication between us, although the instructions from Congress prescribe that nothing shall be done without the participation of the king."   To this Franklin replied : " Nothing has been agreed in the preliminaries contrary to the interests of France ; and no peace is to take place between us and England till you have concluded yours."   He admitted that the commissioners, in not consulting Vergennes, had been guilty of " neglecting a point of *bienséance ;*" but, as this " was not from want of respect to the king," he hoped it would be excused.   The probability is, that as Jay and Adams were extremely jealous of French influence, and full of suspicions (which turned out chimerical) on the subject, Franklin yielded, against his better judgment and inclinations, to a course, his opposition to which would have been misconstrued, and, perhaps, abortive.   Notwithstanding the slight put upon the French court, Vergennes was magnanimous enough, a few days after, to advance another loan of upwards of a million of dollars to the United States. The whole course of the French court towards the people of the United States shows that Franklin did not err when he pronounced it "noble, generous, and sincere."

The treaty signed by the commissioners was duly ratified by Congress, and was received with much approbation by the people of the United States.

Franklin now arranged highly favorable terms for the payment of our debt to France; negotiated a treaty with Sweden, the first power to welcome us into the family of nations; and also a treaty with Prussia, in which he incorporated a humane article against privateering, of which practice he always had the greatest abhorrence, denouncing it as "robbery" and "piracy." On the 13th of May, 1784, the ratifications of a definitive treaty were interchanged between Mr. Hartley on the side of Great Britain, the Count de Vergennes, and Franklin and Jay. In relation to this event, Franklin writes to Charles Thompson, Secretary of Congress: "Thus the great and hazardous enterprise we have been engaged in is, God be praised, happily completed; an event I hardly expected I should live to see. A few years of peace, well improved, will restore and increase our strength; but our future safety will depend on our union and our virtue. Britain will be long watching for advantages, to recover what she has lost. If we do not convince the world that we are a nation to be depended on for fidelity in our treaties,— if we appear negligent in paying our debts, and ungrateful to those who have served and befriended us,— our reputation, and all the strength it is capable of procuring, will be lost, and fresh attacks upon us will be encouraged and promoted by better prospects of success."

At length, to Franklin's repeated applications for a recall, — applications which had long been unheeded, because Congress was well aware of his profound skill in diplomacy, his influence and his patriotic devotion,— a substitute at the French court was, in March 1785, appointed in Mr. Jefferson. "You have come to fill Dr. Franklin's place?" some one asked. "O, no, sir!" replied Jefferson; "no man living can do that; but I am appointed to succeed him."

8*

XI.

FRANKLIN'S public celebrity in France seems to have been almost eclipsed by the social esteem in which he was held in private. "You wish to know how I live," he writes to Mrs. Stevenson, under date of Passy, 1779. "I have abundance of acquaintance; dine abroad six days in seven. Sundays I reserve to dine at home, with such Americans as pass this way; and I then have my grandson Ben, with some other American children, from the school. If being treated with all the politeness of France, and the apparent respect and esteem of all ranks, from the highest to the lowest, can make a man happy, I ought to be so." To a friend in America he writes: "The account you have had of the vogue I am in here has some truth in it. Perhaps few strangers in France have had the good fortune to be so universally popular."

"His company was sought," says Mignet, "not only as the most illustrious, but as the most agreeable, that the times afforded. He inspired his friends with sentiments of tenderness, admiration and respect; nor was his attachment to them less strong. He had an especially affectionate regard for Madame Helvetius,* whom he called ' Our Lady of Auteuil,' and who came every week to dine at least once with him and his little colony at Passy. He had lost his wife in 1779; and, notwithstanding his seventy-six years, he made a proposition of marriage to Madame Helvetius, shortly before the close of the war. But she had refused the hand of Turgot, and did not accept his. Franklin thereupon wrote her a letter, which is a model of wit and grace :

" ' Chagrined,' he writes, ' at your barbarous resolution, pronounced so positively yesterday evening, to remain single during life, in honor of your dear husband, I withdrew to my chamber, fell upon my bed, believed myself dead, and found myself in the Elysian Fields. I was asked if I desired to see any persons in particular. "Lead me," said I, "to the philosophers." "There are two who reside here-

---

* Widow of Helvetius, the celebrated materialist, author of "De L' esprit,' and other works of a similar tendency. She resided at Auteuil.

about, in this garden. They are very good neighbors, and much attached to each other." "Who are they?" "Socrates and Helvetius." "I esteem them both prodigiously; but let me see Helvetius first, as I know a little French, but not a word of Greek."— He received me very courteously, having known me, he said, by reputation, some time. He asked me a thousand things about the war, and the present state of religion, liberty and government, in France. "But you do not inquire," said I, "after your dear Madame Helvetius; and yet she loves you excessively, and it is not an hour ago that I was with her." "Ah!" said he, "you remind me of my former felicity; but one must forget it, if he would be happy here. For several years I could think only of her. At length I am consoled. I have taken another wife,—the most like her that I could find. She is not, it is true, altogether so handsome; but she has as much good sense, a large share of wit, and she loves me devotedly. Her constant study is to please me, and she is gone out this moment to get the choicest nectar and ambrosia to regale me with this evening; remain with me, and you will see her." "I perceive," returned I, "that your ancient companion is more faithful than you; for she has had many excellent offers, all of which she has refused. I confess to you that I myself was in love with her to distraction; but she was inexorable towards me, and rejected me absolutely for love of you." "I condole with you," said he, "for your misfortune; for, in truth, she is a good and beautiful lady, and amiable withal. But the Abbé de la R****, and the Abbé M****, are they not at her house sometimes?" "They certainly are; for not one of your friends has she dropped." "If you had gained over the Abbé M**** (with some good coffee and cream) to speak for you, you would perhaps have succeeded; for he is as subtle a reasoner as Duns Scotus or St. Thomas; he puts his arguments in such strong order that they become almost irresistible. And if the Abbé de la R**** had been bribed (by some fine edition of an old classic) to speak *against* you, that would have been still better; as I always observed, when he advised a thing, she had a strong inclination the other way." As he uttered these words, came in the new Madame Helvetius with the nectar; and

at once I recognized in her my old American spouse, Mrs.
Franklin! I re-claimed her, but she coldly said, "I was a
good wife to you for forty-nine years and four months —
almost half a century; be content with that. I have here
formed a new connection, which shall last forever." Indig-
nant at this refusal of my Eurydice, I forthwith resolved
to quit these ungrateful spirits, and to return to this good
world, to see once more the sun and you. Here I am!
Let us be revenged!' "

This piece of *badinage* was written by Franklin in
French, and addressed to Madame Helvetius. If from this
alone, Mignet's mention of an offer of marriage is derived,
the inference is undoubtedly erroneous. Franklin carried
into his social intercourse with the sex a pleasantry which,
without overstepping the bounds of the most respectful
courtesy, was delightful to those who could appreciate the
worth of a compliment from such a man, and the delicate
humor with which it was masked. John Adams relates
that there was a Mademoiselle de Passy, whom Franklin
used to call his favorite, and his flame, and his love, which
flattered the family, and did not displease the young lady.
She was afterwards betrothed to the celebrated Marquis de
Tonnerre (*tonnerre*, the French for *thunder*). After the
marquis had demanded mademoiselle for a wife, and
obtained her, Madame de Chaumont, who was a wit, the
first time she saw Franklin, cried out, "Hélas! tous les
conducteurs de Monsieur Franklin n'ont pas empêché le
tonnerre de tomber sur Mademoiselle de Passy."— (Alas!
all the conductors of Mr. Franklin have not prevented the
thunder from lighting on Mademoiselle de Passy.)

To Madame Brillon, one of his neighbors at Passy,
Franklin addressed his admirable little story of " The
Whistle," and his ingenious apologue, "The Ephemera."
Of this lady he says : " She is of most respectable character
and pleasing conversation; mistress of an amiable family,
with which I spend an evening twice in every week. She
has, among other elegant accomplishments, that of an excellent musician; and, with her daughters, who sing prettily,
and some friends who play, she kindly entertains me and
my grandson with little concerts, a cup of tea, and a game
of chess. I call this *my opera;* for I rarely go to the

opera at Paris." At Sanoy, twelve miles from Paris, he was entertained with great distinction at a *fête champêtre*, April 12, 1781, by the Count and Countess d'Houdetot. He planted a locust-tree in their garden; and poems were recited, and a song sung in his honor, every stanza of which was delivered by a different member of the company. The third stanza was as follows :

> " Guillaume Tell fut brave, mais sauvage ;
> J'estime plus notre cher Benjamin ;
> De l'Amérique en fixant le destin,
> A table il rit, et c'est là le vrai sage." *

While at Passy, he wrote his " Dialogue with the Gout," one of the most exquisite specimens of moral humor in the language. Various other pieces, which he classed under the name of " Bagatelles," were composed by him at this time by way of diversion amid his graver pursuits. He had always a fondness for his old printer's craft, and seemed proud of his proficiency in it. While residing at Passy, he had a small printing-office fitted up in his house, where he put in type and printed the " bagatelles " which he penned for the amusement of his neighbors.

In the society of Madame Helvetius, his acquaintance was sought by the chiefs of the encyclopedists, D'Alembert and Diderot, the latter of whom was atheistical or deistical according to the state of his health or the weather; a writer who, while he assailed religion, was careful to give his children a religious education. Here, also, was introduced to Franklin the celebrated Turgot, who wrote the Latin epigraph † thenceforth attached to so many engravings of the American sage :

> " Eripuit cœlo fulmen sceptrumque tyrannis."

---

* William Tell was brave but rude ;
More our Benjamin I prize,
Who, while he shapes his country's good,
Smiles at our board, there truly wise.

† " He snatched the lightning from heaven, the sceptre from tyrants."

The Latin line seems to have been suggested by the following, from the " Anti-Lucretius " of the Cardinal de Polignac :

> "Eripuitque Jovi fulmen Phœboque sagittas."

And this would seem to have been partially borrowed from the " Astronomica " of Manilius :

> " Eripuit Jovi fulmen viresque tonandi "

Prints, medallion portraits, and busts of Franklin, were
multiplied throughout France ; and rings, bracelets, canes
and snuff-boxes, bearing his likeness, were worn or carried
quite generally.   Such was the steady modesty of his
nature, however, that he experienced more embarrassment
than gratification from Turgot's brilliant compliment.   In
palliation of it, he wrote to John Jay : " You must know
that the desire of pleasing, by a perpetual rise of compliments, in this polite nation, has so used up all the common
expressions of approbation, that they are become flat and
insipid, and to use them almost implies censure.   Hence
music, that formerly might be sufficiently praised when it
was called *bonne*, to go a little further they called it *excel-
lente*, then *superbe*, *magnifique*, *exquise*, *céleste*, all which
being in their turns worn out, there only remains *divine*;
and, when that is grown as insignificant as its predecessors,
I think they must return to common speech and common
sense."   To a poetaster of the day, Felix Nogaret, who
applied to him for his opinion on a French translation of
Turgot's verse, he replied :

" Passy, 8 March, 1781.

    " SIR : I received the letter you have done me the honor of writing to
me the 2d instant, wherein, after overwhelming me with a flood of compliments, which I can never hope to merit, you request my opinion of your
translation of a Latin verse that has been applied to me. If I were, which
I really am not, sufficiently skilled in your excellent language to be a judge
of its poesy, the supposition of my being the subject must restrain me from
any opinion on that line, except that it ascribes too much to me, especially
in what relates to the tyrant ; the revolution having been the work of
many able and brave men, wherein it is sufficient honor for me if I am
allowed a small share."

    Among the first to welcome Franklin at Paris, was Con-
dorcet, the friend and biographer of both Voltaire and Turgot, and whom John Adams describes as "a philosopher
with a face as pale, or rather as white, as a sheet of paper."
Cabanis, the celebrated physician, and the friend of Mirabeau, Buffon, the " Pliny of France," Raynal, Mably,
Vicq d'Azyr, La Rochefoucauld, the Abbé Morellet, the
Abbé La Roche, Le Roy, Le Veillard, Malesherbes, and
other eminent statesmen and men of letters, were among
the associates or intimate friends of Franklin.   With Mirabeau, before the latter had attained his marvellous reputa-

tion, he seems to have been well acquainted, and gave him a letter of introduction to Benjamin Vaughan, in London. "This will be handed you," he writes, "by Count Mirabeau, son of the Marquis of that name, author of *L'Ami des Hommes*. This gentleman is esteemed here, and I recommend him to your civilities and counsels, particularly with respect to the printing of a piece he has written on the subject of *hereditary nobility*, on occasion of the order of Cincinnati lately attempted to be established in America, which cannot be printed here. I find that some of the best judges think it extremely well written, with great clearness, force and elegance. If you can recommend him to an honest, reasonable bookseller, that will undertake it, you will do him service, and perhaps some to mankind, who are too much bigoted in many countries to that kind of imposition."

We have already seen that he was subjected, in his diplomatic capacity, to numerous applications, which taxed his time and patience exorbitantly. His scientific reputation invited propositions hardly less annoying from speculators and inventors. "The number of wild schemes proposed to me," he writes, "is so great, and they have heretofore taken so much of my time, that I begin to reject all, though possibly *some* of them may be worth notice." Under date of Passy, December 13, 1778, after recording in his diary the visits of three of these experimenters on the same day, he makes the following note: "Received a parcel from an unknown philosopher, who submits to my consideration a memoir on the subject of *elementary fire*, containing experiments in a dark chamber. It seems to be well written, and is in English, with a little tincture of French idiom. I wish to see the experiments, without which I cannot well judge of it." This "unknown philosopher" was afterwards discovered to be Marat, the sanguinary monster, whose atrocities during the revolution roused Charlotte Corday to rid the world of his presence.

Franklin spoke French but indifferently, and his pronunciation was defective. He told John Adams that he was wholly inattentive to the grammar. Madame Geoffrin, to whom, in his visit to France in 1767 or 1769, he brought a letter from David Hume, reported that she could not initiate him into the language. Notwithstanding his advanced age, when he established himself at Passy, he lived to make a great improvement in speaking French, and to enjoy it perfectly in the hearing. In the year 1779, he read a paper on the Aurora Borealis to the Royal Academy of Sciences at Paris, in which he traced the phenomenon to electrical agencies. At times he would be led into amusing misapprehensions, through his difficulty in understanding the language when uttered with rapidity. On one occasion, being present at a sitting of the Lyceum or the Academy, during the delivery of a lecture, and not distinctly understanding the French that was spoken, he thought, in order not to be wanting in politeness, that every time he saw Madame de Bouflers give signs of approbation, he would applaud; but he afterwards found that, without knowing it, he had applauded most vigorously those passages which had been complimentary to himself.

In March, 1784, a royal commission was appointed to investigate the subject of animal magnetism, the marvels of which had been recently disclosed by Mesmer. Franklin was placed at the head of this commission, which numbered Le Roy, Bailly, Guillotin (proposer of the guillotine as an instrument of death), and other men of science and physicians. Some six months were given to an investigation of the subject; but Franklin, through indisposition, was absent from many of the sittings. An attempt was on one occasion made to affect him by the mesmeric passes, but it did not succeed. The commissioners, through Bailly, reported adversely to the claims of Mesmer, but admitted certain phenomena, which they attributed to the agency of the imagination. This was merely giving a vague name to what was inexplicable. Franklin wrote thus cautiously upon the subject, to M. de la Condamine, prior to the action of the commission: "As to the animal magnetism, so much talked of, I must doubt its existence till I can see or feel some effect of it. None of the cures said to be performed by it have fallen under my observation, and there are so many disorders which cure themselves, and such a disposition in mankind to deceive themselves and one another on these occasions, and living long has given me so frequent opportunities of seeing certain remedies cried up as curing everything, and yet soon after totally laid aside as useless.

I cannot but fear that the expectation of great advantage from this new method of treating diseases will prove a delusion. That delusion may, however, and in some cases, be of use while it lasts. There are in every great, rich city a number of persons who are never in health, because they are fond of medicines, and always taking them, whereby they derange the natural functions, and hurt their constitution. If these people can be persuaded to forbear their drugs, in expectation of being cured by only the physician's finger, or an iron rod pointing at them, they may possibly find good effects, though they mistake the cause." At a later period he wrote to Dr. Ingenhousz : "Mesmer is still here, and has still some adherents and some practice. It is surprising how much credulity still subsists in the world. I suppose all the physicians in France put together have not made so much money, during the time he has been here, as he alone has done. And we have now a fresh folly. A magnetizer pretends that he can, by establishing what is called a *rapport* between any person and a *somnambule*, put it in the power of that person to direct the actions of the *somnambule*, by a simple strong volition only, without speaking or making any signs ; and many people daily flock to see this strange operation."

While resident at Passy, Franklin received a present of Cowper's Poems, then beginning to win their way to fame, and he wrote to the donor : " The relish for reading poetry had long since left me ; but there is something so new in the manner, so easy and yet so correct in the language, so clear in the expression, yet concise, and so just in the sentiments, that I have read the whole with great pleasure, and some of the pieces more than once. I beg you to accept my thankful acknowledgments, and to present my respects to the author." Cowper was well pleased with the compliment, coming, as he said, from " one of the first philosophers, one of the most eminent literary characters, as well as one of the most important in the political world, that the present age can boast of ; " and he playfully remarks : " We may now treat the critics as the Archbishop of Toledo treated Gil Blas when he found fault with one of his sermons."

Among the opportunities which Franklin took for employing his official powers in behalf of the cause of humanity and science, was that of instructing American cruisers not to seize Captain Cook's vessel, and granting passports to vessels despatched with relief to the Moravian missions, and alms for sufferers in the West India Colonies. On the publication of "Cook's Voyage," a copy was forwarded to Franklin, with the approbation of the king ; and, subsequently, one of the gold medals struck in honor of Captain Cook by the Royal Society was sent to him.

The period for his departure from France having now arrived, he received from Count Vergennes and other official personages the most cordial assurances of esteem, and regrets at his quitting the country. A French national vessel would have been provided for him, if the minister of marine had been apprized sooner of his intended return home. His many distinguished friends took leave of him, one by one, with marks of the most affectionate interest and regard. To his old friend, David Hartley, he wrote, "in his eightieth year : " "I cannot quit the coasts of Europe without taking leave of my ever dear friend, Mr. Hartley. We were long fellow-laborers in the best of all works, the work of peace. I leave you still in the field, but, having finished my day's task, I am going home *to go to bed*. Wish me a good night's rest, as I do you a pleasant evening. Adieu ! "

He set out from Passy, with his two grandsons and M. Veillard, July 12, 1785. He travelled in one of the queen's litters, borne by two large mules, the muleteer riding another. The journey to Havre occupied six days, and he was entertained on the route with great distinction, by the Cardinal de la Rochefoucauld, M. Holker the banker, and others. At Rouen a deputation from the Academy came with their compliments. From Havre he passed over in a packet-boat to Southampton, where he remained four days. Here he was met by his son, William Temple Franklin,— expatriated on account of his loyalist principles, and in the receipt of a pension from the British government. Here, also, were assembled to welcome him the " good bishop" of St. Asaph, his wife and daughter, Mr. Benjamin Vaughan, and other English friends. On the 27th of July, he embarked in the London packet, Captain Truxton, one of his fellow-passengers being Mr. Houdon, the artist, engaged by him and Mr. Jefferson to make a statue of Washington for the State of Virginia. The bishop and his family accompanied Franklin on board, and remained during the night before the vessel sailed. Finding in the morning that he was still asleep, they left without disturbing him; and, when he awoke, he learned that the company was gone, and the ship under sail.

He was not idle during the voyage. He wrote a paper on "Improvements in Navigation," and another "On Smoky Chimneys." When in the Gulf Stream, he renewed his experiments on the temperature of the water. After a voyage of forty-eight days, he arrived at Philadelphia the 14th of September. "We landed," he says in his journal, "at Market-street wharf, where we were received by a crowd of people with huzzas, and accompanied with acclamations quite to my door. Found my family well. God be praised and thanked for all his mercies!" The ringing of bells and firing of cannon were likewise made to speak a welcome to the returning patriot and sage.

XII.

WELCOMES from public bodies soon followed the outburst of popular affection and enthusiasm. From the Assembly of Pennsylvania, the American Philosophical Society, and the University, he received addresses, to which he sent suitable replies. Washington wrote him the assurance that no one "could salute him with more sincerity or pleasure" than he. Franklin was now very pleasantly situated in his domestic relations, and there was every temptation for him to withdraw from public affairs. "I am got into my *niche*," he writes, "after being kept out of it twenty-four years by foreign employments. It is a very good house, that I built long ago to retire into, without being able till now to enjoy it. I am again surrounded by my friends, with a fine family of grandchildren about my knees, and an affectionate, good daughter and son-in-law to take care of me. And, after fifty years' public service, I have the pleasure to find the esteem of my country with regard to me undiminished."

But he was not allowed to remain long aloof from public business. In a few days after his return, he was elected a member of the Supreme Executive Council of Pennsylvania, and in October he was chosen President of the State, as the executive was styled under the old constitution. He filled this office through the three successive years which the constitution allowed, receiving on his first election all the votes of the Legislature except one, and at the two subsequent elections a unanimous vote. Entertaining a theory that in a republican government there should be no emoluments attached to office, he devoted his salary as president to public purposes. Having been elected one of the delegates from Pennsylvania to the convention for forming the constitution of the United States, which met at Philadelphia, May 1787, he objected in that body to the incorporation of the salary principle in the constitution. "There are two passions," he said, "which have a powerful influence in the affairs of men. These are *ambition* and *avarice;* the love of power and the love of money. Separately, each of these has great force in prompting men to action; but, when united in view of the same object, they have in many minds the most violent effects. Place before the eyes of such men a post of *honor*, that shall at the same time be a place of *profit*, and they will move heaven and earth to obtain it." The country's experience has proved the truth of this; but where shall we find a remedy?

Franklin made no pretensions to oratory; and when he spoke it was with as much simplicity as pith. "The examples of Washington, Franklin and Jefferson," says John Adams, "are enough to show that silence and reserve in public are more efficacious than argumentation or oratory." Where other signal qualities of character and mind are manifested by the individual, the absence of the oratorical accomplishment may not be an obstacle to success; but it must ever be an added charm and power. Franklin introduced a motion into the convention for daily prayers, but it was not adopted. He made the following memorable remarks in its support:

"In the beginning of the contest with Britain, when we were sensible of danger, we had daily prayers in this room for the divine protection. Our prayers, sir, were heard; and they were graciously answered. All of us, who were engaged in the struggle, must have observed frequent instances of a superintending Providence in our favor. To that kind Providence we owe this happy opportunity of consulting in peace on the means of establishing our future national felicity. And have we now forgotten that powerful Friend? or do we imagine we no longer need His assistance; I have lived, sir, a long time; and, the longer I live, the more convincing proofs I see of this truth, *that* God *governs in the affairs of men.* And, if a sparrow cannot fall to the ground without his notice, is it probable that an empire can rise without his aid? We have been assured, sir, in the sacred writings, that ' except the Lord build the house, they labor in vain that build it.' I firmly believe this ; and I also believe, that, without His concurring aid, we shall succeed in this political building no better than the builders of Babel ; we shall be divided by our little, partial, local interests, our projects will be confounded, and we ourselves shall become a reproach and a by-word down to future ages. And, what is worse, mankind may hereafter, from this unfortunate instance, despair of establishing government by human wisdom, and leave it to chance, war and conquest. I therefore beg leave to move, that henceforth prayers, imploring the assistance of Heaven and its blessing on our deliberations, be held in this assembly every morning before we proceed to business ; and that one or more of the clergy of this city be requested to officiate in that service."

There were some features in the constitution of the United States, as finally adopted, which Franklin would have had different. He was in favor of an executive council rather than a single officer as the head of the government ; and he was opposed to salaries. But, in his speech at the close of the convention, he said : " I consent to this constitution because I expect no better, and because I am not sure that it is not the best. The opinions I have had of its *errors* I sacrifice to the public good. I have never whispered a syllable of them abroad." " Much of the strength and efficiency of any government, in procuring and securing happiness to the people, depends on *opinion*, on the general opinion of the goodness of that government, as well as of the wisdom and integrity of its governors. I hope, therefore, for our own sakes, as a part of the people, and for the sake of our posterity, that we shall act heartily and unanimously in recommending this constitution, wherever our influence may extend, and turn our future thoughts and endeavors to the means of having it *well administered.*"

From the commencement of the government, the inattention of Congress to private claims has been a by-word of reproach. Not even the illustrious services of Benjamin Franklin could exempt him from the habitual fate of public creditors. To use his own words, " Though an active man, he

9*

had never gone through so much business during eight years in any part of his life, as during those of his residence in France, between his seventy-second and eightieth years. Before his departure for that country, he had put all the money he could raise — between three and four thousand pounds — into the hands of Congress, thus demonstrating his confidence, and encouraging others to lend their money in support of the cause. He made no bargain for appointments, but was promised, by a vote, the *net* salary of five hundred pounds sterling per annum, his expenses paid, and to be assisted by a secretary, who was to have one thousand pounds per annum, to include all contingencies." Many services, not appertaining to the office of plenipotentiary, were performed by Franklin in France; such as judge of admiralty, consul, and·banker in examining and accepting bills of exchange. His accounts were audited by Mr. Barclay, the agent appointed by Congress; but certain reasonable claims for extra services and assistance were left unadjusted. He repeatedly requested the attention of Congress to these claims, but without success. He was the more anxious, inasmuch as some malevolent persons had insinuated that he was largely indebted to government, and that he avoided a settlement. It was a matter of chagrin to him, to the last, that his appeals for justice were not heeded; and it remains a stigma upon the fair fame of the old Congress, as well as of the first under the new constitution, that these claims were never adjusted.

In the year 1788, Franklin wrote a paper, entitled a "Comparison of the Conduct of the Ancient Jews and the Anti-Federalists of the United States," a satire upon the assailants of the new constitution; also some scientific papers, and a portion of his autobiography. In 1789 he wrote a long memoir relative to the Academy, now the University, of Pennsylvania, and a satirical paper on the Abuses of the Press. He drew up a "Plan for Improving the Condition of the Free Blacks," and wrote an Address to the Public from the "Pennsylvania Society for Promoting the Abolition of Slavery," of which society he was president. He was also president of a "Society for Alleviating the Miseries of Public Prisons." His last published paper appeared in the *Federal Gazette* of March 25, 1790, over the signature of "Historicus," and purported to be a speech delivered in the Divan of Algiers, 1687, by a member of that council, against the petition of a sect called *Erika*, who prayed for the abolition of slavery. It was a parody upon a speech in support of negro slavery by Mr. Jackson, member of Congress from Georgia, and is remarkable as showing that Franklin's intellectual faculties had not deteriorated in his eighty-fourth year. His last public act was the signing, as president of the Abolition Society, a memorial to Congress. His last letter of which any copy has been preserved — and, from its date, probably the last which he wrote — is one addressed, nine days before his decease, to Jefferson, the Secretary of State, upon the subject of the North-eastern Boundary. It is indicative of a mind unimpaired in clearness and strength.

A friendship, founded upon the sincerest mutual esteem, appears to have existed between Franklin and Washington. "I must soon quit this scene," writes the former, in 1780, to the latter; "but you may live to see our country flourish, as it will, amazingly and rapidly, after the war is over; like a field of young Indian corn, which long fair weather and sunshine had enfeebled and discolored, and which in that weak state, by a thunder-gust of violent wind, hail and rain, seemed to be threatened with absolute destruction; yet the storm being past, it recovers fresh verdure, shoots up with double vigor, and delights the eye, not of its owner only, but of every observing traveller." A comparison this which would have graced the lips of Nestor and the page of Homer! "General Washington is the man," writes Franklin in 1788, to his friend Veillard, at Passy, "that all our eyes are fixed on- for president; and what little influence I may have is devoted to him." After bequeathing, in the codicil to his will, his "fine crab-tree walking-stick, with a gold head curiously wrought in the form of the cap of liberty," to Washington, Franklin adds, with one of his felicitous turns of expression, "If it were a sceptre, he has merited it, and would become it." "I am now," he writes September 16, 1789, to Washington, "finishing my eighty-fourth year, and probably with it my career in this life; but, in whatever state of existence I am placed hereafter, if I retain any memory of what has passed here, I shall with it retain the esteem, respect and affection, which have long been, my dear friend, yours, most sincerely." To which Washington, with unwonted warmth and earnestness of expression, replies: "If to be venerated for benevolence, if to be admired for talents, if to be esteemed for patriotism, if to be beloved for philanthropy, can gratify the human mind, you must have the pleasing consolation to know that you have not lived in vain. And I flatter myself that it will not be ranked among the least grateful occurrences of your life to be assured that, so long as I retain my memory, you will be recollected with respect, veneration and affection, by your sincere friend, George Washington."

Very beautiful is the spectacle of the closing years of Franklin's long and laborious life. Though not without his share of physical infirmities, he retained his lively interest in public affairs, his warm social and domestic sympathies, his amenity and serenity of temper, his active and vigorous intellect, his abiding faith in another and a better life. He seems to have realized the wish expressed in another's behalf by Wordsworth:

> " Thy thoughts and feelings shall not die,
>   Nor leave thee, when gray hairs are nigh,
>   A melancholy slave;
>   But an old age serene and bright,
>   And lovely as a Lapland night,
>   Shall lead thee to thy grave."

His correspondence at this time, in the vivacity, humor, justness of thought, and happy reliance on Providence, which it exhibits, is a model of style and mood. To a friend in London he writes, May 18, 1787: "When I consider how many terrible diseases the human body is liable to, I comfort myself that only three incurable ones have fallen to my share, namely, the gout, the stone and old age; and that these have not yet deprived me of my natural cheerfulness, my delight in books, and enjoyment of social conversation." In the next paragraph, alluding to a friend who had been lately married, he says: "After all, wedlock is the natural state of man. A bachelor is not a complete human being. He is like the odd half of a pair of scissors, which has not yet found its fellow, and therefore is not even half so useful as they might be together." Writing to George Whatley May 18, 1787, he says : "You are now seventy-eight and I am eighty-two; you tread fast upon my heels ; but, though you have more strength and spirit, you cannot come up with me till I stop, which must now be soon; for I am grown so old as to have buried most of the friends of my youth, and I now often hear persons whom I knew when children called *old* Mr. Such-a-one, to distinguish them from their sons, now men grown and in business ; so that, by living twelve years beyond David's period, I seem to have intruded myself into the company of posterity, when I ought to have been abed and asleep. Yet had I gone at seventy it would have cut off twelve of the most active years of my life, employed too in matters of the greatest importance; but whether I have been doing good or mischief is for time to discover. I only know that I intended well, and I hope all will end well."

To a friend in France he writes, November 13, 1789 : "It is now more than a year since I have heard from my dear friend Le Roy. What can be the reason ? Are you still living ? Or have the mob of Paris mistaken the head of a monopolizer of knowledge for a monopolizer of corn, and paraded it about the streets ?" And then, gliding from gay to grave, he adds : "Great part of the news we have had from Paris, for near a year past, has been very afflicting. I sincerely wish and pray it may all end well and happy, both for the king and the nation."

To the Rev. John Lothrop, Boston, he writes, May 31, 1788, hopefully and prophetically of the progress of mankind, morally and physically. "I have been long impressed," he says, "with the same sentiments you so well express of the growing felicity of mankind, from the improvements in philosophy, morals, politics and even the conveniences of common living, and the invention and acquisition of new and useful utensils and instruments ; so that I have sometimes almost wished it had been my destiny to be born two or three centuries hence. For invention and improvement are prolific, and beget more of their kind." Shall we believe that this divine thirst for knowledge, which age could not diminish, has ended at the tomb, and that the great discoveries of the last half-century are a blank to the intellect which was their bold precursor, finding delight in kindred triumphs of mind over matter?

"The style of his letters * in general," says Lord Jeffrey, "is excellent. They are chiefly remarkable for great simplicity of language, admirable good sense and ingenuity, and an amiable and inoffensive cheerfulness, that is never overclouded or eclipsed." "There is something extremely amiable in old age, when thus exhibited without querulousness, discontent or impatience, and free, at the same time, from any affected or unbecoming levity." Not only the style of his letters, but of all his published compositions, is a model of plain and unaffected diction, exhibiting an affluence of thought with great economy of words. There is sometimes a pithy sententiousness in his expressions, by which his meaning is conveyed with wonderful precision and expansion; as where, in allusion to the declaratory act of the British Parliament, asserting the *right* to tax Americans, he says: "I will freely spend nineteen shillings in the pound to defend my right of giving or refusing the other shilling; and, after all, if I can not defend that right, I will retire cheerfully with my little family into the boundless woods of America, which are sure to afford freedom and subsistence *to any man who can bait a hook or pull a trigger.*" Of his philosophical writings, Sir Humphrey Davy says: "A singular felicity of induction guided all his researches, and by very small means he established very grand truths. The style and manner of his publication on Electricity are almost as worthy of admiration as the doctrine it contains. He has endeavored to remove all mystery and obscurity from the subject. He has written equally for the uninitiated and for the philosopher; and he has rendered his details amusing as well as perspicuous, elegant as well as simple. Science appears in his language in a dress

---

* Although the number of his letters in existence is sufficient to show that his epistolary industry was remarkable, some of the most valuable have been lost. When he went to France, he left a chest of papers with Mr. Joseph Galloway (of whom see a mention, page 89). Mr. G. joined the enemy, leaving the papers in Philadelphia; and they were rifled and scattered during the occupation of that city by the British. Franklin's own house was occupied by the enemy at the time; and his books and some other articles were carried off.

wonderfully decorous, the best adapted to display her native loveliness."

To his sister, Mrs. Mecom, his letters exhibit invariable kindness and generosity. The following is but one specimen out of many of the substantial nature of his attentions. Under date of November 4, 1787, he writes: "Your bill is honored. It is impossible for me always to guess what you may want, and I hope, therefore, that you will never be shy in letting me know wherein I can help to make your life more comfortable." Even in his charities, he seems to have had an eye to utility in making them stretch as far as possible. While in France, Mr. Nixon, an English clergyman, prisoner on parole, applied to him for pecuniary aid. Franklin sent him a permission to draw on him for five *louis d'ors*, remarking, "Some time or other you may have an opportunity of assisting with an equal sum a stranger who has equal need of it. Do so. By that means you will discharge any obligation you may suppose yourself under to me. *Enjoin him to do the same on occasion.* By pursuing such a practice, much good may be done with little money. Let kind offices go round. Mankind are all of a family."

Inheriting from healthy and temperate parents a constitution favorable to longevity, he attended carefully to the laws of health, and, until the period of his residence in France, took abundant exercise in the open air. "Dr. Franklin," says John Adams, in his diary at Passy, "upon my saying, the other day, that I fancied he did not exercise so much as he was wont, answered, ' Yes, I walk a league every day in my chamber; I walk quick, and for an hour, so that I go a league; I make a point of religion of it.'" It is believed, however, that the confinement required by his official duties led to diseases which abbreviated his life, and prevented its reaching his father's term of eighty-nine years. He was afflicted with gout, to which supervened, in 1782, a severe calculous complaint; and, with occasional intermissions, they became so severe as to confine him, the last twelve months of his life, almost constantly to his bed. In the letter to President Washington already quoted from, he says : "For my own personal ease, I should have died two years ago; but, though those years have been passed in excruciating pain, I am pleased that I have lived them, since they have brought me to see our present situation." "Hitherto this long life has been tolerably happy," he writes, March 2, 1789, to Mrs. Greene, "so that, if I were allowed to live it over again, I would make no objection, only wishing for leave to do, what authors do in a second edition of their works, correct some of my *errata*."

He was symmetrically and compactly formed, though latterly inclining to corpulency. His height was five feet nine or ten inches. His features were an index of the good temper, amenity, cheerfulness and affability, which were his characteristics. John Adams represents him as taciturn on committees and in Congress. In society he was far from being loquacious; but no one possessed a more entertaining fund of conversation, or used it more happily on fitting occasions. Childhood, that "best detector of a gentle heart," was ever welcome to his knee. For the young his manners and his words of sage advice and pleasantry had an indescribable charm. Sir Samuel Romilly, when a young man, called on him at Passy (1782), with a friend. "Dr. Franklin," he writes, "was indulgent enough to converse a good deal with us, whom he observed to be young men very desirous of improving by his conversation. Of all the celebrated persons whom, in my life, I have chanced to see, Dr. F., both from his appearance and his conversation, seemed to me the most remarkable. His venerable, patriarchal appearance, the simplicity of his manners and language, and the novelty of his observations,—at least, the novelty of them at that time to me,—impressed me with an opinion of him as one of the most extraordinary men that ever existed."

In April, 1790, his illness had so increased that the constant attendance of his physician, Dr. John Jones, was required. John Adams mentions a report that, in the opinion of Franklin's "own able physician, Dr. Jones, he fell a sacrifice, at last, not to the stone, but to his own theory, having caught the violent cold which finally choked him, by sitting for some hours at a window, with the cool air blowing upon him." Dr. Jones published an account of Franklin's last illness, in which he makes no mention of any such fact. We subjoin the following extracts from it:

"The stone, with which he had been afflicted for several years, had, for the last twelve months of his life, confined him chiefly to his bed; and, during the extremely painful paroxysms, he was obliged to take large doses of laudanum, to mitigate his tortures. Still, in the intervals of pain, he not only amused himself by reading and conversing cheerfully with his family and a few friends who visited him, but was often employed in doing business of a public as well as of a private nature, with various persons who waited upon him for that purpose; and, in every instance, displayed not only the readiness and disposition to do good which were the distinguishing characteristics of his life, but the fullest and clearest possession of his uncommon abilities. He also not unfrequently indulged in those *jeux d'esprit* and entertaining anecdotes which were the delight of all who heard them.

"About sixteen days before his death, he was seized with a feverish disposition, without any particular symptoms attending it, till the third or fourth day, when he complained of a pain in his left breast, which increased till it became extremely acute, attended by a cough and laborious breathing. During this state, when the severity of his pains drew forth a groan of complaint, he would observe that he was afraid he did not bear them as he ought; acknowledging his grateful sense of the many blessings he had received from the supreme Being, who had raised him from small and low beginnings to such high rank and consideration among men; and made no doubt but that his present afflictions were kindly intended to wean him from a world in which he was no longer fit to act the part assigned him. In this frame of body and mind he continued until five days before his death, when the pain and difficulty of breathing entirely left him, and his family were flattering themselves with the hopes of his recovery; but an imposthume, which had formed in his lungs, suddenly burst, and discharged a quantity of matter, which he continued to throw up while he had power; but, as that failed, the organs of respiration became gradually oppressed; a calm, lethargic state succeeded; and on the 17th instant (April 1790), about

10

eleven o'clock at night, he quietly expired, closing a long and useful life of eighty-four years and three months."

"The evening of his life," says Dr. Rush, "was marked by the same activity of his moral and intellectual powers which distinguished its meridian. His conversation with his family upon the subject of his dissolution was free and cheerful. A few days before he died, he rose from his bed, and begged that it might be made up for him, so that he 'might die in a decent manner.' His daughter told him that she hoped he would recover, and live many years longer. He calmly replied, 'I hope not.' Upon being advised to change his position in bed, that he might breathe easy, he said, ' A dying man can do nothing easy.' "

His attached friend, Mrs. Hewson, once Mary Stevenson, daughter of his London landlady, was " the faithful witness of the closing scene," and has left an interesting account of it. " No repining," she says, "no peevish expression, ever escaped him during a confinement of two years, in which, I believe, if every moment of ease could be added together, the sum would not amount to two whole months. When the pain was not too violent to be amused, he employed himself with his books, his pen, or in conversation with his friends; and upon every occasion displayed the clearness of his intellect and the cheerfulness of his temper. Even when the intervals from pain were so short that his words were frequently interrupted, I have known him to hold a discourse in a sublime strain of piety." "I shall never forget one day that I passed with our friend last summer. I found him in bed in great agony, but when that agony abated a little I asked if I should read to him. He said Yes; and the first book I met with was Johnson's ' Lives of the Poets.' I read the life of Watts, who was a favorite author with Dr. Franklin; and, instead of lulling him to sleep, it roused him to a display of the powers of his memory and his reason. He repeated several of Watts's ' Lyric Poems,' and descanted upon their sublimity in a strain worthy of them and of their pious author. It is natural for us to wish that an attention to some ceremonies had accompanied that religion of the heart which I am convinced Dr. Franklin always possessed; but let us, who feel the benefit of them, continue to practise them, without thinking lightly of that piety which could support pain without a murmur, and meet death without terror."

He had expressed a wish in his will that his body should be buried "with as little expense or ceremony as may be." The funeral took place the 21st of April, and was attended by the members of the city and state governments, the various societies of the city, and some twenty thousand citizens. The bells were muffled and tolled; flags displayed at half-mast; and the consignment of the body to the earth was signalized by peals of artillery. His remains lie in the north-west corner of Christ Church Cemetery, in the city of Philadelphia, by the side of those of his wife. "I wish to be buried," he writes in his will, "by the side of my wife, if it may be; and that a marble stone, to be made by Chambers, six feet long, four feet wide, plain, with only a small moulding round the upper edge, and this inscription:

> BENJAMIN
> AND } FRANKLIN.
> DEBORAH
> 178–

to be placed over us both." His modest wishes have been fulfilled. So well hidden is this grave at the present day, that we have known many native Philadelphians who could not direct one to the place.

The following epitaph, the metaphor in which, though not original, has never before been so well expressed, was written by Franklin when he was about twenty-three years of age:

> "The Body
> of
> Benjamin Franklin,
> Printer
> (Like the cover of an old book,
> Its contents torn out,
> And stript of its lettering and gilding),
> Lies here, food for worms.
> But the work itself shall not be lost,
> For it will, as he believed, appear once more,
> In a new and more elegant edition,
> Revised and corrected
> by
> THE AUTHOR."

Congress, which was in session at New York, took suitable notice of Franklin's death; and, on motion of Mr. Madison, resolved that the members should wear the customary badge of mourning for one month, "as a mark of veneration due to the memory of a citizen whose native genius was not more an ornament to human nature than his various exertions of it have been precious to science, to freedom and to his country." In France high honors were paid. Condorcet eulogized him in the Academy, and Mirabeau from the tribune of the National Assembly. "Antiquity," said the latter, "would have erected altars to this great and powerful genius."

In his will, after distributing his property and various memorials among his kindred * and friends, and the societies of which he was a member, Franklin left one thousand pounds to the city of Philadelphia, and the same sum to the town of Boston, to be put at interest and loaned in small sums to young married mechanics. The advantages which he anticipated from these bequests have not been fully realized. The Philadelphia legacy is now worth about twenty thousand dollars; the Boston legacy had accumulated in 1853 to the sum of fifty-four thousand two hundred and eighty dollars, and will reach, it is estimated, in 1891 (one hundred years from the time the bequest was made), the sum of four hundred thousand dollars, if the average rate of interest continues the same as for the last twenty years. Another donation, of about one hundred pounds, to the town of Boston, to be expended in the purchase of silver medals for the most meritorious pupils in the public schools, has been fruitful of good. The "Franklin medals" are still annually bestowed; and show that the testator could have devised no mode better suited to keep his memory green in the minds of the youth attending the free schools, to which he himself "owed his first instructions in literature."

* There is not now any male descendant of Franklin bearing his name. His grandson, William Temple Franklin, died without issue. His daughter Sarah married Richard Bache in 1767, and their descendants are numerous, six out of seven marrying, namely, Benjamin Franklin Bache, who married Margaret Marcoe ; William, who married Catharine Wistar; Deborah, Wm. J. Duane ; Richard, a daughter of Alexander J. Dallas ; Sarah, Thomas Sargeant.

The prudential maxims, quoted or originated by Franklin in his Almanac, have given an erroneous impression in regard to his character.   If he commended frugality, it was because through that virtue the "glorious privilege of being independent" might be attained.   "A penny saved is a penny earned" was but introductory to the maxim, "Spare, that you may share."   He exercised a wise generosity whenever he had an opportunity to enlarge the comforts or improve the condition of his countrymen.   His devotion to scientific pursuits was entirely free from a mercenary anticipation.   It does not appear that he ever received from them any other returns than of "empty praise;" and yet they must have involved a great sacrifice of time, that might have been converted into lucre.   When he invented his stove, he refused a patent, from which he might have derived a handsome annual income, and gave it freely to the public.   He sought no profit whatever from his published writings, and indicated a singular carelessness in regard to them.   He was continually devising some plan for advancing the comfort and general interests of his fellow-men; at one time establishing a subscription library, and then a hospital; now forming the first fire-engine company in the country, and then a philosophical society; now introducing the yellow willow-tree for making baskets, and then the agricultural use of plaster; now establishing an academy, and then suggesting an improvement in common sewers; now harnessing the lightning, and then contriving a copying machine; now studying the best mode of paving streets, and then planning the union of the Colonies; now suggesting to navigators a mode of testing the water of the Gulf Stream, and then devising a cure for smoky chimneys. It would be difficult to give a complete enumeration of all his contributions to the cause of science and civilization. Alluding to his present of some Rhenish grape-vines to Mr. Quincy, John Adams says: "Thus, he (Franklin) took the trouble to hunt over the city, and not finding vines there, he sends seventy miles into the country, and then sends one bundle by water, and, lest they should miscarry, another by land, to a gentleman whom he owed nothing to and was but little acquainted with, purely for the sake of doing good in the world by propagating the Rhenish vines

10*

through these provinces. . . . . This is an instance, too, of his amazing capacity for business, his memory and resolution. Amidst so much business, as counsellor, postmaster, printer, so many private studies, and so many public avocations, too, to remember such a transient hint, and exert himself so in answer to it, is surprising." The same writer says in his Diary, that when in London he (John Adams) went over Blackfriar's Bridge to see Viny's manufacture of patent wheels made of bent timber; and he adds: "Viny values himself much upon his mechanical invention; is loud in praise of Franklin, who first suggested to him the hint of a bent wheel. Franklin once told me he had seen such a wheel in Holland before he set Viny to work."

The same time given to advancing his own fortunes, that he gave to advancing the general welfare and prosperity of his fellow-men, would have made Franklin a much richer man than he ever lived to be. "Franklin, with all his abilities," says Leigh Hunt, "is but at the head of those who think that man *lives by bread alone.*" A grosser misconception of character was never formed. No man ever did more by his example than Franklin to show the worthlessness of mere sensual, compared with moral and intellectual welfare. Rising from very humble beginnings, he early felt the worth of diligence and economy in his business. But he was never so engrossed in it that he could not give a good share of his time to literary, scientific, musical and social enjoyments, and to public affairs. Having attained a moderate competence, he withdrew from active business, and accepted employments of a public nature, the emoluments of which were comparatively insignificant. While in England, music and science were the occupations of his leisure. He invented the Harmonica, gave musical parties, and pursued his electrical studies with a self-sacrificing zeal. His conceptions of the high destiny of man constantly exercised upon him their elevating effect; and he would speak with enthusiasm of his anticipations of studying the works of the Creator in other worlds and modes of being, and of conferring with the great and good of all ages and climes.

If we take Franklin's own dry and brief account of his days of courtship, we must grant that he seems to have been deficient in the chivalrous sentiment which we look for in a lover. In his nineteenth year he "made some courtship" to Miss Read; but, when he went to England, he "forgot by degrees his engagements" to her, and she married another. Some years afterwards he made "serious courtship" to a young lady who had been recommended to him by his friend Mrs. Godfrey. But, before venturing upon an engagement, he apprized the parents that he expected, with his bride, money enough to pay off an encumbrance upon his printing-office, amounting to about a hundred pounds. The parents demurred, and he abandoned his suit, and turned his attention elsewhere. But the business of a printer being looked on with distrust, he soon found (he tells us) that he "was not to expect money with a wife," unless with such a one as he "should not otherwise think agreeable." The tender passion must have had little sway with him at this time, if it could thus be elevated or depressed according to the graduation of his bride's dowry. Let us judge him, however, by the record of his acts, rather than of his words. Franklin returned to his first love, and married her in spite of many obstacles; and she proved "a good and faithful helpmate."

His playful letter,* in his old age, to Madame Helvetius, in which he imagines a visit to the Elysian Fields, where he found his departed wife the mate of Madame's departed husband, though pervaded by an elegant pleasantry, has been quoted as showing that the sentiment which sanctifies connubial affection, and which would have been proof against a thought of levity, was wanting in his case. But Franklin was a humorist, and, when he gave play to the imaginative faculty, it took the direction of humorous fable or anecdote. If, as his French biographers assert, he seriously made proposals of marriage to Madame Helvetius, he could hardly have made a more gallant retreat, after her rejection of his suit, than under the cover of that ingenious apologue. Towards this lady he seems to have entertained a regard which was deep and genuine, and not without a rose-tint of romance. When upwards of eighty, he wrote to her from Philadelphia: "I stretch my arms towards you,

* See page 90.

in spite of the immensity of ocean that separates us, and await that celestial kiss which I firmly hope, one day, to give you!'"   In a letter about a year before he died, to the Abbé Morellet, he alludes to her as "the good lady whom we all love, and whose remembrance I shall cherish while a breath of life remains."*

With regard to Franklin's religious views, we have a very explicit statement in his letter of March 9, 1790, to President Stiles, of Yale College, from which it would appear that Franklin's creed did not materially differ from that of the Humanitarians of the present day. In this letter he says:

"You desire to know something of my religion. It is the first time I have been questioned upon it. But I cannot take your curiosity amiss, and shall endeavor in a few words to gratify it.   Here is my creed: I believe in one God, the creator of the universe. That he governs it by his providence. That he ought to be worshipped. That the most acceptable service we render to him is doing good to his other children. That the soul of man is immortal, and will be treated with justice in another life respecting its conduct

* Mrs. John Adams dined with Madame Helvetius in 1784, at Dr. Franklin's, and has left her impressions of the lady in a letter to a friend, from which the following is a passage: "She entered the room with a careless, jaunty air. Upon seeing ladies who were strangers to her, she bawled out, 'Ah, mon Dieu! where is Franklin? Why did you not tell me there were ladies here?' You must suppose her speaking all this in French. 'How I look!' said she, taking hold of a chemise made of tiffany, which she had on over a blue lutestring, and which looked as much upon the decay as her beauty, — for she was once a handsome woman. Her hair was frizzled; over it she had a small straw hat, with a dirty-gauze half-handkerchief round it, and a bit of dirtier gauze than ever my maids wore was bowed on behind. She had a black gauze scarf thrown over her shoulders. She ran out of the room; when she returned, the Doctor entered at one door, she at the other; upon which she ran forward to him, caught him by the hand, 'Helas, Franklin!' then gave him a double kiss, one upon each cheek, and another upon his forehead. When we went into the room to dine, she was placed between the Doctor and Mr. Adams. She carried on the chief of the conversation at dinner, frequently locking her hand into the Doctor's, and sometimes spreading her arms upon the backs of both the gentlemen's chairs, then throwing her arm carelessly upon the Doctor's neck. I should have been greatly astonished at this conduct, if the good Doctor had not told me that in this lady I should see a genuine Frenchwoman, wholly free from affectation or stiffness of behavior, and one of the best women in the world. For this I must take the Doctor's word."

in this.   These I take to be the fundamental points in all sound religion, and I regard them as you do, in whatever sect I meet with them.   As to Jesus of Nazareth, my opinion of whom you particularly desire, I think his system of morals and his religion, as he left them to us, the best the world ever saw or is like to see; but I apprehend it has received various corrupting changes, and I have, with most of the present dissenters in England, some doubts as to his divinity; though it is a question I do not dogmatize upon, having never studied it, and think it needless to busy myself with it now, when I expect soon an opportunity of knowing the truth with less trouble. I see no harm, however, in its being believed, if that belief has the good consequence, as probably it has, of making his doctrines more respected and more observed; especially as I do not perceive that the Supreme takes it amiss by distinguishing the believers, in his government of the world, with any peculiar marks of his displeasure.   I shall only add respecting myself, that, having experienced the goodness of that Being in conducting me prosperously through a long life, I have no doubt of its continuance in the next, though without the smallest conceit of meriting such goodness.   My sentiments on this head you will see in the copy of an old letter enclosed."*

Even in the adoption of his religious views, Franklin seems to have been biased by his habitual regard for utility as the primary good.   Finding, at an early period of his experience, that men destitute of religious convictions were unreliable, treacherous and sensual, he came to consider morality as essential to social and individual well-being, and religion as essential to morality : hence he found in the necessities of human nature a warrant for both.   He was penetrated with a vital and abiding conviction of the great realities of a special Providence, and the immortality of the soul.   Expressions that frequently occur in his familiar letters and public speeches indicate that his belief in the agency of Deity in the affairs of nations and individuals, his cheerful certainty in regard to another and a better world, were habits of mind the influence of which was powerful and constant.   Regarding this state of existence as one

---

* Supposed to be that to George Whitefield, page 412.

of preparatory discipline for another, he looked forward with delight to enlarged opportunities of studying the works of the Creator. "It is to me," he writes, in his eighty-first year, "a comfortable reflection, that, since we must live forever in a future state, there is a sufficient stock of amusement in reserve for us to be found in constantly learning something new to eternity, the present quantity of human ignorance infinitely exceeding that of human knowledge."

Of historical theology he seems to have known little. In a letter dated July 18, 1784, he writes of having asked information of the Pope's Nuncio, "whether a Protestant bishop might not be ordained by the Catholic in America." The answer was such as few readers will fail to anticipate : "The thing is impossible."

As a philanthropist, Franklin was bold, consistent, active, and greatly in advance of his age. From his Quaker brethren in Philadelphia he contracted all their zeal in behalf of humanity, although in his mind it put on the aspect of plain, practical beneficence. He was ever foremost in all humane enterprises. He was never misled, through sympathy with a majority, into the support of measures which, though popular, were inconsistent with a high-toned Christian morality. He was the champion of the Indians when to advocate their cause was to displease the many. He was one of the earliest opponents of the slave-trade and slavery. He omitted no opportunity to protest against war and its iniquity, and he branded as piracy the custom of privateering, however sanctioned by international usage. As a statesman and philosopher, his fame is imperishable. As an active benefactor of his race, he is entitled to its lasting gratitude. As one of the founders of the American Union, he must ever be held in honorable remembrance by all who prize American institutions. As the zealous foe to oppression in all its forms, he merits the thankful regard of good men of all ages and climes.

AUTOBIOGRAPHY

OF

BENJAMIN FRANKLIN.

CHAPTER I.*

I HAVE ever had a pleasure in obtaining any little anecdotes of my ancestors. You may remember the inquiries I made among the remains of my relations when you were with me in England, and the journey I undertook for that purpose. Imagining it may be equally agreeable to you to learn the circumstances of *my* life, many of which you are unacquainted with, and expecting the enjoyment of a few weeks' uninterrupted leisure, I sit down to write them. Besides, there are some other inducements that excite me to this undertaking. From the poverty and obscurity in which I was born, and in which I passed my earliest years, I have raised myself to a state of affluence and some degree of celebrity in the world. As constant good fortune has accompanied me even to an advanced period of life, my posterity will perhaps be desirous of learning the means which I employed, and which, thanks to Providence, so well succeeded with me. They may also deem them fit to be imitated, should any of them find themselves in similar circumstances.

This good fortune, when I reflect on it, which is frequently the case, has induced me sometimes to say, that, if it were left

---

* For the convenience of the reader, the Autobiography is divided into chapters. The first part, which closes with the fourth chapter, was addressed, in the form of a letter, from Twyford, the seat of the Bishop of St. Asaph, to Franklin's son, Wm. Franklin, Governor of New Jersey. It bears date 1771.

to my choice, I should have no objection to go over the same life from its beginning to the end; requesting only the advantage authors have of correcting in a second edition the faults of the first. So would I also wish to change some incidents of it, for others more favorable. Notwithstanding, if this condition was denied, I should still accept the offer of re-commencing the same life. But, as this repetition is not to be expected, that which resembles most living one's life over again seems to be to recall all the circumstances of it; and, to render this remembrance more durable, to record them in writing. In thus employing myself, I shall yield to the inclination, so natural to old men, of talking of themselves and their own actions; and I shall indulge it without being tiresome to those who, from respect to my age, might conceive themselves obliged to listen to me, since they will be always free to read me or not.

And, lastly (I may as well confess it, as the denial of it would be believed by nobody), I shall perhaps not a little gratify my own vanity. Indeed, I never heard or saw the introductory words, "Without vanity I may say," &c., but some vain thing immediately followed. Most people dislike vanity in others, whatever share they have of it themselves; but I give it fair quarter wherever I meet with it, being persuaded that it is often productive of good to the possessor, and to others who are within his sphere of action; and therefore in many cases it would not be altogether absurd, if a man were to thank God for his *vanity* among the other comforts of life. And now I speak of thanking God, I desire with all humility to acknowledge that I attribute the mentioned happiness of my past life to his divine providence, which led me to the means I used, and gave the success. My belief of this induces me to *hope*, though I must not *presume*, that the same goodness will still be exercised towards me in continuing that happiness, or enable me to bear a fatal reverse, which I may experience as others have done; the complexion of my future fortune being known to Him only, in whose power it is to bless us, even in our afflictions.

Some notes, which one of my uncles, who had the same curiosity in collecting family anecdotes, once put into my hands, furnished me with several particulars relative to our ancestors. From these notes I learned, that they lived in the same village, — Ecton, in Northamptonshire, — on a freehold of about thirty acres, for at least three hundred years, and how much longer could not be ascertained.

This small estate would not have sufficed for their maintenance without the business of a smith, which had continued in the family down to my uncle's time, the eldest son being always brought up to that employment; a custom which he and my father followed with regard to their eldest sons. When I searched the registers at Ecton, I found an account of their marriages and burials from the year 1555 only, as the registers kept did not commence previous thereto. I, however, learned from it that I was the youngest son of the youngest son for five generations back. My grandfather, Thomas, who was born in 1598, lived at Ecton till he was too old to continue his business, when he retired to Banbury, in Oxfordshire, to the house of his son John, with whom my father served an apprenticeship. There my uncle died and lies buried. We saw his grave-stone in 1758. His eldest son Thomas lived in the house at Ecton, and left it with the land to his only daughter, who, with her husband, one Fisher of Wellingborough, sold it to Mr. Isted, now lord of the manor there. My grandfather had four sons, who grew up; namely, Thomas, John, Benjamin, and Josiah. Being at a distance from my papers, I will give you what account I can of them from memory; and, if my papers are not lost in my absence, you will find among them many more particulars.

Thomas, my eldest uncle, was bred a smith under his father, but, being ingenious, and encouraged in learning, as all his brothers were, by an Esquire Palmer, then the principal inhabitant of that parish, he qualified himself for the bar, and became a considerable man in the county; was chief mover of all public-spirited enterprises for the county or town of Northampton, as well as of his own village, of which many instances were related of him; and he was much taken notice of and patronized by Lord Halifax. He died in 1702, the 6th of January; four years, to a day, before I was born. The recital which some elderly persons made to us of his character, I remember, struck you as something extraordinary, from its similarity with what you knew of me. "Had he died," said you, "four years later, on the same day, one might have supposed a transmigration."

John, my next uncle, was bred a dyer, I believe of wool. Benjamin was bred a silk-dyer, serving an apprenticeship in London. He was an ingenious man. I remember, when I was a boy, he came to my father's in Boston, and resided in the house with us for several years. There was always a particular affection between my father and him, and I was his godson. He lived to a great age. He left behind him two quarto volumes of manuscript, of his own poetry, consisting of fugitive pieces addressed to his friends. He had invented a short-hand of his own, which he taught me, but, not having practised it, I

11

have now forgotten it. He was very pious, and an assiduous attendant at the sermons of the best preachers, which he reduced to writing according to his method, and had thus collected several volumes of them. He was also a good deal of a politician; too much so, perhaps, for his station. There fell lately into my hands, in London, a collection he had made of all the principal political pamphlets relating to public affairs, from the year 1641 to 1717. Many of the volumes are wanting, as appears by their numbering; but there still remain eight volumes in folio, and twenty in quarto and in octavo. A dealer in old books had met with them, and, knowing me by name, having bought books of him, he brought them to me. It would appear that my uncle must have left them here when he went to America, which was about fifty years ago. I found several of his notes in the margins. His grandson, Samuel Franklin, is still living in Boston.*

Our humble family early embraced the reformed religion. Our forefathers continued Protestants through the reign of Mary, when they were sometimes in danger of persecution, on account of their zeal against Popery. They had an English Bible, and, to conceal it and place it in safety, it was fastened open with tapes under and within the cover of a joint stool. When my great-grandfather wished to read it to his family, he placed the joint stool on his knees, and then turned over the leaves under the tapes. One of the children stood at the door to give notice if he saw the apparitor coming, who was an officer of the spiritual court. In that case the stool was turned down again upon its feet, when the Bible remained concealed under it as before. This anecdote I had from Uncle Benjamin. The family continued all of the Church of England till about the end of Charles the Second's reign, when some of the ministers that had been outed for their non-conformity holding conventicles in Northamptonshire, my Uncle Benjamin and my father Josiah adhered to them, and so continued all their lives. The rest of the family remained with the Episcopal Church.

My father married young, and carried his wife with three children to New-England, about 1685. The conventicles being at that time forbidden by law, and frequently disturbed in the meetings, some considerable men of his acquaintances determined to go to that country, and he was prevailed with to accompany them thither, where they expected to enjoy the exercise of their religion with freedom. By the same wife my father had four children more born there, and by a second ten others; in all

---

* His descendants are still living there.

seventeen; of whom I remember to have seen thirteen sitting together at his table, who all grew up to years of maturity and were married. I was the youngest son, and the youngest of all the children except two daughters. I was born in Boston, in New England.* My mother, the second wife of my father, was Abiah Folger, daughter of Peter Folger, one of the first settlers of New England; of whom honorable mention is made by Cotton Mather in his ecclesiastical history of that country, entitled *Magnalia Christi Americana,* as "a godly and learned Englishman," if I remember the words rightly. I was informed he wrote several small occasional works, but only one of them was printed, which I remember to have seen several years since. It was written in 1675. It was in familiar verse, according to the taste of the times and the people, and addressed to the government there. It asserts the liberty of conscience, in behalf of the Anabaptists, the Quakers, and other sectaries that had been persecuted. He attributes to this persecution the Indian wars and other calamities that had befallen the country; regarding them as so many judgments of God to punish so heinous an offence, and exhorting the repeal of those laws, so contrary to charity. This piece appeared to me as written with manly freedom, and a pleasing simplicity. The six last lines I remember, but have forgotten the preceding ones of the stanza;† the purport of them was, that his censures proceeded from good will, and therefore he would be known to be the author:

* In Milk-street, January 17th, or 6th, Old Style. A granite store now occupies the site, having the inscription "Birthplace of Franklin." Franklin's father occupied subsequently a house corner of Hanover and Union streets, which is sometimes claimed as entitled to the distinction of Benjamin's birthplace.

† They are as follow:

> " I am for peace, and not for war,
>   And that's the reason why
> I write more plain than some men do,
>   That use to daub and lie.
> But I shall cease, and set my name
>   To what I here insert;
> Because to be a libeller," &c.

Peter was no poet. He wrote sad doggerel, notwithstanding his descendant's indulgent opinion. The Folgers seem to have been a somewhat unpolished race. " They are wonderfully shy," writes Franklin to his sister, August, 1789. " But I admire their honest plainness of speech. About a year ago I invited two of them to dine with me; their answer was, that they would, if they could not do better. I suppose they did better; for I never saw them afterwards, and so had no opportunity of showing my miff, if I had one."

" Because to be a libeller
    I hate it with my heart.
From Sherbon Town where now I dwell,
    My name I do put here;
Without offence your real friend,
    It is Peter Folger."

My elder brothers were all put apprentices to different trades.
I was put to the grammar school at eight years of age ; my father
intending to devote me, as the tithe of his sons, to the service of
the church. My early readiness in learning to read, — which must
have been very early, as I do not remember when I could not
read, — and the opinion of all his friends that I should certainly
make a good scholar, encouraged him in this purpose of his.
My Uncle Benjamin too approved of it, and proposed to give me
his short-hand volume of sermons to set up with, if I would
learn his short-hand. I continued, however, at the grammar
school rather less than a year, though in that time I had risen
gradually from the middle of the class of that year to be at the
head of the same class, and was removed into the next class,
whence I was to be placed in the third at the end of the year.

But my father, burdened with a numerous family, was unable
without inconvenience to support the expense of a college education. Considering, moreover, as he said to one of his friends in
my presence, the little encouragement that line of life afforded
to those educated for it, he gave up his first intentions, took me
from the grammar school, and sent me to a school for writing
and arithmetic, kept by a then famous man, Mr. George Brown-
well. He was a skilful master, and successful in his profession,
employing the mildest and most encouraging methods. Under
him I learned to write a good hand pretty soon ; but I failed
entirely in arithmetic. At ten years old I was taken to help
my father in his business, which was that of a tallow-chandler
and soap-boiler; a business to which he was not bred, but had
assumed on his arrival in New England, because he found that
his dyeing trade, being in little request, would not maintain his
family. Accordingly, I was employed in cutting wicks for the
candles, filling the moulds for cast candles, attending the shop,
going of errands, &c. I disliked the trade, and had a strong
inclination to go to sea ; but my father declared against it. But,
residing near the water, I was much in it and on it. I learned
to swim well and to manage boats ; and, when embarked with
other boys, I was commonly allowed to govern, especially in any
case of difficulty ; and upon other occasions I was generally the
leader among the boys, and sometimes led them into scrapes, of

which I will mention one instance, as it shows an early project-ing public spirit, though not then justly conducted.

There was a salt marsh, which bounded part of the mill-pond, on the edge of which, at high water, we used to stand to fish for minnows. By much trampling we had made it a mere quag-mire. My proposal was to build a wharf there for us to stand upon; and I showed my comrades a large heap of stones, which were intended for a new house near the marsh, and which would very well suit our purpose. Accordingly in the evening, when the workmen were gone home, I assembled a number of my play-fellows, and we worked diligently like so many emmets, some-times two or three to a stone, till we brought them all to make our little wharf. The next morning, the workmen were sur-prised at missing the stones which had formed our wharf. In-quiry was made after the authors of this transfer; we were dis-covered, complained of, and corrected by our fathers; and, though I demonstrated the utility of our work, mine convinced me that that which was not honest could not be truly useful.

I suppose you may like to know what kind of a man my father was. He had an excellent constitution, was of a middle stature, well set, and very strong. He could draw prettily, and was skilled a little in music. His voice was sonorous and agreeable, so that when he played on his violin, and sung withal, as he was accustomed to do after the business of the day was over, it was extremely agreeable to hear. He had some knowledge of me-chanics, and on occasion was very handy with other tradesmen's tools. But his great excellence was his sound understanding, and his solid judgment in prudential matters, both in private and public affairs. It is true he was never employed in the lat-ter, the numerous family he had to educate, and the straitness of his circumstances, keeping him close to his trade; but I re-member well his being frequently visited by leading men, who consulted him for his opinion in public affairs, and those of the church he belonged to; and who showed a great respect for his judgment and advice. He was also much consulted by private persons about their affairs, when any difficulty occurred, and frequently chosen an arbitrator between contending parties.

At his table he liked to have, as often as he could, some sensible friend or neighbor to converse with; and always took care to start some ingenious or useful topic for discourse, which might tend to improve the minds of his children. By this means he turned our attention to what was good, just and prudent, in the conduct of life; and little or no notice was ever taken of what related to the victuals on the table; whether it was well or

11*

ill dressed, in or out of season, of good or bad flavor, preferable or inferior to this or that other thing of the kind; so that I was brought up in such a perfect inattention to those matters, as to be quite indifferent what kind of food was set before me. Indeed, I am so unobservant of it, that to this day I can scarce tell, a few hours after dinner, of what dishes it consisted. This has been a great convenience to me in travelling, where my companions have been sometimes very unhappy for want of a suitable gratification of their more delicate, because better instructed, tastes and appetites.

My mother had likewise an excellent constitution; she suckled all her ten children. I never knew either my father or mother to have any sickness, but that of which they died; he at eighty-nine, and she at eighty-five years of age. They lie buried together at Boston, where I some years since placed a marble over their grave, with this inscription:

JOSIAH FRANKLIN
and
ABIAH his wife
Lie here interred.
They lived lovingly together in wedlock,
Fifty-five years;
And without an estate, or any gainful employment,
By constant labor, and honest industry
(With God's blessing),
Maintained a large family comfortably;
And brought up thirteen children and seven grandchildren
Reputably.
From this instance, reader,
Be encouraged to diligence in thy calling,
And distrust not Providence.
He was a pious and prudent man,
She a discreet and virtuous woman.
Their youngest son,
In filial regard to their memory,
Places this stone.
J. F. born 1655; died 1744. Æt. 89.
A. F. born 1667; died 1752. Æt. 85.*

By my rambling digressions, I perceive myself to be grown old. I used to write more methodically. But one does not dress for private company as for a public ball. Perhaps it is only negligence.

To return: I continued thus employed in my father's business for two years,—that is, till I was twelve years old; and my brother John, who was bred to that business, having left my

---

* The marble having become dilapidated, the citizens of Boston replaced it in 1827 by a granite obelisk.

father, married, and set up for himself at Rhode Island, there was every appearance that I was destined to supply his place, and become a tallow-chandler. But my dislike to the trade continuing, my father had apprehensions that, if he did not put me to one more agreeable, I should break loose and go to sea, as my brother Josiah had done, to his great vexation. In consequence, he took me to walk with him, and see joiners, bricklayers, turners, braziers, &c., at their work, that he might observe my inclination, and endeavor to fix it on some trade or profession that would keep me on land. It has ever since been a pleasure to me to see good workmen handle their tools. And it has been often useful to me to have learned so much by it as to be able to do some trifling jobs in the house when a workman was not at hand, and to construct little machines for my experiments at the moment when the intention of making these was warm in my mind. My father determined at last for the cutler's trade, and placed me for some days on trial with Samuel, son to my Uncle Benjamin, who was bred to that trade in London, and had just established himself in Boston. But the sum he exacted as a fee for my apprenticeship displeased my father, and I was taken home again.

From my infancy I was passionately fond of reading, and all the money that came into my hands was laid out in the purchasing of books. I was very fond of voyages. My first acquisition was Bunyan's works in separate little volumes. I afterwards sold them to enable me to buy R. Burton's *Historical Collections*. They were small chapmen's books, and cheap; forty volumes in all. My father's little library consisted chiefly of books in polemic divinity, most of which I read. I have often regretted that, at a time when I had such a thirst for knowledge, more proper books had not fallen in my way, since it was resolved I should not be bred to divinity. There was among them Plutarch's *Lives*, which I read abundantly, and I still think that time spent to great advantage. There was also a book of Defoe's, called *An Essay on Projects*, and another of Dr. Mather's, called *An Essay to do Good*, which perhaps gave me a turn of thinking that had an influence on some of the principal future events of my life. This bookish inclination at length determined my father to make me a printer, though he had already one son, James, of that profession.

In 1717 my brother James returned from England with a press and letters, to set up his business in Boston. I liked it much better than that of my father, but still had a hankering for the sea. To prevent the apprehended effect of such an inclination, my father was impatient to have me bound to my brother. I stood out some time, but at last was persuaded and signed the indenture, when I was yet but twelve years old. I was to serve an apprenticeship till I was twenty-one years of age, only I was to be allowed journeymen's wages during the last year. In a little time I made a great progress in the business, and became a useful hand to my brother. I now had access to better books. An acquaintance with the apprentices of booksellers enabled me sometimes to borrow a small one, which I was careful to return soon, and clean. Often I sat up in my chamber reading the greatest part of the night, when the book was borrowed in the evening and to be returned in the morning, lest it should be found missing.

After some time, a merchant, an ingenious, sensible man, Mr. Matthew Adams, who had a pretty collection of books, frequented our printing-office, took notice of me, and invited me to see his library, and very kindly proposed to lend me such books as I chose to read. I now took a strong inclination for poetry, and wrote some little pieces. My brother, supposing it might turn to account, encouraged me, and induced me to compose two occasional ballads. One was called *The Light House Tragedy*, and contained an account of the shipwreck of Captain Worthilake with his two daughters; the other was a sailor's song, on the taking of the famous *Teach*, or *Blackbeard* the pirate. They were wretched stuff, in street-ballad style; and when they were printed, my brother sent me about the town to sell them. The first sold prodigiously, the event being recent, and having made a great noise. This success flattered my vanity; but my father discouraged me by criticizing my performances, and telling me verse-makers were generally beggars. Thus I escaped being a poet, and probably a very bad one; but, as prose writing has been of great use to me in the course of my life, and was a principal means of my advancement, I shall tell you how in such a situation I acquired what little ability I may be supposed to have in that way.

There was another bookish lad in the town, John Collins by name, with whom I was intimately acquainted. We sometimes disputed, and very fond we were of argument, and very desirous of confuting one another; which disputatious turn, by the way, is apt to become a very bad habit, making people often extremely disagreeable in company, by the contradiction that is necessary to bring it into practice; and thence, besides souring and spoiling the conversation, it is productive of disgusts, and perhaps enmities, with those who may have occasion for friendship. I had caught this by reading my father's books of dispute on religion. Persons of good sense, I have since observed, seldom fall into it, except lawyers, university men, and generally men of all sorts who have been bred at Edinburgh.

A question was once, somehow or other, started between Collins and me, on the propriety of educating the female sex in learning, and their abilities for study. He was of opinion that it was improper, and that they were naturally unequal to it. I took the contrary side, perhaps a little for dispute's sake. He was naturally more eloquent, having a greater plenty of words; and sometimes, as I thought, I was vanquished more by his fluency than by the strength of his reasons. As we parted without settling the point, and were not to see one another again for some time, I sat down to put my arguments in writing, which I copied fair and sent to him. He answered, and I replied. Three or four letters on a side had passed, when my father happened to find my papers and read them. Without entering into the subject in dispute, he took occasion to talk to me about my manner of writing; observed, that though I had the advantage of my antagonist in correct spelling and pointing (which he attributed to the printing-house), I fell far short in elegance of expression, in method, and in perspicuity, of which he convinced me by several instances. I saw the justice of his remarks, and thence grew more attentive to my manner of writing, and determined to endeavor to improve my style.

About this time, I met with an odd volume of the *Spectator*. I had never before seen any of them. I bought it, read it over and over, and was much delighted with it. I thought the writing excellent, and wished, if possible, to imitate it. With that view, I took some of the papers, and making short hints of the sentiments in each sentence, laid them by a few days, and then, without looking at the book, tried to complete the papers again, by expressing each hinted sentiment at length, and as fully as it had been expressed before, in any suitable words that should occur to me. Then I compared my *Spectator* with the original, discovered some of my faults, and corrected them. But I found I wanted a stock of words, or a readiness in recollecting and using them, which I thought I should have acquired before that time, if I had gone on making verses; since the continual search for words of the same import, but of different length to suit the measure, or of different sound for the rhyme, would have laid me under a constant necessity of searching for variety, and also have tended to fix that variety in my mind, and make me master of it. Therefore I took some of the tales in the

Spectator and turned them into verse; and, after a time, when I had pretty well forgotten the prose, turned them back again.

I also sometimes jumbled my collection of hints into confusion, and after some weeks endeavored to reduce them into the best order before I began to form the full sentences and complete the subject. This was to teach me method in the arrangement of the thoughts. By comparing my work with the original, I discovered many faults, and corrected them; but I sometimes had the pleasure to fancy that, in certain particulars of small consequence, I had been fortunate enough to improve the method or the language, and this encouraged me to think that I might in time come to be a tolerable English writer; of which I was extremely ambitious. The time I allotted for writing exercises, and for reading, was at night, or before work began in the morning, or on Sundays, when I contrived to be in the printing-house, avoiding as much as I could the constant attendance at public worship, which my father used to exact of me when I was under his care, and which I still continued to consider a duty, though I could not afford time to practise it.

When about sixteen years of age, I happened to meet with a book, written by one Tryon, recommending a vegetable diet. I determined to go into it. My brother, being yet unmarried, did not keep house, but boarded himself and his apprentices in another family. My refusing to eat flesh occasioned an inconvenience, and I was frequently chid for my singularity. I made myself acquainted with Tryon's manner of preparing some of his dishes, such as boiling potatoes or rice, making hasty-pudding, and a few others, and then proposed to my brother, that if he would give me weekly half the money he paid for my board, I would board myself. He instantly agreed to it, and I presently found that I could save half what he paid me. This was an additional fund for buying of books; but I had another advantage in it. My brother and the rest going from the printing-house to their meals, I remained there alone, and, despatching presently my light repast (which was often no more than a biscuit, or a slice of bread, a handful of raisins, or a tart from the pastry cook's, and a glass of water), had the rest of the time, till their return, for study; in which I made the greater progress from that greater clearness of head, and quicker apprehension, which generally attend temperance in eating and drinking. Now it was, that, being on some occasion made ashamed of my ignorance in figures, which I had twice failed learning when at school, I took Cocker's book on Arithmetic, and went through the whole by myself with the greatest ease.

I also read Seller's and Sturmy's book on *Navigation*, which made me acquainted with the little geometry it contains, but I never proceeded far in that science. I read about this time Locke *on Human Understanding*, and *The Art of Thinking* by Messrs. de Port-Royal.

While I was intent on improving my language, I met with an English Grammar (I think it was Greenwood's), having at the end of it two little sketches on the Arts of Rhetoric and Logic, the latter finishing with a dispute in the Socratic method. And, soon after, I procured Xenophon's *Memorable Things of Socrates*, wherein there are many examples of the same method. I was charmed with it, adopted it, dropped my abrupt contradiction and positive argumentation, and put on the humble inquirer. And being then, from reading Shaftesbury and Collins, made a doubter, as I already was in many points of our religious doctrines, I found this method the safest for myself, and very embarrassing to those against whom I used it; therefore I took delight in it, practised it continually, and grew very artful and expert in drawing people, even of superior knowledge, into concessions the consequences of which they did not foresee, entangling them in difficulties out of which they could not extricate themselves, and so obtaining victories that neither myself nor my cause always deserved.

I continued this method some few years, but gradually left it, retaining only the habit of expressing myself in terms of modest diffidence, never using, when I advance anything that may possibly be disputed, the words *certainly, undoubtedly*, or any others that give the air of positiveness to an opinion; but rather saying, *I conceive*, or *apprehend*, a thing to be so and so; *It appears to me*, or *I should not think it, so or so, for such and such reasons ;* or, *I imagine it to be so ;* or, *It is so, if I am not mistaken*. This habit, I believe, has been of great advantage to me, when I have had occasion to inculcate my opinions, and persuade men into measures that I have been from time to time engaged in promoting. And as the chief ends of conversation are to *inform* or to be *informed*, to *please* or to *persuade*, I wish well-meaning and sensible men would not lessen their power of doing good by a positive, assuming manner, that seldom fails to disgust, tends to create opposition, and to defeat most of those purposes for which speech was given to us. In fact, if you wish to instruct others, a positive, dogmatical manner in advancing your sentiments may occasion opposition, and prevent a candid attention. If you desire instruction and improvement from others, you should not at the same time express yourself fixed in your present opinions. Modest and sensible men, who do not love disputation, will leave you undisturbed in the possession of your errors. In adopting such a manner, you can seldom expect to please your hearers, or obtain the concurrence you desire. Pope judiciously observes,

> " Men must be taught as if you taught them not,
> And things unknown proposed as things forgot."

He also recommends it to us

> " To speak, though sure, with seeming diffidence."

And he might have joined with this line that which he has coupled with another, I think less properly, —

> " For want of modesty is want of sense."

If you ask, Why less properly? I must repeat the lines,

> " Immodest words admit of no defence,
> For want of modesty is want of sense."

Now, is not the *want of sense*, where a man is so unfortunate as to want it, some apology for his *want of modesty?* And would not the lines stand more justly thus?

> " Immodest words admit *but* this defence,
> That want of modesty is want of sense."

This, however, I should submit to better judgments.

My brother had, in 1720 or 1721, begun to print a newspaper. It was the second that appeared in America,* and was called the *New England Courant.* The only one before it was the *Boston News-Letter.* I remember his being dissuaded by some of his friends from the undertaking, as not likely to succeed, one newspaper being in their judgment enough for America. At this time, 1771, there are not less than five-and-twenty. He went on, however, with the undertaking. I was employed to carry the papers to the customers, after having worked in composing the types, and printing off the sheets.

He had some ingenious men among his friends, who amused themselves by writing little pieces for this paper, which gained it credit, and made it more in demand, and these gentlemen often visited us. Hearing their conversations, and their accounts of

* A mistake. The *Boston Gazette* and the *American Weekly Mercury,* of Philadelphia, were both of prior origin.

the approbation their papers were received with, I was excited to try my hand among them. But, being still a boy, and suspecting that my brother would object to printing anything of mine in his paper, if he knew it to be mine, I contrived to disguise my hand, and, writing an anonymous paper, I put it at night under the door of the printing-house. It was found in the morning, and communicated to his writing friends, when they called in as usual. They read it, commented on it in my hearing, and I had the exquisite pleasure of finding it met with their approbation, and that, in their different guesses at the author, none were named but men of some character among us for learning and ingenuity. I suppose that I was rather lucky in my judges, and that they were not really so very good as I then believed them to be. Encouraged, however, by this attempt, I wrote and sent in the same way to the press several other pieces, that were equally approved; and I kept my secret till all my fund of sense for such performances was exhausted, and then discovered it, when I began to be considered a little more by my brother's acquaintance.

However, that did not quite please him, as he thought it tended to make me too vain. This might be one occasion of the differences we began to have about this time. Though a brother, he considered himself as my master, and me as his apprentice, and accordingly expected the same services from me as he would from another, while I thought he degraded me too much in some he required of me, who from a brother expected more indulgence. Our disputes were often brought before our father, and I fancy I was either generally in the right, or else a better pleader, because the judgment was generally in my favor. But my brother was passionate, and had often beaten me, which I took extremely amiss; and, thinking my apprenticeship very tedious, I was continually wishing for some opportunity of shortening it, which at length offered in a manner unexpected. Perhaps this harsh and tyrannical treatment of me might be a means of impressing me with the aversion to arbitrary power that has stuck to me through my whole life.

One of the pieces in our newspaper on some political point, which I have now forgotten, gave offence to the Assembly. He was taken up, censured, and imprisoned for a month by the Speaker's warrant, I suppose because he would not discover the author. I too was taken up and examined before the Council; but, though I did not give them any satisfaction, they contented themselves with admonishing me, and dismissed me, considering me perhaps as an apprentice, who was bound to keep his master's

12

secrets. During my brother's confinement, which I resented a good deal, notwithstanding our private differences, I had the management of the paper; and I made bold to give our rulers some rubs in it, which my brother took very kindly, while others began to consider me in an unfavorable light, as a youth that had a turn for libelling and satire.

My brother's discharge was accompanied with an order, and a very odd one, that " *James Franklin* should no longer print the newspaper called *The New England Courant.*" * On a consultation held in our printing-office amongst his friends, what he should do in this conjuncture, it was proposed to elude the order by changing the name of the paper. But my brother, seeing inconveniences in this, came to a conclusion, as a better way, to let the paper in future be printed in the name of *Benjamin Franklin;* and, in order to avoid the censure of the Assembly, that might fall on him as still printing it by his apprentice, he contrived and consented that my old indenture should be returned to me with a discharge on the back of it, to show in case of necessity; and, in order to secure to him the benefit of my service, I should sign new indentures for the remainder of my time, which were to be kept private. A very flimsy scheme it was; however, it was immediately executed, and the paper was printed accordingly, under my name, for several months.

At length, a fresh difference arising between my brother and me, I took upon me to assert my freedom; presuming that he would not venture to produce the new indentures. It was not fair in me to take this advantage, and this I therefore reckon one of the first *errata* of my life; but the unfairness of it weighed little with me when under the impressions of resentment for the blows his passion too often urged him to bestow upon me. Though he was otherwise not an ill-natured man; perhaps I was too saucy and provoking.

When he found I would leave him, he took care to prevent my getting employment in any other printing-house of the town, by going round and speaking to every master, who accordingly refused to give me work. I then thought of going to New York, as the nearest place where there was a printer. And I was rather inclined to leave Boston, when I reflected that I had already made myself a little obnoxious to the governing party,

* An unwarrantable and despotic act; there being nothing libellous, or even reasonably offensive, in any of the articles the publication of which in the *Courant* was thus resented. James Franklin removed soon afterwards to Newport, and established the *Rhode Island Gazette*, Sept. 1732. He died Feb. 1735.

and, from the arbitrary proceedings of the Assembly in my brother's case, it was likely I might, if I stayed, soon bring myself into scrapes ; and further, that my indiscreet disputations about religion began to make me pointed at with horror by good people, as an infidel and atheist. I concluded, therefore, to remove to New York ; but my father now siding with my brother, I was sensible that, if I attempted to go openly, means would be used to prevent me. My friend Collins, therefore, undertook to manage my flight. He agreed with the captain of a New York sloop to take me, under pretence of my being a young man of his acquaintance that had an intrigue with a girl of bad character, whose parents would compel me to marry her, and that I could neither appear or come away publicly. I sold my books to raise a little money, was taken on board the sloop privately, had a fair wind, and in three days found myself at New York, near three hundred miles from my home, at the age of seventeen (October 1723), without the least recommendation, or knowledge of any person in the place, and very little money in my pocket.

The inclination I had had for the sea was by this time done away, or I might now have gratified it. But having another profession, and conceiving myself a pretty good workman, I offered my services to a printer of the place, old Mr. William Bradford, who had been the first printer in Pennsylvania, but had removed thence, in consequence of a quarrel with the Governor, George Keith. He could give me no employment, having little to do, and hands enough already ; but he said, " My son at Philadelphia has lately lost his principal hand, Aquila Rose, by death; if you go thither, I believe he may employ you." Philadelphia was one hundred miles further ; I set out, however, in a boat for Amboy, leaving my chest and things to follow me round by sea.

In crossing the bay, we met with a squall that tore our rotten sails to pieces, prevented our getting into the Kill, and drove us upon Long Island. In our way, a drunken Dutchman, who was a passenger too, fell overboard ; when he was sinking I reached through the water to his shock pate, and drew him up, so that we got him in again. His ducking sobered him a little, and he went to sleep, taking first out of his pocket a book, which he desired I would dry for him. It proved to be my old favorite author, Bunyan's *Pilgrim's Progress*, in Dutch, finely printed on good paper, copper cuts, a dress better than I had ever seen it wear in its own language. I have since found that it has been translated into most of the languages of Europe, and suppose it has been more generally read than any other book, except perhaps the Bible. Honest John was the first that I know of who mixed narration and dialogue; a method of writing very engaging to the reader, who, in the most interesting parts, finds himself, as it were, admitted into the company and present at the conversation. Defoe has imitated him successfully in his *Robinson Crusoe*, in his *Moll Flanders*, and other pieces; and Richardson has done the same in his *Pamela*, &c.

On approaching the island, we found it was in a place where there could be no landing, there being a great surge on the stony beach. So we dropped anchor, and swung out our cable towards the shore. Some people came down to the shore, and hallooed to us, as we did to them; but the wind was so high, and the surge so loud, that we could not understand each other. There were some small boats near the shore, and we made signs, and called to them to fetch us; but they either did not comprehend us, or it was impracticable, so they went off. Night approaching, we had no remedy but to have patience till the wind abated; and in the mean time the boatmen and myself concluded to sleep, if we could; and so we crowded into the hatches, where we joined the Dutchman, who was still wet, and the spray, breaking over the head of our boat, leaked through to us, so that we were soon almost as wet as he. In this manner we lay all night, with very little rest; but, the wind abating the next day, we made a shift to reach Amboy before night; having been thirty hours on the water without victuals, or any drink but a bottle of filthy rum; the water we sailed on being salt.

In the evening I found myself very feverish, and went to bed; but, having read somewhere that cold water drunk plentifully was good for a fever, I followed the prescription, and sweat plentifully most of the night. My fever left me, and in the morning, crossing the ferry, I proceeded on my journey on foot, having fifty miles to go to Burlington, where I was told I should find boats that would carry me the rest of the way to Philadelphia.

CHAPTER II.

Night at an Inn—Arrival in Philadelphia—Meets his future Wife—The
First House he slept in—Engaged by Keimer – Acquaintance with Gov.
Keith—Visit to Boston—His Father's Advice—Visits his Brother John
at Newport—A Lure and an Escape—Stay in New York—An Unruly
Companion—A Great Erratum—Big Promises and Small Fulfilment—
An Uneasy Conscience—Abandons a Vegetable Diet—Mode of Life
with Keimer—Courtship—Acquaintances—Trials at Composition—
Sails for London with Ralph—Looks into the Bag for his Letters of In-
troduction.

IT rained very hard all the day; I was thoroughly soaked,
and by noon a good deal tired; so I stopped at a poor inn,
where I stayed all night, beginning now to wish I had never
left home. I made so miserable a figure, too, that I found, by
the questions asked me, I was suspected to be some runaway in-
dentured servant, and in danger of being taken up on that
suspicion. However, I proceeded next day, and got in the
evening to an inn, within eight or ten miles of Burlington, kept
by one Dr. Brown. He entered into conversation with me while
I took some refreshment, and, finding I had read a little, became
very obliging and friendly. Our acquaintance continued all
the rest of his life. He had been, I imagine, an ambulatory
quack doctor, for there was no town in England, nor any country
in Europe, of which he could not give a very particular account.
He had some letters, and was ingenious, but he was an infidel,
and wickedly undertook, some years after, to turn the Bible into
doggerel verse; as Cotton had formerly done with Virgil. By
this means he set many facts in a ridiculous light, and might
have done mischief with weak minds if his work had been published; but it never was.

At his house I lay that night, and arrived the next morning
at Burlington; but had the mortification to find that the regular boats were gone a little before, and no other expected to go
before Tuesday, this being Saturday. Wherefore I returned to
an old woman in the town, of whom I had bought some ginger-
bread to eat on the water, and asked her advice. She proposed
to lodge me till a passage by some other boat occurred. I
accepted her offer, being much fatigued by travelling on foot.
Understanding I was a printer, she would have had me remain
in that town and follow my business; being ignorant what stock
was necessary to begin with. She was very hospitable, gave me

12*

a dinner of ox-cheek with great good will, accepting only of a
pot of ale in return ; and I thought myself fixed till Tuesday
should come.   However, walking in the evening by the side of
the river, a boat came by, which I found was going towards
Philadelphia, with several people in her.   They took me in, and,
as there was no wind, we rowed all the way; and about midnight, not having yet seen the city, some of the company were
confident we must have passed it, and would row no further ;
others knew not where we were, so we put towards the shore,
got into a creek, landed near an old fence, with the rails of
which we made a fire, the night being cold, in October, and
there we remained till daylight.   Then one of the company
knew the place to be Cooper's Creek, a little above Philadelphia,
which we saw as soon as we got out of the creek, and arrived
there about eight or nine o'clock on the Sunday morning, and
landed at Market-street wharf.

I have been the more particular in this description of my
journey, and shall be so of my first entry into that city, that
you may in your mind compare such unlikely beginnings with
the figure I have since made there.   I was in my working dress,
my best clothes coming round by sea.   I was dirty, from my
being so long in the boat.   My pockets were stuffed out with
shirts and stockings, and I knew no one, nor where to look for
lodging.   Fatigued with walking, rowing, and the want of sleep,
I was very hungry ; and my whole stock of cash consisted in a
single dollar, and about a shilling in copper coin, which I gave
to the boatmen for my passage.   At first they refused it, on
account of my having rowed ; but I insisted on their taking it.
Man is sometimes more generous when he has little money than
when he has plenty ; perhaps to prevent his being thought to
have but little.

I walked towards the top of the street, gazing about till near
Market-street, where I met a boy with bread.   I had often
made a meal of dry bread, and, inquiring where he had bought
it, I went immediately to the baker's he directed me to.   I
asked for biscuits, meaning such as we had at Boston ; that sort,
it seems, was not made in Philadelphia.   I then asked for a
three-penny loaf, and was told they had none.   Not knowing
the different prices, nor the names of the different sorts of bread,
I told him to give me three-penny worth of any sort.   He gave
me accordingly three great puffy rolls.   I was surprised at the
quantity, but took it, and, having no room in my pockets, walked
off with a roll under each arm, and eating the other.   Thus I
went up Market-street as far as Fourth-street, passing by the

door of Mr. Read, my future wife's father; when she, standing at the door, saw me, and thought I made, as I certainly did, a most awkward, ridiculous appearance. Then I turned and went down Chestnut-street and part of Walnut-street, eating my roll all the way, and, coming round, found myself again at Market-street wharf, near the boat I came in, to which I went for a draught of the river water; and, being filled with one of my rolls, gave the other two to a woman and her child that came down the river in the boat with us, and were waiting to go further.

Thus refreshed, I walked again up the street, which by this time had many clean-dressed people in it, who were all walking the same way. I joined them, and thereby was led into the great meeting-house of the Quakers, near the market. I sat down among them, and, after looking round a while and hearing nothing said, being very drowsy through labor and want of rest the preceding night, I fell fast asleep, and continued so till the meeting broke up, when some one was kind enough to rouse me. This, therefore, was the first house I was in, or slept in, in Philadelphia.

I then walked down towards the river, and looking in the faces of every one, I met a young Quaker man whose counte-nance pleased me, and, accosting him, requested he would tell me where a stranger could get a lodging. We were then near the sign of the Three Mariners. "Here," said he, "is a house where they receive strangers, but it is not a reputable one; if thee wilt walk with me, I 'll show thee a better one;" and he conducted me to the Crooked Billet, in Water-street. There I got a dinner; and while I was eating, several questions were asked me; as, from my youth and appearance, I was suspected of being a runaway.

After dinner, my host having shown me to a bed, I laid myself on it without undressing, and slept till six in the evening, when I was called to supper. I went to bed again very early, and slept very soundly till next morning. Then I dressed myself as neat as I could, and went to Andrew Bradford, the printer's. I found in the shop the old man his father, whom I had seen at New York, and who, travelling on horseback, had got to Phila-delphia before me. He introduced me to his son, who received me civilly, gave me a breakfast, but told me he did not at present want a hand, being lately supplied with one; but there was another printer in town, lately set up, one Keimer, who perhaps might employ me; if not, I should be welcome to lodge at his house, and he would give me a little work to do now and then, till fuller business should offer.

The old gentleman said he would go with me to the new printer; and when we found him, "Neighbor," said Bradford, "I have brought to see you a young man of your business; perhaps you may want such a one." He asked me a few questions, put a composing-stick in my hand to see how I worked, and then said he would employ me soon, though he had just then nothing for me to do. And taking old Bradford, whom he had never seen before, to be one of the town's people that had a good will for him, entered into a conversation on his present undertaking and prospects; while Bradford, not discovering that he was the other printer's father, on Keimer's saying he expected soon to get the greatest part of the business into his own hands, drew him on by artful questions, and starting little doubts, to explain all his views, what influence he relied on, and in what manner he intended to proceed. I, who stood by and heard all, saw immediately that one was a crafty old sophister, and the other a true novice. Bradford left me with Keimer, who was greatly surprised when I told him who the old man was.

The printing-house, I found, consisted of an old, damaged press, and a small, worn-out fount of English types, which he was using himself, composing an *Elegy* on Aquila Rose, before mentioned; an ingenious young man, of excellent character, much respected in the town, secretary to the Assembly, and a pretty poet. Keimer made verses too, but very indifferently. He could not be said to *write* them, for his method was to compose them in the types directly out of his head. There being no copy, but one pair of cases, and the *Elegy* probably requiring all the letter, no one could help him. I endeavored to put his press (which he had not yet used, and of which he understood nothing) into order to be worked with; and, promising to come and print off his *Elegy*, as soon as he should have got it ready, I returned to Bradford's, who gave me a little job to do for the present, and there I lodged and dieted. A few days after, Keimer sent for me to print off the *Elegy*. And now he had got another pair of cases, and a pamphlet to reprint, on which he set me to work.

These two printers I found poorly qualified for their business. Bradford had not been bred to it, and was very illiterate; and Keimer, though something of a scholar, was a mere compositor, knowing nothing of press-work. He had been one of the French prophets, and could act their enthusiastic agitations. At this time he did not profess any particular religion, but something of all on occasion ; was very ignorant of the world, and had, as I afterwards found, a good deal of the knave in his composition. He did not like my lodging at Bradford's while I worked with him. He had a house, indeed, but without furniture, so he could not lodge me ; but he got me a lodging at Mr. Read's, before mentioned, who was the owner of his house ; and, my chest of clothes being come by this time, I made rather a more respectable appearance in the eyes of Miss Read than I had done when she first happened to see me eating my roll in the street.

I began now to have some acquaintance among the young people of the town that were lovers of reading, with whom I spent my evenings very pleasantly ; and gained money by my industry and frugality. I lived very contented, and forgot Boston as much as I could, and did not wish it should be known where I resided, except to my friend Collins, who was in the secret, and kept it faithfully. At length, however, an incident happened that occasioned my return home much sooner than I had intended. I had a brother-in-law, Robert Homes, master of a sloop that traded between Boston and Delaware. He being at Newcastle, forty miles below Philadelphia, and hearing of me, wrote me a letter mentioning the grief of my relations and friends in Boston at my abrupt departure, assuring me of their good will to me, and that everything would be accommodated to my mind, if I would return ; to which he entreated me earnestly. I wrote an answer to his letter, thanked him for his advice, but stated my reasons for quitting Boston so fully, and in such a light, as to convince him I was not so much in the wrong as he had apprehended.

Sir William Keith, governor of the province, was then at Newcastle, and Captain Homes, happening to be in company with him when my letter came to hand, spoke to him of me, and showed him the letter. The governor read it, and seemed surprised when he was told my age. He said I appeared a young man of promising parts, and therefore should be encouraged ; the printers at Philadelphia were wretched ones ; and, if I would set up there, he made no doubt I should succeed ; for his part, he would procure me the public business, and do me every other service in his power. This my brother-in-law, Homes, afterwards told me in Boston ; but I knew as yet nothing of it ; when one day, Keimer and I being at work together near the window, we saw the governor and another gentleman (who proved to be Colonel French, of Newcastle, in the province of

Delaware), finely dressed, come directly across the street to our house, and heard them at the door.

Keimer ran down immediately, thinking it a visit to him; but the governor inquired for me, came up, and, with a condescension and politeness I had been quite unused to, made me many compliments, desired to be acquainted with me, blamed me kindly for not having made myself known to him when I first came to the place, and would have me away with him to the tavern, where he was going with Colonel French, to taste, as he said, some excellent madeira. I was not a little surprised, and Keimer stared with astonishment. I went, however, with the governor and Colonel French, to a tavern at the corner of Third-street, and over the madeira he proposed my setting up my business. He stated the probabilities of my success, and both he and Colonel French assured me I should have their interest and influence to obtain for me the public business of both governments. And, as I expressed doubts that my father would assist me in it, Sir William said he would give me a letter to him, in which he would set forth the advantages, and he did not doubt he should determine him to comply. So it was concluded I should return to Boston by the first vessel, with the governor's letter to my father. In the mean time it was to be kept a secret, and I went on working with Keimer as usual. The governor sent for me now and then to dine with him, which I considered a great honor; more particularly as he conversed with me in a most affable, familiar and friendly manner.

About the end of April 1724, a little vessel offered for Boston. I took leave of Keimer, as going to see my friends. The governor gave me an ample letter, saying many flattering things of me to my father, and strongly recommending the project of my setting up at Philadelphia, as a thing that would make my fortune. We struck on a shoal in going down the bay, and sprung a-leak; we had a blustering time at sea, and were obliged to pump almost continually, at which I took my turn. We arrived safe, however, at Boston, in about a fortnight. I had been absent seven months, and my friends had heard nothing of me; for my brother Homes was not yet returned, and had not written about me. My unexpected appearance surprised the family; all were, however, very glad to see me, and made me welcome, except my brother. I went to see him at his printing-house. I was better dressed than ever while in his service, having a genteel new suit from head to foot, a watch, and my pockets lined with near five pounds sterling in silver.

He received me not very frankly, looked me all over, and turned to his work again.

The journeymen were inquisitive where I had been, what sort of a country it was, and how I liked it. I praised it much, and the happy life I led in it, expressing strongly my intention of returning to it; and, one of them asking what kind of money we had there, I produced a handful of silver and spread it before them, which was a kind of *raree-show* they had not been used to, paper being the money of Boston. Then I took an opportunity of letting them see my watch; and lastly (my brother still grum and sullen) gave them a dollar to drink, and took my leave. This visit of mine offended him extremely. For, when my mother some time after spoke to him of a reconciliation, and of her wish to see us on good terms together, and that we might live for the future as brothers, he said I had insulted him in such a manner before his people that he could never forget or forgive it. In this, however, he was mistaken.

My father received the governor's letter with some surprise, but said little of it to me for some time. Captain Homes returning, he showed it to him, and asked him if he knew Sir William Keith, and what kind of man he was; adding that he must be of small discretion, to think of setting a youth up in business who wanted three years to arrive at man's estate. Homes said what he could in favor of the project, but my father was decidedly against it, and at last gave a flat denial. He wrote a civil letter to Sir William, thanking him for the patronage he had so kindly offered me, and declining to assist me as yet in setting up, I being in his opinion too young to be trusted with the management of an undertaking so important, and for which the preparation required a considerable expenditure.

My *old* companion, Collins, who was a clerk in the post-office, pleased with the account I gave him of my new country, determined to go thither also; and, while I waited for my father's determination, he set out before me by land to Rhode Island, leaving his books, which were a pretty collection in mathematics and natural philosophy, to come with mine and me to New York; where he proposed to wait for me.

My father, though he did not approve Sir William's proposition, was yet pleased that I had been able to obtain so advantageous a character from a person of such note where I had resided, and that I had been so industrious and careful as to equip myself so handsomely in so short a time; therefore, seeing no prospect of an accommodation between my brother and me, he gave his consent to my returning again to Philadelphia

advised me to behave respectfully to the people there, endeavor
to obtain the general esteem, and avoid lampooning and libelling,
to which he thought I had too much inclination; telling me
that by steady industry and prudent parsimony I might save
enough, by the time I was one-and-twenty, to set me up; and
that if I came near the matter he would help me out with the
rest. This was all I could obtain, except some small gifts as
tokens of his and my mother's love, when I embarked again for
New York; now with their approbation and their blessing.

The sloop putting in at Newport, Rhode Island, I visited my
brother John, who had been married and settled there some
years. He received me very affectionately, for he always loved
me. A friend of his, one Vernon, having some money due to him
in Pennsylvania, about thirty-five pounds currency, desired I
would recover it for him, and keep it till I had his directions
what to employ it in. Accordingly he gave me an order to
receive it. This business afterwards occasioned me a good deal
of uneasiness.

At Newport we took in a number of passengers, amongst
whom were two young women travelling together, and a sensible,
matron-like Quaker lady, with her servants. I had shown an
obliging disposition to render her some little services, which
probably impressed her with sentiments of good will towards
me; for when she witnessed the daily growing familiarity between the young women and myself, which they appeared to
encourage, she took me aside, and said, "Young man, I am
concerned for thee, as thou hast no friend with thee, and seems
not to know much of the world, or of the snares youth is exposed to; depend upon it, these are very bad women; I can see
it by all their actions; and if thee art not upon thy guard, they
will draw thee into some danger; they are strangers to thee,
and I advise thee, in a friendly concern for thy welfare, to have
no acquaintance with them." As I seemed at first not to think
so ill of them as she did, she mentioned some things she had observed and heard, that had escaped my notice, but now convinced me she was right. I thanked her for her kind advice,
and promised to follow it. When we arrived at New York,
they told me where they lived, and invited me to come and see
them; but I avoided it, and it was well I did. For the next
day the captain missed a silver spoon and some other things,
that had been taken out of his cabin, and, knowing that these
were a couple of strumpets, he got a warrant to search their
lodgings, found the stolen goods, and had the thieves punished.
So though we had escaped a sunken rock, which we scraped

upon in the passage, I thought this escape of rather more importance to me.

At New York I found my friend Collins, who had arrived
there some time before me. We had been intimate from children, and had read the same books together; but he had the
advantage of more time for reading and studying, and a wonderful genius for mathematical learning, in which he far outstripped
me.   While I lived in Boston, most of my hours of leisure for
conversation were spent with him, and he continued a sober as
well as industrious lad; was much respected for his learning by
several of the clergy and other gentlemen, and seemed to promise
making a good figure in life.   But, during my absence, he had
acquired a habit of drinking brandy; and I found by his own
account, as well as that of others, that he had been drunk every
day since his arrival at New York, and behaved himself in a
very extravagant manner.   He had gamed too and lost his
money, so that I was obliged to discharge his lodgings, and
defray his expenses on the road, and at Philadelphia; which
proved a great burden to me.

The then Governor of New York, Burnet (son of Bishop
Burnet), hearing from the captain that one of the passengers
had a great many books on board, desired him to bring me to
see him.   I waited on him, and should have taken Collins with
me, had he been sober.   The governor received me with great
civility, showed me his library, which was a considerable one,
and we had a good deal of conversation relative to books and
authors.   This was the second governor who had done me the
honor to take notice of me; and for a poor boy, like me, it was
very pleasing.

We proceeded to Philadelphia.   I received in the way Vernon's money, without which we could hardly have finished our
journey.   Collins wished to be employed in some counting-
house; but, whether they discovered his dram-drinking by his
breath, or by his behavior, though he had some recommendations, he met with no success in any application, and continued
lodging and boarding at the same house with me, and at my
expense.   Knowing I had that money of Vernon's, he was
continually borrowing of me, still promising repayment as soon
as he should be in business.   At length he had got so much of
it, that I was distressed to think what I should do in case of
being called on to remit it.

His drinking continued, about which we sometimes quarrelled;
for, when a little intoxicated, he was very irritable.   Once, in
a boat on the Delaware with some other young men, he refused

13

to row in his turn. "I will be rowed home," said he. "We will not row you," said I. "You must," said he, "or stay all night on the water, just as you please." The others said, "Let us row, what signifies it?" But, my mind being soured with his other conduct, I continued to refuse. So he swore he would make me row, or throw me overboard; and coming along stepping on the thwarts towards me, when he came up and struck at me, I clapped my head under his thighs, and, rising, pitched him head foremost into the river. I knew he was a good swimmer, and so was under little concern about him; but before he could get round to lay hold of the boat, we had, with a few strokes, pulled her out of his reach; and whenever he drew near the boat, we asked him if he would row, striking a few strokes to slide her away from him. He was ready to stifle with vexation, and obstinately would not promise to row. Finding him at last beginning to tire, we drew him into the boat, and brought him home dripping wet. We hardly exchanged a civil word after this adventure. At length a West India captain, who had a commission to procure a preceptor for the sons of a gentleman at Barbadoes, met with him, and proposed to carry him thither to fill that situation. He accepted, and promised to remit me what he owed me out of the first money he should receive; but I never heard of him after.

The violation of my trust respecting Vernon's money was one of the first great *errata* of my life; and this showed that my father was not much out in his judgment, when he considered me as too young to manage business. But Sir William, on reading his letter, said he was too prudent, that there was a great difference in persons; and discretion did not always accompany years, nor was youth always without it. "But, since he will not set you up, I will do it myself. Give me an inventory of the things necessary to be had from England, and I will send for them. You shall repay me when you are able; I am resolved to have a good printer here, and I am sure you must succeed." This was spoken with such an appearance of cordiality, that I had not the least doubt of his meaning what he said. I had hitherto kept the proposition of my setting up a secret in Philadelphia, and I still kept it. Had it been known that I depended on the governor, probably some friend, that knew him better, would have advised me not to rely on him; as I afterwards heard it as his known character to be liberal of promises, which he never meant to keep. Yet, unsolicited as he was by me, how could I think his generous offers insincere? I believed him one of the best men in the world.

I presented him an inventory of a little printing-house, amounting, by my computation, to about one hundred pounds sterling. He liked it, but asked me if my being on the spot in England to choose the types, and see that everything was good of the kind, might not be of some advantage. "Then," said he, "when there, you may make acquaintance, and establish correspondences in the bookselling and stationery line." I agreed that this might be advantageous. "Then," said he, "get yourself ready to go with *Annis*;" which was the annual ship, and the only one at that time usually passing between London and Philadelphia. But, as it would be some months before *Annis* sailed, I continued working with Keimer, fretting extremely about the money Collins had got from me, and in great apprehensions of being called upon for it by Vernon. This, however, did not happen for some years after.

I believe I have omitted mentioning, that in my first voyage from Boston to Philadelphia, being becalmed off Block Island, our crew employed themselves in catching cod, and hauled up a great number. Till then, I had stuck to my resolution to eat nothing that had had life; and on this occasion I considered, according to my master Tryon, the taking every fish as a kind of unprovoked murder, since none of them had nor could do us any injury that might justify this massacre. All this seemed very reasonable. But I had been formerly a great lover of fish, and, when it came out of the frying-pan, it smelt admirably well. I balanced some time between principle and inclination, till recollecting that, when the fish were opened, I saw smaller fish taken out of their stomachs, then thought I, "If you eat one another, I don't see why we may not eat you.' So I dined upon cod very heartily, and have since continued to eat as other people; returning only now and then occasionally to a vegetable diet. So convenient a thing it is to be a *reasonable creature*, since it enables one to find or make a *reason* for everything one has a mind to do.

Keimer and I lived on a pretty good familiar footing, and agreed tolerably well; for he suspected nothing of my setting up. He retained a great deal of his old enthusiasm, and loved argumentation. We therefore had many disputations. I used to work him so with my Socratic method, and had trepanned him so often by questions apparently so distant from any point we had in hand, yet by degrees leading to the point and bringing him into difficulties and contradictions, that at last he grew ridiculously cautious, and would hardly answer me the most common question, without asking first, "What do you intend to infer from that?" However, it gave him so high an-opinion of my abilities in the confuting way, that he seriously proposed my being his colleague in a project he had of setting up a new sect. He was to preach the doctrines, and I was to confound all opponents. When he came to explain with me upon the doctrines, I found several conundrums which I objected to, unless I might have my way a little too, and introduce some of mine.

Keimer wore his beard at full length, because somewhere in the Mosaic law it is said, "*Thou shalt not mar the corners of thy beard.*" He likewise kept the Seventh day, Sabbath; and these two points were essential with him. I disliked both; but agreed to them on condition of his adopting the doctrine of not using animal food. "I doubt," said he, "my constitution will not bear it." I assured him it would, and that he would be the better for it. He was usually a great eater, and I wished to give myself some diversion in half starving him. He consented to try the practice, if I would keep him company. I did so, and we held it for three months. Our provisions were purchased, cooked, and brought to us regularly by a woman in the neighborhood, who had from me a list of forty dishes, which she prepared for us at different times, in which there entered neither fish, flesh nor fowl. This whim suited me the better at this time from the cheapness of it, not costing us above eighteen pence sterling each per week. I have since kept several lents most strictly, leaving the common diet for that, and that for the common, abruptly, without the least inconvenience. So that, I think, there is little in the advice of making those changes by easy gradations. I went on pleasantly, but poor Keimer suffered grievously, grew tired of the project, longed for the flesh-pots of Egypt, and ordered a roast pig. He invited me and two women friends to dine with him; but, it being brought too soon upon the table, he could not resist the temptation, and ate the whole before we came.

I had made some courtship during this time to Miss Read. I had a great respect and affection for her, and had some reasons to believe she had the same for me; but, as I was about to take a long voyage, and we were both very young,—only a little above eighteen,—it was thought most prudent by her mother to prevent our going too far at present; as a marriage, if it was to take place, would be more convenient after my return, when I should be, as I hoped, set up in my business. Perhaps too she thought my expectations not so well founded as I imagined them to be.

My chief acquaintances at this time were Charles Osborne, Joseph Watson, and James Ralph; all lovers of reading.   The two first were clerks to an eminent scrivener or conveyancer in the town, Charles Brockden; the other was a clerk to a merchant.   Watson was a pious, sensible young man, of great integrity; the others rather more lax in their principles of religion, particularly Ralph, who, as well as Collins, had been unsettled by me; for which they both made me suffer.   Osborne was sensible, candid, frank; sincere and affectionate to his friends, but in literary matters too fond of criticism.   Ralph was ingenious, genteel in his manners, and extremely eloquent; I think I never knew a prettier talker.   Both were great admirers of poetry, and began to try their hands in little pieces. Many pleasant walks we have had together on Sundays in the woods, on the banks of the Schuylkill, where we read to one another, and conferred on what we had read.

Ralph was inclined to give himself up entirely to poetry, not doubting that he might make great proficiency in it, and even make his fortune by it.   He pretended that the greatest poets must, when they first began to write, have committed as many faults as he did.   Osborne endeavored to dissuade him, assured him he had no genius for poetry, and advised him to think of nothing beyond the business he was bred to; that in the mercantile way, though he had no stock, he might by his diligence and punctuality recommend himself to employment as a factor, and in time acquire wherewith to trade on his own account.   I approved, for my part, the amusing one's self with poetry now and then, so far as to improve one's language, but no further.

On this, it was proposed that we should each of us at our next meeting produce a piece of our own composing, in order to improve by our mutual observations, criticisms, and corrections. As language and expression were what we had in view, we excluded all considerations of invention, by agreeing that the task should be a version of the eighteenth Psalm, which describes the descent of a Deity.   When the time of our meeting drew nigh, Ralph called on me first, and let me know his piece was ready.   I told him I had been busy, and, having little inclination, had done nothing.   He then showed me his piece for my opinion, and I much approved it, as it appeared to me to have great merit.   "Now," said he, "Osborne never will allow the least merit in anything of mine, but makes a thousand criticisms out of mere envy.   He is not so jealous of you; I wish therefore you would take this piece and produce it as yours; I will

13*

pretend not to have had time, and so produce nothing. We shall then hear what he will say to it." It was agreed, and I immediately transcribed it, that it might appear in my own hand.

We met; Watson's performance was read: there were some beauties in it, but many defects. Osborne's was read: it was much better; Ralph did it justice; remarked some faults, but applauded the beauties. He himself had nothing to produce. I was backward, seemed desirous of being excused, had not had sufficient time to correct, &c.; but no excuse could be admitted; produce I must. It was read and repeated: Watson and Osborne gave up the contest, and joined in applauding it. Ralph only made some criticisms, and proposed some amendments; but I defended my text. Osborne was severe against Ralph, and told me he was no better able to criticize than compose verses. As these two were returning home, Osborne expressed himself still more strongly in favor of what he thought my production; having before refrained, as he said, lest I should think he meant to flatter me. "But who would have imagined," said he, "that Franklin was capable of such a performance; such painting, such force, such fire! He has even improved on the original. In common conversation he seems to have no choice of words; he hesitates and blunders; and yet, good God, how he writes!" When we next met, Ralph discovered the trick we had played, and Osborne was laughed at.

This transaction fixed Ralph in his resolution of becoming a poet. I did all I could to dissuade him from it, but he continued scribbling verses till Pope cured him.* He became, however, a pretty good prose writer. More of him hereafter. But, as I may not have occasion to mention the other two, I shall just remark here that Watson died in my arms a few years after, much lamented, being the best of our set. Osborne went to the West Indies, where he became an eminent lawyer and

* Ralph stands pilloried to posterity in Pope's somewhat overrated "Dunciad" —

"Silence, ye wolves, while Ralph to Cynthia howls,
And makes Night hideous; answer him, ye owls!"

The allusion here, Pope tells us, is to "a thing" of Ralph's, entitled "Night." He calls him "a low writer," who praised himself in the journals — wholly illiterate, &c From Franklin's account, he was evidently a man of little principle. This did not prevent his becoming a successful political writer. He was pensioned in consideration of his pamphlets in support of the ministry. Having obtained possession of a manuscript belonging to Frederick, Prince of Wales, his pension was increased, shortly before his death, 1762, to six hundred pounds a year, in consequence of his surrender of the manuscripts.

made money, but died young. He and I had made a serious agreement, that the one who happened first to die should, if possible, make a friendly visit to the other, and acquaint him how he found things in that separate state. But he never fulfilled his promise.

The governor, seeming to like my company, had me frequently at his house, and his setting me up was always mentioned as a fixed thing. I was to take with me letters recommendatory to a number of his friends, besides the letter of credit to furnish me with the necessary money for purchasing the press, types, paper, &c. For these letters I was appointed to call at different times, when they were to be ready; but a future time was still named. Thus we went on till the ship, whose departure too had been several times postponed, was on the point of sailing. Then, when I called to take my leave and receive the letters, his secretary, Dr. Baird, came out to me, and said the governor was extremely busy in writing, but would be down at Newcastle before the ship, and then the letters would be delivered to me.

Ralph, though married, and having one child, had determined to accompany me in this voyage. It was thought he intended to establish a correspondence, and obtain goods to sell on commission; but I found after, that, having some cause of discontent with his wife's relations, he proposed to leave her on their hands, and never to return to America. Having taken leave of my friends, and exchanged promises with Miss Read, I quitted Philadelphia, in the ship, which anchored at Newcastle. The governor was there; but when I went to his lodging, his secretary came to me from him, with expressions of the greatest regret that he could not then see me, being engaged in business of the utmost importance; but that he would send the letters to me on board, wishing me heartily a good voyage, and a speedy return, &c. I returned on board a little puzzled, but still not doubting.

Mr. Andrew Hamilton, a celebrated lawyer of Philadelphia, had taken his passage in the same ship for himself and son, with Mr. Denham, a Quaker merchant, and Messrs. Oniam and Russel, masters of an iron-work in Maryland, who had engaged the great cabin; so that Ralph and I were forced to take up with a berth in the steerage, and, none on board knowing us, were considered as ordinary persons. But Mr. Hamilton and his son (it was James, since governor) returned from Newcastle to Philadelphia; the father being recalled by a great fee to plead for a seized ship. And, just before we sailed, Colonel French coming on board, and showing me great respect, I was more taken notice of, and, with my friend Ralph, invited by the other gentlemen to come into the cabin, there being now room. Accordingly we removed thither.

Understanding that Colonel French had brought on board the governor's despatches, I asked the captain for those letters that were to be under my care. He said all were put into the bag together, and he could not then come at them; but, before we landed in England, I should have an opportunity of picking them out; so I was satisfied at present, and we proceeded on our voyage. We had a sociable company in the cabin, and lived uncommonly well, having the addition of all Mr. Hamilton's stores, who had laid in plentifully. In this passage Mr. Denham contracted a friendship for me that continued during his life. The voyage was otherwise not a pleasant one, as we had a great deal of bad weather.

When we came into the channel, the captain kept his word with me, and gave me an opportunity of examining the bag for the governor's letters. I found some upon which my name was put, as under my care. I picked out six or seven, that, by the hand-writing, I thought might be the promised letters, especially as one of them was addressed to Baskett, the king's printer, and another to some stationer.

CHAPTER III.

Arrival in London — Finds his Letters are Worthless — Intimacy with Ralph — Gets Work in a Printing-house — Metaphysical Treatise — Frequents a Club — A Promise to see Sir Isaac Newton — Sir Hans Sloane — A Dangerous Acquaintance — Offends Ralph — Watts's Printing-house — Press-work — Mode of Life — Habits of London Printers — Makes a Reform — A Landlady and a Recluse — Swimming — Anecdote of Mr. Denham — New Employment — Almost a Swimming-teacher — Sir William Wyndham.

WE arrived in London the 24th December, 1724. I waited upon the stationer, who came first in my way, delivering the letter as from Governor Keith. "I don't know such a person," said he; but, opening the letter, "O! this is from Riddlesden. I have lately found him to be a complete rascal, and I will have nothing to do with him, nor receive any letters from him." So, putting the letter into my hand, he turned on his heel and left me to serve some customer. I was surprised to find these were not the governor's letters ; and, after recollecting and comparing circumstances, I began to doubt his sincerity. I found my friend Denham, and opened the whole affair to him. He let me into Keith's character : told me there was not the least probability that he had written any letters for me ; that no one, who knew him, had the smallest dependence on him ; and he laughed at the idea of the governor's giving me a letter of credit, having, as he said, no credit to give. On my expressing some concern about what I should do, he advised me to endeavor getting some employment in the way of my business. "Among the printers here," said he, "you will improve yourself, and, when you return to America, you will set up to greater advantage."

We both of us happened to know, as well as the stationer, that Riddlesden, the attorney, was a very knave. He had half ruined Miss Read's father, by persuading him to be bound for him. By his letter it appeared there was a secret scheme on foot to the prejudice of Mr. Hamilton (supposed to be then coming over with us); that Keith was concerned in it, with Riddlesden. Denham, who was a friend of Hamilton's, thought he ought to be acquainted with it ; so, when he arrived in England, which was soon after, partly from resentment and ill-will to Keith and Riddlesden, and partly from good-will to him, I waited on him, and gave him the letter. He thanked me cordially, the information being of importance to him ; and from that time he became my friend, greatly to my advantage afterwards on many occasions.

But what shall we think of a governor playing such pitiful tricks, and imposing so grossly on a poor ignorant boy? It was a habit he had acquired. He wished to please everybody ; and, having little to give, he gave expectations. He was otherwise an ingenious, sensible man, a pretty good writer, and a good governor for the people ; though not for his constituents, the Proprietaries, whose instructions he sometimes disregarded. Several of our best laws were of his planning, and passed during his administration.

Ralph and I were inseparable companions. We took lodgings together in Little Britain at three shillings and sixpence a week ; as much as we could then afford. He found some relations, but they were poor and unable to assist him. He now let me know his intentions of remaining in London, and that he never meant to return to Philadelphia. He had brought no money with him ; the whole he could muster having been expended in paying his

passage. I had fifteen pistoles; so he borrowed occasionally
of me to subsist, while he was looking out for business. He
first endeavored to get into the playhouse, believing himself
qualified for an actor; but Wilkes,* to whom he applied, advised
him candidly not to think of that employment, as it was impossible he should succeed in it. Then he proposed to Roberts,
a publisher in Pater Noster Row, to write for him a weekly
paper like the *Spectator*, on certain conditions; which Roberts
did not approve. Then he endeavored to get employment as a
hackney writer, to copy for the stationers and lawyers about the
Temple; but could not find a vacancy.

For myself, I immediately got into work at Palmer's, a famous
printing-house in Bartholomew Close, where I continued near a
year. I was pretty diligent, but I spent with Ralph a good
deal of my earnings at plays and public amusements. We had
nearly consumed all my pistoles, and now just rubbed on from
hand to mouth. He seemed quite to have forgotten his wife
and child; and I by degrees my engagements with Miss Read,
to whom I never wrote more than one letter, and that was to let
her know I was not likely soon to return. This was another of
the great *errata* of my life, which I could wish to correct, if I
were to live it over again. In fact, by our expenses, I was constantly kept unable to pay my passage.

At Palmer's I was employed in composing for the second
edition of Wollaston's "*Religion of Nature*." Some of his
reasonings not appearing to me well founded, I wrote a little
metaphysical piece, in which I made remarks on them. It was
entitled, "*A Dissertation on Liberty and Necessity, Pleasure
and Pain*." I inscribed it to my friend Ralph; I printed a
small number. It occasioned my being more considered by Mr.
Palmer as a young man of some ingenuity, though he seriously
expostulated with me upon the principles of my pamphlet, which
to him appeared abominable. My printing this pamphlet was
another *erratum*. While I lodged in Little Britain, I made an
acquaintance with one Wilcox, a bookseller, whose shop was
next door. He had an immense collection of second-hand books.
Circulating libraries were not then in use; but we agreed that,
on certain reasonable terms, which I have now forgotten, I might
take, read and return, any of his books. This I esteemed a
great advantage, and I made as much use of it as I could.

My pamphlet by some means falling into the hands of one
Lyons, a surgeon, author of a book entitled "*The Infallibility*

* A comedian of some note in his day.

of Human Judgment," it occasioned an acquaintance between us. He took great notice of me; called on me often to converse on those subjects; carried me to the Horns, a pale-ale house in —— Lane, Cheapside, and introduced me to Dr. Mandeville, author of the "*Fable of the Bees*," who had a club there, of which he was the soul, — being a most facetious, entertaining companion. Lyons, too, introduced me to Dr. Pemberton, at Batson's Coffee-house, who promised to give me an opportunity, some time or other, of seeing Sir Isaac Newton, of which I was extremely desirous; but this never happened.

I had brought over a few curiosities, among which the principal was a purse made of the *asbestos*, which purifies by fire. Sir Hans Sloane heard of it, came to see me, and invited me to his house in Bloomsbury-square, showed me all his curiosities, and persuaded me to add that to the number; for which he paid me handsomely.

In our house lodged a young woman, a milliner, who, I think, had a shop in the Cloisters. She had been genteelly bred, was sensible, lively, and of a most pleasing conversation. Ralph read plays to her in the evenings, they grew intimate, she took another lodging, and he followed her. They lived together some time; but, he being still out of business, and her income not sufficient to maintain them with her child, he took a resolution of going from London, to try for a country school, which he thought himself well qualified to undertake, as he wrote an excellent hand, and was a master of arithmetic and accounts. This, however, he deemed a business below him; and, confident of future better fortune, when he should be unwilling to have it known that he was once so meanly employed, he changed his name, and did me the honor to assume mine; for I soon after had a letter from him, acquainting me that he was settled in a small village (in Berkshire, I think it was, where he taught reading and writing to ten or a dozen boys, at sixpence each per week); recommending Mrs. T—— to my care, and desiring me to write to him, directing for *Mr. Franklin*, schoolmaster, at such a place.

He continued to write to me frequently, sending me large specimens of an epic poem, which he was then composing, and desiring my remarks and corrections. These I gave him from time to time, but endeavored rather to discourage his proceedings. One of Young's Satires was then just published. I copied and sent him a great part of it, which set in a strong light the folly of pursuing the Muses. All was in vain; sheets of the poem continued to come by every post. In the mean time, Mrs. T——, having on his account lost her friends and business, was often in distresses, and used to send for me, and borrow what money I could spare to help to alleviate them. I grew fond of her company, and, being at that time under no religious restraint, and taking advantage of my importance to her, I attempted to take some liberties with her (another *erratum*), which she repulsed, with a proper degree of resentment. She wrote to Ralph and acquainted him with my conduct; this occasioned a breach between us; and, when he returned to London, he let me know he considered all the obligations he had been under to me as annulled; from which I concluded I was never to expect his repaying the money I had lent him, or that I had advanced for him. This, however, was of little consequence, as he was totally unable; and by the loss of his friendship I found myself relieved from a heavy burden. I now began to think of getting a little beforehand, and, expecting better employment, I left Palmer's to work at Watts's, near Lincoln's Inn Fields, a still greater printing-house. Here I continued all the rest of my stay in London.*

At my first admission into the printing-house I took to working at press, imagining I felt a want of the bodily exercise I had been used to in America, where press-work is mixed with the composing. I drank only water; the other workmen, near fifty in number, were great drinkers of beer. On occasion I carried up and down stairs a large form of types in each hand, when others carried but one in both hands. They wondered to see, from this and several instances, that the *Water-American*, as they called me, was *stronger* than themselves, who drank *strong* beer! We had an ale-house boy, who attended always in the house to supply the workmen. My companion at the press drank every day a pint before breakfast, a pint at breakfast with his bread and cheese, a pint between breakfast and dinner, a pint at dinner, a pint in the afternoon about six o'clock, and another when he had done his day's work. I thought it a detestable custom; but it was necessary, he supposed, to drink *strong* beer that he might be *strong* to labor. I endeavored to convince him that the bodily strength afforded by beer could only be in proportion to the grain or flour of the barley dissolved in the

* In the year 1768, he visited this same printing-office, and, going up to a particular press, said to the men who were working at it: "Come, my friends, we will drink together. It is now forty years since I worked, like you, at this press, as a journeyman printer." Franklin then sent out for a gallon of porter, and drank with them. This press is now in the Patent Office at Washington.

water of which it was made; that there was more flour in a pennyworth of bread; and therefore, if he could eat that with a pint of water, it would give him more strength than a quart of beer. He drank on, however, and had four or five shillings to pay out of his wages, every Saturday night, for that vile liquor; an expense I was free from. And thus these poor devils keep themselves always under.

Watts, after some weeks, desiring to have me in the composing-room, I left the press-men; a new *bien venu* for drink, being five shillings, was demanded of me by the compositors. I thought it an imposition, as I had paid one to the press-men; the master thought so too, and forbade my paying it. I stood out two or three weeks, was accordingly considered as an excommunicate, and had so many little pieces of private malice practised on me, by mixing my sorts, transposing and breaking my matter, &c. &c., if ever I stepped out of the room, — and all ascribed to the *chapel ghost*, which they said ever haunted those not regularly admitted, — that, notwithstanding the master's protection, I found myself obliged to comply and pay the money; convinced of the folly of being on ill terms with those one is to live with continually.

I was now on a fair footing with them, and soon acquired considerable influence. I proposed some reasonable alterations in their *chapel* * laws, and carried them against all opposition. From my example, a great many of them left their muddling breakfast of beer, bread and cheese, finding they could with me be supplied from a neighboring house with a large porringer of hot water-gruel, sprinkled with pepper, crumbled with bread, and a bit of butter in it, for the price of a pint of beer, namely, three halfpence. This was a more comfortable as well as a cheaper breakfast, and kept their heads clearer. Those who continued sotting with their beer all day were often, by not paying, out of credit at the ale-house, and used to make interest with me to get beer; their *light*, as they phrased it, *being out*. I watched the pay-table on Saturday night, and collected what I stood engaged for them, having to pay sometimes near thirty shillings a week on their accounts. This, and my being esteemed a pretty good *riggite*, — that is, a jocular verbal satirist, — supported my consequence in the society. My constant attendance (I never making a *St. Monday*) recommended me to the master; and my uncommon quickness at composing occasioned my being

---

* A printing-house was formerly called a *chapel* in England, from a tradition that printing was first carried on in an old chapel.

14

put upon work of despatch, which was generally better paid. So I went on now very agreeably.

My lodgings in Little Britain being too remote, I found another in Duke-street, opposite to the Romish chapel. It was up three pair of stairs backwards, at an Italian warehouse. A widow lady kept the house; she had a daughter, and a maid-servant, and a journeyman who attended the warehouse, but lodged abroad. After sending to inquire my character at the house where I last lodged, she agreed to take me in at the same rate, three shillings and sixpence a week; cheaper, as she said, from the protection she expected in having a man to lodge in the house. She was a widow, an elderly woman; had been bred a Protestant, being a clergyman's daughter, but was converted to the Catholic religion by her husband, whose memory she much revered; had lived much among people of distinction, and knew a thousand anecdotes of them as far back as the time of Charles the Second. She was lame in her knees with the gout, and therefore seldom stirred out of her room; so sometimes wanted company; and hers was so highly amusing to me, that I was sure to spend an evening with her whenever she desired it. Our supper was only half an anchovy each, on a very little slice of bread and butter, and half a pint of ale between us; but the entertainment was in her conversation. My always keeping good hours, and giving little trouble in the family, made her unwilling to part with me; so that, when I talked of a lodging I had heard of, nearer my business, for two shillings a week, which, intent as I was on saving money, made some difference, she bid me not think of it, for she would abate me two shillings a week for the future; so I remained with her at one shilling and sixpence as long as I stayed in London.

In a garret of her house there lived a maiden lady of seventy, in the most retired manner, of whom my landlady gave me this account: that she was a Roman Catholic; had been sent abroad when young, and lodged in a nunnery with an intent of be-coming a nun; but, the country not agreeing with her, she returned to England, where, there being no nunnery, she had vowed to lead the life of a nun, as near as might be done in those circumstances. Accordingly, she had given all her estate to charitable purposes, reserving only twelve pounds a year to live on; and out of this sum she still gave a part in charity, living herself on water-gruel only, and using no fire but to boil it. She had lived many years in that garret, being permitted to remain there gratis by successive Catholic tenants of the house below, as they deemed it a blessing to have her there. A priest

visited her, to confess her, every day.   "From this, I asked her,"
said my landlady, "how she, as she lived, could possibly find
so much employment for a confessor." "O," said she, "it is
impossible to avoid *vain thoughts*." I was permitted once to
visit her.   She was cheerful and polite, and conversed pleasantly.
The room was clean, but had no other furniture than a mattress,
a table with a crucifix and a book, a stool which she gave me
to sit on, and a picture over the chimney of St. Veronica displaying her handkerchief, with the miraculous figure of Christ's
bleeding face on it, which she explained to me with great
seriousness.   She looked pale, but was never sick; and I give
it as another instance on how small an income life and health
may be supported.

At Watts's printing-house I contracted an acquaintance with
an ingenious young man, one Wygate, who, having wealthy
relations, had been better educated than most printers; was a
tolerable Latinist, spoke French, and loved reading.   I taught
him and a friend of his to swim, at twice going into the river,
and they soon became good swimmers.   They introduced me to
some gentlemen from the country, who went to Chelsea by water,
to see the College and Don Saltero's curiosities.   In our return,
at the request of the company, whose curiosity Wygate had
excited, I stripped and leaped into the river, and swam from
near Chelsea to Blackfriars; performing in the way many feats
of activity, both upon and under the water, that surprised and
pleased those to whom they were novelties.

I had from a child been delighted with this exercise,* had
studied and practised Thevenot's motions and positions, and
added some of my own, — aiming at the graceful and easy, as well
as the useful.   All these I took this occasion of exhibiting to
the company, and was much flattered by their admiration; and
Wygate, who was desirous of becoming a master, grew more and
more attached to me on that account, as well as from the similarity of our studies.   He at length proposed to me travelling
all over Europe together, supporting ourselves everywhere by
working at our business.   I was once inclined to it; but,
mentioning it to my good friend Mr. Denham, with whom I
often spent an hour when I had leisure, he dissuaded me from
it; advising me to think only of returning to Pennsylvania,
which he was now about to do.

* The experiments of Franklin in floating with a kite-string in his hand,
&c., and his sleeping an hour by the watch while floating, are worthy of
note.   He wrote two interesting letters on the art of swimming.

I must record one trait of this good man's character. He had formerly been in business at Bristol, but failed, in debt to a number of people, compounded, and went to America. There, by a close application to business as a merchant, he acquired a plentiful fortune in a few years. Returning to England in the ship with me, he invited his old creditors to an entertainment, at which he thanked them for the easy composition they had favored him with, and, when they expected nothing but the treat, every man at the first remove found under his plate an order on a banker for the full amount of the unpaid remainder, with interest.

He now told me he was about to return to Philadelphia, and should carry over a great quantity of goods, in order to open a store there. He proposed to take me over as clerk, to keep his books, in which he would instruct me, copy his letters, and attend the store. He added, that, as soon as I should be acquainted with mercantile business, he would promote me by sending me with a cargo of flour and bread to the West Indies, and procure me commissions from others which would be profitable; and, if I managed well, would establish me handsomely. The thing pleased me; for I was grown tired of London, remembered with pleasure the happy months I had spent in Pennsylvania, and wished again to see it. Therefore I immediately agreed on the terms of fifty pounds a year, Pennsylvania money; less, indeed, than my then present gettings as a compositor, but affording a better prospect.

I now took leave of printing, as I thought, forever, and was daily employed in my new business, going about with Mr. Denham among the tradesmen to purchase various articles and see them packed up, delivering messages, calling up workmen to despatch, &c.; and when all was on board, I had a few days' leisure. On one of these days, I was, to my surprise, sent for by a great man I knew only by name, Sir William Wyndham; and I waited upon him. He had heard by some means or other of my swimming from Chelsea to Blackfriars, and of my teaching Wygate and another young man to swim in a few hours. He had two sons, about to set out on their travels; he wished to have them first taught swimming, and proposed to gratify me handsomely if I would teach them. They were not yet come to town, and my stay was uncertain; so I could not undertake it. But, from the incident, I thought it likely that, if I were to remain in England and open a swimming-school, I might get a good deal of money; and it struck me so strongly, that, had the overture been made me sooner, probably I should not so soon have returned to America. Many years after, you and I had something of more importance to do with one of these sons of Sir William Wyndham, become Earl of Egremont, which I shall mention in its place.

Thus I passed about eighteen months in London; most part of the time I worked hard at my business, and spent but little upon myself, except in seeing plays and in books. My friend Ralph had kept me poor; he owed me about twenty-seven pounds, which I was now never likely to receive; a great sum out of my small earnings! I loved him, notwithstanding, for he had many amiable qualities. I had improved my knowledge, however, though I had by no means improved my fortune; but I had made some very ingenious acquaintance, whose conversation was of great advantage to me; and I had read considerably.

CHAPTER IV.

Embarks for Philadelphia — Arrival — Illness and Disappointment — Foreman to Keimer — Breaks with him — Resolves to set up for himself — Meredith — Engraves Plates — Views of Religion — His London Dissertation — New Convictions — Types from London — A Partner — A Croaker — The Junto — Writes the Busy-body — Sets up a Newspaper — Friends in need — Dissolves with Partner — Tract on a Paper Currency — Opens a Stationer's Shop — Thrifty Habits — Matrimonial Designs — Miss Read — Marriage — A Subscription Library.

WE sailed from Gravesend on the 23d of July, 1726. For the incidents of the voyage, I refer you to my journal, where you will find them all minutely related. Perhaps the most important part of that journal is the *plan* * to be found in it, which I formed at sea, for regulating the future conduct of my life. It is the more remarkable, as being formed when I was

* The journal in existence does not contain the *plan* here referred to. In a subsequent chapter of this autobiography, a specimen of the "Plan of Order" is given. The journal consists mostly of details of the customary routine of life at sea. Occasionally we have a Franklinian gleam, as in the following passage : "Truth and sincerity have a certain distinguishing native lustre about them, which cannot be counterfeited; they are like fire and flame, that cannot be painted." He rises to enthusiasm as he records, under date of October 11, 1726, his entrance into the Delaware : "The sun enlivens our stiff limbs with his glorious rays of warmth and brightness. The sky looks gay, with here and there a silver cloud. The fresh breezes from the woods refresh us ; the immediate prospect of liberty, after so long and irksome confinement, ravishes us. In short, all things conspire to make this the most joyful day I ever knew."

14*

so young, and yet being pretty faithfully adhered to quite through to old age.

We landed at Philadelphia the 11th of October, where I found sundry alterations. Keith was no longer governor, being superseded by Major Gordon; I met him walking the streets as a common citizen. He seemed a little ashamed at seeing me, and passed without saying anything. I should have been as much ashamed at seeing Miss Read, had not her friends, despairing, with reason, of my return, after the receipt of my letter, persuaded her to marry another, one Rogers, a potter, which was done in my absence. With him, however, she was never happy, and soon parted from him, refusing to cohabit with him, or bear his name, it being now said he had another wife. He was a worthless fellow, though an excellent workman, which was the temptation to her friends. He got into debt, ran away in 1727 or 1728, went to the West Indies, and died there. Keimer had got a better house, a shop well supplied with stationery, plenty of new types, and a number of hands, though none good, and seemed to have a great deal of business.

Mr. Denham took a store in Water-street, where we opened our goods; I attended the business diligently, studied accounts, and grew in a little time expert at selling. We lodged and boarded together; he counselled me as a father, having a sincere regard for me. I respected and loved him, and we might have gone on together very happily; but, in the beginning of February 1727, when I had just passed my twenty-first year, we both were taken ill. My distemper was a pleurisy, which very nearly carried me off. I suffered a good deal, gave up the point in my own mind, and was at the time rather disappointed when I found myself recovering; regretting, in some degree, that I must now, some time or other, have all that disagreeable work to go over again. I forget what Mr. Denham's distemper was; it held him a long time, and at length carried him off. He left me a small legacy in a nuncupative will, as a token of his kindness for me, and he left me once more to the wide world; for the store was taken into the care of his executors, and my employment under him ended.

My brother-in-law, Homes, being now at Philadelphia, advised my return to my business; and Keimer tempted me, with an offer of large wages by the year, to come and take the management of his printing-house, that he might better attend to his stationer's shop. I had heard a bad character of him in London from his wife and her friends, and was not for having any more to do with him. I wished for employment as a merchant's clerk; but, not meeting with any, I closed again with Keimer. I found in his house these hands: Hugh Meredith, a Welsh Pennsylvanian, thirty years of age, bred to country work; he was honest, sensible, a man of experience, and fond of reading, but addicted to drinking. Stephen Potts, a young countryman of full age, bred to the same, of uncommon natural parts, and great wit and humor; but a little idle. These he had agreed with at extreme low wages per week, to be raised a shilling every three months, as they would deserve by improving in their business; and the expectation of these high wages, to come on hereafter, was what he had drawn them in with. Meredith was to work at press, Potts at bookbinding, which he by agreement was to teach them, though he knew neither one nor the other. John ———, a wild Irishman, brought up to no business, whose service, for four years, Keimer had purchased from the captain of a ship; he too was to be made a pressman. George Webb, an Oxford scholar, whose time for four years he had likewise bought, intending him for a compositor, of whom more presently; and David Harry, a country boy, whom he had taken apprentice.

I soon perceived that the intention of engaging me at wages so much higher than he had been used to give was, to have these raw, cheap hands formed through me; and, as soon as I had instructed them, they being all articled to him, he should be able to do without me. I went, however, very cheerfully, put his printing-house in order, which had been in great confusion, and brought his hands by degrees to mind their business and to do it better.

It was an odd thing to find an Oxford scholar in the situation of a bought servant. He was not more than eighteen years of age, and he gave me this account of himself: that he was born in Gloucester, educated at a grammar school, and had been distinguished among the scholars for some apparent superiority in performing his part when they exhibited plays; belonged to the Wits' Club there, and had written some pieces in prose and verse, which were printed in the Gloucester newspapers. Thence was sent to Oxford; there he continued about a year, but not well satisfied; wishing, of all things, to see London, and become a player. At length, receiving his quarterly allowance of fifteen guineas, instead of discharging his debts, he went out of town, hid his gown in a furze-bush, and walked to London; where, having no friend to advise him, he fell into bad company, soon spent his guineas, found no means of being introduced among the players, grew necessitous, pawned his clothes, and wanted bread. Walking the street very hungry, not knowing what to do with himself, a crimp's bill was put into his hand, offering immediate entertainment and encouragement to such as would bind themselves to serve in America. He went directly, signed the indentures, was put into the ship, and came over ; never writing a line to his friends to acquaint them what was become of him. He was lively, witty, good-natured, and a pleasant companion ; but idle, thoughtless, and imprudent to the last degree.

John, the Irishman, soon ran away ; with the rest I began to live very agreeably, for they all respected me the more, as they found Keimer incapable of instructing them, and that from me they learned something daily. My acquaintance with ingenious people in the town increased. We never worked on Saturday, that being Keimer's Sabbath ; so that I had two days for reading. Keimer himself treated me with great civility and apparent regard, and nothing now made me uneasy but my debt to Vernon, which I was yet unable to pay, being hitherto but a poor economist. He, however, kindly made no demand of it.

Our printing-house often wanted sorts, and there was no letter-foundery in America ; I had seen types cast at James's in London, but without much attention to the manner; however, I contrived a mould, and made use of the letters we had as puncheons, struck the matrices in lead, and thus supplied in a pretty tolerable way all deficiencies. I also engraved several things, on occasion ; made the ink ; I was warehouseman, and, in short, quite a *fac-totum*. But, however serviceable I might be, I found that my services became every day of less importance, as the other hands improved in their business ; and, when Keimer paid me a second quarter's wages, he let me know that he felt them too heavy, and thought I should make an abatement. He grew by degrees less civil, put on more the airs of master, frequently found fault, was captious, and seemed ready for an outbreaking. I went on nevertheless with a good deal of patience, thinking that his encumbered circumstances were partly the cause.

At length a trifle snapt our connection ; for, a great noise happening near the court-house, I put my head out of the window to see what was the matter. Keimer, being in the street, looked up and saw me, called out to me in a loud voice and angry tone to mind my business ; adding some reproachful words, that nettled me the more for their publicity ; all the neighbors who were looking out on the same occasion being witnesses how I was treated. He came up immediately into the printing-house, continued the quarrel, high words passed on both sides, he gave me the quarter's warning we had stipulated, expressing a wish that he had not been obliged to so long a warning. I told him his wish was unnecessary, for I would leave him that instant; and so, taking my hat, walked out of doors, desiring Meredith, whom I saw below, to take care of some things I left, and bring them to my lodgings.

Meredith came accordingly in the evening, when we talked my affair over. He had conceived a great regard for me, and was very unwilling that I should leave the house while he remained in it. He dissuaded me from returning to my native country, which I began to think of; he reminded me that Keimer was in debt for all he possessed, that his creditors began to be uneasy; that he kept his shop miserably, sold often without a profit for ready money, and often trusted without keeping accounts; that he must therefore fail, which would make a vacancy I might profit of. I objected my want of money. He then let me know that his father had a high opinion of me, and, from some discourse that had passed between them, he was sure would advance money to set me up, if I would enter into partnership with him. "My time," said he, "will be out with Keimer in the spring; by that time we may have our press and types in from London. I am sensible I am no workman; if you like it, your skill in the business shall be set against the stock I furnish, and we will share the profits equally."

The proposal was agreeable to me, and I consented; his father was in town, and approved of it; the more, as he said I had great influence with his son, had prevailed on him to abstain long from dram-drinking, and he hoped might break him of that wretched habit entirely, when we came to be so closely connected. I gave an inventory to the father, who carried it to a merchant; the things were sent for, the secret was to be kept till they should arrive, and in the mean time I was to get work, if I could, at the other printing-house. But I found no vacancy there, and so remained idle a few days, when Keimer, on a prospect of being employed to print some paper money in New Jersey, which would require cuts and various types, that I only could supply, and apprehending Bradford might engage me and get the job from him, sent me a very civil message, that old friends should not part for a few words the effect of sudden passion, and wishing me to return. Meredith persuaded me to comply, as it would give more opportunity for his improvement under my daily instructions; so I returned, and we went on more smoothly than for some time before. The New Jersey job was obtained; I contrived a copper-plate press for it, the first that had been seen in the country; I cut several ornaments and checks for the bills. We went together to Burlington, where I executed the whole to satisfaction; and he received so large a sum for the work as to be enabled thereby to keep himself longer from ruin.

At Burlington I made acquaintance with many principal people of the province. Several of them had been appointed by the Assembly a committee to attend the press, and take care that no more bills were printed than the law directed. They were, therefore, by turns constantly with us, and generally he who attended brought with him a friend or two for company. My mind having been much more improved by reading than Keimer's, I suppose it was for that reason my conversation seemed to be more valued. They had me to their houses, introduced me to their friends, and showed me much civility; while he, though the master, was a little neglected. In truth, he was an odd creature; ignorant of common life, fond of rudely opposing received opinions, slovenly to extreme dirtiness, enthusiastic in some points of religion, and a little knavish withal.

We continued there near three months; and by that time I could reckon among my acquired friends Judge Allen, Samuel Bustill, the Secretary of the Province, Isaac Pearson, Joseph Cooper, and several of the Smiths, members of Assembly, and Isaac Decow, the Surveyor-General. The latter was a shrewd, sagacious old man, who told me that he began for himself when young by wheeling clay for the brickmakers, learned to write after he was of age, carried the chain for surveyors, who taught him surveying, and he had now, by his industry, acquired a good estate; and, said he, "I foresee that you will soon work this man out of his business, and make a fortune in it at Philadelphia." He had then not the least intimation of my intention to set up there or anywhere else. These friends were afterwards of great use to me, as I occasionally was to some of them. They all continued their regard for me as long as they lived.

Before I enter upon my public appearance in business, it may be well to let you know the then state of my mind with regard to my principles and morals, that you may see how far these influenced the future events of my life. My parents had early given me religious impressions, and brought me through my childhood piously, in the Dissenting way. But I was scarce fifteen, when, after doubting by turns several points, as I found them disputed in the different books I read, I began to doubt of the Revelation itself. Some books against Deism fell into my hands; they were said to be the substance of the sermons which had been preached at Boyle's Lectures. It happened that they wrought an effect on me quite contrary to what was intended by them.   For the arguments of the Deists, which were quoted to be refuted, appeared to me much stronger than the refutations; in short, I soon became a thorough Deist.   My arguments perverted some others, particularly Collins and Ralph; but, each of these having wronged me greatly without the least compunction, and recollecting Keith's conduct towards me (who was another freethinker), and my own towards Vernon and Miss Read, — which at times gave me great trouble, — I began to suspect that this doctrine, though it might be true, was not very useful. My London pamphlet, printed in 1725,* which had for its motto these lines of Dryden :

> " Whatever is, is right.   But purblind man
> Sees but a part o' the chain, the nearest links ;
> His eyes not carrying to that equal beam,
> That poises all above ; "

and which, from the attributes of God, his infinite wisdom, goodness and power, concluded that nothing could possibly be wrong in the world, and that vice and virtue were empty distinctions, no such things existing, appeared now not so clever a performance as I once thought it ; and I doubted whether some error

---

* A copy of this, long supposed to be out of existence, has been recently found in England.   It is an octavo of sixteen pages, entitled " A Discourse on Liberty and Necessity, Pleasure and Pain ; in a letter to a friend." The motto from Dryden, misquoted by Franklin in his Autobiography, is given as follows :

> " Whatever is, is in its causes just,
> Since all things are by fate ; but purblind man
> Sees but a part of the chain, the nearest link ;
> His eyes not carrying to the equal beam
> That poises all above."

The pamphlet, of which only a hundred copies were printed, is addressed " to Mr. J. R." (James Ralph), and commences : " Sir, I have here, according to your request, given you my present thoughts *on the general state of the universe ; "* and concludes : " Truth will be truth, though it sometimes prove mortifying and distasteful."   The attempt was rather presumptuous for a lad of nineteen ; and Franklin lived to be ashamed of it.   He says, in a letter to Benjamin Vaughan, dated November 9, 1779: " In 1730 I wrote a piece on the other side of the question, which began with laying for its foundation this fact, ' *That almost all men in all ages and countries have at times made use of* PRAYER.'   Thence I reasoned that, if all things are ordained, prayer must, among the rest, be ordained.   But, as prayer can procure no change in things that are ordained, praying must then be useless, and an absurdity.   God would, therefore, not ordain praying, if everything else was ordained.   But praying exists; therefore all other things are not ordained, &c.   This pamphlet was never printed, and the manuscript has been long lost.   The great uncertainty I found in metaphysical reasonings disgusted me, and I quitted that kind of reading and study for others more satisfactory."

had not insinuated itself unperceived into my argument, so as to infect all that followed, as is common in metaphysical reasonings.

I grew convinced that *truth, sincerity* and *integrity*, in dealings between man and man, were of the utmost importance to the felicity of life; and I formed written resolutions, which still remain in my journal-book, to practise them ever while I lived. Revelation had, indeed, no weight with me, as such; but I entertained an opinion that, though certain actions might not be bad *because* they were forbidden by it, or good *because* it commanded them, yet probably those actions might be forbidden *because* they were bad for us, or commanded *because* they were beneficial to us, in their own natures, all the circumstances of things considered. And this persuasion, with the kind hand of Providence, or some guardian angel, or accidental favorable circumstances and situations, or all together, preserved me through this dangerous time of youth, and the hazardous situations I was sometimes in among strangers, remote from the eye and advice of my father, free from any *wilful* gross immorality or injustice, that might have been expected from my want of religion. I say *wilful*, because the instances I have mentioned had something of *necessity* in them, from my youth, inexperience, and the knavery of others. I had therefore a tolerable character to begin the world with; I valued it properly, and determined to preserve it.

We had not been long returned to Philadelphia, before the new types arrived from London. We settled with Keimer, and left him by his consent before he heard of it. We found a house to let near the Market, and took it. To lessen the rent, which was then but twenty-four pounds a year, though I have since known it to let for seventy, we took in Thomas Godfrey, a glazier, and his family, who were to pay a considerable part of it to us, and we to board with them. We had scarce opened our letters and put our press in order, before George House, an acquaintance of mine, brought a countryman to us, whom he had met in the street, inquiring for a printer. All our cash was now expended in the variety of particulars we had been obliged to procure, and this countryman's five shillings, being our first-fruits, and coming so seasonably, gave me more pleasure than any crown I have since earned; and the gratitude I felt towards House has made me often more ready than perhaps I otherwise should have been to assist young beginners.

There are croakers in every country, always boding its ruin. Such a one there lived in Philadelphia; a person of note, an elderly man, with a wise look and a very grave manner of speaking; his name was Samuel Mickle. This gentleman, a stranger to me, stopped me one day at my door, and asked me if I was the young man who had lately opened a new printing-house. Being answered in the affirmative, he said he was sorry for me, because it was an expensive undertaking, and the expense would be lost; for Philadelphia was a sinking place, the people already half bankrupts, or near being so; all the appearances of the contrary, such as new buildings and the rise of rents, being, to his certain knowledge, fallacious; for they were, in fact, among the things that would ruin us. Then he gave me such a detail of misfortunes now existing, or that were soon to exist, that he left me half melancholy. Had I known him before I engaged in this business, probably I never should have done it. This person continued to live in this decaying place, and to declaim in the same strain, refusing, for many years, to buy a house there, because all was going to destruction; and, at last, I had the pleasure of seeing him give five times as much for one as he might have bought it for when he first began croaking.

I should have mentioned before that, in the autumn of the preceding year, I had formed most of my ingenious acquaintance into a club for mutual improvement, which we called the JUNTO; we met on Friday evenings. The rules that I drew up required that every member, in his turn, should produce one or more queries on any point of Morals, Politics or Natural Philosophy, to be discussed by the company; and once in three months produce and read an essay of his own writing, on any subject he pleased. Our debates were to be under the direction of a president, and to be conducted in the sincere spirit of inquiry after truth, without fondness for dispute, or desire of victory; and, to prevent warmth, all expressions of positiveness in opinions, or direct contradiction, were after some time made contraband, and prohibited under small pecuniary penalties.

The first members were Joseph Breintnal, a copier of deeds for the scriveners, — a good-natured, friendly, middle-aged man, a great lover of poetry, reading all he could meet with, and writing some that was tolerable; very ingenious in making little knick-knackeries, and of sensible conversation.

Thomas Godfrey, a self-taught mathematician, great in his way, and afterwards inventor of what is now called *Hadley's Quadrant.** But he knew little out of his way, and was not a pleasing companion; as, like most great mathematicians I have

---

* The claim of Godfrey to an invention, the merit of which Hadley surreptitiously obtained by copying Godfrey's instrument, has been fully established.

met with, he expected universal precision in everything said, or was forever denying or distinguishing upon trifles, to the disturbance of all conversation.   He soon left us.

Nicholas Scull, a surveyor, afterwards surveyor-general, who loved books, and sometimes made a few verses.

William Parsons, bred a shoemaker, but, loving reading, had acquired a considerable share of mathematics, which he first studied with a view to astrology, and afterwards laughed at it. He also became surveyor-general.

William Maugridge, joiner, but a most exquisite mechanic, and a solid, sensible man.

Hugh Meredith, Stephen Potts, and George Webb, I have characterized before.

Robert Grace, a young gentleman of some fortune, generous lively, and witty ; a lover of punning, and of his friends.

Lastly, William Coleman, then a merchant's clerk, about my age, who had the coolest, clearest head, the best heart, and the exactest morals, of almost any man I ever met with.   He became afterwards a merchant of great note, and one of our provincial judges.   Our friendship continued without interruption to his death, upwards of forty years; and the club continued almost as long, and was the best school of philosophy, morality and politics, that then existed in the province ; for our queries which were read the week preceding their discussion, put us upon reading with attention on the several subjects, that we might speak more to the purpose ; and here too we acquired better habits of conversation, everything being studied in our rules which might prevent our disgusting each other.   Hence the long continuance of the club, which I shall have frequent occasion to speak further of hereafter.

But my giving this account of it here is to show something of the interest I had, every one of these exerting themselves in recommending business to us.   Breintnal, particularly, procured us from the Quakers the printing of forty sheets of their history, the rest being to be done by Keimer ; and upon these we worked exceedingly hard, for the price was low.   It was a folio, *pro patriâ* size, in pica, with long primer notes.   I composed a sheet a day, and Meredith worked it off at press ; it was often eleven at night, and sometimes later, before I had finished my distribution for the next day's work.   For the little jobs sent in by our other friends now and then put us back.   But, so determined I was to continue doing a sheet a day of the folio, that one night, when, having imposed my forms, I thought my day's work over, one of them, by accident, was broken, and two pages reduced to *pi.* I immediately distributed and composed it over again before I went to bed; and this industry, visible to our neighbors, began to give us character and credit; particularly, I was told, that, mention being made of the new printing-office at the merchants' every-night club, the general opinion was that it must fail, there being already two printers in the place, Keimer and Bradford; but Dr. Baird (whom you and I saw, many years after, at his native place, St. Andrew's in Scotland) gave a contrary opinion. "For the industry of that Franklin," said he, "is superior to anything I ever saw of the kind; I see him still at work when I go home from club, and he is at work again before his neighbors are out of bed." This struck the rest, and we soon after had offers from one of them to supply us with stationery; but as yet we did not choose to engage in shop business.

I mention this industry more particularly and the more freely, though it seems to be talking in my own praise, that those of my posterity who shall read it may know the use of that virtue, when they see its effects in my favor throughout this relation.

George Webb, who had found a female friend that lent him wherewith to purchase his time of Keimer, now came to offer himself as a journeyman to us. We could not then employ him; but I foolishly let him know, as a secret, that I soon intended to begin a newspaper, and might then have work for him. My hopes of success, as I told him, were founded on this: that the then only newspaper, printed by Bradford, was a paltry thing, wretchedly managed, no way entertaining, and yet was profitable to him; I therefore freely thought a good paper would scarcely fail of good encouragement. I requested Webb not to mention it; but he told it to Keimer, who immediately, to be beforehand with me, published proposals for one himself, on which Webb was to be employed. I was vexed at this; and, to counteract them, not being able to commence our paper, I wrote several amusing pieces for Bradford's paper, under the title of the Busy Body, which Breintnal continued some months. By this means the attention of the public was fixed on that paper, and Keimer's proposals, which we burlesqued and ridiculed, were disregarded. He began his paper, however; and, before carrying it on three quarters of a year, with at most only ninety subscribers, he offered it me for a trifle; and I, having been ready some time to go on with it, took it in hand directly; and it proved in a few years extremely profitable to me.*

* This was the *Pennsylvania Gazette*, the publication of which Franklin and Meredith began in 1729. There is a story that some of his subscribers,

I perceive that I am apt to speak in the singular number, though our partnership still continued; it may be that in fact the whole management of the business lay upon me. Meredith was no compositor, a poor pressman, and seldom sober. My friends lamented my connection with him, but I was to make the best of it.

Our first papers made quite a different appearance from any before in the province; a better type, and better printed; but some remarks of my writing, on the dispute then going on between Governor Burnet and the Massachusetts Assembly, struck the principal people, occasioned the paper and the manager of it to be much talked of, and in a few weeks brought them all to be our subscribers.

Their example was followed by many, and our number went on growing continually. This was one of the first good effects of my having learned a little to scribble; another was, that the leading men, seeing a newspaper now in the hands of those who could also handle a pen, thought it convenient to oblige and encourage me. Bradford still printed the votes, and laws, and other public business. He had printed an address of the House to the Governor, in a coarse, blundering manner; we reprinted it elegantly and correctly, and sent one to every member. They were sensible of the difference, it strengthened the hands of our friends in the House, and they voted us their printers for the year ensuing.

Among my friends in the House, I must not forget Mr. Hamilton, before mentioned, who was then returned from England, and had a seat in it. He interested himself for me strongly in that instance, as he did in many others afterwards, continuing his patronage till his death.*

Mr. Vernon, about this time, put me in mind of the debt I owed him, but did not press me. I wrote to him an ingenuous letter of acknowledgment, craving his forbearance a little longer, which he allowed me. As soon as I was able, I paid him the principal with the interest, and many thanks; so that *erratum* was in some degree corrected.†

---

having threatened to " stop their patronage" in consequence of certain sentiments he had advanced, Franklin invited them to dine, and having set before them a coarse meal mixture, known as *sawdust pudding*, on their drawing back from it he remarked, " Gentlemen, a man who can subsist on sawdust pudding need call no man *patron.*"

* I afterwards procured for his son *five hundred pounds.*

† While minister at Paris, he rendered important services to a descendant of Mr. Vernon.

But now another difficulty came upon me, which I had never the least reason to expect. Mr. Meredith's father, who was to have paid for our printing-house, according to the expectations given me, was able to advance only one hundred pounds currency, which had been paid; and a hundred more were due to the merchant, who grew impatient and sued us all. We gave bail, but saw that, if the money could not be raised in time, the suit must soon come to a judgment and execution, and our hopeful prospects must, with us, be ruined; as the press and letters must be sold for payment, perhaps at half price.

In this distress two true friends, whose kindness I have never forgotten, nor ever shall forget while I can remember anything, came to me separately, unknown to each other, and, without any application from me, offered each of them to advance me all the money that should be necessary to enable me to take the whole business upon myself, if that should be practicable; but they did not like my continuing the partnership with Meredith, who, as they said, was often seen drunk in the street, playing at low games in ale-houses, much to our discredit. These two friends were William Coleman and Robert Grace. I told them I could not propose a separation while any prospect remained of the Merediths' fulfilling their part of our agreement; because I thought myself under great obligations to them for what they had done, and would do if they could; but, if they finally failed in their performance, and our partnership must be dissolved, I should then think myself at liberty to accept the assistance of my friends.

Thus the matter rested for some time, when I said to my partner, "Perhaps your father is dissatisfied at the part you have undertaken in this affair of ours, and is unwilling to advance for you and me, what he would for you. If that is the case, tell me, and I will resign the whole to you, and go about my business." "No," said he, "my father has really been disappointed, and is really unable; and I am unwilling to distress him further. I see this is a business I am not fit for. I was bred a farmer, and it was folly in me to come to town, and put myself, at thirty years of age, an apprentice to learn a new trade. Many of our Welsh people are going to settle in North Carolina, where land is cheap. I am inclined to go with them, and follow my old employment; you may find friends to assist you. If you will take the debts of the company upon you, return to my father the hundred pounds he has advanced, pay my little personal debts, and give me thirty pounds and a new saddle, I will relinquish the partnership, and leave the whole in your hands."

15*

I agreed to this proposal; it was drawn up in writing, signed and sealed immediately. I gave him what he demanded, and he went soon after to Carolina; whence he sent me next year two long letters, containing the best account that had been given of that country, the climate, the soil, and husbandry; for in those matters he was very judicious. I printed them in the papers, and they gave great satisfaction to the public.

As soon as he was gone, I recurred to my two friends; and, because I would not give an unkind preference to either, I took half of what each had offered and I wanted of one, and half of the other; paid off the company's debts, and went on with the business in my own name; advertising that the partnership was dissolved. I think this was in or about the year 1729.*

About this time there was a cry among the people for more paper money; only fifteen thousand pounds being extant in the province, and that soon to be sunk. The wealthy inhabitants opposed any addition, being against all paper currency, from the apprehension that it would depreciate, as it had done in New England, to the injury of all creditors. We had discussed this point in our Junto, where I was on the side of an addition; being persuaded that the first small sum struck in 1723 had done much good, by increasing the trade, employment, and number of inhabitants in the province; since I now saw all the old houses inhabited, and many new ones building; whereas I remembered well, when I first walked about the streets of Philadelphia, eating my roll, I saw many of the houses in Walnut-street, between Second and Front streets, with bills on their doors, " *To be let ;* " and many likewise in Chestnut-street and other streets; which made me think the inhabitants of the city were one after another deserting it.

Our debates possessed me so fully of the subject, that I wrote and printed an anonymous pamphlet on it, entitled, " *The Nature and Necessity of a Paper Currency.*" It was well received by the common people in general; but the rich men disliked it, for it increased and strengthened the clamor for more money ; and, they happening to have no writers among them that were able to answer it, their opposition slackened, and the point was carried by a majority in the House. My friends there, who considered I had been of some service, thought fit to reward me by employing me in printing the money; a very profitable job, and a great help to me. This was another advantage gained by my being able to write.

* By the agreement, still extant, it appears that the dissolution took place July 14, 1730.

The utility of this currency became by time and experience so evident, that the principles upon which it was founded were never afterwards much disputed; so that it grew soon to fifty-five thousand pounds, and in 1739 to eighty thousand pounds; trade, building, and inhabitants, all the while increasing. Though I now think there are limits, beyond which the quantity may be hurtful.

I soon after obtained, through my friend Hamilton, the printing of the Newcastle paper money, another profitable job, as I then thought it; small things appearing great to those in small circumstances; and these to me were really great advantages, as they were great encouragements. Mr. Hamilton procured for me also the printing of the laws and votes of that government, which continued in my hands as long as I followed the business.

I now opened a small stationer's shop. I had in it blanks of all kinds; the correctest that ever appeared among us. I was assisted in that by my friend Breintnal. I had also paper, parchment, chapmen's books, &c. One Whitemarsh, a compositor I had known in London, an excellent workman, now came to me, and worked with me constantly and diligently; and I took an apprentice, the son of Aquila Rose.

I began now gradually to pay off the debt I was under for the printing-house. In order to secure my credit and character as a tradesman, I took care not only to be in *reality* industrious and frugal, but to avoid the appearances to the contrary. I dressed plain, and was seen at no places of idle diversion. I never went out a fishing or shooting; a book indeed sometimes debauched me from my work, but that was seldom, was private, and gave no scandal; and, to show that I was not above my business, I sometimes brought home the paper I purchased at the stores through the streets on a wheelbarrow. Thus being esteemed an industrious, thriving young man, and paying duly for what I bought, the merchants who imported stationery solicited my custom; others proposed supplying me with books, and I went on prosperously. In the mean time, Keimer's credit and business declining daily, he was at last forced to sell his printing-house to satisfy his creditors. He went to Barbadoes, and there lived some years in very poor circumstances.

His apprentice, David Harry, whom I had instructed while I worked with him, set up in his place at Philadelphia, having bought his materials. I was at first apprehensive of a powerful rival in Harry, as his friends were very able, and had a good deal of interest. I therefore proposed a partnership to him, which he fortunately for me rejected with scorn. He was very proud, dressed like a gentleman, lived expensively, took much diversion and pleasure abroad, ran in debt, and neglected his business; upon which all business left him, and, finding nothing to do, he followed Keimer to Barbadoes, taking the printing-house with him. There this apprentice employed his former master as a journeyman; they quarrelled often, and Harry went continually behindhand, and at length was obliged to sell his types and return to country work in Pennsylvania. The person who bought them employed Keimer to use them, but a few years after he died.

There remained now no other printer in Philadelphia, but the old Bradford; but he was rich and easy, did a little in the business by straggling hands, but was not anxious about it. However, as he held the post-office, it was imagined he had better opportunities of obtaining news, his paper was thought a better distributer of advertisements than mine, and therefore had many more; which was a profitable thing to him, and a disadvantage to me. For, though I did indeed receive and send papers by the post, yet the public opinion was otherwise; for what I did send was by bribing the riders, who took them privately; Bradford being unkind enough to forbid it, which occasioned some resentment on my part; and I thought so meanly of the practice, that, when I afterwards came into his situation, I took care never to imitate it.

I had hitherto continued to board with Godfrey, who lived in a part of my house with his wife and children, and had one side of the shop for his glazier's business, though he worked little, being always absorbed in his mathematics. Mrs. Godfrey projected a match for me with a relation's daughter, took opportunities of bringing us often together, till a serious courtship on my part ensued; the girl being in herself very deserving. The old folks encouraged me by continual invitations to supper, and by leaving us together, till at length it was time to explain. Mrs. Godfrey managed our little treaty. I let her know that I expected as much money with their daughter as would pay off my remaining debt for the printing-house; which I believe was not then above a hundred pounds. She brought me word they had no such sum to spare; I said they might mortgage their house in the loan-office. The answer to this, after some days, was, that they did not approve the match; that, on inquiry of Bradford, they had been informed the printing business was not a profitable one, the types would soon be worn out and more wanted; that Keimer and David Harry had failed, one after the other, and I should probably soon follow them; and therefore I was forbidden the house, and the daughter was shut up.

Whether this was a real change of sentiment, or only artifice, on a supposition of our being too far engaged in affection to retract, and therefore that we should steal a marriage, which would leave them at liberty to give or withhold what they pleased, I know not. But I suspected the motive, resented it, and went no more. Mrs. Godfrey brought me afterwards some more favorable accounts of their disposition, and would have drawn me on again; but I declared absolutely my resolution to have nothing more to do with that family. This was resented by the Godfreys, we differed, and they removed, leaving me the whole house, and I resolved to take no more inmates.

But this affair having turned my thoughts to marriage, I looked round me and made overtures of acquaintance in other places; but soon found that, the business of a printer being generally thought a poor one, I was not to expect money with a wife, unless with such a one as I should not otherwise think agreeable. In the mean time, that hard to be governed passion of youth had hurried me frequently into intrigues with low women that fell in my way, which were attended with some expense and great inconvenience, besides a continual risk to my health by a distemper, which of all things I dreaded, though by great good luck I escaped it.

A friendly correspondence as neighbors had continued between me and Miss Read's family, who all had a regard for me from the time of my first lodging in their house. I was often invited there and consulted in their affairs, wherein I sometimes was of service. I pitied poor Miss Read's unfortunate situation, who was generally dejected, seldom cheerful, and avoided company. I considered my giddiness and inconstancy when in London as in a great degree the cause of her unhappiness; though the mother was good enough to think the fault more her own than mine, as she had prevented our marrying before I went thither, and persuaded the other match in my absence. Our mutual affection was revived, but there were now great objections to our union. That match was indeed looked upon as invalid, a preceding wife being said to be living in England; but this could not easily be proved, because of the distance, &c.; and, though there was a report of his death, it was not certain. Then, though it should be true, he had left many debts, which his successor might be called upon to pay. We ventured, however, over all these difficulties, and I took her to wife Sept. 1st, 1730. None of the inconveniences happened that we had apprehended;

she proved a good and faithful helpmate, assisted me much by attending to the shop; we throve together, and ever mutually endeavored to make each other happy. Thus I corrected that great *erratum* as well as I could.

About this time, our club meeting, not at a tavern, but in a little room of Mr. Grace's, set apart for that purpose, a proposition was made by me, that, since our books were often referred to in our disquisitions upon the queries, it might be convenient to us to have them all together where we met, that upon occasion they might be consulted; and by thus clubbing our books in a common library, we should, while we liked to keep them together, have each of us the advantage of using the books of all the other members, which would be nearly as beneficial as if each owned the whole. It was liked and agreed to, and we filled one end of the room with such books as we could best spare. The number was not so great as we expected; and, though they had been of great use, yet some inconveniences occurring for want of due care of them, the collection after about a year was separated, and each took his books home again.

And now I set on foot my first project of a public nature, that for a subscription library. I drew up the proposals, got them put into form by our great scrivener, Brockden, and, by the help of my friends in the Junto, procured fifty subscribers of forty shillings each to begin with, and ten shillings a year for fifty years, the term our company was to continue. We afterwards obtained a charter, the company being increased to one hundred. This was the mother of all the North American subscription libraries, now so numerous. It is become a great thing itself, and continually goes on increasing. These libraries have improved the general conversation of the Americans, made the common tradesmen and farmers as intelligent as most gentlemen from other countries, and perhaps have contributed in some degree to the stand so generally made throughout the colonies in defence of their privileges.*

---

* Here the Twyford letter, forming the First Part of the Autobiography, ends. The Second Part, of which the next chapter is the commencement, was begun at Passy, twelve years after the First was written, namely, in 1783. It is preceded by the following paragraphs, referring to letters from Benjamin Vaughan and Abel James, urging Franklin to resume his Autobiography, the First Part of which they had read in manuscript :

"It is some time since I received the above letters, but I have been too busy till now to think of complying with the request they contain. It might, too, be much better done if I were at home among my papers, which would aid my memory, and help to ascertain dates; but my return being uncertain, and having just now a little leisure, I will endeavor to recollect and write what I can; if I live to get home, it may there be corrected and improved.

CHAPTER V.

Second Part of the Autobiography — The Philadelphia Library — A Good Wife — Family Habits — Religious Views — Moral Perfection aimed at — A Group of Virtues — Scheme for their Attainment — Mottoes and Prayers — Story of the Speckled Axe — Result of the Scheme — Project of a Treatise on the Art of Virtue.

AT the time I established myself in Pennsylvania, there was not a good bookseller's shop in any of the colonies to the southward of Boston. In New York and Philadelphia, the printers were indeed stationers, but they sold only paper, almanacs, ballads, and a few common school-books. Those who loved reading were obliged to send for their books from England; the members of the Junto had each a few. We had left the ale-house, where we first met, and hired a room to hold our club in. I proposed that we should all of us bring our books to that room ; where they would not only be ready to consult in our conferences, but become a common benefit, each of us being at liberty to borrow such as he wished to read at home. This was accordingly done, and for some time contented us.

Finding the advantage of this little collection, I proposed to render the benefit from the books more common, by commencing a public subscription library. I drew a sketch of the plan and rules that would be necessary, and got a skilful conveyancer, Mr. Charles Brockden, to put the whole in form of articles of agreement to be subscribed; by which each subscriber engaged to pay a certain sum down for the first purchase of the books, and an annual contribution for increasing them.

So few were the readers at that time in Philadelphia, and the majority of us so poor, that I was not able, with great industry, to find more than fifty persons, mostly young tradesmen, willing to pay down for this purpose forty shillings each, and ten shillings per annum. With this little fund we began. The books were imported ; the library was opened one day in the week for lending them to the subscribers, on their promissory notes to pay double the value if not duly returned. The institution soon manifested its utility, was imitated by other towns,

---

" Not having any copy here of what is already written, I know not whether an account is given of the means I used to establish the Philadelphia public library, - which from a small beginning is now become so considerable, — though I remember to have come down to near the time of that transaction (1730). I will therefore begin here with an account of it, which may be struck out if found to have been already given."

and in other provinces. The libraries were augmented by donations; reading became fashionable; and our people, having no public amusements to divert their attention from study, became better acquainted with books; and in a few years were observed by strangers to be better instructed and more intelligent than people of the same rank generally are in other countries.

When we were about to sign the above-mentioned articles, which were to be binding on us, our heirs, &c., for fifty years, Mr. Brockden, the scrivener, said to us, "You are young men, but it is scarcely probable that any of you will live to see the expiration of the term fixed in the instrument." A number of us, however, are yet living, but the instrument was after a few years rendered null, by a charter that incorporated and gave perpetuity to the company.*

The objections and reluctances I met with, in soliciting the subscriptions, made me soon feel the impropriety of presenting one's self as the proposer of any useful project, that might be supposed to raise one's reputation in the smallest degree above that of one's neighbors, when one has need of their assistance to accomplish that project. I therefore put myself as much as I could out of sight, and stated it as a scheme of a *number of friends*, who had requested me to go about and propose it to such as they thought lovers of reading. In this way my affair went on more smoothly, and I ever after practised it on such occasions; and, from my frequent successes, can heartily recommend it. The present little sacrifice of your vanity will afterwards be amply repaid. If it remains a while uncertain to whom the merit belongs, some one more vain than yourself may be encouraged to claim it, and then even envy will be disposed to do you justice, by plucking those assumed feathers, and restoring them to their right owner.

This library afforded me the means of improvement by constant study, for which I set apart an hour or two each day; and thus repaired in some degree the loss of the learned education my father once intended for me. Reading was the only amusement I allowed myself. I spent no time in taverns, games, or frolics of any kind; and my industry in my business continued as indefatigable as it was necessary. I was indebted for my printing-house; I had a young family coming on to be educated, and I had two competitors to contend with for business, who were established in the place before me.

---

* This library, founded in 1731, was incorporated in 1742. It now numbers upwards of sixty thousand volumes. A marble statue of Franklin, occupying a niche in front of the present building, was presented to the company by Mr. Wm. Bingham. It was executed in Italy at a cost of five hundred guineas.

My circumstances, however, grew daily easier. My original habits of frugality continuing, and my father having, among his instructions to me when a boy, frequently repeated a proverb of Solomon, " *Seest thou a man diligent in his calling, he shall stand before kings, he shall not stand before mean men,*" I thence considered industry as a means of obtaining wealth and distinction, which encouraged me; though I did not think that I should ever literally *stand before kings,* — which, however, has since happened; for I have stood before *five,* and even had the honor of sitting down with one, the King of Denmark, to dinner.*

We have an English proverb that says, " *He that would thrive must ask his wife.*" It was lucky for me that I had one as much disposed to industry and frugality as myself. She assisted me cheerfully in my business, folding and stitching pamphlets, tending shop, purchasing old linen rags for the paper-makers, &c. We kept no idle servants, our table was plain and simple, our furniture of the cheapest. For instance, my break-fast was for a long time bread and milk (no tea), and I ate it out of a twopenny earthen porringer, with a pewter spoon. But mark how luxury will enter families, and make a progress, in spite of principle; being called one morning to breakfast, I found it in a china bowl, with a spoon of silver! They had been bought for me without my knowledge by my wife, and had cost her the enormous sum of three and twenty shillings; for which she had no other excuse or apology to make, but that she thought *her* husband deserved a silver spoon and china bowl as well as any of his neighbors. This was the first appearance of plate and china in our house; which afterwards, in a course of years, as our wealth increased, augmented gradually to several hundred pounds in value.

I had been religiously educated as a Presbyterian; but, though some of the dogmas of that persuasion, such as *the eternal decrees of God, election, reprobation, &c.,* appeared to me unin-telligible, others doubtful, and I early absented myself from the public assemblies of the sect, Sunday being my studying day, I never was without some religious principles. I never doubted, for instance, the existence of a Deity; that he made the world and governed it by his providence; that the most acceptable service of God was the doing good to man; that our souls are immortal; and that all crimes will be punished, and virtue rewarded, either here or hereafter. These I esteemed the essen-

* The king, being on a visit to London, made the acquaintance of Franklin, who dined with him, Oct. 1, 1768, in the company of foreign ambassadors and other persons of distinction.

tials of every religion ; and, being to be found in all the religions we had in our country, I respected them all, though with different degrees of respect, as I found them more or less mixed with other articles, which, without any tendency to inspire, promote, or confirm morality, served principally to divide us, and make us unfriendly to one another. This respect to all, with an opinion that the worst had some good effects, induced me to avoid all discourse that might tend to lessen the good opinion another might have of his own religion ; and as our province increased in people, and new places of worship were continually wanted, and generally erected by voluntary contribution, my mite for such purpose, whatever might be the sect, was never refused.

Though I seldom attended any public worship,* I had still an opinion of its propriety, and of its utility when rightly con-. ducted, and I regularly paid my annual subscription for the support of the only Presbyterian minister or meeting we had in Philadelphia. He used to visit me sometimes as a friend, and admonish me to attend his administrations ; and I was now and then prevailed on to do so, — once for five Sundays successively. Had he been in my opinion a good preacher, perhaps I might have continued, notwithstanding the occasion I had for the Sunday's leisure in my course of study; but his discourses were chiefly either polemic arguments, or explications of the peculiar doctrines of our sect, and were all to me very dry, uninteresting, and unedifying, since not a single moral principle was inculcated or enforced; their aim seeming to be rather to make us *Presbyterians* than *good citizens.*

At length he took for his text that verse of the fourth chapter to the Philippians, "*Finally, brethren, whatsoever things are true, honest, just, pure, lovely, or of good report, if there be any virtue, or any praise, think on these things.*" And I imagined, in a sermon on such a text, we could not miss of having some morality. But he confined himself to five points only, as meant by the apostle: 1. Keeping holy the Sabbath day. 2. Being diligent in reading the holy Scriptures. 3. Attending duly the public worship. 4. Partaking of the Sacrament. 5. Paying a due respect to God's ministers. These might be all good things; but, as they were not the kind of good things that I expected from that text, I despaired of ever meeting with them from any

* In a letter, Nov. 8, 1764, to his daughter, he says: " Go constantly to church, whoever preaches. The act of devotion in the Common Prayer Book is your principal business there, and, if properly attended to, will do more towards amending the heart than sermons generally can do. . . . Yet I do not mean you should despise sermons, even of the preachers you dislike; for the discourse is often much better than the man, as sweet and clear waters come through very dirty earth."

other, was disgusted, and attended his preaching no more.   I had some years before composed a little liturgy, or form of prayer,* for my own private use (in 1728), entitled *Articles of Belief and Acts of Religion*.   I returned to the use of this, and went no more to the public assemblies.   My conduct might be blamable, but I leave it without attempting further to excuse it ; my present purpose being to relate facts, and not to make apologies for them.

It was about this time I conceived the bold and arduous project of arriving at *moral perfection.*   I wished to live without committing any fault at any time, and to conquer all that either natural inclination, custom or company, might lead me into. As I knew, or thought I knew, what was right and wrong, I did not see why I might not *always* do the one and avoid the other. But I soon found I had undertaken a task of more difficulty than I had imagined.   While my attention was taken up and care employed in guarding against one fault, I was often surprised by another ; habit took the advantage of inattention ; inclination was sometimes too strong for reason.   I concluded, at length, that the mere speculative conviction, that it was our interest to be completely virtuous, was not sufficient to prevent our slipping ; and that the contrary habits must be broken, and good ones acquired and established, before we can have any dependence on a steady, uniform rectitude of conduct.   For this purpose, I therefore tried the following method :

In the various enumerations of the *moral virtues* I had met with in my reading, I found the catalogue more or less numerous, as different writers included more or fewer ideas under the same name.   *Temperance*, for example, was by some confined to eating and drinking ; while by others it was extended to mean the moderating every other pleasure, appetite, inclination or passion, bodily or mental, even to our avarice and ambition. I proposed to myself, for the sake of clearness, to use rather more names, with fewer ideas annexed to each, than a few names

* This paper is dated Nov. 20th, 1728 ; and bears the marks of juvenility in the style.   In it Franklin avows his belief in " one supreme, most perfect Being," and prays to " be preserved from atheism, impiety, and profaneness."   The following passage occurs under the head of " Thanks " :

" For peace and liberty, for food and raiment, for corn, and wine, and milk, and every kind of healthful nourishment, — Good God, I thank Thee!

" For the common benefits of air and light, for useful fire and delicious water, — Good God, I thank Thee !

" For knowledge, and literature, and every useful art; for my friends and their prosperity, and for the fewness of my enemies, — Good God, I thank Thee !

" For all thy innumerable benefits; for life, and reason, and the use of speech; for health, and joy, and every pleasant hour, — My Good God, I thank Thee."

with more ideas; and I included, under thirteen names of virtues, all that at that time occurred to me as necessary or desirable; and annexed to each a short precept, which fully expressed the extent I gave to its meaning.

These names of *virtues*, with their precepts, were:

1. TEMPERANCE. — Eat not to dulness; drink not to elevation.

2. SILENCE. — Speak not but what may benefit others or yourself; avoid trifling conversation.

3. ORDER. — Let all your things have their places; let each part of your business have its time.

4. RESOLUTION. — Resolve to perform what you ought; perform without fail what you resolve.

5. FRUGALITY. — Make no expense but to do good to others or yourself; that is, waste nothing.

6. INDUSTRY. — Lose no time; be always employed in something useful; cut off all unnecessary actions.

7. SINCERITY. — Use no hurtful deceit; think innocently and justly; and, if you speak, speak accordingly.

8. JUSTICE. — Wrong none by doing injuries, or omitting the benefits that are your duty.

9. MODERATION. — Avoid extremes; forbear resenting injuries so much as you think they deserve.

10. CLEANLINESS. — Tolerate no uncleanliness in body, clothes, or habitation.

11. TRANQUILLITY. — Be not disturbed at trifles, or at accidents common or unavoidable.

12. CHASTITY. . . . . . .

13. HUMILITY. — Imitate Jesus and Socrates.

My intention being to acquire the *habitude* of all these virtues, I judged it would be well not to distract my attention by attempting the whole at once, but to fix it on *one* of them at a time; and, when I should be master of that, then to proceed to another; and so on, till I should have gone through the thirteen. And, as the previous acquisition of some might facilitate the acquisition of certain others, I arranged them with that view, as they stand above. *Temperance* first, as it tends to procure that coolness and clearness of head, which is so necessary where constant vigilance was to be kept up, and a guard maintained against the unremitting attraction of ancient habits, and the force of perpetual temptations. This being acquired and established, *Silence* would be more easy; and my desire being to gain knowledge at the same time that I improved in virtue, and considering that in conversation it was obtained rather by the use of the ear than of the tongue, and therefore wishing to break a habit I was getting into of prattling, punning and jesting, which only made me acceptable to trifling company, I gave *Silence* the second place. This, and the next, *Order*, I expected would allow me more time for attending to my project and my studies. *Resolution*, once become habitual, would keep me firm in my endeavors to obtain all the subsequent virtues; *Frugality* and *Industry*, relieving me from my remaining debt, and producing affluence and independence, would make more easy the practice of *Sincerity* and *Justice*, &c. &c. Conceiving, then, that, agreeably to the advice of Pythagoras in his *Golden Verses*, daily examination would be necessary, I contrived the following method for conducting the examination :

I made a little book, in which I allotted a page for each of the virtues. I ruled each page with red ink, so as to have seven columns, one for each day of the week, marking each column with a letter for the day. I crossed these columns with thirteen red lines, marking the beginning of each line with the first letter of one of the virtues; on which line, and in its proper column, I might mark, by a little black spot, every fault I found, upon examination, to have been committed respecting that virtue, upon that day.*

FORM OF THE PAGES.

TEMPERANCE.

Eat not to dulness : drink not to elevation.

	Sunday.	Monday.	Tuesday.	Wed'ay.	Thur'ay.	Friday.	Sat'ay.
Temp'ce.							
Silence.	*	*		*		*	
Order.	*	*	*		*	*	*
Resol'n.		*				*	
Frug'ty.		*				*	
Indus'y.			*				
Sincerity							
Justice.							
Moder'n.							
Clean'ss.	·						
Tran'ity.							
Chastity.							
Hum'y.							

* This little book is dated *Sunday, July 1st, 1733.*

*16

I determined to give a week's strict attention to each of the virtues successively. Thus, in the first week, my great guard was to avoid every the least offence against *Temperance;* leaving the other virtues to their ordinary chance, only marking every evening the faults of the day. Thus, if in the first week I could keep my first line, marked T, clear of spots, I supposed the habit of that virtue so much strengthened, and its opposite weakened, that I might venture extending my attention to include the next, and for the following week keep both lines clear of spots. Proceeding thus to the last, I could get through a course complete in thirteen weeks, and four courses in a year. And like him who, having a garden to weed, does not attempt to eradicate all the bad herbs at once, which would exceed his reach and his strength, but works on one of the beds at a time, and, having accomplished the first, proceeds to a second ; so I should have, I hoped, the encouraging pleasure of seeing on my pages the progress made in virtue, by clearing successively my lines of their spots, till, in the end, by a number of courses, I should be happy in viewing a clean book, after a thirteen weeks' daily examination.

This my little book had for its motto these lines from Addison's *Cato:*

> " Here will I hold. If there 's a Power above us
> (And that there is, all nature cries aloud
> Through all her works), He must delight in virtue;
> And that which He delights in must be happy."

Another, from Cicero :

> " O vitæ Philosophia dux ! O virtutum indagatrix expultrixque vitiorum!
> Unus dies, bene et ex præceptis tuis actus, peccanti immortalitati est ante-
> ponendus."

Another, from the Proverbs of Solomon, speaking of wisdom or virtue :

> " Length of days is in her right hand, and in her left hand riches and
> honor. Her ways are ways of pleasantness, and all her paths are peace."

And, conceiving God to be the fountain of wisdom, I thought it right and necessary to solicit his assistance for obtaining it. To this end, I formed the following little prayer, which was prefixed to my tables of examination, for daily use :

> " O powerful Goodness ! bountiful Father ! merciful Guide ! Increase in
> me that wisdom which discovers my truest interest. Strengthen my resolu-
> tion to perform what that wisdom dictates. Accept my kind offices to thy
> other children, as the only return in my power for thy continual favors
> to me."

I used also sometimes a little prayer which I took from Thomson's *Poems*, namely:

> " Father of light and life, thou Good Supreme !
> O teach me what is good: teach me Thyself !
> Save me from folly, vanity, and vice,
> From every low pursuit; and feed my soul
> With knowledge, conscious peace, and virtue pure;
> Sacred, substantial, never-fading bliss ! "

The precept of *Order* requiring that *every part of my business should have its allotted time*, one page in my little book contained the following scheme of employment for the twenty-four hours of a natural day.

SCHEME.

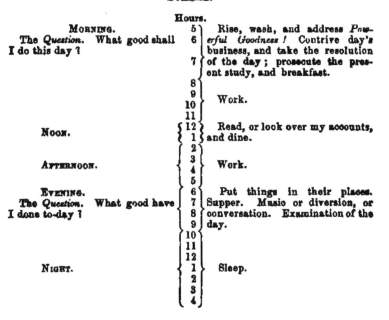

	Hours.	
MORNING.	5	Rise, wash, and address *Powerful Goodness !* Contrive day's business, and take the resolution of the day ; prosecute the present study, and breakfast.
The *Question*. What good shall I do this day ?	6	
	7	
	8	
	9	Work.
	10	
	11	
NOON.	12	Read, or look over my accounts, and dine.
	1	
	2	
AFTERNOON.	3	Work.
	4	
	5	
EVENING.	6	Put things in their places. Supper. Music or diversion, or conversation. Examination of the day.
The *Question*. What good have I done to-day ?	7	
	8	
	9	
	10	
	11	
	12	
NIGHT.	1	Sleep.
	2	
	3	
	4	

I entered upon the execution of this plan for self-examination, and continued it, with occasional intermissions, for some time. I was surprised to find myself so much fuller of faults than I had imagined; but I had the satisfaction of seeing them diminish. To avoid the trouble of renewing now and then my little book, which, by scraping out the marks on the paper of old faults to make room for new ones in a new course, became full of holes, I transferred my tables and precepts to the ivory leaves of a memorandum book, on which the lines were drawn with red ink, that made a durable stain; and on those lines I marked my faults with a black-lead pencil; which marks I could easily wipe out with a wet sponge. After a while I went through one course only in a year; and afterwards only one in several years; till at length I omitted them entirely, being employed in voyages and business abroad, with a multiplicity of affairs, that interfered; but I always carried my little book with me.

My scheme of *Order* gave me the most trouble; and I found that, though it might be practicable where a man's business was such as to leave him the disposition of his time, — that of a journeyman printer, for instance, — it was not possible to be exactly observed by a master, who must mix with the world, and often receive people of business at their own hours. Order, too, with regard to places for things, papers, &c., I found extremely difficult to acquire. I had not been early accustomed to *method*, and, having an exceedingly good memory, I was not so sensible of the inconvenience attending want of method. This article, therefore, cost me much painful attention, and my faults in it vexed me so much, and I made so little progress in amendment, and had such frequent relapses, that I was almost ready to give up the attempt, and content myself with a faulty character in that respect. Like the man, who, in buying an axe of a smith, my neighbor, desired to have the whole of its surface as bright as the edge. The smith consented to grind it bright for him, if he would turn the wheel; he turned while the smith pressed the broad face of the axe hard and heavily on the stone, which made the turning of it very fatiguing. The man came every now and then from the wheel to see how the work went on; and at length would take his axe as it was, without further grinding. "No," said the smith, "turn on, turn on, we shall have it bright by and by; as yet it is only speckled." "Yes," said the man, "but *I think I like a speckled axe best.*" And I believe this may have been the case with many, who, having, for want of some such means as I employed, found the difficulty of obtaining good and breaking bad habits in other points of vice and virtue, have given up the struggle, and concluded that "*a speckled axe is best.*" For something, that pretended to be reason, was every now and then suggesting to me that such extreme nicety as I exacted of myself might be a kind of foppery in morals, which, if it were known, would make me ridiculous; that a perfect character might be attended with the inconvenience of being envied and hated; and that a benevolent man should allow a few faults in himself, to keep his friends in countenance.

In truth, I found myself incorrigible with respect to *Order ;*

and now I am grown old, and my memory bad, I feel very sensibly the want of it. But on the whole, though I never arrived at the perfection I had been so ambitious of obtaining, but fell far short of it, yet I was, by the endeavor, a better and a happier man than I otherwise should have been, if I had not attempted it; as those who aim at perfect writing by imitating the engraved copies, though they never reach the wished-for excellence of those copies, their hand is mended by the endeavor, and is tolerable while it continues fair and legible.

It may be well my posterity should be informed that to this little artifice, with the blessing of God, their ancestor owed the constant felicity of his life, down to his seventy-ninth year, in which this is written. What reverses may attend the remainder is in the hand of Providence; but, if they arrive, the reflection on past happiness enjoyed ought to help his bearing them with more resignation. To *Temperance* he ascribes his long-continued health, and what is still left to him of a good constitution; to *Industry* and *Frugality*, the early easiness of his circumstances and acquisition of his fortune, with all that knowledge that enabled him to be a useful citizen, and obtained for him some degree of reputation among the learned; to *Sincerity* and *Justice*, the confidence of his country, and the honorable employs it conferred upon him; and to the joint influence of the whole mass of the virtues, even in the imperfect state he was able to acquire them, all that evenness of temper, and that cheerfulness in conversation, which makes his company still sought for, and agreeable even to his young acquaintance. I hope, therefore, that some of my descendants may follow the example, and reap the benefit.

It will be remarked that, though my scheme was not wholly without religion, there was in it no mark of any of the distinguishing tenets of any particular sect. I had purposely avoided them; for, being fully persuaded of the utility and excellency of my method, and that it might be serviceable to people in all religions, and intending some time or other to publish it, I would not have anything in it that should prejudice any one, of any sect, against it. I proposed writing a little comment on each virtue, in which I would have shown the advantages of possessing it, and the mischiefs attending its opposite vice; I should have called my book* THE ART OF VIRTUE, because it would have shown the means and manner of obtaining virtue,

---

* In a letter, Nov. 1733, to Lord Kames, he intimates that he has not renounced his plan of completing the work. "I have, from time to time," he says, "made and caused to be made experiments of the method, with

which would have distinguished it from the mere exhortation to
be good, that does not instruct and indicate the means, but is
like the apostle's man of verbal charity, who, without showing
to the naked and hungry how or where they might get clothes
or victuals, only exhorted them to be fed and clothed. *James*
2 : 15, 16.

But it so happened that my intention of writing and publishing this comment was never fulfilled. I had, indeed, from time
to time, put down short hints of the sentiments and reasonings
to be made use of in it; some of which I have still by me; but
the necessary close attention to private business in the earlier
part of life, and public business since, have occasioned my postponing it. For, it being connected in my mind with *a great
and extensive project*, that required the whole man to execute,
and which an unforeseen succession of employs prevented my
attending to, it has hitherto remained unfinished.

In this piece it was my design to explain and enforce this
doctrine, *that vicious actions are not hurtful because they are
forbidden, but forbidden because they are hurtful*, the nature of
man alone considered; that it was, therefore, every one's interest
to be virtuous, who wished to be happy even in this world; and
I should from this circumstance (there being always in the world
a number of rich merchants, nobility, states and princes, who
have need of honest instruments for the management of their
affairs, and such being so rare) have endeavored to convince
young persons that no qualities are so likely to make a poor
man's fortune as those of *probity* and *integrity*.

My list of virtues contained at first but twelve; but a Quaker
friend having kindly informed me that I was generally thought
proud, that my pride showed itself frequently in conversation,—
that I was not content with being in the right when discussing
any point, but was overbearing, and rather insolent, of which he
convinced me by mentioning several instances, — I determined to
endeavor to cure myself, if I could, of this vice or folly, among
the rest; and I added *Humility* to my list, giving an extensive
meaning to the word.

I cannot boast of much success in acquiring the *reality* of
this virtue, but I had a good deal with regard to the appearance
of it. I made it a rule to forbear all direct contradiction to
the sentiments of others, and all positive assertion of my own.
I even forbid myself, agreeably to the old laws of our Junto, the

success. The materials have been growing ever since. The form only is
now to be given; in which I propose employing my first leisure after my
return to my *other* country." He never found the *leisure* he anticipated.

use of every word or expression in the language that imported a fixed opinion; such as *certainly, undoubtedly,* &c., and I adopted instead of them, *I conceive, I apprehend,* or *I imagine,* a thing to be so and so; or it so *appears to me at present.* When another asserted something that I thought an error, I denied myself the pleasure of contradicting him abruptly, and of showing immediately some absurdity in his proposition; and in answering I began by observing that, in certain cases or circumstances, his opinion would be right, but in the present case there *appeared* or *seemed to me* some difference, &c.

I soon found the advantage of this change in my manners; the conversations I engaged in went on more pleasantly. The modest way in which I proposed my opinions procured them a readier reception and less contradiction; I had less mortification when I was found to be in the wrong; and I more easily prevailed with others to give up their mistakes and join with me, when I happened to be in the right.

And this mode, which I at first put on with some violence to natural inclination, became at length easy, and so habitual to me, that perhaps for the last fifty years no one has ever heard a dogmatical expression escape me. And to this habit (after my character of integrity) I think it principally owing that I had early so much weight with my fellow-citizens when I proposed new institutions or alterations in the old; and so much influence in public councils, when I became a member; for I was but a bad speaker, never eloquent, subject to much hesitation in my choice of words, hardly correct in language, and yet I generally carried my point.

In reality, there is perhaps no one of our natural passions so hard to subdue as *pride.* Disguise it, struggle with it, stifle it, mortify it as much as one pleases, it is still alive, and will every now and then peep out and show itself; you will see it, perhaps, often in this history. For, even if I could conceive that I had completely overcome it, I should probably be *proud* of my *humility.**

---

* Here concludes what was written at Passy. In resuming his Autobiography, Franklin prefaced the ensuing chapter with this "Memorandum": "I am now about to write at home (Philadelphia), August 1788, but cannot have the help expected from my papers, many of them being lost in the war. I have, however, found the following." He then proceeds as in the text.

CHAPTER VI.

Plan of a United Party for Virtue — Poor Richard's Almanac — Summary of Maxims — Mode of Conducting his Newspaper — Caution to Young Printers — Hint to Young Women — Rev. Mr. Hemphill — On the Study of Languages — Visit to Boston — To his Brother James at Newport — The Junto — Clerk of the Assembly — Postmaster — Public Reforms — The Watch — Forms the first Fire-company.

HAVING mentioned *a great and extensive project*, which I had conceived, it seems proper that some account should be here given of that project and its object. Its first rise in my mind appears in the following little paper, accidentally preserved, namely:

"*Observations on my reading history, in the Library,* May 9*th,* 1731.

"That the great affairs of the world, the wars, and revolutions, are carried on and effected by parties.

"That the view of these parties is their present general interest, or what they take to be such.

"That the different views of these different parties occasion all confusion.

"That while a party is carrying on a general design, each man has his particular private interest in view.

"That as soon as a party has gained its general point, each member becomes intent upon his particular interest; which, thwarting others, breaks that party into divisions, and occasions more confusion.

"That few in public affairs act from a mere view of the good of their country, whatever they may pretend; and, though their actings bring real good to their country, yet men primarily considered that their own and their country's interests were united, and so did not act from a principle of benevolence.

"That fewer still, in public affairs, act with a view to the good of mankind.

"There seems to me at present to be great occasion for raising a *United Party for Virtue,* by forming the virtuous and good men of all nations into a regular body, to be governed by suitable good and wise rules, which good and wise men may probably be more unanimous in their obedience to than common people are to common laws.

"I at present think that whoever attempts this aright, and is well qualified, cannot fail of pleasing God, and of meeting with success."

Revolving this project in my mind, as to be undertaken hereafter, when my circumstances should afford me the necessary leisure, I put down from time to time, on pieces of paper, such thoughts as occurred to me respecting it. Most of these are lost; but I find one purporting to be the substance of an intended creed, containing, as I thought, the essentials of every known religion, and being free of everything that might shock the professors of any religion. It is expressed in these words, namely:

"That there is one God, who made all things.

"That he governs the world by his providence.

"That he ought to be worshipped by adoration, prayer, and thanksgiving.

"But that the most acceptable service to God is doing good to man.

"That the soul is immortal.

"And that God will certainly reward virtue and punish vice, either here or hereafter."

My ideas at that time were, that the sect should be begun and spread at first among young and single men only; that each person to be initiated should not only declare his assent to such creed, but should have exercised himself with the thirteen weeks' examination and practice of the virtues, as in the before-mentioned model; that the existence of such a society should be kept a secret, till it was become considerable, to prevent solicitations for the admission of improper persons; but that the members should, each of them, search among his acquaintance for ingenious, well-disposed youths, to whom, with prudent caution, the scheme should be gradually communicated. That the members should engage to afford their advice, assistance and support, to each other in promoting one another's interest, business, and advancement in life. That, for distinction, we should be called THE SOCIETY OF THE FREE AND EASY. Free, as being, by the general practice and habits of the virtues, free from the dominion of vice; and particularly, by the practice of industry and frugality, free from debt, which exposes a man to constraint, and a species of slavery to his creditors.

This is as much as I can now recollect of the project, except that I communicated it in part to two young men, who adopted it with some enthusiasm; but my then narrow circumstances, and the necessity I was under of sticking close to my business, occasioned my postponing the further prosecution of it at that time; and my multifarious occupations, public and private, induced me to continue postponing, so that it has been omitted, till I have no longer strength or activity left sufficient for such an enterprise. Though I am still of opinion it was a practicable scheme, and might have been very useful, by forming a great number of good citizens; and I was not discouraged by the seeming magnitude of the undertaking, as I have always thought that one man of tolerable abilities may work great changes, and accomplish great affairs among mankind, if he first forms a good plan; and, cutting off all amusements or other employments, that would divert his attention, makes the execution of that same plan his sole study and business.

In 1732, I first published my Almanac, under the name of *Richard Saunders*; it was continued by me about twenty-five years, and commonly called *Poor Richard's Almanac*.* I endeavored to make it both entertaining and useful, and it accordingly came to be in such demand that I reaped considerable profit from it, vending annually near ten thousand. And observing that it was generally read, scarce any neighborhood in the province being without it, I considered it as a proper vehicle for conveying instruction among the common people, who bought scarcely any other books. I therefore filled all the little spaces that occurred between the remarkable days in the Calendar with proverbial sentences, chiefly such as inculcated industry and frugality, as the means of procuring wealth, and thereby securing virtue; it being more difficult for a man in want to act always honestly, as, to use here one of those proverbs, *it is hard for an empty sack to stand upright*.

These proverbs, which contained the wisdom of many ages and nations, I assembled and formed into a connected discourse prefixed to the Almanac of 1757, as the harangue of a wise old man to the people attending an auction. The bringing all these scattered counsels thus into a focus, enabled them to make greater impressions. The piece, being universally approved, was copied in all the newspapers of the American continent; reprinted in Britain on a large sheet of paper, to be stuck up in houses; two translations were made of it in France, and great numbers bought by the clergy and gentry, to distribute gratis among their poor

* Three editions of the first number were printed before the end of January, 1733. The title-page bears the imprint: " By Richard Saunders, Philomat. Printed and sold by B. Franklin." The humor of these " annuals " is at times rather too broad for modern ears polite. Such was the sale of the work, that new editions had frequently to be put to press. Within the last five years, neat editions, giving the literary portion of several numbers, have been published in New York.

parishioners and tenants. In Pennsylvania, as it discouraged useless expense in foreign superfluities, some thought it had its share of influence in producing that growing plenty of money which was observable for several years after its publication.

I considered my newspaper, also, as another means of communicating instruction, and in that view frequently reprinted in it extracts from the *Spectator*, and other moral writers; and sometimes published little pieces of my own, which had been first composed for reading in our Junto. Of these are a Socratic dialogue, tending to prove that, whatever might be his parts and abilities, a vicious man could not properly be called a man of sense; and a discourse on self-denial, showing that virtue was not secure till its practice became a *habitude*, and was free from the opposition of contrary inclinations. These may be found in the papers about the beginning of 1735.

In the conduct of my newspaper, I carefully excluded all libelling and personal abuse, which is of late years become so disgraceful to our country. Whenever I was solicited to insert anything of that kind, and the writers pleaded, as they generally did, the liberty of the press; and that a newspaper was like a stage-coach, in which any one who would pay had a right to a place; my answer was, that I would print the piece separately if desired, and the author might have as many copies as he pleased to distribute himself; but that I would not take upon me to spread his detraction; and that, having contracted with my subscribers to furnish them with what might be either useful or entertaining, I could not fill their papers with private altercation, in which they had no concern, without doing them manifest injustice. Now, many of our printers make no scruple of gratifying the malice of individuals by false accusations of the fairest characters among ourselves, augmenting animosity even to the producing of duels; and are, moreover, so indiscreet as to print scurrilous reflections on the government of neighboring states, and even on the conduct of our best national allies, which may be attended with the most pernicious consequences. These things I mention as a caution to young printers, and that they may be encouraged not to pollute their presses and disgrace their profession by such infamous practices, but refuse steadily; as they may see, by my example, that such a course of conduct will not, on the whole, be injurious to their interests.

In 1733, I sent one of my journeymen to Charleston, South Carolina, where a printer was wanting. I furnished him with a press and letters, on an agreement of partnership, by which I was to receive one-third of the profits of the business, paying

one-third of the expense.   He was a man of learning, but ignorant in matters of account; and, though he sometimes made me
remittances, I could get no account from him, nor any satisfactory state of our partnership while he lived.   On his decease,
the business was continued by his widow, who, being born and
bred in Holland, where, as I have been informed, the knowledge
of accounts makes a part of female education, she not only sent
me as clear a statement as she could find of the transactions past,
but continued to account with the greatest regularity and exactness every quarter afterwards; and managed the business with
such success, that she not only reputably brought up a family of
children, but, at the expiration of the term, was able to purchase
of me the printing-house, and establish her son in it.

I mention this affair chiefly for the sake of recommending
that branch of education for our young women, as likely to be
of more use to them and their children, in case of widowhood,
than either music or dancing, by preserving them from losses by
imposition of crafty men, and enabling them to continue, perhaps, a profitable mercantile house, with established correspondence, till a son is grown up fit to undertake and go on with it;
to the lasting advantage and enriching of the family.

About the year 1734, there arrived among us a young Presbyterian preacher, named Hemphill, who delivered with a good
voice, and apparently extempore, most excellent discourses;
which drew together considerable numbers, of different persuasions, who joined in admiring them.   Among the rest, I became
one of his constant hearers, his sermons pleasing me, as they
had little of the dogmatical kind, but inculcated strongly the
practice of virtue, or what, in the religious style, are called *good
works*.   Those, however, of our congregation who considered
themselves as orthodox Presbyterians, disapproved his doctrine,
and were joined by most of the old ministers, who arraigned
him of heterodoxy before the synod, in order to have him
silenced.   I became his zealous partisan, and contributed all I
could to raise a party in his favor, and combated for him a while
with some hopes of success.   There was much scribbling, *pro* and
con, upon the occasion; and finding that, though an elegant
preacher, he was but a poor writer, I wrote for him two or three
pamphlets, and a piece in the *Gazette* of April 1735.   Those
pamphlets, as is generally the case with controversial writings,
though eagerly read at the time, were soon out of vogue, and I
question whether a single copy of them now exists.

During the contest, an unlucky occurrence hurt his cause exceedingly.   One of our adversaries having heard him preach a

sermon that was much admired, thought he had somewhere read the sermon before, or at least a part of it. On searching, he found that part quoted at length, in one of the British *Reviews*, from a discourse of Dr. Foster's. This detection gave many of our party disgust, who accordingly abandoned his cause, and occasioned our more speedy discomfiture in the synod. I stuck by him, however; I rather approved his giving us good sermons composed by others, than bad ones of his own manufacture; though the latter was the practice of our common teachers. He afterwards acknowledged to me that none of those he preached were his own; adding, that his memory was such as enabled him to retain and repeat any sermon after once reading only. On our defeat, he left us in search elsewhere of better fortune, and I quitted the congregation, never attending it after; though I continued many years my subscription for the support of its ministers.

I had begun in 1733 to study languages; I soon made myself so much a master of the French as to be able to read the books in that language with ease. I then undertook the Italian. An acquaintance, who was also learning it, used often to tempt me to play chess with him. Finding this took up too much of the time I had to spare for study, I at length refused to play any more, unless on this condition, that the victor in every game should have a right to impose a task, either of parts of the grammar to be got by heart, or in translations, which tasks the vanquished was to perform upon honor, before our next meeting. As we played pretty equally, we thus beat one another into that language. I afterwards, with a little pains-taking, acquired as much of the Spanish as to read their books also.

I have already mentioned that I had only one year's instruction in a Latin school, and that when very young, after which I neglected that language entirely. But, when I had attained an acquaintance with the French, Italian and Spanish, I was surprised to find, on looking over a Latin Testament, that I understood more of that language than I had imagined; which encouraged me to apply myself again to the study of it, and I met with more success, as those preceding languages had greatly smoothed my way.

From these circumstances I have thought there is some inconsistency in our common mode of teaching languages. We are told that it is proper to begin first with the Latin, and, having acquired that, it will be more easy to attain those modern languages which are derived from it; and yet we do not begin with the Greek, in order more easily to acquire the Latin. It is true that, if we can clamber and get to the top of a staircase without using the steps, we shall more easily gain them in descending; but certainly, if we begin with the lowest, we shall with more ease ascend to the top; and I would therefore offer it to the consideration of those who superintend the education of our youth, whether, since many of those who begin with the Latin quit the same after spending some years without having made any great proficiency, and what they have learned becomes almost useless, so that their time has been lost, it would not have been better to have begun with the French, proceeding to the Italian and Latin. For, though after spending the same time they should quit the study of languages, and never arrive at the Latin, they would, however, have acquired another tongue or two, that, being in modern use, might be serviceable to them in common life.

After ten years' absence from Boston, and having become easy in my circumstances, I made a journey thither to visit my relations, which I could not sooner afford. In returning, I called at Newport, to see my brother James, then settled there with his printing-house. Our former differences were forgotten, and our meeting was very cordial and affectionate. He was fast declining in health, and requested me that, in case of his death, which he apprehended not far distant, I would take home his son, then but ten years of age, and bring him up to the printing business. This I accordingly performed, sending him a few years to school before I took him into the office. His mother carried on the business till he was grown up, when I assisted him with an assortment of new types, those of his father being in a manner worn out. Thus it was that I made my brother ample amends for the service I had deprived him of by leaving him so early.

In 1736, I lost one * of my sons, a fine boy of four years old, by the small-pox, taken in the common way. I long regretted him bitterly, and still regret that I had not given it to him by inoculation. This I mention for the sake of parents who omit that operation, on the supposition that they should never forgive themselves if the child died under it; my example showing that the regret may be the same either way, and, therefore, that the safer should be chosen.

Our club, the Junto, was found so useful, and afforded such satisfaction to the members, that some were desirous of introducing their friends, which could not well be done without ex

* See page 89.

ceeding what we had settled as a convenient number; namely, twelve. We had, from the beginning, made it a rule to keep our institution a secret, which was pretty well observed; the intention was, to avoid applications of improper persons for admittance, some of whom, perhaps, we might find it difficult to refuse I was one of those who were against any addition to our number but, instead of it, made in writing a proposal that every member separately should endeavor to form a subordinate club, with the same rules respecting queries, &c., and without informing them of the connection with the Junto. The advantages proposed were, the improvement of so many more young citizens by the use of our institutions; our better acquaintance with the general sentiments of the inhabitants on any occasion, as the Junto member might propose what queries we should desire, and was to report to the Junto what passed at his separate club; the promotion of our particular interests in business by more extensive recommendation, and the increase of our influence in public affairs, and our power of doing good, by spreading through the several clubs the sentiments of the Junto.

The project was approved, and every member undertook to form his club; but they did not all succeed. Five or six only were completed, which were called by different names, as the *Vine*, the *Union*, the *Band*. They were useful to themselves, and afforded us a good deal of amusement, information, and instruction, besides answering, in some considerable degree, our views of influencing the public on particular occasions; of which I shall give some instances, in course of time, as they happened.

My first promotion was my being chosen, in 1736, clerk of the General Assembly. The choice was made that year without opposition; but the year following, when I was again proposed (the choice, like that of the members, being annual), a new member made a long speech against me, in order to favor some other candidate. I was, however, chosen, which was the more agreeable to me, as, besides the pay for the immediate service of clerk, the place gave a better opportunity of keeping up an interest among the members, which secured to me the business of printing the votes, laws, paper money, and other occasional jobs for the public, that, on the whole, were very profitable.

I therefore did not like the opposition of this new member, who was a gentleman of fortune and education, with talents that were likely to give him in time great influence in the House, which indeed afterwards happened. I did not, however, aim at gaining his favor by paying any servile respect to him, but, after some time, took this other method. Having heard that he had in his library a certain very scarce and curious book, I wrote a note to him, expressing my desire of perusing that book, and requesting that he would do me the favor of lending it to me for a few days.   He sent it immediately; and I returned it in about a week with another note, expressing strongly the sense of the favor.   When we next met in the House, he spoke to me, which he had never done before, and with great civility; and he ever after manifested a readiness to serve me on all occasions, so that we became great friends, and our friendship continued to his death.   This is another instance of the truth of an old maxim I had learned, which says, "*He that has once done you a kindness will be more ready to do you another than he whom you yourself have obliged.*"   And it shows how much more profitable it is prudently to remove, than to resent, return and continue, inimical proceedings.

In 1737, Colonel Spotswood, late Governor of Virginia, and then postmaster-general, being dissatisfied with the conduct of his deputy at Philadelphia, respecting some negligence in rendering, and want of exactness in framing, his accounts, took from him the commission and offered it to me.   I accepted it readily, and found it of great advantage; for, though the salary was small, it facilitated the correspondence that improved my newspaper, increased the number demanded, as well as the advertisements to be inserted, so that it came to afford me a considerable income.   My old competitor's newspaper declined proportionably, and I was satisfied, without retaliating his refusal, while postmaster, to permit my papers being carried by the riders. Thus, he suffered greatly from his neglect in due accounting; and I mention it as a lesson to those young men who may be employed in managing affairs for others, that they should always render accounts, and make remittances, with great clearness and punctuality.   The character of observing such a conduct is the most powerful of all recommendations to new employments and increase of business.

I began now to turn my thoughts to public affairs, beginning, however, with small matters.   The city watch was one of the first things that I conceived to want regulation.   It was managed by the constables of the respective wards in turn; the constable summoned a number of housekeepers to attend him for the night.   Those who chose never to attend paid him six shillings a year to be excused, which was supposed to go to hiring substitutes, but was in reality much more than was necessary for that purpose, and made the constableship a place of profit; and the constable, for a little drink, often got such ragamuffins about him as a watch that respectable housekeepers did not choose to mix with. Walking the rounds, too, was often neglected, and most of the nights spent in tippling. I thereupon wrote a paper, to be read in the Junto, representing these irregularities, but insisting more particularly on the inequality of the six shilling tax of the constable, respecting the circumstances of those who paid it; since a poor widow housekeeper, all whose property to be guarded by the watch did not, perhaps, exceed the value of fifty pounds, paid as much as the wealthiest merchant, who had thousands of pounds' worth of goods in his stores.

On the whole, I proposed, as a more effectual watch, the hiring of proper men to serve constantly in the business; and, as a more equitable way of supporting the charge, the levying a tax that should be proportioned to the property. This idea, being approved by the Junto, was communicated to the other clubs, but as originating in each of them; and though the plan was not immediately carried into execution, yet, by preparing the minds of people for the change, it paved the way for the law obtained a few years after, when the members of our clubs were grown into more influence.

About this time I wrote a paper (first to be read in the Junto, but it was afterwards published) on the different accidents and carelessnesses by which houses were set on fire, with cautions against them, and means proposed of avoiding them. This was spoken of as a useful piece, and gave rise to a project, which soon followed it, of forming a company for the more ready extinguishing of fires, and mutual assistance in removing and securing of goods when in danger. Associates in this scheme were presently found, amounting to thirty. Our articles of agreement obliged every member to keep always in good order, and fit for use, a certain number of leathern buckets, with strong bags and baskets (for packing and transporting of goods), which were to be brought to every fire; and we agreed about once a month to spend a social evening together, in discoursing and communicating such ideas as occurred to us, upon the subject of fires, as might be useful in our conduct on such occasions.

The utility of this institution soon appeared, and many more desiring to be admitted than we thought convenient for one company, they were advised to form another, which was accordingly done; and thus went on one new company after another, till they became so numerous as to include most of the inhabitants who were men of property; and now, at the time of my writing this, though upwards of fifty years since its establishment, that which I first formed, called the *Union Fire Company*, still subsists; though the first members are all deceased but one, who is older by a year than I am. The fines that have been paid by members for absence at the monthly meetings have been applied to the purchase of fire-engines, ladders, fire-hooks, and other useful implements for each company; so that I question whether there is a city in the world better provided with the means of putting a stop to beginning conflagrations; and, in fact, since these institutions, the city has never lost by fire more than one or two houses at a time, and the flames have often been extinguished before the house in which they began has been half consumed.

CHAPTER VII.

Arrival of Whitefield — Effects of his Preaching — Church for all Sects — Anecdote — Vindication of Whitefield — His Clear Voice — Elocution improved by Practice — Mistake in Publishing — Franklin's Partnerships in Printing — Proposals for an Academy — A Philosophical Society — Active in Measures for Defence — Chosen Colonel — Proposes a Fast — The Quakers — James Logan — Anecdote of Penn — The Dunkers — The Franklin Fire-place — Refuses a Patent for it.

IN 1739 arrived among us, from Ireland, the Reverend Mr. Whitefield, who had made himself remarkable there as an itinerant preacher. He was at first permitted to preach in some of our churches; but the clergy, taking a dislike to him, soon refused him their pulpits, and he was obliged to preach in the fields. The multitudes of all sects and denominations that attended his sermons were enormous, and it was a matter of speculation to me, who was one of the number, to observe the extraordinary influence of his oratory on his hearers, and how much they admired and respected him, notwithstanding his common abuse of them, by assuring them they were naturally *half beasts and half devils*. It was wonderful to see the change soon made in the manners of our inhabitants. From being thoughtless or indifferent about religion, it seemed as if all the world were growing religious, so that one could not walk through the town in an evening without hearing psalms sung in different families of every street.

And it being found inconvenient to assemble in the open air, subject to its inclemencies, the building of a house to meet in was no sooner proposed, and persons appointed to receive contributions, than sufficient sums were soon received to procure the ground, and erect the building, which was one hundred feet long and seventy broad; and the work was carried on with such spirit as to be finished in a much shorter time than could have been expected. Both house and ground were vested in trustees, expressly for the use of *any preacher of any religious persuasion* who might desire to say something to the people at Philadelphia; the design in building being not to accommodate any particular sect, but the inhabitants in general; so that, even if the Mufti of Constantinople were to send a missionary to preach Mahometanism to us, he would find a pulpit at his service.

Mr. Whitefield, on leaving us, went preaching all the way through the Colonies to Georgia. The settlement of, that province had been lately begun, but, instead of being made with hardy, industrious husbandmen, accustomed to labor,—the only people fit for such an enterprise,—it was with families of broken shop-keepers and other insolvent debtors; many of indolent and idle habits, taken out of the jails, who, being set down in the woods, unqualified for clearing land, and unable to endure the hardships of a new settlement, perished in numbers, leaving many helpless children unprovided for. The sight of their miserable situation inspired the benevolent heart of Mr. Whitefield with the idea of building an Orphan House there, in which they might be supported and educated. Returning northward, he preached up this charity, and made large collections; for his eloquence had a wonderful power over the hearts and purses of his hearers, of which I myself was an instance.

I did not disapprove of the design, but, as Georgia was then destitute of materials and workmen, and it was proposed to send them from Philadelphia at a great expense, I thought it would have been better to have built the house at Philadelphia, and brought the children to it. This I advised; but he was resolute in his first project, rejected my counsel, and I therefore refused to contribute.

I happened soon after to attend one of his sermons, in the course of which I perceived he intended to finish with a collection, and I silently resolved he should get nothing from me. I had in my pocket a handful of copper money, three or four silver dollars, and five pistoles in gold. As he proceeded I began to soften, and concluded to give the copper. Another stroke of his oratory made me ashamed of that, and determined me to give the silver; and he finished so admirably, that I emptied my pocket wholly into the collector's dish, gold and all. At this sermon there was also one of our club, who, being of my

sentiments respecting the building in Georgia, and suspecting a
collection might be intended, had, by precaution, emptied his
pockets before he came from home.   Towards the conclusion of
the discourse, however, he felt a strong inclination to give, and
applied to a neighbor who stood near him to lend him some
money for the purpose.   The request was fortunately made to
perhaps the only man in the company who had the firmness not
to be affected by the preacher.   His answer was, "At any
other time, friend Hopkinson, I would lend to thee freely ; but
not now, for thee seems to be out of thy right senses."

Some of Mr. Whitefield's enemies affected to suppose that he
would apply these collections to his own private emolument;
but I, who was intimately acquainted with him, being employed
in printing his sermons and journals,* never had the least
suspicion of his integrity; but am to this day decidedly of opinion
that he was in all his conduct a perfectly *honest man;* and
methinks my testimony in his favor ought to have the more
weight, as we had no religious connection.   He used, indeed,
sometimes to pray for my conversion, but never had the satisfaction of believing that his prayers were heard.   Ours was a mere
civil friendship, sincere on both sides, and lasted to his death.

The following instance will show the terms on which we stood.
Upon one of his arrivals from England at Boston, he wrote to
me that he should come soon to Philadelphia, but knew not where
he could lodge when there, as he understood his old friend and
host, Mr. Benezet, was removed to Germantown.   My answer
was, "You know my house ; if you can make shift with its scanty
accommodations, you will be most heartily welcome."   He replied,
that if I made that kind offer for *Christ's* sake, I should not
miss of a reward.   And I returned, "Don't let me be mistaken;
it was not for *Christ's* sake, but for *your sake.*"   One of our
common acquaintance jocosely remarked that, knowing it to be
the custom of the saints, when they received any favor, to shift
the burden of the obligation from off their own shoulders, and
place it in heaven, I had contrived to fix it on earth.

The last time I saw Mr. Whitefield was in London, when he
consulted me about his Orphan House concern, and his purpose
of appropriating it to the establishment of a college.

He had a loud and clear voice, and articulated his words so
perfectly that he might be heard and understood at a great distance ; especially as his auditors observed the most perfect
silence.   He preached one evening from the top of the Court

* Franklin's proposals for the publication of them in four volumes, at two
shillings each, may be found in the *Pennsylvania Gazette* of Nov. 15, 1739.

House steps, which are in the middle of Market-street, and on the west side of Second-street, which crosses it at right angles. Both streets were filled with his hearers to a considerable distance. Being among the hindmost in Market-street, I had the curiosity to learn how far he could be heard, by retiring backwards down the street towards the river; and I found his voice distinct till I came near Front-street, when some noise in that street obscured it. Imagining then a semicircle, of which my distance should be the radius, and that it was filled with auditors, to each of whom I allowed two square feet, I computed that he might well be heard by more than thirty thousand. This reconciled me to the newspaper accounts of his having preached to twenty-five thousand people in the fields, and to the history of generals haranguing whole armies, of which I had sometimes doubted.

By hearing him often, I came to distinguish easily between sermons newly composed and those which he had often preached in the course of his travels. His delivery of the latter was so improved by frequent repetition, that every accent, every emphasis, every modulation of voice, was so perfectly well turned and well placed, that, without being interested in the subject, one could not help being pleased with the discourse; a pleasure of much the same kind with that received from an excellent piece of music. This is an advantage itinerant preachers have over those who are stationary, as the latter cannot well improve their delivery of a sermon by so many rehearsals.

His writing and printing from time to time gave great advantage to his enemies; unguarded expressions, and even erroneous opinions, delivered in preaching, might have been afterwards explained or qualified by supposing others that might have accompanied them; or they might have been denied; but *litera scripta manet*. Critics attacked his writings violently, and with so much appearance of reason as to diminish the number of his votaries, and prevent their increase. So that I am satisfied that if he had never written anything he would have left behind him a much more numerous and important sect, and his reputation might in that case have been still growing even after his death; as, there being nothing of his writing on which to found a censure, and give him a lower character, his proselytes would be left at liberty to attribute to him as great a variety of excellences as their enthusiastic admiration might wish him to have possessed.*

* George Whitefield was born in Gloucester, England, in 1714, and died, in 1770, at Newburyport, Mass., where his mortal remains were interred.

18

My business was now constantly augmenting, and my circumstances growing daily easier; my newspaper having become very profitable, as being, for a time, almost the only one in this and the neighboring provinces. I experienced, too, the truth of the observation, *"that after getting the first hundred pounds, it is more easy to get the second;"* money itself being of a prolific nature.

The partnership at Carolina having succeeded, I was encouraged to engage in others, and to promote several of my workmen, who had behaved well, by establishing them in printinghouses in different colonies, on the same terms with that in Carolina. Most of them did well, being enabled, at the end of our term, six years, to purchase the types of me, and go on working for themselves, by which means several families were raised. Partnerships often finish in quarrels; but I was happy in this, that mine were all carried on and ended amicably; owing, I think, a good deal to the precaution of having very explicitly settled, in our articles, everything to be done by or expected from each partner, so that there was nothing to dispute; which precaution I would therefore recommend to all who enter into partnerships; for, whatever esteem partners may have for, and confidence in, each other at the time of the contract, little jealousies and disgusts may arise, with ideas of inequality in the care and burden, business, &c., which are attended often with breach of friendship and of the connection; perhaps with lawsuits, and other disagreeable consequences.

I had, on the whole, abundant reason to be satisfied with my being established in Pennsylvania. There were, however, some things that I regretted, there being no provision for defence, nor for a complete education of youth; no militia, nor any college. I therefore, in 1743, drew up a proposal for establishing an academy; and, at that time, thinking the Reverend Richard Peters, who was out of employ, a fit person to superintend such an institution, I communicated the project to him; but he, having more profitable views in the service of the Proprietors, which succeeded, declined the undertaking; and, not knowing another at that time suitable for such a trust, I let the scheme lie a while dormant. I succeeded better the next year, 1744, in proposing and establishing a *Philosophical Society*. The paper I wrote for that purpose will be found among my writings, if not lost with many others.*

* This institution now has a library of fifteen thousand volumes, and a good collection of minerals, &c. In 1741, Franklin tried the experiment of a monthly magazine, but it did not succeed. It was entitled "The General

With respect to defence, Spain having been several years at war against Great Britain, and being at length joined by France, which brought us into great danger, and the labored and long-continued endeavor of our governor, Thomas, to prevail with our Quaker Assembly to pass a militia law, and make other provisions for the security of the province, having proved abortive, I proposed to try what might be done by a voluntary subscription of the people.   To promote this, I first wrote and published a pamphlet, entitled PLAIN TRUTH, in which I stated our helpless situation in strong lights, with the necessity of union and discipline for our defence, and promised to propose in a few days an association, to be generally signed for that purpose. The pamphlet had a sudden and surprising effect.   I was called upon for the instrument of association.   Having settled the draft of it with a few friends, I appointed a meeting of the citizens in the large building before mentioned.   The house was pretty full; I had prepared a number of printed copies, and provided pens and ink dispersed all over the room.   I harangued them a little on the subject, read the paper, explained it, and then distributed the copies, which were eagerly signed, not the least objection being made.

When the company separated, and the papers were collected, we found above twelve hundred signatures; and, other copies being dispersed in the country, the subscribers amounted at length to upwards of ten thousand.   These all furnished themselves as soon as they could with arms, formed themselves into companies and regiments, chose their own officers, and met every week to be instructed in the manual exercise, and other parts of military discipline.   The women, by subscriptions among themselves, provided silk colors, which they presented to the companies, painted with different devices and mottoes, which I supplied.

The officers of the companies composing the Philadelphia regiment, being met, chose me for their colonel; but, conceiving myself unfit, I declined that station, and recommended Mr. Lawrence, a fine person, and a man of influence, who was accordingly appointed.   I then proposed a lottery to defray the expense of building a battery below the town, and furnished with cannon.   It filled expeditiously, and the battery was soon erected, the merlons being framed of logs, and filled with earth. We bought some old cannon from Boston; but, these not being sufficient, we wrote to London for more, soliciting, at the same

Magazine and Historical Chronicle."   Six numbers were published, when it was discontinued.

time, our Proprietaries for some assistance, though without much expectation of obtaining it.

Meanwhile, Colonel Lawrence, Mr. Allen, Abraham Taylor, and myself, were sent to New York by the associators, commissioned to borrow some cannon of Governor Clinton. He at first refused us peremptorily; but, at a dinner with his council, where there was great drinking of Madeira wine, as the custom of that place then was, he softened by degrees, and said he would lend us six. After a few more bumpers he advanced to ten; and, at length, he very good-naturedly conceded eighteen. They were fine cannon, eighteen-pounders, with their carriages, which were soon transported and mounted on our batteries, where the associators kept a nightly guard while the war lasted; and, among the rest, I regularly took my turn of duty there, as a common soldier.

My activity in these operations was agreeable to the Governor and Council; they took me into confidence, and I was consulted by them in every measure where their concurrence was thought useful to the association. Calling in the aid of religion, I proposed to them the proclaiming a fast, to promote reformation, and implore the blessing of Heaven on our undertaking. They embraced the motion; but, as it was the first fast ever thought of in the province, the secretary had no precedent from which to draw the proclamation. My education in New England, where a fast is proclaimed every year, was here of some advantage; I drew it in the accustomed style; it was translated into German, printed in both languages, and circulated through the province. This gave the clergy of the different sects an opportunity of influencing their congregations to join the association, and it would probably have been general among all but the Quakers, if the peace had not soon intervened.

It was thought by some of my friends that, by my activity in these affairs, I should offend that sect, and thereby lose my interest in the Assembly of the province, where they formed a great majority. A young man, who had likewise some friends in the Assembly, and wished to succeed me as their clerk, acquainted me that it was decided to displace me at the next election; and he, through good-will, advised me to resign, as more consistent with my honor than being turned out. My answer to him was, that I had read or heard of some public man who made it a rule never to ask for an office, and never to refuse one when offered to him. "I approve," said I, "of this rule, and shall practise it with a small addition; I shall never *ask*, never *refuse*, nor ever RESIGN an office. If they will have my office of clerk, to dispose of it to another, they shall take it from me. I will not, by giving it up, lose my right of some time or other making reprisal on my adversaries." I heard, however, no more of this; I was chosen again unanimously as clerk at the next election. Possibly, as they disliked my late intimacy with the members of Council, who had joined the governors in all the disputes about military preparations, with which the House had long been harassed, they might have been pleased if I would voluntarily have left them; but they did not care to displace me on account merely of my zeal for the association, and they could not well give another reason.

Indeed, I had some cause to believe that the defence of the country was not disagreeable to any of them, provided they were not required to assist in it. And I found that a much greater number of them than I could have imagined, though against *offensive* war, were clearly for the *defensive*. Many pamphlets *pro* and *con* were published on the subject, and some by good Quakers in favor of *defence;* which, I believe, convinced most of their young people.

A transaction in our fire-company gave me some insight into their prevailing sentiments. It had been proposed that we should encourage the scheme for building a battery, by laying out the present stock, then about sixty pounds, in tickets of the lottery. By our rules no money could be disposed of till the next meeting after the proposal. The company consisted of thirty members, of whom twenty-two were Quakers, and eight only of other persuasions. We eight punctually attended the meeting; but, though we thought that some of the Quakers would join us, we were by no means sure of a majority. Only one Quaker, Mr. James Morris, appeared to oppose the measure. He expressed much sorrow that it had ever been proposed, as he said *Friends* were all against it, and it would create such discord as might break up the company. We told him that we saw no reason for that; we were the minority, and if *Friends* were against the measure, and out-voted us, we must and should, agreeably to the usage of all societies, submit. When the hour for business arrived, it was moved to put this to the vote; he allowed we might do it by the rules, but, as he could assure us that a number of members intended to be present for the purpose of opposing it, it would be but candid to allow a little time for their appearing.

While we were disputing this, a waiter came to tell me that two gentlemen below desired to speak with me. I went down, and found there two of our Quaker members. They told

18*

me there were eight of them assembled at a tavern just by; that they were determined to come and vote with us if there should be occasion, which they hoped would not be the case, and desired we would not call for their assistance if we could do without it, as their voting for such a measure might embroil them with their elders and friends. Being thus secure of a majority, I went up, and, after a little seeming hesitation, agreed to a delay of another hour. This Mr. Morris allowed to be extremely fair. Not one of his opposing friends appeared, at which he expressed great surprise; and, at the expiration of the hour, we carried the resolution eight to one; and as, of the twenty-two Quakers, eight were ready to vote with us, and thirteen by their absence manifested that they were not inclined to oppose the measure, I afterwards estimated the proportion of Quakers sincerely against defence as one to twenty-one only. For these were all regular members of the society, and in good reputation among them, and who had notice of what was proposed at that meeting.

The honorable and learned Mr. Logan, who had always been of that sect, wrote an address to them, declaring his approbation of *defensive* war, and supported his opinion by many strong arguments. He put into my hands sixty pounds to be laid out in lottery-tickets for the battery, with directions to apply what prizes might be drawn wholly to that service. He told me the following anecdote of his old master, William Penn, respecting defence. He came over from England, when a young man, with that Proprietary, and as his secretary. It was war-time, and their ship was chased by an armed vessel, supposed to be an enemy. Their captain prepared for defence; but told William Penn, and his company of Quakers, that he did not expect their assistance, and they might retire into the cabin; which they did, except James Logan, who chose to stay upon deck, and was quartered to a gun. The supposed enemy proved a friend, so there was no fighting; but when the secretary went down to communicate the intelligence, William Penn rebuked him severely for staying upon deck, and undertaking to assist in defending the vessel, contrary to the principles of Friends; especially as it had not been required by the captain. This reprimand, being before all the company, piqued the secretary, who answered, "I being thy servant, why did thee not order me to come down? But thee was willing enough that I should stay and help to fight the ship, when thee thought there was danger."

My being many years in the Assembly, a majority of which

were constantly Quakers, gave me frequent opportunities of seeing the embarrassment given them by their principle against
war, whenever application was made to them, by order of the
crown, to grant aids for military purposes.   They were unwilling to offend government, on the one hand, by a direct refusal ;
and their friends, the body of the Quakers, on the other, by a
compliance contrary to their principles; using a variety of eva-
sions to avoid complying, and modes of disguising the compliance when it became unavoidable.   The common mode at last
was, to grant money under the phrase of its being *"for the
king's use,"* and never to inquire how it was applied.

But, if the demand was not directly from the crown, that
phrase was found not so proper, and some other was to be invented.   Thus, when powder was wanting (I think it was for the
garrison at Louisburg), and the government of New England
solicited a grant of some from Pennsylvania, which was much
urged on the House by Governor Thomas, they would not grant
money to buy *powder*, because that was an ingredient of war ;
but they voted an aid to New England of three thousand pounds,
to be put into the hands of the governor, and appropriated it
for the purchase of bread, flour, wheat, or *other grain*.   Some
of the Council, desirous of giving the House still further embarrassment, advised the governor not to accept provision, as
not being the thing he had demanded ; but he replied, " I shall
take the money, for I understand very well their meaning ;
other grain is gunpowder ;" which he accordingly bought, and
they never objected to it.

It was in allusion to this fact that, when in our fire-company
we feared the success of our proposal in favor of the lottery,
and I had said to a friend of mine, one of our members, " If we
fail, let us move the purchase of a fire-engine with the money ;
the Quakers can have no objection to that ; and then, if you
nominate me and I you as a committee for that purpose, we will
buy a great gun, which is certainly a *fire-engine ;*" " I see,"
said he, " you have improved by being so long in the Assembly ;
your equivocal project would be just a match for their wheat or
other grain."

Those embarrassments that the Quakers suffered, from having
established and published it as one of their principles that no
kind of war was lawful, and which, being once published, they
could not afterwards, however they might change their minds,
easily get rid of, reminds me of what I think a more prudent
conduct in another sect among us, — that of the Dunkers. I was
acquainted with one of its founders, Michael Welfare, soon after

it appeared. He complained to me that they were grievously
calumniated by the zealots of other persuasions, and charged
with abominable principles and practices, to which they were
utter strangers. I told him this had always been the case with
new sects, and that, to put a stop to such abuse, I imagined it
might be well to publish the articles of their belief, and the
rules of their discipline. He said that it had been proposed
among them, but not agreed to, for this reason : " When we were
first drawn together as a society," said he, " it had pleased God
to enlighten our minds so far as to see that some doctrines,
which were esteemed truths, were errors; and that others, which
we had esteemed errors, were real truths. From time to time,
He has been pleased to afford us further light, and our princi-
ciples have been improving, and our errors diminishing. Now
we are not sure that we are arrived at the end of this pro-
gression, and at the perfection of spiritual or theological knowledge ; and we fear that, if we should once print our confession
of faith, we should feel ourselves as if bound and confined by it,
and perhaps be unwilling to receive further improvement; and
our successors still more so, as conceiving what their elders and
founders had done to be something sacred, never to be departed
from."

This modesty in a sect is perhaps a singular instance in the
history of mankind, every other sect supposing itself in possession of all truth, and that those who differ are so far in the
wrong; like a man travelling in foggy weather ; — those at some
distance before him on the road he sees wrapped up in the fog, as
well as those behind him, and also the people in the fields on
each side; but near him all appear clear, though in truth he is
as much in the fog as any of them. To avoid this kind of
embarrassment, the Quakers have of late years been gradually
declining the public service in the Assembly and in the magistracy,
choosing rather to quit their power than their principles.

In order of time, I should have mentioned before that, having, in 1742, invented an open stove for the better warming of
rooms, and at the same time saving fuel, as the fresh air admitted was warmed in entering, I made a present of the model to
Mr. Robert Grace, one of my early friends, who, having an iron
furnace, found the casting of the plates for these stoves a profitable thing, as they were growing in demand. To promote that
demand, I wrote and published a pamphlet, entitled, "An Account of the New-invented Pennsylvanian Fireplaces; wherein
their Construction and Manner of Operation are particularly
explained; their Advantages above every other Method of

Warming Rooms demonstrated ; and all Objections that have been raised against the Use of them answered and obviated," &c. This pamphlet had a good effect. Governor Thomas was so pleased with the construction of this stove, as described in it, that he offered to give me a patent for the sole vending of them for a term of years ; but I declined it from a principle which has ever weighed with me on such occasions, namely, *That, as we enjoy great advantages from the inventions of others, we should be glad of an opportunity to serve others by any invention of ours ; and this we should do freely and generously.*

An ironmonger in London, however, assuming a good deal of my pamphlet and working it up into his own, and making some small changes in the machine, which rather hurt its operation, got a patent for it there, and made, as I was told, a little fortune by it.   And this is not the only instance of patents taken out of my inventions by others, — though not always with the same success, — which I never contested, as having no desire of profiting by patents myself, and hating disputes.   The use of these fireplaces in very many houses, both here in Pennsylvania and the neighboring states, has been, and is, a great saving of wood to the inhabitants.

CHAPTER VIII.

Moves in the Cause of Education — An Academy — A Trustee — New Partnership — Electrical Experiments — Public Employments — A Member of the Assembly — Commissioner to treat with Indians — The Pennsylvania Hospital — Advice in procuring Subscriptions — Street Paving, Cleaning and Lighting — Project for Cleaning Streets in London — Postmaster-general of America — Honorary Degrees.

PEACE being concluded, and the association business therefore at an end, I turned my thoughts again to the affair of establishing an academy.   The first step I took was to associate in the design a number of active friends, of whom the Junto furnished a good part ; the next was to write and publish a pamphlet, entitled *Proposals relating to the Education of Youth in Pennsylvania.* This I distributed among the principal inhabitants gratis ; and as soon as I could suppose their minds a little prepared by the perusal of it, I set on foot a subscription for opening and supporting an academy.   It was to be paid in quotas yearly for five years ; by so dividing it, I judged the subscription might be larger; **and I** believe it was so, amounting to no less, if I remember right, than five thousand pounds.*

In the introduction to these proposals, I stated their publication not as an act of mine, but of some *public-spirited gentlemen;* avoiding as much as I could, according to my usual rule, the presenting myself to the public as the author of any scheme for their benefit.

The subscribers, to carry the project into immediate execution, chose out of their number twenty-four trustees, and appointed Mr. Francis, then attorney-general, and myself, to draw up constitutions for the government of the academy; which being done and signed, a house was hired, masters engaged, and the schools opened, I think in the same year —1749.

The scholars increasing fast, the house was soon found too small, and we were looking out for a piece of ground properly situated, with intent to build, when accident threw into our way a large house ready built, which, with a few alterations, might well serve our purpose. This was the building before mentioned, erected by the hearers of Mr. Whitefield, and was obtained for us in the following manner.

It is to be noted that, the contributions to this building being made by the people of different sects, care was taken in the nomination of trustees, in whom the building and ground were to be vested, that a predominancy should not be given to any sect, lest in time that predominancy might be a means of appropriating the whole to the use of such sect, contrary to the original intention. It was for this reason that one of each sect was appointed; namely, one Church-of-England man, one Presbyterian, one Baptist, one Moravian, &c., who, in case of vacancy by death, were to fill it by election from among the contributors. The Moravian happened not to please his colleagues, and on his death they resolved to have no other of that sect. The difficulty then was, how to avoid having two of some other sect, by means of the new choice.

Several persons were named, and for that reason not agreed to. At length one mentioned me, with the observation that I was merely an honest man, and of *no sect* at all; which prevailed with them to choose me. The enthusiasm which existed when the

---

* "Other great benefactions for this institution," says Wm. Temple Franklin, " were subsequently obtained, both in America and Great Britain, through the influence of Dr. Franklin; who, on his return to Philadelphia from England, in 1775, carried thence two large gold medals, given by Mr. Sargent, one of his friends, to be bestowed as prizes on such scholars as should distinguish themselves by writing on subjects to be proposed to them by the trustees or governors of the college."

house was built, had long since abated, and its trustees had not been able to procure fresh contributions for paying the ground-rent, and discharging some other debts the building had occa-sioned, which embarrassed them greatly. Being now a member of both boards of trustees, that for the building and that for the academy, I had a good opportunity of negotiating with both, and brought them finally to an agreement, by which the trustees for the building were to cede it to those of the academy; the latter undertaking to discharge the debt, to keep forever open in the building a large hall for occasional preachers, according to the original intention, and maintain a free school for the instruction of poor children.

Writings were accordingly drawn; and, on paying the debts, the trustees of the academy were put in possession of the prem-ises; and, by dividing the great and lofty hall into stories, and different rooms above and below for the several schools, and pur-chasing some additional ground, the whole was soon made fit for our purpose, and the scholars removed into the building. The whole care and trouble of agreeing with the workmen, purchas-ing materials, and superintending the work, fell upon me; and I went through it the more cheerfully, as it did not then inter-fere with my private business; having the year before taken a very able, industrious, and honest partner, Mr. David Hall, with whose character I was well acquainted, as he had worked for me four years. He took off my hands all care of the printing-office, paying me punctually my share of the profits. This partner-ship continued eighteen years, successfully for us both.

The trustees of the academy, after a while, were incorporated by a charter from the governor; their funds were increased by contributions in Britain, and grants of land from the proprieta-ries, to which the Assembly has since made considerable addition; and thus was established the present University of Philadelphia. I have been continued one of its trustees from the beginning, now near forty years, and have had the very great pleasure of seeing a number of the youth, who have received their education in it, distinguished by their improved abilities, serviceable in public stations, and ornaments to their country.

When I was disengaged myself, as above mentioned, from private business, I flattered myself that, by the sufficient though moderate fortune I had acquired, I had found leisure during the rest of my life for philosophical studies and amusements. I pur-chased all Dr. Spence's apparatus, who had come from England to lecture in Philadelphia, and I proceeded in my electrical experiments with great alacrity; but, the public, now considering me as a man of leisure, laid hold of me for their purposes; every part of our civil government, and almost at the same time, imposing some duty upon me.

The governor put me into the commission of the peace; the corporation of the city chose me one of the Common Council, and soon after Alderman; and the citizens at large elected me a burgess, to represent them in the Assembly. This latter station was the more agreeable to me, as I grew at length tired with sitting there to hear the debates, in which, as clerk, I could take no part; and which were often so uninteresting, that I was induced to amuse myself with making magic squares or circles, or anything to avoid weariness; and I conceived my becoming a member would enlarge my power of doing good. I would not, however, insinuate that my ambition was not flattered by all these promotions; it certainly was, for, considering my low beginning, they were great things to me; and they were still more pleasing, as being so many spontaneous testimonies of the public good opinion, and by me entirely unsolicited.

The office of justice of the peace I tried a little, by attending a few courts, and sitting on the bench to hear causes; but finding that more knowledge of the common law than I possessed was necessary to act in that station with credit, I gradually withdrew from it, excusing myself by being obliged to attend the higher duties of a legislator in the Assembly. My election to this trust was repeated every year for ten years, without my ever asking any elector for his vote, or signifying, either directly or indirectly, any desire of being chosen. On taking my seat in the House, my son was appointed their clerk.

The year following, a treaty being to be held with the Indians at Carlisle, the governor sent a message to the House, proposing that they should nominate some of their members, to be joined with some members of Council, as commissioners for that purpose. The House named the Speaker (Mr. Norris) and myself; and, being commissioned, we went to Carlisle, and met the Indians accordingly.

As those people are extremely apt to get drunk, and when so are very quarrelsome and disorderly, we strictly forbade the selling any liquor to them; and, when they complained of this restriction, we told them that, if they continued sober during the treaty, we would give them plenty of rum when the business was over. They promised this, and they kept their promise, because they could get no rum, and the treaty was conducted very orderly, and concluded to mutual satisfaction. They then claimed and received the rum; this was in the afternoon; they were near one hundred men, women and children, and were lodged in temporary cabins, built in the form of a square, just without the town. In the evening, hearing a great noise among them, the commissioners walked to see what was the matter. We found they had made a great bonfire in the middle of the square; they were all drunk, men and women, quarrelling and fighting. Their dark-colored bodies, half naked, seen only by the gloomy light of the bonfire, running after and beating one another with firebrands, accompanied by their horrid yellings, formed a scene the most resembling our ideas of hell that could well be imagined; there was no appeasing the tumult, and we retired to our lodging. At midnight a number of them came thundering at our door, demanding more rum, of which we took no notice.

The next day, sensible they had misbehaved in giving us that disturbance, they sent three of their old counsellors to make their apology. The orator acknowledged the fault, but laid it upon the rum; and then endeavored to excuse the rum, by saying, "The Great Spirit, who made all things, made everything for some use; and whatever use he designed anything for, that use it should always be put to. Now, when he made rum, he said, ' *Let this be for the Indians to get drunk with;* ' and it must be so." And indeed, if it be the design of Providence to extirpate these savages, in order to make room for the cultivators of the earth, it seems not impossible that rum may be the appointed means. It has already annihilated all the tribes who formerly inhabited the sea-coast.

In 1751, Dr. Thomas Bond, a particular friend of mine, conceived the idea of establishing a hospital in Philadelphia (a very beneficent design, which has been ascribed to me, but was originally and truly his) for the reception and cure of poor sick persons, whether inhabitants of the province or strangers. He was zealous and active in endeavoring to procure subscriptions for it; but, the proposal being a novelty in America, and at first not well understood, he met but with little success.

At length he came to me, with the compliment that he found there was no such a thing as carrying a public-spirited project through without my being concerned in it. "For," said he, "I am often asked, by those to whom I propose subscribing, *Have you consulted Franklin on this business? And what does he think of it?* And when I tell them that I have not, supposing it rather out of your line, they do not subscribe, but say *they will consider it.*" I inquired into the nature and probable utility of this scheme, and receiving from him a very satisfactory explanation, I not only subscribed to it myself, but engaged heartily in the design of procuring subscriptions from others. Previously, however, to the solicitation, I endeavored to prepare the minds of the people, by writing on the subject in the newspapers, which was my usual custom in such cases, but which Dr. Bond had omitted.

The subscriptions afterwards were more free and generous; but, beginning to flag, I saw they would be insufficient without some assistance from the Assembly, and therefore proposed to petition for it, which was done. The country members did not at first relish the project; they objected that it could only be serviceable to the city, and therefore the citizens alone should be at the expense of it; and they doubted whether the citizens themselves generally approved of it. My allegation on the contrary, that it met with such approbation as to leave no doubt of our being able to raise two thousand pounds by voluntary donations, they considered it a most extravagant supposition, and utterly impossible.

On this I formed my plan; and, asking leave to bring in a bill for incorporating the contributors according to the prayer of their petition, and granting them a blank sum of money, — which leave was obtained chiefly on the consideration that the House could throw the bill out, if they did not like it, — I drew it so as to make the important clause a conditional one, namely: "And be it enacted, by the authority aforesaid, that, when the said contributors shall have met and chosen their managers and treasurer, and shall have raised by their contributions a capital stock of two thousand pounds' value (the yearly interest of which is to be applied to the accommodation of the sick poor in the said hospital, and of charge for diet, attendance, advice, and medicines), and *shall make the same appear to the satisfaction of the Speaker of the Assembly for the time being;* that then it shall and may be lawful for the said Speaker, and he is hereby required, to sign an order on the provincial treasurer, for the payment of two thousand pounds, in two yearly payments, to the treasurer of the said hospital, to be applied to the founding, building, and finishing of the same."

This condition carried the bill through; for the members who had opposed the grant, and now conceived they might have the credit of being charitable without the expense, agreed to its passage; and then, in soliciting subscriptions among the people, we urged the conditional promise of the law as an additional motive to give, since every man's donation would be doubled; thus the clause worked both ways. The subscriptions accordingly soon exceeded the requisite sum, and we claimed and received the public gift, which enabled us to carry the design into execution. A convenient and handsome building was soon erected ; the institution has, by constant experience, been found useful, and flourishes to this day ; and I do not remember any of my political manœuvres the success of which at the time gave more pleasure, or wherein, after thinking of it, I more easily excused myself for having made some use of cunning.*

It was about this time that another projector, the Reverend Gilbert Tennent, came to me with a request that I would assist him in procuring a subscription for erecting a new meeting-house. It was to be for the use of a congregation he had gathered among the Presbyterians, who were originally disciples of Mr. White-field.   Unwilling to make myself disagreeable to my fellow-citizens by too frequently soliciting their contributions, I absolutely refused.   He then desired I would furnish him with a list of the names of persons I knew by experience to be generous and public-spirited.   I thought it would be unbecoming in me, after their kind compliance with my solicitations, to mark them out to be worried by other beggars, and therefore refused to give such a list.   He then desired I would at least give him my advice.   " That I will readily do," said I ; " and, in the first place, I advise you to apply to all those who you know will give something ; next, to those who you are uncertain whether they will give anything or not, and show them the list of those who have given ; and lastly, do not neglect those who you are sure will give nothing ; for in some of them you may be mistaken." He laughed and thanked me, and said he would take my advice. He did so, for he asked of *everybody ;* and he obtained a much larger sum than he expected, with which he erected the capacious and elegant meeting-house that stands in Arch-street.

Our city, though laid out with a beautiful regularity, the streets large, straight, and crossing each other at right angles, had the disgrace of suffering those streets to remain long unpaved, and in wet weather the wheels of heavy carriages ploughed them into a quagmire, so that it was difficult to cross them, and in dry weather the dust was offensive.   I had lived near what was called the Jersey Market, and saw with pain the inhabitants wading in mud while purchasing their provisions.   A strip of ground down the middle of that market was at length paved with brick, so that, being once in the market, they had firm footing, but were often over shoes in dirt to get there.   By

* The building now occupied by the Pennsylvania Hospital is situated in Pine-street, Philadelphia, between Eighth and Ninth.   It occupies a whole square, having been completed in the year 1804.

talking and writing on the subject, I was at length instrumental in getting the street paved with stone between the market and the brick foot-pavement that was on the side next the houses. This, for some time, gave an easy access to the market, dry-shod; but, the rest of the street not being paved, whenever a carriage came out of the mud upon this pavement, it shook off and left its dirt upon it; and it was soon covered with mire, which was not removed, the city as yet having no scavengers.

After some inquiry, I found a poor, industrious man, who was willing to undertake keeping the pavement clean, by sweeping it twice a week, carrying off the dirt from before all the neighbors' doors, for the sum of sixpence per month, to be paid by each house. I then wrote and printed a paper setting forth the advantages to the neighborhood that might be obtained from this small expense; the greater ease in keeping our houses clean, so much dirt not being brought in by people's feet; the benefit to the shops by more custom, as buyers could more easily get at them, and by not having in windy weather the dust blown in upon their goods, &c. &c. I sent one of these papers to each house, and in a day or two went round to see who would subscribe an agreement to pay these sixpences. It was unanimously signed, and for a time well executed. All the inhabitants of the city were delighted with the cleanliness of the pavement that surrounded the market, it being a convenience to all; and this raised a general desire to have all the streets paved, and made the people more willing to submit to a tax for that purpose.

After some time, I drew a bill for paving the city, and brought it into the Assembly. It was just before I went to England, in 1757, and did not pass till I was gone, and then with an alteration in the mode of assessment, which I thought not for the better, but with an additional provision for lighting as well as paving the streets, which was a great improvement. It was by a private person, the late Mr. John Clifton, giving a sample of the utility of lamps, by placing one at his door, that the people were first impressed with the idea of lighting all the city. The honor of this public benefit has also been ascribed to me, but it belongs truly to that gentleman. I did but follow his example, and have only some merit to claim respecting the form of our lamps, as differing from the globe-lamps we were at first supplied with from London. They were found inconvenient in these respects: they admitted no air below, the smoke therefore did not readily go out above, but circulated in the globe, lodged on its inside, and soon obstructed the light they were intended to afford; giving, besides, the daily trouble of wiping them clean; and an accidental stroke on one of them would demolish it, and render it totally useless. I therefore suggested the composing them of four flat panes, with a long funnel above to draw up the smoke, and crevices admitting the air below to facilitate the ascent of the smoke; by this means they were kept clean, and did not grow dark in a few hours, as the London lamps do, but continued bright till morning; and an accidental stroke would generally break but a single pane, easily repaired.

I have sometimes wondered that the Londoners did not, from the effect holes in the bottom of the globe-lamps used at Vauxhall have in keeping them clean, learn to have such holes in their street-lamps. But, these holes being made for another purpose, namely, to communicate flame more suddenly to the wick by a little flax hanging down through them, the other use, of letting in air, seems not to have been thought of; and therefore, after the lamps have been lit a few hours, the streets of London are very poorly illuminated.

The mention of these improvements puts me in mind of one I proposed, when in London, to Dr. Fothergill, who was among the best men I have known, and a great promoter of useful projects. I had observed that the streets, when dry, were never swept, and the light dust carried away; but it was suffered to accumulate till wet weather reduced it to mud, and then, after lying some days so deep on the pavement that there was no crossing but in paths kept clean by poor people with brooms, it was with great labor raked together and thrown up into carts, open above, the sides of which suffered some of the slush at every jolt on the pavement to shake out and fall, sometimes to the annoyance of foot passengers. The reason given for not sweeping the dusty streets was, that the dust would fly into the windows of shops and houses.

An accidental occurrence had instructed me how much sweeping might be done in a little time. I found at my door in Craven-street, one morning, a poor woman sweeping my pavement with a birch broom; she appeared very pale and feeble, as just come out of a fit of sickness. I asked who employed her to sweep there; she said, "Nobody; but I am poor and in distress, and I sweeps before gentlefolkeses doors, and hopes they will give me something." I bid her sweep the whole street clean, and I would give her a shilling; this was at nine o'clock; at noon she came for the shilling. From the slowness I saw at first in her working, I could scarce believe that the work was done so soon, and sent my servant to examine it who reported that the whole street was swept perfectly clean, and all the dust

19*

placed in the gutter, which was in the middle; and the next rain washed it quite away, so that the pavement, and even the kennel, were perfectly clean.

I then judged that, if that feeble woman could sweep such a street in three hours, a strong, active man might have done it in half the time.   And here let me remark the convenience of having but one gutter in such a narrow street running down its middle, instead of two, one on each side near the footway.   For where all the rain that falls on a street runs from the sides and meets in the middle, it forms there a current strong enough to wash away all the mud it meets with; but, when divided into two channels, it is often too weak to cleanse either, and only makes the mud it finds more fluid; so that the wheels of carriages and feet of horses throw and dash it upon the foot pavement, which is thereby rendered foul and slippery, and sometimes splash it upon those who are walking.   My proposal, communicated to the Doctor, was as follows:

"For the more effectually cleaning and keeping clean the streets of London and Westminster, it is proposed that the several watchmen be contracted with to have the dust swept up in the dry seasons, and the mud raked up at other times, each in the several streets and lanes of his round; that they be furnished with brooms and other proper instruments for these purposes, to be kept at their respective stands, ready to furnish the poor people they may employ in the service.

"That in the dry summer months the dust be all swept up into heaps at proper distances, before the shops and windows of houses are usually opened; when scavengers, with close-covered carts, shall also carry it all away.

"That the mud, when raked up, be not left in heaps to be spread abroad again by the wheels of carriages and trampling of horses; but that the scavengers be provided with bodies of carts, not placed high upon wheels, but low upon sliders, with lattice bottoms, which, being covered with straw, will retain the mud thrown into them, and permit the water to drain from it; whereby it will become much lighter, water making the greatest part of the weight.   These bodies of carts to be placed at convenient distances, and the mud brought to them in wheelbarrows; they remaining where placed till the mud is drained, and then horses brought to draw them away."

I have since had doubts of the practicability of the latter part of this proposal, in all places, on account of the narrowness of some streets, and the difficulty of placing the draining sleds so as not to encumber too much the passage; but I am still of opinion that the former, requiring the dust to be swept up and carried away before the shops are open, is very practicable in the summer, when the days are long; for, in walking through the Strand and Fleet-street one morning at seven o'clock, I observed there was not one shop open, though it had been daylight and the sun up above three hours; the inhabitants of London choosing voluntarily to live much by candle-light, and sleep by sunshine, and yet often complain, a little absurdly, of the duty on candles, and the high price of tallow.

Some may think these trifling matters not worth minding or relating; but, when they consider that, though dust blown into the eyes of a single person, or into a single shop, in a windy day, is but of small importance, yet the great number of the instances in a populous city, and its frequent repetition, gives it weight and consequence, perhaps they will not censure very severely those who bestow some attention to affairs of this seemingly low nature.   Human felicity is produced not so much by great pieces of good fortune that seldom happen, as by little advantages that occur every day.   Thus, if you teach a poor young man to shave himself, and keep his razor in order, you may contribute more to the happiness of his life than in giving him a thousand guineas. This sum may be soon spent, the regret only remaining of having foolishly consumed it; but, in the other case, he escapes the frequent vexation of waiting for barbers, and of their sometimes dirty fingers, offensive breaths, and dull razors; he shaves when most convenient to him, and enjoys daily the pleasure of its being done with a good instrument.   With these sentiments I have hazarded the few preceding pages, hoping they may afford hints, which some time or other may be useful to a city I love,—having lived many years in it very happily,—and perhaps to some of our towns in America.

Having been some time employed by the postmaster-general of America, as his comptroller in regulating the several offices, and bringing the officers to account, I was, upon his death, in 1753, appointed, jointly with Mr. William Hunter, to succeed him, by a commission from the postmaster-general in England.   The American office had hitherto never paid anything to that of Britain.   We were to have six hundred pounds a year between us, if we could make that sum out of the profits of the office. To do this, a variety of improvements was necessary; some of these were inevitably at first expensive; so that in the first four years the office became above nine hundred pounds in debt to us. But it soon after began to repay us; and before I was displaced by a freak of the ministers, of which I shall speak hereafter, we had brought it to yield *three times* as much clear revenue to the crown as the post-office of Ireland. Since that imprudent transaction, they have received from it — not one farthing.

The business of the post-office occasioned my taking a journey this year to New England, where the College of Cambridge, of their own motion, presented me with the degree of Master of Arts. Yale College, in Connecticut, had before made me a similar compliment. Thus, without studying in any college, I came to partake of their honors. They were conferred in consideration of my improvements and discoveries in the electric branch of natural philosophy.*

CHAPTER IX.

Delegate to the Albany Convention — Proposes a Plan of Union — Confers with Gov. Shirley at Boston — Meets Gov. Morris at New York — Anecdote — Proprietary quarrels — War with France — Assists Mr. Quincy, in procuring Supplies — Visits Braddock's Army — Procures Horses and Wagons for it — Character of Braddock — His Defeat — Poor Reward of Franklin's Services.

In 1754, war with France being again apprehended, a congress of commissioners from the different colonies was by an order of the Lords of Trade to be assembled at Albany; there to confer with the chiefs of the Six Nations, concerning the means of defending both their country and ours. Governor Hamilton, having received this order, acquainted the House with it, requesting they would furnish proper presents for the Indians, to be given on this occasion; and naming the speaker (Mr. Norris) and myself to join Mr. John Penn and Mr. Secretary Peters as

---

*In a letter from France, May 1784, Franklin remarks, on revisiting Boston: "I long much to see again my native place, and to lay my bones there. I left it in 1723; I visited it in 1733, 1743, 1753, and 1763. In 1773 I was in England; in 1775 I had a sight of it, but could not enter, it being then in possession of the enemy. I did hope to have been there in 1783, but could not obtain my dismission from this employment here; and now I fear I shall never have that happiness." In a letter, from Philadelphia, May 31, 1788, to the Rev. John Lathrop, Boston, Franklin writes: "It seems probable, though not certain, that I shall hardly again visit *that beloved place*. But I enjoy the company and conversation of its inhabitants, when any of them are so good as to visit me; for, besides their general good sense, which I value, the Boston manner, turn of phrase, and even tone of voice and accent in pronunciation, all please, and seem to refresh and revive me."

commissioners to act for Pennsylvania. The House approved the nomination, and provided the goods for the presents, though they did not much like treating out of the province; and we met the other commissioners at Albany about the middle of June.

In our way thither, I projected and drew up a plan for the union of all the colonies under one government, so far as might be necessary for defence, and other important general purposes. As we passed through New York, I had there shown my project to Mr. James Alexander and Mr. Kennedy, two gentlemen of great knowledge in public affairs; and, being fortified by their approbation, I ventured to lay it before the congress. It then appeared that several of the commissioners had formed plans of the same kind. A previous question was first taken, whether a union should be established, which passed in the affirmative unanimously. A committee was then appointed, one member from each colony, to consider the several plans and report. Mine happened to be preferred, and, with a few amendments, was accordingly reported.

By this plan, the general government was to be administered by a President-general, appointed and supported by the crown; and a grand council was to be chosen by the representatives of the people of the several colonies, met in their respective Assemblies. The debates upon it in Congress went on daily, hand in hand with the Indian business. Many objections and difficulties were started; but at length they were all overcome, and the plan was unanimously agreed to, and copies ordered to be transmitted to the Board of Trade and to the Assemblies of the several provinces. Its fate was singular; the Assemblies did not adopt it, as they all thought there was too much *prerogative* in it; and in England it was judged to have too much of the *democratic*. The Board of Trade did not approve it nor recommend it for the approbation of his majesty; but another scheme was formed, supposed to answer the same purpose better, whereby the governors of the provinces, with some members of their respective councils, were to meet and order the raising of troops, building of forts, &c., and to draw on the treasury of Great Britain for the expense, which was afterwards to be refunded by an act of Parliament laying a tax on America. My plan, with my reasons in support of it, is to be found among my political papers that were printed.

Being the winter following in Boston, I had much conversation with Governor Shirley upon both the plans. Part of what passed between us on this occasion may also be seen among those papers. The different and contrary reasons of dislike to my

plan makes me suspect that it was really the true medium; and
I am still of opinion it would have been happy for both sides
if it had been adopted.   The colonies so united would have been
sufficiently strong to have defended themselves; there would
then have been no need of troops from England; of course, the
subsequent pretext for taxing America, and the bloody contest
it occasioned, would have been avoided.   But such mistakes
are not new; history is full of the errors of states and princes.

> "Look round the habitable world, — how few
> Know their own good, or, knowing it, pursue!"

Those who govern, having much business on their hands, do
not generally like to take the trouble of considering and carrying into execution new projects.   The best public measures are
therefore seldom adopted from previous wisdom, but forced by
the occasion.*

The Governor of Pennsylvania, in sending it down to the
Assembly, expressed his approbation of the plan, "as appearing
to him to be drawn up with great clearness and strength of
judgment, and therefore recommended it as well worthy of their
closest and most serious attention."   The House, however, by
the management of a certain member, took it up when I happened to be absent, which I thought not very fair, and repro-
bated it without paying any attention to it at all, to my no small
mortification.

In my journey to Boston this year, I met at New York with
our new governor, Mr. Morris, just arrived there from England,
with whom I had been before intimately acquainted.   He brought
a commission to supersede Mr. Hamilton, who, tired with the
disputes his Proprietary instructions subjected him to, had resigned.   Mr. Morris asked me if I thought he must expect as
uncomfortable an administration.   I said, "No; you may, on
the contrary, have a very comfortable one, if you will only take
care not to enter into any dispute with the Assembly."   "My
dear friend," said he, pleasantly, "how can you advise my avoiding disputes?   You know I love disputing, it is one of my
greatest pleasures; however, to show the regard I have for your
counsel, I promise you I will, if possible, avoid them."   He had
some reason for loving to dispute, being eloquent, an acute

* "Wm. Penn," says Bancroft, "in 1697 had proposed an annual Congress of all the provinces on the continent of America, with power to regulate commerce.   Franklin revived the great idea, and breathed into it
enduring life.   As he descended the Hudson, the people of New York
thronged about him to welcome him; and he who first entered their city as
a runaway apprentice was revered as the mover of American Union."

sophister, and therefore generally successful in argumentative conversation. He had been brought up to it from a boy, his father, as I have heard, accustoming his children to dispute with one another for his diversion, while sitting at table after dinner, but I think the practice was not wise, for, in the course of my observation, those disputing, contradicting, and confuting people, are generally unfortunate in their affairs. They get victory sometimes, but they never get good will, which would be of more use to them. We parted, he going to Philadelphia, and I to Boston.

In returning I met at New York with the votes of the Assembly of Pennsylvania, by which it appeared that, notwithstanding his promise to me, he and the House were already in high contention; and it was a continual battle between them, as long as he retained the government. I had my share of it; for, as soon as I got back to my seat in the Assembly, I was put on every committee for answering his speeches and messages, and by the committees always desired to make the drafts. Our answers, as well as his messages, were often tart, and sometimes indecently abusive; and, as he knew I wrote for the Assembly, one might have imagined that when we met we could hardly avoid cutting throats. But he was so good-natured a man that no personal difference between him and me was occasioned by the contest, and we often dined together.

One afternoon, in the height of this public quarrel, we met in the street. "Franklin," said he, "you must go home with me and spend the evening; I am to have some company that you will like;" and, taking me by the arm, led me to his house. In gay conversation over our wine, after supper, he told us, jokingly, that he much admired the idea of Sancho Panza, who, when it was proposed to give him a government, requested it might be a government of blacks; as then, if he could not agree with his people, he might sell them. One of his friends, who sat next to me, said, "Franklin, why do you continue to side with those damned Quakers? Had you not better sell them? The Proprietor will give you a good price." "The governor," said I, "has not yet *blacked* them enough." He indeed had labored hard to blacken the Assembly in all his messages, but they wiped off his coloring as fast as he laid it on, and placed it, in return, thick upon his own face; so that, finding he was likely to be *negrofied* himself, he, as well as Mr. Hamilton, grew tired of the contest, and quitted the government.

These public quarrels were all at bottom owing to the Proprietaries, our hereditary governors; who, when any expense was to be incurred for the defence of their province, with incredible meanness instructed their deputies to pass no act for levying the necessary taxes, unless their vast estates were in the same act expressly exonerated; and they had even taken the bonds of these deputies to observe such instructions. The Assemblies for three years held out against this injustice, though constrained to bend at last. At length Captain Denny, who was Governor Morris's successor, ventured to disobey those instructions; how that was brought about I shall show hereafter.

But I am got forward too fast with my story; there are still some transactions to be mentioned, that happened during the administration of Governor Morris.

War being in a manner commenced with France, the government of Massachusetts' Bay projected an attack upon Crown Point, and sent Mr. Quincy to Pennsylvania, and Mr. Pownall, afterwards Governor Pownall, to New York, to solicit assistance. As I was in the Assembly, knew its temper, and was Mr. Quincy's countryman, he applied to me for my influence and assistance. I dictated his address to them, which was well received. They voted an aid of ten thousand pounds, to be laid out in provisions. But, the governor refusing his assent to their bill (which included this, with other sums granted for the use of the crown), unless a clause were inserted exempting the Proprietary estate from bearing any part of the tax that would be necessary, the Assembly, though very desirous of making their grant to New England effectual, were at a loss how to accomplish it. Mr. Quincy labored hard with the governor to obtain his assent, but he was obstinate.

I then suggested a method of doing the business without the governor, by orders on the trustees of the Loan Office, which, by law, the Assembly had the right of drawing. There was indeed little or no money at the time in the office, and therefore I proposed that the orders should be payable in a year, and to bear an interest of five per cent. With these orders I supposed the provisions might easily be purchased. The Assembly, with very little hesitation, adopted the proposal. The orders were immediately printed, and I was one of the committee directed to sign and dispose of them. The fund for paying them was the interest of all the paper currency then extant in the province upon loan, together with the revenue arising from the excise, which being known to be more than sufficient, they obtained credit, and were not only taken in payment for the provisions, but many moneyed people, who had cash lying by them, vested it in those orders, which they found advantageous, as they bore

interest while upon hand, and might, on any occasion, be used
as money. So that they were eagerly all bought up, and, in a
few weeks, none of them was to be seen. Thus this important
affair was by my means completed. Mr. Quincy returned thanks
to the Assembly in a handsome memorial, went home highly
pleased with the success of his embassy, and ever after bore for
me the most cordial and affectionate friendship.

The British government, not choosing to permit the union of
the colonies as proposed at Albany, and to trust that union with
their defence, lest they should thereby grow too military, and
feel their own strength, — suspicion and jealousies at this time being entertained of them, — sent over General Braddock with two
regiments of regular English troops for that purpose. He
landed at Alexandria, in Virginia, and thence marched to Fredericktown, in Maryland, where he halted for carriages. Our
Assembly apprehending, from some information, that he had received violent prejudices against them, as averse to the service,
wished me to wait upon him, not as from them, but as postmaster-
general, under the guise of proposing to settle with him the
mode of conducting with most celerity and certainty the despatches between him and the governors of the several provinces,
with whom he must necessarily have continual correspondence;
and of which they proposed to pay the expense. My son accompanied me on this journey.

We found the general at Fredericktown, waiting impatiently
for the return of those he had sent through the back parts of
Maryland and Virginia to collect wagons. I stayed with him
several days, dined with him daily, and had full opportunities
of removing his prejudices, by the information of what the Assembly had before his arrival actually done, and were still willing to do, to facilitate his operations. When I was about to
depart, the returns of wagons to be obtained were brought in,
by which it appeared that they amounted only to twenty-five,
and not all of those were in serviceable condition. The general
and all the officers were surprised, declared the expedition was
then at an end, being impossible; and exclaimed against the
ministers for ignorantly sending them into a country destitute
of the means of conveying their stores, baggage, &c., not less
than one hundred and fifty wagons being necessary.

I happened to say I thought it was a pity they had not been
landed in Pennsylvania, as in that country almost every farmer
had his wagon. The general eagerly laid hold of my words,
and said, "Then you, sir, who are a man of interest there, can
probably procure them for us; and I beg you will undertake
20

it." I asked what terms were to be offered the owners of the wagons; and I was desired to put on paper the terms that appeared to me necessary. This I did, and they were agreed to, and a commission and instructions accordingly prepared immediately. What those terms were will appear in the advertisement I published as soon as I arrived at Lancaster; which being, from the great and sudden effect it produced, a piece of some curiosity, I shall insert it at length, as follows :

" ADVERTISEMENT.

"Lancaster, April 26th, 1755.

"Whereas, one hundred and fifty wagons, with four horses to each wagon, and fifteen hundred saddle or pack horses, are wanted for the service of his majesty's forces, now about to rendezvous at Will's Creek; and his Excellency, General Braddock, having been pleased to empower me to contract for the hire of the same; I hereby give notice, that I shall attend for that purpose at Lancaster from this day to next Wednesday evening, and at York from next Thursday morning till Friday evening, where I shall be ready to agree for wagons and teams, or single horses, on the following terms, namely: 1. That there shall be paid for each wagon, with four good horses and a driver, fifteen shillings *per diem ;* and for each able horse with a pack-saddle, or other saddle and furniture, two shillings *per diem ;* and for each able horse without a saddle, eighteen pence *per diem.* 2. That the pay commence from the time of their joining the forces at Will's Creek, which must be on or before the 20th of May ensuing ; and that a reasonable allowance be paid over and above for the time necessary for their travelling to Will's Creek and home again after their discharge. 3. Each wagon and team, and every saddle or pack-horse, is to be valued by indifferent persons chosen between me and the owner; and, in case of the loss of any wagon, team or other horse, in the service, the price, according to such valuation, is to be allowed and paid. 4. Seven days' pay is to be advanced and paid in hand by me to the owner of each wagon and team, or horse, at the time of contracting, if required ; and the remainder to be paid by General Braddock, or by the paymaster of the army, at the time of their discharge; or from time to time, as it shall be demanded. 5. No drivers of wagons, or persons taking care of the hired horses, are, on any account, to be called upon to do the duty of soldiers, or be otherwise employed than in conducting or taking care of their carriages or horses. 6. All oats,

Indian corn, or other forage that wagons or horses bring to the camp, more than is necessary for the subsistence of the horses, is to be taken for the use of the army, and a reasonable price paid for the same.

" Note.— My son, William Franklin, is empowered to enter into like contracts with any person in Cumberland County.

" B. FRANKLIN."

" *To the Inhabitants of the Counties of Lancaster, York, and Cumberland.*

" Friends and Countrymen :

" Being occasionally at the camp at Frederick a few days since, I found the general and officers extremely exasperated on account of their not being supplied with horses and carriages, which had been expected · from this province, as most able to furnish them ; but, through the dissensions between our governor and Assembly, money had not been provided, nor any steps taken for that purpose.

" It was proposed to send an armed force immediately into these counties, to seize as many of the best carriages and horses as should be wanted, and compel as many persons into the service as would be necessary to drive and take care of them.

" I apprehended that the progress of British soldiers through these counties, on such an occasion, especially considering the temper they are in, and their resentment against us, would be attended with many and great inconveniences to the inhabitants, and therefore more willingly took the trouble of trying first what might be done by fair and equitable means. The people of these back counties have lately complained to the Assembly that a sufficient currency was wanting ; you have an opportunity of receiving and dividing among you a very considerable sum ; for, if the service of this expedition should continue, as it is more than probable it will, for one hundred and twenty days, the hire of these wagons and horses will amount to upwards of thirty thousand pounds ; which will be paid you in silver and gold, of the king's money.

" The service will be light and easy, for the army will scarce march above twelve miles per day, and the wagons and baggage horses, as they carry those things that are absolutely necessary to the welfare of the army, must march with the army, and no faster ; and are, for the army's sake, always placed where they can be most secure, whether in a march or in a camp.

" If you are really, as I believe you are, good and loyal subjects to his majesty, you may now do a most acceptable service,

and make it easy to yourselves; for three or four of such as
cannot separately spare from the business of their plantations
a wagon and four horses and a driver, may do it together, — one
furnishing the wagon, another one or two horses, and another
the driver, — and divide the pay proportionably between you.
But, if you do not this service to your king and country voluntarily, when such good pay and reasonable terms are offered to
you, your loyalty will be strongly suspected. The king's business
must be done; so many brave troops, come so far for your defence, must not stand idle through your backwardness to do
what may be reasonably expected from you; wagons and horses
must be had; violent measures will probably be used; and you
will be left to seek for a recompense where you can find it, and
your case, perhaps, be little pitied or regarded.

"I have no particular interest in this affair, as, except the
satisfaction of endeavoring to do good, I shall have only my
labor for my pains. If this method of obtaining the wagons
and horses is not likely to succeed, I am obliged to send word
to the general in fourteen days; and I suppose Sir John St.
Clair, the hussar, with a body of soldiers, will immediately enter
the province for the purpose; which I shall be sorry to hear,
because I am very sincerely and truly your friend and well-wisher,

"B. FRANKLIN."

I received of the general about eight hundred pounds, to
be disbursed in advance money to the wagon-owners; but, that
sum being insufficient, I advanced upwards of two hundred
pounds more; and, in two weeks, the one hundred and fifty
wagons, with two hundred and fifty-nine carrying-horses, were on
their march for the camp. The advertisement promised payment
according to the valuation, in case any wagons or horses should
be lost. The owners, however, alleging they did not know General Braddock, or what dependence might be had on his promise,
insisted on my bond for the performance; which I accordingly
gave them.

While I was at the camp, supping one evening with the officers of Colonel Dunbar's regiment, he represented to me his
concern for the subalterns, who, he said, were generally not in
affluence, and could ill afford, in this dear country, to lay in the
stores that might be necessary in so long a march through a
wilderness, where nothing was to be purchased. I commiserated
their case, and resolved to endeavor procuring them some relief.
I said nothing, however, to him of my intention, but wrote the
next morning to the committee of the Assembly who had the

disposition of some public money, warmly recommending the case of these officers to their consideration, and proposing that a present should be sent them of necessaries and refreshments. My son, who had some experience of a camp life, and of its wants, drew up a list for me, which I enclosed in my letter. The committee approved, and used such diligence, that, conducted by my son, the stores arrived at the camp as soon as the wagons. They consisted of twenty parcels, each containing

6 lbs. loaf sugar.	1 Gloucester cheese.
6 do. Muscovado do.	1 keg containing 20 lbs. good butter.
1 do. green tea.	2 dozen old Madeira wine.
1 do. bohea do.	2 gallons Jamaica spirits.
6 do. ground coffee.	1 bottle flower of mustard.
6 do. chocolate.	2 well-cured hams.
½ chest best white biscuit.	½ dozen dried tongues.
½ lb. pepper.	6 lbs. rice.
1 quart white vinegar.	6 lbs. raisins.

These parcels, well packed, were placed on as many horses, each parcel, with the horse, being intended as a present for one officer. They were very thankfully received, and the kindness acknowledged by letters to me, from the colonels of both regiments, in the most grateful terms. The general, too, was highly satisfied with my conduct in procuring him the wagons, and readily paid my account of disbursements; thanking me repeatedly, and requesting my further assistance in sending provisions after him. I undertook this also, and was busily employed in it till we heard of his defeat; advancing for the service, of my own money, upwards of one thousand pounds sterling, of which I sent him an account. It came to his hands, luckily for me, a few days before the battle, and he returned me immediately an order on the paymaster for the round sum of one thousand pounds, leaving the remainder to the next account. I consider this payment as good luck, having never been able to obtain that remainder; of which more hereafter.

This general was, I think, a brave man, and might probably have made a figure as a good officer in some European war. But he had too much self-confidence, too high an opinion of the validity of regular troops, and too mean a one of both Americans and Indians. George Croghan, our Indian interpreter, joined him on his march, with one hundred of those people, who might have been of great use to his army as guides and scouts, if he had treated them kindly; but he slighted and neglected them, and they gradually left him.

In conversation with him one day, he was giving me some account of his intended progress. "After taking Fort Duquesne,"

20*

said he, " I am to proceed to Niagara; and, having taken that, to Frontenac, if the season will allow time, and I suppose it will; for Dequesne can hardly detain me above three or four days, and then I see nothing that can obstruct my march to Niagara." Having before revolved in my mind the long line his army must make in their march by a very narrow road, to be cut for them through the woods and bushes, and also what I had read of a former defeat of fifteen hundred French, who invaded the Illinois country, I had conceived some doubts and some fears for the event of the campaign. But I ventured only to say, " To be sure, sir, if you arrive well before Duquesne, with these fine troops, so well provided with artillery, the fort, though completely fortified, and assisted with a very strong garrison, can probably make but a short resistance. The only danger I apprehend of obstruction to your march is from the ambuscades of the Indians, who, by constant practice, are dexterous in laying and executing them; and the slender line, near four miles long, which your army must make, may expose it to be attacked by surprise in its flanks, and to be cut like a thread into several pieces, which, from their distance, cannot come up in time to support each other."

He smiled at my ignorance, and replied, " These savages may indeed be a formidable enemy to your raw American militia; but upon the king's regular and disciplined troops, sir, it is impossible they should make any impression." I was conscious of an impropriety in my disputing with a military man in matters of his profession, and said no more. The enemy, however, did not take the advantage of his army which I apprehended its long line of march exposed it to, but let it advance without interruption till within nine miles of the place; and then, when more in a body (for it had just passed a river, where the front had halted till all were come over), and in a more open part of the woods than any it had passed, attacked its advanced guard by a heavy fire from behind trees and bushes; which was the first intelligence the general had of an enemy's being near him. This guard being disordered, the general hurried the troops up to their assistance, which was done in great confusion, through wagons, baggage, and cattle; and presently the fire came upon their flank; the officers, being on horseback, were more easily distinguished, picked out as marks, and fell very fast; and the soldiers were crowded together in a huddle, having or hearing no orders, and standing to be shot at till two-thirds of them were killed; and then, being seized with a panic, the remainder fled with precipitation.

The wagoners took each a horse out of his team and scampered; their example was immediately followed by others; so that all the wagons, provisions, artillery and stores, were left to the enemy. The general, being wounded, was brought off with difficulty; his secretary, Mr. Shirley, was killed by his side, and out of eighty-six officers sixty-three were killed or wounded; and seven hundred and fourteen men killed of eleven hundred. These eleven hundred had been picked men from the whole army; the rest had been left behind with Colonel Dunbar, who was to follow with the heavier part of the stores, provisions, and baggage. The flyers, not being pursued, arrived at Dunbar's camp, and the panic they brought with them instantly seized him and all his people. And, though he had now above one thousand men, and the enemy who had beaten Braddock did not at most exceed four hundred Indians and French together, instead of proceeding and endeavoring to recover some of the lost honor, he ordered all the stores, ammunition, &c., to be destroyed, that he might have more horses to assist his flight towards the settlements, and less lumber to remove. He was there met with requests from the Governors of Virginia, Maryland and Pennsylvania, that he would post his troops on the frontiers, so as to afford some protection to the inhabitants; but he continued his hasty march through all the country, not thinking himself safe till he arrived at Philadelphia, where the inhabitants could protect him. This whole transaction gave us Americans the first suspicion that our exalted ideas of the prowess of British regular troops had not been well founded.

In their first march, too, from their landing till they got beyond the settlements, they had plundered and stripped the inhabitants, totally ruining some poor families, besides insulting, abusing, and confining the people, if they remonstrated. This was enough to put us out of conceit of such defenders, if we had really wanted any. How different was the conduct of our French friends in 1781, who, during a march through the most inhabited part of our country, from Rhode Island to Virginia, near seven hundred miles, occasioned not the smallest complaint for the loss of a pig, a chicken, or even an apple.

Captain Orme, who was one of the general's aids-de-camp, and, being grievously wounded, was brought off with him, and continued with him to his death, which happened in a few days, told me that he was totally silent all the first day, and at night only said "Who would have thought it?" That he was silent again the following day, saying only, at last, ' We shall better know how to deal with them another time;" and died in a few minutes after.

The secretary's papers, with all the general's orders, instructions and correspondence, falling into the enemy's hands they selected and translated into French a number of the articles, which they printed, to prove the hostile intentions of the British court before the declaration of war. Among these I saw some letters of the general to the ministry, speaking highly of the great service I had rendered the army, and recommending me to their notice. David Hume, who was some years after secretary to Lord Hertford, when minister in France, and afterwards to General Conway, when secretary of state, told me he had seen among the papers in that office letters from Braddock highly recommending me. But, the expedition having been unfortunate, my service, it seems, was not thought of much value, for those recommendations were never of any use to me.

As to rewards from himself, I asked only one, which was, that he would give orders to his officers not to enlist any more of our bought servants, and that he would discharge such as had been already enlisted. This he readily granted, and several were accordingly returned to their masters, on my application. Dunbar, when the command devolved on him, was not so generous. He being at Philadelphia on his retreat, or rather flight, I applied to him for the discharge of the servants of three poor farmers of Lancaster County that he had enlisted, reminding him of the late general's orders on that head. He promised me that, if the masters would come to him at Trenton, where he should be in a few days, on his march to New York, he would there deliver their men to them. They accordingly were at the expense and trouble of going to Trenton, and there he refused to perform his promise, to their great loss and disappointment.

As soon as the loss of the wagons and horses was generally known, all the owners came upon me for the valuation which I had given bond to pay. Their demands gave me a great deal of trouble. I acquainted them that the money was ready in the paymaster's hands, but the order for paying it must first be obtained from General Shirley; and that I had applied for it, but, he being at a distance, an answer could not soon be received, and they must have patience. All this, however, was not sufficient to satisfy them, and some began to sue me. General Shirley at length relieved me from this terrible situation, by appointing commissioners to examine the claims, and ordering payment. They amounted to near twenty thousand pounds, which to pay would have ruined me.

Before we had the news of this defeat, the two doctors Bond came to me with a subscription paper for raising money to defray

the expense of a grand firework, which it was intended to exhibit
at a rejoicing on receiving the news of our taking Fort Duquesne.
I looked grave, and said it would, I thought, be time enough to
prepare the rejoicing when we knew we should have occasion to
rejoice.   They seemed surprised that I did not immediately comply with their proposal.   "Why, the d—l!" said one of them,
"you surely don't suppose that the fort will not be taken?" "I
don't know that it will not be taken; but I know that the
events of war are subject to great uncertainty."   I gave them
the reasons of my doubting; the subscription was dropped, and
the projectors thereby missed the mortification they would have
undergone if the firework had been prepared.   Dr. Bond, on
some other occasion afterwards, said that he did not like Franklin's forebodings.*

CHAPTER X.

Commissioner for Disbursing Money for Public Defence — His Militia Bill
— Appointed to take Charge of the Frontier and build Forts — March —
Military Preparations — Indian Massacre — Arrival at Gnadenhutten —
New Mode of securing Punctuality at Prayers — The Moravians — Their
Marriages — Colonel Franklin — Journey to Virginia — Offered a Com-
mission as General — Account of his Electrical Discoveries — A Member
of the Royal Society — Receives the Copley Medal.

GOVERNOR MORRIS, who had continually worried the Assembly
with message after message before the defeat of Braddock, to
beat them into the making of acts to raise money for the defence
of the province, without taxing among others the Proprietary
estates, and had rejected all their bills for not having such an
exempting clause, now redoubled his attacks, with more hope of
success, the danger and necessity being greater.   The Assembly,
however, continued firm, believing they had justice on their side,
and that it would be giving up an essential right if they suffered
the governor to amend their money bills.   In one of the last,
indeed, which was for granting fifty thousand pounds, his proposed amendment was only of a single word.   The bill expressed,

---

* About this time Franklin coöperated with other philanthropic citizens
in carrying out a plan for improving the condition of the Germans in
America.

"that all estates real and personal were to be taxed, those of the Proprietaries *not* excepted." His amendment was,—for *not* read *only*. A small, but very material alteration. However, when the news of the disaster reached England, our friends there, whom we had taken care to furnish with all the Assembly's answers to the governor's messages, raised a clamor against the Proprietaries for their meanness and injustice in giving their governor such instructions; some going so far as to say that, by obstructing the defence of their province, they forfeited their right to it. They were intimidated by this; and sent orders to their receiver-general to add five thousand pounds of their money to whatever sum might be given by the Assembly for such purpose.

This, being testified to the House, was accepted in lieu of their share of a general tax, and a new bill was formed with an exempting clause, which passed accordingly. By this act I was appointed one of the commissioners for disposing of the money, sixty thousand pounds. I had been active in modelling the bill, and procuring its passage; and had at the same time drawn one for establishing and disciplining a voluntary militia, which I carried through the House without much difficulty, as care was taken in it to leave the Quakers at liberty. To promote the association necessary to form the militia, I wrote a dialogue stating and answering all the objections I could think of to such a militia; which was printed, and had, as I thought, great effect.

While the several companies in the city and country were forming, and learning their exercise, the governor prevailed with me to take charge of our north-western frontier, which was infested by the enemy, and provide for the defence of the inhabitants by raising troops and building a line of forts. I undertook this military business, though I did not conceive myself well qualified for it. He gave me a commission with full powers, and a parcel of blank commissions for officers, to be given to whom I thought fit. I had but little difficulty in raising men, having soon five hundred and sixty under my command. My son, who had in the preceding war been an officer in the army raised against Canada, was my aid-de-camp, and of great use to me. The Indians had burned Gnadenhutten, a village settled by the Moravians, and massacred the inhabitants; but the place was thought a good situation for one of the forts.

In order to march thither, I assembled the companies at Bethlehem, the chief establishment of these people. I was surprised to find it in so good a posture of defence; the destruction of Gnadenhutten had made them apprehend danger. The princi-

pal buildings were defended by a stockade ; they had purchased
a quantity of arms and ammunition from New York, and had
even placed quantities of small paving-stones between the windows of their high stone houses, for their women to throw them
down upon the heads of any Indians that should attempt to
force into them.   The armed brethren, too, kept watch, and relieved each other on guard, as methodically as in any garrison
town.   In conversation with the bishop, Spangenberg, I mentioned my surprise ; for, knowing they had obtained an act of
Parliament exempting them from military duties in the colonies,
I had supposed they were conscientiously scrupulous of bearing
arms.   He answered me that it was not one of their established
principles, but that at the time of their obtaining that act it
was thought to be a principle with many of their people.   On
this occasion, however, they, to their surprise, found it adopted by
but a few.   It seems they were either deceived in themselves,
or deceived the Parliament ; but common sense, aided by present
danger, will sometimes be too strong for whimsical opinions.

It was the beginning of January when we set out upon this
business of building forts.   I sent one detachment towards the
Minisink, with instructions to erect one for the security of that
upper part of the country ; and another to the lower part, with
similar instructions ; and I concluded to go myself with the rest
of my force to Gnadenhutten, where a fort was thought more
immediately necessary.   The Moravians procured me five wagons
for our tools, stores and baggage.

Just before we left Bethlehem, eleven farmers, who had been
driven from their plantations by the Indians, came to me, requesting a supply of fire-arms, that they might go back and bring
off their cattle.   I gave them each a gun, with suitable ammunition.   We had not marched many miles before it began to rain,
and it continued raining all day ; there were no habitations on
the road to shelter us, till we arrived near night at the house of
a German, where, and in his barn, we were all huddled together, as
wet as water could make us.   It was well we were not attacked
in our march, for our arms were of the most ordinary sort, and
our men could not keep the locks of their guns dry.   The Indians
are dexterous in contrivances for that purpose, which we had
not.   They met that day the eleven poor farmers above mentioned, and killed ten of them.   The one that escaped informed
us that his and his companions' guns would not go off, the prim-
ing being wet with the rain.

The next day being fair, we continued our march, and arrived
at the desolated Gnadenhutten.   There was a mill near, round

which were left several pine boards, with which we soon hutted ourselves; an operation the more necessary at that inclement season, as we had no tents.   Our first work was to bury more effectually the dead we found there, who had been half-interred by the country people.

The next morning our fort was planned and marked out, the circumference measuring four hundred and fifty-five feet, which would require as many palisades to be made, one with another, of a foot diameter each.   Our axes, of which we had seventy, were immediately set to work to cut down trees; and, our men being dexterous in the use of them, great despatch was made. Seeing the trees fall so fast, I had the curiosity to look at my watch when two men began to cut at a pine; in six minutes they had it upon the ground, and I found it of fourteen inches diameter.   Each pine made three palisades of eighteen feet long, pointed at one end.   While these were preparing, our other men dug a trench all round, of three feet deep, in which the palisades were to be planted; and, the bodies being taken off our wagons, and the fore and hind wheels separated by taking out the pin which united the two parts of the perch, we had ten carriages with two horses each, to bring the palisades from the woods to the spot.   When they were set up, our carpenters built a platform of boards all round within, about six feet high, for the men to stand on when to fire through the loop-holes.   We had one swivel gun, which we mounted on one of the angles, and fired it as soon as fixed, to let the Indians know, if any were within hearing, that we had such pieces; and thus our fort—if that name may be given to so miserable a stockade — was finished in a week, though it rained so hard, every other day, that the men could not work.

This gave me occasion to observe that, when men are employed, they are best contented; for on the days they worked they were good-natured and cheerful, and, with the consciousness of having done a good day's work, they spent the evening jollily; but on our idle days they were mutinous and quarrelsome, finding fault with the pork, the bread, &c., and were continually in bad humor; which put me in mind of a sea-captain, whose rule it was to keep his men constantly at work; and when his mate once told him that they had done everything, and there was nothing further to employ them about, "O," said he, "make them scour the anchor."

This kind of fort, however contemptible, is a sufficient defence against Indians, who have no cannon.   Finding ourselves now posted securely, and having a place to retreat to on occasion, we ventured out in parties to scour the adjacent country. We met with no Indians, but we found the places on the neighboring hills where they had lain to watch our proceedings. There was an art in their contrivance of those places that seems worth mentioning. It being winter, a fire was necessary for them; but a common fire on the surface of the ground would, by its light, have discovered their position at a distance. They had therefore dug holes in the ground about three feet diameter, and somewhat deeper; we found where they had with their hatchets cut off the charcoal from the sides of burnt logs lying in the woods. With these coals they had made small fires in the bottom of the holes, and we observed among the weeds and grass the prints of their bodies, made by their lying all round with their legs hanging down in the holes to keep their feet warm; which, with them, is an essential point. This kind of fire, so managed, could not discover them, either by its light, flame, sparks, or even smoke; it appeared that the number was not great, and it seems they saw we were too many to be attacked by them with prospect of advantage.

We had for our chaplain a zealous Presbyterian minister, Mr. Beatty, who complained to me that the men did not generally attend his prayers and exhortations. When they enlisted they were promised, besides pay and provisions, a gill of rum a day, which was punctually served out to them, half in the morning, and the other half in the evening; and I observed they were punctual in attending to receive it; upon which I said to Mr. Beatty, "It is perhaps below the dignity of your profession to act as steward of the rum; but, if you were only to distribute it out after prayers, you would have them all about you." He liked the thought, undertook the task, and, with the help of a few hands to measure out the liquor, executed it to satisfaction; and never were prayers more generally and more punctually attended. So that I think this method preferable to the punishment inflicted by some military laws for non-attendance on divine service.

I had hardly finished this business, and got my fort well stored with provisions, when I received a letter from the governor, acquainting me that he had called the Assembly, and wished my attendance there, if the posture of affairs on the frontiers was such that my remaining there was no longer necessary. My friends, too, of the Assembly, pressing me by their letters to be, if possible, at the meeting, and my three intended forts being now completed, and the inhabitants contented to remain on their farms under that protection, I resolved to return; the more will-

21

ingly, as a New England officer, Colonel Clapham, experienced
in Indian war, being on a visit to our establishment, consented
to accept the command. I gave him a commission, and, parading
the garrison, had it read before them; and introduced him to
them as an officer, who, from his skill in military affairs, was
much more fit to command them than myself; and, giving them
a little exhortation, took my leave. I was escorted as far as
Bethlehem, where I rested a few days, to recover from the fatigue
I had undergone. The first night, lying in a good bed, I could
hardly sleep, it was so different from my hard lodgings on the
floor of a hut at Gnadenhutten, with only a blanket or two.

While at Bethlehem, I inquired a little into the practices of
the Moravians; some of them had accompanied me, and all
were very kind to me. I found they worked for a common
stock, ate at common tables, and slept in common dormitories,
great numbers together. In the dormitories I observed loop-
holes, at certain distances, all along just under the ceiling, which
I thought judiciously placed for change of air. I went to their
church, where I was entertained with good music, the organ being accompanied with violins, hautboys, flutes, clarinets, &c. I
understood their sermons were not usually preached to mixed
congregations of men, women and children, as is our common
practice; but that they assembled sometimes the married men,
at other times their wives, then the young men, the young
women, and the little children; each division by itself. The sermon I heard was to the latter, who came in and were placed in
rows on benches; the boys under the conduct of a young man,
their tutor, and the girls conducted by a young woman. The
discourse seemed well adapted to their capacities, and was delivered in a pleasing, familiar manner, coaxing them, as it were, to
be good. They behaved very orderly, but looked pale and unhealthy; which made me suspect they were kept too much within
doors, or not allowed sufficient exercise.

I inquired concerning the Moravian marriages, whether the
report was true that they were by lot. I was told that lots
were used only in particular cases; that generally, when a young
man found himself disposed to marry, he informed the elders of
his class, who consulted the elder ladies, that governed the young
women. As these elders of the different sexes were well acquainted with the tempers and dispositions of their respective
pupils, they could best judge what matches were suitable, and
their judgments were generally acquiesced in. But if, for example, it should happen that two or three young women were
found to be equally proper for the young man, the lot was then

recurred to. I objected, if the matches are not made by the mutual choice of the parties, some of them may chance to be very unhappy. "And so they may," answered my informer, "if you let the parties choose for themselves." Which indeed I could not deny.

Being returned to Philadelphia, I found the association went on with great success. The inhabitants that were not Quakers, having pretty generally come into it, formed themselves into companies, and chose their captains, lieutenants and ensigns, according to the new law. Dr. Bond visited me, and gave me an account of the pains he had taken to spread a general good liking to the law, and ascribed much to those endeavors. I had the vanity to ascribe all to my *Dialogue;* however, not knowing but that he might be in the right, I let him enjoy his opinion, which I take to be generally the best way in such cases. The officers, meeting, chose me to be colonel of the regiment, which I this time accepted. I forget how many companies we had, but we paraded about twelve hundred well-looking men, with a company of artillery, who had been furnished with six brass fieldpieces, which they had become so expert in the use of as to fire twelve times in a minute. The first time I reviewed my regiment, they accompanied me to my house, and would salute me with some rounds fired before my door, which shook down and broke several glasses of my electrical apparatus. And my new honor proved not much less brittle; for all our commissions were soon after broken, by a repeal of the law in England.

During this short time of my colonelship, being about to set out on a journey to Virginia, the officers of my regiment took it into their heads that it would be proper for them to escort me out of town, as far as the Lower Ferry. Just as I was getting on horseback, they came to my door, between thirty and forty, mounted, and all in their uniforms. I had not been previously acquainted with their project, or I should have prevented it, being naturally averse to the assuming of state on any occasion; and I was a good deal chagrined at their appearance, as I could not avoid their accompanying me. What made it worse was, that, as soon as we began to move, they drew their swords and rode with them naked all the way. Somebody wrote an account of this to the Proprietor, and it gave him great offence. No such honor had been paid to him when in the province, nor to any of his governors; and he said it was only proper to princes of the blood royal, which may be true for aught I know, who was, and still am, ignorant of the etiquette in such cases.

This silly affair, however, greatly increased his rancor against me, which was before considerable, on account of my conduct in the Assembly respecting the exemption of his estate from taxation, which I had always opposed very warmly, and not without severe reflections on the meanness and injustice of contending for it.   He accused me to the ministry, as being the great obstacle to the king's service, preventing, by my influence in the House, the proper form of the bills for raising money ; and he instanced the parade with my officers, as a proof of my having an intention to take the government of the province out of his hands by force.   He also applied to Sir Everard Fawkener, the Postmaster-general, to deprive me of my office.   But it had no other effect than to procure from Sir Everard a gentle admonition.

Notwithstanding the continual wrangle between the governor and the House, in which I, as a member, had so large a share, there still subsisted a civil intercourse between that gentleman and myself, and we never had any personal difference.   I have sometimes since thought that his little or no resentment against me, for the answers it was known I drew up to his messages, might be the effect of professional habit ; and that, being bred a lawyer, he might consider us both as merely advocates for contending clients in a suit,—— he for the Proprietaries, and I for the Assembly.   He would therefore sometimes call, in a friendly way, to advise with me on difficult points ; and sometimes, though not often, take my advice.

We acted in concert to supply Braddock's army with provisions ; and, when the shocking news arrived of his defeat, the governor sent in haste for me, to consult with him on measures for preventing the desertion of the back counties.   I forget now the advice I gave ; but I think it was, that Dunbar should be written to, and prevailed with, if possible, to post his troops on the frontiers for their protection, until, by reinforcements from the colonies, he might be able to proceed in the expedition. And, after my return from the frontier, he would have had me undertake the conduct of such an expedition with provincial troops, for the reduction of Fort Duquesne, Dunbar and his men being otherwise employed ; and he proposed to commission me as general.   I had not so good an opinion of my military abilities as he professed to have, and I believe his professions must have exceeded his real sentiments; but probably he might think that my popularity would facilitate the business with the men, and influence in the Assembly the grant of money to pay for it ; and that, perhaps, without taxing the Proprietary.   Finding me not so forward to engage as he expected, the project was dropped ; and he soon after left the government, being superseded by Captain Denny.

Before I proceed in relating the part I had in public affairs under this new governor's administration, it may not be amiss to give here some account of the rise and progress of my philosophical reputation.

In 1746, being in Boston, I met there with a Dr. Spence, who was lately arrived from Scotland, and showed me some electric experiments. They were imperfectly performed, as he was not very expert; but, being on a subject quite new to me. they equally surprised and pleased me. Soon after my return to Philadelphia, our library company received from Mr. Peter Collinson, Fellow of the Royal Society of London, a present of a glass tube, with some account of the use of it in making such experiments. I eagerly seized the opportunity of repeating what I had seen at Boston; and, by much practice, acquired great readiness in performing those also which we had an account of from England, adding a number of new ones. I say much practice, for my house was continually full, for some time, with persons who came to see these new wonders.

To divide a little this encumbrance among my friends, I caused a number of similar tubes to be blown in our glass-house, with which they furnished themselves, so that we had at length several performers. Among these, the principal was Mr. Kinnersley, an ingenious neighbor, who being out of business, I encouraged him to undertake showing the experiments for money, and drew up for him two lectures, in which the experiments were ranged in such order, and accompanied with explanations in such method, as that the foregoing should assist in comprehending the following. He procured an elegant apparatus for the purpose, in which all the little machines that I had roughly made for myself were neatly formed by instrument makers. His lectures were well attended. and gave great satisfaction; and, after some time, he went through the colonies, exhibiting them in every capital town, and picked up some money. In the West India Islands, indeed, it was with difficulty the experiments could be made, from the general moisture of the air.

Obliged as we were to Mr. Collinson for the present of the tube, &c., I thought it right he should be informed of our success in using it, and wrote him several letters containing accounts of our experiments. He got them read in the Royal Society, where they were not at first thought worth so much notice as to be printed in their *Transactions*. One paper, which I wrote to Mr. Kinnersley, on the sameness of lightning with electricity, I sent to Mr. Mitchel, an acquaintance of mine, and one of the members also of that society; who wrote me word, that it had been read, but was laughed at by the connoisseurs.   The papers however, being shown to Dr. Fothergill, he thought them of too much value to be stifled, and advised the printing of them.   Mr Collinson then gave them to Cave for publication in his *Gentleman's Magazine*; but he chose to print them separately in a pamphlet, and Dr. Fothergill wrote the preface.   Cave, it seems, judged rightly for his profession; for, by the additions that arrived afterwards, they swelled to a quarto volume, which has had five editions, and cost him nothing for copy-money.

It was, however, some time before those papers were much taken notice of in England.   A copy of them happening to fall into the hands of the Count de Buffon, a philosopher deservedly of great reputation in France, and indeed all over Europe, he prevailed with M. Dubourg to translate them into French; and they were printed at Paris.   The publication offended the Abbé Nollet, Preceptor in Natural Philosophy to the Royal Family, and an able experimenter, who had formed and published a theory of electricity, which then had the general vogue.   He could not at first believe that such a work came from America, and said it must have been fabricated by his enemies at Paris, to oppose his system.   Afterwards, having been assured that there really existed such a person as Franklin at Philadelphia, which he had doubted, he wrote and published a volume of Letters, chiefly addressed to me, defending his theory, and denying the verity of my experiments, and of the positions deduced from them.

I once proposed answering the Abbé, and actually began the answer; but, on consideration that my writings contained a description of experiments which any one might repeat and verify, and, if not to be verified, could not be defended; or of observations offered as *conjectures*, and not delivered dogmatically, therefore not laying me under any obligation to defend them; and reflecting that a dispute between two persons, written in different languages, might be lengthened greatly by mistranslations, and thence misconceptions of one another's meaning, — much of one of the Abbé's letters being founded on an error in the translation, — I concluded to let my papers shift for themselves; believing it was better to spend what time I could spare from public business in making new experiments, than in disputing about those already made.   I therefore never answered M. Nollet; and the event gave me no cause to repent my silence; for my friend M. Le Roy, of the Royal Academy of Sciences, took up my cause and refuted him; my book was translated into the Italian, German, and Latin languages; and the doctrine it contained was by degrees generally adopted by the philosophers of Europe, in preference to that of the Abbé; so that he lived to see himself the last of his sect, except Monsieur B——, of Paris, his *élève* and immediate disciple.

What gave my book the more sudden and general celebrity, was the success of one of its proposed experiments, made by Messieurs Dalibard and De Lor at Marly, for drawing lightning from the clouds. This engaged the public attention everywhere. M. De Lor, who had an apparatus for experimental philosophy, and lectured in that branch of science, undertook to repeat what he called the *Philadelphia Experiments;* and, after they were performed before the king and court, all the curious of Paris flocked to see them. I will not swell this narrative with an account of that capital experiment, nor of the infinite pleasure I received in the success of a similar one I made soon after with a kite at Philadelphia, as both are to be found in the histories of electricity.

Dr. Wright, an English physician, when at Paris, wrote to a friend, who was of the Royal Society, an account of the high esteem my experiments were in among the learned abroad, and of their wonder that my writings had been so little noticed in England. The society, on this, resumed the consideration of the letters that had been read to them; and the celebrated Dr. Watson drew up a summary account of them, and of all I had afterwards sent to England on the subject, which he accompanied with some praise of the writer. This summary was then printed in their *Transactions;* and, some members of the society in London, particularly the very ingenious Mr. Canton, having verified the experiment of procuring lightning from the clouds by a pointed rod, and acquainted them with the success, they soon made me more than amends for the slight with which they had before treated me. Without my having made any application for that honor, they chose me a member, and voted that I should be excused the customary payments, which would have amounted to twenty-five guineas; and ever since have given me their *Transactions* gratis.* They also presented me with the gold medal of Sir Godfrey Copley, for the year 1753, the delivery of which was accompanied by a very handsome speech of the president, Lord Macclesfield, wherein I was highly honored.

---

* Subsequently looking at the minutes of the society, Franklin found that the certificate, worded very advantageously for him, was signed by Lord Macclesfield, then President, Lord Parker, and Lord Willoughby; that the election was by a unanimous vote; and, the honor being voluntarily conferred by the society, unsolicited by Franklin, it was thought wrong to demand or receive the usual fees or composition.

CHAPTER XI.

Overtures from Gov. Denny — The Assembly and the Proprietaries — Franklin deputed to go to England as Agent of the Assembly — Discussion before Lord Loudoun — Vexatious Delays — Anecdote — Departure with
his Son for England — Anecdote of Shirley — Incidents of the Voyage —
Arrival in London.

OUR new governor, Captain Denny, brought over for me the
before-mentioned medal from the Royal Society, which he pre
sented to me at an entertainment given him by the city.   He
accompanied it with very polite expressions of his esteem for
me, having, as he said, been long acquainted with my character.
After dinner, when the company, as was customary at that time,
were engaged in drinking, he took me aside into another room,
and acquainted me that he had been advised by his friends in
England to cultivate a friendship with me, as one who was
capable of giving him the best advice, and of contributing most
effectually to the making his administration easy.   That he
therefore desired, of all things, to have a good understanding with
me; and he begged me to be assured of his readiness on all occasions to render me every service that might be in his power.
He said much to me also of the Proprietor's good disposition
towards the province, and of the advantage it would be to us all,
and to me in particular, if the opposition that had been so long
continued to his measures was dropped, and harmony restored
between him and the people; in effecting which, it was thought
no one could be more serviceable than myself; and I might
depend on adequate acknowledgments and recompenses.   The
drinkers, finding we did not return immediately to the table,
sent us a decanter of madeira, which the governor made a liberal
use of, and in proportion became more profuse of his solicitations and promises.

My answers were to this purpose: that my circumstances,
thanks to God, were such as to make Proprietary favors unnecessary to me; and that, being a member of the Assembly,
I could not possibly accept of any; that, however, I had no
personal enmity to the Proprietary, and that whenever the public measures he proposed should appear to be for the good of the
people, no one would espouse and forward them more zealously
than myself; my past opposition having been founded on this,
that the measures which had been urged were evidently intended

to serve the Proprietary interest, with great prejudice to that
of the people. That I was much obliged to him (the governor)
for his profession of regard to me; and that he might rely on
everything in my power to render his administration as easy to
him as possible, hoping, at the same time, that he had not brought
with him the same unfortunate instructions his predecessors had
been hampered with.

On this he did not then explain himself; but, when he afterwards came to do business with the Assembly, they appeared
again, the disputes were renewed, and I was as active as ever in
the opposition, being the penman, first of the request to have a
communication of the instructions, and then of the remarks upon
them, which may be found in the votes of the times, and in the
Historical Review I afterwards published. But between us,
personally, no enmity arose; we were often together; he was a
man of letters, had seen much of the world, and was entertaining and pleasing in conversation. He gave me information that
my old friend Ralph was still alive; that he was esteemed one
of the best political writers in England; had been employed in
the dispute between Prince Frederick and the king, and had
obtained a pension of three hundred pounds a year; that his
reputation was indeed small as a poet, Pope having damned his
poetry in the Dunciad; but his prose was thought as good as
any man's.

The Assembly finally finding the Proprietary obstinately per-
sisted in shackling the deputies with instructions inconsistent not
only with the privileges of the people, but with the service of
the crown, resolved to petition the king against them, and appointed me their agent to go over to England, to present and
support the petition. The House had sent up a bill to the governor, granting a sum of sixty thousand pounds for the king's
use (ten thousand pounds of which was subjected to the orders
of the then general, Lord Loudoun), which the governor, in compliance with his instructions, absolutely refused to pass.

I had agreed with Captain Morris, of the packet at New
York, for my passage, and my stores were put on board, when
Lord Loudoun arrived at Philadelphia, expressly, as he told me,
to endeavor an accommodation between the governor and Assembly, that his majesty's service might not be obstructed by
their dissensions. Accordingly he desired the governor and
myself to meet him, that he might hear what was to be said on
both sides. We met and discussed the business.

In behalf of the Assembly, I urged the various arguments,
that may be found in the public papers of that time, which were

of my writing, and are printed with the minutes of the Assembly; and the governor pleaded his instructions, the bond he had given to observe them, and his ruin if he disobeyed; yet seemed not unwilling to hazard himself, if Lord Loudoun would advise it.   This his lordship did not choose to do, though I once thought I had nearly prevailed with him to do it; but finally he rather chose to urge the compliance of the Assembly; and he entreated me to use my endeavors with them for that purpose, declaring that he would spare none of the king's troops for the defence of our frontiers, and that, if we did not continue to provide for that defence ourselves, they must remain exposed to the enemy.

I acquainted the House with what had passed, and, presenting them with a set of resolutions I had drawn up, declaring our rights, that we did not relinquish our claim to those rights, but only suspended the exercise of them on this occasion through *force*, against which we protested, they at length agreed to drop that bill, and frame another conformable to the Proprietary instructions.   This of course the governor passed, and I was then at liberty to proceed on my voyage.   But in the mean time the packet had sailed with my sea-stores, which was some loss to me, and my only recompense was his lordship's thanks for my service; all the credit of obtaining the accommodation falling to his share.

He set out for New York before me; and, as the time for despatching the packet-boats was at his disposition, and there were two then remaining there, one of which, he said, was to sail very soon, I requested to know the precise time, that I might not miss her by any delay of mine.   The answer was : " I have given out that she is to sail on Saturday next; but I may let you know, *entre nous*, that if you are there by Monday morning you will be in time, but do not delay longer." By some accidental hindrance at a ferry, it was Monday noon before I arrived, and I was much afraid she might have sailed, as the wind was fair; but I was soon made ·easy by the information that she was still in the harbor, and would not move till the next day.

One would imagine that I was now on the very point of departing for Europe.   I thought so; but I was not then so well acquainted with his lordship's character, of which *indecision* was one of the strongest features.   I shall give some instances. It was about the beginning of April that I came to New York, and I think it was near the end of June before we sailed.   There were then two of the packet-boats, which had been long in readiness, but were detained for the general's letters, which were always to be ready *to-morrow*.   Another packet arrived; she too was detained; and before we sailed, a fourth was expected. Ours was the first to be despatched, as having been there longest. Passengers were engaged for all, and some extremely impatient to be gone, and the merchants uneasy about their letters, and for the orders they had given for insurance (it being war-time), and for autumnal goods; but their anxiety availed nothing; his lordship's letters were not ready; and yet whoever waited on him found him always at his desk, pen in hand, and concluded he must needs write abundantly.

Going myself one morning to pay my respects, I found in his antechamber one Innis, a messenger of Philadelphia, who had come thence express with a packet from Governor Denny, for the general. He delivered to me some letters from my friends there, which occasioned my inquiring when he was to return, and where he lodged, that I might send some letters by him. He told me he was ordered to call to-morrow at nine for the general's answer to the governor, and should set off immediately. I put my letters into his hands the same day. A fortnight after, I met him again in the same place. "So, you are soon returned, Innis?" "Returned! no, I am not gone yet." "How so?" "I have called here this and every morning, these two weeks past, for his lordship's letters, and they are not yet ready." "Is it possible, when he is so great a writer; for I see him constantly at his escritoire?" "Yes," said Innis, "but he is like St. George on the signs, *always on horseback, and never rides on.*" This observation of the messenger was, it seems, well founded; for, when in England, I understood that Mr. Pitt, afterwards Lord Chatham, gave it as one reason for removing this general, and sending Generals Amherst and Wolfe, *that the minister never heard from him, and could not know what he was doing.*

In this daily expectation of sailing, and all the three packets going down to Sandy Hook, to join the fleet there, the passengers thought it best to be on board, lest by a sudden order the ships should sail and they be left behind. There, if I remember, we were about six weeks, consuming our sea-stores, and obliged to procure more. At length the fleet sailed, the general and all his army on board, bound to Louisburg, with intent to besiege and take that fortress; and all the packet-boats in company were ordered to attend the general's ship ready to receive his despatches when they should be ready. We were out five days before we got a letter with leave to part; and then our ship quitted the fleet and steered for England. The other two packets he still detained, carried them with him to Halifax, where he stayed some time to exercise the men in sham attacks upon sham forts, then altered his mind as to besieging Louisburg, and returned to New York, with all his troops, together with the two packets above mentioned, and all their passengers! During his absence the French and savages had taken Fort George, on the frontier of that province, and the Indians had massacred many of the garrison after capitulation.

I saw afterwards, in London, Captain Bound, who commanded one of those packets. He told me that, when he had been detained a month, he acquainted his lordship that his ship was grown foul to a degree that must necessarily hinder her fast sailing,—a point of consequence for a packet-boat,— and requested an allowance of time to have her down and clean her bottom. His lordship asked how long time that would require. He answered, three days. The general replied, "If you can do it in one day I give leave, otherwise not; for you must certainly sail the day after to-morrow." So he never obtained leave, though detained afterwards from day to day during full three months.

I saw also in London one of Bonell's passengers, who was so enraged against his lordship for deceiving and detaining him so long in New York, and then carrying him to Halifax and back again, that he swore he would sue him for damages. Whether he did or not, I never heard; but, as he represented it, the injury to his affairs was very considerable.

On the whole, I wondered much how such a man came to be intrusted with so important a business as the conduct of a great army; but, having since seen more of the great world, and the means of obtaining and motives for giving places and employments, my wonder is diminished. General Shirley, on whom the command of the army devolved upon the death of Braddock, would, in my opinion, if continued in place, have made a much better campaign than that of Loudoun, in 1756, which was frivolous, expensive, and disgraceful to our nation beyond conception. For, though Shirley was not bred a soldier, he was sensible and sagacious in himself, and attentive to good advice from others, capable of forming judicious plans, and quick and active in carrying them into execution. Loudoun, instead of defending the colonies with his great army, left them totally exposed, while he paraded idly at Halifax, by which means Fort George was lost; besides, he deranged all our mercantile operations, and distressed our trade by a long embargo on the exportation of provisions, on pretence of keeping supplies from being obtained by the enemy, but in reality for beating down their price in favor of the contractors, in whose profits, it was said, perhaps from suspicion only, he had a share; and, when at length the embargo was taken off, neglecting to send notice of it to Charleston, where the Carolina fleet was detained near three months; and whereby their bottoms were so much damaged by the worm, that a great part of them foundered in their passage home.

Shirley was, I believe, sincerely glad of being relieved from so burdensome a charge as the conduct of an army must be to a man unacquainted with military business. I was at the entertainment given by the city of New York to Lord Loudoun, on his taking upon him the command. Shirley, though thereby superseded, was present also. There was a great company of officers, citizens and strangers, and, some chairs having been borrowed in the neighborhood, there was one among them very low, which fell to the lot of Mr. Shirley. I sat by him, and perceiving it, I said, "They have given you a very low seat." "No matter, Mr. Franklin," said he; "I find *a low seat* the easiest."

While I was, as before mentioned, detained at New York, I received all the accounts of the provisions, &c., that I had furnished to Braddock, some of which accounts could not sooner be obtained from the different persons I had employed to assist in the business. I presented them to Lord Loudoun, desiring to be paid the balance. He caused them to be examined by the proper officer, who, after comparing every article with its voucher, certified them to be right; and his lordship promised to give me an order on the paymaster for the balance due to me. This was, however, put off from time to time; and, though I called often for it by appointment, I did not get it. At length, just before my departure, he told me he had, on better consideration, concluded not to mix his accounts with those of his predecessors. "And you," said he, "when in England, have only to exhibit your accounts to the treasury, and you will be paid immediately."

I mentioned, but without effect, a great and unexpected expense I had been put to by being detained so long at New York, as a reason for my desiring to be presently paid; and, on my observing that it was not right I should be put to any further trouble or delay in obtaining the money I had advanced, as I charged no commission for my service, "O," said he, "you must not think of persuading us that you are no gainer; we understand better those matters, and know that every one concerued in supplying the army finds means in the doing it to fill his own pockets." I assured him that was not my case, and that I had not pocketed a farthing; but he appeared clearly not to believe me; and indeed I afterwards learned that immense fortunes are often made in such employments. As to my balance, I am not paid it to this day, of which more hereafter.

22

Our captain of the packet boasted much, before we sailed, of the swiftness of his ship; unfortunately, when we came to sea, she proved the dullest of ninety-six sail, to his no small mortification. After many conjectures respecting the cause, when we were near another ship almost as dull as ours, which, however, gained upon us, the captain ordered all hands to come aft and stand as near the ensign staff as possible. We were, passengers included, about forty persons. While we stood there, the ship mended her pace, and soon left her neighbor far behind, which proved clearly what our captain suspected, that she was loaded too much by the head. The casks of water, it seems, had been all placed forward; these he therefore ordered to be moved further aft, on which the ship recovered her character, and proved the best sailer in the fleet.

The captain said she had once gone at the rate of thirteen knots, which is accounted thirteen miles per hour. We had on board, as a passenger, Captain Archibald Kennedy, of the Royal Navy, who contended that it was impossible, and that no ship ever sailed so fast, and that there must have been some error in the division of the log-line, or some mistake in heaving the log. A wager ensued between the two captains, to be decided when there should be sufficient wind. Kennedy therefore examined the log-line, and, being satisfied with it, he determined to throw the log himself. Some days after, when the wind was very fair and fresh, and the captain of the packet, Lutwidge, said he believed she then went at the rate of thirteen knots, Kennedy made the experiment, and owned his wager lost.

The foregoing fact I give for the sake of the following observation. It has been remarked as an imperfection in the art of ship-building, that it can never be known till she is tried whether a new ship will or will not be a good sailer; for that the model of a good sailing ship had been exactly followed in a new one, which has been proved, on the contrary, remarkably dull. I apprehend that this may partly be occasioned by the different opinions of seamen respecting the modes of loading, rigging and sailing, of a ship. Each has his method; and the same vessel, laden by the method and orders of one captain, shall sail worse than when by the orders of another. Besides, it scarce ever happens that a ship is formed, fitted for the sea, and sailed, by the same person. One man builds the hull, another rigs her, a third loads and sails her. No one of these has the advantage of knowing all the ideas and experience of the others, and therefore cannot draw just conclusions from a combination of the whole.

Even in the simple operation of sailing when at sea, I have often observed different judgments in the officers who commanded the successive watches, the wind being the same. One would have the sails trimmed sharper or flatter than another; so that they seemed to have no certain rule to govern by. Yet I think a set of experiments might be instituted, — first, to determine the most proper form of the hull for swift sailing; next, the best dimensions and most proper place for the masts; then, the form and quantity of sails, and their position, as the winds may be; and lastly, the disposition of the lading. This is an age of experiments, and I think a set accurately made and combined would be of great use.

We were several times chased in our passage, but outsailed everything, and in thirty days had soundings. We had a good observation, and the captain judged himself so near our port, Falmouth, that, if we made a good run in the night, we might be off the mouth of that harbor in the morning; and by running in the night might escape the notice of the enemy's privateers, who often cruised near the entrance of the channel. Accordingly all the sail was set that we could possibly carry, and, the wind being very fresh and fair, we stood right before it, and made great way. The captain, after his observation, shaped his course, as he thought, so as to pass wide of the Scilly Rocks; but it seems there is sometimes a strong current setting up St. George's Channel, which formerly caused the loss of Sir Cloudesley Shovel's squadron, in 1707. This was probably also the cause of what happened to us.

We had a watchman placed in the bow, to whom they often called, " *Look well out before there ;* " and he as often answered, "*Ay, ay ;*" but perhaps had his eyes shut, and was half asleep, at the time ; they sometimes answering, as is said, mechanically ; for he did not see a light just before us, which had been hid by the studding-sails from the man at the helm, and from the rest of the watch, but by an accidental yaw of the ship was discovered, and occasioned a great alarm, we being very near it; the light appearing to me as large as a cart-wheel. It was midnight, and our captain fast asleep ; but Captain Kennedy, jumping upon deck, and seeing the danger, ordered the ship to wear round, all sails standing ; an operation dangerous to the masts, but it carried us clear, and we avoided shipwreck, for we were running fast on the rocks on which the light was erected. This deliverance impressed me strongly with the utility of lighthouses, and made me resolve to encourage the building some of them in America, if I should live to return thither.

In the morning it was found, by the soundings, that we were near our port, but a thick fog hid the land from our sight. About nine o'clock the fog began to rise, and seemed to be lifted up from the water like the curtain of a theatre, discovering underneath the town of Falmouth, the vessels in the harbor, and the fields that surround it. This was a pleasing spectacle to those who had been long without any other prospect than the uniform view of a vacant ocean; and it gave us the more pleasure, as we were now free from the anxieties which had arisen.*

I set out immediately, with my son, for London, and we only stopped a little by the way to view Stonehenge on Salisbury Plain, and Lord Pembroke's house and gardens, with the very curious antiquities at Wilton. We arrived in London the 27th of July, 1757.†

* In a letter from Franklin to his wife, dated at Falmouth, the 17th of July, 1757, after giving her a similar account of his voyage, escape and landing, he adds : "The bell ringing for church, we went thither immediately, and, with hearts full of gratitude, returned sincere thanks to God for the mercies we had received. Were I a Roman Catholic, perhaps I should on this occasion vow to build a chapel to some saint ; but, as I am not, if I were to vow at all, it should be to build a *lighthouse.*"

† The Autobiography of Franklin terminates here. He had intended resuming it, but was prevented either by the pressure of public business or physical infirmities.

POLITICAL PAPERS.

INTERVIEWS WITH LORD CHATHAM.*

WHEN I came to England in 1757, you may remember I made several attempts to be introduced to Lord Chatham (at that time first minister), on account of my Pennsylvania business, but without success. He was then too great a man, or too much occupied in affairs of greater moment. I was therefore obliged to content myself with a kind of non-apparent and unacknowledged communication, through Mr. Potter and Mr. Wood, his secretaries, who seemed to cultivate an acquaintance with me by their civilities, and drew from me what information I could give relative to the American war, with my sentiments occasionally on measures that were proposed or advised by others, which gave me the opportunity of recommending and enforcing the utility of conquering Canada. I afterwards considered Mr. Pitt as an *inaccessible;* I admired him at a distance, and made no more attempts for a nearer acquaintance. I had only once or twice the satisfaction of hearing, through Lord Shelburne, and I think Lord Stanhope, that he did me the honor of mentioning me sometimes as a person of respectable character.

But, towards the end of August last, returning from Brighthelmstone, I called to visit my friend, Mr. Sargent, at his seat, Halsted, in Kent, agreeable to a former engagement. He let me know that he had promised to conduct me to Lord Stanhope's, at Chevening, who expected I would call on him when I came

---

* On his passage from England in March 1775, in a letter to his son, Franklin committed to paper a statement of his " efforts to effect a reconciliation and prevent a breach between Great Britain and her Colonies." In the introductory memoir we have given an abstract of that portion of this statement relating to the interviews with Lord Howe, Mr. Barclay and others. The passages relating to Lord Chatham possess superior interest, and we have here detached them from the context.

22*

into that neighborhood. We accordingly waited on Lord Stanhope that evening, who told me that Lord Chatham desired to see me, and that Mr. Sargent's house, where I was to lodge, being in the way, he would call for me there the next morning, and carry me to Hayes. This was done accordingly.

That truly great man received me with abundance of civility, inquired particularly into the situation of affairs in America, spoke feelingly of the severity of the late laws against Massachusetts, gave me some account of his speech in opposing them, and expressed great regard and esteem for the people of that country, who he hoped would continue firm and united in defending, by all peaceable and legal means, their constitutional rights. I assured him that I made no doubt they would do so; which he said he was pleased to hear from me, as he was sensible I must be well acquainted with them.   *   *   *

In fine, he expressed much satisfaction in my having called upon him, and particularly in the assurances I had given him that America did not aim at *independence;* adding that he should be glad to see me again as often as might be. I said I should not fail to avail myself of the permission he was pleased to give me, of waiting upon his lordship occasionally, being very sensible of the honor, and of the great advantages and improvement I should reap from his instructive conversation; which indeed was not a mere compliment.   *   *   *

I had promised Lord Chatham to communicate to him the first important news I should receive from America. I therefore sent him the proceedings of the Congress as soon as I received them; but a whole week passed, after I received the petition, before I could, as I wished to do, wait upon him with it, in order to obtain his sentiments on the *whole;* for my time was taken up in meetings with the other agents to consult about presenting the petition, in waiting three different days with them on Lord Dartmouth, in consulting upon and writing letters to the speakers of Assemblies, and other business, which did not allow me a day to go to Hayes.

At last, on Monday the 26th, I got out, and was there about one o'clock; he received me with an affectionate kind of respect that from so great a man was extremely engaging; but the opinion he expressed of the Congress was still more so. They had acted, he said, with so much temper, moderation and wisdom, that he thought it the most honorable assembly of statesmen since those of the ancient Greeks and Romans in the most virtuous times: that there was not in their whole proceedings above one or two things he could have wished otherwise;

perhaps but one, and that was their assertion that the keeping up a standing army in the colonies in time of peace, without consent of their legislatures, was against law; he doubted that was not well founded, and that the law alluded to did not extend to the colonies. The rest he admired and honored; he thought the petition decent, manly, and properly expressed; he inquired much and particularly concerning the state of America, the probability of their perseverance, the difficulties they must meet with in adhering for any long time to their resolutions, the resources they might have to supply the deficiency of commerce; to all which I gave him answers with which he seemed well satisfied. He expressed a great regard and warm affection for that country, with hearty wishes for their prosperity, and that government here might soon come to see its mistakes and rectify them; and intimated that possibly he might, if his health permitted, prepare something for its consideration, when the Parliament should meet after the holidays, on which he should wish to have previously my sentiments.

I mentioned to him the very hazardous state I conceived we were in, by the continuance of the army in Boston; that whatever disposition there might be in the inhabitants to give no just cause of offence to the troops, or in the general to preserve order among them, an unpremeditated, unforeseen quarrel might happen between perhaps a drunken porter and a soldier, that might bring on a riot, tumult and bloodshed, and its consequences produce a breach impossible to be healed; that the army could not possibly answer any good purpose *there*, and might be infinitely mischievous; that no accommodation could be properly proposed and entered into by the Americans while the bayonet was at their breasts; that, to have any agreement binding, all force should be withdrawn. His lordship seemed to think these sentiments had something in them that was reasonable.

From Hayes I went to Halsted, Mr. Sargent's place, to dine, intending thence a visit to Lord Stanhope at Chevening; but, hearing there that his lordship and the family were in town, I staid in Halsted all night, and the next morning went to Chiselhurst to call upon Lord Camden, it being in my way to town. I met his lordship and family in two carriages, just without his gate, going on a visit of congratulation to Lord Chatham and his lady, on the late marriage of their daughter to Lord Mahon, son of Lord Stanhope. They were to be back to dinner; so I agreed to go in, stay dinner, and spend the evening there, and not to return to town till next morning. We had that afternoon and evening a great deal of conversation on American affairs, concerning which he was very inquisitive, and I gave him the best information in my power. I was charmed with his generous and noble sentiments; and had the great pleasure of hearing his full approbation of the proceedings of the Congress, the petition, &c. &c., of which, at his request, I afterwards sent him a copy. He seemed anxious that the Americans should continue to act with the same temper, coolness and wisdom, with which they had hitherto proceeded in most of their public assemblies, in which case he did not doubt they would succeed in establishing their rights, and obtain a solid and durable agreement with the mother country; of the necessity ànd great importance of which agreement, he seemed to have the strongest impressions. * * * *

On the 19th of January, I received a card from Lord Stanhope, acquainting me that Lord Chatham, having a motion to make on the morrow in the House of Lords concerning America, greatly desired that I might be in the House, into which Lord Stanhope would endeavor to procure me admittance. At this time it was a rule of the House that no person could introduce more than one friend. The next morning, his lordship let me know, by another card, that if I attended at two o'clock in the lobby, Lord Chatham would be there about that time, and would himself introduce me. I attended, and met him there accordingly. On my mentioning to him what Lord Stanhope had written to me, he said, " Certainly; and I shall do it with the more pleasure, as I am sure your being present at this day's debate will be of more service to America than mine;" and so, taking me by the arm, was leading me along the passage to the door that enters near the throne, when one of the door-keepers followed, and acquainted him that by the order none were to be carried in at that door, but the eldest sons or brothers of peers; on which he limped back with me to the door near the bar, where were standing a number of gentlemen waiting for the peers who were to introduce them, and some peers waiting for friends they expected to introduce; among whom he delivered me to the door-keepers, saying aloud, "This is Dr. Franklin, whom I would have admitted into the House;" when they readily opened the door for me accordingly. As it had not been publicly known that there was any communication between his lordship and me, this I found occasioned some speculation. His appearance in the house, I observed, caused a kind of bustle among the officers, who were hurried in sending messengers for members,—I suppose those in connection with the ministry, something of importance being expected when that great man appears; it being but seldom that his infirmities permit his attendance. I had great satisfaction in hearing his motion and the debate upon it, which I shall not attempt to give here an account of, as you may find a better in the papers of the time. It was his motion for withdrawing the troops from Boston, as the first step towards an accommodation. The day following, I received a note from Lord Stanhope, expressing that "at the desire of Lord Chatham was sent me enclosed the motion he made in the House of Lords, that I might be possessed of it in the most authentic manner, by the communication of the individual paper which was read to the House by the mover himself." I sent copies of this motion to America, and was the more pleased with it, as I conceived it had partly taken its rise from a hint I had given his lordship in a former conversation. * * * *

I was quite charmed with Lord Chatham's speech in support of his motion. He impressed me with the highest idea of him as a great and most able statesman. Lord Camden, another wonderfully good speaker and close reasoner, joined him in the same argument, as did several other lords, who spoke excellently well; but all availed no more than the whistling of the winds. This motion was rejected. Sixteen Scotch peers, and twenty-four bishops, with all the lords in possession or expectation of places, when they vote together unanimously, as they generally do for ministerial measures, make a dead majority that renders all debating ridiculous in itself, since it can answer no end. Full of the high esteem I had imbibed for Lord Chatham, I wrote back to Lord Stanhope the following note, namely :

" Dr. Franklin presents his best respects to Lord Stanhope, with many thanks to his lordship and Lord Chatham, for the communication of so authentic a copy of the motion. Dr. Franklin is filled with admiration of that truly great man. He has seen, in the course of his life, sometimes eloquence without wisdom, and often wisdom without eloquence ; in the present instance he sees both united, and both, as he thinks, in the highest degree possible.

" *Craven-street, Jan.* 23, 1775."

As, in the course of the debate, some lords in the administration had observed that it was common and easy to censure their measures, but those who did so proposed nothing better, Lord Chatham mentioned that he should not be one of those idle censurers ; that he had thought long and closely upon the subject, and proposed soon to lay before their lordships the result of his meditation, in a plan for healing our differences, and restoring peace to the empire, to which his present notion was preparatory. I much desired to know what his plan was, and intended waiting on him to see if he would communicate it to me; but he went the next morning to Hayes, and I was so much taken up with daily business and company that I could not easily get out to him.

A few days after, however, Lord Mahon called on me, and told me Lord Chatham was very desirous of seeing me; when I promised to be with him the Friday following, several engagements preventing my going sooner. On Friday the 27th, I took a post-chaise about nine o'clock, and got to Hayes about eleven, but my attention being engaged in reading a new pamphlet, the post-boy drove me a mile or two beyond the gate. His lordship, being out an airing in his chariot, had met me before I reached Hayes, unobserved by me, turned and followed me, and, not finding me there, concluded, as he had seen me reading, that I had passed by mistake, and sent a servant after me. He expressed great pleasure at my coming, and acquainted me, in a long conversation, with the outlines of his plan, parts of which he read to me. He said he had communicated it only to Lord Camden, whose advice he much relied on, particularly in the law part; and that he would, as soon as he could get it transcribed, put it into my hands for my opinion and advice, but should show it to no other person before he presented it to the House; and he requested me to make no mention of it, otherwise parts might be misunderstood and blown up beforehand, and others perhaps adopted and produced by ministers as their own. I promised the closest secrecy, and kept my word; not even mentioning to any one that I had seen him. I dined with him, his family only present, and returned to town in the evening.

On the Sunday following, being the 29th, his lordship came to town, and called upon me in Craven-street. He brought with him his plan transcribed, in the form of an act of Parliament, which he put into my hands, requesting me to consider it carefully, and communicate to him such remarks upon it as should occur to me. His reason for desiring to give me that trouble was, as he was pleased to say, that he knew no man so thoroughly acquainted with the subject, or so capable of giving advice upon it; that he thought the errors of ministers in American affairs had been often owing to their not obtaining the best information; that therefore, though he had considered the business thoroughly in all its parts, he was not so confident of his own judgment, but that he came to set it right by mine, as men set their watches by a regulator. He had not determined when he should produce it in the House of Lords; but in the course of our conversation, considering the precarious situation of his health, and that if presenting it was delayed some intelligence might arrive which would make it seem less seasonable, or in all parts not so proper, — or the ministry might engage in different measures, and then say, If you had produced your plan sooner, we might have attended to it, — he concluded to offer it the Wednesday following; and therefore wished to see me upon it the preceding Tuesday, when he would again call upon me, unless I could conveniently come to Hayes.

I chose the latter, in respect to his lordship, and because there was less likelihood of interruptions; and I promised to be with him early, that we might have more time. He staid with me near two hours, his equipage waiting at the door; and being there while people were coming from church, it was much taken notice of and talked of, as at that time was every little circumstance that men thought might possibly any way affect American affairs. Such a visit from so great a man, on so important a business, flattered not a little my vanity; and the honor of it gave me the more pleasure, as it happened on the very day, twelve months, that the ministry had taken so much pains to disgrace me before the privy council.

I applied myself immediately to the reading and considering the plan, of which, when it was afterwards published, I sent you a copy, and therefore need not insert it here. I put down upon paper, as I went along, some short memorandums for my future discourse with him upon it. * * * *

I was at Hayes early on Tuesday, agreeably to my promise, when we entered into consideration of the plan; but, though I staid near four hours, his lordship, in the manner of, I think, all eloquent persons, was so full and diffuse in supporting every particular I questioned, that there was not time to go through half my memorandums; he is not easily interrupted, and I had such pleasure in hearing him, that I found little inclination to interrupt him. Therefore, considering that neither of us had much expectation that the plan would be adopted entirely as it stood; that in the course of its consideration, if it should be received, proper alterations might be introduced; that before it would be settled America should have opportunity to make her objections and propositions of amendment; that, to have it received at all here, it must seem to comply a little with some of the prevailing prejudices of the legislature; that if it was not so perfect as might be wished, it would at least serve as a basis for treaty, and in the mean time prevent mischiefs; and that, as his lordship had determined to offer it the next day, there was not time to make changes and another fair copy,—I therefore ceased my querying; and, though afterwards many people were pleased to do me the honor of supposing I had a considerable share in composing it, I assure you that the addition of a single word only was made at my instance, namely, "*constitutions*," after "charters;" for my filling up, at his request, a blank, with the titles of acts proper to be repealed, which I took from the proceedings of the Congress, was no more than might have been done by any copying clerk.

On Wednesday, Lord Stanhope, at Lord Chatham's request, called upon me, and carried me down to the House of Lords, which was soon very full.   Lord Chatham, in a most excellent speech, introduced, explained, and supported his plan.   When he sat down, Lord Dartmouth rose, and very properly said it contained matter of such weight and magnitude as to require much consideration, and he therefore hoped the noble earl did not expect their lordships to decide upon it by an immediate vote, but would be willing it should lie upon the table for consideration. Lord Chatham answered readily that he expected nothing more. But Lord Sandwich rose, and in a petulant, vehement speech, opposed its being received at all, and gave his opinion that it ought to be immediately *rejected*, with the contempt it deserved; that he could never believe it to be the production of any British peer; that it appeared to him rather *the work of some American ,* and, turning his face towards me, who was leaning on the bar, said he fancied he had in his eye the person who drew it up, one of the bitterest and most mischievous enemies this country had ever known.

This drew the eyes of many lords upon me; but, as I had no inducement to take it to myself, I kept my countenance as immovable as if my features had been made of wood.   Then several other lords of the administration gave their sentiments also for rejecting it, of which opinion, also, was strongly the *wise* Lord Hillsborough; but the Dukes of Richmond and Manchester, Lord Shelburne, Lord Camden, Lord Temple, Lord Lyttleton and others, were for receiving it, some through approbation, and others for the character and dignity of the House.   One lord mentioning, with applause, the candid proposal of one of the ministers, Lord Dartmouth, his lordship rose again, and said, that having since heard the opinions of so many lords against receiving it to lie upon the table for consideration, he had altered his mind, could not accept the praise offered him, for a candor of which he was now ashamed, and should therefore give his voice for rejecting the plan immediately. I am the more particular in this, as it is a trait of that nobleman's character, who, from his office, is supposed to have so great a share in American affairs, but who has in reality no will or judgment of his own, being, with dispositions for the best measures, easily prevailed with to join in the worst.

Lord Chatham, in his reply to Lord Sandwich, took notice of his illiberal insinuation, that the plan was not the person's who proposed it; declared that it was entirely his own, a declaration he thought himself the more obliged to make, as many of their lordships appeared to have so mean an opinion of it; for, if it was so weak or so bad a thing, it was proper in him to take care that no other person should unjustly share in the censure it deserved. That it had been heretofore reckoned his vice not to be apt to take advice; but he made no scruple to declare that, if he were the first minister of this country, and had the care of settling this momentous business, he should not be ashamed of publicly calling to his assistance a person so perfectly acquainted with the whole of American affairs as the gentleman alluded to, and so injuriously reflected on; one, he was pleased to say, whom all Europe held in high estimation for his knowledge and wisdom, and ranked with our Boyles and Newtons; who was an honor, not to the English nation only, but to human nature! I found it harder to stand this extravagant compliment than the preceding equally extravagant abuse; but kept as well as I could an unconcerned countenance, as not conceiving it to relate to me.

To hear so many of these *hereditary* legislators declaiming so vehemently against, not the adopting merely, but even the *consideration*, of a proposal so important in its nature, offered by a person of so weighty a character, one of the first statesmen of the age, who had taken up this country when in the lowest despondency, and conducted it to victory and glory through a war with two of the mightiest kingdoms in Europe; to hear them censuring his plan, not only for their own misunderstandings of what was in it, but for their imaginations of what was not in it, which they would not give themselves an opportunity of rectifying by a second reading; to perceive the total ignorance of the subject in some, the prejudice and passion of others, and the wilful perversion of plain truth in several of the ministers; and, upon the whole, to see it so ignominiously rejected by so great a majority, and so hastily too, in breach of all decency and prudent regard to the character and dignity of their body, as a third part of the national legislature, gave me an exceeding mean opinion of their

23

abilities, and made their claim of sovereignty over three millions of virtuous, sensible people in America seem the greatest of absurdities, since they appeared to have scarce discretion enough to govern a herd of swine. *Hereditary legislators!* thought I. There would be more propriety, because less hazard of mischief, in having (as in some university of Germany) *hereditary professors of mathematics!* But this was a hasty reflection; for the *elected* House of Commons is no better, nor ever will be while the electors receive money for their votes, and pay money wherewith ministers may bribe their representatives when chosen.

A PRUSSIAN EDICT,* ASSUMING CLAIMS OVER BRITAIN.

DANTZIC, Sept. 5, 1773.

WE have long wondered here at the supineness of the English nation under the Prussian impositions upon its trade entering our port. We did not, till lately, know the claims, ancient and modern, that hang over that nation, and therefore could not suspect that it might submit to those impositions from a sense of duty, or from principles of equity. The following edict, just made public, may, if serious, throw some light upon the matter:

"FREDERICK, by the grace of God, King of Prussia, &c., to all present and to come; [*a tous presens et a venir.* — ORIGINAL.] Health! — The peace now enjoyed throughout our dominions having afforded us leisure to apply ourselves to the regulation of commerce, the improvement of our finances, and at the same time the easing of our *domestic* subjects in their taxes: for these causes, and other good considerations us thereunto moving, we hereby make known, that, after having deliberated these affairs in our council, present our dear brothers, and other great officers of the state, members of the same; WE, of our certain knowledge, full power, and authority royal, have made and issued this present edict, namely.

"Whereas it is well known to all the world that the first German settlements made in the island of Britain were by

* See page 55.

colonies of people subjects to our renowned ducal ancestors, and drawn from their dominions, under the conduct of Hengist, Horsa, Hella, Uffa, Cerdicus, Ida, and others; and that the said colonies have flourished under the protection of our august house for ages past, have never been emancipated therefrom, and never-theless have hitherto yielded little profit to the same: and whereas we ourself have in the last war fought for and defended the said colonies against the power of France, and thereby enabled them to make conquests from the said power in America, for which we have not yet received adequate compensation: and whereas it is just and expedient that a revenue should be raised from the said colonies in Britain towards our indemnification; and that those who are descendants of our ancient subjects, and thence still owe us due obedience, should contribute to the replenishing of our royal coffers (as they must have done, had their ances-tors remained in the territories now to us appertaining). WE do therefore hereby ordain and command, that, from and after the date of these presents, there shall be levied and paid to our officers of the *customs*, on all goods, wares and merchandises, and on all grain and other produce of the earth, exported from the said island of Britain, and on all goods of whatever kind imported into the same, a duty of four and a half per cent. *ad valorem*, for the use of us and our successors: And that the said duty may more effectually be collected, we do hereby ordain, that all ships or vessels bound from Great Britain to any other part of the world, or from any other part of the world to Great Britain, shall in their respective voyages touch at our port of Koningsberg, there to be unladen, searched, and charged with the said duties.

" And whereas there hath been from time to time discovered in the said island of Great Britain, by our colonists there, many mines or beds of *iron*-stone: and sundry subjects of our ancient dominion, skilful in converting the said stone into metal, have in time past transported themselves thither, carrying with them and communicating that art; and the inhabitants of the said island, presuming that they had a natural right to make the best use they could of the natural productions of their country, for their own benefit, have not only built furnaces for smelting the said stone into iron, but have erected plating-forges, slitting-mills and steel-furnaces, for the more convenient manufacturing of the same, thereby endangering a diminution of the said manu-facture in our ancient dominion; we do, therefore, hereby fur-ther ordain, that from and after the date hereof no mill nor other engine for slitting or rolling of iron, nor any plating-forge to work with a tilt-hammer, nor any furnace for making steel, shall be erected or continued in the said island of Great Britain; and the lord lieutenant of every county in the said island is hereby commanded, on information of any such erection within his county, to order, and by force to cause the same to be abated and destroyed, as he shall answer the neglect thereof to us at his peril.   But we are nevertheless graciously pleased to permit the inhabitants of the said island to transport their iron into Prussia, there to be manufactured, and to them returned, they paying our Prussian subjects for the workmanship, with all the costs of commission, freight and risk, coming and returning; anything herein contained to the contrary notwithstanding.

"We do not, however, think fit to extend this our indulgence to the article of *wool ;* but, meaning to encourage, not only the manufacturing of woollen cloth, but also the raising of wool, in our ancient dominions, and to prevent both, as much as may be, in our said island, we do hereby absolutely forbid the transportation of wool from thence even to the mother-country, Prussia; and that those islanders may be further and more effectually restrained in making any advantage of their own wool, in the way of manufacture, we command that none shall be carried out of one county into another; nor shall any worsted, bay, or woollen yarn, cloth, says, bays, kerseys, serges, frizes, druggets, cloth-serges, shalloons, or any other drapery stuffs or woollen manufactures whatsoever, made up or mixed with wool in any of the said counties, be carried into any other county, or be water-borne even across the smallest river or creek, on penalty of forfeiture of the same, together with the boats, carriages, horses, &c., that shall be employed in removing them :— Nevertheless, our loving subjects there are hereby permitted (if they think proper) to use all their wool as manure, for the improvement of their lands.

"And whereas the art and mystery of making *hats* hath arrived at great perfection in Prussia, and the making of hats by our remoter subjects ought to be as much as possible restrained; and forasmuch as the islanders before-mentioned, being in possession of wool, beaver, and other furs, have presumptuously conceived they had a right to make some advantage thereof, by manufacturing the same into hats, to the prejudice of our domestic manufacture : we do, therefore, hereby strictly command and ordain, that no hats or felts whatsoever, dyed or undyed, finished or unfinished, shall be loaden or put into or upon any vessel, cart, carriage or horse, to be transported or conveyed out of one county in the said island into another county, or to any ther place whatsoever, by any person or persons whatsoever, on pain of forfeiting the same, with a penalty of five hundred pounds sterling for every offence : Nor shall any hat-maker in any of the said counties employ more than two apprentices, on penalty of five pounds sterling per month ; we intending hereby, that such hat-makers, being so restrained, both in the production and sale of their commodity, may find no advantage in continuing their business : But, lest the said islanders should suffer inconveniency by the want of hats, we are further graciously pleased to permit them to send their beaver furs to Prussia, and we also permit hats made thereof to be exported from Prussia to Britain ; the people thus favored to pay all costs and charges of manufacturing, interest, commission to our merchants, insurance and freight going and returning, as in the case of iron.

" And lastly, being willing further to favor our said colonies in Britain, we do hereby also ordain and command, that all the *thieves*, highway and street robbers, house-breakers, forgerers, murderers, s—d—tes, and villains of every denomination, who have forfeited their lives to the law in Prussia, but whom we, in our great clemency, do not think fit here to hang, shall be emptied out of our jails into the said island of Great Britain for the better peopling of that country.

" We flatter ourselves that these our royal regulations and commands will be thought *just and reasonable* by our much favored colonists in England ; the said regulations being copied from their statutes of 10 & 11 Will. III. c. 10 ; 5 Geo. II. c. 22 ; 23 Geo. II. c. 29 ; 4 Geo. I. c. 11, and from other equitable laws made by their Parliaments, or from instructions given by their princes, or from resolutions of both Houses, entered into for the good government of their *own colonies in Ireland and America.*

" And all persons in the said island are hereby cautioned not to oppose in any wise the execution of this our edict, or any part thereof, such opposition being high treason ; of which all who are suspected shall be transported in fetters from Britain to Prussia, there to be tried and executed according to the Prussian law.

" Such is our pleasure.

" Given at Potsdam, this twenty-fifth day of the month of August, one thousand seven hundred and seventy-three, and in the thirty-third year of our reign.
" By the king, in his council.
" RECHTMÆSSIG, Sec."

23*

Some take this edict to be merely one of the king's *jeux d'esprit* : others suppose it serious, and that he means a quarrel with England : but all here think the assertion it concludes with, " that these regulations are copied from the acts of the English Parliament respecting their colonies," a very injurious one ; it being impossible to believe that a people distinguished for their love of liberty,—a nation so wise, so liberal in its sentiments, so just and equitable towards its neighbors,—should, from mean and injudicious views of petty immediate profit, treat its own children in a manner so arbitrary and tyrannical !

RULES FOR REDUCING A GREAT EMPIRE TO A SMALL ONE ; PRESENTED TO A LATE MINISTER WHEN HE ENTERED UPON HIS ADMINISTRATION.*

An ancient sage valued himself upon this,—that though he could not fiddle, he knew how to make a great city of a little one. The science that I, a modern simpleton, am about to communicate, is the very reverse.

I address myself to all ministers who have the management of extensive dominions, which, from their very greatness, are become troublesome to govern—because the multiplicity of their affairs leaves no time for fiddling.

I.   In the first place, gentlemen, you are to consider that a great empire, like a great cake, is most easily diminished at the edges.   Turn your attention, therefore, first to your *remotest* provinces ; that, as you get rid of them, the next may follow in order.

II.   That the possibility of this separation may always exist, take special care the provinces are *never incorporated with the mother-country ;* that they do not enjoy the same common rights, the same privileges in commerce, and that they are governed by severer laws, all of your enacting, without allowing them any share in the choice of the legislators.   By carefully making and preserving such distinctions, you will (to keep to my simile of the cake) act like a wise gingerbread-baker, who, to facilitate a division, cuts his dough half through in those places where, when baked, he would have it broken to pieces.

* See page 55.

III. Those remote provinces have perhaps been acquired, purchased or conquered, at the sole expense of the settlers or their ancestors, without the aid of the mother-country. If this should happen to increase her strength, by their growing numbers, ready to join in her wars; her commerce, by their growing demand for her manufactures; or her naval power, by greater employment for her ships and seamen,— they may probably suppose some merit in this, and that it entitles them to some favor. You are therefore to *forget it all, or resent it*, as if they had done you injury. If they happen to be zealous whigs, friends of liberty, nurtured in revolution principles, remember all that to their prejudice, and contrive to punish it; for such principles, after a revolution is thoroughly established, are of no more use; they are even odious and abominable.

IV. However peaceably your colonies have submitted to your government, shown their affection to your interests, and patiently borne their grievances, you are to suppose them *always inclined to revolt*, and treat them accordingly. Quarter troops among them, who by their insolence may provoke the rising of mobs, and by their bullets and bayonets suppress them. By this means, like the husband who uses his wife ill from suspicion, you may in time convert your suspicions into realities.

V. Remote provinces must have governors and judges to represent the royal person, and execute everywhere the delegated parts of his office and authority. You, ministers, know that much of the strength of government depends on the opinion of the people, and much of that opinion on the *choice of rulers* placed immediately over them. If you send them wise and good men for governors, who study the interest of the colonists, and advance their prosperity, they will think their king wise and good, and that he wishes the welfare of his subjects. If you send them learned and upright men for judges, they will think him a lover of justice. This may attach your provinces more to his government. You are therefore to be careful who you recommend for those offices. If you can find prodigals who have ruined their fortunes, broken gamesters, or stock-jobbers, these may do well as governors; for they will probably be rapacious, and provoke the people by their extortions. Wrangling proctors and pettifogging lawyers too are not amiss, for they will be forever disputing and quarrelling with their little Parliaments. If withal they should be ignorant, wrong-headed and insolent, so much the better. Attorneys, clerks and Newgate solicitors, will do for chief-justices, especially if they hold their places during your pleasure :— and all will

contribute to impress those ideas of your government that are
proper for a people you would wish to renounce it.

VI.   To confirm these impressions, and strike them deeper,
whenever the injured come to the capital with complaints of mal-
administration, oppression or injustice, *punish such suitors* with
long delay, enormous expense, and a final judgment in favor of
the oppressor.   This will have an admirable effect every way.
The trouble of future complaints will be prevented, and governors
and judges will be encouraged to further acts of oppression and
injustice, and thence the people may become more disaffected,
and at length desperate.

VII.   When such governors have crammed their coffers, and
made themselves so odious to the people that they can no longer
remain among them with safety to their persons, *recall and reward*
them with pensions.   You may make them baronets too, if that
respectable order should not think fit to resent it.   All will contribute to encourage new governors in the same practice, and make
the supreme government detestable.

VIII.   If, when you are engaged in war, your colonies should
vie in liberal aids of men and money against the common enemy,
upon your simple requisition, and give far beyond their abilities,
reflect that a penny taken from them by your power is more
honorable to you than a pound presented by their benevolence;
despise therefore their voluntary grants, and resolve to harass
them with *novel taxes*.   They will probably complain to your
Parliament, that they are taxed by a body in which they have
no representative, and that this is contrary to common right.
They will petition for redress.   Let the Parliament flout their
claims, reject their petitions, refuse even to suffer the reading
of them, and treat the petitioners with the utmost contempt.
Nothing can have a better effect in producing the alienation proposed ; for though many can forgive injuries, none ever forgave
contempt.

IX.   In laying these taxes, *never regard the heavy burdens*
those remote people already undergo, in defending their own frontiers, supporting their own provincial government, making new
roads, building bridges, churches, and other public edifices, which
in old countries have been done to your hands, by your ancestors,
but which occasion constant calls and demands on the purses of
a new people.   Forget the restraint you lay on their trade for
your own benefit, and the advantage a monopoly of this trade gives
your exacting merchants.   Think nothing of the wealth those
merchants and your manufacturers acquire by the colony commerce, their increased ability thereby to pay taxes at home,

their accumulating in the price of their commodities most of those taxes, and so levying them from their consuming customers: all this, and the employment and support of thousands of your poor by the colonists, you are entirely to forget. But remember to make your arbitrary tax more grievous to your provinces, by public declarations importing that your power of taxing them has *no limits*, so that when you take from them without their consent a shilling in the pound, you have a clear right to the other nineteen. This will probably weaken every idea of security in their property, and convince them that under such a government they have nothing they can call their own; which can scarce fail of producing the happiest consequences!

X. Possibly, indeed, some of them might still comfort themselves, and say, "Though we have no property, we have yet something left that is valuable ; we have constitutional *liberty, both of person and of conscience.* This king, these lords, and these commons, who it seems are too remote from us to know us and feel for us, cannot take from us our *habeas corpus* right, or our right of trial by a jury of our neighbors : they cannot deprive us of the exercise of our religion, alter our ecclesiastical constitution, and compel us to be papists if they please, or Mahometans." To annihilate this comfort, begin by laws to perplex their commerce with infinite regulations, impossible to be remembered and observed : ordain seizures of their property for every failure, take away the trial of such property by jury, and give it to arbitrary judges of your own appointing, and of the lowest characters in the country, whose salaries and emoluments are to arise out of the duties or condemnations, and whose appointments are during pleasure. Then let there be a formal declaration of both Houses that opposition to your edicts is treason, and that persons suspected of treason in the provinces may, according to some obsolete law, be seized and sent to the metropolis of the empire for trial ; and pass an act, that those there charged with certain other offences shall be sent away in chains from their friends and country, to be tried in the same manner for felony. Then erect a new court of inquisition among them, accompanied by an armed force, with instructions to transport all such suspected persons, to be ruined by the expense if they bring over evidences to prove their innocence, or be found guilty and hanged if they cannot afford it. And, lest the people should think you cannot possibly go any further, pass another solemn declaratory act, " that kings, lords and commons, had, have, and of right ought to have, full power and authority to make statutes of sufficient force and validity to bind the unrepresented provinces *in all cases whatso-*

ever.'' This will include spiritual with temporal, and, taken together, must operate wonderfully to your purpose, by convincing them that they are at present under a power something like that spoken of in the Scriptures, which can not only kill their bodies, but damn their souls to all eternity, by compelling them, if it pleases, to worship the devil.

XI. To make your taxes more odious, and more likely to procure resistance, send from the capital a *board of officers* to superintend the collection, *composed of the most indiscreet,* ill-bred and insolent, you can find. Let these have large salaries out of the extorted revenue, and live in open grating luxury upon the sweat and blood of the industrious, whom they are to worry continually with groundless and expensive prosecutions, before the above-mentioned arbitrary revenue judges; all at the cost of the party prosecuted, though acquitted, because the king is to pay no costs. Let these men, by your order, be exempted from all the common taxes and burdens of the province, though they and their property are protected by its laws. If any revenue officers are suspected of the least tenderness for the people, discard them. If others are justly complained of, protect and reward them. If any of the under officers behave so as to provoke the people to drub them, promote those to better offices; this will encourage others to procure for themselves such profitable drubbings, by multiplying and enlarging such provocations, — and all will work towards the end you aim at.

XII. Another way to make your tax odious is, to *misapply the produce of it.* If it was originally appropriated for the defence of the provinces, and the better support of government, and the administration of justice where it may be necessary, then apply none of it to that defence, but bestow it, where it is not necessary, in augmenting salaries or pensions to every governor who has distinguished himself by his enmity to the people, and by calumniating them to their sovereign. This will make them pay it more unwillingly, and be more apt to quarrel with those that collect it, and those that imposed it, who will quarrel again with them, — and all shall contribute to your own purpose, of making them weary of your government.

XIII. If the people of any province have been accustomed to *support their own governors and judges* to satisfaction, you are to apprehend that such governors and judges may be thereby influenced to treat the people kindly, and to do them justice. This is another reason for applying part of that revenue in larger salaries to such governors and judges, given, as their commissions are, during *your* pleasure only, forbidding them to take any salaries from their provinces; that thus the people may no longer hope any kindness from their governors, or (in crown cases) and justice from their judges. And, as the money, thus misapplied in one province, is extorted from all, probably all will resent the misapplication.

XIV. If the Parliaments of your provinces should dare to claim rights, or complain of your administration, order them to be harassed with *repeated dissolutions.* If the same men are continually returned by new elections, adjourn their meetings to some country village, where they cannot be accommodated, and there keep them during pleasure; for this, you know, is your prerogative, and an excellent one it is, as you may manage it to promote discontents among the people, diminish their respect, and increase their disaffection.

XV. Convert the brave, honest officers of your *navy* into pimping tide-waiters and colony officers of the *customs.* Let those who in time of war fought gallantly in defence of the commerce of their countrymen in peace be taught to prey upon it. Let them learn to be corrupted by great and real smugglers; but (to show their diligence) scour with armed boats every bay, harbor, river, creek, cove or nook, throughout the coast of your colonies; stop and detain every coaster, every wood-boat, every fisherman; tumble their cargoes and even their ballast inside out, and upside down; and if a pennyworth of pins is found un-entered, let the whole be seized and confiscated. Thus shall the trade of your colonists suffer more from their friends in time of peace than it did from their enemies in war. Then let these boats' crews land upon every farm in their way, rob their orchards, steal their pigs and poultry, and insult the inhabitants. If the injured and exasperated farmers, unable to procure other justice, should attack the aggressors, drub them, and burn their boats, you are to call this *high treason and rebellion,* order fleets and armies into their country, and threaten to carry all the offenders three thousand miles to be hanged, drawn, and quartered. — O! this will work admirably.

XVI. If you are told of *discontents* in your colonies, never believe that they are general, or that you have given occasion for them; therefore do not think of applying any remedy, or of changing any offensive measure. Redress no grievance, lest they should be encouraged to demand the redress of some other grievance. Grant no request that is just and reasonable, lest they should make another, that is unreasonable. Take all your informations of the state of the colonies from your governors and officers in enmity with them. Encourage and reward these leasing-makers, secrete their lying accusations, lest they should be confuted, but act upon them as the clearest evidence, and believe nothing you hear from the friends of the people. Suppose all *their* complaints to be invented and promoted by a few factious demagogues, whom, if you could catch and hang, all would be quiet. Catch and hang a few of them accordingly, and the blood of the martyrs shall work miracles in favor of your purpose.

XVII. If you see *rival nations* rejoicing at the prospect of your disunion with your provinces, and endeavoring to promote it, — if they translate, publish and applaud, all the complaints of your discontented colonies, at the same time privately stimulating you to severer measures, — let not that alarm or offend you. Why should it, since you all mean the same thing?

XVIII. If any colony should, *at their own charge, erect a fortress*, to secure their *port* against the fleets of a foreign enemy, get your governor to betray that fortress into your hands. Never think of paying what it cost the country, for that would look, at least, like some regard for justice ; but turn it into a citadel, to awe the inhabitants and curb their commerce. If they should have lodged in such fortress the very arms they bought and used to aid you in your conquests, seize them all ; it will provoke like ingratitude, added to robbery. One admirable effect of these operations will be, to discourage every other colony from erecting such defences, and so their and your enemies may more easily invade them, to the great disgrace of your government, and of course the furtherance of your project.

XIX. Send armies into their country, under pretence of protecting the inhabitants ; but, instead of garrisoning the forts on their frontiers with those troops, to prevent incursions, demolish those forts, and order the troops into the heart of the country, that the savages may be encouraged to attack the frontiers, and that the troops may be protected by the inhabitants ; this will seem to proceed from your *ill-will or your ignorance*, and contribute further to produce and strengthen an opinion among them that you are no longer fit to govern them.

XX. Lastly, invest the *general of your army in the provinces* with great and unconstitutional powers, and free him from the control of even your own civil governors. Let him have troops enough under his command, with all the fortresses in his possession, and who knows but (like some provincial generals in the Roman empire, and encouraged by the universal discontent you have produced) he may take it into his head to set up for himself? If he should, and you have carefully practised these few excellent rules of mine, take my word for it, all the provinces will immediately join him ; and you will that day (if you have not done it sooner) get rid of the trouble of governing them, and all the plagues attending their commerce and connection from thenceforth and forever.

AN ALGERINE SPEECH.

To the Editor of the Federal Gazette.

March 23, 1790.

SIR : Reading last night in your excellent paper the speech of Mr Jackson in Congress, against their meddling with the affair of slavery, or attempting to mend the condition of the slaves, it put me in mind of a similar one made about one hundred years since, by Side Mehemed Ibrahim, a member of the Divan of Algiers, which may be seen in Martin's account of his consulship, *Anno* 1687. It was against granting the petition of the sect called *Erika* or *Purists*, who prayed for the abolition of piracy and slavery, as being unjust. Mr. Jackson does not quote it, — perhaps he has not seen it. If, therefore, some of its reasonings are to be found in his eloquent speech, it may only show that men's interests and intellects operate and are operated on with surprising similarity in all countries and climates, whenever they are under similar circumstances. The African's speech, as translated, is as follows :

"*Allah Bismillah, &c.*
"*God is great, and Mahomet is his prophet.*
"Have these *Erika* considered the consequences of granting their petition? If we cease our cruises against the Christians, how shall we be furnished with the commodities their countries produce, and which are so necessary for us? If we forbear to make slaves of their people, who, in this hot climate, are to cultivate our lands? Who are to perform the common labors of our city, and in our families? Must we not then be our own slaves? And is there not more compassion and more favor due to us as Mosselmen than to these Christian dogs?

"We have now about fifty thousand slaves in and near Algiers; this number, if not kept up by fresh supplies, will soon diminish and be gradually annihilated. If we then cease taking and plundering the infidel ships, and making slaves of the seamen and passengers, our lands will become of no value for want of cultivation, the rents of houses in the city will sink one-

24

half, and the revenue of government arising from its share of
prizes be totally destroyed! And for what? To gratify the
whims of a whimsical sect, who would have us not only forbear
making more slaves, but even to manumit those we have! But
who is to indemnify their masters for the loss? Will the state
do it? Is our treasury sufficient? Will the *Erika* do it? Can
they do it? Or would they, to do what they think justice to
the slaves, do a greater injustice to the owners?

" And, if we set our slaves free, what is to be done with them?
Few of them will return to their countries; they know too well
the greater hardships they must there be subject to; they will
not embrace our holy religion; they will not adopt our manners;
our people will not pollute ourselves by intermarrying with them.
Must we maintain them as beggars in our streets, or suffer our
properties to be the prey of their pillage? for men accustomed
to slavery will not work for a livelihood when not compelled.
And what is there so pitiable in their present condition? Were
they not slaves in their own countries? Are not Spain, Portu-
gal, France, and the Italian States, governed by despots, who
hold all their subjects in slavery, without exception? Even
England treats its sailors as slaves; for they are, whenever the
government pleases, seized, and confined in ships of war, con-
demned not only to work, but to fight, for small wages, or a mere
subsistence, not better than our slaves are allowed by us.

" Is their condition, then, made worse by their falling into our
hands? No, they have only exchanged one slavery for another,
and I may say a better; for here they are brought into a land
where the sun of Islamism gives forth its light, and shines in
full splendor, and they have an opportunity of making themselves acquainted with the true doctrine, and thereby saving
their immortal souls. Those who remain at home have not that
happiness. Sending the slaves home, then, would be sending
them out of light into darkness. I repeat the question, What is
to be done with them? I have heard it suggested that they
may be planted in the wilderness, where there is plenty of land
for them to subsist on, and where they may flourish as a free
state; but they are, I doubt, too little disposed to labor without
compulsion, as well as too ignorant, to establish a good government; and the wild Arabs would soon molest and destroy or again
enslave them. While serving us, we take care to provide them
with everything, and they are treated with humanity. The
laborers in their own country are, as I am well informed, worse
fed, lodged, and clothed. The condition of most of them is
therefore already mended, and requires no further improvement.

Here their lives are in safety. They are not liable to be impressed for soldiers, and forced to cut one another's Christian throats, as in the wars of their own countries.

"If some of the religious mad bigots who now tease us with their silly petitions have, in a fit of blind zeal, freed their slaves, it was not generosity, it was not humanity, that moved them to the action; it was from the conscious burden of a load of sins, and a hope, from the supposed merits of so good a work, to be excused from damnation. How grossly are they mistaken to suppose slavery to be disallowed by the Koran! Are not the two precepts, to quote no more, ' *Masters, treat your slaves with kindness ; slaves, serve your masters with cheerfulness and fidelity,*' clear proofs to the contrary? Nor can the plundering of infidels be in that sacred book forbidden, since it is well known from it that God has given the world, and all that it contains, to his faithful Mosselmen, who are to enjoy it of right, as fast as they conquer it.

"Let us, then, hear no more of this detestable proposition, the manumission of Christian slaves, the adoption of which would, by depreciating our lands and houses, and thereby depriving so many good citizens of their properties, create universal discontent, and provoke insurrections, to the endangering of government, and producing general confusion. I have therefore no doubt but this wise council will prefer the comfort and happiness of a whole nation of true believers to the whim of a few *Erika*, and dismiss their petition."

The result was, as *Martin* tells us, that the Divan came to this resolution : "The doctrine that plundering and enslaving the Christians is unjust is at best *problematical ;* but that it is the interest of this state to continue the practice is clear ; — therefore let the petition be rejected."

And it was rejected accordingly.

And since like motives are apt to produce in the minds of men like opinions and resolutions, may we not, Mr. Brown, venture to predict, from this account, that the petitions to the Parliament of England for abolishing the slave-trade, to say nothing of other legislatures, and the debates upon them, will have a similar conclusion?

I am, sir, your constant reader and humble servant,

HISTORICUS.

ON GRATITUDE TO THE MINISTRY.

To the Printer of the Public Advertiser.

[Supposed date, LONDON, 1772.]

SIR : Your correspondent Britannicus inveighs violently against Dr. Franklin for his ingratitude to the ministry of this nation, who have conferred upon him so many favors. They gave him the post-office of America, they made his son a governor, and they offered him a post of five hundred a year in the salt office if he would relinquish the interests of his country ; but he has had the wickedness to continue true to it, and is as much an American as ever. As it is a settled point in government here that every man has his price, 'tis plain they are bunglers in their business, and have not given him enough. Their master has as much reason to be angry with them as Rodrigue, in the play, with his apothecary, for not effectually poisoning Pandolpho, and they must probably make use of the apothecary's justification, namely :

—

" SCENE IV.

" *Rodrigue and Fell the Apothecary.*

" *Rodrigue.* You promised to have this Pandolpho upon his bier in less than a week ; 'tis more than a month since, and he still walks and stares me in the face.

" *Fell.* True ; and yet I have done my best endeavors. In various ways I have given the miscreant as much poison as would have killed an elephant. He has swallowed dose after dose ; far from hurting him, he seems the better for it. He hath a wonderfully strong constitution. I find I cannot kill him but by cutting his throat, and that, as I take it, is not my business.

" *Rodrigue.* Then it must be mine."

PHILOSOPHICAL.*

[TO PETER COLLINSON, LONDON.]

THE ELECTRICAL KITE.

PHILADELPHIA, Oct. 16, 1752.

As FREQUENT mention is made in public papers from Europe of the success of the Philadelphia experiment for drawing the electric fire from clouds by means of pointed rods of iron erected

---

* We have already quoted (page 106) the high and authoritative estimate placed upon Franklin's philosophical writings by Sir Humphrey Davy. Lord Jeffrey, in the *Edinburgh Review*, remarks upon them as follows: "The most ingenious and profound explanations are suggested, as if they were the most natural and obvious way of accounting for the phenomena; and the author seems to value himself so little on his most important discoveries, that it is necessary to compare him with others before we can form a just notion of his merits. As he seems to be conscious of no exertion, he feels no partiality for any part of his speculations, and never seeks to raise the reader's ideas of their importance by any arts of declamation or eloquence. Indeed, the habitual precision of his conceptions, and his invariable practice of referring to specific facts and observations, secured him, in a great measure, both from extravagant conjectures, in which too many naturalists have indulged, and from the zeal and enthusiasm which seem so naturally to be engendered in their defence. He was by no means averse to give scope to his imagination in suggesting a variety of explanations of obscure and unmanageable phenomena; but he never allowed himself to confound these vague and conjectural theories with the solid results of experience and observation. In his meteorological papers, and in his observations upon heat and light, there is a great deal of such bold and original suggestion; but the author evidently sets little value on them, and has no sooner disburdened his mind of the impressions from which they proceeded, than he seems to dismiss them entirely from his consideration, and turns to the legitimate philosophy of experiment with unabated diligence and humility. As an instance of this disposition, we may quote part of a letter to the Abbé Soulavie upon a new theory of the earth, which he proposes and dismisses, without concern or anxiety, in the course of a few sentences; *though, if the idea had fallen on the brain of an European philosopher, it might have germinated into a volume of eloquence*, like Buffon's, or an infinite array of paragraphs and observations, like those of Parkinson or Dr Hutton."

24*

on high buildings, &c., it may be agreeable to the curious to be informed that the same experiment has succeeded in Philadelphia, though made in a different and more easy manner, which is as follows :

Make a small cross of two light strips of cedar, the arms so long as to reach to the four corners of a large thin silk handkerchief when extended ; tie the corners of the handkerchief to the extremities of the cross, so you have the body of a kite ; which being properly accommodated with a tail, loop and string, will rise in the air like those made of paper ; but this, being of silk, is fitter to bear the wet and wind of a thunder-gust without tearing. To the top of the upright stick of the cross is to be fixed a very sharp-pointed wire, rising a foot or more above the wood. To the end of the twine next the hand is to be tied a silk ribbon, and where the silk and twine join a key may be fastened.

This kite is to be raised when a thunder-gust appears to be coming on, and the person who holds the string must stand within a door or window, or under some cover, so that the silk ribbon may not be wet ; and care must be taken that the twine does not touch the frame of the door or window. As soon as any of the thunder-clouds come over the kite, the pointed wire will draw the electric fire from them, and the kite, with all the twine, will be electrified, and the loose filaments of the twine will stand out every way, and be attracted by an approaching finger. And when the rain has wetted the kite and twine, so that it can conduct the electric fire freely, you will find it stream out plentifully from the key on the approach of your knuckle. At this key the vial may be charged ; and from electric fire thus obtained spirits may be kindled, and all the other electric experiments be performed which are usually done by the help of a rubbed glass globe or tube, and thereby the sameness of the electric matter with that of lightning completely demonstrated.

* In 1747, Franklin wrote, in reference to his electrical pursuits, to Peter Collinson : " I never was before engaged in any study that so totally engrossed my attention and time as this has lately done ; for, what with making experiments when I can be alone, and repeating them to my friends and acquaintance, who, from the novelty of the thing, come continually in crowds to see them, I have during some months past had little leisure for anything else." Collinson wrote to him from London, in 1753 : " The King of France strictly commands the Abbé Mazéas to write a letter in the politest terms to the Royal Society, to return the king's thanks and compliments, in an express manner, to Mr. Franklin, of Pennsylvania, for his useful discoveries in electricity, and the application of pointed rods to prevent the terrible effects of thunder-storms."

VARIOUS EXPERIMENTS — TREATMENT OF INVENTORS.

PHILADELPHIA, March 18, 1775.

YOUR question, how I came first to think of proposing the experiment of drawing down the lightning, in order to ascertain its sameness with the electric fluid, I cannot answer better than by giving you an extract from the minutes I used to keep of the experiments I made, with memorandums of such as I purposed to make, the reasons for making them, and the observations that arose upon them, from which minutes my letters were afterwards drawn. By this extract you will see that the thought was not so much " an out-of-the-way one " but that it might have occurred to an electrician.

" *Nov.* 7, 1749. — Electrical fluid agrees with lightning in these particulars : 1. Giving light. 2. Color of the light. 3. Crooked direction. 4. Swift motion. 5. Being conducted by metals. 6. Crack or noise in exploding. 7. Subsisting in water or ice. 8. Rending bodies it passes through. 9. Destroying animals. 10. Melting metals. 11. Firing inflammable substances. 12. Sulphureous smell. —The electric fluid is attracted by points. — We do not know whether this property is in lightning. — But, since they agree in all the particulars wherein we can already compare them, is it not probable they agree likewise in this? Let the experiment be made."

I wish I could give you any satisfaction in the article of clouds. I am still at a loss about the manner in which they become charged with electricity ; no hypothesis I have yet formed perfectly satisfying me. Some time since, I heated very hot a brass plate two feet square, and placed it on an electric stand. From the plate a wire extended horizontally four or five feet, and, at the end of it, hung, by linen threads, a pair of cork balls. I then repeatedly sprinkled water over the plate, that it might be raised from it in vapor, hoping that if the vapor either carried off the electricity of the plate, or left behind it that of the water (one of which I supposed it must do, if, like the clouds, it became electrized itself, either positively or negatively), I should perceive and determine it by the separation of the balls, and by finding whether they were positive or negative ; but no alteration was made at all, nor could I perceive that the steam was itself electrized, though I have still some suspicion that the steam was not fully examined, and I think the experiment should be repeated. Whether the first state-of electrized clouds is positive or negative, if I could find the cause of that, I should be at no loss about the other; for either is easily deduced from the other, as one state is easily produced by the other. A strongly positive cloud may drive out of a neighboring cloud much of its natural quantity of the electric fluid, and, passing by it, leave it in a negative state. In the same way, a strongly negative cloud may occasion a neighboring cloud to draw into itself from others an additional quantity, and, passing by it, leave it in a positive state. How these effects may be produced you will easily conceive, on perusing and considering the experiments in the enclosed paper; and from them too it appears probable that every change from positive to negative, and from negative to positive, that during a thunder-gust we see in the cork balls annexed to the apparatus, is not owing to the presence of clouds in the same state, but often to the absence of positive or negative clouds, that, having just passed, leave the rod in the opposite state.

The knocking down of the six men was performed with two of my large jars not fully charged. I laid one end of my discharging-rod upon the head of the first; he laid his hand upon the head of the second; the second his hand on the head of the third, and so to the last, who held in his hand the chain that was connected with the outside of the jars. When they were thus placed, I applied the other end of my rod to the prime conductor, and they all dropped together. When they got up, they all declared they had not felt any stroke, and wondered how they came to fall; nor did any of them either hear the crack, or see the light of it. You suppose it a dangerous experiment; but I had once suffered the same myself, receiving, by accident, an equal stroke through my head, that struck me down, without hurting me; and I had seen a young woman who was about to be electrified through the feet (for some indisposition) receive a greater charge through the head, by inadvertently stooping forward to look at the placing of her feet, till her forehead (as she was very tall) came too near my prime conductor: she dropped, but instantly got up again, complaining of nothing. A person so struck sinks down doubled, or folded together as it were, the joints losing their strength and stiffness at once, so that he drops on the spot where he stood instantly, and there is no previous staggering, nor does he ever fall lengthwise. Too great a charge might, indeed, kill a man; but I have not yet seen any hurt done by it. It would certainly, as you observe, be the easiest of all deaths.

The experiment you have heard so imperfect an account of is

merely this : I electrified a silver pint can, on an electric stand, and then lowered into it a cork ball of about an inch diameter, hanging by a silk string, till the cork touched the bottom of the can. The cork was not attracted to the inside of the can as it would have been to the outside; and though it touched the bottom, yet when drawn out it was not found to be electrified by that touch, as it would have been by touching the outside. The fact is singular. You require the reason; I do not know it. Perhaps you may discover it, and then you will be so good as to communicate it to me.* I find a frank acknowledgment of one's ignorance is not only the easiest way to get rid of a difficulty, but the likeliest way to obtain information, and therefore I practise it; I think it an honest policy. Those who affect to be thought to know everything, and so undertake to explain everything, often remain long ignorant of many things that others could and would instruct them in, if they appeared less conceited.

The treatment your friend has met with is so common, that no man who knows what the world is, and ever has been, should expect to escape it.

There are everywhere a number of people, who, being totally destitute of any inventive faculty themselves, do not readily conceive that others may possess it; they think of inventions as of miracles, — there might be such formerly, but they are ceased. With these, every one who offers a new invention is deemed a pretender; he had it from some other country, or from some book; a man of *their own acquaintance*, one who has no more sense than themselves, could not possibly, in their opinion, have been the inventor of anything. They are confirmed, too, in these sentiments, by frequent instances of pretensions to invention, which vanity is daily producing. That vanity too, though an incitement to invention, is, at the same time, the pest of inventors. Jealousy and envy deny the merit or the novelty of your invention; but vanity, when the novelty and merit are established, claims it for its own. The smaller your invention is, the more mortification you receive in having the credit of it disputed with you by a rival, whom the jealousy and envy of others are ready to support against you, at least so far as to make the point doubtful.† It is not in itself of importance

---

* Dr. Franklin afterwards thought that, possibly, the mutual repulsion of the inner opposite sides of the electrized might prevent the accumulating of an electric atmosphere upon them, and occasion it to stand chiefly on the outside; but recommended it to the further examination of the curious.

† We have heard of persons in Philadelphia, even at the present day, who deny to Franklin the merit of his electrical discoveries.

enough for a dispute; no one would think your proofs and reasons worth their attention; and yet, if you do not dispute the point, and demonstrate your right, you not only lose the credit of being in that instance *ingenious*, but you suffer the disgrace of not being *ingenuous*,— not only of being a plagiary, but of being a plagiary for trifles. Had the invention been greater, it would have disgraced you less; for men have not so contemptible an idea of him that robs for gold on the highway as of him that can pick pockets for half-pence and farthings.

Thus, through envy, jealousy, and the vanity of competitors for fame, the origin of many of the most extraordinary inventions, though produced within but a few centuries past, is involved in doubt and uncertainty. We scarce know to whom we are indebted for the *compass*, and for *spectacles;* nor have even *paper* and *printing*, that record everything else, been able to preserve with certainty the name and reputation of their inventors. One would not, therefore, of all faculties or qualities of the mind, wish, for a friend, or a child, that he should have that of invention. For his attempts to benefit mankind in that way, however well imagined, if they do not succeed, expose him, though very unjustly, to general ridicule and contempt; and, if they do succeed, to envy, robbery, and abuse.

——————

[TO MR. KINNERSLEY.]

FIRE IN BODIES — EXPERIMENT.

LONDON, Feb. 20, 1762.

How many ways there are of kindling fire, or producing heat in bodies! By the sun's rays, by collision, by friction, by hammering, by putrefaction, by fermentation, by mixtures of fluids, by mixtures of solids with fluids, and by electricity. And yet the fire, when produced, though in different bodies it may differ in circumstances, as in color, vehemence, &c., yet in the same bodies it is generally the same. Does not this seem to indicate that the fire existed in the body, though in a quiescent state, before it was by any of these means excited, disengaged, and brought forth to action and to view? May it not constitute a part, and even a principal part, of the solid substance of bodies?

If this should be the case, kindling fire in a body would be nothing more than developing this inflammable principle, and setting it at liberty to act in separating the parts of that body, which then exhibits the appearances of scorching, melting, burning, &c.   When a man lights a hundred candles from the flame of one, without diminishing that flame, can it be properly said to have *communicated* all that fire?   When a single spark from a flint, applied to a magazine of gunpowder, is immediately attended with this consequence, that the whole is in flame, exploding with immense violence, could all this fire exist first in the spark?   We cannot conceive it.

And thus we seem led to this supposition, — that there is fire enough in all bodies to singe, melt, or burn them, whenever it is, by any means, set at liberty, so that it may exert itself upon them, or be disengaged from them.   This liberty seems to be afforded it by the passage of electricity through them, which we know can and does, of itself, separate the parts even of water; and perhaps the immediate appearances of fire are only the effects of such separations.   If so, there would be no need of supposing that the electric fluid *heats itself* by the swiftness of its motion, or heats bodies by the resistance it meets with in passing through them.   They would only be heated in proportion as such separation could be more easily made.   Thus a melting heat cannot be given to a large wire in the flame of a candle, though it may to a small one; and this not because the large wire resists *less* that action of the flame which tends to separate its parts, but because it resists it *more* than the smaller wire; or because the force, being divided among more parts, acts weaker on each.

This reminds me, however, of a little experiment I have frequently made, that shows, at one operation, the different effects of the same quantity of electric fluid passing through different quantities of metal.   A strip of tin-foil, three inches long, a quarter of an inch wide at one end, and tapering all the way to a sharp point at the other, fixed between two pieces of glass, and having the electricity of a large glass jar sent through it, will not be discomposed in the broadest part; towards the middle will appear melted in spots; where narrower, it will be quite melted; and about half an inch of it next the point will be reduced to smoke.

PROTECTION FROM LIGHTNING.

PARIS, Sept. 1767.

EXPERIMENTS made in electricity first gave philosophers a suspicion that the matter of lightning was the same with the electric matter.   Experiments afterwards made on lightning obtained from the clouds by pointed rods, received into bottles, and subjected to every trial, have since proved this suspicion to be perfectly well founded, and that whatever properties we find in electricity are also the properties of lightning.

This matter of lightning, or of electricity, is an extreme subtle fluid, penetrating other bodies, and subsisting in them, equally diffused.

When, by any operation of art or nature, there happens to be a greater proportion of this fluid in one body than in another, the body which has most will communicate to that which has least, till the proportion becomes equal ; provided the distance between them be not too great ; or, if it is too great, till there be proper conductors to convey it from one to the other.

If the communication be through the air without any conductor, a bright light is seen between the bodies, and a sound is heard.   In our small experiments, we call this light and sound the electric spark and snap ; but in the great operations of nature the light is what we call *lightning*, and the sound (produced at the same time, though generally arriving later at our ears than the light does to our eyes) is, with its echoes, called *thunder*.

If the communication of this fluid is by a conductor, it may be without either light or sound, the subtle fluid passing in the substance of the conductor.

If the conductor be good and of sufficient bigness, the fluid passes through it without hurting it.   If otherwise, it is damaged or destroyed.

All metals, and water, are good conductors.   Other bodies may become conductors by having some quantity of water in them, as wood, and other materials used in building ; but not having much water in them, they are not good conductors, and, therefore, are often damaged in the operation.

Glass, wax, silk, wool, hair, feathers, and even wood, perfectly dry, are non-conductors ; that is, they resist instead of facilitating the passage of this subtle fluid.

When this fluid has an opportunity of passing through two conductors, — one good and sufficient, as of metal, the other not so good, — it passes in the best, and will follow it in any direction.

The distance at which a body charged with this fluid will discharge itself suddenly, striking through the air into another body that is not charged, or not so highly charged, is different according to the quantity of the fluid, the dimensions and form of the bodies themselves, and the state of the air between them. This distance, whatever it happens to be, between any two bodies, is called their *striking distance*, as, till they come within that distance of each other, no stroke will be made.

The clouds have often more of this fluid in proportion than the earth; in which case, as soon as they come near enough (that is, within the striking distance) or meet with a conductor, the fluid quits them and strikes into the earth. A cloud fully charged with this fluid, if so high as to be beyond the striking distance from the earth, passes quietly, without making noise or giving light, unless it meets with other clouds that have less.

Tall trees and lofty buildings, as the towers and spires of churches, become sometimes conductors between the clouds and the earth; but not being good ones, — that is, not conveying the fluid freely, — they are often damaged.

Buildings that have their roofs covered with lead, or other metal, the spouts of metal continued from the roof into the ground to carry off the water, are never hurt by lightning, as, whenever it falls on such a building, it passes in the metals, and not in the walls.

When other buildings happen to be within the striking distance from such clouds, the fluid passes in the walls, whether of wood, brick or stone, quitting the walls only when it can find better conductors near them, as metal rods, bolts, and hinges of windows or doors, gilding on wainscot or frames of pictures, the silvering on the backs of looking-glasses, the wires for bells, and the bodies of animals, as containing watery fluids. And, in passing through the house, it follows the direction of these conductors, taking as many in its way as can assist it in its passage, whether in a straight or crooked line, leaping from one to the other, if not far distant from each other, only rending the wall in the spaces where these partial good conductors are too distant from each other.

An iron rod being placed on the outside of a building, from the highest part continued down into the moist earth, in any direction, straight or crooked, following the form of the roof or parts of the building, will receive the lightning at its upper end, attracting it so as to prevent its striking any other part; and, affording it a good conveyance into the earth, will prevent its damaging any part of the building.

25

A small quantity of metal is found able to conduct a great quantity of this fluid. A wire no bigger than a goose-quill has been known to conduct (with safety to the building as far as the wire was continued) a quantity of lightning that did prodigious damage both above and below it; and probably larger rods are not necessary, though it is common in America to make them of half an inch, some of three-quarters, or an inch diameter.

The rod may be fastened to the wall, chimney, &c., with staples of iron. The lightning will not leave the rod (a good conductor) to pass into the wall (a bad conductor) through those staples. It would rather, if any were in the walls, pass out of it into the rod, to get more readily by that conductor into the earth.

If the building be very large and extensive, two or more rods may be placed at different parts, for greater security.

Small ragged parts of clouds, suspended in the air between the great body of clouds and the earth (like leaf-gold in electrical experiments), often serve as partial conductors for the lightning, which proceeds from one of them to another, and by their help comes within the striking distance to the earth or a building. It therefore strikes through those conductors a building that would otherwise be out of the striking distance.

Long sharp points communicating with the earth, and presented to such parts of clouds, drawing silently from them the fluid they are charged with, they are then attracted to the cloud, and may leave the distance so great as to be beyond the reach of striking.

It is therefore that we elevate the upper end of the rod six or eight feet above the highest part of the building, tapering it gradually to a fine sharp point, which is gilt to prevent its rusting.

Thus the pointed rod either prevents a stroke from the cloud, or, if a stroke is made, conducts it to the earth with safety to the building.

The lower end of the rod should enter the earth so deep as to come at the moist part, perhaps two or three feet; and if bent when under the surface so as to go in a horizontal line six or eight feet from the wall, and then bent again downwards three or four feet, it will prevent damage to any of the stones of the foundation.

A person apprehensive of danger from lightning, happening during the time of thunder to be in a house not so secured, will do well to avoid sitting near the chimney, near a looking-glass, or any gilt pictures or wainscot ; the safest place is the middle of the room (so it be not under a metal lustre suspended by a chain), sitting in one chair and laying the feet up in another. It is still safer to bring two or three mattresses or beds into the middle of the room, and, folding them up double, place the chair upon them ; for they not being so good conductors as the walls, the lightning will not choose an interrupted course through the air of the room and the bedding, when it can go through a continued better conductor, the wall. But where it can be had, a hammock or swinging bed, suspended by silk cords equally distant from the walls on every side, and from the ceiling and floor above and below, affords the safest situation a person can have in any room whatever, and what indeed may be deemed quite free from danger of any stroke by lightning.

[TO JOHN PRINGLE, M.D.]

ON THE EFFECTS OF ELECTRICITY IN PARALYTIC CASES.

CRAVEN-STREET, Dec. 21, 1757.

IN compliance with your request, I send you the following account of what I can at present recollect relating to the effects of electricity in paralytic cases, which have fallen under my observation.

Some years since, when the newspapers made mention of great cures performed in Italy and Germany by means of electricity, a number of paralytics were brought to me from different parts of Pennsylvania, and the neighboring provinces, to be electrized, which I did for them at their request. My method was, to place the patient first in a chair on an electric stool, and draw a number of large strong sparks from all parts of the affected limb or side. Then I fully charged two six-gallon glass jars, each of which had about three square feet of surface coated ; and sent the united shock of these through the affected limb or limbs, repeating the stroke commonly three times each day. The first thing observed was an immediate greater sensible warmth in the lame limbs that had received the stroke than in the others; and the next morning the patients usually related that they had in the night felt a pricking sensation in the flesh of the paralytic limbs ; and would sometimes show a number of small red spots, which they supposed were occasioned by those prickings. The limbs, too, were found more capable of voluntary motion, and seemed to receive strength.

A man, for instance, who could not the first day lift the lame hand from off his knee, would the next day raise it four or five inches, the third day higher, and on the fifth day was able, but with a feeble, languid motion, to take off his hat. These appearances gave great spirits to the patients, and made them hope a perfect cure; but I do not remember that I ever saw any amendment after the fifth day; which the patients perceiving, and finding the shocks pretty severe, they became discouraged, went home, and in a short time relapsed; so that I never knew any advantage from electricity in palsies that was permanent. And how far the apparent temporary advantage might arise from the exercise in the patient's journey, and coming daily to my house, or from the spirits given by the hope of success, enabling them to exert more strength in moving their limbs, I will not pretend to say.

Perhaps some permanent advantage might have been obtained, if the electric shocks had been accompanied with proper medicine and regimen, under the direction of a skilful physician. It may be, too, that a few great strokes, as given in my method, may not be so proper as many small ones; since, by the account from Scotland of a case in which two hundred shocks from a vial were given daily, it seems that a perfect cure has been made. As to any uncommon strength supposed to be in the machine used in that case, I imagine it could have no share in the effect produced, since the strength of the shock from charged glass is in proportion to the quantity of surface of the glass coated; so that my shock from those large jars, must have been much greater than any that could be received from a vial held in the hand.

[TO DR. PERCIVAL MANCHESTER.]

METEOROLOGICAL IMAGINATIONS AND CONJECTURES.

PASSY, May 1784.

THERE seems to be a region higher, in the air over all countries, where it is always winter, where frost exists continually, since in the midst of summer, on the surface of the earth, ice falls often from above in the form of hail.

Hailstones, of the great weight we sometimes find them, did

not probably acquire their magnitude before they began to descend. The air, being eight hundred times rarer than water, is unable to support it but in the shape of vapor, a state in which its particles are separated. As soon as they are condensed by the cold of the upper region so as to form a drop, that drop begins to fall. I˘ it freezes into a grain of ice, that ice descends. In descending, both the drop of water and the grain of ice are augmented by particles of the vapor they pass through in falling, and which they condense by coldness, and attach to themselves.

It is possible that, in summer, much of what is rain when it arrives at the surface of the earth might have been snow when it began its descent; but, being thawed in passing through the warm air near the surface, it is changed from snow into rain.

How immensely cold must be the original particle of hail, which forms the centre of the future hailstone, since it is capable of communicating sufficient cold, if I may so speak, to freeze all the mass of vapor condensed round it, and form a lump of perhaps six or eight ounces in weight!

When, in summer time, the sun is high, and continues long every day above the horizon, his rays strike the earth more directly, and with longer continuance, than in the winter; hence the surface is more heated, and to a greater depth, by the effect of those rays.

When rain falls on the heated earth, and soaks down into it, it carries down with it a great part of the heat, which by that means descends still deeper.

The mass of earth, to the depth of perhaps thirty feet, being thus heated to a certain degree, continues to retain its heat for some time. Thus the first snows that fall in the beginning of winter seldom lie long on the surface, but are soon melted, and soon absorbed. After which, the winds that blow over the country on which the snows had fallen are not rendered so cold as they would have been, by those snows, if they had remained, and thus the approach of the severity of winter is retarded, and the extreme degree of its cold is not always at the time we might expect it, namely, when the sun is at its greatest distance, and the day shortest, but some time after that period, according to the English proverb, which says, "as the day lengthens, the cold strengthens;" the causes of refrigeration continuing to operate, while the sun returns too slowly, and his force continues too weak, to counteract them.

During several of the months of the year 1783, when the effects of the sun's rays to heat the earth in these northern

25*

regions should have been the greatest, there existed a constant fog over all Europe, and great part of North America. This fog was of a permanent nature : it was dry, and the rays of the sun seemed to have little effect towards dissipating it, as they easily do a moist fog, arising from water. They were indeed rendered so faint, in passing through it, that when collected in the focus of a burning-glass they would scarce kindle brown paper. Of course, their summer effect in heating the earth was exceedingly diminished.

Hence the surface was early frozen.

Hence the first snows remained on it unmelted, and received continual additions.

Hence perhaps the winter of 1783–4 was more severe than any that had happened for many years.

The cause of this universal fog is not yet ascertained. Whether it was adventitious to this earth, and merely a smoke proceeding from the consumption by fire of some of those great burning balls or globes which we happen to meet with in our rapid course round the sun, and which are sometimes seen to kindle and be destroyed in passing our atmosphere, and whose smoke might be attracted and retained by our earth ; or whether it was the vast quantity of smoke, long continuing to issue during the summer from Hecla, in Iceland, and that other volcano which arose out of the sea near that island, which smoke might be spread by various winds over the northern part of the world, is yet uncertain.

It seems, however, worth the inquiry, whether other hard winters, recorded in history, were preceded by similar permanent and widely-extended summer fogs. Because, if found to be so, men might from such fogs conjecture the probability of a succeeding hard winter, and of the damage to be expected by the breaking up of frozen rivers in the spring, and take such measures as are possible and practicable to secure themselves and effects from the mischiefs that attended the last.

[TO DR. LINING, AT CHARLESTON.]

ON COLD PRODUCED BY EVAPORATION.

NEW YORK, April 14, 1757.

IT is a long time since I had the pleasure of a line from you; and, indeed, the troubles of our country, with the hurry of business I have been engaged in on that account, have made me so bad a correspondent, that I ought not to expect punctuality in others.

But, being about to embark for England, I could not quit the continent without paying my respects to you, and, at the same time, taking leave to introduce to your acquaintance a gentleman of learning and merit, Colonel Henry Bouquet, who does me the favor to present you this letter, and with whom I am sure you will be much pleased.

Professor Simpson, of Glasgow, lately communicated to me some curious experiments of a physician of his acquaintance, by which it appeared that an extraordinary degree of cold, even to freezing, might be produced by evaporation. I have not had leisure to repeat and examine more than the first and easiest of them, namely: Wet the ball of a thermometer by a feather dipped in spirit of wine, which has been kept in the same room, and has, of course, the same degree of heat or cold.   The mercury sinks presently three or four degrees, and the quicker if during the evaporation you blow on the ball with bellows ; a second wetting and blowing, when the mercury is down, carries it yet lower.   I think I did not get it lower than five or six degrees from where it naturally stood, which was at that time sixty.   But it is said that, a vessel of water being placed in another somewhat larger, containing spirit, in such a manner that the vessel of water is surrounded with the spirit, and both placed under the receiver of an air-pump, on exhausting the air, the spirit, evaporating, leaves such a degree of cold as to freeze the water, though the thermometer in the open air stands many degrees above the freezing point.

I know not how this phenomena is to be accounted for ; but it gives me occasion to mention some loose notions relating to heat and cold which I have for some time entertained, but not yet reduced into any form.   Allowing common fire, as well as electrical, to be a fluid capable of permeating other bodies, and seeking an equilibrium, I imagine some bodies are better fitted by nature to be conductors of that fluid than others; and that generally those which are the best conductors of the electric fluid are also the best conductors of this ; and è contra.

Thus, a body which is a good conductor of fire readily receives it into its substance, and conducts it through the whole to all the parts, as metals and water do ; and if two bodies, both good conductors, one heated and the other in its common state, are brought into contact with each other, the body which has most fire readily communicates of it to that which had least, and that which had least readily receives it, till an equilibrium is produced. Thus, if you take a dollar between your fingers with one hand, and a piece of wood of the same dimensions with the other, and bring both at the same time to the flame of a candle, you will find yourself obliged to drop the dollar before you drop the wood, because it conducts the heat of the candle sooner to your flesh. Thus, if a silver tea-pot had a handle of the same metal, it would conduct the heat from the water to the hand, and become too hot to be used; we therefore give to a metal tea-pot a handle of wood, which is not so good a conductor as metal. But a china or stone tea-pot, being in some degree of the nature of glass, which is not a good conductor of heat, may have a handle of the same stuff. Thus, also, a damp, moist air shall make a man more sensible of cold, or chill him more, than a dry air that is colder; because a moist air is fitter to receive and conduct away the heat of his body. This fluid, entering bodies in great quantity, first expands them by separating their parts a little; afterwards, by further separating their parts, it renders solids fluid, and at length dissipates their parts in air. Take this fluid from melted lead, or from water, the parts cohere again, — the first grows solid, the latter becomes ice; and this is sooner done by the means of good conductors.

Thus, if you take, as I have done, a square bar of lead, four inches long and one inch thick, together with three pieces of wood planed to the same dimensions, and lay them on a smooth board, fixed so as not to be easily separated or moved, and pour into the cavity they form as much melted lead as will fill it, you will see the melted lead chill and become firm on the side next the leaden bar, some time before it chills on the other three sides, in contact with the wooden bars, though before the lead was poured in they might all be supposed to have the same degree of heat and coldness, as they had been exposed in the same room to the same air. You will likewise observe that the leaden bar, as it has cooled the melted lead more than the wooden bars have done, so it is itself more heated by the melted lead. There is a certain quantity of this fluid called fire in every living human body, which fluid, being in due proportion, keeps the parts of the flesh and blood at such a just distance from each other as that the flesh and nerves are supple, and the blood fit for circulation. If part of this due proportion of fire be conducted away, by means of a contact with other bodies, as air, water or metals, the parts of our skin and flesh that come into such contact first draw more near together than is agreeable, and give that sensation which we call cold ; and, if too much be conveyed away, the body stiffens, the blood ceases to flow, and death ensues.

On the other hand, if too much of this fluid be communicated to the flesh, the parts are separated too far, and pain ensues, as when they are separated by a pin or lancet. The sensation that the separation by fire occasions we call heat or burning. My desk on which I now write, and the lock of my desk, are both exposed to the same temperature of the air, and have therefore the same degree of heat or cold : yet, if I lay my hand successively on the wood and on the metal, the latter feels much the coldest ; not that it is really so, but, being a better conductor, it more readily than the wood takes away and draws into itself the fire that was in my skin. Accordingly, if I lay one hand part on the lock and part on the wood, and, after it has laid on some time, I feel both parts with my other hand, I find the part that has been in contact with the lock very sensibly colder to the touch than the part that lay on the wood.

How a living animal obtains its quantity of this fluid called fire is a curious question. I have shown that some bodies (as metals) have a power of attracting it stronger than others ; and I have sometimes suspected that a living body had some power of attracting out of the air, or other bodies, the heat it wanted. Thus, metals hammered, or repeatedly bent, grow hot in the beat or hammered part. But, when I consider that air in contact with the body cools it ; that the surrounding air is rather heated by its contact with the body ; that every breath of cooler air drawn in carries off part of the body's heat when it passes out again ; that therefore there must be in the body a fund for producing it, or otherwise the animal would soon grow cold, — I have been rather inclined to think that the fluid *fire*, as well as the fluid *air*, is attracted by plants in their growth, and becomes consolidated with the other materials of which they are formed, and makes a great part of their substance ; that when they come to be digested, and to suffer in the vessels a kind of fermentation, part of the fire, as well as part of the air, recovers its fluid active state again, and diffuses itself in the body, digesting and separating it ; that the fire so reproduced, by digesting and separation, continually leaving the body, its place is supplied by fresh quantities, arising from the continual separation ; that whatever quickens the motion of the fluids in an animal quickens the separation, and reproduces more of the fire, as exercise ; that all the fire emitted by wood, and other combustibles, when burning, existed in them before, in a solid state, being only discovered when separating ; that some fossils, as sulphur, sea-coal, &c., contain a great deal of solid fire ;

and that, in short, what escapes and is dissipated in the burning
of bodies, besides water and earth, is generally the air and fire
that before made parts of the solid.   Thus I imagine that animal heat arises by or from a kind of fermentation in the juices
of the body, in the same manner as heat arises in the liquors
preparing for distillation, wherein there is a separation of the
spirituous from the watery and earthly parts.   And it is remarkable that the liquor in a distiller's vat, when in its highest and
best state of fermentation, as I have been informed, has the same
degree of heat with the human body : that is, about 94 or 96.

Thus, as by a constant supply of fuel in a chimney you keep
a warm room, so, by a constant supply of food in the stomach,
you keep a warm body ; only, where little exercise is used, the
heat may possibly be conducted away too fast ; in which case, such
materials are to be used for clothing and bedding, against the
effects of an immediate contact of the air, as are, in themselves,
bad conductors of heat, and consequently prevent its being communicated through their substance to the air.   Hence what is
called *warmth* in wool, and its preference on that account to
linen, wool not being so good a conductor ; and hence all the
natural coverings of animals, to keep them warm, are such as
retain and confine the natural heat in the body, by being bad
conductors, such as wool, hair, feathers, and the silk by which the
silk-worm, in its tender embryo state, is first clothed.   Clothing thus considered does not make a man warm by *giving* warmth,
but by *preventing* the too quick dissipation of the heat produced
in his body, and so occasioning an accumulation.

There is another curious question I will just venture to touch
upon, namely : Whence arises the sudden extraordinary degree
of cold perceptible on mixing some chemical liquors, and even on
mixing salt and snow, where the composition appears colder than
the coldest of the ingredients ? I have never seen the chemical mixtures made, but salt and snow I have often mixed myself, and am
fully satisfied that the composition feels much colder to the touch,
and lowers the mercury in the thermometer more, than either ingredient would do separately.   I suppose, with others, that cold
is nothing more than the absence of heat or fire.   Now, if the
quantity of fire before contained or diffused in the snow and salt
was expelled in the uniting of the two matters, it must be driven
away either through the air or the vessel containing them.   If it
is driven off through the air, it must warm the air, and a thermometer held over the mixture, without touching it, would discover the heat by the rising of the mercury, as it must, and
always does, in warm air.

This, indeed, I have not tried, but I should guess it would rather be driven off through the vessel, especially if the vessel be metal, as being a better conductor than air ; and so one should find the basin warmer after such mixture. But, on the contrary, the vessel grows cold, and even water, in which the vessel is sometimes placed for the experiment, freezes into hard ice on the basin. Now, I know not how to account for this otherwise than by supposing that the composition is a better conductor of fire than the ingredients separately, and, like the lock compared with the wood, has a stronger power of attracting fire, and does accordingly attract it suddenly from the fingers, or a thermometer put into it, from the basin that contains it, and from the water in contact with the outside of the basin ; so that the fingers have the sensation of extreme cold, by being deprived of much of their natural fire ; the thermometer sinks, by having part of its fire drawn out of the mercury ; the basin grows colder to the touch, as by having its fire drawn into the mixture it is become more capable of drawing and receiving it from the hand ; and through the basin the water loses its fire that kept its fluid, so it becomes ice One would expect that, from all this attracted acquisition of fire to the composition, it should become warmer ; and, in fact, the snow and salt dissolve at the same time into water, without freezing.

————

LONDON, June 17, 1758.

IN a former letter I mentioned the experiment for cooling bodies by evaporation, and that I had, by repeatedly wetting the thermometer with common spirits, brought the mercury down five or six degrees. Being lately at Cambridge, and mentioning this in conversation with Dr. Hadley, professor of chemistry there, he proposed repeating the experiments with ether, instead of common spirits, as the ether is much quicker in evaporation. We accordingly went to his chamber, where he had both ether and a thermometer. By dipping first the ball of the thermometer into the ether, it appeared that the ether was precisely of the same temperament with the thermometer, which stood then at 65 ; for it made no alteration in the height of the little column of mercury. But when the thermometer was taken out of the ether, and the ether, with which the ball was wet, began to evaporate, the mercury sunk several degrees. The wetting was then repeated by a feather that had been dipped into the ether, when the mercury sunk still lower.

We continued this operation, one of us wetting the ball, and another of the company blowing on it with the bellows, to quicken the evaporation, the mercury sinking all the time, till it came down to 7, which is twenty-five degrees below the freezing point, when we left off. Soon after it passed the freezing point, a thin coat of ice began to cover the ball. Whether this was water collected and condensed by the coldness of the ball, from the moisture in the air, or from our breath; or whether the feather, when dipped into the ether, might not sometimes go through it, and bring up some of the water that was under it, I am not certain; perhaps all might contribute. The ice continued increasing till we ended the experiment, when it appeared near a quarter of an inch thick all over the ball, with a number of small spicula, pointing outwards.

From this experiment one may see the possibility of freezing a man to death on a warm summer's day, if he were to stand in a passage through which the wind blew briskly, and to be wet frequently with ether, a spirit that is more inflammable than brandy or common spirits of wine.

It is but within these few years that the European philosophers seem to have known this power in nature of cooling bodies by evaporation. But in the East they have long been acquainted with it. A friend tells me there is a passage in Bernier's Travels through Hindostan, written near one hundred years ago, that mentions it as a practice (in travelling over dry deserts in that hot climate) to carry water in flasks wrapt in wet woollen cloths, and hung on the shady side of the camel, or carriage, but in the free air; whereby, as the cloths gradually grow drier, the water contained in the flasks is made cool. They have likewise a kind of earthen pots, unglazed, which let the water gradually and slowly ooze through their pores, so as to keep the outside a little wet, notwithstanding the continual evaporation, which gives great coldness to the vessel, and the water contained in it. Even our common sailors seem to have had some notion of this property; for I remember that, being at sea when I was a youth, I observed one of the sailors, during a calm in the night, often wetting his finger in his mouth, and then holding it up in the air, to discover, as he said, if the air had any motion, and from which side it came; and this he expected to do, by finding one side of his finger grow suddenly cold, and from that side he should look for the next wind; which I then laughed at, as a fancy.

May not several phenomena, hitherto unconsidered or unaccounted for, be explained by this property? During the hot Sunday at Philadelphia, in June 1750, when the thermometer was up at 100 in the shade, and I sat in my chamber without exercise, only reading or writing, with no other clothes on than a shirt, and a pair of long linen drawers, the windows all open, and a brisk wind blowing through the house, the sweat ran off the backs of my hands, and my shirt was often so wet as to induce me to call for dry ones to put on. In this situation, one might have expected that the natural heat of the body (96), added to the heat of the air (100), should jointly have created or produced a much greater degree of heat in the body; but the fact was, that my body never grew so hot as the air that surrounded it, or the inanimate bodies immersed in the same air. For I remember well that the desk, when I laid my arm upon it; a chair, when I sat down in it; and a dry shirt out of the drawer, when I put it on, all felt exceedingly warm to me, as if they had been warmed before a fire. And I suppose a dead body would have acquired the temperature of the air, though a living one, by continual sweating, and by the evaporation of that sweat, was kept cold.

May not this be a reason why our reapers in Pennsylvania, working in the open field, in the clear hot sunshine common in our harvest-time, find themselves well able to go through that labor, without being much incommoded by the heat, while they continue to sweat, and while they supply matter for keeping up that sweat by drinking frequently of a thin evaporable liquor, water mixed with rum; but, if the sweat stops, they drop, and sometimes die suddenly, if a sweating is not again brought on by drinking that liquor, or, as some rather choose in that case, a kind of hot punch, made with water, mixed with honey, and a considerable proportion of vinegar? May there not be in negroes a quicker evaporation of the perspirable matter from their skins and lungs, which, by cooling them more, enables them to bear the sun's heat better than whites do? (if this is a fact, as it is said to be; for the alleged necessity of having negroes, rather than whites, to work in the West India fields, is founded upon it) though the color of their skins would otherwise make them more sensible of the sun's heat, since black cloth heats much sooner, and more, in the sun, than white cloth. I am persuaded, from several instances happening within my knowledge, that they do not bear cold weather so well as the whites; they will perish when exposed to a less degree of it, and are more apt to have their limbs frost-bitten; and may not this be from the same cause? Would not the earth grow much hotter under the summer sun, if a constant evaporation from its surface, greater as the sun shines stronger, did not, by tending to

26

cool it, balance in some degree the warmer effects of the sun's rays? Is it not owing to the constant evaporation from the surface of every leaf, that trees, though shone on by the sun, are always, even the leaves themselves, cool to our sense? at least, much cooler than they would otherwise be? May it not be owing to this that fanning ourselves when warm does really cool us, though the air is itself warm that we drive with the fan upon our faces; for the atmosphere round, and next to our bodies, having imbibed as much of the perspired vapor as it can well contain, receives no more, and the evaporation is therefore checked and retarded, till we drive away that atmosphere, and bring drier air in its place, that will receive the vapor, and therefore facilitate and increase the evaporation? Certain it is, that mere blowing of air on a dry body does not cool it, as any one may satisfy himself, by blowing with a bellows on the dry ball of a thermometer;—the mercury will not fall; if it moves at all, it rather rises, as being warmed by the friction of the air on its surface.

To these queries of imagination, I will only add one practical observation : that, wherever it is thought proper to give ease, in cases of painful inflammation of- the flesh (as from burnings, or the like), by cooling the part, linen cloths, wet with spirit, and applied to the part inflamed, will produce the coolness required better than if wet with water, and will continue it longer. For water, though cold when first applied, will soon acquire warmth from the flesh, as it does not evaporate fast enough; but the cloths wet with spirit will continue cold as long as any spirit is left to keep up the evaporation, the parts warmed escaping as soon as they are warmed, and carrying off the heat with them.

SALT WATER RENDERED FRESH BY DISTILLATION — METHOD OF RELIEVING THIRST BY SEA-WATER.

CRAVEN-STREET, August 10, 1761.

WE are to set out this week for Holland, where we may possibly spend a month, but purpose to be at home again before the coronation. I could not go without taking leave of you by a line at least, when I am so many letters in your debt.

In yours of May 19, which I have before me, you speak of the ease with which salt water may be made fresh by distillation, supposing it to be, as I had said, that in evaporation the air would take up water, but not the salt that was mixed with it. It is true that distilled sea-water will not be salt, but there are other disagreeable qualities that rise with the water in distillation ; which indeed several besides Dr. Hales have endeavored by some means to prevent, but as yet their methods have not been brought much into use.

I have a singular opinion on this subject, which I will venture to communicate to you, though I doubt you will rank it among my whims. It is certain that the skin has *imbibing* as well as *discharging* pores; witness the effects of a blistering-plaster, &c. I have read that a man, hired by a physician to stand by way of experiment in the open air naked during a moist night, weighed near three pounds heavier in the morning.

I have often observed myself, that, however thirsty I may have been before going into the water to swim, I am never long so in the water. These imbibing pores, however, are very fine,—perhaps fine enough in filtering to separate salt from water ; for though I have soaked (by swimming, when a boy) several hours in the day for several days successively in salt water, I never found my blood and juices salted by that means, so as to make me thirsty or feel a salt taste in my mouth ; and it is remarkable that the flesh of sea-fish, though bred in salt water, is not salt.

Hence I imagine, that if people at sea, distressed by thirst, when their fresh water is unfortunately spent, would make bathing-tubs of their empty water-casks, and, filling them with sea-water, sit in them an hour or two each day, they might be greatly relieved. Perhaps keeping their clothes constantly wet might have an almost equal effect, and this without danger of catching cold. Men do not catch cold by wet clothes at sea. Damp but not wet linen may possibly give colds, but no one catches cold by bathing, and no clothes can be wetter than water itself. Why damp clothes should then occasion colds, is a curious question, the discussion of which I reserve for a future letter, or some future conversation.

[TO MISS STEVENSON.]

TENDENCY OF RIVERS TO THE SEA — EFFECTS OF THE
SUN'S RAYS ON CLOTHS OF DIFFERENT COLORS.

September 20, 1761.

MY DEAR FRIEND: It is, as you observed in our late conversation, a very general opinion that *all rivers run into the sea*,
or deposit their waters there. 'T is a kind of audacity to call
such general opinions in question, and may subject one to censure. But we must hazard something in what we think the
cause of truth; and, if we propose our objections modestly, we
shall, though mistaken, deserve a censure less severe than when
we are both mistaken and insolent.

That some rivers run into the sea is beyond a doubt: such,
for instance, are the Amazon, and I think the Oronoco and the
Mississippi. The proof is, that their waters are fresh quite to
the sea, and out to some distance from the land. Our question
is, whether the fresh waters of those rivers whose beds are filled
with salt water to a considerable distance up from the sea (as
the Thames, the Delaware, and the rivers that communicate with
Chesapeake Bay in Virginia) do ever arrive at the sea? And,
as I suspect they do not, I am now to acquaint you with my
reasons; or, if they are not allowed to be reasons, my conceptions at least, of this matter.

The common supply of rivers is from springs, which draw
their origin from rain that has soaked into the earth. The
union of a number of springs forms a river. The waters, as they
run, exposed to the sun, air and wind, are continually evaporating. Hence in travelling one may often see where a river runs,
by a long bluish mist over it, though we are at such a distance
as not to see the river itself. The quantity of this evaporation
is greater or less, in proportion to the surface exposed by the
same quantity of water to those causes of evaporation. While
the river runs in a narrow, confined channel in the upper, hilly
country, only a small surface is exposed; a greater, as the river
widens. Now, if a river ends in a lake, as some do, whereby its
waters are spread so wide as that the evaporation is equal to
the sum of all its springs, that lake will never overflow: — and
if, instead of ending in a lake, it was drawn into greater length
as a river, so as to expose a surface equal in the whole to that
lake, the evaporation would be equal, and such river would end
as a canal; when the ignorant might suppose, as they actually

do in such cases, that the river loses itself by running under ground, whereas in truth it has run up into the air.

Now, how many rivers that are open to the sea widen much before they arrive at it, not merely by the additional waters they receive, but by having their course stopped by the opposing flood-tide; by being turned back twice in twenty-four hours, and by finding broader beds in the low, flat countries to dilate themselves in; hence the evaporation of the fresh water is proportionably increased, so that in some rivers it may equal the springs of supply In such cases, the salt water comes up the river, and meets the fresh in that part where, if there were a wall or bank of earth across, from side to side, the river would form a lake, — fuller indeed at some times than at others, according to the seasons, but whose evaporation would, one time with another, be equal to its supply.

When the communication between the two kinds of water is open, this supposed wall of separation may be conceived as a movable one, which is not only pushed some miles higher up the river by every flood-tide from the sea, and carried down again as far by every tide of ebb, but which has even this space of vibration removed nearer to the sea in wet seasons, when the springs and brooks in the upper country are augmented by the falling rains, so as to swell the river, and further from the sea in dry seasons.

Within a few miles above and below this movable line of separation, the different waters mix a little, partly by their motion to and fro, and partly from the greater specific gravity of the salt water, which inclines it to run under the fresh, while the fresh water, being lighter, runs over the salt.

Cast your eye on the map of North America, and observe the Bay of Chesapeake in Virginia, mentioned above; you will see communicating with it by their mouths the great rivers Susquehanna, Potomac, Rappahannock, York and James, besides a number of smaller streams, each as big as the Thames. It has been proposed by philosophical writers, that, to compute how much water any river discharges into the sea in a given time, we should measure its depth and swiftness at any part above the tide; as, for the Thames, at Kingston or Windsor. But can one imagine that if all the water of those vast rivers went to the sea, it would not first have pushed the salt water out of that narrow-mouthed bay, and filled it with fresh? The Susquehanna alone would seem to be sufficient for this, if it were not for the loss by evaporation. And yet that bay is salt quite up to Annapolis.

26*

As to our other subject, the different degrees of heat imbibed from the sun's rays by cloths of different colors, since I cannot find the notes of my experiment to send you, I must give it as well as I can from memory.

But first let me mention an experiment you may easily make yourself. Walk but a quarter of an hour in your garden when the sun shines, with a part of your dress white, and a part black; then apply your hand to them alternately, and you will find a very great difference in their warmth. The black will be quite hot to the touch, the white still cool.

Another. Try to fire the paper with a burning-glass. If it is white, you will not easily burn it; but, if you bring the focus to a black spot, or upon letters, written or printed, the paper will immediately be on fire under the letters.

Thus fullers and dyers find black cloths, of equal thickness with white ones, and hung out equally wet, dry in the sun much sooner than the white, being more readily heated by the sun's rays. It is the same before a fire; the heat of which sooner penetrates black stockings than white ones, and so is apt sooner to burn a man's shins. Also, beer much sooner warms in a black mug set before the fire than in a white one, or in a bright silver tankard.

My experiment was this. I took a number of little square pieces of broadcloth from a tailor's pattern-card, of various colors. There were black, deep blue, lighter blue, green, purple, red, yellow, white, and other colors or shades of colors. I laid them all out upon the snow in a bright sunshiny morning. In a few hours (I cannot now be exact as to the time) the black, being warmed most by the sun, was sunk so low as to be below the stroke of the sun's rays; the dark blue almost as low, the lighter blue not quite so much as the dark, the other colors less as they were lighter; and the quite white remained on the surface of the snow, not having entered it at all.

What signifies philosophy that does not apply to some use? May we not learn from hence that black clothes are not so fit to wear in a hot, sunny climate or season as white ones, because in such clothes the body is more heated by the sun when we walk abroad, and are at the same time heated by the exercise, which double heat is apt to bring on putrid, dangerous fevers? That soldiers and seamen, who must march and labor in the sun, should in the East or West Indies have an uniform of white? That summer hats, for men or women, should be white, as repelling that heat which gives headaches to many, and to some the fatal stroke that the French call the *coup de soleil*? That the ladies' summer hats, however, should be lined with black, as not reverberating on their faces those rays which are reflected upwards from the earth or water? That the putting a white cap of paper or linen *within* the crown of a black hat, as some do, will not keep out the heat, though it would if placed *without?* That fruit-walls, being blacked, may receive so much heat from the sun in the day-time as to continue warm in some degree through the night, and thereby preserve the fruit from frosts, or forward its growth? — with sundry other particulars of less or greater importance, that will occur from time to time to attentive minds.

[TO THE SAME.]

EFFECT OF AIR ON THE BAROMETER — THE STUDY OF INSECTS.

CRAVEN-STREET, June 11, 1760.

'T is a very sensible question you ask, How the air can affect the barometer, when its opening appears covered with wood? If indeed it was so closely covered as to admit of no communication of the outward air to the surface of the mercury, the change of weight in the air could not possibly affect it. But the least crevice is sufficient for the purpose; a pin-hole will do the business. And, if you could look behind the frame towhich your barometer is fixed, you would certainly find some small opening.

There are indeed some barometers in which the body of mercury at the lower end is contained in a close leather bag, and so the air cannot come into immediate contact with the mercury; yet the same effect is produced. For, the leather being flexible, when the bag is pressed by any additional weight of air it contracts, and the mercury is forced up into the tube; when the air becomes lighter, and its pressure less, the weight of the mercury prevails, and it descends again into the bag.

Your observation on what you have lately read concerning insects is very just and solid. Superficial minds are apt to despise those who make that part of the creation their study, as mere triflers; but certainly the world has been much obliged to them. Under the care and management of man, the labors of the little silk-worm afford employment and subsistence to thousands of families, and become an immense article of commerce. The bee, too,

yields us its delicious honey, and its wax useful to a multitude
of purposes.   Another insect, it is said, produces the cochineal,
from whence we have our rich scarlet dye.   The usefulness of
the cantharides, or Spanish flies, in medicine, is known to all,
and thousands owe their lives to that knowledge.   By human
industry and observation, other properties of other insects may
possibly be hereafter discovered, and of equal utility.   A
thorough acquaintance with the nature of these little creatures
may also enable mankind to prevent the increase of such as are
noxious, or secure us against the mischiefs they occasion.

These things doubtless your books make mention of: I can
only add a particular late instance, which I had from a Swedish
gentleman of good credit.   In the green timber intended for
ship-building at the king's yard in that country, a kind of worms
were found, which every year became more numerous and more
pernicious, so that the ships were greatly damaged before they
came into use.   The king sent Linnæus, the great naturalist,
from Stockholm, to inquire into the affair, and see if the mischief
was capable of any remedy.   He found, on examination, that
the worm was produced from a small egg, deposited in the little
roughnesses on the surface of the wood, by a particular kind of
fly or beetle; from whence the worm, as soon as it was hatched,
began to eat into the substance of the wood, and after some time
came out again a fly of the parent kind, and so the species increased.   The season in which the fly laid its eggs Linnæus
knew to be about a fortnight (I think) in the month of May, and
at no other time in the year.   He therefore advised, that some
days before that season all the green timber should be thrown
into the water, and kept under water till the season was over.
Which being done by the king's order, the flies, missing the usual
nests, could not increase; and the species was either destroyed
or went elsewhere, and the wood was effectually preserved; for
after the first year it became too dry and hard for their purpose.

There is, however, a prudent moderation to be used in studies
of this kind.   The knowledge of nature may be ornamental, and
it may be useful; but if, to attain an eminence in that, we neglect
the knowledge and practice of essential duties, we deserve repre-
hension.   For there is no rank in natural knowledge of equal
dignity and importance with that of being a good parent, a good
child, a good husband or wife, a good neighbor or friend, a good
subject or citizen, — that is, in short, a good Christian.   Nicholas
Gimcrack, therefore, who neglected the care of his family to
pursue butterflies, was a just object of ridicule, and we must
give him up as fair game to the satirist.

[TO DR. JOSEPH PRIESTLEY.]

EFFECT OF VEGETATION ON NOXIOUS AIR.

THAT the vegetable creation should restore the air which is spoiled by the animal part of it, looks like a rational system, and seems to be of a piece with the rest. Thus fire purifies water, all the world over. It purifies it by distillation, when it raises it in vapors, and lets it fall in rain; and further still by filtration, when, keeping it fluid, it suffers that rain to percolate the earth. We knew before that putrid animal substances were converted into sweet vegetables when mixed with the earth, and applied as manure; and now, it seems, that the same putrid substances, mixed with the air, have a similar effect. The strong thriving state of your mint, in putrid air, seems to show that the air is mended by taking something from it, and not by adding to it.

I hope this will give some check to the rage of destroying trees that grow near houses, which has accompanied our late improvements in gardening, from an opinion of their being unwholesome. I am certain, from long observation, that there is nothing unhealthy in the air of woods; for we Americans have everywhere our country habitations in the midst of woods, and no people on earth enjoy better health, or are more prolific.

[TO OLIVER NEALE.]

THE ART OF SWIMMING.

I CANNOT be of opinion with you, that it is too late in life for you to learn to swim. The river near the bottom of your garden affords a most convenient place for the purpose. And, as your new employment requires your being often on the water, of which you have such a dread, I think you would do well to make the trial; nothing being so likely to remove those apprehensions as the consciousness of an ability to swim to the shore in case of an accident, or of supporting yourself in the water till a boat could come to take you up.

I do not know how far corks or bladders may be useful in learning to swim, having never seen much trial of them. Possibly they may be of service in supporting the body while you are learning what is called the stroke, or that manner of drawing in and striking out the hands and feet that is necessary to produce progressive motion. But you will be no swimmer till you can place some confidence in the power of the water to support you; I would therefore advise the acquiring that confidence in the first place; especially as I have known several who, by a little of the practice necessary for that purpose, have insensibly acquired the stroke, taught as it were by nature.

The practice I mean is this. Choosing a place where the water deepens gradually, walk coolly into it till it is up to your breast, then turn round, your face to the shore, and throw an egg into the water between you and the shore. It will sink to the bottom, and be easily seen there, as your water is clear. It must lie in water so deep as that you cannot reach it to take it up but by diving for it. To encourage yourself in order to do this, reflect that your progress will be from deeper to shallower water, and that at any time you may, by bringing your legs under you, and standing on the bottom, raise your head far above the water. Then plunge under it with your eyes open, throwing yourself towards the egg, and endeavoring by the action of your hands and feet against the water to get forward till within reach of it. In this attempt you will find that the water buoys you up against your inclination; that it is not so easy a thing to sink as you imagined; that you cannot, but by active force, get down to the egg. Thus you feel the power of the water to support you, and learn to confide in that power; while your endeavors to overcome it, and to reach the egg, teach you the manner of acting on the water with your feet and hands, which action is afterwards used in swimming to support your head higher above water, or to go forward through it.

I would the more earnestly press you to the trial of this method, because, though I think I satisfied you that your body is lighter than water, and that you might float in it a long time with your mouth free for breathing, if you would put yourself in a proper posture, and would be still and forbear struggling; yet till you have obtained this experimental confidence in the water, I cannot depend on your having the necessary presence of mind to recollect that posture and directions I gave you relating to it. The surprise may put all out of your mind. For though we value ourselves on being reasonable knowing creatures, reason and knowledge seem on such occasions to be of little use to us; and the brutes, to whom we allow scarce a glimmering of either, appear to have the advantage of us.

I will, however, take this opportunity of repeating those particulars to you which I mentioned in our last conversation, as, by perusing them at your leisure, you may possibly imprint them so in your memory as on occasion to be of some use to you.

1. That though the legs, arms, and head of a human body, being solid parts, are specifically something heavier than fresh water, yet the trunk, particularly the upper part, from its hollowness, is so much lighter than water as that the whole of the body taken together is too light to sink wholly under water, but some part will remain above, until the lungs become filled with water, which happens from drawing water into them instead of air, when a person in the fright attempts breathing while the mouth and nostrils are under water.

2. That the legs and arms are specifically lighter than salt water, and will be supported by it; so that a human body would not sink in salt water, though the lungs were filled as above, but from the greater specific gravity of the head.

3. That, therefore, a person throwing himself on his back in salt water, and extending his arms, may easily lie so as to keep his mouth and nostrils free for breathing; and by a small motion of his hands may prevent turning, if he should perceive any tendency to it.

4. That in fresh water, if a man throws himself on his back, near the surface, he cannot long continue in that situation but by proper action of his hands on the water. If he uses no such action, the legs and lower part of the body will gradually sink till he comes into an upright position, in which he will continue suspended, the hollow of the breast keeping the head uppermost.

5. But if, in this erect position, the head is kept upright above the shoulders, as when we stand on the ground, the immersion will, by the weight of that part of the head that is out of water, reach above the mouth and nostrils, perhaps a little above the eyes, so that a man cannot long remain suspended in water with his head in that position.

6. The body continuing suspended as before, and upright, if the head be leaned quite back, so that the face looks upwards, all the back part of the head being then under water, and its weight consequently in a great measure supported by it, the face will remain above water quite free for breathing, will rise an inch higher every inspiration, and sink as much every expiration, but never so low that the water may come over the mouth.

7. If, therefore, a person unacquainted with swimming, and falling accidentally into the water, could have presence of mind sufficient to avoid struggling and plunging, and to let the body take this natural position, he might continue long safe from drowning, till perhaps help would come. For, as to the clothes,

their additional weight while immersed is very inconsiderable, the water supporting it, though, when he comes out of the water, he would find them very heavy indeed.

But, as I said before, I would not advise you or any one to depend on having this presence of mind on such an occasion, but learn fairly to swim; as I wish all men were taught to do in their youth. They would, on many occurrences, be the safer for having that skill, and on many more the happier, as freer from painful apprehensions of danger, to say nothing of the enjoyment in so delightful and wholesome an exercise. Soldiers particularly should, methinks, all be taught to swim; it might be of frequent use, either in surprising an enemy, or saving themselves. And, if I had now boys to educate, I should prefer those schools (other things being equal) where an opportunity was afforded for acquiring so advantageous an art, which, once learned, is never forgotten.

[TO M. DUBOURG.]

BATHING AND SWIMMING.*

I AM apprehensive that I shall not be able to find leisure for making all the disquisitions and experiments which would be desirable on this subject. I must, therefore, content myself with a few remarks.

The specific gravity of some human bodies, in comparison to that of water, has been examined by Mr. Robinson, in the Philosophical Transactions, volume 50, page 30, for the year 1757. He asserts that fat persons, with small bones, float most easily upon the water.

The diving-bell is accurately described in the Transactions.

When I was a boy, I made two oval palettes, each about ten inches long, and six broad, with a hole for the thumb, in order to retain it fast in the palm of my hand. They much resembled a painter's palettes. In swimming, I pushed the edges of these forward, and I struck the water with their flat surfaces as I drew them back. I remember I swam faster by means of these palettes, but they fatigued my wrists. I also fitted to the soles of my feet a kind of sandals; but I was not satisfied with them, because I observed that the stroke is partly given by the inside

---

* This, and the four following extracts of letters to M. Dubourg, are re-translated from the French edition of Dr. Franklin's works.

of the feet and the ankles, and not entirely with the soles of the feet.

We have here waistcoats for swimming, which are made of double sail-cloth, with small pieces of cork quilted in between them.

I know nothing of the *scaphandre* of M. de la Chapelle.

I know, by experience, that it is a great comfort to a swimmer, who has a considerable distance to go, to turn himself sometimes on his back, and to vary in other respects the means of procuring a progressive motion.

When he is seized with the cramp in the leg, the method of driving it away is to give to the parts affected a sudden, vigorous and violent shock ; which he may do in the air as he swims on his back.

During the great heats of summer there is no danger in bathing, however warm we may be, in rivers which have been thoroughly warmed by the sun. But to throw one's self into cold spring water, when the body has been heated by exercise in the sun, is an imprudence which may prove fatal. I once knew an instance of four young men, who, having worked at harvest in the heat of the day, with a view of refreshing themselves, plunged into a spring of cold water ; two died upon the spot, a third the next morning, and the fourth recovered with great difficulty. A copious draught of cold water, in similar circumstances, is frequently attended with the same effect in North America.

The exercise of swimming is one of the most healthy and agreeable in the world. After having swam for an hour or two in the evening, one sleeps coolly the whole night, even during the most ardent heat of summer. Perhaps, the pores being cleansed, the insensible perspiration increases, and occasions this coolness. It is certain that much swimming is the means of stopping a diarrhœa, and even of producing a constipation. With respect to those who do not know how to swim, or who are affected with a diarrhœa at a season which does not permit them to use that exercise, a warm bath, by cleansing and purifying the skin, is found very salutary, and often effects a radical cure. I speak from my own experience, frequently repeated, and that of others to whom I have recommended this.

You will not be displeased if I conclude these hasty remarks by informing you that, as the ordinary method of swimming is reduced to the act of rowing with the arms and legs, and is consequently a laborious and fatiguing operation when the space of water to be crossed is considerable, there is a method in which a

27

swimmer may pass to great distances with much facility, by means of a sail. This discovery I fortunately made by accident, and in the following manner.

When I was a boy I amused myself one day with flying a paper kite; and, approaching the bank of a pond, which was near a mile broad, I tied the string to a stake, and the kite ascended to a very considerable height above the pond, while I was swimming. In a little time, being desirous of amusing myself with my kite, and enjoying at the same time the pleasure of swimming, I returned; and, loosing from the stake the string with the little stick which was fastened to it, went again into the water, where I found that, lying on my back and holding the stick in my hands, I was drawn along the surface of the water in a very agreeable manner. Having then engaged another boy to carry my clothes round the pond, to a place which I pointed out to him on the other side, I began to cross the pond with my kite, which carried me quite over without the least fatigue, and with the greatest pleasure imaginable. I was only obliged occasionally to halt a little in my course, and resist its progress, when it appeared that, by following too quick, I lowered the kite too much; by doing which occasionally, I made it rise again. I have never since that time practised this singular mode of swimming, though I think it not impossible to cross in this manner from Dover to Calais. The packet-boat, however, is still preferable.

[TO THE SAME.]
ON THE FREE USE OF AIR.

LONDON, July 28, 1760.

I GREATLY approve the epithet which you give, in your letter of the 8th of June, to the new method of treating the small-pox, which you call the *tonic* or bracing method; I will take occasion, from it, to mention a practice to which I have accustomed myself. You know the cold bath has long been in vogue here as a tonic; but the shock of the cold water has always appeared to me, generally speaking, as too violent, and I have found it much more agreeable to my constitution to bathe in another element, — I mean cold air. With this view, I rise almost every morning, and sit in my chamber without any clothes whatever, half an hour or an hour, according to the season, either reading or writing. This practice is not in the least painful, but, on the contrary, agreeable; and, if I return to bed afterwards, before I dress myself, as sometimes happens, I make a supplement to my night's rest of one or two hours of the most pleasing sleep that can be imagined. I find no ill consequences whatever resulting from it, and that at least it does not injure my health, if it does not in fact contribute much to its preservation. I shall therefore call it for the future a *bracing* or *tonic* bath.

[TO THE SAME.]

ON THE CAUSES OF COLDS.

March 10, 1773.

I SHALL not attempt to explain why damp clothes occasion colds, rather than wet ones, because I doubt the fact; I imagine that neither the one nor the other contribute to this effect, and that the causes of colds are totally independent of wet, and even of cold. I propose writing a short paper on this subject, the first moment of leisure I have at my disposal. In the mean time I can only say, that, having some suspicions that the common notion, which attributes to cold the property of stopping the pores and obstructing perspiration, was ill-founded, I engaged a young physician, who is making some experiments with Sanctorius's balance, to estimate the different proportions of his perspiration, when remaining one hour quite naked, and another warmly clothed. He pursued the experiment in this alternate manner for eight hours successively, and found his perspiration almost double during those hours in which he was naked.

[TO THE ABBÉ SOULAVIE.*]

THEORY OF THE EARTH.

[Read in the American Philosophical Society, November 21, 1788.]

PASSY, September 22, 1788.

I RETURN the papers, with some corrections. I did not find coal mines under the calcareous rock in Derbyshire. I only

---

* Occasioned by his sending me some notes he had taken of what I had said to him in conversation on the Theory of the Earth. I wrote it to set him right in some points wherein he had mistaken my meaning. B. F.

remarked that at the lowest part of that rocky mountain which was in sight there were oyster-shells mixed in the stone; and, part of the high county of Derby being probably as much above the level of the sea as the coal mines of Whitehaven were below it, it seemed a proof that there had been a great *boulversement* in the surface of that island, some part of it having been depressed under the sea, and other parts, which had been under it, being raised above it. Such changes in the superficial parts of the globe seemed to me unlikely to happen, if the earth were solid to the centre. I therefore imagined that the internal parts might be a fluid more dense, and of greater specific gravity, than any of the solids we are acquainted with, which, therefore, might swim in or upon that fluid.

Thus the surface of the globe would be a shell, capable of being broken and disordered by the violent movements of the fluid on which it rested. And, as air has been compressed by art so as to be twice as dense as water, in which case, if such air and water could be contained in a strong glass vessel, the air would be seen to take the lowest place, and the water to float above and upon it; and as we know not yet the degree of density to which air may be compressed, and M. Amontons calculated that, its density increasing as it approached the centre, in the same proportion as above the surface, it would at the depth of ―――― leagues be heavier than gold; possibly the dense fluid occupying the internal parts of the globe might be air compressed. And as the force of expansion in dense air when heated is in proportion to its density, this central air might afford another agent to move the surface, as well as be of use in keeping alive the subterraneous fires; though, as you observe, the sudden rarefaction of water coming into contact without those fires, may also be an agent sufficiently strong for that purpose, when acting between the incumbent earth and the fluid on which it rests.

If one might indulge imagination in supposing how such a globe was formed, I should conceive that, all the elements in separate particles being originally mixed in confusion, and occupying a great space, they would (as soon as the Almighty fiat ordained gravity, or the mutual attraction of certain parts, and the mutual repulsion of others, to exist) all move to their common centre: that the air, being a fluid whose parts repel each other, though drawn to the common centre by their gravity, would be densest towards the centre, and rarer as more remote; consequently all matters lighter than the central parts of that air, and immersed in it, would recede from the centre, and rise till they arrived at that region of the air which was of the same specific gravity with themselves, where they would rest; while other matter, mixed with the lighter air, would descend, and the two meeting would form the shell of the first earth, leaving the upper atmosphere nearly clear.

The original movement of the parts towards their common centre would naturally form a whirl there; which would continue upon the turning of the new-formed globe upon its axis, and the greatest diameter of the shell would be in its equator. If by any accident afterwards the axis should be changed, the dense internal fluid, by altering its form, must burst the shell, and throw all its substance into the confusion in which we find it.

I will not trouble you at present with my fancies concerning the manner of forming the rest of our system.   Superior beings smile at our theories, and at our presumption in making them. I will just mention that your observations on the ferruginous nature of the lava which is thrown out from the depths of our volcanoes gave me great pleasure.   It has long been a supposition of mine, that the iron contained in the surface of the globe has made it capable of becoming, as it is, a great magnet; that the fluid of magnetism perhaps exists in all space; so that there is a magnetical north and south of the universe, as well as of this globe, and that if it were possible for a man to fly from star to star, he might govern his course by the compass; that it was by the power of this general magnetism this globe became a particular magnet.   In soft or hot iron the fluid of magnetism is naturally diffused equally; when within the influence of the magnet it is drawn to one end of the iron, made denser there, and rarer at the other.   While the iron continues soft and hot, it is only a temporary magnet; if it cools or grows hard in that situation, it becomes a permanent one, the magnetic fluid not easily resuming its equilibrium.   Perhaps it may be owing to the permanent magnetism of this globe, which it had not at first, that its axis is at present kept parallel to itself, and not liable to the changes it formerly suffered, which occasioned the rupture of its shell, the submersions and emersions of its lands, and the confusion of its seasons.   The present polar and equatorial diameters differing from each other near ten leagues, it is easy to conceive, in case some power should shift the axis gradually, and place it in the present equator, and make the new equator pass through the present poles, what a sinking of the waters would happen in the present equatorial regions, and what a rising in the present polar regions; so that vast tracts would be discovered that now are under water, and others covered that are now dry, the water rising and sinking in the different extremes near five leagues. Such an operation as this possibly occasioned much of Europe, and among the rest this mountain of Passy on which I live, — and which is composed of limestone, rock and sea-shells, — to be abandoned by the sea, and to change its ancient climate, which seems to have been a hot one.

The globe being now become a perfect magnet, we are, perhaps, safe from any change of its axis. But we are still subject to the accidents on the surface which are occasioned by a wave in the internal ponderous fluid; and such a wave is producible by the sudden violent explosion you mention, happening from the junction of water and fire under the earth, which not only lifts the incumbent earth that is over the explosion, but, impressing with the same force the fluid under it, creates a wave, that may run a thousand leagues, lifting, and thereby shaking successively, all the countries under which it passes.

I know not whether I have expressed myself so clearly as not to get out of your sight in these reveries. If they occasion any new inquiries, and produce a better hypothesis, they will not be quite useless. You see I have given a loose to imagination; but I approve much more your method of philosophizing, which proceeds upon actual observation, makes a collection of facts, and concludes no further than those facts will warrant. In my present circumstances that mode of studying the nature of the globe is out of my power, and therefore I have permitted myself to wander a little in the wilds of fancy.

P. S. I have heard that chemists can by their art decompose stone and wood, extracting a considerable quantity of water from the one, and air from the other. It seems natural to conclude from this that water and air were ingredients in their original composition; for men cannot make new matter of any kind. In the same manner may we not suppose that when we consume combustibles of all kinds, and produce heat or light, we do not create that heat or light, but only decompose a substance which received it originally as a part of its composition? Heat may be thus considered as originally in a fluid state; but, attracted by organized bodies in their growth, becomes a part of the solid. Besides this, I can conceive that in the first assemblage of the articles of which this earth is composed each brought its portion of the loose heat that had been connected with it, and the whole, when pressed together, produced the internal fire that still subsists.

[TO DAVID RITTENHOUSE.]

NEW AND CURIOUS THEORY OF LIGHT AND HEAT.

[Read in the American Philosophical Society, November 20, 1788.]

UNIVERSAL space, as far as we know of it, seems to be filled with a subtle fluid, whose motion or vibration is called light.

This fluid may possibly be the same with that which, being attracted by and entering into other more solid matter, dilates the substance by separating the constituent particles, and so rendering some solids fluid, and maintaining the fluidity of others; of which fluid when our bodies are totally deprived, they are said to be frozen; when they have a proper quantity, they are in health, and fit to perform all their functions, — it is then called natural heat; when too much, it is called fever; and when forced into the body in too great a quantity from without, it gives pain, by separating and destroying the flesh, and is then called burning, and the fluid so entering and acting is called fire.

While organized bodies, animal or vegetable, are augmenting in growth, or are supplying their continual waste, is not this done by attracting and consolidating this fluid called fire, so as to form of it a part of their substance? And is it not a separation of the parts of such substance, which, dissolving its solid state, sets that subtle fluid at liberty, when it again makes its appearance as fire?

For the power of man relative to matter seems limited to the separating or mixing the various kinds of it, or changing its form and appearance by different compositions of it; but does not extend to the making or creating new matter, or annihilating the old. Thus, if fire be an original element or kind of matter, its quantity is fixed and permanent in the universe. We cannot destroy any part of it, or make addition to it; we can only separate it from that which confines it, and so set it at liberty; as when we put wood in a situation to be burnt, or transfer it from one solid to another; as when we make lime by burning stone, a part of the fire dislodged in the fuel being left in the stone. May not this fluid, when at liberty, be capable of penetrating and entering into all bodies, organized or not, quitting easily in totality those not organized, and quitting easily in part those which are, — the part assumed and fixed remaining till the body is dissolved?

Is it not this fluid which keeps asunder the particles of air, permitting them to approach, or separating them more, in proportion as its quantity is diminished or augmented?

Is it not the greater gravity of the particles of air which forces the particles of this fluid to mount with the matters to which it is attached, as smoke or vapor?

Does it not seem to have a greater affinity with water, since it will quit a solid to unite with that fluid, and go off with it in vapor, leaving the solid cold to the touch, and the degree measurable by the thermometer?

The vapor rises attached to this fluid, but at a certain height they separate, and the vapor descends in rain, retaining but little of it in snow, or hail less. What becomes of that fluid? Does it rise above our atmosphere, and mix with the universal mass of the same kind?

Or does a spherical stratum of it, denser, as less mixed with air, attracted by this globe, and repelled or pushed up only to a certain height from its surface by the greater weight of air, remain there surrounding the globe, and proceeding with it round the sun?

In such case, as there may be a continuity or communication of this fluid through the air quite down to the earth, is it not by the vibrations given to it by the sun that light appears to us? And may it not be that every one of the infinitely small vibrations, striking common matter with a certain force, enters its substance, is held there by attraction, and augmented by succeeding vibrations, till the matter has received as much as their force can drive into it?

Is it not thus that the surface of this globe is continually heated by such repeated vibrations in the day, and cooled by the escape of the heat when those vibrations are discontinued in the night, or intercepted and reflected by clouds?

Is it not thus that fire is amassed, and makes the greatest part of the substance of combustible bodies?

Perhaps, when this globe was first formed, and its original particles took their place at certain distances from the centre, in proportion to their greater or less gravity, the fluid fire, attracted towards that centre, might in great part be obliged, as lightest, to take place above the rest, and thus form the sphere of fire above supposed, which would afterwards be continually diminishing by the substance it afforded to organized bodies, and the quantity restored to it again by the burning or other separating of the parts of those bodies.

Is not the natural heat of animals thus produced, by separating in digestion the parts of food, and setting their fire at liberty?

Is it not this sphere of fire which kindles the wandering globes that sometimes pass through it in our course round the

sun, have their surface kindled by it, and burst when their included air is greatly rarefied by the heat on their burning surfaces?

May it not have been from such considerations that the
ancient philosophers supposed a sphere of fire to exist above the
air of our atmosphere?

[TO M. DUBOURG.]

ON THE PREVAILING DOCTRINES OF LIFE AND DEATH.

YOUR observations on the causes of death, and the experiments which you propose for recalling to life those who appear
to be killed by lightning, demonstrate equally your sagacity and
your humanity. It appears that the doctrines of life and death
in general are yet but little understood.

A toad buried in sand will live, it is said, till the sand
becomes petrified; and then, being enclosed in the stone, it may
still live for we know not how many ages. The facts which are
cited in support of this opinion are too numerous, and too circumstantial, not to deserve a certain degree of credit. As we
are accustomed to see all the animals with which we are
acquainted eat and drink, it appears to us difficult to conceive
how a toad can be supported in such a dungeon; but, if we
reflect that the necessity of nourishment which animals experience in their ordinary state proceeds from the continual waste
of their substance by perspiration, it will appear less incredible
that some animals in a torpid state, perspiring less because they
use no exercise, should have less need of aliment; and that
others, which are covered with scales or shells, which stop perspiration, such as land and sea turtles, serpents, and some species of fish, should be able to subsist a considerable time without
any nourishment whatever.

A plant, with its flowers, fades and dies immediately, if
exposed to the air without having its root immersed in a humid
soil, from which it may draw a sufficient quantity of moisture
to supply that which exhales from its substance and is carried
off continually by the air. Perhaps, however, if it were buried
in quicksilver, it might preserve for a considerable space of
time its vegetable life, its smell and color. If this be the case,
it might prove a commodious method of transporting from distant countries those delicate plants which are unable to sustain

the inclemency of the weather at sea, and which require partic ular care and attention.

I have seen an instance of common flies preserved in a manner somewhat similar. They had been drowned in Madeira wine, apparently about the time when it was bottled in Virginia, to be sent hither (to London). At the opening of one of the bottles, at the house of a friend where I then was, three drowned flies fell into the first glass that was filled. Having heard it remarked that drowned flies were capable of being revived by the rays of the sun, I proposed making the experiment upon these: they were therefore exposed to the sun upon a sieve which had been employed to strain them out of the wine. In less than three hours, two of them began by degrees to recover life. They commenced by some convulsive motions of the thighs, and at length they raised themselves upon their legs, wiped their eyes with their fore-feet, beat and brushed their wings with their hind-feet, and soon after began to fly, finding themselves in Old England without knowing how they came thither. The third continued lifeless till sunset, when, losing all hopes of him, he was thrown away.

I wish it were possible, from this instance, to invent a method of embalming drowned persons in such a manner that they may be recalled to life at any period, however distant; for, having a very ardent desire to see and observe the state of America an hundred years hence, I should prefer to any ordinary death the being immersed in a cask of Madeira wine, with a few friends, till that time, to be then recalled to life by the solar warmth of my dear country! But since, in all probability, we live in an age too early, and too near the infancy of science, to hope to see such an art brought in our time to its perfection, I must for the present content myself with the treat which you are so kind as to promise me, of the resurrection of a fowl or a turkey-cock.

[TO JOHN INGENHOUSZ.]

ON SMOKY CHIMNEYS.*

AT SEA, August 1785.

THOSE who would be acquainted with this subject should begin by considering on what principle smoke ascends in any

* This paper has been somewhat abridged from the original, as have others in this collection under the head of Philosophical.

chimney. At first many are apt to think that smoke is in its
nature and of itself specifically lighter than air, and rises in it
for the same reason that cork rises in water. These see no case
why smoke should not rise in the chimney, though the room be
ever so close. Others think there is a power in chimneys to
draw up the smoke, and that there are different forms of chimneys which afford more or less of this power. These amuse
themselves with searching for the best form. The equal dimensions of a funnel in its whole length is not thought artificial
enough, and it is made, for fancied reasons, sometimes tapering
and narrowing from below upwards, and sometimes the contrary, &c.

A simple experiment or two may serve to give more correct
ideas. Having lit a pipe of tobacco, plunge the stem to the
bottom of a decanter half filled with cold water; then, putting
a rag over the bowl, blow through it and make the smoke
descend in the stem of the pipe, from the end of which it will
rise in bubbles through the water; and, being thus cooled, will
not afterwards rise to go out through the neck of the decanter,
but remain spreading itself, and resting on the surface of the
water. This shows that smoke is really heavier than air, and
that it is carried upwards only when attached to, or acted upon,
by air that is heated, and thereby rarefied and rendered specifically lighter than the air in its neighborhood.

Smoke being rarely seen but in company with heated air,
and its upward motion being visible, though that of the rarefied
air that drives it is not so, has naturally given rise to the error.

I need not explain to you, my learned friend, what is meant
by rarefied air; but, if you make the public use you propose of
this letter, it may fall into the hands of some who are unacquainted with the term and with the thing. These then may
be told, that air is a fluid which has weight as well as others,
though about eight hundred times lighter than water. That
heat makes the particles of air recede from each other and take
up more space, so that the same weight of air heated will have
more bulk than equal weights of cold air which may surround
it, and in that case must rise, being forced upwards by such
colder and heavier air, which presses to get under it and take
its place. That air is so rarefied or expanded by heat may be
proved to their comprehension, by a lank blown bladder, which,
laid before a fire, will soon swell, grow tight, and burst.

What is it, then, which makes a *smoky chimney*, — that is, a
chimney which, instead of conveying up all the smoke, discharges a part of it into the room, offending the eyes and damaging the furniture?

The causes of this effect, which have fallen under my observation, amount to *nine*, differing from each other, and, therefore requiring different remedies.

1. *Smoky chimneys in a new house are such, frequently, from mere want of air.*

Remedies. — When you find, on trial, that opening the door or a window enables the chimney to carry up all the smoke, you may be sure that want of air *from without* was the cause of its smoking. I say *from without*, to guard you against a common mistake of those who may tell you the room is large, contains abundance of air, sufficient to supply any chimney, and therefore it cannot be that the chimney wants air. These reasoners are ignorant that the largeness of a room, if tight, is in this case of small importance, since it cannot part with a chimney full of air without occasioning so much vacuum; which it requires a great force to effect, and could not be borne if effected.

2. A second cause of the smoking of chimneys is *their openings in the room being too large;* that is, too wide, too high, or both. Architects in general have no other ideas of proportion in the opening of a chimney than what relate to symmetry and beauty respecting the dimensions of the room; while its true proportion, respecting its function and utility, depends on quite other principles; and they might as properly proportion the step in a staircase to the height of the story, instead of the natural elevation of men's legs in mounting. The proportion, then, to be regarded is, what relates to the height of the funnel.

Remedy. — As different circumstances frequently mix themselves in these matters, it is difficult to give precise dimensions for the openings of all chimneys. Our fathers made them generally much too large: we have lessened them; but they are often still of greater dimension than they should be, the human eye not being easily reconciled to sudden and great changes. If you suspect that your chimney smokes from the too great dimension of its opening, contract it by placing movable boards so as to lower and narrow it gradually, till you find the smoke no longer issues into the room. The proportion so found will be that which is proper for that chimney, and you may employ the bricklayer or mason to reduce it accordingly. However, as, in building new houses, something must be sometimes hazarded, I would make the openings in my lower rooms about thirty inches square and eighteen deep, and those in the upper only eighteen inches square and not quite so deep; the intermediate ones diminishing in proportion as the height of funnel diminished. In the larger opening, billets of two feet long, or half the common length of cord-wood, may be burnt conveniently; and for the smaller such wood may be sawed into thirds. Where coals are the fuel, the grates will be proportioned to the openings. The same depth is nearly necessary to all, the funnels being all made of a size proper to admit a chimney-sweeper. If, in large and elegant rooms, custom or fancy should require the appearance of a large chimney, it may be formed of extensive marginal decorations, in marble, &c. In time, perhaps, that which is fittest in the nature of things may come to be thought handsomest. But at present, when men and women in different countries show themselves dissatisfied with the forms God has given to their heads, waists and feet, and pretend to shape them more perfectly, it is hardly to be expected that they will be content always with the best form of a chimney. And there are some, I know, so bigoted to the fancy of a large noble opening, that rather than change it they would submit to have damaged furniture, sore eyes, and skins almost smoked to bacon.

3. Another cause of smoky chimneys is *too short a funnel.* This happens necessarily in some cases, as where a chimney is required in a low building; for, if the funnel be raised high above the roof, in order to strengthen its draft, it is then in danger of being blown down, and crushing the roof in its fall.

Remedies. — Contract the opening of the chimney, so as to oblige all the entering air to pass through or very near the fire; whereby it will be more heated and rarefied, the funnel itself be more warmed, and its contents have more of what may be called the force of levity, so as to rise strongly and maintain a good draft at the opening.

Or you may in some cases, to advantage, build additional stories over the low building, which will support a high funnel.

4. Another very common cause of the smoking of chimneys is *their overpowering one another.* For instance, if there be two chimneys in one large room, and you make fires in both of them, the doors and windows close shut, you will find that the greater and stronger fire shall overpower the weaker, and draw air down its funnel to supply its own demand; which air, descending in the weaker funnel, will drive down its smoke, and force it into the room. If, instead of being in one room, the two chimneys are in two different rooms communicating by a door, the case is the same whenever that door is open. In a very tight house, I have known a kitchen chimney on the lowest floor, when it had a great fire in it, overpower any other chimney in the house, and draw air and smoke into its room as often as the door was opened communicating with the staircase.

28

Remedy. — Take care that every room has the means of supplying itself from without with the air its chimney may require, so that no one of them may be obliged to borrow from another, nor under the necessity of lending. A variety of these means have been already described.

5. Another cause of smoking is *when the tops of chimneys are commanded by higher buildings, or by a hill*, so that the wind blowing over such eminences falls like water over a dam, sometimes almost perpendicularly on the tops of the chimneys that lie in its way, and beats down the smoke contained in them.

Remedy. — That commonly applied to this case is a turn-cap made of tin or plate iron, covering the chimney above and on three sides, open on one side, turning on a spindle, and which, being guided or governed by a vane, always presents its back to the current. This, I believe, may be generally effectual, though not certain, as there may be cases in which it will not succeed. Raising your funnels, if practicable, so as their tops may be higher, or at least equal with the commanding eminence, is more to be depended on. But the turning-cap, being easier and cheaper, should first be tried.

6. There is another case of command, the reverse of that last mentioned. It is where the commanding eminence is further from the wind than the chimney commanded.

Remedy. — I know of but one, which is to raise such funnel higher than the roof, supporting it, if necessary, by iron bars. For a turn-cap in this case has no effect, the dammed up air pressing down through it, in whatever position the wind may have placed its opening.

7. Chimneys, otherwise drawing well, are sometimes made to smoke by *the improper and inconvenient situation of a door*. The *remedies* are obvious and easy. Either put an intervening screen from the wall round great part of the fireplace; or, which is perhaps preferable, shift the hinges of your door, so as it may open the other way, and when open throw the air along the other wall.

8. A room that has no fire in its chimney is sometimes filled with *smoke, which is received at the top of its funnel, and descends into the room.* The *remedy* is to have a sliding plate that will shut perfectly the offending funnel.

9. Chimneys which generally draw well do nevertheless sometimes give smoke into the rooms, *it being driven down by strong winds passing over the tops of their funnels*, though not

descending from any commanding eminence. This case is most frequent where the funnel is short, and the opening turned from the wind. It is the more grievous when it happens to be a cold wind that produces the effect, because, when you most want your fire, you are sometimes obliged to extinguish it.

Remedies. — In some places, particularly in Venice, where they have not stacks of chimneys, but single flues, the custom is, to open or widen the top of the flue rounding in the true form of a funnel; which some think may prevent the effect just mentioned, for that the wind blowing over one of the edges into the funnel may be slanted out again on the other side by its form. I have had no experience of this; but I have lived in a windy country, where the contrary is practised, the tops of the flues being *narrowed* inwards, so as to form a slit for the issue of the smoke, long as the breadth of the funnel, and only four inches wide. This seems to have been contrived on a supposition that the entry of the wind would thereby be obstructed, and, perhaps, it might have been imagined that the whole force of the rising warm air being condensed, as it were, in the narrow opening, would thereby be strengthened, so as to overcome the resistance of the wind. This, however, did not always succeed; for when the wind was at north-east and blew fresh the smoke was forced down by fits into the room I commonly sat in, so as to oblige me to shift the fire into another. The position of the slit in this funnel was, indeed, north-east and south-west. Perhaps, if it had lain across the wind, the effect might have been different. But on this I can give no certainty. It seems a matter proper to be referred to experiment. Possibly a turn-cap might have been serviceable, but it was not tried.

Chimneys have not been long in use in England. I formerly saw a book printed in the time of Queen Elizabeth, which remarked the then modern improvements of living, and mentioned among others the convenience of chimneys. " Our forefathers," said the author, " had no chimneys. There was in each dwelling-house only one place for a fire, and the smoke went out through a hole in the roof; but now there is scarce a gentleman's house in England that has not at least one chimney in it." When there was but one chimney, its top might then be opened as a funnel; and, perhaps, borrowing the form from the Venetians, it was then the flue of a chimney got that name.

Such is now the growth of luxury, that in both England and France we must have a chimney for every room; and in some houses every possessor of a chamber, and almost every servant, will have a fire; so that, the flues being necessarily built in stacks, the opening of each as a funnel is impracticable. This change of manners soon consumed the fire-wood of England, and will soon render fuel extremely scarce and dear in France, if the use of coals be not introduced in the latter kingdom, as it has been in the former, where it at first met with opposition; for there is extant in the records of one of Queen Elizabeth's Parliaments a motion made by a member, reciting, "That many dyers, brewers, smiths, and other artificers of London, had, of late, taken to the use of pit-coal for their fires, instead of wood, which filled the air with noxious vapors and smoke, very prejudicial to the health, particularly of persons coming out of the country; and therefore moving that a law might pass to prohibit the use of such fuel (at least during the session of Parliament) by those artificers."

It seems it was not then commonly used in private houses. Its supposed unwholesomeness was an objection. Luckily, the inhabitants of London have got over that objection, and now think it rather contributes to render their air salubrious, as they have had no general pestilential disorder since the general use of coals, when, before it, such were frequent. Paris still burns wood at an enormous expense, continually augmenting; the inhabitants having still that prejudice to overcome. In Germany you are happy in the use of stoves, which save fuel wonderfully: your people are very ingenious in the management of fire, but they may still learn something in that art from the Chinese, whose country, being greatly populous and fully cultivated, has little room left for the growth of wood, and, having not much other fuel that is good, have been forced upon many inventions, during a course of ages, for making a little fire go as far as possible.

I have thus gone through all the common causes of the smoking of chimneys that I can at present recollect as having fallen under my observation; communicating the remedies that I have known successfully used for the different cases, together with the principles on which both the disease and the remedy depend, and confessing my ignorance wherever I have been sensible of it. You will do well, if you publish, as you propose, this letter, to add in notes, or, as you please, such observations as may have occurred to your attentive mind; and, if other philosophers will do the same, this part of science, though humble, yet of great utility, may in time be perfected. For many years past, I have rarely met with a case of a smoky chimney which has not been solvable on these principles, and cured by these remedies, where people have been willing to apply them;

which is indeed not always the case, for many have prejudices in favor of the nostrums of pretending chimney doctors and fumists, and some have conceits and fancies of their own, which they rather choose to try than to lengthen a funnel, alter the size of an opening, or admit air into a room, however necessary; for some are as much afraid of fresh air as persons in the hydrophobia are of fresh water.

I myself had formerly this prejudice, this *aërophobia*, as I now account it; and, dreading the supposed dangerous effects of cool air, I considered it as an enemy, and closed with extreme care every crevice in the rooms I inhabited. Experience has convinced me of my error. I now look upon fresh air as a friend; I even sleep with an open window. I am persuaded that no common air from without is so unwholesome as the air within a close room that has been often breathed and not changed. Moist air, too, which formerly I thought pernicious, gives me now no apprehensions; for, considering that no dampness of air applied to the outside of my skin can be equal to what is applied to and touches it within, my whole body being full of moisture, and finding that I can lie two hours in a bath twice a week, covered with water, which certainly is much damper than any air can be, and this for years together, without catching cold, or being in any other manner disordered by it, I no longer dread mere moisture, either in air or in sheets or shirts; and I find it of importance to the happiness of life, the being freed from vain terrors, especially of objects that we are every day exposed inevitably to meet with.

You physicians have of late happily discovered, after a contrary opinion had prevailed some ages, that fresh and cool air does good to persons in the small-pox and other fevers. It is to be hoped that in another century or two we may all find out that it is not bad even for people in health. And, as to moist air, here I am at this present writing in a ship with above forty persons, who have had no other but moist air to breathe for six weeks past; everything we touch is damp, and nothing dries, yet we are all as healthy as we should be on the mountains of Switzerland, whose inhabitants are not more so than those of Bermuda or St. Helena, islands on whose rocks the waves are dashed into millions of particles, which fill the air with damp, but produce no diseases, the moisture being pure, unmixed with the poisonous vapors arising from putrid marshes and stagnant pools, in which many insects die and corrupt the water. These places only, in my opinion, — which, however, I submit to yours, — afford unwholesome air; and, that it is not the mere water contained in damp air, but the volatile particles of corrupted animal matter mixed with that water, which renders such air pernicious to those who breathe it.   And I imagine it a cause of the same kind that renders the air in close rooms, where the perspirable matter is breathed over and over again by a number of assembled people, so hurtful to health.   After being in such a situation, many find themselves affected by that *febricula* which the English alone call *a cold*, and, perhaps from the name, imagine that they caught the malady by *going out* of the room, when it was in fact by being in it.

You begin to think that I wander from my subject, and go out of my depth.   So I return again to my chimneys.

We have of late many lectures in experimental philosophy. I have wished that some of them would study this branch of that science, and give experiments in it as a part of their lectures.   The addition to their present apparatus need not be very expensive.   A number of little representations of rooms, composed each of five panes of sash-glass, framed in wood at the corners, with proportionable doors, and movable glass chimneys, with openings of different sizes, and different lengths of funnel, and some of the rooms so contrived as to communicate on occasion with others, so as to form different combinations, and exemplify different cases; with quantities of green wax taper cut into pieces of an inch and half, sixteen of which, stuck together in a square, and lit, would make a strong fire for a little glass chimney, and, blown out, would continue to burn, and give smoke as long as desired.   With such an apparatus, all the operations of smoke and rarefied air in rooms and chimneys might be seen through their transparent sides; and the effect of wind on chimneys, commanded or otherwise, might be shown by letting the entering air blow upon them through an opened window of the lecturer's chamber, where it would be constant while he kept a good fire in his chimney.   By the help of such lectures our fumists would become better instructed.   At present, they have generally but one remedy, which perhaps they have known effectual in some one case of smoky chimneys; and they apply that indiscriminately to all the other causes, without success, — but not without expense to their employers.

With all the science, however, that a man shall suppose himself possessed of in this article, he may sometimes meet with cases that may puzzle him.   I once lodged in a house at London, which, in a little room, had a single chimney and funnel. The opening was very small, yet it did not keep in the smoke, and all attempts to have a fire in this room were fruitless.   I could not imagine the reason, till at length observing that the chamber over it, which had no fireplace in it, was always filled with smoke when a fire was kindled below, and that the smoke came through the cracks and crevices of the wainscot, I had the wainscot taken down, and discovered that the funnel which went up behind it had a crack many feet in length, and wide enough to admit my arm, — a breach very dangerous with regard to fire, and occasioned probably by an apparent irregular settling of one side of the house. The air, entering this breach freely, destroyed the drawing force of the funnel. The remedy would have been filling up the breach, or rather rebuilding the funnel; but the landlord rather chose to stop up the chimney.

Another puzzling case I met with at a friend's country-house near London. His best room had a chimney in which, he told me, he never could have a fire, for all the smoke came out into the room. I flattered myself I could easily find the cause, and prescribe the cure. I had a fire made there, and found it as he said. I opened the door, and perceived it was not want of air. I made a temporary contraction of the opening of the chimney, and found that it was not its being too large that caused the smoke to issue. I went out and looked up at the top of the chimney; its funnel was joined in the same stack with others, some of them shorter, that drew very well, and I saw nothing to prevent its doing the same. In fine, after every other examination I could think of, I was obliged to own the insufficiency of my skill. But my friend, who made no pretensions to such kind of knowledge, afterwards discovered the cause himself. He got to the top of the funnel by a ladder, and, looking down, found it filled with twigs and straw cemented by earth, and lined with feathers. It seems the house, after being built, had stood empty some years before he occupied it; and he concluded that some large birds had taken advantage of its retired situation to make their nest there. The rubbish, considerable in quantity, being removed, and the funnel cleared, the chimney drew well and gave satisfaction.

In general, smoke is a very tractable thing, easily governed and directed, when one knows the principles, and is well informed of the circumstances. You know I made it *descend* in my Pennsylvania stove.

Much more of the prosperity of a winter country depends on the plenty and cheapness of fuel than is generally imagined. In travelling, I have observed that in those parts where the inhabitants can have neither wood, nor coal, nor turf, but at excessive prices, the working people live in miserable hovels, are ragged, and have nothing comfortable about them. But when fuel is cheap (or where they have the art of managing it to advantage) they are well furnished with necessaries, and have decent habitations. The obvious reason is, that the working hours of such people are the profitable hours, and they who cannot afford sufficient fuel have fewer such hours in the twenty-four than those who have it cheap and plenty ; for much of the domestic work of poor women, — such as spinning, sewing, knitting, — and of the men in those manufactures that require little bodily exercise, cannot well be performed where the fingers are numbed with cold ; those people, therefore, in cold weather, are induced to go to bed sooner, and lie longer in a morning, than they would do if they could have good fires or warm stoves to sit by ; and their hours of work are not sufficient to produce the means of comfortable subsistence. Those public works, therefore, such as roads, canals, &c., by which fuel may be brought cheap into such countries from distant places, are of great utility ; and those who promote them may be reckoned among the benefactors of mankind.

I have great pleasure in having thus complied with your request, and in the reflection that the friendship you honor me with, and in which I have ever been so happy, has continued so many years without the smallest interruption. Our distance from each other is now augmented, and nature must soon put an end to the possibility of my continuing our correspondence ; but, if consciousness and memory remain in a future state, my esteem and respect for you, my dear friend, will be everlasting.

MORAL AND MISCELLANEOUS.

ON SEARCHING AFTER HIDDEN TREASURES.*

THERE are amongst us great numbers of honest artificers and laboring people, who, fed with a vain hope of growing suddenly rich, neglect their business almost to the ruining of themselves and families, and voluntarily endure abundance of fatigue in a fruitless search after imaginary hidden treasures. They wander through the woods and bushes by day, to discover the marks and signs; at midnight they repair to those hopeful spots with spades and pickaxes; full of expectation, they labor violently, trembling at the same time in every joint through fear of certain malicious demons, who are said to haunt and guard the places. At length, a mighty hole is dug, and perhaps several cart-loads of earth thrown out; but, alas, no keg or iron pot is found! no seaman's chest, ornamented with Spanish pistoles or weighty pieces of eight! Then they conclude that, through some mistake in the procedure, some rash word spoke, or some rule of art neglected, the guardian spirit had power to sink it deeper into the earth, and convey it out of his reach. Yet when a man is once thus infatuated, he is so far from being discouraged by ill-success, that he is rather animated to double his industry, and will try again and again, in a hundred different places, in hopes at last of meeting with some lucky hit, that shall at once sufficiently reward them for all their expense of time and labor.

This odd humor of digging for money, through a belief that much has been hid by pirates formerly frequenting the river, has for several years been mighty prevalent among us; insomuch that you can hardly walk half a mile out of the town on any

---

* This paper is from a series of essays entitled "The Busy Body," of which Franklin gives some account in his Autobiography. They are mostly in imitation of the *Spectator*, and were written when he was about twenty-three years of age. They are, for the most part, such "unconsidered trifles" as he must have taken little pride in preserving.

side, without observing several pits dug with that design, and
perhaps some lately opened.   Men otherwise of very good sense
have been drawn into this practice through an overrunning desire of hidden wealth, and an easy credulity of what they so
earnestly wished might be true ; while the rational and almost
certain methods of acquiring riches by industry and frugality
are neglected or forgotten.   There seems to be some peculiar
charm in the conceit of finding money, and, if the sands of the
Schuylkill were so much mined with small grains of gold that a
man might in a day's time, with care and application, get together to the value of half a crown, I make no question but we
should find several people employed there that can with ease
earn five shillings a day at their proper trades.

Many are the idle stories told of the private success of some
people, by which others are encouraged to proceed ; and the
astrologers, with whom the country swarms at this time, are
either in the belief of these things themselves, or find their
advantage in persuading others to believe them ; for they are
often consulted about the critical times for digging, the methods
of laying the spirit, and the like whimseys, which renders them
very necessary to, and very much caressed by, the poor, deluded
money-hunters.

There is certainly something very bewitching in the pursuit
after mines of gold and silver, and other valuable metals, and
many have been ruined by it.   A sea-captain of my acquaintance
used to blame the English for envying Spain their mines of silver, and too much despising and overlooking the advantages of
their own industry and manufactures.   "For my part," says he,
"I esteem the banks of Newfoundland to be a more valuable
possession than the mountains of Potosi ; and, when I have
been there on the fishing account, I have looked upon every cod
pulled up into the vessel as a certain quantity of silver ore,
which required only carrying to the next Spanish port to be
coined into pieces of eight; not to mention the national profit
of fitting out and employing such a number of ships and seamen."

Let honest Peter Buckram, who has long without success
been a searcher after hidden money, reflect on this, and be re-
claimed from this unaccountable folly ; let him consider that
every stitch he takes when he is on his shop-board is picking up
a part of a grain of gold, that will in a few days' time amount
to a pistole ; and let Faber think the same of every nail he
drives, or every stroke with his plane ; such thoughts may make
them industrious, and of consequence in time they may be

wealthy. But how absurd it is to neglect a certain profit for such a ridiculous whimsey; to spend whole days at the George tavern in company with an idle pretender to astrology, contriving schemes to discover what was never hidden, and forgetting how carelessly business is managed at home in their absence: to leave their wives and a warm bed at midnight (no matter if rain, hail, snow, or blow a hurricane, provided that be the critical hour) and fatigue themselves with the violent exercise of digging for what they shall never find, and perhaps getting a cold that may cost their lives, or at least disordering themselves so as to be fit for no business besides for some days after! Surely this is nothing less than the most egregious folly and madness.

I shall conclude with the words of my discreet friend, Agricola, of Chester county, when he gave his son a good plantation: "My son," says he, "I give thee now a valuable parcel of land; I assure thee I have found a considerable quantity of gold by digging there; thee mayest do the same; but thee must carefully observe this, — never to dig more than plough deep."

ADVANTAGES OF VERACITY.

Veritas luce clarior.

A FRIEND of mine was the other day cheapening some trifles at a shopkeeper's, and after a few words they agreed on a price. At the tying up of the parcels he had purchased, the mistress of the shop told him that people were growing very hard, for she actually lost by everything she sold. How, then, is it possible, said my friend, that you can keep on your business. Indeed, sir, answered she, I must of necessity shut my doors, had I not a very great trade. The reason, said my friend (with a sneer), is admirable.

There are a great many retailers who falsely imagine that being *historical* (the modern phrase for lying) is much for their advantage; and some of them have a saying, *that it is a pity lying is a sin, it is so useful in trade;* though, if they would examine into the reason why a number of shopkeepers raise considerable estates, while others who have set out with better fortunes have become bankrupts, they would find that the former made up with truth, diligence and probity, what they were deficient of in stock; while the latter have been guilty of imposing on such customers as they found had no skill in the quality of their goods.

The former character raises a credit which supplies the want of fortune, and their fair dealing brings them customers; whereas none will return to buy of him by whom he has been once imposed upon. If people in trade would judge rightly, we might buy blindfolded, and they would save both to themselves and customers the unpleasantness of *haggling*.

Though there are numbers of shopkeepers who scorn the mean vice of lying, and whose word may very safely be relied on, yet there are too many who will endeavor, and, backing their falsities with asseverations, pawn their salvation to raise their prices.

As example works more than precept, and my sole view being the good and interest of my countrymen, whom I could wish to see without any vice or folly, I shall offer an example of the veneration bestowed on truth and abhorrence of falsehood among the ancients.

Augustus, triumphing over Mark Antony and Cleopatra, among other captives who accompanied them brought to Rome a priest of about sixty years old. The Senate, being informed that this man had never been detected in a falsehood, and was believed never to have told a lie, not only restored him to liberty, but made him a High Priest, and caused a statue to be erected to his honor. The priest thus honored was an Egyptian, and an enemy to Rome; but his virtue removed all obstacles.

Pamphilius was a Roman citizen whose body upon his death was forbidden sepulture, his estate was confiscated, his house razed, and his wife and children banished the Roman territories, wholly for his having been a notorious and inveterate liar.

Could there be greater demonstrations of respect for truth than these of the Romans, who elevated an enemy to the greatest honors, and exposed the family of a citizen to the greatest contumely?

There can be no excuse for lying; neither is there anything equally despicable and dangerous as a liar, no man being safe who associates with him; for, *he who will lie will swear to it,* says the proverb, and such a one may endanger my life, turn my family out of doors, and ruin my reputation, whenever he shall find it his interest; and if a man will lie and swear to it in his shop to obtain a trifle, why should we doubt his doing so when he may hope to make a fortune by his perjury? The crime is in itself so mean, that to call a man a liar is esteemed everywhere an affront not to be forgiven.

If any have lenity enough to allow the dealers an excuse for this bad practice, I believe they will allow none for the gentleman who is addicted to this vice, and must look upon him with contempt. That the world does so is visible by the derision with which his name is treated whenever it is mentioned.

The philosopher Epimenides gave the Rhodians this description of Truth: She is the companion of the gods, the joy of heaven, the light of the earth, the pedestal of justice, and the basis of good policy.

Eschines told the same people that Truth was a virtue without which force was enfeebled, justice corrupted, humility became dissimulation, patience intolerable, chastity a dissembler, liberty lost, and pity superfluous.

Pharmanes the philosopher told the Romans that Truth was the centre on which all things rested: a chart to sail by, a remedy for all evils, and a light to the whole world.

Anaxarchus, speaking of Truth, said it was health incapable of sickness, life not subject to death, an elixir that healeth all, a sun not to be obscured, a moon without eclipse, an herb which never withereth, a gate that is never closed, and a path which never fatigues the traveller.

But, if we are blind to the beauties of truth, it is astonishing that we should not open our eyes to the inconvenience of falsity. A man given to romance must be always on his guard for fear of contradicting and exposing himself to derision; for the most *historical* would avoid the odious character, though it is impossible, with the utmost circumspection, to travel long on this route without detection, and shame and confusion follow. Whereas he who is a votary of truth never hesitates for an answer, has never to rack his invention to make the sequel quadrate with the beginning of his story, nor obliged to burden his memory with minute circumstances, since truth speaks easily what it recollects, and repeats openly and frequently without varying facts, which liars cannot always do, even though gifted with a good memory.

[From the *Pennsylvania Gazette*, Nov. 20, 1735.]

ON TRUE HAPPINESS.

THE desire of happiness is in general so natural, that all the world are in pursuit of it; all have this one end solely in view, though they take such different methods to attain it, and are so much divided in their notions of what it consists of.

29

As evil can never be preferred, and though evil is often the effect of our own choice, yet we never desire it but under the appearance of an imaginary good.

Many things we indulge ourselves in may be considered by us as evils, and yet be desirable; but then, they are only considered as evils in their effects and consequences, not as evils at present, and attended with immediate misery.

Reason represents things to us, not only as they are at present, but as they are in their whole nature and tendency: passion only regards them in the former light; when this governs us, we are regardless of the future, and are only affected by the present.

It is impossible for us ever to enjoy ourselves rightly, if our conduct be not such as to preserve the harmony and order of our faculties, and the original frame and constitution of our minds: all true happiness, as all that is truly beautiful, can only result from order.

Whilst there is a conflict betwixt the two principles of *passion* and *reason*, we must be miserable in proportion to the ardor of the struggle; and when the victory is gained, and reason is so far subdued as seldom to trouble us with its remonstrances, the happiness we have then attained is not the happiness of our rational nature, but the happiness only of the inferior and sensual part of us; and consequently a very low and imperfect happiness, compared with that which the other would have afforded us.

If we reflect upon any one passion and disposition of mind abstracted from virtue, we shall soon see the disconnection between that and true solid happiness. It is of the very essence, for instance, of envy to be uneasy and disquieted; pride meets with provocations and disturbances upon almost every occasion; covetousness is ever attended with solicitude and anxiety; ambition has its disappointments to sour us, but never the good fortune to satisfy us; its appetite grows the keener by indulgence, and all we can gratify it with at present serves but the more to inflame its insatiable desires.

The passions, by being too much conversant with earthly objects, can never fix in us a proper composure, and acquiescence of mind. Nothing but an indifference to the things of this world, an entire submission to the will of Providence here, and a well-grounded expectation of happiness hereafter, can give us a true satisfactory enjoyment of ourselves. Virtue is the best guard against the many unavoidable evils incident to us; nothing better alleviates the weight of the afflictions, or gives a truer relish of the blessings of human life.

What is without us has not the least connection with happiness, only so far as the preservation of our lives and health depends upon it ; health of body, though so far necessary that we cannot be perfectly happy without it, is not sufficient to make us happy of itself. Happiness springs immediately from the mind ; health is but to be considered as a condition or circumstance, without which this happiness cannot be tasted pure and unabated.

Virtue is the best preservative of health, as it prescribes temperance, and such a regulation of our passions as is most conducive to the well-being of the animal economy. So that it is at the same time the only true happiness of the mind, and the best means of preserving the health of the body.

If our desires are for the things of this world, they are never to be satisfied. If our great view is upon those of the next, the expectation of them is an infinitely higher satisfaction than the enjoyment of those of the present.

There is no true happiness, then, but in a virtuous and self-approving conduct ; unless our actions will bear the test of our sober judgments and reflections upon them, they are not the actions, and consequently not the happiness, of a rational being.

[From the *Pennsylvania Gazette*, Feb. 18, 1734.]

ON SELF-DENIAL.

It is commonly asserted that *without self-denial there is no virtue ;* and that the greater the self-denial is, the greater is the virtue.

If it were said that he who cannot deny himself anything he inclines to, though he knows it will be to his hurt, has not the virtue of resolution or fortitude, it would be intelligible enough ; but, as it stands, the proposition seems obscure or erroneous.

Let us consider some of the virtues singly.

If a man has no inclination to wrong people in his dealings, — if he feels no temptation to it, and therefore never does it, — can it be said that he is not a just man ? If he is a just man, has he not the virtue of justice ?

If to a certain man idle diversions have nothing in them that is tempting, and therefore he never relaxes his application to business for their sake, is he not an industrious man; or has he not the virtue of industry?

I might in like manner instance in all the rest of the virtues; but, to make the thing short, as it is certain that the more we strive against the temptation to any vice, and practise the contrary virtue, the weaker will that temptation be, and the stronger will be that habit, till at length the temptation hath no force, or entirely vanishes, does it follow from thence that in our endeavors to overcome vice we grow continually less and less virtuous, till at length we have no virtue at all?

If self-denial be the essence of virtue, then it follows that the man who is naturally temperate, just, &c., is not virtuous, but that, in order to be virtuous, he must, in spite of his natural inclinations, wrong his neighbors, and eat and drink, &c., to excess.

But perhaps it may be said, by the word *virtue*, in the above assertion, is meant *merit*, and so it should stand; thus without self-denial there is no merit, and the greater the self-denial the greater the merit.

The self-denial here meant must be when our inclinations are towards vice, or else it would still be nonsense.

By merit is understood desert; and when we say a man merits, we mean that he deserves praise or reward.

We do not pretend to merit anything of God; for he is above our service, and the benefits he confers on us are the effects of his goodness and bounty.

All our merit, then, is with regard to one another, and from one to another.

Taking, then, the proposition as it stands:

If a man does me a service from a natural benevolent inclination, does he deserve less of me than another who does me the like kindness against his inclination?

If I have two journeymen, one naturally industrious, the other idle, but both perform a day's work equally good, ought I to give the latter the most wages?

Indeed, lazy workmen are commonly observed to be more extravagant in their demands than the industrious; for, if they have not more for their work, they cannot live as well as the industrious. But, though it be true to a proverb that *lazy folks take the most pains*, does it follow that they deserve the *most money?* If you were to employ servants in affairs of trust, would you pay more wages to one you knew was naturally honest, than for one naturally roguish, but who had lately acted honestly; for currents whose natural channels are dammed up, till a new course is by time worn sufficiently deep, and become natural, are apt to break

their banks   If one servant is more valuable than another, has
he not more merit than the other ? and yet this is not on account
of superior self-denial.

Is a patriot not praiseworthy, if public spirit is natural to him ?
Is a pacing horse less valuable for being a natural pacer ?

Nor, in my opinion, has any man less merit for having in general naturally virtuous inclinations.

The truth is, that temperance, justice, charity, &c., are virtues
whether practised with or against our inclinations ; and the man
who practises them merits our love and esteem ; and self-denial
is neither good nor bad, but as it is applied.   He that denies a
vicious inclination is virtuous in proportion to his resolution ; but
the most perfect virtue is above all temptation, such as the virtue
of the saints in heaven : and he who does any foolish, indecent,
or wicked thing, merely because it is contrary to his inclination,
like some mad enthusiasts I have read of, who ran about in public naked under the notion of taking up the cross, is not prac-
tising the reasonable science of virtue, but is lunatic.

Newcastle, February 5.

[From Poor Richard's Almanac, 1742.]

RIVALSHIP IN ALMANAC-MAKING.

Courteous Reader : This is the ninth year of my endeavors
to serve thee in the capacity of a calendar-writer.   The encouragement I have met with must be ascribed, in a great measure,
to your charity, excited by the open, honest declaration I made
of my poverty at my first appearance.   This my brother *Phi-
lomaths* could, without being conjurers, discover ; and *Poor
Richard's* success has produced ye a *Poor Will*, and a *Poor
Robin ;* and, no doubt, *Poor John*, &c., will follow, and we shall
all be, *in name*, what some folks say we are already in *fact*, a
parcel of *poor almanac-makers*.

During the course of these nine years, what buffetings have I
not sustained !   The fraternity have been all in arms.   Honest
Titan, deceased, was raised, and made to abuse his old friend.
Both authors and printers were angry.   Hard names, and many,
were bestowed on me.   *They denied me to be the author of my
own works ;* declared there never was any such person ; asserted
that I was dead sixty years ago ; prognosticated my death to
happen within a twelvemonth ; with many other malicious incon-

sistencies, the effects of blind passion, envy at my success, and a vain hope of depriving me, dear reader, of thy wonted countenance and favor. *Who knows him?* they cry: *Where does he live?*

But what is that to them? If I delight in a private life, have they any right to drag me out of my retirement? I have good reason for concealing the place of my abode. It is time for an old man, as I am, to think of preparing for his great remove. The perpetual teasing of both neighbors and strangers, to calculate nativities, give judgments on schemes, and erect figures, discover thieves, detect horse-dealers, describe the route of runaways and strayed cattle; the crowd of visitors with a thousand trifling questions, — *Will my ship return safe? Will my mare win the race? Will her next colt be a pacer? When will my wife die? Who shall be my husband? And HOW LONG first? When is the best time to cut hair, trim cocks or sow salad?* — these and the like impertinences I have now neither taste nor leisure for. I have had enough of them. All that these angry folks can say will never provoke me to tell them where I live — I would eat my nails first.

My last adversary is *J. J——n*, philomat, who *declares and protests* (in his preface, 1741) that the *false prophecy put in my almanac concerning him, the year before, is altogether* false and untrue, *and that I am one of Baal's false prophets.* This *false, false prophecy* he speaks of, related to his reconciliation with the Church of Rome; which, notwithstanding his declaring and protesting, is, I fear, too true. Two-things in his elegiac verses confirm me in this suspicion. He calls the first of November *All-Hallows day.* Reader, does not this smell of popery? Does it in the least savor of the pure language of Friends? But the plainest thing is, his adoration of saints, which he confesses to be his practice, in these words, page 4:

> "When any trouble did me befall,
>   To my dear *Mary* then I would call."

Did he think the whole world were so stupid as not to take notice of this? So ignorant as not to know that all Catholics pay the highest regard to the *Virgin Mary?* Ah! friend *John*, we must allow you to be a poet, but you are certainly no Protestant. I could heartily wish your religion was as good as your verses.

RICHARD SAUNDERS.

THE WASTE OF LIFE.

ANERGUS was a gentleman of a good estate; he was bred to no business, and could not contrive how to waste his hours agreeably. He had no relish for any of the proper works of life, nor any taste at all for the improvements of the mind; he spent generally ten hours of the four-and-twenty in his bed; he dozed away two or three more on his couch, and as many were dissolved in good liquor every evening, if he met with company of his own humor. Five or six of the next he sauntered away with much indolence: the chief business of them was to contrive his meals, and to feed his fancy beforehand with the promise of a dinner and supper; not that he was so very a glutton, or so entirely devoted to appetite; but chiefly because he knew not how to employ his thoughts better, he let them rove about the sustenance of his body. Thus he had made a shift to wear off ten years since the paternal estate fell into his hands; and yet, according to the abuse of words in our day, he was called a man of virtue, because he was scarce ever known to be quite drunk, nor was his nature much inclined to lewdness.

One evening, as he was musing along, his thoughts happened to take a most unusual turn; for they cast a glance backward, and began to reflect on his manner of life. He bethought himself what a number of living beings had been made a sacrifice to support his carcass, and how much corn and wine had been mingled with those offerings. He had not quite lost all the arithmetic that he learned when he was a boy, and he set himself to compute what he had devoured since he came to the age of man.

" About a dozen feathered creatures, small and great, have, one week with another," said he, " given up their lives to prolong mine, which in ten years amounts to at least six thousand.

" Fifty sheep have been sacrificed in a year, with half a hecatomb of black cattle, that I might have the choicest part offered weekly upon my table. Thus a thousand beasts out of the flock and the herd have been slain in ten years' time to feed me, besides what the forest has supplied me with. Many hundreds of fishes have, in all their varieties, been robbed of life for my repast, and of the smaller fry as many thousands.

" A measure of corn would hardly afford fine flour enough for a month's provision, and this arises to above six score bushels; and many hogsheads of ale and wine, and other liquors, have passed through this body of mine, this wretched strainer of meat and drink.

" And what have I done, all this time, for God or *man?*   What a vast profusion of good things upon an useless life and a worthless liver !   There is not the meanest creature among all these which I have devoured but hath answered the end of its creation better than I.   It was made to support human nature, and it hath done so.   Every crab and oyster I have eat, and every grain of corn I have devoured, hath filled up its place in the rank of beings with more propriety and honor than I have done.   O, shameful waste of life and time ! "

In short, he carried on his moral reflections with so just and severe a force of reason, as constrained him to change his whole course of life, to break off his follies at once, and to apply himself to gain some useful knowledge, when he was more than thirty years of age ; he lived many following years, with the character of a worthy man, and an excellent Christian ; he performed the kind offices of a good neighbor at home, and made a shining figure as a patriot in the senate-house ; he died with a peaceful conscience, and the tears of his country were dropped upon his tomb.

The world, that knew the whole series of his life, stood amazed at the mighty change.   They beheld him as a wonder of reformation, while he himself confessed and adored the divine power and mercy, which had transformed him from a brute to a man.

But this was a single instance ; and we may almost venture to write MIRACLE upon it.   Are there not numbers of both sexes, among our young gentry, in this degenerate age, whose lives thus run to utter waste, without the least tendency to usefulness ?

When I meet with persons of such a worthless character as this, it brings to my mind some scraps of Horace :

> " Nos numerus sumus, et fruges consumere nati.
> ————————————————Alcinoique Juventus
> Cui pulchrum fuit in Medios dormire dies," &c.

PARAPHRASE.

> " There are a number of us creep
> Into this world, to eat and sleep ;
> And know no reason why they 're born
> But merely to consume the corn,
> Devour the cattle, fowl and fish,
> And leave behind an empty dish :
> Though crows and ravens do the same,
> Unlucky birds of hateful name ;
> Ravens or crows might fill their places,
> And swallow corn or carcasses.
> Then, if their tomb-stone, when they die,
> Ben't taught to flatter and to lie,
> There 's nothing better will be said,
> Than that they 've eat up all their bread,
> Drank up all their drink, and gone to bed."

There are other fragments of that heathen poet, which occur on such occasions · one in the first of his satires, the other in the last of his epistles, which seem to represent life only as a season of luxury :

> " ————Exacto contentus tempore vitæ
> Cedat uti conviva satur————
> Lusisti satus, edisti satis atque bibisti ;
> Tempus abire tibi "

Which may be thus put into English :

> " Life 's but a feast : and when we die,
> Horace would say, if he were by,
> Friend, thou hast eat and drank enough,
> 'T is time now to be marching off :
> Then like a well-fed guest depart,
> With cheerful looks and ease at heart,
> Bid all your friends good-night, and say
> You 've done the business of the day."

————

[From the *Pennsylvania Gazette*, June 23, 1730.]

DIALOGUE I.

BETWEEN PHILOCLES AND HORATIO, MEETING ACCIDENTALLY IN THE FIELDS, CONCERNING VIRTUE AND PLEASURE.

Philocles. My friend Horatio! I am very glad to see you ; prithee how came such a man as you alone? and musing too? What misfortune in your pleasures has sent you to philosophy for relief?

Horatio. You guess very right, my dear Philocles : we pleasure-hunters are never without them ; and yet, so enchanting is the game, we cannot quit the chase. How calm and undisturbed is your life, how free from present embarrassments and future cares! I know you love me, and look with compassion upon my conduct : show me, then, the path which leads up to that constant and invariable good, which I have heard you so beautifully describe, and which you seem so fully to possess.

Phil. There are few men in the world I value more than you, Horatio ; for, amidst all your foibles, and painful pursuits of pleasure, I have oft observed in you an honest heart, and a mind strongly bent towards virtue. I wish, from my soul, I could assist you in acting steadily the part of a reasonable creature : for, if you would not think it a paradox, I should tell you I love you better than you do yourself.

Hor. A paradox, indeed! Better than I do myself! when I love my dear self so well, that I love everything else for my own sake.

Phil. He only loves himself well who rightly and judiciously loves himself.

Hor. What do you mean by that, Philocles? You men of reason and virtue are always dealing in mysteries, though you laugh at them when the church makes them. I think he loves himself very well, and very judiciously too, as you call it, who allows himself to do whatever he pleases.

Phil. What! though it be to the ruin and destruction of that very self which he loves so well? That man alone loves himself rightly who procures the greatest possible good to himself through the whole of his existence, and so pursues pleasure as not to give for it more than it is worth.

Hor. That depends all upon opinion. Who shall judge what the pleasure is worth? Suppose a pleasing form of the fair kind strikes me so much that I can enjoy nothing without the enjoyment of that one object? Or, that pleasure in general is so favorite a mistress, that I will take her as men do their wives, for better, for worse, — minding no consequences, nor regarding what is to come? Why should I not do it?

Phil. Suppose, Horatio, that a friend of yours entered into the world, about two-and-twenty, with a healthful, vigorous body, and a fair, plentiful estate of about five hundred pounds a year; and yet, before he had reached thirty, should, by following his pleasures, and not, as you say, duly regarding consequences, have run out of his estate, and disabled his body to that degree that he had neither the means nor capacity of enjoyment left, nor anything else to do but wisely shoot himself through the head to be at rest, — what would you say to this unfortunate man's conduct? Is it wrong by opinion or fancy only, or is there really a right and wrong in the case? Is not one opinion of life and action juster than another, or one sort of conduct preferable to another? Or, does that miserable son of pleasure appear as reasonable and lovely a being, in your eyes, as a man who, by prudently and rightly gratifying his natural passions, had preserved his body in full health, and his estate entire, and enjoyed both to a good old age, and then died with a thankful heart for the good things he had received, and with an entire submission to the will of Him who first called him into being? Say, Horatio! are these men equally wise and happy? And is everything to be measured by mere fancy and opinion, without considering whether that fancy or opinion be right?

Hor. Hardly so, neither, I think; yet sure the wise and good Author of nature could never make us to plague us. He could never give us passions, on purpose to subdue and conquer them; or produce this self of mine, or any other self, only that it may be denied; for that is denying the works of the great Creator himself. Self-denial, then, which is what I suppose you mean by prudence, seems to me not only absurd, but very dishonorable to that supreme wisdom and goodness which is supposed to make so ridiculous and contradictory a creature, that must be always fighting with himself in order to be at rest, and undergo voluntary hardships in order to be happy. Are we created sick, only to be commanded to be sound? Are we born under one law, our passions, and yet bound to another, that of reason? Answer me, Philocles, for I am warmly concerned for the honor of nature, the mother of us all.

Phil. I find, Horatio, my two characters have frighted you; so that you decline the trial of what is good by reason, and had rather make a bold attack upon Providence; the usual way of you gentlemen of fashion, who, when, by living in defiance of the eternal rules of reason, you have plunged yourself into a thousand difficulties, endeavor to make yourselves easy by throwing the burden upon nature. You are, Horatio, in a very miserable condition indeed; for you say you cannot be happy if you control your passions, and you feel yourself miserable by an unrestrained gratification of them; so that here is evil, irremediable evil, either way.

Hor. That is very true, — at least, it appears so to me. Pray what have you to say, Philocles, in honor of nature or Providence? Methinks, I am in pain for her; how do you rescue her? poor lady!

Phil. This, my dear Horatio, I have to say: that what you find fault with and clamor against as the most terrible evil in the world, self-denial, is really the greatest good, and the highest self-gratification. If indeed you use the word in the sense of some weak, sour moralists, and much weaker divines, you will have just reason to laugh at it; but, if you take it as understood by philosophers, and men of sense, you will presently see her charms, and fly to her embraces, notwithstanding her demure looks, as absolutely necessary to produce even your own darling sole good, pleasure; for self-denial is never a duty, or a reasonable action, but as it is a natural means of procuring more pleasure than you can taste without it; so that this grave, saint-like guide to happiness, as rough and dreadful as she has been made to appear, is in truth the kindest and most beautiful mistress in the world.

Hor. Prithee, Philocles, do not wrap yourself in allegory and metaphor: why do you tease me thus? I long to be satisfied what is this philosophical self-denial — the necessity and reason of it; I am impatient, and all on fire. Explain, therefore, in your beautiful, natural, easy way of reasoning, what I am to understand by this grave lady of yours, with so forbidding, downcast looks, and yet so absolutely necessary to my pleasures. I stand ready to embrace her; for, you know, pleasure I court under all shapes and forms.

Phil. Attend, then, and you will see the reason of this philosophical self-denial. There can be no absolute perfection in any creature, because every creature is derived from something of a superior existence, and dependent on that source for its own existence; no created being can be all-wise, all-good, and all-powerful, because his powers and capacities are finite and limited; consequently, whatever is created must, in its own nature, be subject to error, irregularity, excess, and imperfectness. All intelligent rational agents find in themselves a power of judging what kind of beings they are, what actions are proper to preserve them, and what consequences will generally attend them; what pleasures they are formed for, and to what degree their natures are capable of receiving them. All we have to do, then, Horatio, is to consider, when we are surprised with a new object, and passionately desire to enjoy it, whether the gratifying that passion be consistent with the gratifying other passion and appetites, equal, if not more necessary to us. And whether it consists with our happiness to-morrow, next week, or next year; for, as we all wish to live, we are obliged, by reason, to take as much care for our future as our present happiness, and not build one upon the ruins of the other; but, if through the strength and power of a present passion, and through want of attending to consequences, we have erred and exceeded the bounds which nature or reason have set us, we are then, for our own sakes, to refrain or deny ourselves a present momentary pleasure, for a future constant and durable one; so that this philosophical self-denial is only refusing to do an action which you strongly desire, because it is inconsistent with your health, convenience, or circumstances in the world; or, in other words, because it would cost you more than it was worth. You would lose by it, as a man of pleasure. Thus you see, Horatio, that self-denial is not only the most reasonable, but the most pleasant thing in the world.

Hor. We are just coming into town, so that we cannot pursue this argument any further at present. You have said a great deal for Nature, Providence and Reason: happy are they who can follow such divine guides!

Phil. Horatio, good-night: I wish you wise in your pleasures.

Hor. I wish, Philocles, I could be as wise in my pleasures as you are pleasantly wise. Your wisdom is agreeable, your virtue is amiable, and your philosophy the highest luxury. Adieu, thou enchanting reasoner!

[From the *Pennsylvania Gazette*, July 9, 1730.]

DIALOGUE II.

BETWEEN PHILOCLES AND HORATIO, CONCERNING VIRTUE AND PLEASURE.

Philocles. Dear Horatio, where hast thou been, these three or four months? What new adventures have you fallen upon since I met you in these delightful, all-inspiring fields, and wondered how such a pleasure-hunter as you could bear being alone?

Horatio. O, Philocles! thou best of friends, because a friend to reason and virtue! I am very glad to see you: do not you remember I told you then that some misfortunes in my pleasures had sent me to philosophy for relief? But now, I do assure you, I can, without a sigh, leave other pleasures for those of philosophy: I can hear the word reason mentioned, and virtue praised, without laughing. Do not I bid fair for conversion, think you?

Phil. Very fair, Horatio; for I remember the time when reason, virtue and pleasure, were the same thing with you: when you counted nothing good but what pleased, nor any thing reasonable but what you gained by; when you made a jest of a mind, and the pleasures of reflection; and elegantly placed your sole happiness, like the rest of the animal creation, in the gratification of sense.

Hor. I did so; but, in our last conversation, when walking upon the brow of this hill, and looking down on that broad, rapid river, and yon widely-extended, beautifully-varied plain, you taught me another doctrine: you showed me that self-denial, which above all things I abhorred, was really the greatest good, and the highest self-gratification, and absolutely necessary to produce even my own darling sole good, Pleasure.

Phil. True: I told you that self-denial was never a duty but

30

when it was a natural means of procuring more pleasure than we could taste without it: that, as we all strongly desire to live, and to live only to enjoy, we should take as much care about our future as our present happiness, and not build one upon the ruins of the other: that we should look to the end, and regard consequences: and if, through want of attention, we had erred, and exceeded the bounds which nature had set us, we were then obliged, for our own sakes, to refrain or deny ourselves a present momentary pleasure, for a future constant and durable good.

Hor. You have shown, Philocles, that self-denial, which weak or interested men have rendered the most forbidding, really the most delightful and amiable, the most reasonable pleasant thing in the world. In a word, if I understand you aright, self-denial is, in truth, self-recognizing, self-acknowledging, or self-owning. But now, my friend, you are to form another promise, and show me the path which leads to that constant durable and invariable good, which I have you so beautifully describe, and which you seem so fully possess. Is not this good of yours a mere chimera? Can anything be constant in a world which is eternally changing, and what appears to exist by an everlasting revolution of one thing into another, and where everything without us and everything within us in perpetual motion? What is this constant durable good, that of yours? Prithee satisfy my soul; for I am all on fire, and impatient to enjoy her. Produce this eternal blooming goddess, with never-fading charms, and see whether I will not embrace her with as much eagerness and rapture as you.

Phil. You seem enthusiastically warm, Horatio; I will wait till you are cool enough to attend to the sober, dispassionate voice of reason.

Hor. You mistake me, my dear Philocles; my warmth is not so great as to run away with my reason: it is only just raised enough to open my faculties, and fit them to receive those eternal truths, and that durable good, which you so triumphantly boast of. Begin, then, — I am prepared.

Phil. I will, I believe; Horatio, with all your scepticism about you, you will allow that good to be constant which is never absent from you, and that to be durable which never ends but with your being.

Hor. Yes, — go on.

Phil. That can never be the good of a creature which when present the creature may be miserable, and when absent is certainly so.

Hor. I think not; but pray explain what you mean, for I am not much used to this abstract way of reasoning.

Phil. I mean all the pleasures of sense. The good of man cannot consist in the mere pleasures of sense; because, when any one of those objects which you love is absent, or cannot be come at, you are certainly miserable; and, if the faculty be impaired, though the object be present, you cannot enjoy it. So that this sensual good depends upon a thousand things without and within you, and all out of your power. Can this, then, be the good of man? Say, Horatio, what think you, — is not this a checkered, fleeting, fantastical good? Can that, in any propriety of speech, be called the good of man, which, even while he is tasting, he may be miserable; and which, when he cannot taste, he is necessarily so? Can that be our good which costs us a great deal of pains to obtain, which cloys in possessing, for which we must wait the return of appetite before we can enjoy again? Or, is that our good which we can come at without difficulty, which is heightened by possession, which never ends in weariness and disappointment, and which the more we enjoy the better qualified we are to enjoy on?

Hor. The latter, I think; but why do you torment me thus? Philocles, show me this good immediately.

Phil. I have showed you what it is not; it is not sensual, but it is rational and moral good. It is doing all the good we can to others by acts of humanity, friendship, generosity and benevolence: this is that constant and durable good, which will afford contentment and satisfaction always alike, without variation or diminution. I speak to your experience now, Horatio. Did you ever find yourself weary of relieving the miserable, or of raising the distressed into life or happiness? Or, rather, do not you find the pleasure grow upon you by repetition, and that it is greater in reflection than in the act itself? Is there a pleasure upon earth to be compared with that which arises from the sense of making others happy? Can this pleasure ever be absent, or ever end but with your being? Does it not always accompany you? Doth not it lie down and rise with you, live as long as you live, give you consolation in the article of death, and remain with you in that gloomy hour when all other things are going to forsake you, or you them?

Hor. How glowingly you paint, Philocles! Methinks Horatio is amongst the enthusiasts. I feel the passion, I am enchantingly convinced; but I do not know why, overborne by something stronger than reason. Sure, some divinity speaks within me; but prithee, Philocles, give me coolly the cause why this rational and moral good so infinitely excels the mere natural or sensual.

Phil. I think, Horatio, that I have clearly shown you the difference between merely natural or sensual good and rational or moral good. Natural or sensual pleasure continues no longer than the action itself; but this divine or moral pleasure continues when the action is over, and swells and grows upon your hand by reflection : the one is inconstant, unsatisfying, of short duration, and attended with numberless ills; the other is constant, yields full satisfaction, is durable, and no evils preceding, accompanying or following it. But, if you inquire further into the cause of this difference, and would know why the moral pleasures are greater than the sensual, perhaps the reason is the same as in all other creatures, — that their happiness or chief good consists in acting up to their chief faculty, or that faculty which distinguishes them from all creatures of a different species. The chief faculty in man is his reason; and, consequently, his chief good, or that which may be justly called his good, consists not merely in action, but in reasonable action. By reasonable actions we understand those actions which are preservative of the human kind, and naturally tend to produce real and unmixed happiness; and these actions, by way of distinction, we call actions morally good.

Hor. You speak very clearly, Philocles; but, that no difficulty may remain upon your mind, pray tell me what is the real difference between natural good and evil and moral good and evil; for I know several people who use the terms without ideas.

Phil. That may be : the difference lies only in this, — that natural good and evil are pleasure and pain, moral good and evil are pleasure or pain produced with intention and design. For, it is the intention only that makes the agent morally good or bad.

Hor. But may not a man, with a very good intention, do an evil action ?

Phil. Yes; but then he errs in his judgment, though his design be good. If his error is invincible, or such as, all things considered, he could not help, he is inculpable ; but, if it arose through want of diligence in forming his judgment about the nature of human actions, he is immoral and culpable.

Hor. I find, then, that, in order to please ourselves rightly, or to do good to others morally, we should take great care of our opinions.

Phil. Nothing concerns you more; for, as the happiness or real good of men consists in right action, and right action cannot be produced without right opinion, it behoves us, above all things in this world, to take care that our own opinions of things be according to the nature of things. The foundation of all virtue and happiness is thinking rightly. He who sees an action is right, — that is, naturally tending to good, — and does it because of that tendency, he only is a moral man ; and he alone is capable of that constant, durable and invariable good, which has been the subject of this conversation.

Hor. How, my dear philosophical guide, shall I be able to know, and determine certainly, what is right and wrong in life ?

Phil. As easily as you distinguish a circle from a square, or light from darkness. Look, Horatio, into the sacred book of nature; read your own nature, and view the relation which other men stand in to you and you to them, and you will immediately see what constitutes human happiness, and consequently what is right.

Hor. We are just coming into town, and can say no more at present. You are my good genius, Philocles : you have showed me what is good ; you have redeemed me from the slavery and misery of folly and vice, and made me a free and happy being.

Phil. Then am I the happiest man in the world. Be you steady, Horatio; never depart from reason and virtue.

Hor. Sooner will I lose my existence. Good-night, Philocles.

Phil. Adieu, dear Horatio.

POOR RICHARD'S ALMANAC.

THE WAY TO WEALTH, AS CLEARLY SHOWN IN THE PREFACE OF AN OLD PENNSYLVANIA ALMANAC, ENTITLED, "POOR RICHARD IMPROVED." *

COURTEOUS READER : I have heard that nothing gives an author so great pleasure as to find his works respectfully quoted by others. Judge, then, how much I must have been gratified by an incident I am going to relate to you. I stopped my horse, lately, where a great number of people were collected, at an

---

* Dr. Franklin for many years published the Pennsylvania Almanac, purporting to be the work of *Richard Saunders,* and furnished it with various sentences and proverbs, having relation chiefly to " industry, attention to one's own business, and frugality." These sentences and proverbs he collected and digested in the above preface.

30*

auction of merchant's goods. The hour of the sale not being come, they were conversing on the badness of the times; and one of the company called to a plain, clean old man, with white locks, "Pray, Father Abraham, what think you of the times? Will not these heavy taxes quite ruin the country? How shall we ever be able to pay them? What would you advise us to do?"

Father Abraham stood up, and replied, "If you would have my advice, I will give it to you in short; 'for a word to the wise is enough,' as poor Richard says."

They joined in desiring him to speak his mind; and, gathering round him, he proceeded as follows:

"Friends," says he, "the taxes are, indeed, very heavy, and, if those laid on by the government were the only ones we had to pay, we might more easily discharge them; but we have many others, and much more grievous to some of us. We are taxed twice as much by our idleness, three times as much by our pride, and four times as much by our folly; and from these taxes the commissioners cannot ease or deliver us, by allowing an abatement. However, let us hearken to good advice, and something may be done for us. 'God helps them that help themselves,' as poor Richard says.

"1. It would be thought a hard government that should tax its people one-tenth part of their time, to be employed in its service; but idleness taxes many of us much more; sloth, by bringing on diseases, absolutely shortens life. 'Sloth, like rust, consumes faster than labor wears, while the used key is always bright,' as poor Richard says. 'But dost thou love life? then do not squander time, for that is the stuff life is made of,' as poor Richard says. How much more than is necessary do we spend in sleep! forgetting that 'the sleeping fox catches no poultry, and that there will be sleeping enough in the grave,' as poor Richard says.

"'If time be of all things the most precious, wasting time must be,' as poor Richard says, 'the greatest prodigality;' since, as he elsewhere tells us, 'lost time is never found again, and what we call time enough always proves little enough.' Let us then up and be doing, and doing to the purpose; so by diligence shall we do more with less perplexity. 'Sloth makes all things difficult, but industry all easy; and he that riseth late must trot all day and shall scarce overtake his business at night; while laziness travels so slowly, that poverty soon overtakes him. Drive thy business, let not that drive thee; and early to bed, and early to rise, makes a man healthy, wealthy, and wise,' as poor Richard says.

"So what signifies wishing and hoping for better times? We may make these times better, if we bestir ourselves. 'Industry need not wish, and he that lives upon hope will die fasting. There are no gains without pains; then help hands, for I have no lands,' or, if I have, they are smartly taxed. 'He that hath a trade hath an estate; and, he that hath a calling hath an office of profit and honor,' as poor Richard says. But then the trade must be worked at, and the calling well followed, or neither the estate nor the office will enable us to pay our taxes. If we are industrious, we shall never starve; for, 'at the working-man's house hunger looks in, but dares not enter.' Nor will the bailiff or the constable enter; for 'industry pays debts, while despair increaseth them.' What though you have found no treasure, nor has any rich relation left you a legacy; 'diligence is the mother of good luck, and God gives all things to industry. Then plough deep, while sluggards sleep, and you shall have corn to sell and to keep.' Work while it is called to-day; for you know not how much you may be hindered to-morrow. 'One to-day is worth two to-morrows,' as poor Richard says; and, further, 'never leave that till to-morrow which you can do to-day.' If you were a servant, would you not be ashamed that a good master should catch you idle? Are you then your own masters? Be ashamed to catch yourself idle, when there is so much to be done for yourself, your family, your country, and your king. Handle your tools without mittens; remember that 'the cat in gloves catches no mice,' as poor Richard says. It is true, there is much to be done, and perhaps you are weak-handed; but stick to it steadily, and you will see great effects, for 'constant dropping wears away stones; and, by diligence and patience the mouse ate in two the cable; and little strokes fell great oaks.'

"Methinks I hear some of you say, 'Must a man afford himself no leisure?' I will tell thee, my friend, what poor Richard says. 'Employ thy time well, if thou meanest to gain leisure; and, since thou art not sure of a minute, throw not away an hour.' Leisure is time for doing something useful; this leisure the diligent man will obtain, but the lazy man never; for 'a life of leisure and a life of laziness are two things. Many, without labor, would live by their wits only, but they break for want of stock;' whereas industry gives comfort, and plenty, and respect. 'Fly pleasures, and they will follow you. The diligent spinner has a large shift; and, now I have a sheep and a cow, every one bids me good-morrow.'

"2. But, with our industry, we must likewise be steady, set-

tled and careful, and oversee our own affairs with our own eyes,
and not trust too much to others ; for, as poor Richard says,

> ' I never saw an oft-removéd tree,
> Nor yet an oft-removéd family,
> That throve so well as those that settled be.'

And again, 'three removes is as bad as a fire;' and again,
'keep thy shop, and thy shop will keep thee;' and again, 'if
you would have your business done, go, — if not, send.' And
again,

> ' He that by the plough would thrive
> Himself must either hold or drive.'

And again, ' the eye of a master will do more work than both
his hands;' and again, 'want of care does us more damage
than want of knowledge;' and again, 'not to oversee workmen
is to leave them your purse open.' Trusting too much to others'
care is the ruin of many ; for, ' in the affairs of this world, men
are saved, not by faith, but by the want of it ;' but a man's own
care is profitable ; for, ' if you would have a faithful servant,
and one that you like, serve yourself. A little neglect may
breed great mischief; for want of a nail the shoe was lost, and
for want of a shoe the horse was lost, and for want of a horse
the rider was lost,' being overtaken and slain by the enemy; all
for want of a little care about a horse-shoe nail.

"3. So much for industry, my friends, and attention to
one's own business. But to these we must add frugality, if we
would make our industry more certainly successful. A man
may, if he knows not how to save as he gets, 'keep his nose all
his life to the grindstone, and die not worth a groat at last. A
fat kitchen makes a lean will ;' and

> ' Many estates are spent in the getting,
> Since women for tea forsook spinning and knitting,
> And men for punch forsook hewing and splitting.'

" ' If you would be wealthy, think of saving, as well as of getting. The Indies have not made Spain rich, because her outgoes
are greater than her incomes.'

"Away, then, with your expensive follies, and you will not
then have so much cause to complain of hard times, heavy taxes,
and chargeable families; for

> ' Women and wine, game and deceit,
> Make the wealth small, and the want great.'

" And further, ' what maintains one vice would bring up two
children.' You may think, perhaps, that a little tea, or a little

punch now and then, diet a little more costly, clothes a little finer, and a little entertainment now and then, can be no great matter. But remember, 'many a little makes a mickle.' Beware of little expenses; 'a small leak will sink a great ship,' as poor Richard says; and again, 'who dainties love shall beggars prove;' and, moreover, 'fools make feasts, and wise men eat them.'

"Here you are all got together to this sale of fineries and knick-knacks. You call them *goods;* but, if you do not take care, they will prove *evils* to some of you. You expect they will be sold cheap, and perhaps they may, for less than they cost; but, if you have no occasion for them, they must be dear to you. Remember what poor Richard says, 'buy what thou hast no need of, and ere long thou shalt sell thy necessaries.' And again, 'at a great pennyworth pause a while.' He means that perhaps the cheapness is apparent only, and not real; or the bargain, by straitening thee in thy business, may do thee more harm than good. For, in another place he says, 'many have been ruined by buying good pennyworths.' Again, 'it is foolish to lay out money in a purchase of repentance;' and yet this folly is practised every day at auctions, for want of minding the almanac. Many a one, for the sake of finery on the back, have gone with a hungry belly, and half starved their families; 'silks and satins, scarlet and velvets, put out the kitchen fire,' as poor Richard says. These are not the necessaries of life, they can scarcely be called the conveniences; and yet, only because they look pretty, how many want to have them! By these and other extravagances, the genteel are reduced to poverty, and forced to borrow of those whom they formerly despised, but who, through industry and frugality, have maintained their standing; in which case it appears plainly that 'a ploughman on his legs is higher than a gentleman on his knees,' as poor Richard says. Perhaps they have had a small estate left them, which they knew not the getting of; they think 'it is day, and it will never be night;' that a little to be spent out of so much is not worth minding; but 'always taking out of the meal-tub, and never putting in, soon comes to the bottom,' as poor Richard says; and then, 'when the well is dry, they know the worth of water.' But this they might have known before, if they had taken his advice: 'if you would know the value of money, go and try to borrow some; for he that goes a borrowing goes a sorrowing,' as poor Richard says; and indeed so does he that lends to such people, when he goes to get it again. Poor Dick further advises, and says,

'Fond pride of dress is sure a curse ;
    Ere fancy you consult, consult your purse.'

And again, 'pride is as loud a beggar as want, and a great
deal more saucy.' When you have bought one fine thing, you
must buy ten more, that your appearance may be all of a piece;
but poor Dick says, ' it is easier to suppress the first desire than
to satisfy all that follow it;' and it is as truly folly for the poor
to ape the rich, as for the frog to swell in order to equal the ox.

'Vessels large may venture more,
    But little boats should keep near shore.'

It is, however, a folly soon punished; for, as poor Richard says,
'pride that dines on vanity sups on contempt; pride break-
fasted with plenty, dined with poverty, and supped with infamy.'
And, after all, of what use is this pride of appearance, for which
so much is risked, so much is suffered? It cannot promote
health, nor ease pain; it makes no increase of merit in the person; it creates envy, it hastens misfortune.

"But what madness must it be to *run in debt* for these superfluities! We are offered by the terms of this sale six months'
credit; and that perhaps has induced some of us to attend it,
because we cannot spare the ready money, and hope now to be
fine without it. But, ah! think what you do when you run in
debt; you give to another power over your liberty. If you cannot pay at the time, you will be ashamed to see your creditor,
you will be in fear when you speak to him, when you will make
poor, pitiful, sneaking excuses, and by degrees come to lose
your veracity, and sink into base, downright lying; for 'the
second vice is lying, the *first* is running in debt,' as poor Richard
says; and again, to the same purpose, ' lying rides upon debt's
back;' whereas a free-born Englishman ought not to be ashamed
nor afraid to see or speak to any man living. But poverty often
deprives a man of all spirit and virtue. 'It is hard for an
empty bag to stand upright.' What would you think of that
prince, or of that government, who should issue an edict forbidding you to dress like a gentleman or gentlewoman, on pain of
imprisonment or servitude? Would you not say that you were
free, have a right to dress as you please, and that such an edict
would be a breach of your privileges, and such a government
tyrannical? And yet, you are about to put yourself under that
tyranny when you run in debt for such dress. Your creditor has
authority, at his pleasure, to deprive you of your liberty, by confining you in jail for life, or by selling you for a servant, if you
should not be able to pay him. When you have got your bargain, you may, perhaps, think little of payment; but, as poor

Richard says, 'creditors have better memories than debtors; creditors are a superstitious sect, great observers of set days and times.' The day comes round before you are aware, and the demand is made before you are prepared to satisfy it; or, if you bear your debt in mind, the term, which at first seemed so long, will, as it lessens, appear extremely short; time will seem to have added wings to his heels, as well as his shoulders. 'Those have a short Lent who owe money to be paid at Easter.' At present, perhaps, you may think yourselves in thriving circumstances, and that you can bear a little extravagance without injury; but

> ' For age and want save while you may, —
> No morning sun lasts a whole day.'

Gain may be temporary and uncertain, but ever, while you live, expense is constant and certain; and 'it is easier to build two chimneys than to keep one in fuel,' as poor Richard says: so, 'rather go to bed supperless than rise in debt.'

> ' Get what you can, and what you get hold,
> 'T is the stone that will turn all your lead into gold.'

And, when you have got the philosopher's stone, sure you will no longer complain of bad times, or the difficulty of paying taxes.

"4. This doctrine, my friends, is reason and wisdom: but, after all, do not depend too much upon your own industry, and frugality and prudence, though excellent things; for they may all be blasted without the blessing of Heaven; and therefore ask that blessing humbly, and be not uncharitable to those that at present seem to want it, but comfort and help them. Remember Job suffered, and was afterwards prosperous.

"And now, to conclude, 'experience keeps a dear school, but fools will learn in no other,' as poor Richard says, and scarce in that; for, it is true, 'we may give advice, but we cannot give conduct:' however, remember this, 'they that will not be counselled cannot be helped;' and further, that 'if you will not hear reason she will surely rap your knuckles,' as poor Richard says."

Thus the old gentleman ended his harangue. The people heard it, and approved the doctrine; and immediately practised the contrary, just as if it had been a common sermon; for the auction opened, and they began to buy extravagantly. I found the good man had thoroughly studied my almanacs, and digested all I had dropped on those topics during the course of twenty-five years. The frequent mention he made of me must have tired any one else; but my vanity was wonderfully delighted with it, though I was conscious that not a tenth part of the wisdom was my own which he ascribed to me, but rather the gleanings that I had made of the sense of all ages and nations. However, I resolved to be the better for the echo of it; and, though I had at first determined to buy stuff for a new coat, I went away resolved to wear my old one a little longer. Reader, if thou wilt do the same, thy profit will be as great as

RICHARD SAUNDERS.

ADVICE TO A YOUNG TRADESMAN.

WRITTEN ANNO 1748.

As you have desired it of me, I write the following hints, which have been of service to me, and may, if observed, be so to you.

Remember that *time* is money. He that can earn ten shillings a day by his labor, and goes abroad or sits idle one-half that day, though he spend but sixpence during his diversion or idleness, ought not to reckon *that* the only expense; he has really spent, or rather thrown away, five shillings besides.

Remember that *credit* is money. If a man lets his money lie in my hands after it is due, he gives me the interest, or so much as I can make of it, during that time. This amounts to a considerable sum where a man has good and large credit, and makes good use of it.

Remember that money is of a prolific generating nature. Money can beget money, and its offspring can beget more, and so on. Five shillings turned is six, turned again it is seven and three-pence, and so on till it becomes a hundred pounds. The more there is of it, the more it produces every turning, so that the profits rise quicker and quicker. He that kills a breeding sow destroys all her offspring to the thousandth generation. He that murders a crown destroys all that it might have produced, even scores of pounds.

Remember that six pounds a year is but a groat a day. For this little sum (which may be daily wasted either in time or expense unperceived) a man of credit may, on his own security, have the constant possession and use of a hundred pounds. So much in stock, briskly turned by an industrious man, produces great advantage.

Remember this saying, "the good paymaster is lord of another man's purse." He that is known to pay punctually and exactly to the time he promises may at any time, and on any occasion, raise all the money his friends can spare. This is sometimes of great use. After industry and frugality, nothing contributes more to the raising of a young man in the world than punctuality and justice in all his dealings : therefore, never keep borrowed money an hour beyond the time you promised, lest a disappointment shut up your friend's purse forever.

The most trifling actions that affect a man's credit are to be regarded. The sound of your hammer at five in the morning, or nine at night, heard by a creditor, makes him easy six months longer; but, if he sees you at a billiard-table, or hears your voice at a tavern, when you should be at work, he sends for his money the next day, demands it before he can receive it in a lump.

It shows, besides, that you are mindful of what you owe; it makes you appear a careful as well as an honest man, and that still increases your credit.

Beware of thinking all your own that you possess, and of living accordingly. It is a mistake that many people who have credit fall into. To prevent this, keep an exact account, for some time, both of your expenses and your income. If you take the pains at first to mention particulars, it will have this good effect: you will discover how wonderfully small trifling expenses mount up to large sums, and will discern what might have been and may for the future be saved, without occasioning any great inconvenience.

In short, the way to wealth, if you desire it, is as plain as the way to market. It depends chiefly on two words, *industry* and *frugality ;* that is, waste neither *time* nor *money*, but make the best use of both. Without industry and frugality nothing will do, and with them everything. He that gets all he can honestly, and saves all he gets (necessary expenses excepted), will certainly become *rich* — if that Being who governs the world, to whom all should look for a blessing on their honest endeavors, doth not, in his wise providence, otherwise determine.

HINTS NECESSARY TO THOSE THAT WOULD BE RICH.

WRITTEN ANNO 1736.

THE use of money is all the advantage there is in having money.

For six pounds a year you may have the use of one hundred
31

pounds, provided you are a man of known prudence and honesty.

He that spends a groat a day idly spends idly above six pounds a year, which is the price for the use of one hundred pounds.

He that wastes idly a groat's worth of his time per day, one day with another, wastes the privilege of using one hundred pounds each day.

He that idly loses five shillings' worth of time loses five shillings, and might as prudently throw five shillings into the sea.

He that loses five shillings not only loses that sum, but all the advantage that might be made by turning it in dealing, which, by the time that a young man becomes old, will amount to a considerable sum of money.

Again: he that sells upon credit asks a price for what he sells equivalent to the principal and interest of his money for the time he is to be kept out of it; therefore, he that buys upon credit pays interest for what he buys, and he that pays ready money might let that money out to use: so that he that possesses anything he bought pays interest for the use of it.

Yet, in buying goods, it is best to pay ready money, because he that sells upon credit expects to lose five per cent. by bad debts; therefore, he charges on all he sells upon credit an advance that shall make up that deficiency.

Those who pay for what they buy upon credit pay their share of this advance.

He that pays ready money escapes, or may escape, that charge.

> " A penny saved is two-pence clear,
> A pin a day 's a groat a year."

THE HANDSOME AND DEFORMED LEG.

There are two sorts of people in the world, who, with equal degrees of health and wealth and the other comforts of life, become, the one happy, and the other miserable. This arises very much from the different views in which they consider things, persons and events, and the effect of those different views upon their own minds.

In whatever situation men can be placed, they may find conveniences and inconveniences; in whatever company, they may find persons and conversation more or less pleasing; at what-

ever table, they may meet with meats and drinks of better and
worse taste, dishes better and worse dressed; in whatever climate, they will find good and bad weather; under whatever
government, they may find good and bad laws, and good and
bad administration of those laws; in whatever poem, or work
of genius, they may see faults and beauties; in almost every
face and every person, they may discover fine features and
defects, good and bad qualities.

Under these circumstances, the two sorts of people above
mentioned fix their attention,—those who are disposed to be
happy on the conveniences of things, the pleasant parts of conversation, the well-dressed dishes, the goodness of the wines, the
fine weather, &c., and enjoy all with cheerfulness. Those who
are to be unhappy think and speak only of the contraries.
Hence, they are continually discontented themselves, and, by
their remarks, sour the pleasures of society, offend personally
many people, and make themselves everywhere disagreeable.

If this turn of mind was founded in nature, such unhappy
persons would be the more to be pitied. But, as the disposition
to criticize and to be disgusted is, perhaps, taken up originally
by imitation, and is, unawares, grown into a habit, which, though
at present strong, may nevertheless be cured when those who
have it are convinced of its bad effects on their felicity, I hope
this little admonition may be of service to them, and put them
on changing a habit, which, though in the exercise it is chiefly
an act of imagination, yet has serious consequences in life, as
it brings on real griefs and misfortunes. For, as many are
offended by and nobody loves this sort of people, no one shows
them more than the most common civility and respect, and
scarcely that; and this frequently puts them out of humor, and
draws them into disputes and contentions. If they aim at
obtaining some advantage in rank or fortune, nobody wishes
them success, or will stir a step, or speak a word, to favor their
pretensions. If they incur public censure or disgrace, no one
will defend or excuse, and many join to aggravate their misconduct, and render them completely odious.

If these people will not change this bad habit, and conde-
scend to be pleased with what is pleasing, without fretting
themselves and others about the contraries, it is good for others
to avoid an acquaintance with them, which is always disagreeable, and sometimes very inconvenient, especially when one
finds one's self entangled in their quarrels.

An old philosophical friend of mine was grown from experience very cautious in this particular, and carefully avoided any

intimacy with such people. He had, like other philosophers, a thermometer to show him the heat of the weather, and a barometer to mark when it was likely to prove good or bad; but, there being no instrument invented to discover, at first sight, this unpleasing disposition in a person, he, for that purpose, made use of his legs; one of which was remarkably handsome, the other, by some accident, crooked and deformed. If a stranger, at the first interview, regarded his ugly leg more than his handsome one, he doubted him. If he spoke of it, and took no notice of the handsome leg, that was sufficient to determine my philosopher to have no further acquaintance with him. Everybody has not this two-legged instrument; but every one, with a little attention, may observe signs of that carping, fault-finding disposition, and take the same resolution of avoiding the acquaintance of those infected with it. I therefore advise those critical, querulous, discontented, unhappy people, that, if they wish to be respected and beloved by others, and happy in themselves, they should *leave off looking at the ugly leg.*

THE SAVAGES OF NORTH AMERICA.

SAVAGES we call them, because their manners differ from ours, which we think the perfection of civility; they think the same of theirs.

Perhaps, if we could examine the manners of different nations with impartiality, we should find no people so rude as to be without any rules of politeness, nor any so polite as not to have some remains of rudeness.

The Indian men, when young, are hunters and warriors; when old, councillors; for all their government is by the council or advice of the sages; there is no force, there are no prisons, no officers to compel obedience, or inflict punishment. Hence, they generally study oratory,— the best speaker having the most influence. The Indian women till the ground, dress the food, nurse and bring up the children, and preserve and hand down to posterity the memory of public transactions. These employments of men and women are accounted natural and honorable. Having few artificial wants, they have abundance of leisure for improvement by conversation.

Our laborious manner of life, compared with theirs, they esteem slavish and base; and the learning on which we value ourselves they regard as frivolous and useless. An instance of this occurred at the treaty of Lancaster, in Pennsylvania, anno 1744, between the government of Virginia and the Six Nations. After the principal business was settled, the commissioners from Virginia acquainted the Indians, by a speech, that there was at Williamsburg a college, with a fund, for educating Indian youth; and that, if the chiefs of the Six Nations would send down half a dozen of their sons to that college, the government would take care that they should be well provided for, and instructed in all the learning of the white people.

It is one of the Indian rules of politeness not to answer a public proposition the same day that it is made; they think it would be treating it as a light matter, and that they show it respect by taking time to consider it, as of a matter important. They therefore deferred their answer till the day following; when their speaker began by expressing their deep sense of the kindness of the Virginia government, in making them that offer; "for we know," says he, "that you highly esteem the kind of learning taught in those colleges, and that the maintenance of our young men, while with you, would be very expensive to you; we are convinced, therefore, that you mean to do us good by your proposal, and we thank you heartily. But you, who are wise, must know that different nations have different conceptions of things; and you will therefore not take it amiss if our ideas of this kind of education happen not to be the same with yours. We have had some experience of it; several of our young people were formerly brought up at the colleges of the northern provinces; they were instructed in all your sciences, but when they came back to us they were bad runners, ignorant of every means of living in the woods, unable to bear either cold or hunger, knew neither how to build a cabin, take a deer, or kill an enemy, spoke our language imperfectly, — were therefore neither fit for hunters, warriors, nor councillors; they were totally good for nothing. We are, however, not the less obliged by your kind offer, though we decline accepting it; and, to show our grateful sense of it, if the gentlemen of Virginia will send us a dozen of their sons, we will take great care of their education, instruct them in all we know, and make *men* of them."

Having frequent occasions to hold public councils, they have acquired great order and decency in conducting them. The old men sit in the foremost ranks, the warriors in the next, and the women and children in the hindmost. The business of the women is to take exact notice of what passes, imprint it in their

31*

memories,— for they have no writing,— and communicate it to their children. They are the records of the council, and they preserve the tradition of the stipulations in treaties a hundred years back; which, when we compare with our writings, we always find exact. He that would speak rises. The rest observe a profound silence. When he has finished and sits down, they leave him five or six minutes to recollect, that, if he has omitted anything he intended to say, or has anything to add, he may rise again and deliver it. To interrupt another, even in common conversation, is reckoned highly indecent. How different this is from the conduct of a polite British House of Commons, where scarce a day passes without some confusion, that makes the speaker hoarse in calling *to order ;* and how different from the mode of conversation in many polite companies of Europe, where, if you do not deliver your sentence with great rapidity, you are cut off in the middle of it by the impatient loquacity of those you converse with, and never suffered to finish it!

The politeness of these savages in conversation is indeed carried to excess, since it does not permit them to contradict or deny the truth of what is asserted in their presence. By this means they indeed avoid disputes; but then it becomes difficult to know their minds, or what impression you make upon them. The missionaries who have attempted to convert them to Christianity all complain of this as one of the great difficulties of their mission. The Indians hear with patience the truths of the gospel explained to them, and give their usual tokens of assent and approbation; you would think they were convinced. No such matter. It is mere civility.

A Swedish minister, having assembled the chiefs of the Susquehanna Indians, made a sermon to them, acquainting them with the principal historical facts on which our religion is founded; such as the fall of our first parents by eating an apple, the coming of Christ to repair the mischief, his miracles and suffering, &c. When he had finished, an Indian orator stood up to thank him. "What you have told us," says he, "is all very good. It is indeed bad to eat apples. It is better to make them all into cider. We are much obliged by your kindness in coming so far to tell us those things which you have heard from your mothers. In return, I will tell you some of those we have heard from ours.

"In the beginning, our fathers had only the flesh of animals to subsist on, and, if their hunting was unsuccessful, they were starving. Two of our young hunters, having killed a deer, made a fire in the woods to broil some parts of it. When they were about to satisfy their hunger they beheld a beautiful young woman descend from the clouds, and seat herself on that hill which you see yonder among the Blue Mountains. They said to each other, ' It is a spirit that perhaps has smelt our broiling venison, and wishes to eat of it ; let us offer some to her.' They presented her with the tongue : she was pleased with the taste of it, and said, ' Your kindness shall be rewarded ; come to this place after thirteen moons, and you shall find something that will be of great benefit in nourishing you and your children to the latest generations.' They did so, and, to their surprise, found plants they had never seen before, but which, from that ancient time, have been constantly cultivated among us, to our great advantage. Where her right hand had touched the ground they found maize, where her left hand had touched it they found kidney-beans, and where her backside had sat on it they found tobacco."

The good missionary, disgusted with this idle tale, said : " What I delivered to you were sacred truths ; but what you tell me is mere fable, fiction and falsehood."

The Indian, offended, replied : " My brother, it seems your friends have not done you justice in your education ; they have not well instructed you in the rules of common civility. You saw that we, who understand and practise those rules, believed all your stories ; why do you refuse to believe ours ? "

When any of them come into our towns, our people are apt to crowd round them, gaze upon them, and incommode them where they desire to be private ; this they esteem great rudeness, and the effect of the want of instruction in the rules of civility and good manners. " We have," say they, " as much curiosity as you, and when you come into our towns we wish for opportunities of looking at you; but for this purpose we hide ourselves behind bushes where you are to pass, and never intrude ourselves into your company."

Their manner of entering one another's villages has likewise its rules. It is reckoned uncivil, in travelling strangers, to enter a village abruptly, without giving notice of their approach. Therefore, as soon as they arrive within hearing, they stop and halloa, remaining there till invited to enter. Two old men usually come out to them, and lead them in. There is in every village a vacant dwelling, called the stranger's house. Here they are placed, while the old men go round from hut to hut, acquainting the inhabitants that strangers are arrived, who are probably hungry and weary ; and every one sends them what he can spare of victuals, and skins to repose on. When the strangers are refreshed, pipes and tobacco are brought; and then, but not before, conversation begins, with inquiries who they are, whither bound, what news, &c., and it usually ends with offers of service, if the strangers have occasion for guides, or any necessaries for continuing their journey; and nothing is exacted for the entertainment.

The same hospitality, esteemed among them as a principal virtue, is practised by private persons; of which *Conrad Weiser*, our interpreter, gave me the following instance. He had been naturalized among the Six Nations, and spoke well the Mohawk language. In going through the Indian country, to carry a message from our governor to the council at Onondaga, he called at the habitation of Canassetego, an old acquaintance, who embraced him, spread furs for him to sit on, and placed before him some boiled beans and venison, and mixed some rum and water for his drink. When he was well refreshed, and had lit his pipe, Canassetego began to converse with him; asked how he had fared the many years since they had seen each other, whence he then came, what occasioned the journey, &c. Conrad answered all his questions, and, when the discourse began to flag, the Indian, to continue it, said: "Conrad, you have lived long among the white people, and know something of their customs; I have been sometimes at Albany, and have observed that once in seven days they shut up their shops, and assemble all in the great house; tell me what it is for. What do they do there?"

"They meet there," says Conrad, "to hear and learn *good things.*"

"I do not doubt," says the Indian, "that they tell you so; they have told me the same; but I doubt the truth of what they say, and I will tell you my reasons. I went lately to Albany, to sell my skins, and buy blankets, knives, powder, rum, &c. You know I used generally to deal with Hans Hanson, but I was a little inclined this time to try some other merchants. However, I called first upon Hans, and asked him what he would give for beaver. He said he could not give any more than four shillings a pound; but, says he, I cannot talk on business now; this is the day when we meet together to learn *good things*, and I am going to meeting. So I thought to myself, since I cannot do any business to-day, I may as well go to the meeting too, and I went with him.

"There stood up a man in black, and began to talk to the people very angrily. I did not understand what he said; but, perceiving that he looked much at me and at Hanson, I imagined he was angry at seeing me there; so I went out, sat down near the house, struck fire, and lit my pipe, waiting till the meeting should break up. I thought, too, that the man had mentioned something of beaver, and I suspected it might be the subject of their meeting. So, when they came out, I accosted my merchant. 'Well, Hans,' says I, 'I hope you have agreed to give more than four shillings a pound?' 'No,' says he, 'I cannot give so much; I cannot give more than three shillings and sixpence. I then spoke to several other dealers; but they all sung the same song, — three and sixpence, — three and sixpence. This made it clear to me that my suspicion was right; and that, whatever they pretended of meeting to learn *good things*, the real purpose was to consult how to cheat Indians in the price of beaver. Consider but a little, Conrad, and you must be of my opinion. If they met so often to learn *good things*, they would certainly have learned some before this time. But they are still ignorant. You know our practice.

"If a white man, in travelling through our country, enters one of our cabins, we all treat him as I do you; we dry him if he is wet, we warm him if he is cold, and give him meat and drink that he may allay his thirst and hunger, and we spread soft furs for him to rest and sleep on: we demand nothing in return. But, if I go into a white man's house at Albany, and ask for victuals and drink, they say, 'Where is your money?' and, if I have none, they say, 'Get out, you Indian dog!' You see they have not yet learned those little *good things* that we need no meetings to be instructed in, because our mothers taught them to us, when we were children; and, therefore, it is impossible their meetings should be, as they say, for any such purpose, or have any such effect; they are only to contrive *the cheating of Indians in the price of beaver.*"

DIALOGUE BETWEEN FRANKLIN AND THE GOUT.

Midnight, October 22, 1780.

Franklin. Eh! O! Eh! What have I done to merit these cruel sufferings?

Gout. Many things; you have ate and drank too freely, and too much indulged those legs of yours in their indolence.

Franklin. Who is it that accuses me?

Gout. It is I, even I, the Gout.

Franklin. What! my enemy in person?

Gout. No, not your enemy.

Franklin. I repeat it, — my enemy; for, you would not only torment my body to death, but ruin my good name; you reproach me as a glutton and a tippler; now, all the world that knows me will allow that I am neither the one nor the other.

Gout. The world may think as it pleases; it is always very complaisant to itself, and sometimes to its friends; but I very well know that the quantity of meat and drink proper for a man, who takes a reasonable degree of exercise, would be too much for another, who never takes any.

Franklin. I take —Eh! O! — as much exercise — Eh! — as I can, Madam Gout. You know my sedentary state; and, on that account, it would seem, Madam Gout, as if you might spare me a little, seeing it is not altogether my own fault.

Gout. Not a jot; your rhetoric and your politeness are thrown away; your apology avails nothing. If your situation in life is a sedentary one, your amusements, your recreations, at least, should be active. You ought to walk or ride; or, if the weather prevents that, play at billiards. But let us examine your course of life. While the mornings are long, and you have leisure to go abroad, what do you do? Why, instead of gaining an appetite for breakfast by salutary exercise, you amuse yourself with books, pamphlets or newspapers, which commonly are not worth the reading. Yet you eat an inordinate breakfast: four dishes of tea, with cream, and one or two buttered toasts, with slices of hung beef, which I fancy are not things the most easily digested. Immediately afterward, you sit down to write at your desk, or converse with persons who apply to you on business. Thus the time passes till one, without any kind of bodily exercise. But all this I could pardon, in regard, as you say, to your sedentary condition. But what is your practice after dinner? Walking in the beautiful gardens of those friends with whom you have dined would be the choice of men of sense; yours is to be fixed down to chess, where you are found engaged for two or three hours! This is your perpetual recreation, which is the least eligible of any for a sedentary man, because, instead of accelerating the motion of the fluids, the rigid attention it requires helps to retard the circulation and obstruct internal secretions. Wrapt in the speculations of this wretched game, you destroy your constitution. What can be expected from such a course of living, but a body replete with stagnant humors, ready to fall a prey to all kinds of dangerous maladies, if I, the Gout, did not occasionally bring you relief by agitating those humors, and so purifying or dissipating them? If it was in some nook or alley in Paris, deprived of walks, that you played a while at chess after dinner, this might be excusable; but the same taste prevails with you in Passy, Auteuil, Montmartre, or Sanoy, places where there are the finest gardens and walks, a pure air, beautiful women, and most agreeable and instructive conversation; all which you might enjoy by frequenting the walks. But these are rejected for this abominable game of chess. Fie, then, Mr. Franklin! But amidst my instructions, I had almost forgotten to administer my wholesome corrections; so take that twinge, — and that!

Franklin. O! Eh! O! O-o-o-o! As much instruction as you please, Madam Gout, and as many reproaches; but pray, Madam, a truce with your corrections!

Gout. No, sir, no, — I will not abate a particle of what is so much for your good, — therefore —

Franklin. O! E-h-h-h! — It is not fair to say I take no exercise, when I do very often, going out to dine and returning in my carriage.

Gout. That, of all imaginable exercises, is the most slight and insignificant, if you allude to the motion of a carriage suspended on springs. By observing the degree of heat obtained by different kinds of motion, we may form an estimate of the quantity of exercise given by each. Thus, for example, if you turn out to walk in winter with cold feet, in an hour's time you will be in a glow all over; ride on horseback, the same effect will scarcely be perceived by four hours' round trotting; but, if you loll in a carriage, such as you have mentioned, you may travel all day, and gladly enter the last inn to warm your feet by a fire. Flatter yourself, then, no longer, that half an hour's airing in your carriage deserves the name of exercise. Providence has appointed few to roll in carriages, while He has given to all a pair of legs, which are machines infinitely more commodious and serviceable. Be grateful, then, and make a proper use of yours. Would you know how they forward the circulation of your fluids, in the very action of transporting you from place to place; — observe, when you walk, that all your weight is alternately thrown from one leg to the other; this occasions a great pressure on the vessels of the foot, and repels their contents; when relieved by the weight being thrown on the other foot, the vessels of the first are allowed to replenish, and, by a return of the weight, this repulsion again succeeds; thus accelerating the circulation of the blood. The heat produced in any given time depends on the degree of this acceleration ; the fluids are shaken, the humors attenuated, the secretions facilitated, and all goes well; the cheeks are ruddy, and health is established. Behold your fair friend at Auteuil ; * a lady who received from bounteous nature more really useful science than half a dozen such pretenders to philosophy as you have been able to extract from all your books. When she honors you with a visit it is on foot. She walks all hours of the day, and leaves indolence and its concomitant maladies, to be endured by her horses. In this see at once the preservative of her health and personal charms. But, when you go to Auteuil, you must have your carriage, though it is no further from Passy to Auteuil than from Auteuil to Passy.

Franklin. Your reasonings grow very tiresome.

Gout. I stand corrected. I will be silent, and continue my office ; take that, and that !

Franklin. O! O-o-o! Talk on, I pray you!

Gout. No, no; I have a good number of twinges for you to-night, and you may be sure of some more to-morrow.

Franklin. What, with such a fever! I shall go distracted. O! Eh! Can no one bear it for me?

Gout. Ask that of your horses; they have served you faithfully.

Franklin. How can you so cruelly sport with my torments?

Gout. Sport! I am very serious. I have here a list of offences against your own health distinctly written, and can justify every stroke inflicted on you.

Franklin. Read it, then.

Gout. It is too long a detail ; but I will briefly mention some particulars.

Franklin. Proceed. I am all attention.

Gout. Do you remember how often you have promised yourself, the following morning, a walk in the grove of Boulogne, in the garden de la Muette, or in your own garden, and have violated your promise, alleging, at one time, it was too cold, at another too warm, too windy, too moist, or what else you pleased; when in truth it was too nothing but your insuperable love of ease?

Franklin. That, I confess, may have happened occasionally, — probably ten times in a year.

Gout. Your confession is very far short of the truth; the gross amount is one hundred and ninety-nine times.

Franklin. Is it possible ?

Gout. So possible, that it is fact; you may rely on the

---

* Madame Helvetius.

accuracy of my statement.   You know Mr. Brillon's gardens, and what fine walks they contain; you know the handsome flight of an hundred steps, which lead from the terrace above to the lawn below.   You have been in the practice of visiting this amiable family twice a week, after dinner, and it is a maxim of your own that "a man may take as much exercise in walking a mile, up and down stairs, as in ten on level ground."   What an opportunity was here for you to have had exercise in both these ways!   Did you embrace it, and how often?

Franklin.   I cannot immediately answer that question.

Gout.   I will do it for you; not once.

Franklin.   Not once?

Gout.   Even so.   During the summer you went there at six o'clock.   You found the charming lady, with her lovely children and friends, eager to walk with you and entertain you with their agreeable conversation; and what has been your choice?   Why, to sit on the terrace, satisfying yourself with the fine prospect, and passing your eye over the beauties of the garden below, without taking one step to descend and walk about in them.   On the contrary, you call for tea and the chess-board; and lo! you are occupied in your seat till nine o'clock, and that besides two hours' play after dinner; and then, instead of walking home, which would have bestirred you a little, you step into your carriage.   How absurd to suppose that all this carelessness can be reconcilable with health, without my interposition'

Franklin.   I am convinced now of the justness of poor Richard's remark, that "Our debts and our sins are always greater than we think for."

Gout.   So it is.   You philosophers are sages in your maxims, and fools in your conduct.

Franklin.   But do you charge, among my crimes, that I return in a carriage from Mr. Brillon's?

Gout.   Certainly; for, having been seated all the while, you cannot object the fatigue of the day, and cannot want, therefore, the relief of a carriage.

Franklin.   What, then, would you have me do with my carriage?

Gout.   Burn it, if you choose; you would at least get heat out of it once in this way.   Or, if you dislike that proposal, here's another for you: observe the poor peasants, who work in the vineyards and grounds about the vilages of Passy, Auteuil, Chaillot, &c.; you may find every day, among these deserving creatures, four or five old men and women, bent and perhaps crippled by weight of years, and too long and too great labor.

32

After a most fatiguing day, these people have to trudge a mile or two to their smoky huts. Order your coachman to set them down. This is an act that will be good for your soul; and, at the same time, after your visit to the Brillons, if you return on foot, that will be good for your body.

Franklin. Ah! how tiresome you are!

Gout. Well, then. to my office; it should not be forgotten that I am your physician. There!

Franklin. O-o-o-o! what a devil of a physician!

Gout. How ungrateful you are to say so! Is it not I who, in the character of your physician, have saved you from the palsy, dropsy, and apoplexy? one or other of which would have done for you long ago, but for me.

Franklin. I submit, and thank you for the past, but entreat the discontinuance of your visits for the future; for, in my mind, one had better die than be cured so dolefully. Permit me just to hint that I have also not been unfriendly to *you*. I never feed physician or quack of any kind, to enter the list against you; if, then, you do not leave me to my repose, it may be said you are ungrateful too.

Gout. I can scarcely acknowledge that as any objection. As to quacks, I despise them; they may kill you, indeed, but cannot injure me. And, as to regular physicians, they are at last convinced that the gout, in such a subject as you are, is no disease, but a remedy; and wherefore cure a remedy? — but to our business, — there!

Franklin. O! O! — for Heaven's sake leave me; and I promise faithfully never more to play at chess, but to take exercise daily, and live temperately.

Gout. I know you too well. You promise fair; but, after a few months of good health, you will return to your old habits; your fine promises will be forgotten, like the forms of the last year's clouds. Let us, then, finish the account, and I will go. But I leave you with an assurance of visiting you again at a proper time and place; for my object is your good, and you are sensible now that I am your *real friend*.

[TO MADAME BRILLON.]

THE WHISTLE.

PASSY, 10 November, 1779.

I RECEIVED my dear friend's two letters, one for Wednesday and one for Saturday. This is again Wednesday. I do not deserve one for to-day, because I have not answered the former. But, indolent as I am, and averse to writing, the fear of having no more of your pleasing epistles, if I do not contribute to the correspondence, obliges me to take up my pen; and, as Mr. B. has kindly sent me word that he sets out to-morrow to see you, instead of spending this Wednesday evening, as I have done its namesakes, in your delightful company, I sit down to spend it in thinking of you, in writing to you, and in reading over and over again your letters.

I am charmed with your description of Paradise, and with your plan of living there; and I approve much of your conclusion, that, in the mean time, we should draw all the good we can from this world. In my opinion, we might all draw more good from it than we do, and suffer less evil, if we would take care not to give too much for *whistles*. For to me it seems that most of the unhappy people we meet with are become so by neglect of that caution.

You ask what I mean? You love stories, and will excuse my telling one of myself.

When I was a child of seven years old, my friends, on a holiday, filled my pocket with coppers. I went directly to a shop where they sold toys for children; and, being charmed with the sound of a *whistle*, that I met by the way in the hands of another boy, I voluntarily offered and gave all my money for one. I then came home, and went whistling all over the house, much pleased with my *whistle*, but disturbing all the family. My brothers, and sisters, and cousins, understanding the bargain I had made, told me I had given four times as much for it as it was worth; put me in mind what good things I might have bought with the rest of the money; and laughed at me so much for my folly, that I cried with vexation, and the reflection gave me more chagrin than the *whistle* gave me pleasure.

This, however, was afterwards of use to me, the impression continuing on my mind; so that often, when I was tempted to buy some unnecessary thing, I said to myself, *Don't give too much for the whistle;* and I saved my money.

As I grew up, came into the world, and observed the actions

of men, I thought I met with many, very many, who *gave too much for the whistle.*

When I saw one too ambitious of court favor, sacrificing his time in attendance on levees, his repose, his liberty, his virtue, and perhaps his friends, to attain it, I have said to myself, *This man gives too much for his whistle.*

When I saw another fond of popularity, constantly employing himself in political bustles, neglecting his own affairs, and ruining them by that neglect, *He pays, indeed,* said I, *too much for his whistle.*

If I knew a miser, who gave up every kind of comfortable living, all the pleasure of doing good to others, all the esteem of his fellow-citizens, and the joys of benevolent friendship, for the sake of accumulating wealth, *Poor man,* said I, *you pay too much for your whistle.*

When I met with a man of pleasure, sacrificing every laudable improvement of the mind, or of his fortune, to mere corporeal sensations, and ruining his health in their pursuit, *Mistaken man,* said I, *you are providing pain for yourself, instead of pleasure ; you give too much for your whistle.*

If I see one fond of appearance, or fine clothes, fine houses, fine furniture, fine equipages, all above his fortune, for which he contracts debts, and ends his career in a prison, *Alas !* say I, *he has paid dear, very dear, for his whistle.*

When I see a beautiful, sweet-tempered girl married to an ill-natured brute of a husband, *What a pity,* say I, *that she should pay so much for a whistle !*

In short, I conceive that great part of the miseries of mankind are brought upon them by the false estimates they have made of the value of things, and by their *giving too much for their whistles.*

Yet I ought to have charity for these unhappy people, when I consider that, with all this wisdom of which I am boasting, there are certain things in the world so tempting, — for example, the apples of King John, which happily are not to be bought; for, if they were put to sale by auction, I might very easily be led to ruin myself in the purchase, and find that I had once more given too much for the *whistle.*

Adieu, my dear friend, and believe me ever yours, very sincerely and with unalterable affection,   B. FRANKLIN.

QUESTIONS FOR THE JUNTO.*

HAVE you read over these queries this morning, in order to consider what you might have to offer the Junto touching any one of them? namely:

1. Have you met with anything, in the author you last read, remarkable, or suitable to be communicated to the Junto? Particularly in history, morality, poetry, physic, travels, mechanic arts, or other parts of knowledge?

2. What new story have you lately heard, agreeable for telling in conversation?

3. Hath any citizen in your knowledge failed in his business lately, and what have you heard of the cause?

---

* For some account of this club, see chapter IV. of the Autobiography. The graver pursuits of the Junto were sometimes varied with music and song. The following song was composed for one of their meetings by Franklin. In one of his letters he applies it to his wife:

MY PLAIN COUNTRY JOAN.

Of their Chloes and Phyllises poets may prate,
   I sing my plain country Joan,
These twelve years my wife, still the joy of my life,—
   Blest day that I made her my own!

Not a word of her face, of her shape, or her air,
   Or of flames, or of darts, you shall hear;
I beauty admire, but virtue I prize,
   That fades not in seventy year.

Am I loaded with care, she takes off a large share,
   That the burden ne'er makes me to reel;
Does good fortune arrive, the joy of my wife
   Quite doubles the pleasure I feel.

She defends my good name, even whem I'm to blame,
   Firm friend as to man e'er was given;
Her compassionate breast feels for all the distressed,
   Which draws down more blessings from heaven.

In health a companion delightful and dear,
   Still easy, engaging, and free;
In sickness no less than the carefulest nurse,
   As tender as tender can be.

In peace and good order my household she guides,
   Right careful to save what I gain;
Yet cheerfully spends, and smiles on the friends
   I've the pleasure to entertain.

Some faults have we all, and so has my Joan,
   But then they're exceedingly small,
And, now I'm grown used to them, so like my own,
   I scarcely can see them at all.

4. Have you lately heard of any citizen's thriving well, and by what means?

5. Have you lately heard how any present rich man, here or elsewhere, got his estate?

6. Do you know of a fellow-citizen who has lately done a worthy action, deserving praise and imitation: or who has lately committed an error, proper for us to be warned against and avoid?

7. What unhappy effects of intemperance have you lately observed or heard? of imprudence? of passion? or of any other vice or folly?

8. What happy effects of temperance? of prudence? of moderation? or of any other virtue?

> Were the finest young princess, with millions in purse,
> To be had in exchange for my Joan,
> I could not get a better, but might get a worse,
> So I'll stick to my dearest old Joan.

The following song was probably written by Franklin during his second visit to England:

THE MOTHER COUNTRY.

> We have an old mother that peevish is grown;
> She snubs us like children that scarce walk alone;
> She forgets we're grown up, and have sense of our own;
> Which nobody can deny, deny,
> Which nobody can deny.

> If we don't obey orders, whatever the case,
> She frowns, and she chides, and she loses all pati-
> Ence, and sometimes she hits us a slap in the face;
> Which nobody can deny, &c.

> Her orders so odd are, we often suspect
> That age has impaired her sound intellect;
> But still an old mother should have due respect;
> Which nobody can deny, &c.

> Let's bear with her humors as well as we can;
> But why should we bear the abuse of her man?
> When servants make mischief, they earn the rattan;
> Which nobody should deny, &c.

> Know, too, ye bad neighbors, who aim to divide
> The sons from the mother, that still she's our pride;
> And if ye attack her, we're all of her side;
> Which nobody can deny, &c.

> We'll join in her law-suits, to baffle all those
> Who, to get what she has, will be often her foes;
> For we know it must all be our own, when she goes;
> Which nobody can deny, deny,
> Which nobody can deny.

9. Have you, or any of your acquaintance, been lately sick or wounded ? If so, what remedies were used, and what were their effects ?

10. Who do you know that are shortly going voyages or journeys, if one should have occasion to send by them ?

11. Do you think of anything at present in which the Junto may be serviceable to *mankind*, to their country, to their friends, or to themselves ?

12. Hath any deserving stranger arrived in town since last meeting, that you heard of ? and what have you heard or observed of his character or merits ? and whether, think you, it lies in the power of the Junto to oblige him, or encourage him as he deserves ?

13. Do you know of any deserving young beginner lately set up, whom it lies in the power of the Junto any way to encourage ?

14. Have you lately observed any defect in the laws of your *country*, of which it would be proper to move the legislature for an amendment ? or do you know of any beneficial law that is wanting ?

15. Have you lately observed any encroachment on the just liberties of the people ?

16. Hath anybody attacked your reputation lately ? and what can the Junto do towards securing it ?

17. Is there any man whose friendship you want, and which the Junto, or any of them, can procure for you ?

18. Have you lately heard any member's character attacked, and how have you defended it ?

19. Hath any man injured you, from whom it is in the power of the Junto to procure redress ?

20. In what manner can the Junto, or any of them, assist you in any of your honorable designs ?

21. Have you any weighty affair in hand, in which you think the advice of the Junto may be of service ?

22. What benefits have you lately received from any man not present ?

23. Is there any difficulty in matters of opinion, of justice, and injustice, which you would gladly have discussed at this time ?

24. Do you see anything amiss in the present customs or proceedings of the Junto, which might be amended ?

Any person to be qualified, to stand up, and lay his hand on his breast, and be asked these questions, namely :

1. Have you any particular disrespect to any present members?

Answer. I have not.

2. Do you sincerely declare that you love mankind in general, of what profession or religion soever?

Answer. I do.

3. Do you think any person ought to be harmed in his body, name or goods, for mere speculative opinions, or his external way of worship?

Answer. No.

4. Do you love truth for truth's sake; and will you endeavor impartially to find and receive it yourself, and communicate it to others?

Answer. Yes.

Questions discussed by the Club.

Is *sound* an entity or body?

How may the phenomena of vapors be explained?

Is self-interest the rudder that steers mankind, the universal monarch to whom all are tributaries?

Which is the best form of government, and what was that form which first prevailed among mankind?

Can any one particular form of government suit all mankind?

What is the reason that the tides rise higher in the Bay of Fundy than the Bay of Delaware?

Is the emission of paper money safe?

What is the reason that men of the greatest knowledge are not the most happy?

How may the possessions of the lakes be improved to our advantage?

Why are tumultuous, uneasy sensations united with our desires?

Whether it ought to be the aim of philosophy to eradicate the passions.

How may smoky chimneys be best cured?

Why does the flame of a candle tend upwards in a spire?

Which is least criminal, a *bad* action joined with a *good* intention, or a *good* action with a *bad* intention?

Is it inconsistent with the principles of liberty, in a free government, to punish a man as a libeller when he speaks the truth?

THE INTERNAL STATE OF AMERICA.

BEING A TRUE DESCRIPTION OF THE INTEREST AND POLICY OF THAT VAST CONTINENT.

THERE is a tradition that, in the planting of New England, the first settlers met with many difficulties and hardships, as is generally the case when a civilized people attempt establishing themselves in a wilderness country. Being piously disposed, they sought relief from Heaven, by laying their wants and distresses before the Lord in frequent set days of fasting and prayer. Constant meditation and discourse on these subjects kept their minds gloomy and discontented ; and, like the children of Israel, there were many disposed to return to that Egypt which persecution had induced them to abandon. At length, when it was proposed in the assembly to proclaim another fast, a farmer of plain sense rose and remarked, that the inconveniences they suffered, and concerning which they had so often wearied Heaven with their complaints, were not so great as they might have expected, and were diminishing every day as the colony strengthened ; that the earth began to reward their labor, and to furnish liberally for their subsistence ; that the seas and rivers were found full of fish, the air sweet, the climate healthy ; and, above all, that they were there in the full enjoyment of liberty, civil and religious. He therefore thought that reflecting and conversing on these subjects would be more comfortable, as tending more to make them contented with their situation ; and that it would be more becoming the gratitude they owed to the Divine Being, if, instead of a fast, they should proclaim a thanksgiving. His advice was taken ; and, from that day to this, they have, in every year, observed circumstances of public felicity sufficient to furnish employment for a thanksgiving day, which is therefore constantly ordered and religiously observed.

I see in the public newspapers of different states frequent complaints of *hard times, deadness of trade, scarcity of money, &c.* It is not my intention to assert or maintain that these complaints are entirely without foundation. There can be no country or nation existing in which there will not be some people so circumstanced as to find it hard to gain a livelihood : people who are not in the way of any profitable trade, and with whom money is scarce, because they have nothing to give in exchange for it; and it is always in the power of a small number to make a great clamor. But, let us take a cool view of the general state of our affairs, and perhaps the prospect will appear less gloomy than has been imagined.

32*

The great business of the continent is agriculture. For one artisan, or merchant, I suppose we have at least one hundred farmers, by far the greatest part cultivators of their own fertile lands, from whence many of them draw not only the food necessary for their subsistence, but the materials of their clothing, so as to need very few foreign supplies ; while they have a surplus of productions to dispose of, whereby wealth·is gradually accumulated. Such has been the goodness of Divine Providence to these regions, and so favorable the climate, that, since the three or four years of hardship in the first settlement of our fathers here, a famine or scarcity has never been heard of amongst us ; on the contrary, though some years may have been more and others less plentiful, there has always been provision enough for ourselves, and a quantity to spare for exportation. And, although the crops of last year were generally good, never was the farmer better paid for the part he can spare commerce, as the published price-currents abundantly testify. The lands he possesses are also continually rising in value with the increase of population ; and, on the whole, he is enabled to give such good wages to those who work for him, that all who are acquainted with the Old World must agree, that in no part of it are the laboring poor so generally well fed, well clothed, well lodged, and well paid, as in the United States of America.

If we enter the cities, we find that, since the Revolution, the owners of houses and lots of ground have had their interest vastly augmented in value ; rents have risen to an astonishing height, and thence encouragement to increase building, which gives employment to an abundance of workmen, as does also the increased luxury and splendor of living of the inhabitants, thus made richer. These workmen all demand and obtain much higher wages than any other part of the world would afford them, and are paid in ready money. This class of people therefore do not, or ought not, to complain of hard times ; and they make a very considerable part of the city inhabitants.

At the distance I live from our American fisheries, I cannot speak of them with any degree of certainty ; but I have not heard that the labor of the valuable race of men employed in them is worse paid, or that they meet with less success, than before the Revolution. The whalemen, indeed, have been deprived of one market for their oil ; but another, I hear, is opening for them, which it is hoped may be equally advantageous ; and the demand is constantly increasing for their spermaceti candles, which therefore bear a much higher price than formerly.

There remain the merchants and shop-keepers. Of these,

though they make but a small part of the wnole nation, the number is considerable, — too great, indeed, for the business they are employed in ; for the consumption of goods in every country has its limits, the faculties of the people, that is, their ability to buy and pay, being equal only to a certain quantity of merchandise. If merchants calculate amiss on this proportion, and import too much, they will of course find the sale dull for the overplus, and some of them will say that trade languishes.   They should, and doubtless will, grow wiser by experience, and import less.   If too many artificers in town and farmers from the country, flattering themselves with the idea of leading easier lives, turn shop-keepers, the whole natural quantity of that business divided among them all may afford too small a share for each, and occasion complaints that trade is dead; these may also suppose that it is owing to scarcity of money, while, in fact, it is not so much from the fewness of buyers as from the excessive number of sellers that the mischief arises ; and, if every shop-keeping farmer and mechanic would return to the use of his plough and working-tools, there would remain of widows, and other women, shop-keepers sufficient for the business, which might then afford them a comfortable maintenance.

Whoever has travelled through the various parts of Europe, and observed how small is the proportion of people in affluence or easy circumstances there, compared with those in poverty and misery, — the few rich and haughty landlords, the multitude of poor, abject, rack-rented, tithe-paying tenants, and half-paid and half-starved ragged laborers, — and views here the happy mediocrity that so generally prevails throughout these states, where the cultivator works for himself, and supports his family in decent plenty, will, methinks, see abundant reason to bless Divine Providence for the evident and great difference in our favor, and be convinced that no nation known to us enjoys a greater share of human felicity.

It is true that in some of the states there are parties and discords ; but, let us look back, and ask if we were ever without them.   Such will exist wherever there is liberty ; and perhaps they help to preserve it.   By the collision of different sentiments, sparks of truth are struck out, and political light is obtained. The different factions, which at present divide us, aim all at the public good : the differences are only about the various modes of promoting it.   Things, actions, measures, and objects of all kinds, present themselves to the minds of men in such a variety of lights, that it is not possible we should all think alike at the same time on every subject, when hardly the same man retains at all times the same ideas of it. Parties are therefore the common lot of humanity; and ours are by no means more mischievous or less beneficial than those of other countries, nations and ages, enjoying in the same degree the great blessing of political liberty.

Some, indeed, among us are not so much grieved for the present state of our affairs as apprehensive for the future. The growth of luxury alarms them, and they think we are, from that alone, in the high road to ruin. They observe that no revenue is sufficient without economy, and that the most plentiful income of a whole people from the natural productions of their country may be dissipated in vain and needless expenses, and poverty be introduced in the place of affluence. This may be possible. It, however, rarely happens: for there seems to be in every nation a greater proportion of industry and frugality, which tend to enrich, than of idleness and prodigality, which occasion poverty; so that, upon the whole, there is a continual accumulation.

Reflect what Spain, Gaul, Germany and Britain, were in the time of the Romans, inhabited by people little richer than our savages; and consider the wealth they at present possess, in numerous well-built cities, improved farms, rich movables, magazines stocked with valuable manufactures, to say nothing of plate, jewels, and coined money; and all this notwithstanding their bad, wasting, plundering governments, and their mad, destructive wars; and yet luxury and extravagant living has never suffered much restraint in those countries. Then consider the great proportion of industrious, frugal farmers inhabiting the interior parts of these American States, and of whom the body of our nation consists, and judge whether it is possible that the luxury of our sea-ports can be sufficient to ruin such a country. If the importation of foreign luxuries could ruin a people, we should probably have been ruined long ago; for the British nation claimed a right, and practised it, of importing among us not only the superfluities of their own production, but those of every nation under heaven; we bought and consumed them, and yet we flourished and grew rich. At present our independent governments may do what we could not then do, — discourage by heavy duties, or prevent by heavy prohibitions, such importations, and thereby grow richer; if, indeed, — which may admit of dispute, — the desire of adorning ourselves with fine clothes, possessing fine furniture, with elegant houses, &c., is not, by strongly inciting to labor and industry, the occasion of producing a greater value than is consumed in the gratification of that desire

The agriculture and fisheries of the United States are the great sources of our increasing wealth. He that puts a seed into the earth is recompensed, perhaps, by receiving forty out of it; and he who draws a fish out of our water draws up a piece of silver.

Let us (and there is no doubt but we shall) be attentive to these, and then the power of rivals, with all their restraining and prohibiting acts, cannot much hurt us. We are sons of the earth and seas; and, like Antæus in the fable, if, in wrestling with a Hercules, we now and then receive a fall, the touch of our parents will communicate to us fresh strength and vigor to renew the contest.

[From the *Pennsylvania Gazette*, No. 409, Oct. 14, 1736.]

ON DISCOVERIES.

THE world, but a few ages since, was in a very poor condition as to trade and navigation, nor indeed were they much better in other matters of useful knowledge. It was a green-headed time. Every useful improvement was hid from them; they had neither looked into heaven nor earth, into the sea nor land, as has been done since. They had philosophy without experiments, mathematics without instruments, geometry without scale, astronomy without demonstration.

They made war without powder, shot, cannon or mortars; nay, the mob made their bonfires without squibs or crackers. They went to sea without compass, and sailed without the needle. They viewed the stars without telescopes, and measured latitudes without observation. Learning had no printing-press, writing no paper, and paper no ink; the lover was forced to send his mistress a deal board for a love-letter, and a billet-doux might be the size of an ordinary trencher. They were clothed without manufacture, and their richest robes were the skins of the most formidable monsters; they carried on trade without books, and correspondence without posts; their merchants kept no accounts, their shop-keepers no cash-books; they had surgery without anatomy, and physicians without the *materia medica*; they gave emetics without ipecacuanha, drew blisters without cantharides, and cured agues without the bark.

As for geographical discoveries, they had neither seen the North Cape nor the Cape of Good Hope south. All the discovered inhabited world which they knew and conversed with was circumscribed within very narrow limits, namely, France, Britain, Spain, Italy, Germany and Greece; the Lesser Asia,

33

the west part of Persia, Arabia, the north parts of Africa, and the islands of the Mediterranean Sea; and this was the whole world to them; — not that even these countries were fully known, neither, and several parts of them not inquired into at all. Germany was known little further than the banks of the Elbe; Poland as little beyond the Vistula, or Hungary a little beyond the Danube; Muscovy, or Russia, perfectly unknown, as much as China beyond it, and India only by a little commerce upon the coast about Surat and Malabar; Africa had been more unknown, but, by the ruin of the Carthagenians, all the western coast of it was sunk out of knowledge again, and forgotten; the northern coast of Africa, in the Mediterranean, remained known, and that was all, for the Saracens, overrunning the nations which were planted there, ruined commerce as well as religion; the Baltic Sea was not discovered, nor even the navigation of it known, for the Teutonic knights came not thither till the 13th century.

America was not heard of, nor so much as a suggestion in the minds of men that any part of the world lay that way. The coasts of Greenland or Spitzbergen, and the whale-fishing, not known; the best navigators in the world, at that time, would have fled from a whale with much more fright and horror than from the devil in the most terrible shapes they had been told he appeared in.

The coasts of Angola, Congo, the Gold and the Grain coasts, on the west side of Africa, from whence since that time such immense wealth has been drawn, not discovered, nor the least inquiry made after them. All the East India and China trade, not only undiscovered, but out of the reach of expectation! Coffee and tea (those modern blessings of mankind) had never been heard of: all the unbounded ocean we now call the South Sea was hid and unknown: all the Atlantic Ocean, beyond the mouth of the Straits, was frightful and terrible in the distant prospect, nor durst any one peep into it, otherwise than as they might creep along the coast of Africa towards Sallee, or Santa Cruz. The North Sea was hid in a veil of impenetrable darkness; the White Sea, or Archangel, was a very modern discovery, not found out till Sir Hugh Willoughby doubled the North Cape, and paid dear for the adventure, being frozen to death with all his crew on the coast of Lapland, while his companion's ship, with the famous Mr. Chancellor, went on to the Gulf of Russia, called the White Sea, where no Christian strangers had ever been before him.

In these narrow circumstances stood the world's knowledge at the beginning of the fifteenth century, when men of genius began to look abroad and about them. Now, as it was wonderful to see a world so full of people, and people so capable of improving, yet so stupid and so blind, so ignorant and so perfectly unimproved, it was wonderful to see with what a general alacrity they took the alarm almost all together ; preparing themselves, as it were, on a sudden, by a general inspiration, to spread knowledge through the earth, and to search into everything that it was impossible to uncover.

How surprising is it to look back, so little a way behind us, and see that even in less than two hundred years all this (now so self-wise) part of the world did not so much as know whether there was any such place as a Russia, a China, a Guinea, a Greenland, or a North Cape ! That, as to America, it was never supposed there was any such place; neither had the world, though they stood upon the shoulders of four thousand years' experience, the least thought so much as that there was any land that way !

As they were ignorant of places, so of things also ; so vast are the improvements of science, that all our knowledge of mathematics, of nature, of the brightest part of human wisdom, had their admission among us within these two last centuries.

What was the world, then, before ? And to what were the heads and hands of mankind applied ? The rich had no commerce, the poor no employment; war and the sword was the great field of honor, — the stage of preferment, — and you have scarce a man eminent in the world for anything before that time, but for a furious, outrageous falling upon his fellow-creatures, like Nimrod and his successors of modern memory.

The world is now daily increasing in experimental knowledge ; and let no man flatter the age with pretending we have arrived to a perfection of discoveries.

> " What 's now discovered only serves to show
> That nothing 's known, to what is yet to know."

POSITIONS TO BE EXAMINED CONCERNING NATIONAL WEALTH.

1. ALL food or subsistence for mankind arise from the earth or waters.

2. Necessaries of life that are not food, and all other con-

veniences, have their value estimated by the proportion of food consumed while we are employed in procuring them.

3. A small people, with a large territory, may subsist on the productions of nature, with no other labor than of gathering the vegetables and catching the animals.

4. A large people, with a small territory, finds these insufficient, and, to subsist, must labor the earth to make it produce greater quantities of vegetable food suitable for the nourishment of men, and of the animals they intend to eat.

5. From this labor arises a *great increase* of vegetable and animal food, and of materials for clothing, as flax, wool, silk, &c. The superfluity of these is wealth. With this wealth we pay for the labor employed in building our houses, cities, &c., which are, therefore, only subsistence thus metamorphosed.

6. *Manufactures* are only *another shape* into which so much provisions and subsistence are turned as were equal in value to the manufactures produced. This appears, from hence, that the manufacturer does not, in fact, obtain from the employer for his labor *more* than a mere subsistence, including raiment, fuel and shelter : all which derive their value from the provisions consumed in procuring them.

7. The produce of the earth, thus converted into manufactures, may be more easily carried to distant markets than before such conversion.

8. *Fair commerce* is where equal values are exchanged for equal, the expense of transport included. Thus, if it costs A in England as much labor and charge to raise a bushel of wheat as it costs B in France to produce four gallons of wine, then are four gallons of wine the fair exchange for a bushel of wheat, A and B meeting at half distance with their commodities to make the exchange. The advantage of this fair commerce is that each party increases the number of his enjoyments, having, instead of wheat alone, or wine alone, the use of both wheat and wine.

9. Where the labor and expense of producing both commodities are known to both parties, bargains will generally be fair and equal. Where they are known to one party only, bargains will often be unequal, knowledge taking its advantage of ignorance.

10. Thus he that carries one thousand bushels of wheat abroad to sell may not probably obtain so great a profit thereon as if he had first turned the wheat into manufactures, by subsisting therewith the workmen while producing those manufactures : since there are many expediting and facilitating methods

of working not generally known ; and strangers to the manufactures, though they know pretty well the expense of raising wheat, are unacquainted with those short methods of working, and thence, being apt to suppose more labor employed in the manufactures than there really is, are more easily imposed on in their value, and induced to allow more for them than they are honestly worth.

11. Thus the advantage of having manufactures in a country does not consist, as is commonly supposed, in their highly advancing the value of rough materials, of which they are formed ; since, though sixpenny-worth of flax may be worth twenty shillings when worked into lace, yet the very cause of its being worth twenty shillings is, that, besides the flax, it has cost nineteen shillings and sixpence in subsistence to the manufacturer. But the advantage of manufactures is, that under their shape provisions may be more easily carried to a foreign market, and by their means our traders may more easily cheat strangers. Few, where it is not made, are judges of the value of lace. The importer may demand forty, and perhaps get thirty shillings, for that which cost him but twenty.

12. Finally, there seem to be but three ways for a nation to acquire wealth. The first is by *war*, as the Romans did, by plundering their conquered neighbors. This is *robbery*. The second by *commerce*, which is generally *cheating*. The third by *agriculture*, the only *honest way*, wherein man receives a real increase of the seed thrown into the ground, in a kind of continual miracle, wrought by the hand of God, in his favor, as a reward for his innocent life and his virtuous industry.

April 4, 1769.

[From the *Pennsylvania Gazette*, April 8, 1736.]

GOVERNMENT.

An ancient sage of the law * says, — the king can do no wrong ; for if he doeth wrong he is not the king.† And, in another place, — when the king doth justice he is God's vicar, but when he doth unjustly he is the agent of the devil.‡ The politeness

* *Bracton* de leg. Angl. An author of great weight, contemporary with Henry III.
† Rex non facit injuriam, qui si facit injuriam, non est rex.
‡ Dum facit justitiam vicarius est regis æterni minister autere diaboli dum declinet ad injuriam.

of the latter times has given a softer turn to the expression. It
is now said, *the king can do no wrong, but his ministers may.*
In allusion to this, the Parliament of 1741 declared they made
war against the king for the king's service. But his majesty
affirmed that such a distinction was absurd; though, by the way,
his own creed contained a greater absurdity, for he believed he
had an authority from God to oppress the subjects, whom by the
same authority he was obliged to cherish and defend. Aristotle
calls all princes tyrants, from the moment they set up an interest
different from that of their subjects; and this is the only definition he gives us of tyranny. Our own countrymen, before cited,
and the sagacious Greek, both agree on this point, that a governor who acts contrary to the ends of government loses the
title bestowed on him at his institution. It would be highly improper to give the same name to things of different qualities,
or that produce different effects; matter, while it communicates
heat, is generally called *fire*, but when the flames are extinguished
the appellation is changed. Sometimes, indeed, the same
sound serves to express things of a contrary nature; but that
only denotes a defect, or poverty in the language.

A wicked prince imagines that the crown receives a new
lustre from absolute power, whereas every step he takes to
obtain it is a forfeiture of the crown.

His conduct is as foolish as it is detestable; he aims at glory
and power, and treads the path that leads to dishonor and contempt; he is a plague to his country, and deceives himself.

During the inglorious reigns of the Stuarts (except a part of
Queen Anne's) it was a perpetual struggle between them and the
people; those endeavoring to subvert, and these bravely opposing the subverters of liberty. What were the consequences?
One lost his life on the scaffold, another was banished. The
memory of all of them stinks in the nostrils of every true lover
of his country; and their history stains with indelible blots the
English annals.

The reign of Queen Elizabeth furnishes a beautiful contrast.
All her views centred in one object, which was the public
good. She made it her study to gain the love of her subjects,
not by flattery or little soothing arts, but by rendering them
substantial favors. It was far from her policy to encroach on
their privileges; she augmented and secured them.

And it is remarked to her eternal honor that the acts presented to her for her royal approbation (forty or fifty of a session
of Parliament) were signed without any examining further than
the titles. This wise and good queen only reigned for her peo-

ple, and knew that it was absurd to imagine they would promote anything contrary to their own interests, which she so studiously endeavored to advance.   On the other hand, when this queen asked money of the Parliament, they frequently gave her more than she demanded, and never inquired how it was disposed of, except for form's sake, being fully convinced she would not employ it but for the general welfare.   Happy princess, happy people! what harmony, what mutual confidence!   Seconded by the hearts and purses of her subjects, she crushed the exorbitant power of Spain, which threatened destruction to England and chains to all Europe.   That monarchy has ever since pined under the stroke, so that now, when we send a man-of-war or two to the West Indies, it puts her into such a panic fright, that if the galleons can steal home she sings *Te Deum* as for a victory.

This is a true picture of governments; its reverse is *tyranny*.

MORALS OF CHESS.

PLAYING at chess is the most ancient and most universal game known among men; for its original is beyond the memory of history, and it has, for numberless ages, been the amusement of all the civilized nations of Asia, the Persians, the Indians, and the Chinese.   Europe has had it above a thousand years; the Spaniards have spread it over their part of America; and it has lately begun to make its appearance in the United States.   It is so interesting in itself as not to need the view of gain to induce engaging in it, and thence it is seldom played for money.   Those, therefore, who have leisure for such diversions, cannot find one that is more innocent; and the following piece, written with a view to correct (among a few young friends) some little improprieties in the practice of it, shows at the same time that it may, in its effects on the mind, be not merely innocent, but advantageous to the vanquished as well as the victor:

The game of chess is not merely an idle amusement.   Several very valuable qualities of the mind, useful in the course of human life, are to be acquired or strengthened by it, so as to become habits, ready on all occasions.   For life is a kind of chess, in which we have often points to gain, and competitors or adversaries to contend with, and in which there is a vast variety of good and evil events, that are in some degree the effects of prudence or the want of it. By playing at chess, then, we may learn,

I. *Foresight*, which looks a little into futurity, and considers the consequences that may attend an action; for it is continually occurring to the player, "If I move this piece, what will be the advantage of my new situation? What use can my adversary make of it to annoy me? What other moves can I make to support it, and to defend myself from his attacks?"

II. *Circumspection*, which surveys the whole chess-board or scene of action; the relations of the several pieces and situations, the dangers they are respectively exposed to, the several possibilities of their aiding each other, the probabilities that the adversary may make this or that move, and attack this or the other piece, and what different means can be used to avoid his stroke, or turn its consequences against him.

III. *Caution*, not to make our moves too hastily. This habit is best acquired by observing strictly the laws of the game; such as, "If you touch a piece, you must move it somewhere; if you set it down, you must let it stand;" and it is therefore best that these rules should be observed, as the game thereby becomes more the image of human life, and particularly of war; in which, if you have incautiously put yourself into a bad and dangerous position, you cannot obtain your enemy's leave to withdraw your troops, and place them more securely, but you must abide all the consequences of your rashness.

And, lastly, we learn by chess the habit of *not being discouraged by present appearances in the state of our affairs*, the habit of *hoping for a favorable change*, and that of *persevering in the search of resources*. The game is so full of events, there is such a variety of turns in it, the fortune of it is so subject to sudden vicissitudes, and one so frequently, after long contemplation, discovers the means of extricating one's self from a supposed insurmountable difficulty, that one is encouraged to continue the contest to the last, in hopes of victory by our own skill, or at least of getting a stale mate, by the negligence of our adversary. And, whoever considers, what in chess he often sees instances of, that particular pieces of success are apt to produce presumption, and its consequent inattention, by which the losses may be recovered, will learn not to be too much discouraged by the present success of his adversary, nor to despair of final good fortune upon every little check he receives in the pursuit of it.

That we may therefore be induced more frequently to choose this beneficial amusement, in preference to others which are not attended with the same advantages, every circumstance which may increase the pleasures of it should be regarded ; and every action or word that is unfair, disrespectful, or that in any way may give uneasiness, should be avoided, as contrary to the immediate intention of both the players, which is to pass the time agreeably.

Therefore, first, if it is agreed to play according to the strict rules, then those rules are to be exactly observed by both parties, and should not be insisted on for one side, while deviated from by the other, for this is not equitable.

Secondly, if it is agreed not to observe the rules exactly, but one party demands indulgences, he should then be as willing to allow them to the other.

Thirdly, no false move should ever be made to extricate yourself out of difficulty, or to gain an advantage. There can be no pleasure in playing with a person once detected in such unfair practice.

Fourthly, if your adversary is long in playing, you ought not to hurry him, or express any uneasiness at his delay. You should not sing, nor whistle, nor look at your watch, nor take up a book to read, nor make a tapping with your feet on the floor, or with your fingers on the table, nor do anything that may disturb his attention. For all these things displease ; and they do not show your skill in playing, but your craftiness or your rudeness.

Fifthly, you ought not to endeavor to amuse and deceive your adversary, by pretending to have made bad moves, and saying that you have now lost the game, in order to make him secure and careless, and inattentive to your schemes ; for this is fraud and deceit, not skill in the game.

Sixthly, you must not, when you have gained a victory, use any triumphing or insulting expression, nor show too much pleasure ; but endeavor to console your adversary, and make him less dissatisfied with himself, by every kind of civil expression that may be used with truth, such as, "You understand the game better than I, but you are a little inattentive ;" or, "You play too fast ;" or, "You had the best of the game, but something happened to divert your thoughts, and that turned it in my favor."

Seventhly, if you are a spectator while others play, observe the most perfect silence. For, if you give advice, you offend both parties, — him against whom you give it, because it may cause the loss of his game ; him in whose favor you give it, because, though it be good, and he follows it, he loses the pleasure he might have had, if you had permitted him to think until it had occurred to himself. Even after a move or moves, you must not, by replacing the pieces, show how they might have been placed better; for that displeases, and may occasion disputes and doubts about their true situation. All talking to the players lessens or diverts their attention, and is therefore unpleasing. Nor should you give the least hint to either party, by any kind of noise or motion. If you do, you are unworthy to be a spectator. If you have a mind to exercise or show your judgment, do it in playing your own game, when you have an opportunity, — not in criticizing, or meddling with, or counselling the play of others.

Lastly, if the game is not to be played rigorously, according to the rules above mentioned, then moderate your desire of victory over your adversary, and be pleased with one over yourself. Snatch not eagerly at every advantage offered by his unskilfulness or inattention; but point out to him kindly that by such a move he places or leaves a piece in danger and unsupported; that by another he will put his king in a perilous situation, &c. By this generous civility (so opposite to the unfairness above forbidden) you may, indeed, happen to lose the game to your opponent; but you will win what is better, his esteem, his respect, and his affection, together with the silent approbation and good-will of impartial spectators.

A PARABLE ON PERSECUTION.

1. AND it came to pass, after these things, that Abraham sat in the door of his tent about the going down of the sun.

2. And behold a man, bowed with age, came from the way of the wilderness, leaning on a staff.

3. And Abraham rose and met him, and said, "Turn in, I pray thee, and wash thy feet, and tarry all night, and thou shalt arise early in the morning and go on thy way."

4. But the man said, "Nay, for I will abide under this tree."

5. And Abraham pressed him greatly; so he turned, and they went into the tent, and Abraham baked unleavened bread, and they did eat.

6. And when Abraham saw that the man blessed not God, he said unto him, "Wherefore dost thou not worship the most high God, creator of heaven and earth?"

7. And the man answered and said, "I do not worship the

God thou speakest of, neither do I call upon his name; for I have made to myself a god, which abideth always in my house, and provideth me with all things."

8. And Abraham's zeal was kindled against the man, and he arose and drove him forth with blows into the wilderness.

9. And at midnight God called upon Abraham, saying, " Abraham, where is the stranger ?"

10. And Abraham answered and said, " Lord, he would not worship thee, neither would he call upon thy name ; therefore I have driven him out before my face into the wilderness."

11. And God said, "Have I borne with him these hundred ninety and eight years, and clothed him, notwithstanding his rebellion against me ; and couldst not thou, that art thyself a sinner, bear with him one night ?"

12. And Abraham said, " Let not the anger of the Lord wax hot against his servant ; lo, I have sinned ; forgive me, I pray thee."

13. And Abraham arose, and went forth into the wilderness, and sought diligently for the man, and found him, and returned with him to the tent ; and when he had entreated him kindly, he sent him away on the morrow with gifts.

14. And God spake unto Abraham, saying, " For this thy sin shall thy seed be afflicted four hundred years in a strange land.

15. " But for thy repentance will I deliver them ; and they shall come forth with power and gladness of heart, and with much substance." *

* The above parable was published by Lord Kames, in his " Sketches of the History of Man," with the following remark in relation to it : " It was communicated to me by Dr. Franklin, of Philadelphia, a man who makes a great figure in the learned world, and who would still make a greater figure for benevolence and candor, were virtue as much regarded in this declining age as knowledge." An absurd charge of plagiarism was brought against Franklin because of this parable, published without his knowledge, and for which he had never claimed originality. In a letter dated November 2, 1789, to Benjamin Vaughan, he says : " The truth is, that I never published the parable, and never claimed more credit from it than what related to the style, and the addition of the concluding threatening and promise. The pub'ishing of it by Lord Kames, without my consent, deprived me of a good deal of amusement, which I used to take in reading it by heart out of any Bible, and obtaining the remarks of the scripturians upon it, which were sometimes very diverting : not but that it is in itself, on account of the importance of its moral, well worth being made known to all mankind." The substance of the story is as old as the day of the Persian poet Saadi. It is also related by Jeremy Taylor.

A PARABLE ON BROTHERLY LOVE.

1. In those days there was no worker of iron in all the land. And the merchants of Midian passed by with their camels, bearing spices, and myrrh, and balm, and wares of iron.

2. And Reuben bought an axe of the Ishmaelite merchants, which he prized highly, for there was none in his father's house.

3. And Simeon said unto Reuben his brother, "Lend me, I pray thee, thine axe." But he refused, and would not.

4. And Levi also said unto him, "My brother, lend me, I pray thee, thine axe;" and he refused him also.

5. Then came Judah unto Reuben, and entreated him, saying, "Lo, thou lovest me, and I have always loved thee; do not refuse me the use of thine axe."

6. But Reuben turned from him, and refused him likewise.

7. Now it came to pass that Reuben hewed timber on the bank of the river, and his axe fell therein, and he could by no means find it.

8. But Simeon, Levi and Judah, had sent a messenger after the Ishmaelites with money, and had bought for themselves each an axe.

9. Then came Reuben unto Simeon, and said, "Lo, I have lost mine axe, and my work is unfinished; lend me thine, I pray thee."

10. And Simeon answered him, saying, "Thou wouldst not lend me thine axe, therefore will I not lend thee mine."

11. Then he went unto Levi, and said unto him, "My brother, thou knowest my loss and my necessity; lend me, I pray thee, thine axe."

12. And Levi reproached him, saying, "Thou wouldst not lend me thine axe when I desired it; but I will be better than thou, and will lend thee mine."

13. And Reuben was grieved at the rebuke of Levi, and, being ashamed, turned from him, and took not the axe, but sought his brother Judah.

14. And, as he drew near, Judah beheld his countenance as it were covered with grief and shame; and he prevented him, saying, "My brother, I know thy loss; but why should it trouble thee? Lo, have I not an axe that will serve both thee and me? Take it, I pray thee, and use it as thine own."

15. And Reuben fell on his neck, and kissed him, with tears, saying, "Thy kindness is great, but thy goodness in forgiving me is greater. Thou art indeed my brother, and whilst I live will I surely love thee."

12. And Judah said, "Let us also love our other brethren; behold, are we not all of one blood?"

17. And Joseph saw these things, and reported them to his father Jacob.

18. And Jacob said, "Reuben did wrong, but he repented; Simeon also did wrong; and Levi was not altogether blameless.

19. "But the heart of Judah is princely. Judah hath the soul of a king. His father's children shall bow down before him, and he shall rule over his brethren."

[TO MADAME BRILLON, OF PASSY.]

THE EPHEMERA; AN EMBLEM OF HUMAN LIFE.

WRITTEN IN 1778.

You may remember, my dear friend, that when we lately spent that happy day in the delightful garden and sweet society of the Moulin Joly, I stopped a little in one of our walks, and stayed some time behind the company. We had been shown numberless skeletons of a kind of little fly, called an ephemera, whose successive generations, we were told, were bred and expired within the day. I happened to see a living company of them on a leaf, who appeared to be engaged in conversation. You know I understand all the inferior animal tongues. My too great application to the study of them is the best excuse I can give for the little progress I have made in your charming language. I listened, through curiosity, to the discourse of these little creatures; but, as they, in their national vivacity, spoke three or four together, I could make but little of their conversation. I found, however, by some broken expressions that I heard now and then, they were disputing warmly on the merits of two foreign musicians, one a *cousin*, the other a *moscheto;* in which dispute they spent their time, seemingly as regardless of the shortness of life as if they had been sure of living a month. Happy people! thought I; you are certainly under a wise, just, and mild government, since you have no public grievances to complain of, nor any subject of contention but the perfections and imperfections of foreign music. I turned my head from them to an old gray-headed one, who was single on another leaf, and talking to himself. Being amused with his soliloquy, I put it down in writing, in hopes it will likewise amuse her to

34

whom I am so much indebted for the most pleasing of all amusements, her delicious company and heavenly harmony.

"It was," said he, "the opinion of learned philosophers of
our race, who lived and flourished long before my time, that
this vast world, the Moulin Joly, could not itself subsist more
than eighteen hours; and I think there was some foundation for
that opinion, since, by the apparent motion of the great luminary
that gives life to all nature, and which in my time has evidently
declined considerably towards the ocean at the end of our earth,
it must then finish its course, be extinguished in the waters that
surround us, and leave the world in cold and darkness, necessarily producing universal death and destruction. I have lived
seven of those hours, — a great age, being no less than four hundred and twenty minutes of time. How very few of us continue
so long! I have seen generations born, flourish and expire.
My present friends are the children and grand-children of the
friends of my youth, who are now, alas, no more! And I must
soon follow them; for, by the course of nature, though still in
health, I cannot expect to live above seven or eight minutes
longer. What now avails all my toil and labor, in amassing
honey-dew on this leaf, which I cannot live to enjoy! What
the political strugles I have been engaged in, for the good of
my compatriot inhabitants of this bush, or my philosophical
studies for the benefit of our race in general! for, in politics,
what can laws do without morals? Our present race of ephemeræ will in a course of minutes become corrupt, like those of
other and older bushes, and consequently as wretched. And
in philosophy how small our progress! Alas! art is long,
and life is short! My friends would comfort me with the idea
of a name, they say, I shall leave behind me; and they tell me
I have lived long enough to nature and to glory. But what
will fame be to an ephemera who no longer exists? And what
will become of all history in the eighteenth hour, when the
world itself, even the whole Moulin Joly, shall come to its end,
and be buried in universal ruin?"

To me, after all my eager pursuits, no solid pleasures now
remain, but the reflection of a long life spent in meaning well,
the sensible conversation of a few good lady ephemeræ, and
now and then a kind smile and a tune from the ever amiable
Brillante.

A DIALOGUE

BETWEEN BRITAIN, FRANCE, SPAIN, HOLLAND, SAXONY, AND AMERICA.*

Britain. Sister of Spain, I have a favor to ask of you. My subjects in America are disobedient, and I am about to chastise them; I beg you will not furnish them with any arms or ammunition.

Spain. Have you forgotten, then, that when my subjects in the Low Countries rebelled against me, you not only furnished them with military stores, but joined them with an army and a fleet? I wonder how you can have the impudence to ask such a favor of me, or the folly to expect it!

Britain. You, my dear sister France, will surely not refuse me this favor.

France. Did you not assist my rebel Huguenots with a fleet and an army at Rochelle? And have you not lately aided, privately and sneakingly, my rebel subjects in Corsica? And do you not at this instant keep their chief pensioned, and ready to head a fresh revolt there, whenever you can find or make an opportunity? Dear sister, you must be a little silly!

Britain. Honest Holland! You see it is remembered I was once your friend; you will therefore be mine on this occasion. I know, indeed, you are accustomed to smuggle with these rebels of mine. I will wink at that; sell them as much tea as you please, to enervate the rascals, since they will not take it of me; but, for God's sake, don't supply them with any arms!

Holland. 'T is true you assisted me against Philip, my tyrant of Spain; but have I not assisted you against one of your tyrants,† and enabled you to expel him? Surely that account, as we merchants say, is *balanced*, and I am nothing in your debt. I have, indeed, some complaints against *you*, for endeavoring to starve me by your *Navigation Acts;* but, being peaceably disposed, I do not quarrel with you for that. I shall only go on quietly with my own business. Trade is my profession; 't is all I have to subsist on. And, let me tell you, I shall make no scruple (on the prospect of a good market for that commodity) even to send my ships to Hell, and supply the Devil with brimstone. For, you must know, I can insure in London against the burning of my sails.

* This satirical piece was written soon after Franklin's arrival in France, as commissioner, at the beginning of the Revolutionary war.
† James the Second.

America to Britain. Why, you old bloodthirsty bully ! You, who have been everywhere vaunting your own prowess, and defaming the Americans as poltroons ! You, who have boasted of being able to march over all their bellies with a single regiment ! You, who by fraud have possessed yourself of their strongest fortress, and all the arms they had stored up in it ! You, who have a disciplined army in their country, intrenched to the teeth, and provided with everything ! Do *you* run about begging all Europe not to supply those poor people with a little powder and shot ? Do you mean, then, to fall upon them naked and unarmed, and butcher them in cold blood ? Is this your courage ? Is this your magnanimity ?

Britain. O ! you wicked — Whig — Presbyterian — Serpent ! Have you the impudence to appear before me, after all your disobedience ? Surrender immediately all your liberties and properties into my hands, or I will cut you to pieces ! Was it for this that I planted your country at so great an expense ? That I protected you in your infancy, and defended you against all your enemies ?

America. I shall not surrender my liberty and property, but with my life. It is not true that my country was planted at your expense. Your own records * refute that falsehood to your face. Nor did you ever afford me a man or a shilling to defend me against the Indians, the only enemies I had upon my own account. But, when you have quarrelled with all Europe, and drawn me with you into all your broils, then you value yourself upon protecting me from the enemies you have made for me. I have no natural cause of difference with Spain, France or Holland, and yet by turns I have joined with you in wars against them all. You would not suffer me to make or keep a separate peace with any of them, though I might easily have done it to great advantage. Does your protecting me in those wars give you a right to fleece me ? If so, as I fought for you, as well as you for me, it gives me a proportionable right to fleece you. What think you of an American law to make a monopoly of you and your commerce, as you have done by your laws of me and mine ? Content yourself with that monopoly if you are wise, and learn justice if you would be respected !

* See the Journals of the House of Commons, 1642, namely :

"*Die Veneris, Martii* 10°, 1642.

"Whereas, the plantations in New England have, by the blessing of Almighty God, had good and prosperous success *without any public charge to this State,*" &c.

Britain. You impudent b——h! Am not I your mother country? Is not that a sufficient title to your respect and obedience?

Saxony. Mother country! Ha! ha! ha! What respect have *you* the front to claim as a mother country? You know that *I* am *your* mother country, and yet you pay me none. Nay, it is but the other day that you hired ruffians * to rob me on the highway,† and burn my house!‡ For shame! Hide your face, and hold your tongue! If you continue this conduct, you will make yourself the contempt of Europe!

Britain. O Lord! Where are my friends?

France, Spain, Holland and Saxony, all together. Friends! Believe us, you have none; nor ever will have any, till you mend your manners. How can we, who are your neighbors, have any regard for you, or expect any equity from you, should your power increase, when we see how basely and unjustly you have used both your *own mother and your own children?*

EXTRACTS.

ON DUELS.

FORMERLY, when duels were used to determine law-suits, from an opinion that Providence would in every instance favor truth and right with victory, they were excusable. At present, they decide nothing. A man says something, which another tells him is a lie. They fight; but, whichever is killed, the point in dispute remains unsettled. To this purpose they have a pleasant little story here. A gentleman in a coffee-house desired another to sit further from him. "Why so?" "Because, sir, you stink." "That is an affront, and you must fight me." "I will fight you, if you insist upon it; but I do not see how that will mend the matter. For, if you kill me, I shall stink too; and if I kill you, you will stink, if possible, worse than you do at present." How can such miserable sinners as we are entertain so much pride as to conceit that every offence against our imagined honor merits *death?* These petty princes in their own opinion would call that sovereign a tyrant who should put one of them to death for

* Prussians.
† They entered and raised contributions in Saxony.
‡ And they burnt the fine suburbs of Dresden, the capital of Saxony.

a little uncivil language, though pointed at his sacred person; yet every one of them makes himself judge in his own cause, condemns the offender without a jury, and undertakes himself to be the executioner.

SIMPLICITY IN WRITING.

How shall we judge of the goodness of a writing? or what qualities should a writing on any subject have, to be good and perfect in its kind?

Answer. To be good it ought to have a tendency to benefit the reader, by improving his virtue or his knowledge. The method should be just; that is, it should proceed regularly from things known to things unknown, distinctly, clearly, and without confusion. The words used should be the most expressive that the language affords, provided they are the most generally understood. Nothing should be expressed in two words that can as well be expressed in one; that is, no synonyms should be used, but the whole be as short as possible, consistent with clearness. The words should be so placed as to be agreeable to the ear in reading: summarily, it should be smooth, clear and short; for the contrary qualities are displeasing.

ADVANTAGES OF THE PRESS.

The ancient Roman and Greek orators could only speak to the number of citizens capable of being assembled within the reach of their voice; their writings had little effect, because the bulk of the people could not read. Now by the press we can speak to nations; and good books, and well-written pamphlets, have great and general influence. The facility with which the same truths may be repeatedly enforced by placing them in different lights, in *newspapers* which are everywhere read, gives a great chance of establishing them. And we now find that it is not only right to strike while the iron is hot, but that it is very practicable to heat it by continual striking.

CORRESPONDENCE.

[TO JOSIAH FRANKLIN, BOSTON.]

A Man's Religion to be judged of by its Fruits — Freemasons.

PHILADELPHIA, April 13, 1738.

HONORED FATHER: I have your favors of the 21st of March, in which you both seem concerned lest I have imbibed some erroneous opinions. Doubtless I have my share, and when the natural weakness and imperfection of human understanding is considered, the unavoidable influence of education, custom, books and company, upon our ways of thinking, I imagine a man must have a good deal of vanity who believes, and a good deal of boldness who affirms, that all the doctrines he holds are true, and all he rejects are false. And, perhaps, the same may be justly said of every sect, church, and society of men, when they assume to themselves that infallibility which they deny to the pope and councils.

I think opinions should be judged of by their influences and effects; and if man holds none that tend to make him less virtuous or more vicious, it may be concluded he holds none that are dangerous, — which, I hope, is the case with me.

I am sorry you should have any uneasiness on my account, and, if it were a thing possible for one to alter his opinions in order to please another's, I know none whom I ought more willingly to oblige in that respect than yourselves. But, since it is no more in a man's power to *think* than to *look* like another, methinks all that should be expected from me is to keep my mind open to conviction; to hear patiently, and examine attentively, whatever is offered me for that end; and, if after all I continue in the same errors, I believe your usual charity will induce you rather to pity and excuse than blame me: in the mean time your care and concern for me is what I am very thankful for.

My mother grieves that one of her sons is an Arian, another

an Arminian; what an Arminian or an Arian is, I cannot say that I very well know. The truth is, I make such distinctions very little my study. I think vital religion has always suffered when orthodoxy is more regarded than virtue; and the Scriptures assure me that at the last day we shall not be examined what we *thought*, but what we *did;* and our recommendation will not be that we said, *Lord! Lord!* but that we did good to our fellow-creatures. See Matt. xx.

As to the freemasons, I know no way of giving my mother a better account of them than she seems to have at present (since it is not allowed that women should be admitted into that secret society). She has, I must confess, on that account, some reason to be displeased with it; but, for anything else, I must entreat her to suspend her judgment till she is better informed, unless she will believe me when I assure her that they are in general a very harmless sort of people, and have no principles or practices that are inconsistent with religion and good manners.

We have had great rains here lately, which, with the thawing of snow in the mountains back of our country, has made vast floods in our rivers, and, by carrying away bridges, boats, &c., made travelling almost impracticable for a week past; so that our post has entirely missed making one trip.

I hear nothing of Dr. Crook, nor can I learn any such person has ever been here.

I hope my sister Jenny's child is by this time recovered. I am your dutiful son,   B. FRANKLIN.

[TO MISS JANE FRANKLIN.]*

On presenting a Spinning-wheel.

PHILADELPHIA, January 6, 1726–7.

DEAR SISTER: I am highly pleased with the account Captain Freeman gives me of you. I always judged, by your behavior when a child, that you would make a good, agreeable woman; and you know you were ever my peculiar favorite. I have been thinking what would be a suitable present for me to make, and for you to receive, as I hear you are grown a celebrated beauty. I had almost determined on a tea-table, but when I considered that the character of a good house-wife was

---

* Afterwards Mrs. Mecom. She was fifteen years old at the above date

far preferable to that of being only a pretty gentlewoman, I concluded to send you a *spinning-wheel*, which I hope you will accept as a small token of my sincere love and affection.

Sister, farewell, and remember that modesty, as it makes the most homely virgin amiable and charming, so the want of it infallibly renders the most perfect beauty disagreeable and odious. But when that brightest of female virtues shines among other perfections of body and mind in the same person, it makes the woman more lovely than an angel. Excuse this freedom, and use the same with me. I am, dear Jenny, your loving brother. B. FRANKLIN.

[TO THE SAME.]

Religious Notions — Doctrine and Worship.

PHILADELPHIA, July 28, 1743.

DEAREST SISTER JENNY: I took your admonition very kindly, and was far from being offended at you for it. If I say anything about it to you, 'tis only to rectify some wrong opinions you seem to have entertained of me; and this I do only because they give you some uneasiness, which I am unwilling to be the occasion of. You express yourself as if you thought I was against worshipping of God, and doubt that good works would merit heaven; which are both fancies of your own, I think, without foundation. I am so far from thinking that God is not to be worshipped, that I have composed and wrote a whole book of devotions for my own use; and I imagine there are few if any in the world so weak as to imagine that the little good we can do here can merit so vast a reward hereafter.

There are some things in your New England doctrine and worship which I do not agree with; but I do not therefore condemn them, or desire to shake your belief or practice of them. We may dislike things that are nevertheless right in themselves; I would only have you make me the same allowance, and have a better opinion both of morality and your brother. Read the pages of Mr. Edwards's late book, entitled, "Some Thoughts concerning the present Revival of Religion in New England," from 367 to 375, and, when you judge of others, if you can perceive the fruit to be good, don't terrify yourself that the tree may be evil; but be assured it is not so, for you know who has said, "Men do not gather grapes off thorns, and figs off thistles."

I have not time to add, but that I shall always be your affectionate brother,   B. FRANKLIN.

P. S. It was not kind in you, when your sister commended good works, to suppose she intended it a reproach to you. 'T was very far from her thoughts.

[TO JAMES READ.]

On Differences between Man and Wife.

Saturday morning, 17 August, 1745.

DEAR JEMMY: I have been reading your letter over again, and, since you desire an answer, I sit down to write you one; yet, as I write in the market, it will, I believe, be but a short one, though I may be long about it. I approve of your method of writing one's mind, when one is too warm to speak it with temper: but, being quite cool myself in this affair, I might as well speak as write, if I had an opportunity.

Are you an attorney by profession, and do you know no better how to choose a proper court in which to bring your action? Would you submit to the decision of a husband a cause between you and his wife? Don't you know that all wives are in the right? It may be you don't, for you are yet but a young husband. But see, on this head, the learned Coke, that oracle of the law, in his chapter *De Jur. Marit. Angl.* I advise you not to bring it to trial; for, if you do, you will certainly be cast.

Frequent interruptions make it impossible for me to go through all your letter. I have only time to remind you of the saying of that excellent old philosopher, Socrates, *that, in differences among friends, they that make the first concessions are the wisest;* and to hint to you that you are in danger of losing that honor in the present case, if you are not very speedy in your acknowledgments, which I persuade myself you will be, when you consider the sex of your adversary.

Your visits never had but one thing disagreeable in them; that is, they were always too short. I shall exceedingly regret the loss of them, unless you continue, as you have begun, to make it up to me by long letters.

I am, dear Jemmy, with sincere love to our dearest Suky, your very affectionate friend and cousin,   B. FRANKLIN.

[TO PETER COLLINSON.]

English Poor Laws — Amending the Scheme of Providence — Anec-
dotes — Aversion from Labor among American Indians — Germans
in Pennsylvania — Their Peculiarities — Hopes for England.

PHILADELPHIA, 9 May, 1753.

SIR: I thank you for the kind and judicious remarks you
have made on my little piece. I have often observed with wonder the temper of the poorer English laborers which you mention,
and acknowledge it to be pretty general. When any of them happen to come here, where labor is much better paid than in England, their industry seems to diminish in equal proportion. But
it is not so with the German laborers. They retain the habitual
industry and frugality they bring with them, and, receiving higher
wages, an accumulation arises that makes them all rich. When
I consider that the English are the offspring of Germans, that
the climate they live in is much of the same temperature, and
when I see nothing in nature that should create this difference,
I am tempted to suspect it must arise from the constitution; and
I have sometimes doubted whether the laws peculiar to England,
which *compel the rich to maintain the poor*, have not given the
latter a dependence that very much lessens the care of providing
against the wants of old age.

I have heard it remarked that the poor in Protestant countries,
on the continent of Europe, are generally more industrious than
those of Popish countries. May not the more numerous foundations in the latter for relief of the poor have some effect
towards rendering them less provident? To relieve the misfortunes of our fellow-creatures is concurring with the Deity; it is
godlike; but, if we provide encouragement for laziness, and
support for folly, may we not be found fighting against the order
of God and nature, which perhaps has appointed want and misery
as the proper punishments for and cautions against, as well as
necessary consequences of idleness and extravagance? Whenever we attempt to amend the scheme of Providence, and to in-
terfere with the government of the world, we had need be very
circumspect, lest we do more harm than good. In New England
they once thought blackbirds useless, and mischievous to the corn.
They made efforts to destroy them. The consequence was, the
blackbirds were diminished; but a kind of worm which devoured
their grass, and which the blackbirds used to feed on, increased
prodigiously; then, finding their loss in grass much greater than
their saving in corn, they wished again for their blackbirds.

We had here some years since a Transylvanian Tartar, who

had travelled much in the East, and came hither merely to see the West, intending to go home through the Spanish West Indies, China, &c.   He asked me, one day, what I thought might be the reason that so many and such numerous nations as the Tartars in Europe and Asia, the Indians in America, and the Negroes in Africa, continued a wandering, careless life, and refused to live in cities, and cultivate the arts they saw practised by the civilized parts of mankind.   While I was considering what answer to make him, he said, in his broken English, " God make man for Paradise.   He make him for live lazy.   Man make God angry. God turn him out of Paradise, and bid workee.   Man no love workee ; he want to go to Paradise again ; he want to live lazy. So all mankind love lazy."   However this may be, it seems certain that the hope of becoming at some time of life free from the necessity of care and labor, together with fear and penury, are the main springs of most people's industry.   To those, indeed, who have been educated in elegant plenty, even the provision made for the poor may appear misery ; but to those who have scarce ever been better provided for, such provision may seem quite good and sufficient.   These latter, then, have nothing to fear worse than their present condition, and scarce hope for anything better than a parish maintenance.   So that there is only the difficulty of getting that maintenance allowed while they are able to work, or a little shame they suppose attending it, that can induce them to work at all ; and what they do will only be from hand to mouth.

The proneness of human nature to a life of ease, of freedom from care and labor, appears strongly in the little success that has hitherto attended every attempt to civilize our American Indians.   In their present way of living, almost all their wants are supplied by the spontaneous productions of nature, with the addition of very little labor, if hunting and fishing may indeed be called labor, where game is so plenty.   They visit us frequently, and see the advantages that arts, sciences, and compact societies, procure us.   They are not deficient in natural understanding ; and yet they have never shown any inclination to change their manner of life for ours, or to learn any of our arts.   When an Indian child has been brought up among us, taught our language, and habituated to our customs, yet, if he goes to see his relatives, and makes one Indian ramble with them, there is no persuading him ever to return.   And that this is not natural to them merely as Indians, but as men, is plain from this, — that when white persons, of either sex, have been taken prisoners by the Indians, and lived a while with them, though ransomed by their friends, and treated with all imaginable tenderness, to prevail with them to stay among the English, yet in a short time they become disgusted with our manner of life, and the care and pains that are necessary to support it, and take the first opportunity of escaping again into the woods, from whence there is no redeeming them. One instance I remember to have heard, where the person was brought home to possess a good estate; but, finding some care necessary to keep it together, he relinquished it to a younger brother, reserving to himself nothing but a gun and a match-coat, with which he took his way again into the wilderness.

So that I am apt to imagine that close societies, subsisting by labor and art, arose first not from choice, but from necessity, when numbers, being driven by war from their hunting-grounds, and prevented by seas, or by other nations, from obtaining other hunting-grounds, were crowded together into some narrow territories, which without labor could not afford them food. However, as matters now stand with us, care and industry seem absolutely necessary to our well-being. They should therefore have every encouragement we can invent, and not one motive to diligence be subtracted; and the support of the poor should not be by maintaining them in idleness, but by employing them in some kind of labor suited to their abilities of body, as I am informed begins to be of late the practice in many parts of England, where workhouses are erected for that purpose. If these were general, I should think the poor would be more careful, and work voluntarily to lay up something for themselves against a rainy day, rather than run the risk of being obliged to work at the pleasure of others for a bare subsistence, and that too under confinement.

The little value Indians set on what we prize so highly, under the name of learning, appears from a pleasant passage that happened some years since at a treaty between some colonies and the Six Nations. When everything had been settled to the satisfaction of both sides, and nothing remained but a mutual exchange of civilities, the English commissioners told the Indians that they had in their country a college for the instruction of youth, who were there taught various languages, arts and sciences; that there was a particular foundation in favor of the Indians, to defray the expense of the education of any of their sons who should desire to take the benefit of it; and said, if the Indians would accept the offer, the English would take half a dozen of their brightest lads, and bring them up in the best manner. The Indians, after consulting on the proposals, replied that it was re-

35

membered that some of their youths had formerly been educated
at that college, but that it had been observed that for a long time
after they returned to their friends *they were absolutely good
for nothing;* being neither acquainted with the true methods of
killing deer, catching beavers, or surprising an enemy. The
proposition they looked on, however, as a mark of kindness and
good-will of the English to the Indian nations, which merited a
grateful return; and therefore, if the English gentlemen would
send a dozen or two of their children to Onondago, the Great
Council would take care of their education, bring them up in
what was really the best manner, and make men of them.

I am perfectly of your mind, that measures of great temper
are necessary with the Germans; and am not without apprehensions that, through their indiscretion, or ours, or both, great disorders may one day arise among us. Those who come hither are
generally the most stupid of their own nation, and, as ignorance
is often attended with credulity when knavery would mislead it,
and with suspicion when honesty would set it right, — and as few
of the English understand the German language, and so cannot
address them either from the press or the pulpit, — it is almost
impossible to remove any prejudices they may entertain. Their
clergy have very little influence on the people, who seem to take
a pleasure in abusing and discharging the minister on every trivial
occasion. Not being used to liberty, they know not how to make
a modest use of it. And, as Kolben says of the young Hottentots, that they are not esteemed men until they have shown their
manhood by *beating their mothers,* so these seem not to think themselves free till they can feel their liberty in abusing and insulting
their teachers. Thus they are under no restraint from ecclesiastical government; they behave, however, submissively enough at
present to the civil government, which I wish they may continue
to do, for I remember when they modestly declined intermeddling
in our elections, but now they come in droves and carry all before
them, except in one or two counties.

Few of their children in the country know English. They import many books from Germany; and of the six printing-houses
in the province two are entirely German, two half-German half-
English, and but two entirely English. They have one German
newspaper, and one half-German. Advertisements intended to
be general are now printed in Dutch and English. The signs in
our streets have inscriptions in both languages, and in some places
only German. They begin of late to make all their bonds and
other legal instruments in their own language, which (though I

think it ought not to be) are allowed good in our courts, where the German business so increases that there is continued need of interpreters; and I suppose in a few years they will also be necessary in the Assembly, to te'l one-half of our legislators what the other half say.

In short, unless the stream of 'heir importation could be turned from this to other colonies, as you very judiciously propose, they will soon so outnumber us that all the advantages we have will, in my opinion, be not able to preserve our language, and even our government will become precarious. The French, who watch all advantages, are now themselves making a German settlement, back of us, in the Illinois country, and by means of these Germans they may in time come to an understanding with ours; and, indeed, in the last war our Germans showed a general disposition that seemed to bode us no good. For, when the English who were not Quakers, alarmed by the danger arising from the defenceless state of our country, entered unanimously into an association, and within this government and the low counties raised, armed, and disciplined near ten thousand men, the Germans, except a very few in proportion to their number, refused to engage in it, giving out, one amongst another, and even in print, that, if they were quiet, the French, should they take the country, would not molest them; at the same time abusing the Philadelphians for fitting out privateers against the enemy, and representing the trouble, hazard and expense, of defending the province, as a greater inconvenience than any that might be expected from a change of government. Yet I am not for refusing to admit them entirely into our colonies. All that seems to me necessary is, to distribute them more equally, mix them with the English, establish English schools where they are now too thick-settled; and take some care to prevent the practice, lately fallen into by some of the ship-owners, of sweeping the German jails to make up the number of their passengers. I say, I am not against the admission of Germans in general, for they have their virtues. Their industry and frugality are exemplary. They are excellent husbandmen, and contribute greatly to the improvement of a country.

I pray God to preserve long to Great Britain the English laws, manners, liberties, and religion. Notwithstanding the complaints so frequent in your public papers of the prevailing corruption and degeneracy of the people, I know you have a great deal of virtue still subsisting among you, and I hope the constitution is not so near a dissolution as some seem to apprehend. I do not think you are generally become such slaves to your vices as to draw down the *justice* Milton speaks of, when he says, that——*

Good Works — On Meriting Heaven — Prayers and Deeds — Example of Christ.

PHILADELPHIA, June 6, 1753.

SIR: I received your kind letter of the 2d instant, and am glad to hear that you increase in strength; I hope you will continue mending, till you recover your former health and firmness. Let me know whether you still use the cold bath, and what effect it has.

As to the kindness you mention, I wish it could have been of more service to you. But, if it had, the only thanks I should desire is, that you would always be equally ready to serve any other person that may need your assistance, and so let good offices go round; for mankind are all of a family.

For my own part, when I am employed in serving others, I do not look upon myself as conferring favors, but as paying debts. In my travels, and since my settlement, I have received much kindness from men to whom I shall never have any opportunity of making the least direct return; and numberless mercies from God, who is infinitely above being benefited by our services. Those kindnesses from men I can, therefore, only return on their fellow-men; and I can only show my gratitude for these mercies from God by a readiness to help his other children and my brethren. For, I do not think that thanks and compliments, though repeated weekly, can discharge our real obligations to each other, and much less those to our Creator.

You will see in this my notion of good works, — that I am far from expecting to merit heaven by them. By heaven we under-

---

* The original MS. ends thus abruptly. It is conjectured that the following is the passage from Milton alluded to :

" Yet sometimes nations will decline so low
From virtue, which is reason, that no wrong,
But justice, and some fatal curse annexed,
Deprives them of their outward liberty,
Their inward lost."   *Paradise Lost*, xii. 97.

* The substance of this letter was communicated subsequently to other correspondents. For an account of Franklin's acquaintance with Whitefield, see the Autobiography.

stand a state of happiness, infinite in degree, and eternal in duration; I can do nothing to deserve such rewards. He that for giving a draught of water to a thirsty person should expect to be paid with a good plantation, would be modest in his demands, compared with those who think they deserve heaven for the little good they do on earth. Even the mixed, imperfect pleasures we enjoy in this world are rather from God's goodness than our merit; how much more such happiness of heaven! For my part, I have not the vanity to think I deserve it, the folly to expect it, nor the ambition to desire it; but content myself in submitting to the will and disposal of that God who made me, who has hitherto preserved and blessed me, and in whose fatherly goodness I may well confide, that he will never make me miserable, and that even the afflictions I may at any time suffer shall tend to my benefit.

The faith you mention has certainly its use in the world; I do not desire to see it diminished, nor would I endeavor to lessen it in any man; but I wish it were more productive of good works than I have generally seen it. I mean real good works; works of kindness, charity, mercy and public spirit; not holiday-keeping, sermon reading or hearing, performing church ceremonies, or making long prayers, filled with flatteries and compliments, despised even by wise men, and much less capable of pleasing the Deity. The worship of God is a duty; the hearing and reading of sermons may be useful; but, if men rest in hearing and praying, as too many do, it is as if a tree should value itself on being watered and putting forth leaves, though it never produced any fruit.

Your great Master thought much less of these outward appearances and professions than many of his modern disciples. He preferred the *doers* of the word to the mere *hearers ;* the son that seemingly refused to obey his father, and yet performed his commands, to him that professed his readiness, but neglected the work; the heretical but charitable Samaritan, to the uncharitable though orthodox priest and sanctified Levite; and those who gave food to the hungry, drink to the thirsty, raiment to the naked, entertainment to the stranger, and relief to the sick, though they never heard of his name, he declares shall in the last day be accepted; when those who cry Lord! Lord! who value themselves upon their faith, though great enough to perform miracles, but have neglected good works, shall be rejected. He professed that he came, not to call the righteous, but sinners, to repentance; which implied his modest opinion that there were some in his time so good that they need not hear even him for

35*

improvement; but, nowadays, we have scarce a little parson that does not think it the duty of every man within his reach to sit under his petty ministrations, and that whoever omits them offends God.

I wish to such more humility, and to you health and happiness; being   B. FRANKLIN.

PHILADELPHIA, 4 March, 1775.

DEAR KATY: Your kind letter of January 20th is but just come to hand, and I take this first opportunity of acknowledging the favor. It gives me great pleasure to hear that you got home safe and well that day. I thought too much was hazarded when I saw you put off to sea in that very little skiff, tossed by every wave. But the call was strong and just, a sick parent. I stood on the shore, and looked after you, till I could no longer distinguish you, even with my glass; then returned to your sister's, praying for your safe passage. Towards evening, all agreed that you must certainly be arrived before that time, the weather having been so favorable; which made me more easy and cheerful, for I had been truly concerned for you.

I left New England slowly, and with great reluctance. Short days' journeys, and loitering visits on the road, manifested my unwillingness to quit a country in which I drew my first breath, spent my earliest and most pleasant days, and had now received so many fresh marks of the people's goodness and benevolence, in the kind and affectionate treatment I had everywhere met with. I almost forgot I had a *home*, till I was more than half-way towards it; till I had, one by one, parted with all my New England friends, and was got into the western borders of Connecticut, among mere strangers. Then, like an old man, who, having buried all he loved in this world, begins to think of heaven, I began to think of and wish for home; and, as I drew nearer, I found the attraction stronger and stronger. My diligence and speed increased with my impatience. I drove on violently, and made such long stretches that a very few days brought me to my own house, and to the arms of my good old wife and children, where I remain, thanks to God, at present well and happy.

Persons subject to the *hyp* complain of the north-east wind as increasing their malady; but, since you promised to send me

kisses in that wind, and I find you as good as your word, it is to
me the gayest wind that blows, and gives me the best spirits.
I write this during a north-east storm of snow, the greatest we
have had this winter. Your favors come mixed with the snowy
fleeces, which are pure as your virgin innocence, white as your
lovely bosom, and — as cold. But let it warm towards some
worthy young man, and may Heaven bless you both with every
kind of happiness!

I desired Miss Anna Ward to send you over a little book I
left with her, for your amusement in that lonely island. My
respects to your good father and mother and sister. Let me
often hear of your welfare, since it is not likely I shall ever
again have the pleasure of seeing you. Accept mine and my
wife's sincere thanks, for the many civilities I receive from you
and your relations; and do me the justice to believe me, dear girl,
your affectionate, faithful friend, and humble servant,

B. FRANKLIN.

P. S. My respectful compliments to your good brother Ward,
and sister; and to the agreeable family of the Wards at Newport, when you see them. Adieu.

[TO MISS CATHERINE RAY.]

PHILADELPHIA, 11 September, 1755.

BEGONE, business, for an hour at least, and let me chat a little
with my Katy.

I have now before me, my dear girl, three of your favors,
namely, of March the 3d, March the 30th, and May the 1st.
The first I received just before I set out on a long journey,
and the others while I was on that journey, which held me near
six weeks. Since my return, I have been in such a perpetual
hurry of public affairs of various kinds, as renders it impracticable for me to keep up my private correspondences, even those
that afforded me the greatest pleasure.

You ask, in your last, how I do, and what I am doing, and
whether everybody loves me yet, and why I make them do so.

In regard to the first, I can say, thanks to God, that I do not
remember I was ever better. I still relish all the pleasures of
life that a temperate man can in reason desire, and through
favor I have them all in my power. This happy situation shall

continue as long as God pleases, who knows what is best for his
creatures, and I hope will enable me to bear with patience and
dutiful submission any change he may think fit to make, that is
less agreeable.   As to the second question, I must confess (but
don't you be jealous), that many more people love me now than
ever did before; for, since I saw you, I have been enabled to do
some general services to the country, and to the army, for which
both have thanked and praised me, and say they love me. They
say so, as you used to do; and, if I were to ask any favors of
them, they would, perhaps, as readily refuse me; so that I find
little real advantage in being beloved, but it pleases my humor.

Now it is near four months since I have been favored with a
single line from you; but I will not be angry with you, because
it is my fault.   I ran in debt to you three or four letters; and,
as I did not pay, you would not trust me any more, and you
had some reason.   But, believe me, I am honest; and, though I
should never make equal returns, you shall see I will keep fair
accounts.   Equal returns I can never make, though I should
write to you by every post; for the pleasure I receive from one
of yours is more than you can have from two of mine.   The
small news, the domestic occurrences among our friends, the
natural pictures you draw of persons, the sensible observations
and reflections you make, and the easy, chatty manner in which
you express everything, all contribute to heighten the pleasure;
and the more as they remind me of those hours and miles that
we talked away so agreeably, even in a winter journey, a wrong
road, and a soaking shower.

I long to hear whether you have continued ever since in that
monastery;* or have broke into the world again, doing pretty
mischief; how the lady Wards do, and how many of them are
married, or about it; what is become of Mr. B—— and Mr.
L——, and what the state of your heart is at this instant.
But that, perhaps, I ought not to know; and, therefore, I will
not conjure, as you sometimes say I do.   If I could conjure,
it should be to know what was that *oddest question about me that
ever was thought of*, which you tell me a lady had just sent to
ask you.

I commend your prudent resolutions, in the article of granting favors to lovers.   But, if I were courting you, I could not
hardly approve such conduct.   I should even be malicious
enough to say you were too *knowing*, and tell you the old story
of the Girl and the Miller.   I enclose you the songs you write

* Block Island.

for, and with them your Spanish letter, with a translation. I honor that honest Spaniard for loving you. It showed the goodness of his taste and judgment. But you must forget him, and bless some worthy young Englishman.

You have spun a long thread, five thousand and twenty-two yards. It will reach almost from Rhode Island hither. I wish I had hold of one end of it, to pull you to me. But you would break it rather than come. The cords of love and friendship are longer and stronger, and in times past have drawn me further,—even back from England to Philadelphia. I guess that some of the same kind will one day draw you out of that island.

I was extremely pleased with the ——— you sent me. The Irish people, who have seen it, say it is the right sort; but I cannot learn that we have anything like it here. The cheeses, particularly one of them, were excellent. All our friends have tasted it, and all agree that it exceeds any English cheese they ever tasted. Mrs. Franklin was very proud that a young lady should have so much regard for her old husband as to send him such a present. We talk of you every time it comes to table. She is sure you are a sensible girl, and a notable housewife, and talks of bequeathing me to you as a legacy; but I ought to wish you a better, and hope she will live these hundred years; for we are grown old together, and, if she has any faults, I am so used to them that I don't perceive them; as the song says,

> "Some faults we have all, and so has my Joan,
>   But then they're exceedingly small,
> And, now I'm grown used to them, so like my own
>   I scarcely can see them at all,
>   My dear friends,
>   I scarcely can see them at all."

Indeed, I begin to think she has none, as I think of you. And, since she is willing I should love you as much as you are willing to be loved by me, let us join in wishing the old lady a long life and a happy.

With her respectful compliments to you, to your good mother and sisters, present mine, though unknown; and believe me to be, dear girl, your affectionate friend and humble servant,

B. FRANKLIN.

P. S. Sally says, "Papa, my love to Miss Katy." If it was not quite unreasonable, I should desire you to write to me every post, whether you hear from me or not. As to your spelling, don't let those laughing girls put you out of conceit with it. It is the best in the world, for every letter of it stands for something.

On the Death of his Brother, John Franklin.

PHILADELPHIA, 23 February, 1756.

— I condole with you. We have lost a most dear and valuable relation. But it is the will of God and nature that these mortal bodies be laid aside when the soul is to enter into real life. This is rather an embryo state, a preparation for living. A man is not completely born until he be dead. Why, then, should we grieve that a new child is born among the immortals a new member added to their happy society?

We are spirits. That bodies should be lent us, while they can afford us pleasure, assist us in acquiring knowledge, or in doing good to our fellow-creatures, is a kind and benevolent act of God. When they become unfit for these purposes, and afford us pain instead of pleasure, instead of an aid become an encumbrance, and answer none of the intentions for which they were given, it is equally kind and benevolent that a way is provided by which we may get rid of them. Death is that way. We ourselves, in some cases, prudently choose a partial death. A mangled, painful limb, which cannot be restored, we willingly cut off. He who plucks out a tooth parts with it freely, since the pain goes with it; and he who quits the whole body parts at once with all pains, and possibilities of pains and diseases, which it was liable to, or capable of making him suffer.

Our friend and we were invited abroad on a party of pleasure, which is to last forever. His chair was ready first, and he is gone before us. We could not all conveniently start together; and why should you and I be grieved at this, since we are soon to follow, and know where to find him? Adieu.

B. FRANKLIN.

[TO HIS WIFE.]
Humorous Rebuke.

" EASTON, Saturday morning, Nov. 13, 1756.

MY DEAR CHILD : I wrote to you a few days since, by a special messenger, and enclosed letters for all our wives and sweethearts, expecting to hear from you by his return, and to have the north-

---

* John Franklin married a second wife, by the name of Hubbard, a widow. Miss E. Hubbard, to whom this letter was addressed, was her daughter by a former marriage.

ern newspapers and English letters, per the packet; but he is just now returned without a scrap for poor us. So I had a good mind not to write to you by this opportunity; but I never can be ill-natured enough, even when there is the most occasion. The messenger says he left the letters at your house, and saw you afterwards at Mr. Dentie's and told you when he would go, and that he lodged at Honey's, next door to you, and yet you did not write; so let Goody Smith give one more just judgment, and say what should be done to you; I think I won't tell you that we are well, nor that we expect to return about the middle of the week, nor will I send you a word of news; that's poz. My duty to mother, love to the children, and to Miss Betsey and Gracey, &c. &c. B. Franklin.

P. S. — I have *scratched out the loving words*, being writ in haste, by mistake, when I *forgot I was angry.*

[TO LORD KAMES.]

His Lordship's Principles of Equity — Franklin's Plan of Writing The Art of Virtue.

London, May 3, 1760.

My dear Lord: I have endeavored to comply with your request in writing something on the present situation of our affairs in America, in order to give more correct notions of the British interest, with regard to the colonies, than those I found many sensible men possessed of. Enclosed you have the production, such as it is. I wish it may, in any degree, be of service to the public. I shall, at least, hope this from it, for my own part, — that you will consider it as a letter from me to you, and take its length as some excuse for being so long a-coming.

I am now reading with great pleasure and improvement your excellent work, *The Principles of Equity.* It will be of the greatest advantage to the judges in our colonies, not only in those which have courts of chancery, but also in those which, having no such courts, are obliged to mix equity with common law. It will be of more service to the colony judges, as few of them have been bred to the law. I have sent a book to a particular friend, one of the judges of the Supreme Court in Pennsylvania.

I will shortly send you a copy of the chapter you are pleased to mention in so obliging a manner; and shall be extremely obliged in receiving a copy of the collection of *Maxims for the*

Conduct of Life, which you are preparing for the use of your children. I purpose, likewise, a little work for the benefit of youth, to be called the *Art of Virtue*.* From the title, I think you will hardly conjecture what the nature of such a book may be. I must, therefore, explain it a little. Many people lead bad lives, that would gladly lead good ones, but know not *how* to make the change. They have frequently *resolved* and *endeavored* it, but in vain; because their endeavors have not been properly conducted. To expect people to be good, to be just, to be temperate, &c., without *showing* them *how* they should *become* so, seems like the ineffectual charity mentioned by the apostle, which consisted in saying to the hungry, the cold and the naked, be ye fed, be ye warmed, be ye clothed, without showing them how they should get food, fire or clothing.

Most people have, naturally, *some* virtues, but none have naturally *all* the virtues. To *acquire* those that are wanting, and secure what we acquire, as well as those we have naturally, is the subject of *an art*. It is as properly an art as painting, navigation or architecture. If a man would become a painter, navigator or architect, it is not enough that he is *advised* to be one, that he is *convinced* by the arguments of his adviser that it would be for his advantage to be one, and that he resolves to be one; but he must also be taught the principles of the art, be shown all the methods of working, and how to acquire the habits of using properly all the instruments; and thus, regularly and gradually, he arrives, by practice, at some perfection in the art. If he does not proceed thus, he is apt to meet with difficulties that discourage him, and make him drop the pursuit.

My *Art of Virtue* has also its instruments, and teaches the manner of using them. Christians are directed to have faith in Christ, as the effectual means of obtaining the change they desire. It may, when sufficiently strong, be effectual with many : for a full opinion that a teacher is infinitely wise, good and powerful, and that he will certainly reward and punish the obedient and disobedient, must give great weight to his precepts, and make them much more attended to by his disciples. But many have this faith in so weak a degree, that it does not produce the effect. Our *Art of Virtue* may, therefore, be of great service to those whose faith is, unhappily, not so strong, and may come in aid of its weakness. Such as are naturally well disposed, and have been carefully educated, so that good habits have been early established, and bad ones prevented, have less

---

* The plan was never carried out. See some account of it in the Autobiography.

noed of this art; but all may be more or less benefited by it. It is, in short, to be adapted for universal use. I imagine what I have now been writing will seem to savor of great presumption; I must, therefore, speedily finish my little piece, and communicate the manuscript to you, that you may judge whether it is possible to make good such pretensions. I shall, at the same time, hope for the benefit of your corrections.

B. FRANKLIN.

[TO MISS MARY STEVENSON.]

Advice in Reading.

CRAVEN-STREET, May 16, 1760.

I SEND my good girl the books I mentioned to her last night. I beg her to accept of them as a small mark of my esteem and friendship. They are written in the familiar, easy manner for which the French are so remarkable, and afford a good deal of philosophic and practical knowledge, unembarrassed with the dry mathematics used by more exact reasoners, but which is apt to discourage young beginners.

I would advise you to read with a pen in your hand, and enter in a little book short hints of what you find that is curious, or that may be useful; for this will be the best method of imprinting such particulars in your memory, where they will be ready, either for practice on some future occasion, if they are matters of utility, or, at least, to adorn and improve your conversation, if they are rather points of curiosity; and, as many of the terms of science are such as you cannot have met with in your common reading, and may therefore be unacquainted with, I think it would be well for you to have a good dictionary at hand, to consult immediately when you meet with a word you do not comprehend the precise meaning of.

This may, at first, seem troublesome and interrupting; but it is a trouble that will daily diminish, as you will daily find less and less occasion for your dictionary, as you become more acquainted with the terms; and, in the mean time, you will read with more satisfaction, because with more understanding. When any point occurs in which you would be glad to have further information than your book affords you, I beg you would not in the least apprehend that I should think it a trouble to receive and answer your questions. It will be a pleasure, and no trouble,

36

For though I may not be able, out of my own little stock of knowledge, to afford you what you require, I can easily direct you to the books where it may most readily be found.   Adieu, and believe me ever, my dear friend,

B. FRANKLIN

[TO GEORGE WHITEFIELD.]
Trust in Providence.

PHILADELPHIA, 19 June, 1764.

DEAR FRIEND : I received your favors of the 21st past, and of the 3d instant, and immediately sent the enclosed as directed.

Your frequently repeated wishes for my eternal, as well as my temporal happiness, are very obliging, and I can only thank you for them and offer you mine in return.   I have myself no doubt that I shall enjoy as much of both as is proper for me.   That Being who gave me existence, and through almost three-score years has been continually showering his favors upon me, whose very chastisements have been blessings to me, — can I doubt that He loves me ?   And, if He loves me, can I doubt that He will go on to take care of me, not only here, but hereafter ?   This to some may seem presumption ; to me it appears the best-grounded hope, — hope of the future built on experience of the past.

By the accounts I have of your late labors, I conclude your health is mended by your journey, which gives me pleasure. Mrs. Franklin presents her cordial respects, with, dear sir, your affectionate humble servant,   B. FRANKLIN.

P. S.   We hope you will not be deterred from visiting your friends here by the bugbear Boston account of the unhealthiness of Philadelphia.

[TO THE EDITOR OF A LONDON NEWSPAPER.]
Satirical Defence of Newspaper Paragraphs and their False Reports.

Monday, 20 May, 1765.

SIR: In your paper of Wednesday last, an ingenious correspondent, who calls himself THE SPECTATOR, and dates from *Pimlico*, under the guise of good-will to news-writers, whom he calls a "useful body of men in this great city," has, in my opinion, artfully attempted to turn them and their works into ridicule, wherein, if he could succed, great injury might be done to the public, as well as to these good people.

Supposing, sir, that the "*we hears*" they give us of this or the other intended tour or voyage of this and the other great personage were mere inventions, yet they at least offer us an innocent amusement while we read, and useful matter for conversation when we are disposed to converse.

Englishmen, sir, are too apt to be silent when they have nothing to say, and too apt to be sullen when they are silent; and when they are sullen, to hang themselves. But, by these *we hears*, we are supplied with abundant funds for discourse. We discuss the motives for such voyages, the probability of their being undertaken, and the practicability of their execution. Here we display our judgment in politics, our knowledge of the interests of princes, and our skill in geography, and (if we have it) show our dexterity in argumentation. In the mean time, the tedious hour is killed, we go home pleased with the applauses we have received from others, or at least with those we give to ourselves; we sleep soundly, and live on, to the comfort of our families. But, sir, I beg leave to say that all the articles of news that seem improbable are not mere inventions. Some of them, I can assure you on the faith of a traveller, are serious truths. And here, quitting Mr. Spectator of Pimlico, give me leave to instance the various accounts the news-writers have given us, with so much honest zeal for the welfare of *Poor Old England*, of the establishing manufactures in the colonies to the prejudice of those of the kingdom. It is objected by superficial readers, who yet pretend to some knowledge of those countries, that such establishments are not only improbable, but impossible, for that their sheep have but little wool, not in the whole sufficient for a pair of stockings a year to each inhabitant; that, from the universal dearness of labor among them, the working of iron, and other materials, except in a few coarse instances, is impracticable to any advantage.

Dear sir, do not let us suffer ourselves to be amused with such groundless objections. The very tails of the American sheep are so laden with wool that each has a little car or wagon, on four little wheels, to support and keep it from trailing on the ground. Would they caulk their ships, would they even litter their horses with wool, if it were not both plenty and cheap? And what signifies the dearness of labor, when an English shilling passes for five-and-twenty? Their engaging three hundred silk-throwsters here in one week for New York was treated as a fable, because, forsooth, they have "no silk there to throw." Those who make this objection perhaps do not know that at the same time the agents from the King of Spain were at Quebec to contract for one thousand pieces of cannon to be made there for the fortification of Mexico, and at New York engaging the usual supply of woollen floor-carpets for their West India houses, other agents from the Emperor of China were at Boston treating about an exchange of raw silk for wool, to be carried in Chinese junks through the Straits of Magellan.

And yet all this is as certainly true as the account, said to be from Quebec, in all the papers of last week, that the inhabitants of Canada are making preparations for a cod and whale fishery this "summer in the upper lakes." Ignorant people may object, that the upper lakes are fresh, and that cod and whales are salt-water fish; but let them know, sir, that cod, like other fish, when attacked by their enemies, fly into any water where they can be safest; that whales, when they have a mind to eat cod, pursue them wherever they fly; and that the grand leap of the whale in the chase up the Falls of Niagara is esteemed, by all who have seen it, as one of the finest spectacles in nature. Really, sir, the world is grown too incredulous. It is like the pendulum, ever swinging from one extreme to another. Formerly everything printed was believed, because it was in print. Now things seem to be disbelieved for just the very same reason. Wise men wonder at the present growth of infidelity. They should have considered, when they taught people to doubt the authority of newspapers and the truth of predictions in the almanacs, that the next step might be a disbelief of the well-vouched accounts of ghosts and witches, and doubts even of the truths of the Creed.

Thus much I thought it necessary to say in favor of an honest set of writers, whose comfortable living depends on collecting and supplying the printers with news at the small price of sixpence an article, and who always show their regard to truth by contradicting in a subsequent article such as are wrong, for another sixpence, to the great satisfaction and improvement of us coffee-house students in history and politics, and all future Livys, Rapins, Robertsons, Humes and Macaulays, who may be sincerely inclined to furnish the world with that *rara avis*, a true history. I am, sir, your humble servant, A TRAVELLER.

[TO MRS. DEBORAH FRANKLIN.]

State of his Affairs — Proposed Marriage of his Daughter.

LONDON, June 22, 1767.

MY DEAR CHILD : Captain Falconer is arrived, and came yesterday to see me and bring my letters. I was extremely glad of yours, because I had none by the packet. It seems now as if I should stay here another winter, and therefore I must leave it to your judgment to act in the affair of our daughter's match as shall seem best. If you think it a suitable one, I suppose the sooner it is completed the better. In that case, I would advise that you do not make an expensive feasting wedding, but conduct everything with frugality and economy, which our circumstances now require to be observed in all our expenses. For, since my partnership with Mr. Hall has expired, a great source of our income is cut off; and, if I should lose the post-office, which, among the many changes here, is far from being unlikely, we should be reduced to our rents and interest of money for a subsistence, which will by no means afford the chargeable housekeeping and entertainments we have been used to.

For my own part, I live here as frugally as possible, not to be destitute of the comforts of life, making no dinners for anybody, and contenting myself with a single dish when I dine at home ; and yet such is the dearness of living here in every article, that my expenses amaze me. I see, too, by the sums you have received in my absence, that yours are very great ; and I am very sensible that your situation naturally brings you a great many visitors, which occasions an expense not easily to be avoided, especially when one has been long in the practice and habit of it. But, when people's incomes are lessened, if they cannot proportionably lessen their outgoings, they must come to poverty. If we were young enough to begin business again, it might be another matter ; but I doubt we are past it, and business not well managed ruins one faster than no business. In short, with frugality and prudent care we may subsist decently on what we have, and leave it entire to our children ; but without such care we shall not be able to keep it together ; it will melt away like butter in the sunshine, and we may live long enough to feel the miserable consequences of our indiscretion.

I know very little of the gentleman or his character, nor can I at this distance. I hope his expectations are not great of any fortune to be had with our daughter before our death. I can only say that, if he proves a good husband to her and a good

86*

son to me, he shall find me as good a father as I can be: but at present I suppose you would agree with me, that we cannot do more than fit her out handsomely in clothes and furniture, not exceeding in the whole five hundred pounds in value. For the rest, they must depend, as you and I did, on their own industry and care, as what remains in our hands will be barely sufficient for our support, and not enough for them when it comes to be divided at our decease.

Sally Franklin is well. Her father, who had not seen her for a twelvemonth, came lately and took her home with him for a few weeks to see her friends. He is very desirous I should take her with me to America.

I suppose the blue room is too blue, the wood being of the same color with the paper, and so looks too dark. I would have you finish it as soon as you can, thus: paint the wainscot a dead white, paper the walls blue, and tack the gilt border round just above the surbase and under the cornice. If the paper is not equally colored when pasted on, let it be brushed over again with the same color, and let the *papier maché* musical figures be tacked to the middle of the ceiling. When this is done, I think it will look very well.

I am glad to hear that Sally keeps up and increases the number of her friends. The best wishes of a fond father for her happiness always attend her. I am, my dear Debby, your affectionate husband, B. FRANKLIN.

[TO MISS MARY STEVENSON.]

Visit to Paris — French Women and Fashions — King and Queen — Versailles — Paris — French Politeness — Travelling.

PARIS, 14 September, 1767.

DEAR POLLY: I am always pleased with a letter from you, and I flatter myself you may be sometimes pleased in receiving one from me, though it should be of little importance, such as this, which is to consist of a few occasional remarks made here and in my journey hither.

Soon after I left you in that agreeable society at Bromley, I took the resolution of making a trip with Sir John Pringle into France. We set out on the 28th past. All the way to Dover we were furnished with post-chaises, hung so as to lean forward, the top coming down over one's eyes, like a hood, as if to prevent one's seeing the country; which being one of my great pleasures, I was engaged in perpetual disputes with the inn-keepers, ostlers and postilions, about getting the straps taken up a hole or two before, and let down as much behind, they insisting that the chaise leaning forward was an ease to the horses, and that the contrary would kill them. I suppose the chaise leaning forward looks to them like a willingness to go forward, and that its hanging back shows reluctance. They added other reasons, that were no reasons at all, and made me, as upon a hundred other occasions, almost wish that mankind had never been endowed with a reasoning faculty, since they know so little how to make use of it, and so often mislead themselves by it, and that they had been furnished with a good sensible instinct instead of it.

At Dover, the next morning, we embarked for Calais, with a number of passengers, who had never before been at sea. They would previously make a hearty breakfast, because, if the wind should fail, we might not get over till supper-time. Doubtless they thought that when they had paid for their breakfast they had a right to it, and that when they had swallowed it they were sure of it. But they had scarce been out half an hour before the sea laid claim to it, and they were obliged to deliver it up. So that it seems there are uncertainties even beyond those between the cup and the lip. If ever you go to sea, take my advice, and live sparingly a day or two beforehand. The sickness, if any, will be lighter and sooner over. We got to Calais that evening.

Various impositions we suffered from boatmen, porters and the like, on both sides the water. I know not which are most rapacious, the English or French; but the latter have, with their knavery, most politeness.

The roads we found equally good with ours in England, in some places paved with smooth stones, like our new streets, for many miles together, and rows of trees on each side, and yet there are no turnpikes. But then the poor peasants complained to us grievously that they were obliged to work upon the roads full two months in the year, without being paid for their labor. Whether this is truth, or whether, like Englishmen, they grumble, cause or no cause, I have not yet been able fully to inform myself.

The women we saw at Calais, on the road, at Boulogne, and in the inns and villages, were generally of dark complexions; but, arriving at Abbeville, we found a sudden change, a multitude of both women and men in that place appearing remarkably fair. Whether this is owing to a small colony of spinners, woolcombers and weavers, brought hither from Holland with the woollen manufactory about sixty years ago, or to their being less exposed to the sun than in other places, their business keeping them much within doors, I know not. Perhaps, as in some other cases, different causes may club in producing the effect, but the effect itself is certain. Never was I in a place of greater industry, wheels and looms going in every house.

As soon as we left Abbeville, the swarthiness returned. I speak generally; for here are some fair women at Paris, who, I think, are not whitened by art. As to rouge, they don't pretend to imitate nature in laying it on. There is no gradual diminution of the color, from the full bloom in the middle of the cheek to the faint tint near the sides, nor does it show itself differently in different faces. I have not had the honor of being at any lady's toilet to see how it is laid on, but I fancy I can tell you how it is or may be done. Cut a hole of three inches diameter in a piece of paper; place it on the side of your face in such a manner as that the top of the hole may be just under the eye; then, with a brush dipped in the color, paint face and paper together; so, when the paper is taken off, there will remain a round patch of red exactly the form of the hole. This is the mode, from the actresses on the stage upwards, through all ranks of ladies, to the princesses of the blood; but it stops there, the queen not using it, having, in the serenity, complacence and benignity, that shine so eminently in, or rather through her countenance, sufficient beauty, though now an old woman, to do extremely well without it.

You see I speak of the queen as if I had seen her; and so I have, for you must know I have been at court. We went to Versailles last Sunday, and had the honor of being presented to the king; he spoke to both of us very graciously and very cheerfully, is a handsome man, has a very lively look, and appears younger than he is. In the evening we were at the *Grand Couvert*, where the family sup in public. The table was half a hollow square, the service gold. When either made a sign for drink, the word was given by one of the waiters: *A boire pour le Roi*, or, *A boire pour la Reine*. Then two persons came from within, the one with wine and the other with water in *carafes*; each drank a little glass of what he brought, and then put both the *carafes* with a glass on a salver, and then presented it. Their distance from each other was such as that other chairs might have been placed between any two of them. An officer of the court brought us up through the crowd of spectators, and placed Sir John so as to stand between the queen and Madame Victoire. The king talked a good deal to Sir John, asking many questions about our royal family; and did me too the honor of taking some notice of me; that is saying enough, for I would not have you think me so much pleased with this king and queen as to have a whit less regard than I used to have for ours. No Frenchman shall go beyond me in thinking my own king and queen the very best in the world, and the most amiable.

Versailles has had infinite sums laid out in building it and supplying it with water. Some say the expenses exceeded eighty millions sterling. The range of buildings is immense; the garden-front most magnificent, all of hewn stone; the number of statues, figures, urns, &c., in marble and bronze of exquisite workmanship, is beyond conception. But the water-works are out of repair, and so is great part of the front next the town, looking, with its shabby, half-brick walls, and broken windows, not much better than the houses in Durham Yard. There is, in short, both at Versailles and Paris, a prodigious mixture of magnificence and negligence, with every kind of elegance except that of cleanliness, and what we call *tidiness*. Though I must do Paris the justice to say that in two points of cleanliness they exceed us. The water they drink, though from the river, they render as pure as that of the best spring, by filtering it through cisterns filled with sand; and the streets, with constant sweeping, are fit to walk in, though there is no paved foot-path. Accordingly, many well-dressed people are constantly seen walking in them. The crowd of coaches and chairs, for this reason, is not so great. Men, as well as women, carry umbrellas in their hands, which they extend in case of rain or too much sun; and, a man with an umbrella not taking up more than three foot square, or nine square feet of the street, when, if in a coach, he would take up two hundred and forty square feet, you can easily conceive that, though the streets here are narrow, they may be much less encumbered. They are extremely well paved, and the stones, being generally cubes, when worn on one side may be turned and become new.

The civilities we everywhere receive give us the strongest impressions of the French politeness. It seems to be a point settled here universally that strangers are to be treated with respect; and one has just the same deference shown one here by being a stranger as in England by being a lady. The custom-house officers at Port St. Denis, as we entered Paris, were about to seize two dozen of excellent Bordeaux wine given us at Boulogne, and which we brought with us; but, as soon as they found

we were strangers, it was immediately remitted on that account.
At the church of Notre Dame, where we went to see a magnificent illumination, with figures, &c., for the deceased Dauphin-
ess, we found an immense crowd, who were kept out by guards;
but, the officer being told that we were strangers from England, he immediately admitted us, accompanied and showed us
everything. Why don't we practise this urbanity to French-
men? Why should they be allowed to outdo us in anything?

Here is an exhibition of painting, like ours in London, to
which multitudes flock daily. I am not connoisseur enough to
judge which has most merit. Every night, Sundays not excepted, here are plays or operas; and, though the weather has
been hot, and the houses full, one is not incommoded by the
heat so much as with us in winter. They must have some way
of changing the air that we are not acquainted with. I shall
inquire into it.

Travelling is one way of lengthening life,—at least, in appearance. It is but about a fortnight since we left London, but the
variety of scenes we have gone through makes it seem equal to
six months living in one place. Perhaps I have suffered a
greater change, too, in my own person, than I could have done
in six years at home. I had not been here six days before my
tailor and perruquier had transformed me into a Frenchman.
Only think what a figure I make in a little bag-wig and with
naked ears! They told me I was become twenty years younger,
and looked very gallant.

This letter shall cost you a shilling, and you may consider it
cheap, when you reflect that it has cost me at least fifty guineas
to get into the situation that enables me to write it. Besides, I
might, if I had stayed at home, have won perhaps two shillings
of you at cribbage. By the way, now I mention cards, let me
tell you that quadrille is now out of fashion here, and English
whist all the mode at Paris and the court.

And pray look upon it as no small matter that, surrounded
as I am by the glories of the world, and amusements of all
sorts, I remember you, and Dolly, and all the dear good folks at
Bromley. It is true, I cannot help it, but must and ever shall
remember you all with pleasure.

Need I add that I am particularly, my dear good friend,
yours, most affectionately,   B. FRANKLIN.

[TO LORD KAMES.]

Use of Oxen in Agriculture — Congratulations — Political Prospects.

LONDON, February 21, 1769.

MY DEAR FRIEND: I received your excellent paper on the preferable use of oxen in agriculture, and have put it in the way of being communicated to the public here. I have observed in America that the farmers are more thriving in those parts of the country where horned cattle are used than in those where the labor is done by horses. The latter are said to require twice the quantity of land to maintain them, and, after all, are not good to eat; at least, we don't think them so.

Here is a waste of land that might afford subsistence for so many of the human species. Perhaps it was for this reason that the Hebrew law-giver, having promised that the children of Israel should be as numerous as the sands of the sea, not only took care to secure the health of individuals, by regulating their diet, that they might be fitter for producing children, but also forbid their using horses, as those animals would lessen the quantity of subsistence for men. Thus we find, when they took any horses from their enemies, they destroyed them; and, in the commandments, where the labor of the ox and ass is mentioned and forbidden on the Sabbath, there is no mention of the horse, probably, because they were to have none; and, by the great armies suddenly raised in that small territory they inhabited, it appears to have been very full of people.*

Food is *always* necessary to *all*, and much the greatest part of the labor of mankind is employed in raising provisions for the mouth. Is not this kind of labor, then, the fittest to be the standard by which to measure the values of all other labor, and, consequently, of all other things, whose value depends on the labor of making or procuring them? May not even gold and silver be thus valued? If the labor of the farmer in producing a bushel of wheat be equal to the labor of the miner in producing an ounce of silver, will not the bushel of wheat just measure the value of the ounce of silver? The miner must eat: the farmer, indeed, can live without the ounce of silver, and so,

---

* There is not in the Jewish law any express prohibition against the use of horses; it is only enjoined that the kings should not multiply the breed, or carry on trade with Egypt for the purchase of horses. (Deut. 17 : 16.) Solomon was the first of the Kings of Judah who disregarded this ordinance. He had forty thousand stalls of horses, which he brought out of Egypt. (1 Kings 4: 26 and 10: 28.) From this time downwards, horses were in constant use in the Jewish armies. It is true that the country, from its rocky surface and unfertile soil, was extremely unfit for the maintenance of those animals. — *Note by Lord Kames.*

perhaps, will have some advantage in settling the price. But these discussions I leave to you, as being more able to manage them; only, I will send you a little scrap I wrote, some time since, on the laws prohibiting foreign commodities.

I congratulate you on your election as President of the Edinburgh Society. I think I formerly took notice to you, in conversation, that I thought there had been some similarity in our fortunes, and the circumstances of our lives. This is a fresh instance, for by letters just received I find that I was, about the same time, chosen President of our American Philosophical Society, established at Philadelphia.

I have sent by sea, to the care of Mr. Alexander, a little box, containing a few copies of the late edition of my books, for my friends in Scotland. One is directed for you, and one for your society, which I beg that you and they would accept as a small mark of my respect. With the sincerest esteem and regard, B. FRANKLIN.

P. S. I am sorry my letter of 1767, concerning the American disputes, miscarried. I now send you a copy of it from my book. The examination mentioned in it you have, probably, seen. Things daily wear a worse aspect, and tend more and more to a breach and final separation.

[TO JOHN ALLEYNE.]

On Early Marriages.

CRAVEN-STREET, August 9, 1768.

DEAR JACK: You desire, you say, my impartial thoughts on the subject of an early marriage, by way of answer to the numberless objections that have been made by numerous persons to your own. You may remember, when you consulted me on the occasion, that I thought youth, on both sides, to be no objection. Indeed, from the marriages that have fallen under my observation, I am rather inclined to think that early ones stand the best chance of happiness. The temper and habits of the young are not yet become so stiff and uncomplying as when more advanced in life; they form more easily to each other, and hence many occasions of disgust are removed. And, if youth has less of that prudence which is necessary to manage a family, yet the parents and elder friends of young married persons are generally at hand to afford their advice, which amply supplies that defect; and by early marriage youth is sooner formed to regular and useful life; and, possibly, some of those accidents or connections that might have injured the constitution, or reputation, or both, are thereby happily prevented.

Particular circumstances of particular persons may, possibly, sometimes make it prudent to delay entering into that state; but, in general, when nature has rendered our bodies fit for it, the presumption is in nature's favor, that she has not judged amiss in making us desire it. Late marriages are often attended, too, with this further inconvenience, that there is not the same chance that the parents shall live to see their offspring educated. " *Late children*," says the Spanish proverb, "*are early orphans.*" A melancholy reflection to those whose case it may be!

With us in America, marriages are generally in the morning of life; our children are therefore educated and settled in the world by noon; and thus, our business being done, we have an afternoon and evening of cheerful leisure to ourselves, such as our friend at present enjoys. By these early marriages we are blessed with more children; and from the mode among us, founded by nature, of every mother suckling and nursing her own child, more of them are raised. Thence the swift progress of population among us, unparalleled in Europe. In fine, I am glad you are married, and congratulate you most cordially upon it. You are now in the way of becoming a useful citizen; and you have escaped the unnatural state of celibacy for life, — the fate of many here, who never intended it, but who, having too long postponed the change of their condition, find at length that it is too late to think of it, and so live all their lives in a situation that greatly lessens a man's value. An odd volume of a set of books bears not the value of its proportion to the set: what think you of the odd half of a pair of scissors? it can't well cut anything; it may possibly serve to scrape a trencher.

Pray make my compliments and best wishes acceptable to your bride. I am old and heavy, or I should ere this have presented them in person. I shall make but small use of the old man's privilege, that of giving advice to younger friends. Treat your wife always with respect; it will procure respect to you, not only from her, but from all that observe it. Never use a slighting expression to her, even in jest; for slights in jest, after frequent bandyings, are apt to end in angry earnest. Be studious in your profession, and you will be learned. Be industrious and frugal, and you will be rich. Be sober and temperate, and you will be healthy. Be in general virtuous, and you will

37

be happy.   At least, you will, by such conduct, stand the best chance for such consequences.

I pray God to bless you both; being ever your affectionate friend,   B. FRANKLIN.

The Boston Resolutions — Parliamentary Anecdote.

LONDON, Dec. 19, 1768.

DEAR SIR: The resolutions of the Boston people concerning trade make a great noise here. Parliament has not yet taken notice of them, but the newspapers are in full cry against America.   Colonel Onslow told me at court, last Sunday, that I could not conceive how much the friends of America were run upon and hurt by them, and how much the Grenvillians triumphed. I have just written a paper for next Tuesday's *Chronicle*, to extenuate matters a little.

Mentioning Colonel Onslow, reminds me of something that passed at the beginning of this session in the House between him and Mr. Grenville. The latter had been raving against America, as traitorous, rebellious, &c., when the former, who has always been its firm friend, stood up and gravely said that in reading the Roman history he found it was a custom among that wise and magnanimous people, whenever the Senate was informed of any discontent in the provinces, to send two or three of their body into the discontented provinces, to inquire into the grievances complained of, and report to the Senate, that mild measures might be used to remedy what was amiss, before any severe steps were taken to enforce obedience. That this example he thought worthy our imitation in the present state of our colonies, for he did so far agree with the honorable gentleman that spoke just before him as to allow there were great discontents among them. He should therefore beg leave to move that two or three members of Parliament be appointed to go over to New England on this service. And, that it might not be supposed he was for imposing burdens on others that he would not be willing to bear himself, he did at the same time declare his own willingness, if the House should think fit to appoint them, to go over thither *with that honorable gentleman.* Upon this there was a great laugh, which continued some time, and was rather increased by Mr. Grenville's asking, "Will the gentleman engage that I shall be safe there? Can I be assured that I shall be allowed to come back again to make the report?" As soon as the laugh was so far subsided as that Mr. Onslow could be heard again, he added, "I cannot absolutely engage for the honorable gentleman's safe return; but, if he goes thither upon this service, I am strongly of opinion the *event* will contribute greatly to the future quiet of both countries." On which the laugh was renewed and redoubled.

If our people should follow the Boston example in entering into resolutions of frugality and industry, full as necessary for us as for them, I hope they will, among other things, give this reason, — that 't is to enable them more speedily and effectually to discharge their debts to Great Britain; this will soften a little, and at the same time appear honorable, and like ourselves.

Yours, &c.,   B. FRANKLIN.

[TO WILLIAM FRANKLIN.]

Riots in London.

LONDON, April 16, 1768

DEAR SON: Since my last, — a long one, of March 13th, — nothing has been talked or thought of here but elections. There have been amazing contests all over the kingdom, *twenty* or *thirty thousand pounds* of a side spent in several places, and inconceivable mischief done by debauching the people and making them idle, besides the immediate actual mischief done by drunken mad mobs to houses, windows, &c. The scenes have been horrible. London was illuminated two nights running at the command of the mob, for the success of Wilkes, in the Middlesex election: the second night exceeded anything of the kind ever seen here on the greatest occasions of rejoicing; as even the small cross streets, lanes, courts, and other out-of-the-way places, were all in a blaze with lights, and the principal streets all night long, as the mobs went round again after two o'clock, and obliged people who had extinguished their candles to light them again. Those who refused had all their windows destroyed. The damage done and expense of candles has been computed at *fifty thousand pounds;* it must have been great, though, probably, not so much.

The ferment is not yet over, for he has promised to surrender himself to the court next Wednesday, and another tumult is then expected; and what the upshot will be no one can yet foresee. 'T is really an extraordinary event to see an outlaw and an exile, of bad personal character, not worth a farthing, come over from France, set himself up as candidate for the capital of the kingdom, miss his election only by being too late in his application, and immediately carrying it for the principal county.

The mob (spirited up by numbers of different ballads sung or roared in every street), requiring gentlemen and ladies of all ranks, as they passed in their carriages, to shout for Wilkes and liberty, marking the same words on all their coaches with chalk, and No. 45 * on every door: which extends a vast way along the roads into the country. I went last week to Winchester, and observed that for fifteen miles out of town there was scarce a door or window-shutter next the road unmarked; and this continued here and there quite to Winchester, which is sixty-four miles.   B. FRANKLIN.

Riots in London — Wilkes — Divisions among the Ministry — The Church in America.

LONDON, May 14, 1768.

DEAR SIR: I received your favor of March 13th, and am extremely concerned at the disorders on our frontiers, and at the debility or wicked connivance of our government and magistrates, which must make property, and even life, more and more insecure among us, if some effectual remedy is not speedily applied. I have laid all the accounts before the ministry here. I wish I could procure more attention to them. I have urged over and over the necessity of the change we desire; but this country itself being at present in a situation very little better, weakens our argument that a royal government would be better managed and safer to live under than that of a proprietary. Even this capital, the residence of the king, is now a daily scene of lawless riot and confusion. Mobs patrolling the streets at noon-day, some knocking all down that will not roar for Wilkes and liberty; courts of justice afraid to give judgment against him; coal-heavers and porters pulling down the houses of coal-merchants, that refuse to give them more wages; sawyers destroying saw-

---

* The number of the *North Briton* containing the libel for which Wilkes was prosecuted.

mills; sailors unrigging all the outward bound ships, and suffering none to sail till merchants agree to raise their pay; watermen destroying private boats and threatening bridges; soldiers firing among the mobs and killing men, women and children, which seems only to have produced an universal sullenness, that looks like a great black cloud coming on, ready to burst in a general tempest.

What the event will be, God only knows. But some punishment seems preparing for a people who are ungratefully abusing the best constitution and the best king any nation was ever blessed with, intent on nothing but luxury, licentiousness, power, places, pensions, and plunder; while the ministry, divided in their councils, with little regard for each other, worried by perpetual oppositions, in continual apprehension of changes, intent on securing popularity in case they should lose favor, have for some years past had little time or inclination to attend to our small affairs, whose remoteness makes them appear still smaller.

The bishops here are very desirous of securing the Church of England in America, and promoting its interest and enlargement by sending one of their order thither: but, though they have long solicited this point with government here, they have not as yet been able to obtain it. So apprehensive are ministers of engaging in any novel measure.

I hope soon to have an opportunity of conferring with you, and therefore say no more at present on this subject.

B. FRANKLIN.

[TO JOSEPH GALLOWAY.]

The Wilkes Riots — More Mischief Brewing — Preparations for Return.

LONDON, May 14, 1768.

DEAR SIR: I received your favor of March 31st. It is now, with the messages, &c., in the hands of the minister, so that I cannot be more particular at present in answering it than to say I should have a melancholy prospect in going home to such public confusion, if I did not leave greater confusion behind me.

The newspapers, and my letter of this day to Mr. Ross, will inform you of the miserable situation this country is in. While I am writing, a great mob of coal-porters fill the street, carrying a wretch of their business upon poles to be ducked, and otherwise punished at their pleasure, for working at the old wages.

All respect to law and government seems to be lost among the common people, who are moreover continually inflamed by seditious scribblers to trample on authority, and everything that used to keep them in order.

The Parliament is now sitting, but will not continue long together, nor undertake any material business. The court of king's bench postponed giving sentence against Wilkes on his outlawry till the next term, intimidated, as some say, by his popularity, and willing to get rid of the affair for a time, till it should be seen what the Parliament would conclude as to his membership. The Commons, at least some of them, resent that conduct, which has thrown a burden on them it might have eased them of, by pillorying or punishing him in some infamous manner, that would have given better ground for expelling him the House. His friends complain of it as a delay of justice, say the court knew the outlawry to be defective, and that they must finally pronounce it void, but would punish him by long confinement. Great mobs of his adherents have assembled before the prison, the guards have fired on them : it is said five or six are killed, and sixteen or seventeen are wounded, and some circumstances have attended this military execution, such as its being done by the Scotch regiment, the pursuing a lad, and killing him at his father's house, &c. &c., that exasperate people exceedingly, and more mischief seems brewing. Several of the soldiers are imprisoned. If they are not hanged, it is feared there will be more and greater mobs; and, if they are, that no soldier will assist in suppressing any mob hereafter. The prospect either way is gloomy. It is said the English soldiers cannot be confided in to act against these mobs, being suspected as rather inclined to favor and join them.

I am preparing for my return, and hope for the pleasure of finding you well, when I shall have an opportunity of communicating to you more particularly the state of things here relating to our American affairs, which I cannot so well do by letter. I enclose you a report of Sir M. L., counsel to the Board of Trade, on one of your late acts. I suppose it has had its effect, so that the repeal will be of little consequence.

In the mean time I am, with sincere esteem and affection, sir, your most obedient and most humble servant,

B. FRANKLIN.

[TO MISS MARY STEVENSON.]
Advice on Family Matters.

LONDON, October, 1768.

I SEE very clearly the unhappiness of your situation, and that it does not arise from any fault in you. I pity you most sincerely. I should not, however, have thought of giving you advice on this occasion, if you had not requested it, believing, as I do, that your own good sense is more than sufficient to direct you in every point of duty to others and yourself. If, then, I should advise you to anything that may be contrary to your own opinion, do not imagine that I shall condemn you if you do not follow such advice. I shall only think that, from a better acquaintance with circumstances, you form a better judgment of what is fit for you to do.

Now, I conceive, with you, that ———, both from her affection to you and from the long habit of having you with her, would really be miserable without you. Her temper, perhaps, was never of the best; and, when that is the case, age seldom mends it. Much of her unhappiness must arise from thence; and, since wrong turns of mind, when confirmed by time, are almost as little in our power to cure as those of the body, I think, with you, that her case is a compassionable one.

If she had, through her own imprudence, brought on herself any grievous sickness, I know you would think it your duty to attend and nurse her with filial tenderness, even were your own health to be endangered by it. Your apprehension, therefore, is right, that it may be your duty to live with her, though inconsistent with your happiness and your interest; but this can only mean present interest and present happiness, for I think your future greater and more lasting interest and happiness will arise from the reflection that you have done your duty, and from the high rank you will ever hold in the esteem of all that know you, for having persevered in doing that duty under so many and great discouragements.

My advice, then, must be, that you return to her as soon as the time proposed for your visit is expired; and that you continue, by every means in your power, to make the remainder of her days as comfortable to her as possible. Invent amusements for her; be pleased when she accepts of them, and patient when she perhaps peevishly rejects them. I know this is hard, but I think you are equal to it; not from any servility of temper, but from abundant goodness. In the mean time, all your friends, sensible of your present uncomfortable situation, should endeavor to ease your burden, by acting in concert with you, and to give her as many opportunities as possible of enjoying the pleasures of society, for your sake.

Nothing is more apt to sour the temper of aged people than the apprehension that they are neglected; and they are extremely apt to entertain such suspicions. It was therefore that I proposed asking her to be of our late party; but, your mother disliking it, the motion was dropped, as some others have been, by my too great easiness, contrary to my judgment. Not but that I was sensible her being with us might have lessened our pleasure, but I hoped it might have prevented you some pain.

In fine, nothing can contribute to true happiness that is inconsistent with duty, nor can a course of action conformable to it be finally without an ample reward. For God governs; and He is *good.* I pray Him to direct you; and, indeed, you will never be without his direction, if you humbly ask it, and show yourself always ready to obey it. Farewell, *my* dear friend, and belive me ever sincerely and affectionately *yours,*

B. FRANKLIN.

[TO A FRIEND.]*

The Difficulties between England and her Colonies — Ends of Providence.

LONDON, 28 November, 1768.

DEAR SIR: I received your obliging favor of the 12th instant. Your sentiments of the importance of the present dispute between Great Britain and the colonies appear to me extremely just. There is nothing I wish for more than to see it amicably and equitably settled.

But Providence will bring about its own ends by its own means; and, if it intends the downfall of a nation, that nation will be so blinded by its pride and other passions as not to see its danger, or how its fall may be prevented.

Being born and bred in one of the countries, and having lived long and made many agreeable connections of friendship in the other, I wish all prosperity to both; but I have talked and written so much and so long on the subject, that my acquaintance are weary of hearing, and the public of reading any more of it,

---

* The name of the person to whom this letter was written is not known.

which begins to make me weary of talking and writing; especially as I do not find that I have gained any point, in either country, except that of rendering myself suspected by my impartiality,—in England of being too much an American, and in America of being too much an Englishman. Your opinion, however, weighs with me, and encourages me to try one effort more, in a full though concise statement of facts, accompanied with arguments drawn from those facts, to be published about the meeting of Parliament, after the holidays. If any good may be done, I shall rejoice; but at present I almost despair.

Have you ever seen the barometer so low as of late? The 22d instant, mine was at 28·41, and yet the weather fine and fair. With sincere esteem, I am, dear friend, yours, affectionately, B. FRANKLIN.

[TO MISS MARY STEVENSON.]

Mother and Daughter — Reason and Enthusiasm.

Saturday Evening, 2 September, 1769.

JUST come home from a venison feast, where I have drunk more than a philosopher ought, I find my dear Polly's cheerful, chatty letter, that exhilarates me more than all the wine.

Your good mother says there is no occasion for any intercession of mine in your behalf. She is sensible that she is more in fault than her daughter. She received an affectionate, tender letter from you, and she has not answered it, though she intended to do it; but her head, not her heart, has been bad, and unfitted her for writing. She owns that she is not so good a subject as you are, and that she is more unwilling to pay tribute to Cæsar, and has less objection to smuggling; but it is not, she says, mere selfishness or avarice; it is rather an honest resentment at the waste of those taxes in pensions, salaries, perquisites, contracts, and other emoluments for the benefit of people she does not love, and who do not deserve such advantages, because — I suppose — because they are not of her party.

Present my respects to your good landlord and his family. I honor them for their conscientious aversion to illicit trading. There are those in the world who would not wrong a neighbor, but make no scruple of cheating the king. The reverse, however, does not hold; for, whoever scruples cheating the king will certainly not wrong his neighbor.

You ought not to wish yourself an enthusiast. They have, indeed, their imaginary satisfactions and pleasures, but these are often balanced by imaginary pains and mortification. You can continue to be a good girl, and thereby lay a solid foundation for expected future happiness, without the enthusiasm that may perhaps be necessary to some others. As those beings who have a good sensible instinct have no need of reason, so those who have reason to regulate their actions have no occasion for enthusiasm. However, there are certain circumstances in life, sometimes, where it is perhaps best not to hearken to reason. For instance : possibly, if the truth were known, I have reason to be jealous of this same insinuating, handsome young physician ; but, as it flatters more my vanity, and therefore gives me more pleasure, to suppose you were in spirits on account of my safe return, I shall turn a deaf ear to reason in this case, as I have done, with success, in twenty others. But I am sure you will always give me reason enough to continue ever your affectionate friend, B. FRANKLIN.

P. S. Our love to Mrs. Tickell. We shall long for your return. Your Dolly was well last Tuesday ; the girls were there on a visit to her ; I mean at Bromley. Adieu. No time now to give you any account of my French journey.

[TO MRS. JANE MECOM.]

On Resigning his Office — Theories of Preëxistence.

LONDON, 30 December, 1770.

DEAR SISTER: This ship staying longer than was expected, gives me an opportunity of writing to you, which I thought I must have missed, when I desired Cousin Williams to excuse me to you. I received your kind letter of September 25th by the young gentlemen, who, by their discreet behavior, have recommended themselves very much to me, and many of my acquaintance. Josiah has attained his heart's desire, of being under the tuition of Mr. Stanley, who, though he had long left off teaching, kindly undertook, at my request, to instruct him, and is much pleased with his quickness of apprehension, and the progress he makes; and Jonathan appears a very valuable young man, sober, regular, and inclined to industry and frugality, which are promising signs of success in business. I am very happy in their company.

As to the rumor you mention (which was, as Josiah tells me, that I had been deprived of my place in the post-office, on account of a letter I wrote to Philadelphia), it might have this foundation,— that some of the ministry had been displeased on my writing such letters, and there were really some thoughts among them of showing that displeasure in that manner. But I had some friends, too, who, unrequested by me, advised the contrary; and my enemies were forced to content themselves with abusing me plentifully in the newspapers, and endeavoring to provoke me to resign. In this they are not likely to succeed, I being deficient in that Christian virtue of resignation. If they would have my office, they must take it.

I have heard of some great man whose rule it was, with regard to offices, *never to ask for them, and never to refuse them ;* to which I have always added, in my own practice, *never to resign them.* As I told my friends, I rose to that office through a long course of service in the inferior degrees of it. Before my time, through bad management, it never produced the salary annexed to it; and when I received it no salary was to be allowed, if the office did not produce it. During the first four years, it was so far from defraying itself that it became nine hundred and fifty pounds sterling in debt to me and my colleague. I had been chiefly instrumental in bringing it to its present flourishing state, and therefore thought I had some kind of right to it. I had hitherto executed the duties of it faithfully, and to the perfect satisfaction of my superiors, which I thought was all that should be expected of me on that account. As to the letters complained of, it was true I did write them, and they were written in compliance with another duty, that to my country ; a duty quite distinct from that of postmaster.

My conduct in this respect was exactly similar to that I held on a similar occasion, but a few years ago, when the then ministry were ready to hug me for the assistance I afforded them in repealing a former revenue act. My sentiments were still the same, that no such acts should be made here for America ; or, if made, should, as soon as possible, be repealed ; and I thought it should not be expected of me to change my political opinions every time his Majesty thought fit to change his ministers. This was my language on the occasion ; and I have lately heard, that, though I was thought much ·to blame, it being understood that every man who holds an office should act with the ministry, whether agreeable or not to his own judgment, yet, in consideration of the goodness of my private character (as they were pleased to compliment me), the office was not to be taken from me.

Possibly they may still change their minds, and remove me; but no apprehension of that sort will, I trust, make the least alteration in my political conduct. My rule, in which I have always found satisfaction, is, never to turn aside in public affairs through views of private interest, but to go straight forward in doing what appears to me right at the time, leaving the consequences with Providence. What, in my younger days, enabled me more easily to walk upright, was, that I had a trade, and that I knew I could live upon little; and thence (never having had views of making a fortune), I was free from avarice, and contented with the plentiful supplies my business afforded me. And now it is still more easy for me to preserve my freedom and integrity, when I consider that I am almost at the end of my journey, and therefore need less to complete the expense of it; and that what I now possess, through the blessing of God, may, with tolerable economy, be sufficient for me (great misfortunes excepted), though I should add nothing more to it by any office or employment whatsoever.

I send you, by this opportunity, the two books you wrote for. They cost three shillings apiece. When I was first in London, about forty-five years since, I knew a person who had an opinion something like your author's. Her name was Ilive, a printer's widow. She died soon after I left England, and by her *will* obliged her son to deliver publicly, in Salters' Hall, a solemn discourse, the purport of which was to prove that this world is the true hell, or place of punishment for the spirits who had transgressed in a better state, and were sent here to suffer for their sins, in animals of all sorts. It is long since I saw the discourse, which was printed. I think a good deal of scripture was cited in it, and that the supposition was, that, though we now remembered nothing of such a preëxistent state, yet after death we might recollect it, and remember the punishments we had suffered, so as to be the better for them; and others, who had not yet offended, might now behold and be warned by our sufferings.

In fact, we see here that every lower animal has its enemy, with proper inclinations, faculties and weapons, to terrify, wound and destroy it; and that men, who are uppermost, are devils to one another; so that, on the established doctrine of the goodness and justice of the great Creator, this apparent state of general and systematical mischief seemed to demand some such supposition as Mrs. Ilive's, to account for it consistently with the honor of the Deity. But our reasoning powers, when employed about what may have been before our existence here, or shall be after it, cannot go far, for want of history and facts. Revelation, only, can give us the necessary information; and that, in the first of these points especially, has been very sparingly afforded us.

I hope you continue to correspond with your friends at Philadelphia. My love to your children; and believe me ever your affectionate brother, B. FRANKLIN.

[TO SAMUEL COOPER.]

Minutes of a Remarkable Conference with Lord Hillsborough.

LONDON, 5 February, 1771.

DEAR SIR: I have just received your kind favor of January 1st by Mr. Bowdoin, to whom I should be glad to render any service here. I wrote to you some weeks since, in answer to yours of July and November, expressing my sentiments without the least reserve on points that require free discussion, as I know I can confide in your prudence not to hurt my usefulness here, by making me more obnoxious than I must necessarily be from that known attachment to the American interest, which my duty, as well as inclination, demands of me.

In the same confidence, I send you the enclosed extract from my journal, containing a late conference between the Secretary * and your friend, in which you will see a little of his temper. It is one of the many instances of his behavior and conduct that have given me the very mean opinion I entertain of his abilities and fitness for his station. His character is conceit, wrongheadedness, obstinacy and passion. Those who would speak most favorably of him allow all this; they only add, that he is an honest man, and means well. If that be true, as perhaps it may, I wish him a better place, where only honesty and well-meaning are required, and where his other qualities can do no harm. Had the war taken place, I have reason to believe he would have been removed. He had, I think, some apprehensions of it himself at the time I was with him. I hope, however, that our affairs will not much longer be perplexed and embarrassed by his perverse and senseless management. I have since heard that his lordship took great offence at some of my last words, which he calls extremely rude and abusive. He

* Lord Hillsborough.

38

assured a friend of mine that they were equivalent to telling him, to his face, that the colonies could expect neither favor nor justice during his administration. I find he did not mistake me.

It is true, as you have heard, that some of my letters to America have been echoed back hither; but that has not been the case with any that were written to you. Great umbrage was taken, but chiefly by Lord Hillsborough, who was disposed before to be angry with me, and therefore the inconvenience was the less; and, whatever the consequences are of his displeasure, putting all my offences together, I must bear them as well as I can. Not but that, if there is to be war between us, I shall do my best to defend myself and annoy my adversary, little regarding the story of the Earthen Pot and Brazen Pitcher. One encouragement I have, the knowledge that he is not a whit better liked by his colleagues in the ministry than he is by me; that he cannot probably continue where he is much longer; and that he can scarce be succeeded by anybody who will not like me the better for his having been at variance with me.

Pray continue writing to me, as you find opportunity. Your candid, clear and well-written letters, be assured, are of great use. With the highest esteem, I am, my dear friend, &c.,

B. FRANKLIN.

Minutes of the Conference mentioned in the preceding Letter.

Wednesday, 16 January, 1771.

I went this morning to wait on Lord Hillsborough. The porter at first denied his lordship, on which I left my name, and drove off. But, before the coach got out of the square, the coachman heard a call, turned and went back to the door, when the porter came and said, "His lordship will see you, sir." I was shown into the levee-room, where I found Governor Bernard, who, I understand, attends there constantly. Several other gentlemen were there attending, with whom I sat down a few minutes, when Secretary Pownall * came out to us, and said his lordship desired I would come in.

I was pleased with this ready admission and preference, having sometimes waited three or four hours for my turn; and, being pleased, I could more easily put on the open, cheerful countenance that my friends advised me to wear. His lordship came towards me and said: " I was dressing, in order to go to court; but, hearing that you were at the door, who are a man of

* John Pownall, Secretary to the Board of Trade, and brother to Governor Pownall.

business, I determined to see you immediately." I thanked his lordship, and said that my business at present was not much ; it was only to pay my respects to his lordship, and to acquaint him with my appointment by the House of Representatives of Massachusetts Bay to be their agent here, in which station, if I could be of any service — (I was going on to say, "to the public, I should be very happy;" but his lordship, whose countenance changed at my naming that province, cut me short by saying, with something between a smile and a sneer,)

L. H. I must set you right there, Mr. Franklin ; you are not agent.

B. F. Why, my lord ?

L. H. You are not appointed.

B. F. I do not understand your lordship ; I have the appointment in my pocket.

L. H. You are mistaken ; I have later and better advices. I have a letter from Governor Hutchinson ; he would not give his assent to the bill.

B. F. There was no bill, my lord ; it was a vote of the House.

L. H. There was a bill presented to the governor, for the purpose of appointing you and another, — one Dr. Lee, I think he is called, — to which the governor refused his assent.

B. F. I cannot understand this, my lord ; I think there must be some mistake in it. Is your lordship quite sure that you have such a letter ?

L. H. I will convince you of it directly. (*Rings the bell.*) Mr. Pownall will come in and satisfy you.

B. F. It is not necessary that I should now detain your lordship from dressing. You are going to court. I will wait on your lordship another time.

L. H. No, stay : he will come immediately. (*To the servant.*) Tell Mr. Pownall I want him.

(*Mr. Pownall comes in.*)

L. H. Have not you at hand Governor Hutchinson's letter, mentioning his refusing his assent to the bill for appointing Dr. Franklin agent ?

Sec. P. My lord ?

L. H. Is there not such a letter ?

Sec. P. No, my lord ; there is a letter relating to some bill for the payment of a salary to Mr. De Berdt, and I think to some other agent, to which the governor had refused his assent.

L. H. And is there nothing in the letter to the purpose I mention ?

Sec. P. No, my lord.

B. F. I thought it could not well be, my lord, as my letters are by the last ships, and they mention no such thing. Here is the authentic copy of the vote of the House appointing me, in which there is no mention of any act intended. Will your lordship please to look at it? (*With seeming unwillingness he takes it, but does not look into it.*)

L. H. An information of this kind is not properly brought to me as Secretary of State. The Board of Trade is the proper place.

B. F. I will leave the paper, then, with Mr. Pownall, to be ——

L. H. (*Hastily.*) To what end would you leave it with him?

B. F. To be entered on the minutes of that Board, as usual.

L. H. (*Angrily.*) It shall not be entered there! No such paper shall be entered there, while I have anything to do with the business of that Board! The House of Representatives has no right to appoint an agent. We shall take no notice of any agents but such as are appointed by acts of Assembly, to which the governor gives his assent. We have had confusion enough already. Here is one agent appointed by the Council, another by the House of Representatives. Which of these is agent for the province? Who are we to hear in provincial affairs? An agent appointed by act of Assembly we can understand. No other will be attended to for the future, I can assure you!

B. F. I cannot conceive, my lord, why the consent of the governor should be thought necessary to the appointment of an agent for the people. It seems to me that ——

L. H. (*With a mixed look of anger and contempt.*) I shall not enter into a dispute with you, sir, upon this subject.

B. F. I beg your lordship's pardon; I do not presume to dispute with your lordship; I would only say that it seems to me that every body of men, who cannot appear in person where business relating to them may be transacted, should have a right to appear by an agent. The concurrence of the governor does not seem to me necessary. It is the business of the people that is to be done; he is not one of them; he is himself an agent.

L. H. (*Hastily.*) Whose agent is he?

B. F. The king's, my lord.

L. H. No such matter. He is one of the corporation by the province charter. No agent can be appointed but by an act, nor any act pass without his assent. Besides, this proceeding is directly contrary to express instructions.

B. F. I did not know there had been such instructions. I am not concerned in any offence against them, and ——

L. H. Yes, your offering such a paper to be entered is an offence against them. (*Folding it up again without having read a word of it.*) No such appointment shall be entered. When I came into the administration of American affairs, I found them in great disorder. By *my firmness* they are now something mended; and, while I have the honor to hold the seals, I shall continue the same conduct the same *firmness.* I think my duty to the master I serve, and to the government of this nation, requires it of me. If that conduct is not approved, *they* may take my office from me when they please. I shall make them a bow and thank them. I shall resign with pleasure. That gentleman knows it (*pointing to Mr. Pownall*); but while I continue in it I shall resolutely persevere in the same FIRMNESS. (*Spoken with great warmth, and turning pale in his discourse, as if he was angry at something or somebody besides the agent, and of more consequence to himself.*)

B. F. (*Reaching out his hand for the paper, which his lordship returned to him.*) I beg your lordship's pardon for taking up so much of your time. It is, I believe, of no great importance whether the appointment is acknowledged or not; for I have not the least conception that an agent can *at present* be of any use to any of the colonies. I shall therefore give your lordship no further trouble. (*Withdrew.*)

[TO JOSHUA BABCOCK.]

Agriculture the most Honorable Employment — Condition of the Poor in Ireland — Savage Life and Civilization.

LONDON, 13 January, 1772.

DEAR SIR: It was with great pleasure I learnt, by Mr. Marchant, that you and Mrs. Babcock and all your good family continue well and happy. I hope I shall find you all in the same state when I next come your way, and take shelter, as often heretofore, under your hospitable roof. The colonel, I am told, continues an active and able farmer; the most honorable of all employments, in my opinion, as being the most useful in itself, and rendering the man most independent. My namesake, his son, will soon, I hope, be able to drive the plough for him.

I have lately made a tour through Ireland and Scotland. In those countries a small part of the society are landlords, great

38*

noblemen, and gentlemen, extremely opulent, living in the highest affluence and magnificence.   The bulk of the people are tenants, extremely poor, living in the most sordid wretchedness, in dirty hovels of mud and straw, and clothed only in rags.

I thought often of the happiness of New England, where every man is a freeholder, has a vote in public affairs, lives in a tidy, warm house, has plenty of good food and fuel, with whole clothes from head to foot, the manufacture, perhaps, of his own family.   Long may they continue in this situation ! But, if they should ever envy the trade of these countries, I can put them in a way to obtain a share of it.   Let them, with three-fourths of the people of Ireland, live the year round on potatoes and buttermilk, without shirts ; then may their merchants export beef, butter, and linen.   Let them, with the generality of the common people of Scotland, go barefoot ; then may they make large exports in shoes and stockings, and, if they will be content to wear rags, like the spinners and weavers of England, they may make cloths and stuffs for all parts of the world.

Further, if my countrymen should ever wish for the honor of having among them a gentry enormously wealthy, let them sell their farms and pay racked rents ; the scale of the landlords will rise, as that of the tenants is depressed, who will soon become poor, tattered, dirty, and abject in spirit.   Had I never been in the American colonies, but were to form my judgment of civil society by what I have lately seen, I should never advise a nation of savages to admit of civilization ; for I assure you that, in the possession and enjoyment of the various comforts of life, compared to these people every Indian is a gentleman, and the effect of this kind of civil society seems to be the depressing multitudes below the savage state, that a few may be raised above it.   My best wishes attend you and yours, being ever, with great esteem, &c.,   B. FRANKLIN.

[TO SAMUEL FRANKLIN.]

How to choose a Wife.

LONDON, 13 January, 1772.

DEAR COUSIN : I received your kind letter of November 8th, and rejoice to hear of the continued welfare of you and your good wife and four daughters.   I hope they will all get good husbands. I dare say they will be educated so as to deserve them.

I knew a wise old man who used to advise his young friends to choose wives out of a bunch; for where there were many daughters, he said, they improved each other, and from emulation acquired more accomplishments, knew more, could do more, and were not spoiled by parental fondness, as single children often are. Yours have my best wishes and blessing, if that can be of any value.

I received a very polite letter from your friend, Mr. Bowen, relating to the print. Please to present him my respectful compliments. I am just returned from a long journey. Your affectionate cousin,   B. FRANKLIN.

[TO WILLIAM FRANKLIN.]

Modes of Exercise — Importance to Health.

LONDON, 19 August, 1772.

DEAR SON: IN yours of May 14th you acquaint me with your indisposition, which gave me great concern. The resolution you have taken to use more exercise is extremely proper; and I hope you will steadily perform it. It is of the greatest importance to prevent diseases, since the cure of them by physic is so very precarious.

In considering the different kinds of exercise, I have thought that the *quantum* of each is to be judged of, not by time or by distance, but by the degree of warmth it produces in the body. Thus, when I observe, if I am cold when I get into a carriage in a morning, I may ride all day without being warmed by it; that, if on horseback my feet are cold, I may ride some hours before they become warm; but, if I am ever so cold on foot, I cannot walk an hour briskly without glowing from head to foot by the quickened circulation; I have been ready to say (using round numbers, without regard to exactness, but merely to make a great difference), that there is more exercise in *one* mile's riding on horseback than *five* in a coach, and more in *one* mile's walking on foot than in *five* on horseback; to which I may add, that there is more in walking *one* mile up and down stairs than in *five* on a level floor.

The two latter exercises may be had within doors, when the weather discourages going abroad; and the last may be had when one is pinched for time, as containing a great quantity of exercise in a handful of minutes. The dumb bell is another exercise of the latter compendious kind. By the use of it I have in forty swings quickened my pulse from sixty to one hundred beats in a minute, counted by a second watch; and I suppose the warmth generally increases with quickness of pulse.

B. FRANKLIN.

[TO JOSEPH PRIESTLEY.]

Moral Algebra, for arriving at Decisions in Doubtful Cases.

LONDON, 19 September, 1772.

DEAR SIR: In the affair of so much importance to you, wherein you ask my advice, I cannot, for want of sufficient premises, counsel you *what* to determine; but, if you please, I will tell you *how*. When those difficult cases occur, they are difficult chiefly because, while we have them under consideration, all the reasons *pro* and *con* are not present to the mind at the same time; but sometimes one set present themselves, and at other times another, the first being out of sight. Hence the various purposes or inclinations that alternately prevail, and the uncertainty that perplexes us.

To get over this, my way is, to divide half a sheet of paper by a line into two columns, writing over the one *pro*, and over the other *con;* then, during three or four days' consideration, I put down under the different heads short hints of the different motives that at different times occur to me, *for* or *against* the measure. When I have thus got them all together in one view, I endeavor to estimate their respective weights; and, where I find two (one on each side) that seem equal, I strike them both out. If I find a reason *pro* equal to some *two* reasons *con*, I strike out the *three*. If I judge some *two* reasons *con* equal to some *three* reasons *pro*, I strike out the *five;* and, thus proceeding, I find at length where the *balance* lies; and if, after a day or two of further consideration, nothing new that is of importance occurs on either side, I come to a determination accordingly. And, though the weight of reasons cannot be taken with the precision of algebraic quantities, yet, when each is thus considered separately and comparatively, and the whole lies before me, I think I can judge better, and am less liable to make a rash step; and in fact I have found great advantage from this kind of equation, in what may be called *moral* or *prudential algebra.*

Wishing sincerely that you may determine for the best, I am ever, my dear friend, yours, most affectionately,

B. FRANKLIN.

[TO THE SAME.]

The Philosopher's Stone — Wickedness of the American War.

PARIS, 27 January, 1777.

DEAR SIR : I received your very kind letter, of February last, some time in September. Major Carleton, who was so kind as to forward it to me, had not an opportunity of doing it sooner. I rejoice to hear of your continual progress in those useful discoveries; I find that you have set all the philosophers of Europe at work upon *fixed air ;* and it is with great pleasure I observe how high you stand in their opinion, for I enjoy my friends' fame as my own.

The hint you gave me, jocularly, that you did not quite despair of the *philosopher's stone,* draws from me a request that, when you have found it, you will take care to lose it again ; for I believe in my conscience that mankind are wicked enough to continue slaughtering one another as long as they can find money to pay the butchers. But, of all the wars in my time, this on the part of England appears to me the wickedest; having no cause but malice against liberty, and the jealousy of commerce. And I think the crime seems likely to meet with its proper punishment, — a total loss of her own liberty, and the destruction of her own commerce.

I suppose you would like to know something of the state of affairs in America. In all probability, we shall be much stronger the next campaign than we were in the last ; better armed, better disciplined, and with more ammunition. When I was at the camp before Boston, the army had not five rounds of powder a man. This was kept a secret even from our people. The world wondered that we so seldom fired a cannon; we could not afford it ; — but we now make powder in plenty.

To me it seems, as it has always done, that this war must end in our favor, and in the ruin of Britain, if she does not speedily put an end to it. An English gentleman here the other day, in company with some French, remarked that it was folly in France not to make war immediately. *And in England,* replied one of them, *not to make peace.*

Do not believe the reports you hear of our internal divisions We are, I believe, as much united as any people ever were, and as firmly. B. FRANKLIN.

Providence Rules — National Characteristics — American Superfluities.

PASSY, 22 April, 1779.

DEAR SIR: I received your very kind letter by Mr. Bradford, who appears a very sensible and amiable young gentleman, to whom I should with pleasure render any services in my power, upon your much-respected recommendation; but I understand he returns immediately.

It is with great sincerity I join you in acknowledging and admiring the dispensations of Providence in our favor. America has only to be thankful, and to persevere. God will finish his work, and establish their freedom; and the lovers of liberty will flock from all parts of Europe, with their fortunes, to participate with us of that freedom, as soon as peace is restored.

I am exceedingly pleased with your account of the French politeness and civility, as it appeared among the officers and people of their fleet. They have certainly advanced in those respects many degrees beyond the English. I find them here a most amiable nation to live with. The Spaniards are by common opinion supposed to be cruel, the English proud, the Scotch insolent, the Dutch avaricious, &c.; but I think the French have no national vice ascribed to them. They have some frivolities, but they are harmless. To dress their heads so that a hat cannot be put on them, and then wear their hats under their arms, and to fill their noses with tobacco, may be called follies, perhaps, but they are not vices. They are only the effects of the tyranny of custom. In short, there is nothing wanting in the character of a Frenchman that belongs to that of an agreeable and worthy man. There are only some trifles surplus, or which might be spared.

Will you permit me, while I do them this justice, to hint a little censure on our own country people, which I do in good will, wishing the cause removed? You know the necessity we are under of supplies from Europe, and the difficulty we have at present in making returns. The interest bills would do a good deal towards purchasing arms, ammunition, clothing, sail-cloth, and other necessaries for defence. Upon inquiry of those who present these bills to me for acceptance, what the money is to be laid out in, I find that most of it is for superfluities, and more than half of it for tea. How unhappily in this instance the folly of our people and the avidity of our merchants concur to weaken and impoverish our country! I formerly computed that we consumed before the war, in that single article, the value of five hundred thousand pounds sterling annually. Much of this was saved by stopping the use of it. I honored the virtuous resolution of our women in foregoing that little gratification, and I lament that such virtue should be of so short duration. Five hundred thousand pounds sterling, annually laid out in defending ourselves, or annoying our enemies, would have great effect. With what face can we ask aids and subsidies from our friends, while we are wasting our own wealth in such prodigality? With great and sincere esteem, I have the honor to be, dear sir, &c., B. FRANKLIN.

[TO JOSEPH PRIESTLEY.]

Progress of Science — All Situations have their Inconveniences — Illustrative Anecdote.

PASSY, 8 February, 1780.

DEAR SIR: Your kind letter of September 27th came to hand but very lately, the bearer having stayed long in Holland. I always rejoice to hear of your being still employed in experimental researches into nature, and of the success you meet with. The rapid progress *true* science now makes occasions my regretting sometimes that I was born so soon. It is impossible to imagine the height to which may be carried in a thousand years the power of man over matter. We may, perhaps, learn to deprive large masses of their gravity, and give them absolute levity, for the sake of easy transport. Agriculture may diminish its labor and double its produce; all diseases may by sure means be prevented or cured, not excepting even that of old age, and our lives lengthened at pleasure even beyond the antediluvian standard. O that moral science were in as fair a way of improvement! that men would cease to be wolves to one another, and that human beings would at length learn what they now improperly call humanity!

I am glad my little paper on the *Aurora Borealis* pleased. If it should occasion further inquiry, and so produce a better hypothesis, it will not be wholly useless. I am ever, with the greatest and most sincere esteem, dear sir, &c.,

B. FRANKLIN.

Enclosed in the foregoing Letter ; being an Answer to a separate Paper received from Dr. Priestley.

I have considered the situation of that person very attentively. I think that, with a little help from the *Moral Algebra,** he might form a better judgment than any other person can form for him. But, since my opinion seems to be desired, I give it for continuing to the end of the term, under all the present disagreeable circumstances. The connection will then die a natural death. No reason will be expected to be given for the separation, and, of course, no offence taken at reasons given ; the friendship may still subsist, and in some other way be useful. The time diminishes daily, and is usefully employed. All human situations have their inconveniences ; we *feel* those that we find in the present, and we neither *feel* nor *see* those that exist in another. Hence we make frequent and troublesome changes without amendment, and often for the worse.

In my youth, I was passenger in a little sloop, descending the river Delaware. There being no wind, we were obliged, when the ebb was spent, to cast anchor, and wait for the next. The heat of the sun on the vessel was excessive, the company strangers to me, and not very agreeable. Near the river-side I saw what I took to be a pleasant green meadow, in the middle of which was a large shady tree, where, it struck my fancy, I could sit and read (having a book in my pocket), and pass the time agreeably till the tide turned. I therefore prevailed with the captain to put me ashore. Being landed, I found the greatest part of my meadow was really a marsh, in crossing which, to come at my tree, I was up to my knees in mire ; and I had not placed myself under its shade five minutes, before the mosquitoes in swarms found me out, attacked my legs, hands and face, and made my reading and my rest impossible ; so that I returned to the beach, and called for the boat to come and take me on board again, where I was obliged to bear the heat I had strove to quit, and also the laugh of the company. Simi-

---

* See letter to Dr. Priestley, dated September 19th, 1772, p. 452.

lar cases in the affairs of life have since frequently fallen under my observation.

I have had thoughts of a college for him in America. I know no one who might be more useful to the public in the instruction of youth. But there are possible unpleasantnesses in that situation; it cannot be obtained but by a too hazardous voyage at this time for a family; and the time for experiments would be all otherwise engaged.*

PASSY, 8 October, 1780.

IT is long, very long, my dear friend, since I had the great pleasure of hearing from you, and receiving any of your very pleasing letters. But it is my fault. I have long omitted my part of the correspondence. Those who love to receive letters should write letters. I wish I could safely promise an amendment of that fault. But, besides the indolence attending age, and growing upon us with it, my time is engrossed by too much business, and I have too many inducements to postpone doing what I feel I ought to do for my own sake, and what I can never resolve to omit entirely.

Your translations from Horace, as far as I can judge of poetry and translations, are very good. That of the *Quò, quò scelesti ruitis?* is so suitable to the times, that the conclusion (in your version) seems to threaten like a prophecy; and, methinks, there is at least some appearance of danger that it may be fulfilled. I am unhappily an enemy, yet I think there has been enough of blood spilt, and I wish what is left in the veins of that once-loved people may be spared by a peace solid and everlasting.

It is a great while since I have heard anything of the *good bishop*. Strange that so simple a character should sufficiently distinguish one of that sacred body! *Donnez-moi de ses nouvelles.* I have been some time flattered with the expectation of seeing the countenance of that most honored and ever beloved

---

* The advice contained in this paper related to Dr. Priestley himself, who had engaged to live with Lord Shelburne, as his librarian, at a salary of about three hundred pounds per annum, for a certain number of years; but, before the term had expired, he became dissatisfied with his situation, and requested counsel from Dr. Franklin on the subject.

friend, delineated by your pencil. The portrait is said to have been long on the way, but is not yet arrived; nor can I hear where it is.

Indolent as I have confessed myself to be, I could not, you see, miss this good and safe opportunity of sending you a few lines, with my best wishes for your happiness, and that of the whole dear and amiable family in whose sweet society I have spent so many happy hours. Mr. Jones * tells me he shall have a pleasure in being the bearer of my letter, of which I make no doubt. I learn from him that to your drawing, and music, and painting, and poetry, and Latin, you have added a proficiency in chess; so that you are, as the French say, *remplie de talens.* May they and you fall to the lot of one that shall duly value them, and love you as much as I do! Adieu.

                                                B. FRANKLIN.

<hr>

[TO FRANCIS HOPKINSON.]
On Planting Trees — Newspaper Abuse.

                                        PASSY, 24 December, 1782.

DEAR SIR : I thank you for your ingenious paper in favor of the trees. I own I now wish we had two rows of them in every one of our streets. The comfortable shelter they would afford us when walking, from our burning summer suns, and the greater coolness of our walls and pavements, would, I conceive, in the improved health of the inhabitants, amply compensate the loss of a house now and then by fire, if such should be the consequence. But a tree is soon felled: and, as axes are at hand in every neighborhood, may be down before the engines arrive.

You do well to avoid being concerned in the pieces of personal abuse, so scandalously common in our newspapers, that I am afraid to lend any of them here, until I have examined and laid aside such as would disgrace us, and subject us among strangers to a reflection like that used by a gentleman in a coffee-house to two quarrellers, who, after a mutually free use of the words *rogue, villain, rascal, scoundrel,* &c., seemed as if they would refer their dispute to him : " I know nothing of you, or your affairs," said he ; " I only perceive *that you know one another.*"

---

* Afterwards the celebrated Sir William Jones

The conductor of a newspaper should, methinks, consider himself as in some degree the guardian of his country's reputation, and refuse to insert such writings as may hurt it. If people will print their abuses of one another, let them do it in little pamphlets, and distribute them where they think proper. It is absurd to trouble all the world with them, and unjust to subscribers in distant places to stuff their papers with matters so unprofitable and so disagreeable. With sincere esteem and affection, I am, &c., B. FRANKLIN.

[TO MRS. MARY HEWSON.]

On the Death of Friends — Folly of War — Protracted Friendship.

PASSY, 27 January, 1783.

—— THE departure of my dearest friend,* which I learn from your last letter, greatly affects me. To meet with her once more in this life was one of the principal motives of my proposing to visit England again, before my return to America. The last year carried off my friends Dr. Pringle, Dr. Fothergill, Lord Kames, and Lord le Despencer. This has begun to take away the rest, and strikes the hardest. Thus the ties I had to that country, and indeed to the world in general, are loosened one by one, and I shall soon have no attachment left to make me unwilling to follow.

I intended writing when I sent the eleven books, but I lost the time in looking for the twelfth. I wrote with that; and hope it came to hand. I therein asked your counsel about my coming to England. On reflection, I think I can, from my knowledge of your prudence, foresee what it will be, namely, not to come too soon, lest it should seem braving and insulting some who ought to be respected. I shall, therefore, omit the journey till I am near going to America, and then just step over to take leave of my friends, and spend a few days with you. I purpose bringing Ben with me, and perhaps may leave him under your care.

At length we are in peace, God be praised, and long, very long, may it continue! All wars are follies, — very expensive and very mischievous ones. When will mankind be convinced of this, and agree to settle their differences by arbitration? Were they to do it, even by the cast of a die, it would be better than by fighting and destroying each other.

* Mrs. Stevenson, the mother of Mrs. Hewson.

Spring is coming on, when travelling will be delightful. Can you not, when you see your children all at school, make a little party and take a trip hither? I have now a large house, delightfully situated, in which I could accommodate you and two or three friends; and I am but half an hour's drive from Paris.

In looking forward twenty-five years seem a long period, but in looking back how short! Could you imagine that it is now full a quarter of a century since we were first acquainted? It was in 1757. During the greatest part of the time, I lived in the same house with my dear deceased friend, your mother; of course, you and I conversed with each other much and often. It is to all our honors that in all that time we never had among us the smallest misunderstanding. Our friendship has been all clear sunshine, without the least cloud in its hemisphere. Let me conclude by saying to you, what I have had too frequent occasions to say to my other remaining old friends, "The fewer we become, the more let us love one another." Adieu, and believe me ever yours, most affectionately, **B. FRANKLIN.**

[TO JOHN SARGENT.]
Gratitude to Providence — Matrimony, &c.

PASSY, 27 January, 1783.

MY DEAR FRIEND: I received and read the letter you was so kind as to write to me the third instant, with a great deal of pleasure, as it informed me of the welfare of a family whom I have so long esteemed and loved, and to whom I am under so many obligations, which I shall ever remember. Our correspondence has been interrupted by that abominable war. I neither expected letters from you, nor would I hazard putting you in danger by writing any to you. We can now communicate freely; and, next to the happiness of seeing and embracing you all again at Halstead, will be that of hearing frequently of your health and prosperity.

Mrs. Sargent and the good lady, her mother, are very kind in wishing me more happy years. I ought to be satisfied with those Providence has already been pleased to afford me, being now in my seventy-eighth; a long life to pass without any uncommon misfortune, the greater part of it in health and vigor of mind and body, near fifty years of it in continued possession of the confidence of my country, in public employments, and enjoying the esteem and affectionate friendly regard of many wise and good men and women, in every country where I have resided. For these mercies and blessings I desire to be thankful to God, whose protection I have hitherto had; and I hope for its continuance to the end, which now cannot be far distant.

The account you give me of your family is pleasing, except that your eldest son continues so long unmarried. I hope he does not intend to live and die in celibacy. The wheel of life, that has rolled down to him from Adam without interruption, should not stop with him. I would not have one dead, unbearing branch in the genealogical tree of the Sargents. The married state is, after all our jokes the happiest, being conformable to our natures. Man and woman have each of them qualities and tempers in which the other is deficient, and which in union contribute to the common felicity. Single and separate, they are not the complete human being; they are like the odd halves of scissors; they cannot answer the end of their formation.

I am concerned at the losses you have suffered by the war. You are still young and active enough to retrieve them; and peace, I hope, will afford the opportunity.

You mention nothing of my good friend Mrs. Deane, or her amiable sisters, whom I saw with you, nor of Mr. Chambers. I hope they are all well and happy. Present my respects to Mrs. Sargent, whom I love very much, and believe me ever, my dear friend, yours, most affectionately, B. FRANKLIN.

[TO SIR JOSEPH BANKS.]

Against War.

PASSY, 27 July, 1783.

DEAR SIR: I received your very kind letter by Dr. Blagden, and esteem myself much honored by your friendly remembrance. I have been too much and too closely engaged in public affairs, since his being here, to enjoy all the benefit of his conversation you were so good as to intend me. I hope soon to have more leisure, and to spend a part of it in those studies that are much more agreeable to me than political operations.

I join with you most cordially in rejoicing at the return of peace. I hope it will be lasting, and that mankind will at length, as they call themselves reasonable creatures, have reason and sense enough to settle their differences without cutting throats; for, in my opinion, *there never was a good war, or a bad peace*. What vast additions to the conveniences and comforts of living might mankind have acquired, if the money spent in wars had been employed in works of public utility ! What an extension of agriculture, even to the tops of our mountains; what rivers rendered navigable, or joined by canals; what bridges, aqueducts, new roads, and other public works, edifices and improvements, rendering England a complete paradise, might have been obtained by spending those millions in doing good, which in the last war have been spent in doing mischief, — in bringing misery into thousands of families, and destroying the lives of so many thousands of working people, who might have performed the useful labor !

I am pleased with the late astronomical discoveries made by our Society.* Furnished as all Europe now is with academies of science, with nice instruments and the spirit of experiment, the progress of human knowledge will be rapid, and discoveries made of which we have at present no conception. I begin to be almost sorry I was born so soon, since I cannot have the happiness of knowing what will be known one hundred years hence.

I wish continued success to the labors of the Royal Society, and that you may long adorn their chair; being, with the highest esteem, dear sir, &o., B. FRANKLIN.

P. S. Dr. Blagden will acquaint you with the experiment of a vast globe sent up into the air, much talked of here, and which, if prosecuted, may furnish means of new knowledge.

[TO JONATHAN SHIPLEY.]
On the Establishment of Peace.

PASSY, 17 March, 1783.

I RECEIVED with great pleasure my dear and respected friend's letter of the 5th instant, as it informed me of the welfare of a family I so much esteem and love.

The clamor against the peace in your Parliament would alarm me for its duration, if I were not of opinion, with you, that the attack is rather against the minister. I am confident none of the opposition would have made a better peace for England, if

* The Royal Society of London.

they had been in his place; at least, I am sure that Lord Stormont, who seems loudest in railing at it, is not the man that could have mended it. My reasons I will give you when I have, what I hope to have, the great happiness of seeing you once more, and conversing with you.

They talk much of there being no *reciprocity* in our treaty. They think nothing, then, of our passing over in silence the atrocities committed by their troops, and demanding no satisfaction for their wanton burnings and devastations of our fair towns and countries. They have heretofore confessed the war to be unjust, and nothing is plainer in reasoning than that the mischiefs done in an unjust war should be repaired. Can Englishmen be so partial to themselves as to imagine they have a right to plunder and destroy as much as they please, and then, without satisfying for the injuries they have done, to have peace on equal terms? We were favorable, and did not demand what justice entitled us to. We shall probably be blamed for it by our constituents; and I still think it would be the interest of England voluntarily to offer reparation of those injuries, and effect it as much as may be in her power. But this is an interest she will never see.

Let us now forgive and forget. Let each country seek its advancement in its own internal advantages of arts and agriculture, not in retarding or preventing the prosperity of the other. America will, with God's blessing, become a great and happy country; and England, if she has at length gained wisdom, will have gained something more valuable, and more essential to her prosperity, than all she has lost, and will still be a great and respectable nation. Her great disease at present is the number and enormous salaries and emoluments of office. Avarice and ambition are strong passions, and, separately, act with great force on the human mind; but, when both are united, and may be gratified in the same object, their violence is almost irresistible, and they hurry men headlong into factions and contentions, destructive of all good government. As long, therefore, as these great emoluments subsist, your Parliament will be a stormy sea, and your public councils confounded by private interests. But it requires much public spirit and virtue to abolish them; more, perhaps, than can now be found in a nation so long corrupted. I am, &c., B. FRANKLIN.

*The Order of the Cincinnati — Ascending and Descending Honors —
Absurdity of the System of Hereditary Nobility.*

PASSY, January 26, 1784.

MY DEAR CHILD: Your care in sending me the newspapers
is very agreeable to me. I received by Captain Barney those
relating to the *Cincinnati*. My opinion of the institution cannot be of much importance. I only wonder that, when the
united wisdom of our nation had, in the articles of confederation, manifested their dislike of establishing ranks of nobility,
by authority either of the congress or of any particular state, a
number of private persons should think proper to distinguish
themselves and their posterity from their fellow-citizens, and
for an order of *hereditary knights*, in direct opposition to the
solemnly-declared sense of their country. I imagine it must be
likewise contrary to the good sense of most of those drawn into
it by the persuasion of its projectors, who have been too much
struck with the ribands and crosses they have seen hanging to
the button-holes of foreign officers. And I suppose those who
disapprove of it have not hitherto given it much opposition,
from a principle somewhat like that of your good mother, relating to punctilious persons, who are always exacting little observ-
ances of respect, that, "*if people can be pleased with small
matters, it is a pity but they should have them.*"

In this view, perhaps, I should not myself, if my advice had
been asked, have objected to their wearing their riband and
badge themselves according to their fancy, though I certainly
should to the entailing it as an honor on their posterity. For,
honor worthily obtained (as that, for example, of our officers) is
in its nature a *personal* thing, and incommunicable to any but
those who had some share in obtaining it. Thus, among the
Chinese, the most ancient, and, from long experience, the wisest
of nations, honor does not *descend*, but *ascends*. If a man, from
his learning, his wisdom, or his valor, is promoted by the emperor to the rank of mandarin, his parents are immediately
entitled to all the same ceremonies of respect from the people
that are established as due to the mandarin himself; on the
supposition that it must have been *owing to the education, instruction and good example, afforded him by his parents,* that he
was rendered capable of serving the public.

This *ascending* honor is therefore useful to the state, as it
encourages parents to give their children a good and virtuous

education. But the *descending honor*, to a posterity who could have no share in obtaining it, is not only groundless and absurd, but often hurtful to that posterity, since it is apt to make them proud, disdaining to be employed in useful arts, and thence falling into poverty, and all the meannesses, servility and wretchedness, attending it; which is the present case with much of what is called the *noblesse* in Europe. Or, if to keep up the dignity of the family estates are entailed entire on the eldest male heir, another pest to industry and improvement of the country is introduced, which will be followed by all the odious mixture of pride, and beggary, and idleness, that have half depopulated and decultivated Spain, occasioning continual extinction of families by the discouragements of marriage, and neglect in the improvement of estates.

I wish, therefore, that the Cincinnati, if they must go on with their project, would direct the badges of their order to be worn by their fathers and mothers, instead of handing them down to their children. It would be a good precedent, and might have good effects. It would also be a kind of obedience to the fifth commandment, in which God enjoins us to *honor our father and mother*, but has nowhere directed us to honor our *children*. And certainly no mode of honoring those immediate authors of our being can be more effectual than that of doing praiseworthy actions, which reflect honor on those who gave us our education; or more becoming than that of manifesting, by some public expression or token, that it is to their instruction and example we ascribe the merit of those actions.

But the absurdity of *descending honors* is not a mere matter of philosophical opinion; it is capable of mathematical demonstration. A man's son, for instance, is but half of his family, the other half belonging to the family of his wife. His son, too, marrying into another family, his share in the grandson is but a fourth; in the great-grandson, by the same process, is but an eighth; in the next generation, a sixteenth; the next, a thirty-second; the next, a sixty-fourth; the next, a hundred and twenty-eighth; the next, a two hundred and fifty-sixth; and the next, a five hundred and twelfth. Thus, in nine generations, which will not require more than three hundred years (no very great antiquity for a family), our present chevalier of the order of Cincinnatus's share in the then existing knight will be but a five hundred and twelfth part; which, allowing the present certain fidelity of American wives to be insured down through all those nine generations, is so small a consideration, that methinks no reasonable man would hazard, for the sake of it, the disa-

greeable consequences of the jealousy, envy and ill-will, of his
countrymen.

Let us go back with our calculation from this young noble,
the five hundreth and twelfth part of the present knight, through
his nine generations, till we return to the year of the institution.
He must have had a father and mother,—they are two; each of
them had a father and mother,—they are four.   Those of the
next preceding generation will be eight, the next sixteen, the
next thirty-two, the next sixty-four, the next one hundred and
twenty-eight, the next two hundred and fifty-six, and the ninth
in this retrocession five hundred and twelve, who must be now
existing, and all contribute their proportion of this future *Chevalier de Cincinnatus*.   These, with the rest, make together as
follows :

$$
\begin{array}{r}
2 \\
4 \\
8 \\
16 \\
32 \\
64 \\
128 \\
256 \\
512 \\
\hline
\end{array}
$$

Total . $\overline{1022}$

One thousand and twenty-two men and women contributors to
the formation of one knight! And, if we are to have a thousand
of these future knights, there must be now and hereafter existing one million and twenty-two thousand fathers and mothers,
who are to contribute to their production ; unless a part of the
number are employed in making more knights than one.   Let
us strike off, then, the twenty-two thousand, on the supposition
of this double employ, and then consider whether, after a reasonable estimation of the number of rogues, and fools, and
scoundrels, and prostitutes, that are mixed with and help to
make up necessarily their million of predecessors, posterity will
have much reason to boast of the noble blood of the then existing set of chevaliers of Cincinnatus.

The future genealogists, too, of these chevaliers, in proving
the lineal descent of their honor through so many generations
(even supposing honor capable in its nature of descending),
will only prove the small share of this honor which can be
justly claimed by any one of them, since the above simple process in arithmetic makes it quite plain and clear that, in pro-

portion as the antiquity of the family shall augment, the right to the honor of the ancestor will diminish; and a few generations more would reduce it to something so small as to be very near an absolute nullity. I hope, therefore, that the order will drop this part of their project, and content themselves, as the knights of the Garter, Bath, Thistle, St. Louis, and other orders of Europe do, with a life enjoyment of their little badge and riband, and let the distinction die with those who have merited it. This, I imagine, will give no offence. For my own part, I shall think it a convenience, when I go into company where there may be faces unknown to me, if I discover by this badge the persons who merit some particular expression of my respect; and it will save modest virtue the trouble of calling for our regard, by awkward, roundabout intimations of having been heretofore employed as officers in the continental service.

The gentleman who made the voyage to France, to provide the ribands and medals, has executed his commission. To me they seem tolerably done; but all such things are criticized. Some find fault with the Latin, as wanting classical elegance and correctness; and, since our nine universities were not able to furnish better Latin, it was a pity, they say, that the mottoes had not been in English. Others object to the title, as not properly assumable by any but General Washington, and a few others who served without pay. Others object to the bald eagle, as looking too much like a *dindon* or turkey. For my own part, I wish the bald eagle had not been chosen as the representative of our country; he is a bird of bad moral character: he does not get his living honestly: you may have seen him perched on some dead tree, where, too lazy to fish for himself, he watches the labor of the fishing-hawk; and when that diligent bird has at length taken a fish, and is bearing it to his nest for the support of his mate and young ones, the bald eagle pursues him, and takes it from him. With all this injustice, he is never in good case, but, like those among men who live by sharping and robbing, he is generally poor, and often very lousy. Besides, he is a rank coward: the little *king-bird*, not bigger than a sparrow, attacks him boldly, and drives him out of the district. He is, therefore, by no means a proper emblem for the brave and honest Cincinnati of America, who have driven all the *king-birds* from our country; though exactly fit for that order of knights which the French call *Chevaliers d'Industrie*.

I am, on this account, not displeased that the figure is not known as a bald eagle, but looks more like a turkey. For, in truth, the turkey is in comparison a much more respectable

bird, and withal a true original native of America.   Eagles
have been found in all countries, but the turkey was peculiar to
ours ; the first of the species seen in Europe being brought to
France by the Jesuits from Canada, and served up at the wed-
ding-table of Charles IX.   He is besides (though a little vain
and silly, 't is true, but not the worse emblem for that) a bird of
courage, and would not hesitate to attack a grenadier of the
British Guards who should presume to invade his farm-yard
with a red coat on.

I shall not enter into the criticisms made upon their Latin.
The gallant officers of America may not have the merit of being
great scholars, but they undoubtedly merit much as brave soldiers from their country, which should, therefore, not leave them
merely to *fame* for their *virtutis premium*, which is one of their
Latin mottoes.   Their *esto perpetua* — another — is an excellent
wish, if they meant it for their country ; bad, if intended for
their order.   The States should not only restore to them the
omnia of their first motto,* which many of them have left and
lost, but pay them justly, and reward them generously.   They
should not be suffered to remain, with all their new-created
chivalry, *entirely* in the situation of the gentleman in the story
which their *omnia reliquit* reminds me of.   You know everything makes me recollect some story.   He had built a very fine
house, and thereby much impaired his fortune.   He had a pride,
however, in showing it to his acquaintance.   One of them, after
viewing it all, remarked a motto over the door — O͞IA VANITAS.
"Whát," says he, "is the meaning of this O͞IA ? 'T is a word I don't
understand."   "I will tell you," said the gentleman : "I had a
mind to have the motto cut on a piece of smooth marble, but there
was not room for it, between the ornaments, to be put in characters large enough to be read.   I therefore made use of a contraction, anciently very common in Latin manuscripts, whereby
the *m*'s and *n*'s in words are omitted, and the omission noted by
a little dash above, which you may see there, so that the word is
omnia — OMNIA VANITAS."   "O," said his friend, "I now comprehend the meaning of your motto, — it relates to your edifice, and
signifies that if you have abridged your *omnia*, you have nevertheless left your VANITAS legible at full length."   I am, as ever,
your affectionate father,   B. FRANKLIN.

---

* Omnia reliquit servare rempublicam.

[TO DR. MATHER, BOSTON.]

Cotton Mather — Anecdote — On visiting Boston.

PASSY, May 12, 1784.

REV. SIR: I received your kind letter, with your excellent advice to the people of the United States, which I read with great pleasure, and hope it will be duly regarded. Such writings, though they may be lightly passed over by many readers, yet, if they make a deep impression on one active mind in a hundred, the effects may be considerable. Permit me to mention one little instance, which, though it relates to myself, will not be quite uninteresting to you. When I was a boy I met with a book entitled "*Essays to do Good*," which, I think, was written by your father. It had been so little regarded by a former possessor that several leaves of it were torn out, but the remainder gave me such a turn of thinking as to have an influence on my conduct through life; for I have always set a greater value on the character of a *doer of good* than on any other kind of reputation; and if I have been, as you seem to think, a useful citizen, the public owes the advantage of it to that book.

You mention your being in your seventy-eighth year: I am in my seventy-ninth; we are grown old together. It is now more than sixty years since I left Boston, but I remember well both your father and grandfather, having heard them both in the pulpit, and seen them in their houses. The last time I saw your father was in the beginning of 1724, when I visited him after my first trip to Pennsylvania. He received me in his library, and, on my taking leave, showed me a shorter way out of the house through a narrow passage, which was crossed by a beam overhead. We were still talking as I withdrew, he accompanying me behind, and I turning partly towards him, when he said, hastily, " *Stoop, stoop!* " I did not understand him till I felt my head hit against the beam. He was a man that never missed any occasion of giving instruction, and upon this he said to me, " *You are young, and have the world before you: STOOP as you go through it, and you may miss many hard thumps.*" This advice, thus beat into my head, has frequently been of use to me; and I often think of it, when I see pride mortified, and misfortunes brought upon people, by their carrying their heads too high.

I long much to see again my native place, and to lay my bones there. I left it in 1723; I visited it in 1733, 1743, 1753, and 1763. In 1773 I was in England; in 1775 I had a
40

sight of it, but could not enter, it being in possession of the enemy. I did hope to have been there in 1783, but could not obtain my dismission from this employment here; and now I fear I shall never have that happiness. My best wishes, however, attend my dear country. *Esto perpetua.* It is now blest with an excellent constitution; may it last forever!

This powerful monarchy continues its friendship for the United States. It is a friendship of the utmost importance to our security, and should be carefully cultivated. Britain has not yet well digested the loss of its dominion over us, and has still at times some flattering hopes of recovering it. Accidents may increase those hopes, and encourage dangerous attempts. A breach between us and France would infallibly bring the English again upon our backs; and yet we have some wild heads among our countrymen, who are endeavoring to weaken that connection! Let us preserve our reputation by performing our engagements; our credit, by fulfilling our contracts; and friends, by gratitude and kindness; for we know not how soon we may again have occasion for all of them. With great and sincere esteem, I have the honor to be, &c., B. FRANKLIN.

[TO B. VAUGHAN.]

American Extravagance — Anecdote — Commerce — Forest Lands — Elements of Wealth.

PASSY, July 26, 1784.

* * * You ask "what remedy I have for the growing luxury of my country, which gives so much *offence to all English travellers,* without exception." I answer that I think it exaggerated, and that travellers are not good judges whether our luxury is growing or diminishing. Our people are hospitable, and have indeed too much pride in displaying upon their tables before strangers the plenty and variety that our country affords. They have the vanity too of sometimes borrowing one another's plate to entertain more splendidly. Strangers, being invited from house to house, meeting every day with a feast, imagine what they see is the ordinary way of living of all the families where they dine, when perhaps each family lives a week after upon the remains of the dinner given.

It is, I own, a folly in our people to give *such offence to English travellers.* The first part of the proverb is thereby verified, that *fools make feasts.* I wish in this case the other were as true, — *and wise men eat them.* These travellers might, one would think, find some fault they could more decently reproach us with than that of our excessive civility to them as strangers.

I have not, indeed, yet thought of a remedy for luxury; I am not sure that in a great state it is capable of a remedy, nor that the evil is in itself always so great as it is represented. Suppose we include in the definition of luxury all unnecessary expense, and then let us consider whether laws to prevent such expense are possible to be executed in a great country, and whether, if they could be executed, our people generally would be happier, or even richer. Is not the hope of one day being able to purchase and enjoy luxuries a great spur to labor and industry? May not luxury therefore produce more than it consumes, if without such a spur people would be, as they are naturally enough inclined to be, lazy and indolent? To this purpose, I remember a circumstance.

The skipper of a shallop, employed between Cape May and Philadelphia, had done us some small service, for which he refused pay. My wife, understanding that he had a daughter, sent her as a present a new-fashioned cap. Three years after, the skipper being at my house, with an old farmer of Cape May, his passenger, he mentioned the cap, and how much his daughter had been pleased with it. " But," said he, " it proved a dear cap to our congregation." " How so?" " When my daughter appeared in it at meeting, it was so much admired that all the girls resolved to get such caps from Philadelphia; and my wife and I computed that the whole could not cost less than a hundred pounds." " True," said the farmer, " but you do not tell all the story. I think the cap was nevertheless an advantage to us; for it was the first thing that set our girls upon knitting worsted mittens for sale at Philadelphia, that they might have wherewithal to buy caps and ribbons there; and you know that *that* industry has continued, and is likely to continue and increase to a much greater value, and answer better purposes." Upon the whole, I was more reconciled to this little piece of luxury, since not only the girls were made happier by having fine caps, but the Philadelphians by the supply of warm mittens.

In our commercial towns upon the sea-coast, fortunes will occasionally be made. Some of those who grow rich will be prudent, live within bounds, and preserve what they have gained for their posterity. Others, fond of showing their wealth, will be extravagant and ruin themselves. Laws cannot prevent this, and perhaps it is not always an evil to the public. A shilling spent idly by a fool may be picked up by a wiser person, who knows better what to do with it: it is therefore not lost.

A vain, silly fellow builds a fine house, furnishes it richly, lives in it expensively, and in a few years ruins himself; but the masons, carpenters, smiths, and other honest tradesmen, have been by his employ assisted in maintaining and raising their families; the farmer has been paid for his labor and encouraged, and the estate is now in better hands. In some cases, indeed, certain modes of luxury may be a public evil, in the same manner as it is a private one. If there be a nation, for instance, that exports its beef and linen to pay for its importations of claret and porter, while a great part of its people live upon potatoes and wear no shirts, wherein does it differ from the sot who lets his family starve, and sells his clothes to buy drink? Our American commerce is, I confess, a little in this way. We sell our victuals to your islands for rum and sugar; the substantial necessaries of life for superfluities. But we have plenty and live well, nevertheless, though by being soberer we might be richer.

By the by, here is just issued an *arrêt* of council, taking off all the duties upon the exportation of brandies, which, it is said, will render them cheaper in America than your rum; in which case there is no doubt but they will be preferred, and we shall be better able to bear your restrictions on our commerce. There are views here, by augmenting their settlements, of being able to supply the growing people of America with the sugar that may be wanted there. On the whole, I believe England will get as little by the commercial war she has begun with us as she did by the military. But to return to luxury.

The vast quantity of forest lands we have yet to clear and put in order for cultivation will for a long time keep the body of our nation laborious and frugal. Forming an opinion of our people and their manners by what is seen among the inhabitants of the seaports, is judging from an improper sample. The people of the trading towns may be rich and luxurious, while the country possesses all the virtues that tend to private happiness and public prosperity. Those towns are not much regarded by the country; they are hardly considered as an essential part of the States; and the experience of the last war has shown that their being in possession of the enemy did not necessarily draw on the subjection of the country, which bravely continued to maintain its freedom and independence, notwithstanding.

It has been computed, by some political arithmetician, that if every man and woman would work four hours each day in something useful, that labor would produce sufficient to procure all the necessaries and comforts of life ; want and misery would be banished out of the world, and the rest of the twenty-four hours might be leisure and pleasure.

What, then, occasions so much want and misery ? It is the employment of men and women in works that produce neither the necessaries nor conveniences of life ; who, with those who do nothing, consume the necessaries raised by the laborious. To explain this.

The first elements of wealth are obtained by labor from the earth and waters. I have land, and raise corn : with this I feed a family that does nothing, — my corn will be consumed, and at the end of the year I shall be no richer than I was at the beginning. But if, while I feed them, I employ them, some in spinning, others in hewing timber and sawing boards, others in making bricks, &c., for building, the value of my corn will be arrested, and remain with me, and at the end of the year we may all be better clothed and better lodged. And if, instead of employing a man I feed in making bricks, I employ him in fiddling for me, the corn he eats is gone, and no part of his manufacture remains to augment the wealth and the conveniences of the family ; I shall therefore be the poorer for this fiddling-man, unless the rest of my family work more, or eat less, to make up the deficiency he occasions.

Look round the world, and see the millions employed in doing nothing, or in something that amounts to nothing, when the necessaries and conveniences of life are in question. What is the bulk of commerce, for which we fight and destroy each other, but the toil of millions for superfluities, to the great hazard and loss of many lives by the constant dangers of the sea ? How much labor spent in building and fitting great ships to go to China and Arabia for tea and for coffee, to the West Indies for sugar, to America for tobacco ! These things cannot be called the necessaries of life, for our ancestors lived very comfortably without them.

A question may be asked, Could all these people now employed in raising, making or carrying superfluities, be subsisted by raising necessaries ? I think they might. The world is large, and a great part of it still uncultivated. Many hundred millions of acres in Asia, Africa and America, are still forest, and a great deal even in Europe. On one hundred acres of this forest a man might become a substantial farmer, and one hundred thousand men employed in clearing each his hundred acres (instead of being, as they are, French hair-dressers) would hardly brighten a spot big enough to be visible from the moon (unless

40*

with Herschell's telescope), so vast are the regions still in the world unimproved.

'T is, however, some comfort to reflect that, upon the whole, the quantity of industry and prudence among mankind exceeds the quantity of idleness and folly. Hence the increase of good buildings, farms cultivated, and populous cities filled with wealth, all over Europe, which a few ages since were only to be found on the coasts of the Mediterranean, And this, notwithstanding the mad wars continually raging, by which are often destroyed in one year the works of many years' peace; so that we may hope that the luxury of a few merchants on the sea-coast will not be the ruin of America.

One reflection more, and I will end this long, rambling letter. Almost all the parts of our bodies require some expense. The feet demand shoes, the legs stockings, the rest of the body clothing, and the belly a good deal of victuals. *Our* eyes, though exceedingly useful, ask, when reasonable, only the cheap assistance of *spectacles*, which could not much impair our finances. But THE EYES OF OTHER PEOPLE are the eyes that ruin us. If all but myself were blind, I should want neither fine clothes, fine houses, nor fine furniture. B. FRANKLIN.

P. S. This will be delivered to you by my grandson. I am persuaded you will afford him your civilities and counsels. Please to accept a little present of books I send by him, curious for the beauty of the impression.

[TO WILLIAM STRAHAN, M.P.]

On visiting England — Public Salaries — Vagrancy of Congress — The War — British Disdain for Yankees — Consequences — Evidences of Providence — Comparison of Fortunes — English Copyrights in America — Emigration.

PASSY, August 19, 1784.

DEAR FRIEND: I received your kind letter of April 17. You will have the goodness to place my delay in answering to the account of indisposition and business, and excuse it. I have now that letter before me; and my grandson, whom you may formerly remember a little scholar at Mr. Elphinston's, purposing to set out in a day or two on a visit to his father in London, I sit down to scribble a little to you, first recommending him as a worthy young man to your civilities and counsels.

You press me much to come to England. I am not without strong inducements to do so ; the fund of knowledge you promise to communicate to me is, in addition to them, no small one. At present it is impracticable. But, when my grandson returns, come with him. We will talk the matter over, and perhaps you may take me back with you. I have a bed at your service, and will try to make your residence, while you can stay with us, as agreeable to you, if possible, as I am sure it will be to me.

You do not " approve the annihilation of profitable places ; for you do not see why a statesman who does his business well should not be paid for his labor as well as any other workman." Agreed. But why more than any other workman ? The less the salary, the greater the honor. In so great a nation there are many rich enough to afford giving their time to the public ; and there are, I make no doubt, many wise and able men who would take as much pleasure in governing for nothing as they do in playing of chess for nothing. It would be one of the noblest amusements.

That this opinion is not chimerical the country I now live in affords a proof ; its whole civil and criminal law administration being done for nothing, or in some sense for less than nothing, since the members of its judiciary parliaments buy their places, and do not make more than three per cent. for their money by their fees and emoluments, while the legal interest is five ; so that, in fact, they give two per cent. to be allowed to govern, and all their time and trouble into the bargain. Thus *profit*, one motive for desiring place, being abolished, there remains only *ambition ;* and that being in some degree balanced by *loss*, you may easily conceive that there will not be very violent factions and contentions for such places, nor much of the mischief to the country that attends your factions, which have often occasioned wars, and overloaded you with debts impayable.

I allow you all the force of your joke upon the vagrancy of our Congress. They have a right to sit *where* they please, of which perhaps they have made too much use by shifting too often. But they have two other rights, — those of sitting *when* they please, and as *long* as they please, in which methinks they have the advantage of your Parliament ; for they cannot be dissolved by the breath of a minister, or sent packing as you were the other day, when it was your earnest desire to have remained longer together.

You " fairly acknowledge that the late war terminated quite contrary to your expectation." Your expectation was ill-founded ; for you would not believe your old friend, who told you repeatedly that by those measures England would lose her colonies, as Epictetus warned in vain his master that he would break his leg. You believed rather the tales you heard of our poltroonery and impotence of body and mind. Do you not remember the story you told me of the Scotch sergeant who met with a party of forty American soldiers, and, though alone, disarmed them all, and brought them in prisoners? — a story almost as improbable as that of an Irishman, who pretended to have alone taken and brought in five of the enemy, by *surrounding* them. And yet, my friend, sensible and judicious as you are, but partaking of the general infatuation, you seemed to believe it. The word *general* puts me in mind of a general — your General Clarke, who had the folly to say in my hearing, at Sir John Pringle's, that with a thousand British grenadiers he would undertake to go from one end of America to the other, and geld all the males, partly by force and partly by a little coaxing. It is plain he took us for a species of animals very little superior to brutes. The Parliament too believed the stories of another foolish general, — I forget his name, — that the Yankees never *felt bold*. Yankee was understood to be a sort of Yahoo, and the Parliament did not think the petitions of such creatures were fit to be received and read in so wise an assembly.

What was the consequence of this monstrous pride and insolence? You first sent small armies to subdue us, believing them more than sufficient; but soon found yourselves obliged to send greater. These, whenever they ventured to penetrate our country beyond the protection of their ships, were either repulsed and obliged to scamper out, or were surrounded, beaten, and taken prisoners. An American planter, who had never seen Europe, was chosen by us to command our troops, and continued during the whole war. This man sent home to you, one after another, five of your best generals, baffled, their heads bare of laurels, disgraced even in the opinion of their employers. Your contempt of our understandings, in comparison with your own, appeared to be not much better founded than that of our courage, if we may judge by this circumstance, that in whatever court of Europe a Yankee negotiator appeared the wise British minister was routed, put in a passion, picked a quarrel with your friends, and was sent home with a flea in his ear.

But after all, my dear friend, do not imagine that I am vain enough to ascribe our success to any superiority in any of those points. I am too well acquainted with all the springs and levers of our machine, not to see that our human means were unequal to our undertaking, and that, if it had not been for the justice of our cause, and the consequent interposition of Providence, in which we had faith, we must have been ruined. If I had ever before been an atheist, I should now have been convinced of the being and government of a Deity! It is he that abases the proud and favors the humble. May we never forget his goodness to us, and may our future conduct manifest our gratitude!

But let us leave these serious reflections, and converse with our usual pleasantry. I remember your observing once to me, as we sat together in the House of Commons, that no two journeymen-printers within your knowledge had met with such success in the world as ourselves. You were then at the head of your profession, and soon afterwards became a member of Parliament. I was an agent for a few provinces, and now act for them all. But we have risen by different modes.

I, as a republican printer, always liked a form well *planed down;* being averse to those *overbearing* letters that hold their heads so *high* as to hinder their neighbors from appearing. You, as a monarchist, chose to work upon *crown* paper, and found it profitable; while I worked upon *pro patria* (often indeed called *fools-cap*) with no less advantage. Both our *heaps hold out* very well, and we seem likely to make a pretty good *day's work* of it.

With regard to public affairs (to continue in the same style), it seems to me that your *compositors* in your *chapel* do not *cast off their copy well*, nor perfectly understand *imposing*: their *forms* too are continually pestered by the *outs* and *doubles* that are not easy to be *corrected*. And I think they were wrong in laying aside some *faces*, and particularly certain *head-pieces*, that would have been both useful and ornamental. But, courage! The business may still flourish with good management, and the master become as rich as any of the company.

By the way, the rapid growth and extension of the English language in America must become greatly advantageous to the booksellers and holders of copyrights in England. A vast audience is assembling there for English authors, ancient, present and future, our people doubling every twenty years; and this will demand large, and of course profitable impressions of your most valuable books. I would therefore, if I possessed such rights, entail them, if such a thing be practicable, upon my posterity; for their worth will be continually augmenting. This may look a little like advice, and yet I have drank no *Madeira* these six months. The subject, however, leads me to another thought, which is, that you do wrong to discourage the emigration of Englishmen to America.

In my piece on population I have proved, I think, that emigration does not diminish but multiplies a nation. You will not

have the fewer at home for those that go abroad ; and, as every
man who comes among us and takes up a piece of land becomes
a citizen, and by our constitution has a voice in elections, and a
share in the government of the country, why should you be
against acquiring by this fair means a repossession of it, and leave
it to be taken by foreigners of all nations and languages, who by
their numbers may drown and stifle the English, which otherwise
would probably become, in the course of two centuries, the most
extensive language in the world, the Spanish only excepted ? It
is a fact that the Irish emigrants and their children are now in
possession of the government of Pennsylvania, by their majority
in the Assembly, as well as of a great part of the territory ; and
I remember well the first ship that brought any of them over.
I am ever, my dear friend, yours, most affectionately,

B. FRANKLIN.

[TO GEORGE WHATLEY.]

*Privileges of Old Age — On a Good Epitaph — Reasons for Confidence
in a Future State — The American Constitution —
England — Anecdote.*

PASSY, May 23, 1785.

DEAR OLD FRIEND: I sent you a few lines the other day,
with the medallion, when I should have written more, but was
prevented by the coming in of a *bavard*, who worried me till
evening. I bore with him, and now you are to bear with me,
for I shall probably *bavarder* in answering your letter.

I am not acquainted with the saying of Alphonsus, which you
allude to as a sanctification of your rigidity in refusing to allow
me the plea of old age as an excuse for my want of exactness
in correspondence. What was that saying? You do not, it
seems, feel any occasion for such an excuse, though you are, as
you say, rising seventy-five. But I am rising (perhaps more
properly falling) eighty, and I leave the excuse with you till you
arrive at that age ; perhaps you may then be more sensible of
its validity, and see fit to use it for yourself.

I must agree with you, that the gout is bad, and that the stone
is worse. I am happy in not having them both together, and I
join in your prayer that you may live till you die without
either. But I doubt the author of the epitaph you send me was
a little mistaken, when he, speaking of the world, says that

" he ne'er cared a pin
What they said or may say of the mortal within."

It is so natural to wish to be well spoken of, whether alive or dead, that I imagine he could not be quite exempt from that desire ; and that at least he wished to be thought a wit, or he would not have given himself the trouble of writing so good an epitaph to leave behind him. Was it not as worthy of his care that the world should say he was an honest and a good man ? I like better the concluding sentiment in the old song called *The Old Man's Wish*, wherein, after wishing for a warm house in a country town, an easy horse, some good authors, ingenious and cheerful companions, a pudding on Sundays, with stout ale, and a bottle of Burgundy, &c. &c., in separate stanzas, each ending with this burden,

> " May I govern my passions with absolute sway,
> Grow wiser and better as my strength wears away,
> Without gout or stone, by a gentle decay, — "

he adds,

> " With a courage undaunted may I face my last day ;
> And when I am gone may the better sort say,
> ' In the morning when sober, in the evening when mellow,
> He 's gone, and has not left behind him his fellow.
> For he governed his passions,' &c."

But what signifies our wishing ? Things happen, after all, as they will happen. I have sung that *wishing song* a thousand times when I was young, and now find at four-score that the three contraries have befallen me, being subject to the gout, and the stone, and not being yet master of all my passions. Like the proud girl in my country, who wished and resolved not to marry a parson, nor a Presbyterian, nor an Irishman, and at length found herself married to an Irish Presbyterian parson. You see I have some reason to wish that in a future state I may not only be *as well as I was*, but a little better. And I hope it : for I too, with your poet, *trust in God*. And when I observe that there is great frugality as well as wisdom in His works, since he has been evidently sparing both of labor and materials ; for by the various wonderful inventions of propagation he has provided for the continual peopling his world with plants and animals, without being at the trouble of repeated new creations ; and by the natural reduction of compound substances to their original elements, capable of being employed in new compositions, he has prevented the necessity of creating new matter ; so that the earth, water, air, and perhaps fire. which, being compounded from wood, do, when the wood is dissolved, return, and again become air, earth, fire and water ; — I say, that when I see nothing annihilated, and not even a drop of water wasted, I cannot suspect the annihilation of souls, or believe that He will suffer the daily waste of millions of minds ready made, that now exist, and put himself to the continual trouble of making new ones. Thus finding myself to exist in the world, I believe I shall in some shape or other always exist; and, with all the inconveniences human life is liable to, I shall not object to a new edition of mine, — hoping, however, that the errata of the last may be corrected. * * * * *

The Philadelphia bank goes on, as I hear, very well. What you call the Cincinnati institution is no institution of our government, but a private convention among the officers of our late army, and so universally disliked by the people that it is supposed it will be dropped. It was considered as an attempt to establish something like an hereditary rank or nobility. I hold, with you, that it was wrong; may I add, that all descending honors are wrong and absurd, — that the honor of virtuous actions appertains only to him that performs them, and is in its nature incommunicable. If it were communicable by descent, it must also be divisible among the descendants; and, the more ancient the family, the less would be found existing in any one branch of it, — to say nothing of the greater chance of unlucky interruptions.

Our constitution seems not to be well understood with you. If the Congress were a permanent body, there would be more reason in being jealous of giving it powers. But its members are chosen annually, cannot be chosen more than three years successively, nor more than three years in seven; and any of them may be recalled at any time, whenever their constituents shall be dissatisfied with their conduct. They are of the people, and return again to mix with the people, having no more durable preëminence than the different grains of sand in an hourglass. Such an assembly cannot easily become dangerous to liberty. They are the servants of the people, sent together to do the people's business, and promote the public welfare; their powers must be sufficient, or their duties cannot be performed. They have no profitable appointments, but a mere payment of daily wages, such as are scarcely equivalent to their expenses; so that, having no chance for great places and enormous salaries or pensions, as in some countries, there is no canvassing or bribing for elections.

I wish Old England were as happy in its government, but I do not see it. Your people, however, think their constitution the best in the world, and affect to despise ours. It is comfortable to have a good opinion of one's self, and of everything that belongs to us; to think one's own religion, king and wife, the best of all possible wives, kings, or religions. I remember three Greenlanders, who had travelled two years in Europe, under the care of some Moravian missionaries, and had visited Germany, Denmark, Holland, and England; when I asked them at Philadelphia (where they were in their way home) whether, now they had seen how much more commodiously the white people lived by the help of the arts, they would not choose to remain among us, their answer was, that they were pleased with having had an opportunity of seeing so many fine things, *but they chose to* LIVE *in their own country*. Which country, by the way, consisted of rock only; for the Moravians were obliged to carry earth in their ship from New York for the purpose of making a cabbage-garden! * * * *

We shall always be ready to take your children, if you send them to us. I only wonder that, since London draws to itself and consumes such numbers of your country people, the country should not, to supply their places, want and willingly receive the children you have to dispose of. That circumstance, together with the multitude who voluntarily part with their freedom as men to serve for a time as lackeys, or for life as soldiers, in consideration of small wages, seems to me proof that your island is over-peopled. And yet it is afraid of emigrations!

B. FRANKLIN.

[TO MRS. MARY HEWSON, LONDON.]

Recovery of an Old Letter — Life in Philadelphia — Cards — Consolation for Idleness — Public Amusements — Family Matters.

PHILADELPHIA, May 6, 1786.

MY DEAR FRIEND : A long winter has passed, and I have not had the pleasure of a line from you, acquainting me with your and your children's welfare, since I left England. I suppose you have been in Yorkshire, out of the way and knowledge of opportunities; for I will not think you have forgotten me.

To make me some amends, I received, a few days past, a large packet from Mr. Williams, dated September 1776, near ten years since, containing three letters from you, one of December 12, 1775. This packet had been received by Mr. Bache after my departure for France, lay dormant among his papers during all my absence, and has just now broke out upon me *like words* that had been, as somebody says, *congealed in northern air.* Therein I find all the pleasing little family history of your children. How William had begun to spell, overcoming by strength of memory all the difficulty occasioned by the common wretched alphabet, while you were convinced of the utility of our new one; how Tom, genius-like, struck out new paths, and, relinquishing the old names of the letters, called U *bell* and P *bottle ;* how Eliza began to grow jolly,—that is, fat and hand-some, resembling Aunt Rooke, whom I used to call *my lovely ;* together with all the *then* news of Lady Blunt's having produced at length a boy ; of Dolly's being well, and of poor good Cath-erine's decease; of your affairs with Muir and Atkinson, and of their contract for feeding the fish in the channel ; of the Vinys, and their jaunt to Cambridge in the long carriages ; of Dolly's journey to Wales with Mr. Scot ; of the Wilkes's, the Pearces, Elphinston, &c. &c. ; concluding with a kind of promise that as soon as the Ministry and Congress agreed to make peace I should have you with me in America. That peace has been some time made, but, alas! the promise is not yet fulfilled. And why is it not fulfilled ? *

I have found my family here in health, good circumstances, and well respected by their fellow-citizens. The companions of my youth are, indeed, almost all departed, but I find an agreeable society among their children and grandchildren. I have public business enough to preserve me from *ennui*, and private amuse-ment besides, in conversation, books, my garden, *and cribbage.* Considering our well-furnished, plentiful market as the best of gardens, I am turning mine, in the midst of which my house stands, into grass-plats, and gravel-walks, with trees and flower-ing shrubs. Cards we sometimes play here in long winter even-ings, but it is as they play at chess,—not for money, but for honor, or the pleasure of beating one another. This will not be quite a novelty to you, as you may remember we played together in that manner during the winter you helped me to pass so agreea-bly at Passy. I have, indeed, now and then a little compunction in reflecting that I spend time so idly ; but another reflection comes to relieve me [*whispering*], "You know the soul is im-mortal ; why, then, should you be such a niggard of a little time, when you have a whole eternity before you?" So, being easily convinced, and, like other reasonable creatures, satisfied with a

---

* Mrs. Hewson (once Miss Mary Stevenson, and daughter of Franklin's London landlady) removed, in 1786, with her family, to Philadelphia where one of her sons became a successful physician.

small reason when it is in favor of doing what I have a mind to do, I shuffle the cards again, and begin another game.

As to public amusements, we have neither plays nor operas, but we had yesterday a kind of oratorio. as you will see by the enclosed paper; and we have assemblies, balls and concerts, besides little parties at one another's houses, in which there is sometimes dancing, and frequently good music; so that we jog on in life as pleasantly as you do in England, anywhere but in London; for there you have plays performed by good actors. That, however, is, I think, the only advantage London has over Philadelphia.

Temple has turned his thoughts to agriculture, which he pursues ardently, being in possession of a fine farm that his father lately conveyed to him. Ben is finishing his studies at college, and continues to behave as well as when you knew him, so that I still think he will make you a good son. His younger brothers and sisters are also all promising, appearing to have good tempers and dispositions, as well as good constitutions. As to myself, I think my general health and spirits rather better than when you saw me, and the particular malady I then complained of continues tolerable. With sincere and very great esteem, I am ever, my dear friend, yours, most affectionately,

B. FRANKLIN.

P. S. My children and grandchildren join with me in best wishes for you and yours. My love to my godson, to Eliza, and to honest Tom. They will all find agreeable companions here. Love to Dolly, and tell her she will do well to come with you.

[TO MRS. JANE MECOM.]

Phonography Anticipated.

PHILADELPHIA, 4 July, 1786.

—— You need not be concerned, in writing to me, about your bad spelling; for, in my opinion, as our alphabet now stands, the bad spelling, or what is called so, is generally the best, as conforming to the sound of the letters and of the words. To give you an instance. A gentleman received a letter, in which were these words: " *Not finding Brown at hom, I delivered your meseg to his yf.*" The gentleman, finding it bad spelling, and therefore not very intelligible, called his lady to help

him read it. Between them they picked out the meaning of all
but the *yf*, which they could not understand. The lady proposed calling her chambermaid, "Because Betty," says she,
"has the best knack at reading bad spelling of any one I
know." Betty came, and was surprised that neither Sir nor
Madam could tell what *yf* was. "Why," says she, "*y f* spells
wife; what else can it spell?"   And, indeed, it is a much better as well as shorter method of spelling *wife* than *doubleyou,
i, ef, e,* which in reality spell *doubleyifey.*

There is much rejoicing in town to-day, it being the anniver-
sary of the Declaration of Independence, which we signed this
day ten years, and thereby hazarded lives and fortunes. God
was pleased to put a favorable end to the contest much sooner
than we had reason to expect. His name be praised. Adieu.

B. FRANKLIN.

[TO MISS ***.]

The Art of procuring Pleasant Dreams.

As a great part of our life is spent in sleep, during which we
have sometimes pleasant and sometimes painful dreams, it becomes of some consequence to obtain the one kind and avoid the
other ; for, whether real or imaginary, pain is pain, and pleasure
is pleasure. If we can sleep without dreaming, it is well that
painful dreams are avoided. If, while we sleep, we can have
any pleasing dream, it is, as the French say, *autant de gagné,*
so much added to the pleasure of life.

To this end, it is, in the first place, necessary to be careful in
preserving health, by due exercise and great temperance ; for, in
sickness, the imagination is disturbed, and disagreeable, sometimes terrible ideas are apt to present themselves. Exercise
should precede meals, not immediately follow them; the first
promotes, the latter, unless moderate, obstructs digestion. If,
after exercise, we feed sparingly, the digestion will be easy and
good, the body lightsome, the temper cheerful, and all the animal
functions performed agreeably. Sleep, when it follows, will be
natural and undisturbed ; while indolence, with full feeding,
occasions nightmares and horrors inexpressible; we fall from
precipices, are assaulted by wild beasts, murderers and demons,
and experience every variety of distress. Observe, however,
that the quantities of food and exercise are relative things ;
those who move much may, and indeed ought to eat more ; those

who use little exercise should eat little. In general, mankind, since the improvement of cookery, eat about twice as much as nature requires. Suppers are not bad, if we have not dined; but restless nights naturally follow hearty suppers, after full dinners. Indeed, as there is a difference in constitutions, some rest well after these meals; it costs them only a frightful dream and an apoplexy, after which they sleep till doomsday. Nothing is more common in the newspapers than instances of people who, after eating a hearty supper, are found dead abed in the morning.

Another means of preserving health, to be attended to, is the having a constant supply of fresh air in your bed-chamber. It has been a great mistake, the sleeping in rooms exactly closed, and in beds surrounded by curtains. No outward air that may come in to you is so unwholesome as the unchanged air, often breathed, of a close chamber. As boiling water does not grow hotter by longer boiling, if the particles that receive greater heat can escape, so living bodies do not putrefy, if the particles, so fast as they become putrid, can be thrown off. Nature expels them by the pores of the skin and the lungs, and in a free, open air they are carried off; but in a close room we receive them again and again, though they become more and more corrupt. A number of persons crowded into a small room thus spoil the air in a few minutes, and even render it mortal, as in the Black Hole at Calcutta. A single person is said to spoil only a gallon of air per minute, and therefore requires a longer time to spoil a chamber-full; but it is done, however, in proportion, and many putrid disorders hence have their origin. It is recorded of Methusalem, who, being the longest liver, may be supposed to have best preserved his health, that he slept always in the open air; for, when he had lived five hundred years, an angel said to him, "Arise, Methusalem, and build thee an house, for thou shalt live yet five hundred years longer." But Methusalem answered, and said, "If I am to live but five hundred years longer, it is not worth while to build me an house; I will sleep in the air, as I have been used to do." Physicians, after having for ages contended that the sick should not be indulged with fresh air, have at length discovered that it may do them good. It is therefore to be hoped, that they may in time discover, likewise, that it is not hurtful to those who are in health, and that we may be then cured of the *aërophobia*, that at present distresses weak minds, and makes them choose to be stifled and poisoned, rather than leave open the window of a bed-chamber, or put down the glass of a coach.

41*

Confined air, when saturated with perspirable matter, will not receive more; and that matter must remain in our bodies, and occasion diseases; but it gives some previous notice of its being about to be hurtful, by producing certain uneasinesses, slight indeed at first, such as with regard to the lungs is a trifling sensation, and to the pores of the skin a kind of restlessness, which is difficult to describe, and few that feel it know the cause of it. But we may recollect that, sometimes, on waking in the night, we have, if warmly covered, found it difficult to get asleep again. We turn often, without finding repose in any position. This fidgetiness (to use a vulgar expression, for want of a better) is occasioned wholly by an uneasiness in the skin, owing to the retention of the perspirable matter, the bed-clothes having received their quantity, and, being saturated, refusing to take any more. To become sensible of this by an experiment, let a person keep his position in the bed, but throw off the bed-clothes, and suffer fresh air to approach the part uncovered of his body; he will then feel that part suddenly refreshed; for the air will immediately relieve the skin, by receiving, licking up, and carrying off, the load of perspirable matter that incommoded it. For every portion of cool air that approaches the warm skin, in receiving its part of that vapor, receives therewith a degree of heat that rarefies and renders it lighter, when it will be pushed away with its burthen, by cooler and therefore heavier fresh air, which for a moment supplies its place, and then, being likewise changed and warmed, gives way to a succeeding quantity. This is the order of nature, to prevent animals being infected by their own perspiration. He will now be sensible of the difference between the part exposed to the air, and that which, remaining sunk in the bed, denies the air access; for this part now manifests its uneasiness more distinctly by the comparison, and the seat of the uneasiness is more plainly perceived than when the whole surface of the body was affected by it.

Here, then, is one great and general cause of unpleasing dreams. For, when the body is uneasy, the mind will be disturbed by it, and disagreeable ideas of various kinds will in sleep be the natural consequences. The remedies, preventive and curative, follow.

1. By eating moderately (as before advised, for health's sake), less perspirable matter is produced in a given time; hence the bed-clothes receive it longer before they are saturated, and we may therefore sleep longer before we are made uneasy by their refusing to receive any more.

2. By using thinner and more porous bed-clothes, which will

suffer the perspirable matter more easily to pass through them, we are less incommoded, such being longer tolerable.

3. When you are awakened by this uneasiness, and find you cannot easily sleep again, get out of bed, beat up and turn your pillow, shake the bed-clothes well, with at least twenty shakes, then throw the bed open and leave it to cool; in the mean while, continuing undressed, walk about your chamber till your skin has had time to discharge its load, which it will do sooner as the air may be drier and colder. When you begin to feel the cold air unpleasant, then return to your bed, and you will soon fall asleep, and your sleep will be sweet and pleasant. All the scenes presented to your fancy will be too of the pleasing kind. I am often as agreeably entertained with them as by the scenery of an opera. If you happen to be too indolent to get out of bed, you may, instead of it, lift up your bed-clothes with one arm and leg, so as to draw in a good deal of fresh air, and by letting them fall force it out again. This, repeated twenty times, will so clear them of the perspirable matter they have imbibed as to permit your sleeping well for some time afterwards. But this latter method is not equal to the former.

Those who do not love trouble, and can afford to have two beds, will find great luxury in rising, when they wake in a hot bed, and going into the cool one. Such shifting of beds would also be of great service to persons ill of a fever, as it refreshes and frequently procures sleep. A very large bed, that will admit a removal so distant from the first situation as to be cool and sweet, may in a degree answer the same end.

One or two observations more will conclude this little piece. Care must be taken, when you lie down, to dispose your pillow so as to suit your manner of placing your head, and to be perfectly easy; then place your limbs so as not to bear inconveniently hard upon one another, as, for instance, the joints of your ankles; for, though a bad position may at first give but little pain and be hardly noticed, yet a continuance will render it less tolerable, and the uneasiness may come on while you are asleep, and disturb your imagination. These are the rules of the art. But, though they will generally prove effectual in producing the end intended, there is a case in which the most punctual observance of them will be totally fruitless. I need not mention the case to you, my dear friend, but my account of the art would be imperfect without it. The case is, when the person who desires to have pleasant dreams has not taken care to preserve, what is necessary above all things,

A GOOD CONSCIENCE.

On his Arguments against a Particular Providence, &c.

[Without date.]

DEAR SIR : I have read your manuscript with some attention. By the argument it contains against a particular Providence, though you allow a general Providence, you strike at the foundations of all religion. For, without the belief of a Providence, that takes cognizance of, guards and guides, and may favor particular persons, there is no motive to worship a Deity, to fear his displeasure, or to pray for his protection.

I will not enter into any discussion of your principles, though you seem to desire it. At present I shall only give you my opinion, that, though your reasonings are subtle, and may prevail with some readers, you will not succeed so as to change the general sentiments of mankind on that subject, and the consequence of printing this piece will be, a great deal of odium drawn upon yourself, mischief to you, and no benefit to others. He that spits against the wind spits in his own face.

But, were you to succeed, do you imagine any good would be done by it ? You yourself may find it easy to live a virtuous life without the assistance afforded by religion ; you having a clear perception of the advantages of virtue, and the disadvantages of vice, and possessing a strength of resolution sufficient to enable you to resist common temptations. But think how great a portion of mankind consists of weak and ignorant men and women, and of inexperienced, inconsiderate youth of both sexes, who have need of the motives of religion to restrain them from vice, to support their virtue, and retain them in the practice of it till it becomes *habitual*, which is the great point for its security. And, perhaps, you are indebted to her originally — that is, to your religious education — for the habits of virtue upon which you now justly value yourself. You might easily display your excellent talents of reasoning upon a less hazardous subject, and thereby obtain a rank with our most distinguished authors. For among us it is not necessary, as among the Hottentots, *that a youth, to be raised into the company of men, should prove his manhood by beating his mother.*

I would advise you therefore not to attempt unchaining the tiger, but to burn this piece before it is seen by any other person, whereby you will save yourself a great deal of mortifica-

---

* There is little doubt that this letter was addressed to Paine, although it was originally published without the name of the person to whom it was directed.

tion from the enemies it may raise against you, and perhaps a good deal of regret and repentance. If men are so wicked *with religion*, what would they be if *without it?* I intend this letter itself as a *proof* of my friendship, and therefore add no *professions* to it; but subscribe simply yours, B. FRANKLIN.

[TO THE EDITORS OF THE PENNSYLVANIA GAZETTE.]

On Party Abuse — Newspaper Scurrility.

MESSRS. HALL AND SELLERS: I lately heard remark that, on examination of the *Pennsylvania Gazette* for fifty years from its commencement, it appeared that during that long period scarce one libellous piece had ever appeared in it. This generally chaste conduct of your paper is much to its reputation; for it has long been the opinion of sober, judicious people, that nothing is more likely to endanger the liberty of the press than the abuse of that liberty by employing it in personal accusation, detraction and calumny. The excesses some of our papers have been guilty of in this particular have set this State in a bad light abroad, as appears by the following letter, which I wish you to publish, not merely to show your own disapprobation of the practice, but as a caution to others of the profession throughout the United States. For I have seen an European newspaper, in which the editor, who had been charged with frequently calumniating the Americans, justifies himself by saying "that he had published nothing disgraceful to us, which he had not taken from our own printed papers." I am, &c., A. B.

"NEW YORK, March 30, 1788.

'DEAR FRIEND: My gout has at length left me, after five months' painful confinement. It afforded me, however, the leisure to read, or hear read, all the packets of your newspapers which you so kindly sent for my amusement.

"Mrs. W. has partaken of it; she likes to read the advertisements; but she remarks some kind of *inconsistency* in the announcing so many diversions for almost every evening in the week, and such quantities to be sold of expensive superfluities, fineries, and luxuries *just imported*, in a country that at the same time fills its papers with complaints of *hard times* and want of money.

"I tell her that such complaints are common to all times and all countries, and were made even in Solomon's time, when, as we are told, silver was as plenty in Jerusalem as the stones in the street, and yet even then there were people that grumbled, so as to incur this censure from that knowing prince : *Say not thou that the former times were better than these; for thou dost not inquire rightly concerning that matter.*

"But the *inconsistence* that strikes me the most is that between the name of your city, *Philadelphia, brotherly love,* and the spirit of rancor, malice and *hatred,* that breathes in its newspapers. For I learn from those papers that your state is divided into parties: that each ascribes all the public operations of the other to vicious motives; that they do not even suspect one another of the smallest degree of honesty; that the anti-federalists are such merely from the fear of losing power, places or emoluments, which they have in possession or in expectation ; that the federalists are a set of *conspirators,* who aim at establishing a tyranny over the persons and property of their countrymen, and to live in splendor on the plunder of the people. I learn, too, that your justices of the peace, though chosen by their neighbors, make a villanous trade of their office, and promote discord to augment fees, and fleece their electors ; and that this would not be mended by placing the choice in the executive council, who, with interested or party views, are continually making as improper appointments. Witness a '*petty fiddler, sycophant and scoundrel,*' appointed judge of the Admiralty; '*an old woman and fomenter of sedition*' to be another of the judges, and '*a Jeffries*' chief-justice, &c. &c. ; with '*two harpies,*' the comptroller and naval officers, to prey upon the merchants and deprive them of their property by force of arms, &c.

"I am informed also, by these papers, that your General Assembly, though the annual choice of the people, shows no regard to their rights, but, from sinister views or ignorance, makes laws in direct violation of the constitution, to divest the inhabitants of their property, and give it to strangers and intruders ; and, that the Council, either fearing the resentment of their constituents, or plotting to enslave them, had projected to disarm them, and given orders for that purpose ; and, finally, that your president, the unanimous joint choice of the Council and Assembly, is '*an old rogue,*' who gave his assent to the federal constitution merely to avoid refunding money he had purloined from the United States.

"There is, indeed, a good deal of manifest *inconsistency* in all this ; and yet, a stranger seeing it in your own prints, though he does not believe it all, may probably believe enough of it to conclude that Pennsylvania is peopled by a set of the most unprincipled, wicked, rascally and quarrelsome scoundrels upon the face of the globe. I have sometimes, indeed, suspected that these papers are the manufacture of foreign enemies among you, who write with a view of disgracing your country, and making you appear contemptible and detestable all the world over; but then I wonder at the indiscretion of your printers in publishing such writings! There is, however, one of your *inconsistencies* that consoles me a little, which is, that, though *living* you give one another the characters of devils, *dead* you are all angels! It is delightful, when any of you die, to read what good husbands, good fathers, good friends, good citizens, and good Christians you were, concluding with a scrap of poetry that places you, with certainty, every one in heaven. So that I think Pennsylvania a good country *to die in*, though a very bad one to live in."

[TO CHARLES THOMPSON.]

PHILADELPHIA, December 29, 1788.

DEAR OLD FRIEND: Enclosed I send a letter to the President of Congress for the time being, which, if you find nothing improper in it, or that in regard to me you could wish changed or amended, I would request you to present. I rely much on your friendly counsel, as you must be better acquainted with persons and circumstances than I am; and I suppose there will be time enough before the new Congress is formed to make any alterations you may advise, though, if presented at all, it should be to the old one.

In the copy of my letter to Mr. Barclay, you may observe, that mention is made of some " considerable articles which I have not charged in my accounts with Congress, but on which I should expect from their equity some consideration." That you may have some information what those articles are, I enclose also a " *Sketch of my Services to the United States,* " wherein you will find mention of the *extra services* I performed that do not appertain to the office of plenipotentiary, namely, as judge of admiralty, as consul before the arrival of Mr. Barclay, as banker in examining and accepting the multitude of bills of exchange, and as secretary for several years, — none being sent to me, though other ministers were allowed such assistance.

I must own I did hope that, as it is customary in Europe to make some liberal provision for ministers when they return home from foreign service, the Congress would at least have been kind enough to have shown their approbation of my conduct by a grant of a small tract of land in their western country, which might have been of use and some honor to my posterity. And I cannot but still think they will do something of the kind for me whenever they shall be pleased to take my services into consideration, as I see by their minutes that they have allowed Mr. Lee handsomely for his services in England, before his appointment to France, in which services I and Mr. Bollan coöperated with him, but have had no such allowance; and, since his return, he has been very properly rewarded with a good place, as well as my friend Mr. Jay: though these are trifling compensations in comparison with what was granted by the king to M. Gérard on his return from America, — but how different is what has happened to me! On my return from England in 1775, the Congress bestowed on me the office of Postmaster-general, for which I was very thankful. It was indeed an office I had some kind of right to, as having previously greatly enlarged the revenue of the post, by the regulations I had contrived and established, while I possessed it under the crown. When I was sent to France, I left it in the hands of my son-in-law, who was to act as my deputy. But, soon after my departure, it was taken from me, and given to Mr. Hazard. When the English ministry formerly thought fit to deprive me of the office, they left me, however, the privilege of receiving and sending my letters free of postage, which is the usage when a postmaster is not displaced for misconduct in the office; but in America I have ever since had the postage demanded of me, which since my return from France has amounted to above fifty pounds, much of it occasioned by my having acted as minister there.

When I took my grandson, William Temple Franklin, with me to France, I purposed, after giving him the French language, to educate him in the study and practice of the law. But, by the repeated expectations given me of a secretary, and constant disappointments, I was induced, and indeed obliged, to retain him with me, to assist in the secretary's office; which disappointments continued till my return, by which time so many years of the opportunity of his studying the law were lost, and his habits of life became so different, that it appeared no longer advisable; and I then considering him as brought up in the diplomatic line, and well qualified by his knowledge in that branch for the employ of a secretary at least (in which opinion I was not alone, for three of my colleagues, without the smallest solicitation from me, chose him secretary of the negotiation for treaties, which they had been empowered to do), I took the liberty of recommending him to the Congress for their protection. This was the only favor I ever asked of them; and the only answer I received was a resolution superseding him, and appointing Col. Humphreys in his place, a gentleman who, though he might have indeed a good deal of military merit, certainly had none in the diplomatic line, and had neither the French language, nor the experience, nor the address, proper to qualify him for such an employment.

This is all to yourself only as a private friend; for I have not, nor ever shall, make any public complaint; and, even if I could have foreseen such unkind treatment from Congress, their refusing me thanks would not in the least have abated my zeal for the cause, and ardor in support of it. I know something of the nature of such changeable assemblies, and how little successors know of the services that have been rendered to the corps before their admission, or feel themselves obliged by such services; and what effect in obliterating a sense of them, during the absence of the servant in a distant country, the artful and reiterated malevolent insinuations of one or two envious and malicious persons may have on the minds of members, even of the most equitable, candid and honorable dispositions; and, therefore, I will pass these reflections into oblivion.

My good friend, excuse, if you can, the trouble of this letter; and, if the reproach thrown on republics, that *they are apt to be ungrateful*, should ever unfortunately be verified with respect to *your* services, remember that you have a right to unbosom yourself in communicating your griefs to your ancient friend, and most obedient humble servant, B. FRANKLIN.

CHARLES THOMPSON, *Esq., Sec'y to Congress.*

Sketch of the Services of B. Franklin to the United States of America.

In England he combated the Stamp Act, and his writings in the papers against it, with his examination in Parliament, were thought to have contributed much to its repeal.

He opposed the Duty Act, and, though he could not prevent its passing, he obtained of Mr. Townshend an omission of several articles, particularly salt.

42

In the subsequent difference he wrote and published many papers refuting the claim of Parliament to tax the colonies.

He opposed all the oppressive acts.

He had two secret negotiations with the ministers for their repeal, of which he has written a narrative. In this he offered payment for the destroyed tea, at his own risk, in case they were repealed.

He was joined with Messrs. Bollan and Lee in all the applications to government for that purpose. Printed several pamphlets, at his own considerable expense, against the then measures of government, whereby he rendered himself obnoxious, was disgraced before the Privy Council, deprived of a place in the post-office of three hundred pounds sterling a year, and obliged to resign his agencies, namely:

Of Pennsylvania, ...	500*l.*
Of Massachusetts, ...	400
Of New Jersey, ...	100
Of Georgia, ...	200
	1200

In the whole, fifteen hundred pounds sterling per annum.

Orders were sent to the king's governors not to sign any warrants on the treasury for the orders of his salaries; and, though he was not actually dismissed by the colonies that employed him, yet, thinking the known malice of the court against him rendered him less likely than others to manage their affairs to their advantage, he judged it to be his duty to withdraw from their service, and leave it open for less exceptionable persons, which saved them the necessity of removing him.

Returning to America, he encouraged the Revolution; was appointed chairman of the committee of safety, where he projected the *chevaux de frize* for securing Philadelphia, then the residence of Congress.

Was sent by Congress to head-quarters near Boston, with Messrs. Harrison and Lynch, in 1775, to settle some affairs with the northern governments and General Washington.

In the spring of 1776, was sent to Canada with Messrs. Chase and Carrol, passing the lakes while they were not yet free from ice. In Canada was, with his colleagues, instrumental in redressing sundry grievances, and thereby reconciling the people more to our cause. He there advanced to General Arnold and other servants of Congress, then in extreme necessity, three hundred and fifty-three pounds in gold out of his own pocket, on the credit of Congress, which was a great service at that juncture, in procuring provisions for our army.

Being, at the time he was ordered on this service, upwards of seventy years of age, he suffered in his health by the hardships of this journey, lodging in the woods, &c., in so inclement a season; but, being recovered, the Congress in the same year ordered him to France. Before his departure, he put all the money he could raise — between three and four thousand pounds — into their hands; which, demonstrating his confidence, encouraged others to lend their money in support of the cause.

He made no bargain for appointments, but was promised, by a vote, the *net* salary of five hundred pounds sterling per annum, his expenses paid, and to be assisted by a secretary, who was to have one thousand pounds per annum, to include all contingencies.

When the Pennsylvania Assembly sent him to England, in 1764, on the same salary, they allowed him one year's advance for his passage, and in consideration of the prejudice to his private affairs that must be occasioned by his sudden departure and absence. He has had no such allowance from Congress, was badly accommodated in a miserable vessel, improper for those northern seas (and which actually foundered in her return), was badly fed, so that on his arrival he had scarce strength to stand.

His services to the States as commissioner, and afterwards as minister plenipotentiary, are known to Congress, as may appear in his correspondence. His *extra services* may not be so well known, and therefore may be here mentioned. No secretary ever arriving, the business was in part before, and entirely when the other commissioners left him, executed by himself, with the help of his grandson, who at first was only allowed clothes, board and lodging, and afterwards a salary never exceeding three hundred pounds a year (except while he served as secretary to the commissioners for peace), by which difference in salary, continued many years, the Congress saved, *if they accept it, seven hundred pounds sterling a year.*

He served as *consul* entirely several years, till the arrival of Mr. Barclay, and even after, as that gentleman was obliged to be much and long absent in Holland, Flanders and England; during which absence what business of the kind occurred still came to Mr. Franklin.

He served, though without any special commission for the purpose, as a *judge of admiralty;* for, the Congress having sent him a quantity of blank commissions for privateers, he granted them to cruisers fitted out in the ports of France, some of them manned by old smugglers, who knew every creek on the coast of England, and, running all round the island, distressed the British coasting trade exceedingly, and raised their general insurance. One of those privateers alone, the *Black Prince*, took in the course of a year seventy-five sail! All the papers taken in each prize brought in were in virtue of an order of council sent up to Mr. Franklin, who was to examine them, judge of the legality of the capture, and write to the admiralty of the port that he found the prize good, and that the sale might be permitted. These papers, which are very voluminous, he has to produce.

He served also as *merchant*, to make purchases, and direct the shipping of stores to a very great value, for which he has charged no commission.

But the part of his service which was the most fatiguing and confining was that of receiving and accepting, after a due and necessary examination, the bills of exchange drawn by Congress for interest-money, to the amount of *two million and a half of livres annually!* multitudes of the bills very small, each of which, the smallest, gave as much trouble in examining, as the largest. And this careful examination was found absolutely necessary, from the constant frauds attempted by presenting *seconds* and *thirds* for payment after the *firsts* had been discharged. As these bills were arriving more or less by every ship and every post, they required constant attendance. Mr. Franklin could make no journey for exercise, as had been annually his custom, and the confinement brought on a malady that is likely to afflict him while he lives.

In short, though he has always been an active man, he never went through so much business during eight years, in any part of his life, as during those of his residence in France; which, however, he did not decline till he saw peace happily made, and found himself in the eightieth year of his age; when, if ever, a man has some right to expect repose.

[TO DAVID HARTLEY.]

State of his Health — Convulsions in France.

PHILADELPHIA, Dec. 4, 1789.

MY VERY DEAR FRIEND: I received your favor of August last. Your kind condolences, on the painful state of my health, are very obliging. I am thankful to God, however, that, among the numerous ills human life is subject to, one only of any importance is fallen to my lot, and that so late as almost to insure that it can be but of short duration.

The convulsions in France are attended with some disagreeable circumstances ; but, if by the struggle she obtains and secures for the nation its future liberty, and a good constitution, a few years' enjoyment of those blessings will amply repair all the damages their acquisition may have occasioned. God grant that not only the love of liberty, but a thorough knowledge of the rights of man, may pervade all the nations of the earth, so that a philosopher may set his foot anywhere on its surface and say, This is my country !

Your wishes for a cordial and perpetual friendship between Britain and her ancient colonies are manifested continually in every one of your letters to me ; something of my disposition on the same subject may appear to you in casting your eye over the enclosed paper. I do not by this opportunity send you any of our Gazettes ; because the postage from Liverpool would be more than they are worth. I can only add my best wishes of every kind of felicity for the three Hartleys, to whom I have the honor of being an affectionate friend and most obedient humble servant,   B. FRANKLIN.

[TO WILLIAM FRANKLIN.]

On Political Differences with his Son.

PASSY, 16 August, 1784.

DEAR SON : I received your letter of the 22d ultimo, and am glad to find that you desire to revive the affectionate intercourse that formerly existed between us. It will be very agreeable to me ; indeed, nothing has ever hurt me so much, and affected me with such keen sensations, as to find myself deserted in my old age by my only son ; and not only deserted, but to find him taking up arms against me in a cause wherein my good fame, fortune and life, were all at stake. You conceived, you say, that your duty to your king and regard for your country required this. I ought not to blame you for differing in sentiment with me in public affairs. We are men, all subject to errors. Our opinions are not in our own power ; they are formed and governed much by circumstances, that are often as inexplicable as they are irresistible. Your situation was such that few would have

42*

censured your remaining neuter, though there are natural duties which precede political ones, and cannot be extinguished by them.

This is a disagreeable subject. I drop it; and we will endeavor, as you propose, mutually to forget what has happened relating to it, as well as we can.   *   *   *

                                        B. FRANKLIN.

[TO NOAH WEBSTER.]

Innovations in the English Language — The Latin and the French — Fashions in Printing — Use of Capital Letters, Italics, &c.

                          PHILADELPHIA, Dec. 26, 1789.

DEAR SIR: I received some time since your "*Dissertations on the English Language.*" The book was not accompanied by any letter or message informing me to whom I am obliged for it, but I suppose it is to yourself. It is an excellent work, and will be greatly useful in turning the thoughts of our countrymen to correct writing. Please to accept my thanks for the great honor you have done me in its dedication. I ought to have made this acknowledgment sooner, but much indisposition prevented me.

I cannot but applaud your zeal for preserving the purity of our language, both in its expressions and pronunciation, and in correcting the popular errors several of our States are continually falling into with respect to both. Give me leave to mention some of them, though possibly they may have already occurred to you. I wish, however, in some future publication of yours, you would set a discountenancing mark upon them. The first I remember is the word *improved*. When I left New England, in the year 1723, this word had never been used among us, as far as I know, but in the sense of *ameliorated*, or made better, except once in a very old book of Dr. Mather's, entitled *Remarkable Providences*. As that eminent man wrote a very obscure hand, I remember that when I read that word in his book, used instead of the word *imployed*, I conjectured it was an error of the printer, who had mistaken a too short *l* in the writing for an *r*, and a *y* with too short a tail for a *v*; whereby *imployed* was converted into *improved*.

But when I returned to Boston, in 1733, I found this change had obtained favor, and was then become common; for I met with it often in perusing the newspapers, where it frequently made an appearance very ridiculous. Such, for instance, as the advertisement of a country house to be sold, which had been many years *improved* as a tavern; and, in the character of a deceased country gentleman, that he had been for more than thirty years *improved* as a justice of peace. This use of the word *improved* is peculiar to New England, and not to be met with among any other speakers of English, either on this or the other side of the water.

During my late absence in France, I find that several other new words have been introduced into our parliamentary language; for example, I find a verb formed from the substantive *notice*: *I should not have* NOTICED *this, were it not that the gentleman*, &c. Also another verb from the substantive *advocate*: *The gentleman who* ADVOCATES, *or has* ADVOCATED, *that motion*, &c. Another from the substantive *progress*, the most awkward and abominable of the three: *The committee having* PROGRESSED, *resolved to adjourn.* The word *opposed*, though not a new word, I find used in a new manner, as, *The gentlemen who are* OPPOSED *to this measure*, — to which I have also myself always been OPPOSED. If you should happen to be of my opinion with respect to these innovations, you will use your authority in reprobating them.

The Latin language, long the vehicle used in distributing knowledge among the different nations of Europe, is daily more and more neglected; and one of the modern tongues, namely, the French, seems in point of universality to have supplied its place. It is spoken in all the courts of Europe; and most of the literati, those even who do not speak it, have acquired knowledge enough of it to enable them easily to read the books that are written in it. This gives a considerable advantage to that nation; it enables its authors to inculcate and spread throughout other nations such sentiments and opinions on important points as are most conducive to its interests, or which may contribute to its reputation, by promoting the common interests of mankind. It is perhaps owing to its being written in French that Voltaire's Treatise on Toleration has had so sudden and so great an effect on the bigotry of Europe as almost entirely to disarm it. The general use of the French language has likewise a very advantageous effect on the profits of the bookselling branch of commerce, it being well known that the more copies can be sold that are struck off from one composition of types, the profits increase in a much greater proportion than they do in making a great number of pieces in any other kind of manufacture. And at present there is no capital town in

Europe without a French bookseller's shop corresponding with Paris.

Our English bids fair to obtain the second place. The great body of excellent printed sermons in our language, and the freedom of our writings on political subjects, have induced a number of divines of different sects and nations, as well as gentlemen concerned in public affairs, to study it; so far, at least, as to read it.   And, if we were to endeavor the facilitating its progress, the study of our tongue might become much more general. Those who have employed some parts of their time in learning a new language have frequently observed that, while their acquaintance with it was imperfect, difficulties small in themselves operated as great ones in obstructing their progress. A book, for example, ill printed, or a pronunciation in speaking not well articulated, would render a sentence unintelligible which, from a clear print or a distinct speaker, would have been immediately comprehended. If, therefore, we would have the benefit of seeing our language more known among mankind, we should endeavor to remove all the difficulties, however small, that discourage the learning it.

But I am sorry to observe that of late years those difficulties, instead of being diminished, have been augmented. In examining the English books that were printed between the Restoration and the accession of George the Second, we may observe that all *substantives* were begun with a capital, in which we imitated our mother tongue, the German. This was more particularly useful to those who were not well acquainted with the English; there being such a prodigious number of our words that are both *verbs* and *substantives*, and spelled in the same manner, though often accented differently in the pronunciation.

This method has, by the fancy of printers, of late years been laid aside, from an idea that suppressing the capitals shows the character to greater advantage; those letters prominent above the line disturbing its even, regular appearance. The effect of this change is so considerable, that a learned man of France, who used to read our books, though not perfectly acquainted with our language, in conversation with me on the subject of our authors, attributed the greater obscurity he found in our modern books, compared with those of the period above mentioned, to change of style for the worse in our writers; of which mistake I convinced him, by marking for him each *substantive* with a capital in a paragraph, which he then easily understood, though before he could not comprehend it. This shows the inconvenience of that pretended improvement.

From the same fondness for an even and uniform appearance of characters in the line, the printers have of late banished also the Italic types, in which words of importance to be attended to in the sense of the sentence, and words on which an emphasis should be put in reading, used to be printed. And lately another fancy has induced some printers to use the short round *s* instead of the long one, which formerly served well to distinguish a word readily by its varied appearance. Certainly the omitting this prominent letter makes the line appear more even, but renders it less immediately legible; as the paring all men's noses might smooth and level their faces, but would render their physiognomies less distinguishable.

Add to all these improvements *backwards* another modern fancy, that gray printing is more beautiful than black; hence the English new books are printed in so dim a character as to be read with difficulty by old eyes, unless in a very strong light and with good glasses. Whoever compares a volume of the *Gentleman's Magazine*, printed between the years 1731 and 1740, with one of those printed in the last ten years, will be convinced of the much greater degree of perspicuity given by black ink than by gray. Lord Chesterfield pleasantly remarked this difference to Faulkner, the printer of the *Dublin Journal*, who was vainly making encomiums on his own paper, as the most complete of any in the world. "But, Mr. Faulkner," said my lord, "don't you think it might be still further improved by using paper and ink not quite so near of a color?" For all these reasons, I cannot but wish that our American printers would, in their editions, avoid these fancied improvements, and thereby render their works more agreeable to foreigners in Europe, to the great advantage of our bookselling commerce.

Further, to be more sensible of the advantage of clear and distinct printing, let us consider the assistance it affords in reading well aloud to an auditory. In so doing, the eye generally slides forward three or four words before the voice. If the sight clearly distinguishes what the coming words are, it gives time to order the modulation of the voice to express them properly. But, if they are obscurely printed, or disguised by omitting the capitals and long *s*'s or otherwise, the reader is apt to modulate wrong; and, finding he has done so, he is obliged to go back and begin the sentence again, which lessens the pleasure of the hearers.

This leads me to mention an old error in our mode of printing. We are sensible that when a question is met with in reading there is a proper variation to be used in the management of the voice. We have therefore a point called an interrogation affixed to the question, in order to distinguish it. But this is absurdly placed at its end; so that the reader does not discover it till he finds he has wrongly modulated his voice, and is therefore obliged to begin again the sentence. To prevent this, the Spanish printers, more sensibly, place an interrogation at the beginning as well as at the end of a question. We have another error of the same kind in printing plays, where something often occurs that is marked as spoken *aside*. But the word *aside* is placed at the end of the speech, when it ought to precede it, as a direction to the reader, that he may govern his voice accordingly. The practice of our ladies in meeting five or six together to form a little busy party, where each is employed in some useful work while one reads to them, is so commendable in itself, that it deserves the attention of authors and printers to make it as pleasing as possible, both to the reader and hearers.

After these general observations, permit me to make one, that I imagine may regard your interests. It is that *your* spelling-book is miserably printed here, so as in many places to be scarcely legible, and on wretched paper. If this is not attended to, and the new one lately advertised as coming out should be preferable in these respects, it may hurt the future sale of yours.

I congratulate you on your marriage, of which the news-papers inform me. My best wishes attend you, being, with sincere esteem, sir, your most obedient and most humble servant,

B. FRANKLIN.

Check Out More Titles From HardPress Classics Series In
this collection we are offering thousands of classic and hard
to find books. This series spans a vast array of subjects – so
you are bound to find something of interest to enjoy reading
and learning about.

Subjects:
Architecture
Art
Biography & Autobiography
Body, Mind &Spirit
Children & Young Adult
Dramas
Education
Fiction
History
Language Arts & Disciplines
Law
Literary Collections
Music
Poetry
Psychology
Science
…and many more.

Visit us at www.hardpress.net

Im TheStory

personalised classic books

"Beautiful gift.. lovely finish.
My Niece loves it, so precious!"

Helen R Brumfieldon

⭐⭐⭐⭐⭐

UNIQUE GIFT

FOR KIDS, PARTNERS
AND FRIENDS

Timeless books such as:

Kids

Alice in Wonderland • The Jungle Book • The Wonderful Wizard of Oz
Peter and Wendy • Robin Hood • The Prince and The Pauper
The Railway Children • Treasure Island • A Christmas Carol

Adults

Romeo and Juliet • Dracula

Highly Customizable

Change Books Title

Replace Characters Names with yours

Upload Photo (on inside page)

Add Inscriptions

Visit
Im TheStory .com
and order yours today!